CRIMINAL BEHAVIOR

CRIMINAL BEHAVIOR

A Psychosocial Approach

THIRD EDITION

CURT R. BARTOL

Castleton State College

PRENTICE HALL, Englewood Cliffs, New Jersey 07632

Library of Congress Cataloging-in-Publication Data

Bartol, Curt R.
    Criminal behavior : a psychosocial approach / Curt R. Bartol. --
3rd ed.
        p.   cm.
    Includes bibliographical references.
    ISBN 0-13-192766-3
    1. Criminal psychology.   2. Criminal behavior--United States.
I. Title.
HV6080.B37 1991
    364.3--dc20   90-31830
                                                      CIP

Editorial/production supervision
  and interior design: *Mary Kathryn Leclercq*
Cover design: *Lundgren Graphics*
Manufacturing buyer: *Ed O'Dougherty*

 © 1991, 1986, 1980 by Prentice-Hall, Inc.
A Simon & Schuster Company
Englewood Cliffs, New Jersey 07632

Printed in the United States of America
10 9 8 7 6

ISBN   0-13-192766-3

Prentice-Hall International (UK) Limited, *London*
Prentice-Hall of Australia Pty. Limited, *Sydney*
Prentice-Hall Canada Inc., *Toronto*
Prentice-Hall Hispanoamericana, S.A., *Mexico*
Prentice-Hall of India Private Limited, *New Delhi*
Prentice-Hall of Japan, Inc., *Tokyo*
Simon & Schuster Asia Pte. Ltd., *Singapore*
Editora Prentice-Hall do Brasil, Ltda., *Rio de Janeiro*

*To Madelene, Jake,
Germaine, and Roland*

Contents

Preface

This is a textbook about criminal behavior from a psychological perspective. Classical and contemporary research and theory on the psychology of crime are reviewed as comprehensively and accurately as possible, with particular emphasis on repetitive, serious offending. Increasingly, psychological research on crime is focusing on cognitive aspects. Specifically, psychologists are directing more attention toward offenders' perceptions, beliefs, reasoning, and attitudes and the processes that contribute to their versions of the world. Therefore, the new challenge of psychological criminology is the systematic integration and organization of the complex interaction of cognitive, motivational, and affective processes. This discernible shift is reflected throughout the pages of this text.

Discouragingly, the many texts on criminology continue to misunderstand or fail to integrate the psychological perspective adequately or accurately. Authors continue to regard "psychology" from a classical Freudian viewpoint, often combined with a vague biological–genetic "trait" or dispositional focus. Occasionally, "learning" is described but often in an overly simplistic and dated fashion. This state of affairs is troubling because psychology is the "core discipline" in the understanding of criminal *behavior*.

This certainly does *not* mean that sociology, political science, or other disciplines have little to contribute toward the understanding of crime. The repetitive message throughout this text is that the study of crime must be *interdisciplinary*, with the various disciplines examining different levels of events. Therefore, adequate theory, sound research, and effective application require solid knowledge about the many *levels* of events that influence the person's life course, running from the individual, to the family, peers, schools, neighborhood, community, and the society as a whole. This text concentrates on the individual level of explanation, but with full recognition and respect for the powerful and dynamic interplay of ecological, social, economic, and political factors.

Several major changes have been made from the previous two editions. The effects of crime on *victims* have been given more emphasis throughout the text. The text also concentrates more on recent research examining the effectiveness of treatment and rehabilitative strategies on criminal behavior. Chapter 12, "Correctional Psychology," reflects this shift in focus and describes the growing research activity on the classification, diagnosis, prediction, treatment, and coping of inmates. A previous chapter on female crime has been deleted in favor of integrating material on women throughout the text. Chapter 9, "Sexual Offenses," has been completely rewritten to reflect substantial changes in the field since the last edition. If there is one area of criminal behavior where psychologists have jumped to the forefront in the past decade, it is in the understanding, diagnosis, and treatment of the sexual offender. An important section on family violence has been added to Chapter 8, "Criminal Homicide and Assault." Chapter 5, "Juvenile Delinquency," has been revised extensively to reflect recent shifts in that field.

The section on "arson" in Chapter 10, "Property Crimes and Crimes Against the Public Order," has been extensively revised and updated. New research and theory has also been added to the sections on burglary and shoplifting in that chapter. New material has been added to Chapter 11, "Drugs and Crime," including new sections on PCPs and crack.

As in the second edition, this text's organization runs from broad, theoretical positions on criminal behavior to specific criminal offenses. Biological positions are presented in the early chapters, while environmental, learning, and cognitive viewpoints come later. The material continues to be heavily referenced so that interested readers can document and decide for themselves the validity of the research conducted and the statements made. As a result of increases in international research and commentary on the the psychological factors on criminal behavior, the text also has acquired a more international flavor.

The major goal is that students of criminal behavior will, as a result of reading this text, avoid oversimplified, prejudicial, dogmatic answers to the complex issues involved in crime. If, after studying the text with an open mind, the reader puts it down seeking additional information, and if the reader has developed an avid interest in discovering better answers, then this text will have fulfilled its purpose.

ACKNOWLEDGMENTS

This material in this text has been tested in the classroom for over ten years. During these years, many students have made comments and suggestions for improvement. To them, I am very grateful. I would also like to thank the reviewers, Edward Ryan of Mansfield University and William E. Thornton of Loyola University, who have made suggestions during the text's continuing development. I would also like to express my appreciation to the staff members of Prentice Hall who have helped in making it all possible. Special thanks are due to production editor Katy Leclercq who orchestrated the many technical aspects of this text with ease and much competence.

Curt R. Bartol

CHAPTER ONE
Introduction

Crime intrigues people. Sometimes it attracts us, sometimes it repels us, occasionally it does both at once. It can amuse, as when we hear about capers and practical jokes that presumably do not harm anyone. It can frighten, if we believe that what happened to one victim might happen to us. Crime can also anger, as when a beloved community member is brutally killed. Violent crime in particular draws attention; consider the rampant excitement and fear in a neighborhood or small town when news of a local murder hits the street.

While interest in crime has always been high, understanding why it occurs and what to do about it has always been a problem. Public officials, politicians, "experts," and streetcorner philosophers continue to offer simple and incomplete solutions for obliterating crime: police patrols, closed-circuit TV, street lights, sturdy locks, judo classes, stiff penalties, speedy imprisonment, or capital punishment. Academe invariably offers abstract interpretations and suggestions, which often have little practical value. As in most areas of human behavior, there is no shortage of experts, but there are few effective solutions.

Our inability to prevent crime is partly due to our problems under-standing criminal behavior, a complex phenomenon. Because crime is complex, explanations of crime require complicated, involved answers. Psychological research indicates that most people have limited tolerance for complexity and ambiguity. People apparently want simple, straightforward answers, no matter how complex the issue. Parents become impatient when psychologists answer questions about child rearing by saying, "It depends"—on the situation, on the parents' reactions to it, on any number of possible variables. This preference for simplicity helps to explain the popularity of do-it-yourself, 100-easy-ways-to-a-better-life books.

This text presents criminal behavior as a vastly complex, poorly understood phenomenon. Readers looking for simple solutions will either have to reorient their thinking, set the text aside, or read it in dismay. There is no all-encompassing psychological explanation for crime, any more than there is a sociological, anthropological, psychiatric, economic, or historic one. In fact, it is unlikely that psychology or any other discipline can formulate basic "truths" about crime without help from other disciplines and areas of research. Unfortunately, much interdisciplinary disinterest (and some animosity) exists among the social science disciplines that study crime. Yet, criminology needs all the help it can get to explain and control criminal behavior. An integration of the data, theory, and general viewpoints of each discipline is crucial.

To review accurately and adequately the plethora of studies and theories from each relevant discipline is far beyond the scope of this text, however. Our focus is the psychological perspective, although other viewpoints also will be described. To date, psychology has been neither fairly represented nor adequately integrated in criminological literature, partly because until recently few psychologists have been interested in studying crime. Research in forensic psychology, a specialty concerned with the many psychological aspects of the judicial process, has increased dramatically over the past two decades, signalling a late-blooming interest in the study of crime itself.

The primary aim of this text is to assess the impact of this recent psychological research, compare it with traditional approaches, and offer a theoretical framework for the study of crime. We cannot begin to do this without first calling attention to philosophical questions that underlie any study of human behavior.

PERSPECTIVES ON HUMAN NATURE

A society's social, political, and economic structures are based on fundamental premises about human beings, their inherent tendencies, abilities, weaknesses, and preferences (Nelson, 1975). Eisenberg (1972) notes that theories of education, political science, economics, and criminology, as well as the policies of a government, are based on implicit assumptions about the nature of humankind. Where crime is at issue, a society which believes that humans are by nature aggressive and violent will have different methods of social control than a society which believes they are by nature peaceful, loving, and friendly. A society committed to an innate violence viewpoint may be forced to accept the position that little can be done to change this biological destiny. In that case, the solution to crime is not to re-educate or train criminals, improve opportunities, or reduce poverty, but rather to make criminal behavior less appealing to the perpetrator. Harsh criminal penalties, target hardening, and a de-emphasis on the individual rights of the criminal reflect this viewpoint, although it would be misleading to suggest that everyone who advocates being tough on criminals subscribes to the innate violence theory.

If we shift our focus away from society as a whole and toward the researchers and theorists who may directly influence social policies, perspectives about human nature become even more relevant. If researchers and theorists believe that humans are fundamentally animal in needs, urges, motives, and overall behavior, they will explain crime very differently from those who believe that humans are different in kind from animals. If they believe that human activity is usually *controlled* or determined by the social environment or driven by internal dispositions (personality), their explanations and solutions will be very different from those of others who believe that humans are self-determined and act primarily on the basis of free will.

Perspectives on human nature not only dictate explanations of crime but also may act as self-fulfilling prophecies. The belief that humans are innately untrustworthy, self-centered, or violent may promote behavior and interactions that support this belief. In other words, if we do not trust people, we may unknowingly set up situations of distrust whereby others not only act distrustfully but also distrust us in turn. By example and by provocation, we actually generate the behavior we condemn.

Thus, a researcher's perspective on human nature not only influences his or her explanations of crime but also may become self-fulfilling. It may strongly affect the research questions asked, the design of the research, the way it is conducted, and the interpretation of the data. Theoretical perspective even influences what research literature will be read. Totally objective research, which presumes the unbiased eye of the scientist and nonsubjective empirical questioning, is extremely difficult to conduct. The dispassionate approach expected of all scientists and researchers may be contaminated by their preconceptions and theoretical notions. This is especially true for social scientists because, in essence, they are studying themselves—an enterprise that lends itself to high levels of subjectivity.

For the foregoing reasons it is important to examine some divergent premises about human nature before delving into explanations of criminal behavior. We do not assert which positions are correct and incorrect, only that different viewpoints color explanations and conclusions about crime.

The two most important philosophical issues about crime and human nature are: (1) the extent to which humans differ from subhumans or animals, especially the primates; and (2) the locus of responsibility for human actions and conduct. The first issue raises the question, "Are we different in *degree* from animals or different *in kind?*" The second issue raises the two-pronged question, "To what extent should individuals be held responsible for their criminal conduct, and to what extent is behavior determined by a combination of internal and external factors?" In the following pages we will explore these questions in more detail, beginning with differences between humans and subhumans. We are indebted to the American philosopher Mortimer J. Adler, who expounded on this issue in his 1967 book, *The Difference of Man and the Difference It Makes*, for influencing much of the following material.

Difference in Kind versus Difference in Degree

A large segment of the psychological and psychiatric research on criminal behavior is dominated by the belief that human beings are basically animals, controlled by a myriad of biological urges, drives, and needs. Further, many scientists believe that if we observe and study the animal kingdom, especially the primates, we will understand why people act violently. Some theorists and writers call human beings the "predator ape," the "killer ape," or the "king of the jungle." They contend that humans are creatures without natural weapons, but whose brain development has propelled them to produce technological weaponry far outstripping any internal propensities for reducing aggression.

The writings of Charles Darwin (1809–1882) have had an extensive impact on this view of contemporary humans. Darwin's main thesis was that humans are fundamentally animals, developed from a common biological ancestry along with all animals and other living things. Long before Darwin, many philosophers and scholars considered humans to be animals— and not very good ones at that. Niccolo Machiavelli (1469–1527), for example, reduced humans to the status of animals governed by force and fraud (Bock, 1980). Thomas Hobbes (1588–1679) emphasized that humans are basically mean-spirited, brutish animals (Bock, 1980).

Darwin's distinctive influence on contemporary thinkers was his contention that humans should be placed on a *single* continuum along with all the *brute* animals. Other philosophers, scientists, and scholars before Darwin had placed humans on a continuum, but it was one representing *rational* animals. Brute animals and other living things were placed on different continua. Aristotle, for example, constructed multiple continua representing rational animals, brute animals, and plants. Darwin, however, legitimized the difference in degree perspective by placing humans along a single continuum of all living things.

The Darwinian perspective is important today because many social scientists, especially psychologists, believe that careful study of this single continuum will enable us to understand human nature, why we do what we do, and therefore, why some of us are criminals. Investigations of anthropoid apes, mice, rats, and pigeons will help us discover basic natural laws of behavior. This position is illustrated in the work of the sociobiologist Edward O. Wilson, including *Sociobiology* (1976) and *On Human Nature* (1978). The Darwinian position also contends that criminal behavior, especially when it is aggressive and violent, reflects the vestiges of the primordial jungle.

Darwin believed that life evolved in continuous ascent by degrees from its lowest to highest forms. All diverse types of life, including those now extinct, have been connected by this developmental sequence. Thus, humankind differs only in gradients or *degrees* from the animal kingdom.

Contemporary post-Darwinian positions agree with Darwin's tenets but add another component: Humans differ in kind *superficially* from other animals. That is, intellectually humans *appear* to differ in kind from all animals in the known universe. Humans can certainly do a lot more than other animals, because our brain is far more organically complex than the brains of subhumans. But the post-Darwinians explain this by introducing the concept of *critical threshold*. At a certain point in the evolutionary development of the human brain, it crossed a critical threshold of complexity, beyond which its intellectual functions expanded dramatically. Still, humans are basically animal in origin, influenced and controlled by the same biochemical and physical forces and motives inherent in all creatures. Even though we appear to differ in kind, even though we can perform complex intellectual activities, we still differ in degree from our infrahuman brethren. Most contemporary psychological, biological, and psychiatric theories of criminal behavior, and many sociological ones, are built on this foundation. As Eysenck (1983, p. 51) asserts: "Little improvement is likely until it is realized that humans are biosocial animals, linked with the animal kingdom through millions of years of evolution . . ."

The second perspective on human nature, that humans differ in kind from subhumans, is becoming more popular. Respected neurobiologists and pioneer brain researchers like Sir John Eccles (Eccles & Robinson, 1984), Roger Sperry (1983), and Wilder Penfield (1975) have concluded that humans differ radically in kind from all other animals in our known universe. Along with many other theorists, they believe that we must introduce a new power or force to account for human thought and consciousness. The concept of the physical, organic brain, operating as the sole determinant of human consciousness and cognitive functioning according to the laws of physics, chemistry, and biology, is simply not enough. The terms *cognitive functioning* or *cognition* refer to the internal mediation processes that take place within the brain (or mind). The difference-in-kind orientation agrees that the organic brain is a *necessary* condition for human thought, but does not accept it as a *sufficient* condition. We *do* need the intact, healthy brain to think, but we also need to introduce something else to explain human thought completely.

How do these two perspectives on human nature influence the study of criminal behavior? The difference-in-degrees position explains criminal behavior as a reflection of natural laws within the animal kingdom, laws that can be discovered through carefully designed research conducted either in animal habitats or in the laboratory, where irrelevant variables can be controlled. Most researchers who assume this generalizability from animals to humans also embrace the critical threshold position. A difference-in-kind orientation argues that comparing humans to animals, either implicitly or explicitly, does not advance our understanding of crime, because humans are radically different from inhumans in one or more important ways. They differ in their ability to think about the future, remember the past in the absence of external stimuli, and consider alternatives for each action.

Conceptual thinking is the core of the difference-in-kind approach. More specifically, human thought, because of concepts that are integrated and organized within the mind, enables us to transcend the immediate environment. These internal concepts extend us not only to objects and events in the remote past and remote future but also to things and events that are not time-bound at all, such as those we find in our daydreams and fantasies. Conceptual thinking produces, among other things, tools, an abstract language, and a culture that can be transmitted from generation to generation.

Animal or perceptual thinking, by contrast, is confined to the perceptual present. Animals can learn, experience, generalize, discriminate, solve problems through trial and error, and even show signs of "insight," but much of the research evidence to date suggests that they cannot think about objects or events that are not perceptually present. Perceptual thinking operates in the presence of appropriate sensory stimuli, never in their absence. The relevant stimuli must be both present and perceived. Although humans also have perceptual thinking, it is not quite the same since it is invariably influenced by conceptual thinking.

According to the difference-in-kind perspective, we will understand crime better if we study and build theories based on the human qualities that are radically different from subhuman features. Regarded this way, criminal behavior becomes a *uniquely human attribute generated solely by the conceptual thinking of the human being.* To suggest that nature or our biological ancestry may be to blame—even partially—for the way we are is to distract our attention from a more viable explanation of behavior.

Determinism versus Free Will

The second crucial perspective on human nature, more complex than the first, focuses on *causes* of behavior; it is most often referred to as the *determinism* debate. For our purposes, *determinism* will refer to the *nature* and *location* of the *causes* of behavior. In other words, what factors cause (determine) behavior, and where are they located? Are they within ourselves? Are they biological factors or drives over which we have little or no control? What causes criminal behavior? Is it the social environment of parents, peers, institutions, and organizations or the biological environment of urges and needs? If both, which is more important? Do mental processes cause criminal behavior?

The foregoing questions may remind you of the nature versus nurture debate, which considers whether our genetic, biological makeup (nature) or our environment (nurture) has the greater influence on us. Questions about determinism are similar, but determinism is a broader concept that takes into account both the immediate neurophysiological factors (rather than simply genetics), and the influences of the immediate environment (rather than simply past experiences). The nature-nurture issue is more oriented toward past events and prior genetic influences provided at conception, birth, and during early development. In evaluating determinism, we are concerned not only with the possible influences of the past on criminal behavior, but also with the present circumstances that influence that behavior. Moreover, determinism is future-related as well.

To say that determinism is an important topic when we discuss crime is to understate. If behavior, including criminal behavior, follows the rules and principles of a lawful, orderly universe, careful study will eventually reveal these principles. This means that we should in time be able to predict, modify, and control criminal behavior. If, on the other hand, human behavior does *not* follow the rules of the physical universe, we will be forced to revise our thinking and look for new explanations of why criminal behavior occurs. Moreover, if the causes of behavior exist primarily within the individual (internal determinism), we are correct in trying to change the behavior of individual criminals. If, on the other hand, the causes of behavior exist primarily within the social environment (external determinism), we should change society to better fit the needs of all individuals. *Internal determinism* is the belief that we are driven by powerful instinctual drives or biological needs; *external determinism* is the belief that we are little more than complicated robots, responding reflexively or automatically to environmental stimuli. Both internal determinism (also called *dispositional psychology*) and external determinism (also called *situational psychology*) reflect a passive view of humankind. Human beings are not seen as active, responsible agents but as helpless, powerless reactors (Chein, 1962).

Many gradients of determinism are recognized in contemporary psychology, but for the present we will discuss two categories: *Hard* and *soft* determinism. *Hard* determinism is the belief that *all* behavior—whether animal or human—is caused (or determined) by forces or events that follow the laws of the universe. Everything we do has a cause, and often we are not aware of it. Causes may exist within the environment (external stimuli) or within the self (internal stimuli). The important thing to remember is that the hard determinists believe that these causes operate according to the natural laws of the universe, independent of direct human control or free will. According to this view, we may *think* we are self-determined, but everything we do, think, or believe actually follows the causal laws of nature. Stated differently, every event has a cause, independent of the individual's wishes. To hard determinists, then, self-control is an illusion. We do not control what happens to us, but instead respond lawfully to life's events and stimuli.

Furthermore, hard determinists do not accept chance or accidental events. The behavior of the man who walks into a restaurant and begins randomly shooting everyone in sight is determined by forces outside his control. Moreover, according to hard determinists, once we understand what causes events in our world, we will be able to predict events, including human behavior, with 100 percent accuracy. If we had understood *all* of the external and internal forces working on the restaurant killer, we would have predicted his outburst with 100 percent accuracy. The key word is *all*, because in order to be 100 percent accurate we must understand all contributing factors. Hard determinists believe that 100 percent accurate prediction is *possible*, but has not yet been attained because we simply do not yet know enough about all the antecedent conditions that impinge on our lives. Someday, however, with carefully conducted research, the hard determinists believe we will.

Soft determinism takes a more moderate position: While there are many controlling forces or events in our lives, there is also a considerable amount of *self*-determination, free will, or personal responsibility. Some soft determinists say we directly control most of our actions. Others say most of what we do is caused by external events, but we can exercise some self-control over our behavior and its consequences. Because of this element of self-control or self-determination, no human being can tell how another will inevitably behave. Human beings are less than 100 percent predictable and, according to some psychologists, *substantially* less than 100 percent predictable. This issue will be very important when we discuss predictions of dangerousness and violent behavior in chapter six.

Another way of conceiving of determinism, rather than dichotomizing it into hard or soft categories, is to consider its location or *locus* of control. That is, the causes of behavior may be either in the environment or within the person. If within the person, they may be either biological or psychological.

If you believe that the primary determining factor of human behavior is the environment (e.g., society), you are endorsing physical determinism or *situationism*. Psychologists who opt for this approach look for the stimuli in the external environment that provoke (cause) relevant responses or behavior patterns. Thus, a situationist argues that criminal conduct results from one or a combination of variables found in society or the immediate

environment—for example, reinforcements, the media, institutions, organizations, parents, peer groups. A classic example of situationism is behaviorism, which posits that all behavior can be understood by considering
stimuli in the environment in combination with rewards and punishments
received from that environment. To use a simplistic example, Erik embez-
zles *because* his aged father's medical expenses are prohibitive (stimulus)
and the money Erik pilfers allows him to maintain his father in a high-
quality nursing home (reward). Situationists do, however, acknowledge a
variety of stimuli, acting in combination to produce the criminal behavior.

On the other hand, if you believe that something within the *person* is
the chief determinant of behavior, you endorse individual determinism or
dispositional theory. Dispositionists look to inner conflicts, beliefs, drives, personal needs, traits, or memories to explain behavior. They see criminal
behavior as the result of some inherent and/or learned predisposition or
tendency existing in each of us, probably in varying degrees.

Dispositional theory can be further subdivided into biological and
psychological determinism. *Biological* determinism holds that human behavior is determined at least partly—and perhaps to a great extent—by
heredity, bodily constitution or physique, physiological factors, or characteristics of the nervous system. Certain physical, biological, and neurological features predispose some of us to be more inclined to engage in certain
behavior patterns, such as aggression. Biological determinists usually believe that these features are modified, limited, or enhanced by our interactions with the outside world. A propensity for aggression could be altered
by nutrition or by culture or the social milieu. A culture that encourages
aggressive action is more likely to bring out innate, biological aggressive
tendencies than one that discourages it.

Psychological determinism is similar, but it argues that psychological
factors are more crucial than biological, neurological ones. Freudians, neo-
Freudians, and other psychodynamically oriented personality theorists fit
into this category. They believe that human behavior is largely determined
by conscious and unconscious forces, urges, conflicts, or motives. Therefore, a psychodynamically oriented dispositional theorist may argue that
criminal behavior results from some unresolved, unconscious conflict.
Trait personality theorists, on the other hand, believe that human behavior
can be attributed to stable, relatively enduring ways of thinking, behaving,
and feeling. Some theorists define traits as constructs or labels that summarize these consistencies in behavior. Others assume that traits exist in tangible form, such as a mental structure, within the person.

Finally, those who believe that situational and dispositional variables
are equally responsible for behavior are called *interactionists*. To them, both
individual and environmental factors play crucial roles in determining behavior. We will deal with this interactionist position in greater detail in
chapter four.

The behavioral and social sciences are built on a strong assumption of determinism, a fundamental working hypothesis of all contemporary scientific methods. Whether the researchers and theorists are hard or soft determinists, whether they believe that the causes of behavior are within the person or in the environment, their goal is similar: to discover the predictable, consistent forces, principles, or laws that are assumed to exist. Without this assumption of determinism, there would be no logical need for the social and behavioral sciences as presently conceived. Nevertheless, most behavioral and social scientists are not hard determinists. Scientists may be hard, scientific determinists in their research endeavors, but in their daily lives they may conceive of themselves and others as active agents who largely control their environments by exercising free choice.

Some scholars, however, suggest that determinism is dominant and pervasive, not only in the social and behavioral sciences, but also in most contemporary scientific assumptions about human nature. Consider the following remark by psychologist R. B. MacLeod: "The 20th century conception of man, represented by Western science, is silently dominated by Newtonian and Darwinian assumptions. Newton and Darwin have become eponyms" (MacLeod, 1970, p. 209).

Darwinism, as we have discussed, relates to the assumption that humans differ in degree from animals. What are Newtonian assumptions? Essentially, they represent hard determinism. Sir Isaac Newton (1642–1727) described the universe as a majestic, clockwork-like machine that follows a *single* set of rules. This mechanical conception embodied complete determinism: *All* things have a physical, identifiable cause. In this sense, Newtonian conceptions of human nature allow only hard determinism. If *A*, then we have 100 percent *B* inevitably.

The Newtonian conception of humankind, however, did not originate with Newton himself but with John Locke (1632–1704), one of his great admirers. In his 1690 *Essay Concerning Human Understanding*, published three years after Newton's *Principia*, Locke tried to do for the human mind what Newton had done for the physical world (MacLeod, 1970). Locke wanted to create a science of the mind analogous to the science of physical things. He believed that the human mind follows the same basic laws of the universe as the physical world. If we know all the relevant antecedent conditions in the physical world (if *A*), we should be able to predict (and control) the results of these antecedent conditions (then *B*). Similarly, if we know all the relevant antecedent conditions of human behavior, we should be able to predict (and control) that behavior, including criminal behavior.

Thus, the Newtonian view of human nature assumes that human behavior is completely lawful; it follows the same laws of the universe as do all physical things. Furthermore, all knowledge, including scientific knowledge, must be derived from sense experience through sensory channels. Science must emphasize facts and their collection through methods highly dependent on the senses, such as sight and sound, and science must reject all speculative and spiritual sources of knowledge. This way of thinking about the world is often called *positivism*, a concept we will cover shortly.

Therefore, during the eighteenth century, a belief in a rigorous and exact science of human nature began to develop and has endured to the present. The scientific method was considered as valid in the study of human beings as in the study of the physical sciences. Inherent in this position is the firm, deterministic belief that everything happens according to the orderly laws of the universe. In its purest form, this deterministic perspective sees human behavior as lawful, and free will or free choice as a myth. Even when modified to recognize free will, however, the determinism paradigm sees human behavior as influenced strongly by forces or stimuli outside the individual.

THEORIES OF CRIME

Criminological literature, whether psychological, sociological, or psychiatric in bent, has traditionally been divided into three broad schools of thought about the causes of crime: The *classical* and *neoclassical* schools, and *positivism*. Recently, a fourth school, *new* or *radical criminology*, has emerged.

Centuries ago, criminal behavior was believed to be the result of evil spirits and demons. Guilt and innocence were established by a variety of procedures that presumably called forth the supernatural allies of the accused. The accused were innocent if they could survive an ordeal or if miraculous signs appeared. They were guilty if they died at the stake or if omens were associated with them. Punishment, under the guise of treatment, often consisted of exorcism; if that failed, the criminal was banished, either through exile or by execution.

In the eighteenth century, this "spiritual" determinism began to give way to the belief that humans are rational creatures with free will, who seek happiness and pleasure and avoid unhappiness and pain. The *classical* school of criminological thought developed at this time, spearheaded by Jeremy Bentham (1748–1832) and Cesare Beccaria (1738–1794). Today, Bentham and Beccaria are best remembered for their thoughts on appropriate punishment as a deterrent to criminal behavior. Bentham suggested that, to reduce crime, society should administer a degree of punishment (pain) just sufficient to offset the potential gains (pleasure) of the criminal behavior. In fact, he is credited with coining the phrase, "Let the punishment fit the crime." Beccaria objected to the existing practices of administering justice, which he saw as capricious and extremely biased, and to unnecessarily harsh and barbaric punishments.

Writers describing the classical school often conclude that it championed free will and rational thought. It supposedly placed humans on a continuum of rational thought, as did earlier philosophers like Aristotle, who conceived of separate continua for brute and rational animals. It is assumed, also, that Bentham, Beccaria, and their followers believed that humans act with total free will. But the classical school actually argued that people are *driven* toward the acquisition of pleasure and the avoidance of pain, independent of any freedom of will. Bentham wrote: "Nature has placed mankind under the governance of two sovereign masters, *pain* and *pleasure*" (cited in McReynolds, 1968, p. 241). The belief that humans are driven or controlled by internal needs overwhelmingly dictated by nature is determinism, or at least soft determinism. Moreover, Bentham apparently believed that all individuals are *inherently* motivated to seek pleasure and avoid pain, without exception, in all situations (McReynolds, 1968). Although he did not elaborate on this underlying hedonistic principle, it appears that even Bentham's notion of free will included a good dose of biological determinism.

The neoclassical school does not represent any break with the classical view of human nature (Vold, 1958); it merely challenges the classical position of absolute free will, which as we have just seen is not as absolute as it is assumed to be. Specifically, neoclassicists argue that free will can be diminished by pathology, incompetence, mental disorder, or other conditions that may mitigate personal responsibility. Whereas the classicists had maintained that humans are totally responsible for their actions, the neoclassicists will say, "Not always."

Positivism is a vague term with multiple interpretations and is rarely used in psychology. Some criminologists, however, use it with some regularity. It refers to the scientific philosophy that the only way to obtain knowledge about our world is through the senses, principally through observation. Only immediately observable phenomena advance knowledge; speculation and reliance on immaterial factors do not. The brain, therefore, should be studied as a physical entity with tangible qualities. Positivists reject any use of "mentalisms" or things that cannot be directly observed (such as mental processes and cognitions). They favor the procedures of collecting and correlating facts to obtain accurate descriptions of the world. A contemporary example of a pure positivist in psychology is B. F. Skinner, who argues that the single most important goal of a psychological science is to find lawful relationships between observable variables. We will elaborate on Skinner's ideas and work in chapter four.

The positive school began at a time when the logic and basic methodology of objective, empirical science was becoming well established (Vold, 1958). It was also a time when Darwinism dominated intellectual discussions about human nature. The writings of one of the earliest positivists, Cesare Lombroso, reflect both his philosophy of science (positivism) and the Darwinian philosophy of human nature that flourished during the last half of the nineteenth century. Lombroso's work, which will be discussed in the next chapter, represents both a biological deterministic perspective and a difference-in-degree orientation toward the explanation of crime. Lombroso believed, especially during the early phases of his career, that criminals were ape-like, primitive creatures, incapable of living normally in society. Because they represented the link between modern humans and apes, their physical characteristics could be observed, measured, analyzed, and catalogued scientifically. Once all the discerning features of criminality had been identified, criminal behavior could be predicted simply through careful observation and measurement.

Positivism continued to develop through the work of Lombroso's pupil Enrico Ferri (1856–1928), Raffaele Garofalo (1852–1934), and their followers, a group which came to be called the Italian school. Although we will not summarize its contributions here, it is important to remember that this Italian positive school of criminological thought is characterized by determinism—especially hard, biological determinism. Because of its heavy reliance on the senses to gather observable facts and measurements, it represents the beginnings of modern scientific criminology.

The positivistic orientation, with its exclusive or near exclusive reliance on observable facts, continues to be prominent in the study of crime today. As the criminologist George B. Vold (1958, p. 39) asserted, "All contemporary scientific criminology is positivistic in method and in basic formulations." We should, however, distinguish between the early Italian positive school of thought, as characterized by Lombroso, Garofalo, and Ferri, and contemporary positivism as a philosophy of science, which insists on empirical evidence, concentrates on only what is overtly observable, and values the controlled experiment as the primary source of the most valid knowledge.

PERSPECTIVES IN CRIMINOLOGY

Our main concern in this text is with *psychological* principles, concepts, theory, and research relevant to criminal behavior. However, it is important to recognize contributions of other disciplines, especially sociology and psychiatry, to the study of crime. As noted earlier, criminology needs all the help it can get in its struggle to understand, explain, and prevent criminal behavior.

It is not easy to make sharp demarcations between psychology, sociology, and psychiatry, since they overlap considerably in focus. Sometimes, what distinguishes a given theory as sociological, psychological, or psychiatric is simply the stated professional affiliation of its proponent. The reader should also realize that condensing any major discipline into a few pages hardly does it justice. To obtain a more adequate overview, the interested reader should consult texts and articles within those disciplines.

Sociological Criminology

Sociological criminology is often divided into two major perspectives, the structural and the processual (Reid, 1985). The *structural* viewpoint studies crime as it relates to the social structure or organization of society. It is primarily concerned with discovering conditions within a society that lead to or cultivate criminal behavior. Structuralists ask, "What social factors cause crime?" They usually answer by describing demographic characteristics of criminal groups, including their ecological and economic features. For example, the structural approach provides the information that most persons convicted of homicide in the United States are young, black, inner-city males, or that women consistently commit fewer violent crimes than men.

The *processual* approach is concerned with *how* people become criminal. Sociological process theories generally emphasize the way individuals learn behavior, both criminal and noncriminal. Alternately, they may focus on elements that bond people to conventional society and therefore prevent them from breaking its laws. Still other processual theorists are concerned not so much with the initial criminal act, but with reactions of society that help maintain criminal or deviant behavior. Among the prominent process theories are Edwin H. Sutherland's theory of differential association, Ronald L. Akers's theory of differential association-reinforcement, the social control theory of Travis Hirschi, and the labelling perspective outlined by Howard Becker and Edwin Schur. Since some process theories overlap considerably with psychological social learning theory, they will be reintroduced in chapter four.

Another approach to sociological criminology is to divide it into functionalist and conflict perspectives. The *functionalist* viewpoint dominated early sociological criminology, particularly through the work of Robert K. Merton, and continues to live in modified form in contemporary theory. It rests on the writings of Emile Durkheim (1858–1917), who believed that crime was essential to the maintenance of a healthy society, serving to identify and validate what was morally acceptable. According to functionalists, individuals become criminals because they have not been adequately socialized to the rules of society. Implicit is the assumption that there are common values in society and that criminal law, which is essentially a consensus of what is not acceptable to society, represents these common values.

Conflict theory is a recent and highly controversial development in sociological criminology. Realizing that the conflict perspective is multidimensional and accommodates a variety of differing positions, the underlying theme is that the crime problem is a manifestation of the conflict between those who have power and those who do not. To the conflict theorists, criminal law, rather than serving society as a whole, is constructed and maintained for the convenience of the few who possess economic and political power.

The conflict perspective has splintered into diverse, sometimes overlapping schools, which have been called Marxist, left-wing, critical, and socialist perspectives. All of these theoretical approaches defy neat distinctions. Two moderately divergent arguments can be identified in conflict theory concerning the question, "Who has the power?" (Inciardi, 1980). One position, called radical criminology, claims that a closely knit ruling class, bent on the exploitation of the masses, not only has the power but can also be blamed for most of the crime. To the radical criminologist, the principal cause of crime and social conflict is the economic division between the capitalist and the worker. Since the powerful capitalists control the wealth, the methods of production, and essentially the power, they are able to write their own interests and values into the criminal law. The ultimate goal of the powerful capitalists, therefore, is to keep the powerless suppressed and their own power and interests protected. Although some of the powerless are forced into crime as a means of survival, they are often stymied and punished by the criminal law. Therefore, the causes of criminal behavior do not reside within the individual; they are inherent in the social order of a particular society. Since crime is a by-product of capitalism, radical criminologists believe that the only effective way of ridding society of crime is to do away with capitalism and embrace socialism.

Conflict criminology differs from the radical position in that it considers the division of power in society normal and acceptable. While radical criminology sees society as consisting of two basic classes, conflict criminology sees a pluralistic society as producing conflicting interests and values between competing groups. According to the conflict perspective, crime is inevitable because it is a natural outcome of clashing interests between different groups with different viewpoints. Therefore, conflict criminologists do not believe that crime control can be achieved with radical changes in the socioeconomic order nor with the redistribution of wealth and power in any pluralistic society characterized by competing groups of differing subcultures and values.

Ruth Kornhauser (1978) suggests still another way to dichotomize sociological criminology, maintaining that all of its theories fall into either a social disorganization or a cultural deviance framework. After advancing a scholarly critical assessment of a variety of sociological theories on juvenile delinquency, Kornhauser concludes that most promising are those that focus on an individual's weakened bonds to a society that does not effectively allow him or her to achieve its goals.

Although we have offered but a cursory look at sociological criminology, it is quite obvious that the sociological perspective of crime emphasizes the role of major social factors outside the individual in the genesis of criminal behavior. This is quite different from the psychological and psychiatric perspectives, both of which are centered on the individual rather than major social or societal factors.

Psychological Criminology

Psychology is the science of behavior and mental processes. Psychological criminology, then, is the science of the behavior and mental processes of the criminal. While sociological criminology focuses on groups and society as a whole, psychological criminology focuses on individual criminal behavior—how it is acquired, evoked, maintained, and modified. Both environmental and personality influences on criminal behavior are considered, along with the mental processes that mediate that behavior. In this context, *personality* refers to all the biological, psychological traits, and cognitive features of the human being that psychologists have identified as important in the mediation and control of behavior. This, however, is a broad definition intended to encompass many varied viewpoints about personality.

In the past, psychologists assumed that they could best understand human behavior by searching for stable, consistent personality dispositions or traits that exert widely generalized effects on behavior (Mischel, 1973). Many psychologists studying crime, therefore, assumed they should search for *the* personality traits or variables underlying criminal behavior. They paid little attention to the person's environment or situation. Presumably, once personality variables were identified, it would be possible to determine and predict which individual was most likely to engage in criminal behavior. As you will learn, the search for the personality of the murderer, rapist, or psychopathic killer has not been fruitful. Psychologists who provide law enforcement agencies with profiles of the rapist still at large, based solely on personality variables, are at best engaging in unvalidated clinical judgment and unsubstantiated hunches. However, psychologists *can* offer statistical probability about some demographic and behavioral patterns of certain offenders. For example, they might determine, roughly, that a rapist is probably young, white, unemployed, from the area, and so forth. They might also offer *possible* motives for the attack, based on research findings and accompanied by the necessary caveats.

It is important to keep in mind that psychology has been heavily immersed in the Darwinian and Newtonian perspectives of human nature, at least since the turn of the century. Two most influential figures in the psychology of the past 100 years, B. F. Skinner and Sigmund Freud, were strongly influenced by these two perspectives of humankind. Recently, there has been a notable shift toward cognitive and social learning approaches, which are much less deterministic. While reading the material that follows, you should try to decide whether humans are different in kind or different in degree from animals. Your choice will have great bearing on your perceptions of criminal behavior and on your proposed solutions to the crime problem.

Psychiatric Criminology

The terms *psychology* and *psychiatry* are often confused by the layperson and even by professionals and scholars in other disciplines. Psychiatric concepts and theories are often believed to be accepted tenets in the field of psychology. In reality, the two professions often see things quite differently, even though there are commonalities.

American psychiatric criminology, also called *forensic psychiatry*, continues to be dominated by a psychodynamic tradition that embraces a variety of psychoanalytic positions. The father of the psychoanalytical theory of human behavior was the physician-neurologist Sigmund Freud (1856–1939), whose followers are called *Freudians*. Many contemporary psychoanalysts subscribe to a modified version of the orthodox Freudian position and are therefore called *neo-Freudians*. Still other psychoanalysts follow the tenets of Alfred Adler and Carl Jung, who broke away from Freud and formed schools of their own. Collectively, all psychoanalytic positions form the psychodynamic school, which explains behavior in terms of motives and drives.

The orthodox psychoanalytic position assumes that we must delve into the abysses of human personality to find unconscious determinants of human behavior, including criminal behavior. Consider the following comments by two forensic psychiatrists. "The criminal rarely knows completely the reasons for his conduct" (Abrahamsen, 1952, p. 21). "Every criminal is such by reason of unconscious forces within him . . . " (Roche, 1958, p. 25). Psychoanalytic and psychodynamic theories acknowledge that behavior varies across situations. However, they conclude that there are enduring and generalized underlying dynamic or motivational dispositions that account for this diversity. "Surface" behaviors indirectly signal or symbolize dynamic, underlying attributes. Psychological defenses distort and disguise the "true" meaning of external or observed behaviors. The trained clinician, therefore, must interpret the significance of these external behaviors, since the actor is not aware of their purpose.

The psychoanalytic or psychodynamic position strongly endorses the view that the prime determinant of human behavior lies within the person and that after the first few years of life the environment plays a very minor role. Consequently, criminal behavior is believed to spring from within, primarily dictated by the biological urges of the unconscious. The environment, culture, or society cannot be held responsible for crime rates; biopsychological needs and urges within the individual are the culprits. Thus, the Darwinian orientation and the difference-in-degree perspective pervade the psychoanalytic school as well as forensic psychiatry in general.

A major reason for studying criminal behavior is to try to predict it, since prediction would help us both to prevent and to control crime. However, reviews of the relevant research have consistently shown that psychodynamically oriented clinicians have been able to predict behavior no better than their behaviorally oriented colleagues (Mischel, 1968, 1973). Furthermore, the psychodynamic school does not engender hard data, partly because its concepts are ambiguous (presumably residing in the intangible recesses of the mind) and not conducive to empirical or scientific examination. The vagaries of the id, the ego, the superego, unconscious urges and impulses, behavioral symbolism, and psychosexual development as explanations of crime are well know to most criminologists, and they hold a dominant place in forensic psychiatry. However, they are not accepted by most contemporary psychologists. In fact, most Freudian and neo-Freudian concepts have never found a secure place in mainstream psychology, especially within the academic realm.

It would be highly incorrect to assume that psychiatry is strictly psychodynamic in orientation, however. A large number of psychiatrists do not accept many of the traditional psychodynamic or psychoanalytical tenets, and some psychologists do. Again, there is more overlap between the professions than some clinicians like to admit. The point here is to emphasize that the terms *forensic psychiatry* and *psychiatric criminology* will be reserved throughout this text for the traditional psychiatric approach to crime, which has been heavily influenced by psychoanalytic theory.

A DEFINITION OF CRIMINAL BEHAVIOR

In a text of this nature, one initial task must be to define criminal behavior and determine the object of our study. It is not easy to do this, since we are confronted with definitional as well as methodological dilemmas. Not only must we decide how to define crime and the criminal, but we must also struggle with the many statistical problems associated with crime reporting and interpretation.

Crime itself is "an intentional act in violation of the criminal law committed without defense or excuse, and penalized by the state as a felony or misdemeanor" (Tappan, 1947, p. 100). Criminal behavior, therefore, is intentional behavior which violates a criminal code, intentional in that it did not occur accidentally or under duress. To be held criminally responsible, a person must have known what he or she was doing during the criminal act and must have known that it was wrong. Obviously, this legal definition encompasses a great variety of acts, ranging from homicide to minor traffic violations.

In a text of this type, we are confronted with several dilemmas. Should we restrict ourselves to a legal definition and study only those individuals who have been convicted of crime? Or should we include individuals who indulge in antisocial behaviors but have not been detected by the criminal justice system? Perhaps our study should include persons predisposed to be criminal, if such persons can be identified. As a review of criminology textbooks and literature attests, there is no universal agreement as to what group or groups should be targeted for study.

If we abide strictly by the legal definition of crime and base research and discussion only on those people who have committed crimes, do we consider only those who have been convicted and incarcerated, or do we include those who have probably broken the criminal law but are not convicted? Even by conservative estimates, 36 to 40 million persons—16 to 18 percent of the total U.S. population—have *arrest* records for nontraffic offenses (U.S. Department of Justice, 1988). Furthermore, how can we include individuals who violate the law but escape detection or those who come to the attention of law enforcement officials but are never arrested?

Trying to study criminal behavior on the basis of incidence presents other problems for social scientists. Incidence of crime is usually measured in one of three ways:

1. official police reports of arrests and convictions, such as those tabulated and forwarded to the FBI for publication in its annual national statistical report on crime, the *Uniform Crime Reports* (UCR);
2. self-report studies, where members of a sample population are asked what offenses they have committed and how often; and
3. national or regional victimization studies, which sample a population of households or businesses asking respondents how often they have been victims of specified crimes.

Crime Reports

The Federal Bureau of Investigation's *Uniform Crime Reports* (UCR), compiled since 1930, is the most-cited source of U.S. crime statistics. The UCR is an annual document (released to the public sometime between late July and early September) containing arrest information received on a voluntary basis from law enforcement agencies throughout the United States. While the first UCR was published with fewer than 1,000 agencies reporting, the 1988 UCR data collection was based on 9,970 agencies representing about 90 percent of the total U.S. population. The UCR divides crimes according to whether they are reported, recorded, or cleared by arrest in relation to various geographical regions of the country. Crimes are also categorized according to seriousness. Serious crimes are called *index* crimes; nonserious crimes are *nonindex* crimes. Index crimes include criminal homicide, forcible rape, robbery, aggravated assault, burglary, larceny-theft, motor vehicle theft, and arson. We will define these crimes more specifically when we cover them in the following chapters. Examples of nonindex crimes include vandalism, carrying weapons, and buying, receiving, and possessing stolen property.

The UCR divides offenders by age, sex, and race, but not by social class or socioeconomic status. Figure 1-1, based on 1984 through 1988 UCR data, shows that arrest rates for serious property crimes peak at around age seventeen or eighteen, just before the age range where many courts begin prosecuting offenders as adults. With increasing age, and particularly after age twenty, property arrests decline dramatically. On the other hand, arrests for violent crime gradually peak and show a gradual decline with age. The UCR also provides data on the number of law enforcement officers killed or assaulted, and some characteristics of homicide victims.

Official crime statistics, like those of the FBI, are generally believed to underestimate most criminal offenses and are routinely criticized for errors and omissions. The total number of criminal offenses committed, known as

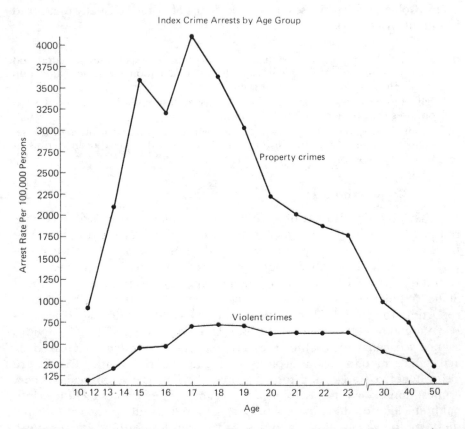

FIGURE 1-1   Index crime arrests by age group. (Based on data from FBI *Uniform Crime Reports,* four-year average, 1984–1988.)

the *dark figure*, will probably never be known, but estimates from a victimization survey conducted by the U.S. Census Bureau suggest that out of every 100 offenses committed, 72 are never recorded in the official statistics (Skogan, 1977). However, Skogan also notes that most unreported violations appear to be minor property offenses rather than more serious crimes.

Self-Report Studies

Many researchers believe that self-report (SR) studies provide a more accurate estimate of actual offenses than do local police or UCR statistics, even though individuals may inflate or deflate reports of their criminal activity. In a dated but important SR survey (Wallerstein and Wyle, 1947), 1,698 persons were asked to indicate on a list of forty-nine criminal offenses which, if any, they had committed. The list included felonies and misdemeanors but excluded traffic violations. Ninety-one percent of the nearly 1,700 respondents admitted they had committed one or more offenses for which they might have received jail or prison sentences. The average number of offenses for each person was eighteen. None of the sample had served an actual prison sentence. This study suggests that most people have broken the criminal law at some point in their lives.

In another study by Short and Nye (1957), 3,000 high school students, with a guarantee of anonymity, were administered questionnaires about their unlawful actions. Not only did the results confirm the high incidence of unlawful behavior reported by the Wallerstein and Wyle study, but it also showed that the unlawful conduct was evenly distributed across all socioeconomic classes. Even if the offenses were not serious ones, if these SR studies are representative, violations of the law are common across all levels of society, at least among young people.

Most SR investigations focus on delinquency rather than adult offending. The SR data are gathered either through interviews (personal or telephone) or questionnaires. In most SR measures, subjects are asked to indicate whether they have engaged in any of the listed illegal activities and, if so, how often. Nettler (1984), in his review of the SR research, concludes that, according to SR data:

1. Almost everyone, by his or her own admission, has violated some criminal law;
2. the amount of "hidden crime" (the dark figure) is enormous; and
3. most of the infractions are minor.

The last point is an important one because it is the basis for much of the criticism directed at SR studies. Most of the offenses included in a majority of SR questionnaires are relatively minor ones—so minor that they are likely to distort one's impressions of criminal offending unless the content of the questions are known. For example, the questionnaire used by Short and Nye was a twenty-three-item delinquency scale which included such questions as to whether one has ever defied his or her parents' authority (to their face). Realize, of course, that the researchers were asking high school students (grades nine through twelve) questions that technically were violations of the law for youth at that time (called *status offenses*). Other items included if one has ever skipped school without a legitimate excuse, taken little things (worth less than $2), bought or drank beer, wine, or liquor, had sexual relations with persons of the opposite sex or the same sex, or gone hunting or fishing without a license. More "serious" violations listed were running away from home, fist fights, gang fights, taking a car for a drive without the owner's knowledge (including parents'), use of narcotic drugs, theft (over $50), and vandalism.

Recent SR studies, responding to the criticisms of earlier investigations, have directed their questions at more serious criminal activities. Still, we must be careful about drawing far-reaching conclusions based on the information from SR research unless the nature of the questions is known, as well as who was asked, why, and how. At this point, however, SR studies do suggest that minor criminal activity is extensive and widespread, at least among youth. Furthermore, SR studies continually show that the number of individuals involved in serious crimes is relatively small, but those few who do engage in serious criminal activity commit a lot of crimes. Moreover, persistent, repetitive offenders do not specialize in any one crime (such as larceny) but show considerable versatility in criminal involvement, committing a wide variety of offenses, violent as well as nonviolent. We will discuss this behavioral pattern in more detail in chapter five.

Victimization Surveys

Additional sources of data on criminal offending are victimization surveys. One of the more ambitious surveys in recent years has been the National Crime Survey (NCS). The Bureau of Census interviews, on a staggered schedule, a large national sample of households (approximately 49,000) representing 101,000 persons over the age of twelve. The households are asked about crimes they experienced during the previous six months.

The NCS was begun by the President's Commission on Law Enforcement and Administration of Justice in 1966. The Commission wanted to supplement the UCR because of the widespread dissatisfaction with and distrust of the accuracy of this source. After considerable experimentation and a variety of pilot projects to test methods and their feasibility, the NCS was fully implemented in 1973, and is funded by the Bureau of Justice Statistics. The survey is currently designed to measure the extent to which households and individuals are victims of rape, robbery, assault, burglary, motor vehicle theft, and larceny. It also provides many details about the victims (such as age, race, sex, education, income, and whether the victim and the offender were related to each other) and about the crimes themselves (such as time and place of occurrence, whether or not reported to police, use of weapons, occurrence of injury, and economic consequences) (U.S. Department of Justice, 1988).

According to NCS data, 35 million victimizations occurred in 1985 (U.S. Department of Justice, 1988). About 5.5 million households were burglarized, and another 8.8 million had something stolen (e.g., a bike left on the front lawn). The NCS also reported that 1.6 million individuals were victims of aggravated assault (assailant inflicted, intended, or threatened to inflict serious bodily harm), and nearly a million individuals said they had been victims of a robbery. Over 13 million individuals had something stolen during the year.

Victimization surveys are now considered an excellent source of information about crime incidents, independent of data collected by law enforcement agencies throughout the country. Often, the offending trends reported through NCS data procedures differ substantially from those found in police data (Ohlin & Tonry, 1989).

Throughout the course of this text we will refer to victimization studies in order to get a better grasp on criminal activity as well as to learn how crime affects victims. In many instances, however, we will use surveys conducted by researchers independent of the NCS.

Offenders the Text Will Focus On

Some argue (e.g., Sellin, 1970; Tappan, 1947) that one who engages in undetected criminal activity is not a criminal in the strictest or operational sense, because a criminal is by definition one who has been detected, arrested, and convicted. However, from a psychological point of view, we encounter problems when we limit ourselves to studying persons legally defined as criminals. Legal classifications are determined by what society, at some point in time, considers socially harmful or, in some cases, morally wrong. Therefore, because each society has a different and changing set of values, what may be judged a criminal act in one may not meet the criteria in another, or even in the same society at a later time. Many states in the U.S. differ significantly in their criminal codes and are continually revising them. Chemical (drug) possession, prostitution, and dissemination of obscene material are examples of activities that generate ever-changing statutes, and if not changing statutes, selective enforcement.

Members of every society (and consequently every society's judicial system) perceive and process violators of the criminal code with some discrimination, so that the offender's background, social status, personality, motivation, sex, age, race, and legal counsel, as well as the circumstances surrounding the offense, all may affect the legal process. It is highly likely that individuals who have been arrested, convicted, and incarcerated represent a distinctly different sample from those who participate in illegal activity but avoid detection, conviction, or incarceration.

Approximately one-fifth of those arrested go to trial, according to Sarbin (1979), who describes the legal process of "becoming a criminal." First, the agents of social control (usually the police) attach a label of "suspect" to the individual. Next, the agents may decide that the suspect should be "arrested." Third, the arrested party may be charged with a crime, at which point he or she becomes a "defendant." Fourth, the defendant may be tried and convicted, at which point he or she becomes a felon. Finally, the felon may be incarcerated in a correctional facility and be labeled a "convict," "inmate," "prisoner," or "criminal." At each step in the process Sarbin uses the word "may," acknowledging the funnelling effect which allows fewer and fewer individuals to reach each subsequent step in the criminal justice process. Hart and Sacks (1958) called this the "great pyramid of legal order," and Galanter (1974) called it the "legal iceberg." Hundreds of thousands of individuals get filtered out, for a variety of reasons.

One reason is the error and subjectivity that cannot realistically be removed from determinations of guilt or innocence. Another is the sentencing process. It has been demonstrated that the characteristics of the victim may influence how much punishment is assigned to the offender. Landy and Aronson (1969) report evidence that if the victim is a respectable citizen (i.e., successful and altruistic), the offender will receive a stiffer sentence than if the case involves an "unrespectable" victim (i.e., despicable and dishonest). Jones and Aronson (1973) found that defendants who raped a married woman or virgin were more likely to receive longer sentences than defendants who raped a divorced woman. It has also been found that the more serious a traffic accident the greater the tendency for jurors to believe that the principals involved were at fault and negligent (Walster, 1966). Such discrepancies in sentencing have led to widespread demands for determinate sentencing, where the punishment is carefully calibrated to the offense and there is less room for discretion on the part of judges or juries.

The aforementioned studies support Lerner's hypothesis (1970, 1980) that people need to believe they live in a *just world* where the undeserving are appropriately deprived or punished. This just-world hypothesis predicts, for example, that some victims of rape, assault, or homicide are assumed by many people to have gotten what they deserved or asked for. The implications of this hypothesis in relation to juries' determinations of guilt, and therefore to the determination of who are criminals, are obvious.

It is generally acknowledged, therefore, that incarcerated individuals are not representative of the "true" criminal population. Yet, with rare exceptions, researchers studying the "criminal mind" use as subjects only those individuals who have reached the final stage of the legal process, inmates in correctional institutions. Consequently, if we discuss only legally determined criminals, we will be neglecting a considerable segment of the population that actually breaks the law. To some extent, we have little choice but to do just that. Because this text is based on research, the kinds and amounts of available empirical data dictate to a great extent what will be covered. On the other hand, we can go beyond this point and study the *behavior* that generally qualifies as criminal. From this perspective, we can include the vast body of psychological research that deals with such areas as aggression, "deviant" sexual behavior, and moral development. However, our focus will be on the *persistent, repetitive offender,* whether detected or undetected by the criminal justice system. In other words, in this text we will concentrate on the individual who has frequently committed serious crime or antisocial acts over an extended period of time (at least several years).

SCOPE OF THE TEXT

This text begins with broad theoretical issues surrounding the origins of criminal behavior. Chapters two and three concentrate on biology and Pavlovian classical conditioning as primary factors in the acquisition of criminal behavior. We include classic and well-cited studies and major theories related to both the biological and classical conditioning perspectives. In chapters four and five, we give greater attention to learning factors and the environmental determinants of criminal behavior. In this sense, the early part of the text progresses from internal or dispositional theories through environmental or situational theories of criminal behavior, and toward a combination of both. Ultimately, we place heavy emphasis on the internal cognitive or mediational processes that take place in the human brain (or mind).

Chapter six focuses on the mentally disordered offender and considers the extent of his or her involvement in crime. Up to this point, the text has been predominantly theoretical. With chapter seven, we set the stage for discussion of specific offenses, beginning with violent crimes. Chapter seven presents in broad terms some of the instigators and regulators of violence. Chapter eight continues this theme with its focus on homicide and aggravated assault and its attempt to offer psychological explanations for these violent offenses.

We continue the review of specific offenses by examining sexual offenses in chapter nine and property offenses in chapter ten. In chapter eleven, we assess the validity of the relationship between drugs and crime. Finally, chapter twelve focuses on the treatment and prevention of criminal behavior.

CHAPTER TWO
Origins of Criminal Behavior: Biological Factors

Many—perhaps most—contemporary students of criminology would agree with the following statement: "Genetics may play a role in criminality, but it is only an insignificant one. There is little doubt that environment is the principal determinant and cause of criminal behavior." Poverty, high unemployment, poor education, overpopulation, and group values that deviate from society's norms are often considered the major culprits producing crime. Heredity-based physiological components are scoffed at, and their possible role as causal agents in criminality is often dismissed.

Why so? Perhaps because accepting heredity as a factor in criminal behavior implies that criminal acts are unavoidable, inevitable consequences of the "bad seed," "bad blood," or "mark of Cain." Heredity is destiny. Little can be done to prevent the ill-fated person from becoming a criminal. A classic illustration of this viewpoint is Cesare Lombroso's doctrine (1911) that some criminals are born that way.

Most behavioral scientists—and many social scientists—recognize, however, that behavioral traits result from an *interaction* of hereditary and environmental factors. We no longer ask whether behavior is due to heredity or environment; we agree that both are involved in a complex way. However, researchers usually focus on one or the other for intensive study.

In this chapter, we will discuss the work of psychologists who study heredity and biopsychology as factors in the genesis of criminal behavior.

Biopsychologists, as they are called, try to determine which genetic and physiological variables play a part in criminal behavior, how important they are, and what can be done to modify them. Biopsychologists do not believe that genetic or physiological components are the sole causal agents. Most would say that understanding the social environment is as important as understanding the biological one. However, they have chosen to concentrate on the biological elements. We will introduce their work and assess their results after we have taken a brief look at the history of biopsychological research in criminality.

THE BORN CRIMINAL

A pioneer researcher on the relationship between crime, genetics, and personality was Cesare Lombroso (1836–1909), the Italian physician and self-termed criminal anthropologist introduced in chapter one. Lombroso's original and basic premise, published in *L'Uomo Delinquente* [*Criminal Man*] in 1876, was that some people are born with strong, innate predispositions to behave antisocially. He was greatly influenced by the views that Charles Darwin expounded in *The Descent of Man*, especially the notion that some people are genetically closer to their primitive ancestry than others (Savitz, 1972). The criminal, Lombroso believed, represented a separate species that had not yet evolved sufficiently toward the more "advanced" *homo sapiens*; this species was genetically somewhere between modern humans and their primitive origins in physical and psychological makeup. He called this evolutionarily retarded species *homo delinquens* and considered those individuals mutations or natural accidents living among civilized humans.

Lombroso collected extensive data on the physical measurements of Italian prisoners and Italian military personnel (noncriminals). He concluded that the criminal was distinguished by certain physical anomalies: An asymmetrical skull, flattened nose, large ears, fat lips, enormous jaws, high cheekbones, and mongolian eye characteristics (1972). Moreover, *homo delinquens*, also derisively called the "born criminal," had an affinity for tattoos, "cruel games," and orgies, and had a peculiar primitive slang, all believed to be behavioral throwbacks to savage, undeveloped human or subhuman species. Lombroso maintained that the born criminal's art works were often faithful reproductions of the first crude artistic attempts of primitive people. The implications were that this primitive creature, who instinctively demonstrated behaviors useful in the wild in the millennia past, could not adjust socially and morally to the demands of modern times.

L'Uomo Delinquente went through several revisions, and by 1897 it had grown to three volumes comprising 1,903 pages. With each edition Lombroso modified his theory from the dogmatic one of 1876 to a more flexible but still basically genetic version. For example, early Lombrosian theory asserted that *all* criminals met the physical dimensions and psychological characteristics outlined. Later, possibly responding to criticism, Lombroso concluded that the born criminal actually accounted for only about one-third of the criminal population (Lombroso-Ferrero, 1972). The other two-thirds comprised a wide assortment of criminal types. Lombroso also suggested at this point that environmental factors were significant in the development of certain types of crime (Wolfgang, 1972). In 1911, Gina Lombroso summarized her father's last work and translated it into English. Still another rendition, *Crime: Its Causes and Remedies*, was published a year later.

According to Cesare Lombroso, offenders who were not born criminals fell into one of six categories. *Habitual* or professional criminals violated the law systematically and engaged in crime as a trade or occupation. The degrading influence of prisons (which Lombroso called "criminal universities"), including daily contact with other hard-core prisoners, played a significant role in the development of this offender. A second type was the *juridicial criminal*, who violated the law not because of any "natural depravity" but simply from lack of prudence, care, or forethought—the impulsive type. *Criminals of passion* violated the law because of their "intense love, honor, noble ambition, or patriotism." They may have murdered to defend their honor, their loved ones, or their country. *Criminaloids* had "weak natures" and were highly susceptible to good and bad examples. They had innate characteristics very similar to those of born criminals, but the environment was an important determinant of their criminal action. *Born criminals*, by contrast, were dictated by strong organic predispositions to crime. Lombroso also recognized the *morally insane* and *hysteric* criminal types.

Born criminals, the biologically predisposed, exhibited a lack of guilt or remorse for any wrongdoing (although they often alleged repentance) and a peculiar inability to learn the distinction between good and evil. Lombroso reported that they did not develop close friendships and were likely to betray companions and accomplices. They displayed "exaggerated notions of their own importance," were impulsive, cruel, and had a high tolerance for pain.

Lombroso at first considered the female offender to be very similar to the male offender, both in physical appearance and psychologically (Wolfgang, 1972). Singling out prostitution as representative of female crime, he saw it as an atavism (a throwback to primitive times) and suggested that most prostitutes were born criminals who lacked a "mother sense." He later modified this view. On second thought, the born criminal woman did not clearly exhibit the same physical anomalies as the male born criminal. Psychologically, however, she was more terrible and cruel than any man, almost monster-like (Wolfgang, 1972). Lombroso based this on his belief that women in general have many traits in common with children, such as revenge, jealousy, and an inclination toward "vengeances of a refined cruelty."

Lombroso had a devoted following, which, as we noted in chapter one, became known as the Italian school of criminology. His outrageous pronouncements often embarrassed other criminologists, however, and they sought ways to refute him. In 1913, Charles Goring (1913/1972) published an influential monograph reporting the results of a study comparing the physical measurements of 3,000 English convicts to those of an equal number of nonconvicts. He had not found the significant physical differences reported by Lombroso. Goring's research was plagued by numerous methodological flaws, as were Lombroso's own investigations. Nevertheless, it proved devastating to the Lombrosian position. Armed with Goring's findings and eager to put the genetics and crime issue to rest, many criminologists quickly wrote the born criminal's obituary.

Although opinion varies about the value of Lombroso's contributions, there is little doubt that he had considerable impact on research directed at the relationship between genetics and the criminal personality. The late Stephen Shafer (1976, pp. 41–42), for example, suggested that Cesare Lombroso could easily be called the father of modern criminology because his theories have stimulated research and empirical investigations on the criminal's personality as well as the social environment. Abrahamsen (1960, pp. 6–7) comments that Lombroso will be remembered "for disproving the assumption that a criminal committed a criminal act because his will was free and so was unquestionably responsible for his act." Abrahamsen agrees that Lombroso paved the way for examining the criminal personality. Wolfgang (1972, p. 287) states: "The clinical, psychological and psychiatric analyses of today that report data on personality traits . . . are similar to, but much more refined and sophisticated than many of the findings reported by Lombroso."

PHYSIQUE AND CRIME

Theorists have linked physical characteristics with personality ever since Hippocrates outlined a typology of physiques and tried to relate them to personality. He also introduced the concept of humors, or body fluids, which presumably influenced personality (Hall & Lindzey, 1970). The modern course in constitutional psychology was set by the German psychiatrist Emil Kretschmer (1925), who distinguished four types of body structures and tried to connect them to specific mental disorders. He called one physique the *pyknic* and noted that it was characterized by a short, fat stature. A second type, exhibiting height and very thin features, was the *leptosomatic* or *aesthenic*. The muscular, vigorous physique was called the *athletic* type. The fourth, the *dysplastic*, represented an incongruous mixture of different physiques in different parts of the body, making it appear "rare, surprising and ugly" (Hall & Lindzey, 1970).

More pertinent to our discussion of crime is the theory of William H. Sheldon (Sheldon & Stevens, 1942; Sheldon, Hartl, & McDermott, 1949), who developed a similar but superior classification of body type in the United States and related physique to delinquency. Sheldon's method is called *somatotyping*. After extensively collecting and documenting physical measurements, Sheldon found he could delineate three basic body builds: the endomorphic (fat and soft), ectomorphic (thin and fragile), and meso-morphic (muscular and hard) (see Figure 2-1). The reader with some background in embryology will recognize that the terms refer to layers of the embryo. The endodermal embryonic layer develops primarily into the digestive viscera, and thus individuals who are plump (endomorphs) are tied to the digestive system. The mesodermal layer of the embryo develops into muscle; therefore, the tough, muscular body, well-equipped for strenuous activity, is labeled the mesomorph. The ectodermal layer is developmentally responsible for the nervous system. The ectomorph has a large brain and central nervous system compared to the rest of his or her body, which is usually tall and thin.

We should emphasize that Sheldon avoided making sharp distinctions between body types or somatotypes. People were scored on the basis of three seven-point scales corresponding to the three somatotypes, with a 7 indicating that they were exclusively that body type. This was a rare occurrence, however. For example, a "pure" mesomorph would have a somatotype of 1-7-1, with the 1s denoting that he or she was devoid of that particular body build. A 3-2-5 person would be primarily ectomorphic (5), but have some features of endomorphs (3) and mesomorphs (2). The average body build would be assigned a 4-4-4 index, indicating constitutional balance.

Sheldon found a strong correlation between personality (or temperament) and somatotype—in other words, he linked certain personality types with certain body types. One personality loves comfort, food, affection, and people. This type is usually even tempered and easy to get along with. Sheldon labeled this disposition *viscertonia* and, as you might have guessed, he connected it closely to the basic endomorph. A second personality type ordinarily needs vigorous physical activity, risk taking, and adventure. A person with this temperament, according to Sheldon, is more likely to be indifferent to pain and aggressive, callous, even ruthless in relationships with others. This cluster of personality traits was called *somatotonia* and was linked with the mesomorph. *Cerebrotonia* labels the person who is inhibited,

	PHYSIQUE	TEMPERAMENT

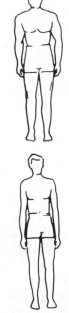

7-1-1   Endomorphic   Viscerotonic
             (soft and round)   (sociable, loves to eat)

1-1-7   Ectomorphic   Cerebrotonic
             (fragile and thin)   (restrained, introverted)

1-7-1   Mesomorphic   Somatotonic
             (muscular and   (adventurous,
             triangular)   competitive)

4-4-4   Balanced   Some mixture

FIGURE 2-1 Sheldon's somatotypes in relation to physique and temperament.

reserved, self-conscious, and afraid of people; it correlates highly with the ectomorphic body build.

Sheldon began to test his theory in 1939 by exploring the relationship between delinquency and physique. His first study involved nearly 400 boys in a residential rehabilitation home. Biographical sketches—family background, medical history, mental and educational performance, and delinquent behavior—were collected for each boy, and they were all assigned somatotype ratings. Sheldon studied his delinquents for eight years, comparing them to a group of male college students. He found that the college men generally clustered around the "average" somatotype of 4-4-4. Delinquents, on the other hand, tended to be heavily mesomorphic, but there were also signs of endomorphy. Ectomorphs were rare in the delinquent group. On the basis of his study, Sheldon concluded that there were definite somatotypic and temperamental differences between delinquent and nondelinquent males.

Subsequent investigations (primarily on males) provided additional, although not very strong, support for Sheldon's findings. Glueck and Glueck (1950, 1956) found that mesomorphs were proportionately over-represented in the delinquent population (60 percent, with 30 percent endomorphs). In general, their findings established that delinquent boys were larger and stronger than nondelinquent boys. In another study, Cortes and Gatti (1972) reported that delinquent subjects (100 boys adjudicated delinquent by the courts) were much more mesomorphic than nondelinquents (100 male high school seniors). Fifty-seven percent of their delinquent group could be easily classified as mesomorphic compared to 19 percent of the nondelinquents. These percentages roughly correspond to those cited by Glueck and Glueck (1950) in their study of 500 youths. Hartl, Monnelly and Elderkin (1982) claim that, in their 30 year follow up of Sheldon's original group, the relationship between mesomorphs and antisocial behavior still holds.

Later, more sophisticated research reached different results. McCandless, Persons, and Roberts (1972) found physique unrelated to either self-reported delinquency or the seriousness of the criminal offenses. Wadsworth (1979), using data from the British National Survey, reported that delinquents, especially those who committed serious offenses, were generally *smaller* in stature and appeared to reach puberty later than their nondelinquent peers. While no somatotyping was done, the results suggest that the delinquents were not mesomorphs, since mesomorphs reportedly reach puberty before the other body types (Rutter & Giller, 1984). Finally, in their longitudinal study of working-class boys in London, West and Farrington (1973) reported little association between delinquency and either height-weight ratios or physical strength.

Wilson and Herrnstein (1985, p. 90) in their influential but controversial book, *Crime and Human Nature*, concluded that the evidence on the relationship between physique and crime "leaves no doubt that constitutional traits correlate with criminal behavior." Some of the evidence does *suggest* a relationship between body build and crime, but there is also a significant amount of evidence that indicates that there may be no relationship. Thus, the research is equivocal and far from conclusive. While it may make logical sense to argue that the mesomorph's physique, because it is so muscular and strong, is well suited for involvement in aggressive or antisocial acts, much more sophisticated and well-executed research needs to be conducted before we can get a better understanding of the physique-crime connection.

Attractiveness

Some researchers have studied physical features, such as facial characteristics, and related them to body build, criminal activity, or treatment by the criminal justice system. Staffieri (1967) found that body build significantly influenced whether one was judged attractive, with mesomorphs generally receiving the highest ratings. Cavior and Howard (1973), concentrating on facial features, found that both black and white delinquents were rated significantly less attractive than nondelinquents. Moreover, correctional personnel often comment that inmates, as a group, have "uglier" faces than the general population. Perhaps facial unattractiveness plays a role in the development of crime and/or increases the probability of being adjudicated delinquent by the courts. Research has found that attractive children are favored by adults and other children. In fact, attractive children are less negatively evaluated than less attractive children, even when they have committed identical antisocial acts (Dion, 1972; Dion, Berscheid, & Walster, 1972). In one study using a simulated jury, good-looking criminals were treated more gently and were considered less dangerous than a comparable group of unattractive criminals (Sigall & Ostrove, 1978).

The thesis that physical unattractiveness might have something to do with criminal behavior has sometimes been applied to rehabilitation. In the mid-1970s, corrective surgery was offered to inmates with facial deformities at Rikers Island, as part of a pilot project testing the value of plastic surgery as a rehabilitative measure (Kurtzberg et al., 1978). The surgery was to be performed just prior to prison release. After extensive medical and psychological screening, 425 inmates were divided into four groups. Depending on his group, the inmate would receive either surgery, counseling, both, or neither (the control group).

The results, though complex, showed some support for the benefits of a new image. The offenders who seemed to benefit most from the intervention were nonaddicts who received surgery; they were substantially less likely to engage in crime during a one-year follow-up period than a comparable group of offenders who received no surgery. Interestingly, the group which received counseling alone committed more detected crime during the follow-up period than even the group which had neither counseling nor surgery. Although the study's results are not clearcut, they do suggest that physical improvements also improve prisoner self-image and the likelihood of acceptance by others. Possibly, the individual with the improved appearance has less need to defend or prove his or her worth through crime or to react aggressively to slights or challenges. And, possibly, the slights and challenges are fewer in number.

Minor Physical Anomalies (MPAs)

In recent years, there has been renewed interest in the relationship between physical attributes and temperament. Specifically, some researchers have focused on minor physical anomalies—such as asymmetrical ears, soft and pliable ears, curved fifth fingers, ocular hypertelorism (widely spaced eyes), multiple hair whorls, webbed toes, furrowed tongue—and learning disabilities, hyperactivity, schizophrenia, aggressiveness, and clumsiness. These minor physical anomalies, or MPAs, seem to correlate (albeit weakly) with some temperamental and behavioral attributes in children. For example, high numbers of MPAs are found in active, aggressive, and impulsive preschool boys (Paulhus & Martin, 1986) and in boys demonstrating conduct disorders (Halverson & Victor, 1976). MPAs are generally not noticed either by people who have them or by others. They are discernible only to trained observers and do not significantly interfere with attractiveness. The occurrence of MPAs is hypothesized to be associated with teratogenic factors (factors that produce physical defects in the developing embryo) operating within the first trimester of pregnancy.

The assumption is that the same teratogenic factors which produce minor physical abnormalities also affect the central nervous system in a way that contributes to behavioral problems and developmental deviations. Presumably, hyperactivity, impulsiveness, restlessness, and inattentiveness are all potential reflections of central nervous system defects that go hand-in-hand with MPAs. While the hypothesis connecting MPAs with a propensity toward delinquent or criminal behavior is interesting, no research has been attempted to test the hypothesis directly. Moreover, Paulhus and Martin (1986) did *not* find the number of MPAs related to self-reported aggressiveness and impulsivity in either male or female college students. Clearly, much more research is needed before further conclusions can be advanced.

TWIN STUDIES

One way to determine the role of genetics in criminality is to compare the incidence and type of criminal convictions among identical and fraternal twins. Fraternal twins (also called dizygotic twins) develop from two different fertilized eggs and are no more genetically alike than ordinary siblings. Identical twins (monozygotic twins) develop from a single egg; they are always the same sex and share all the same genes. Theoretically, the twin method of research assumes that similar environments exert similar influences on each member of a twin set. Therefore, differences are presumably due to genetic factors.

Some investigators suggest that identical twins are so physically alike that they probably elicit similar social responses from their environment, more so than fraternal twins. In this sense, they are more likely to develop similar personalities. There may be merit to this viewpoint, but research does not yet support it. Rather, some research has found that identical twins reared apart are more alike in some personality attributes than are identicals reared in the same home environment (Shields, 1962; Canter, 1973). When reared together, identicals may make a conscious effort to accentuate their individual identities, whereas when reared apart they may have less need to be different.

Concordance, a key concept in twin study research, is the genetics term for the degree to which related pairs of subjects both show a particular behavior or condition. It is usually expressed in percentages. Assume that we want to determine the concordance of intelligence among twenty pairs of identical twins and twenty pairs of fraternals. If we find that ten pairs of the identical twins have approximately the same IQ score, but only five pairs of the fraternals obtain the same score, our concordance is 50 percent for identicals, 25 percent for fraternals. The concordance for identicals would be twice that of fraternals, suggesting that hereditary factors play an important role in intelligence. If, however, the two concordances were about the same, we would conclude that genetics is irrelevant, at least as represented in our sample and measured by our methods.

Numerous twin studies using this concordance method have strongly indicated that heredity is a powerful determinant of intelligence, schizophrenia, depressions, neurotic disorders, alcoholism, and criminal behavior (Claridge, 1973; Rosenthal, 1970, 1971; McClearn & DeFries, 1973; Hetherington & Parke, 1975). The first such study relative to criminality was reported by the Munich physician Johannes Lange (1929) in his book *Crime As Destiny* (Rosenthal, 1971; Christiansen, 1977a). The title reflects Lange's Lombrosian conviction that criminal conduct is a predetermined fate dictated by heredity. He found a criminality concordance of 77 percent for thirteen pairs of adult identical twins and only 12 percent for seventeen pairs of adult fraternal twins. Auguste Marcel Legras (1932) then found a 100 percent criminal concordance for five pairs of identicals. Note that both of these studies used small samples. Subsequent studies, using more sophisticated designs and methods of twin identification and sampling, continued to find a substantially higher criminal concordance for identical twins when compared to fraternals. The levels were not as high as those reported by either Lange or Legras, however. Table 2-1 summarizes rele-

TABLE 2-1   Summary of Twin-Criminality Studies Showing Pairs and Concordance Rates

RESEARCHER	IDENTICAL TWINS			FRATERNAL TWINS		
	NO. OF PAIRS	PAIRS CONCOR- DANT	PERCENT	NO. OF PAIRS	PAIRS CONCOR- DANT	PERCENT
Lange (1929)	13	10	77	17	2	12
Legras (1932)	4	4	100	5	0	0
Rosanoff (1934)	37	25	68	60	6	10
Kranz (1936)	31	20	65	43	20	53
Stumpfl (1936)	18	11	61	19	7	37
Borgstrom (1939)	4	3	75	5	2	40
Rosanoff et al. (1941)	45	35	78	27	6	18
Yoshimasu (1961)	28	17	61	18	2	11
Yoshimasu (1965)	28	14	50	26	0	0
Hayashi (1967)	15	11	73	5	3	60
Dalgaard & Kringlen (1976)	31	8	26	54	8	15
Christiansen (1977b)						
Males	71	25	35	120	15	13
Females	14	2	21	27	2	8
Totals	339	185	55	426	73	17

vant investigations of criminal concordance. Although these tabulated investigations differed in method and definitions of criminality, the combined concordance levels demonstrate that, where criminal behavior is concerned, identical twins seem better matched than fraternal twins.

Hans Eysenck reviewed other twin studies, found similar concordances, and concluded: "Thus concordance is found over four times as frequently in identicals as in fraternals, a finding which seems to put beyond any doubt that heredity plays an extremely important part in the genesis of criminal behaviour" (Eysenck, 1973, p. 167). Rosenthal, however, injects a word of caution, stressing the many pitfalls of the concordance twin method and the ramifications of using different legal definitions of criminality. Nevertheless, he allows, ". . . it is clearly not possible to rule out the potential fact that genetic factors may indeed be the primary source of the higher concordance rate in MZ (identical) as compared to DZ (fraternal) twins" (Rosenthal, 1975, p. 10).

Eysenck further complicates the issue by suggesting that twin studies may actually have *deflated* the true concordance rate, since it is likely that identical twins were often confused with fraternal twins, especially in the earlier studies. If the twins are of the same sex, it is difficult to distinguish identicals from fraternals from appearance alone. Today, blood type, fingerprints (which are highly similar but not identical), and various genetically determined serum proteins allow differentiation. Since these methods were not available to earlier investigators, Eysenck contends that mixups may have confounded the results. However, the concordance rates may just as easily have been inflated as deflated.

As Table 2-1 reveals, twin studies have not *invariably* found high criminal concordance rates in favor of identical twins. One study, by Dalgaard and Kringlen (1976), found no significant difference at all between identicals and fraternals. The Dalgaard-Kringlen sample included all the registered male twins born in Norway between 1921 and 1930. However, 32 percent of the sample were deleted from the analysis for various reasons, which might have affected the results. Also, the label *criminal* was applied to traffic violations, military offenses, and treason during World War II as well as to all actions against the penal code. This was a broader definition than that used in most twin studies. The late Karl O. Christiansen, who devoted much of his research work to twin studies, was at a loss to explain the lack of significant differences reported by Dalgaard and Kringlen. He advocated an additional study to determine whether "some special conditions exist in Norway that would dampen the expression of genetic factors . . . " (Christiansen, 1977a, p. 82).

Overall, despite procedural and definitional problems and except for the Dalgaard-Kringlen data, the studies examining concordance rates among twins have consistently indicated higher concordance for identicals. This clearly *suggests* that it might be wise to consider heredity a significant component in criminality. This is not to say, however, that it is the sole or even the most important causal factor of criminality.

ADOPTION STUDIES

Another method used to identify crucial variables in the interaction between heredity and environment is the adoption study, which helps identify environments most conducive to criminality. There have been exceedingly few such investigations, however, and those few have been fraught with methodological problems.

One of the first adoption studies was carried out in Denmark by Schulsinger (1972), who explored the incidence of psychopathy in the biological relatives of adopted adults. Schulsinger compared fifty-seven adopted adults whom he diagnosed psychopathic to a control group of fifty-seven nonpsychopathic adopted adults. The two groups were matched for sex, age, social class, and age of transfer to the adopting family. The study's direct implications for criminal behavior are questionable, because Schulsinger defined psychopathy by his own loose criteria. Individuals who were "impulse ridden" and who exhibited "acting-out behavior" qualified.

As we will see in chapter three, these descriptions do not necessarily connote either psychopathy or criminality.

Schulsinger found that 3.9 percent of the biological relatives of psychopathic adoptees could also be classified as psychopathic, whereas only 1.4 percent of the control group's biological relatives could. The results just failed to reach statistical significance, indicating that we should be very cautious about accepting their implications. It is interesting, though, that psychopathy—even given its loose definition—was about two and a half times greater in the family backgrounds of acting-out adoptees.

Crowe (1974) conducted a better-designed study, a follow-up of fifty-two persons relinquished for early adoption by female offenders. Ninety percent of the biological mothers were felons at the time of the adoptive placement, the most common offenses being forgery and passing bad checks. Twenty-five of the adoptees were female, and all were white. Another fifty-two adoptees with no evidence of criminal family background were selected as a control group and matched for sex, race, and age at the time of adoption.

For the follow-up phase of the study, Crowe selected thirty-seven index and thirty-seven control subjects who had by then reached age eighteen. (*Index* subjects in research are those subjects who are of major concern.) Seven of the index adoptees had arrest records, as adults, all seven had at least one conviction, four had multiple arrests, two had multiple convictions, and three were felons. Of the thirty-seven matching controls, two had adult arrest records, and only one of these had been convicted. Each subject's personality was diagnosed by three clinicians based on test results and data gathered in an interview; no family background was included. The clinicians made their diagnoses independently of one another and without knowing the subject's group. Six of the adoptees born of female offenders were labeled "antisocial personality"; one control group subject was labeled "probable antisocial personality."

Crowe found a positive correlation between the tendency of the index group to be antisocial and two other variables: the child's age at the time of adoptive placement, and the length of time the child had spent in temporary care (orphanages and foster homes) prior to that placement. The older the child of an offender upon adoptive placement and the longer the temporary placement, the more likely would the child grow up antisocial. The control group members were not affected by these conditions. This suggests either that the two adoptee groups responded differently to similar environmental conditions or that the adoption agency placed the offspring of female offenders in less desirable homes—and there was no indication that this selective placement had occurred.

Hutchings and Mednick (1975) also conducted a study examining the effects of genetics and environment. They reasoned that if there is a genetic basis for criminality, then there should be a significant relationship be tween the criminal tendencies of biological parents and those of their children who were adopted by someone else. In 1971, using Copenhagen adoption files, Hutchings and Mednick identified 1,145 male adoptees, who by then were thirty to forty-four years old. They were matched with an equal number of nonadoptee controls on sex, age, occupational status of fathers, and residence. The researchers learned that 185 adoptees (16.2 percent) had criminal records, compared to 105 nonadoptees (8.9 percent). A check on the biological fathers of the adoptees revealed that they were nearly three times more likely to be involved in criminal activity than were either the adoptees' adoptive fathers or the fathers of the nonadopted controls. Furthermore, there was a significant relationship between the criminality of the sons and that of the fathers. Where the biological father had a criminal record and the adoptive father had none, a significant number of adoptees still became criminal (22 percent); but where the biological father had no record and the adoptive father had a criminal record, the number of adoptees who pursued criminal activities was lower (11.5 percent). If both the biological and adoptive fathers were criminal, the chances were much greater that the adoptee would also be criminal than if only one man was criminal. Hutchings and Mednick concluded that genetic factors continue to exert strong influences in the tendency toward criminality, even though environmental factors also play important roles.

One serious limitation to the Hutchings-Mednick data, as well as to any adoption study, is that agencies often try to match the adopted child with the adoptive family on the basis of the child's biological and socioeconomic background. The Crowe study involving the children of offenders found no evidence of this, but the Danish agency used in the Hutchings-Mednick investigation confirmed that this was done. To their credit, the researchers not only recognized this problem, but also admonished that extrapolations to American society should be made cautiously, since Danish society is more homogeneous in cultural values and race.

The most comprehensive adoption study to date was conducted by Mednick, Gabrielli, and Hutchings (1984, 1987). These researchers compared the court convictions of 14,427 adoptees (adopted between the years 1927 and 1947) in a small European country with conviction records of their biological and adoptive parents. The study showed a significant relationship between the conviction history of the adoptees (for both males and females) and their biological parents. Specifically, if either biological parent had been convicted of a crime, the risk of criminality in the adoptee (the biological child) increased significantly. This relationship was especially strong for male adoptees who were chronic or persistent offenders. As we might expect, chronic offenders accounted for a disproportionate share of the total offending for the entire cohort. Interestingly, there was no evidence that the type of crime committed by the biological parent had any relation to the type of crime committed by the biological child. Both the

biological parent and biological child tended to engage in crime but selected different kinds of crime. There was also no indication that the
adopted children knew about the criminality of their biological parents.
The researchers concluded that some factor transmitted by criminal parents increased the probability that their children would engage in criminal
behavior. Elsewhere, Gabrielli and Mednick (1983, p. 63) commented, "It is
reasonable . . . to conclude that some people inherit biological characteristics which permit them to be antisocial more readily than others."

In summary, twin and adoption studies suggest that genetic components may contribute significantly to a *tendency* to become criminal, but they
have also found that environment is highly important (see Ellis, 1982, for a
review of this interaction). The available data so far indicate that some
people may be born with a biological predisposition to behavior that runs
counter to social values and norms, and that environmental factors may
either inhibit or stimulate it. To help pinpoint this possible predisposition,
we turn now to the theory and research of the British psychologist Hans J.
Eysenck.

EYSENCK'S THEORY OF PERSONALITY AND CRIME

Hans J. Eysenck (Eysenck & Gudjonsson, 1989) is convinced that sociological theory has little to offer toward the understanding and treatment of
crime. "In many ways we disagree with various sociological theories that
have become so popular since World War II but which, we believe, are
fundamentally erroneous and counter to fact" (Eysenck & Gudjonsson,
1989, p. 1). Instead, Eysenck argues that psychological knowledge provides
the key answers and strategies for the prevention of criminal behavior. "We
believe that psychology is a fundamental discipline which underlies any
advances we may make in the prevention of crime, and the treatment of
criminals" (Eysenck & Gudjonsson, 1989, p. ix). Not only will psychology
lead the way toward the solution of crime, Eysenck tells us, but the neurological underpinnings of personality are one of the prime determinants
of antisocial and criminal behavior.

Eysenck (1977) proposes that criminal behavior is the result of an
interaction between certain environmental conditions and *inherited* features
of the nervous system. He believes that a comprehensive theory of criminality must allow for an examination of the neurological makeup and the
unique socialization history of each individual. Statements that crime is
caused by social conditions such as poverty, poor education, or unemployment are as inaccurate as hereditary and biological explanations. "Crime
cannot be understood in terms of heredity alone, but it can also not be
understood in terms of environment alone" (Eysenck, 1973, p. 171). Eysenck also suggests that different combinations of environmental, neu-

robiological, and personality factors give rise to different types of crime (Eysenck & Eysenck, 1970). This position implies that different person-alities are more susceptible to certain crimes than others, an issue we will return to shortly.

Unlike most contemporary theories of crime, Eysenck's theory places heavy emphasis on genetic predispositions toward criminal conduct, or at least toward antisocial behavior. It is important to note at the outset that he is not suggesting that individuals are *born* criminal, but rather that some people are born with nervous system characteristics that are significantly different from the general population and that affect their ability to con-form to social expectancies and rules. "It is not crime itself or criminality that is innate; it is certain peculiarities of the central and autonomic ner-vous system that react with the environment, with upbringing, and many other environment factors to increase the probability that a given person would act in a certain antisocial manner" (Eysenck & Gudjonsson, 1989, p. 7). Eysenck isolates features of the central and autonomic nervous systems to account for a substantial portion of the differences found in personality in general. The way each individual's nervous system functions may be as unique as his or her personality characteristics. Carrying this a step further, we could posit that some nervous systems are more likely to engage in criminal activity because of their reactivity, sensitivity, and excitability.

Based on a series of empirical studies and statistical analysis, Eysenck argues that there are four higher order factors of personality—one higher order factor for ability called "g" (general intelligence), and three higher order factors for temperament, called *extraversion, neuroticism,* and *psychot-icism.* Eysenck believes that the ability factor is an important factor in the cause of criminality, but is less important than the temperament factors. He writes, "we may conclude that intelligence is a factor in the causation of criminality but that its contribution is probably smaller than one might have thought at first" (Eysenck & Gudjonsson, 1989, p. 50).

Most of the research on crime and personality has focused on extra-version and neuroticism, which are essentially the core concepts of Ey-senckian theory. Eysenck did not identify psychoticism until he found a need to account for behaviors not fully explained by extraversion or neuro-ticism.

Eysenck visualizes each of the three temperament or personality fac-tors on a continuum, with the neuroticism and extraversion lines at right angles and intersecting. Psychoticism is on a separate continuum. Most people fall in the intermediate or midpoint area of each, and people rarely are at either extreme (see Figure 2-2; most people fall within the square). The extraversion dimension runs from the extreme pole extraversion to the extreme introversion, with the middle range called ambiversion. Thus, depending on where a person falls on this dimension, that person may be an extravert, introvert, or ambivert. The neuroticism continuum runs from

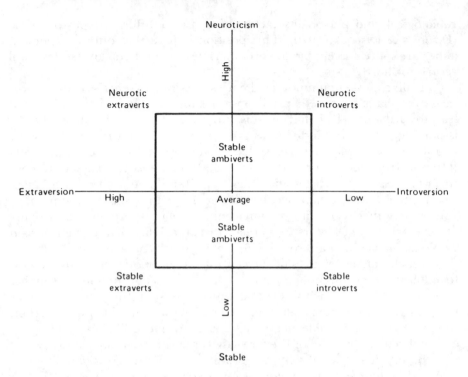

FIGURE 2-2 Illustration of Eysenck's personality dimensions for neuroticism and extraversion.

the polar ends of neuroticism to stability, with no middle label. Psychoticism runs from tough-mindedness (high psychoticism) to tender-mindedness (low psychoticism), also with no label for the middle majority. The extraversion dimension is believed to reflect basic functions of the central nervous system (CNS), which consists of the brain and spinal cord, while neuroticism represents functions of the peripheral nervous system (nerve pathways outside the central nervous system). As yet, neither Eysenck nor other researchers have postulated a nervous system mechanism for psychoticism.

Eysenck developed several self-report questionnaires to measure these personality variables, the best known being the British Maudsley Personality Inventory (MPI) and its American editions, the Eysenck Personality Inventory (EPI) and the Eysenck Personality Questionnaire (EPQ). The questionnaires have stimulated extensive research to explore both their validity and Eysenck's concept of personality. Overall, worldwide research has supported the general theory, but when it is applied to criminality, the support begins to crumble. We will review some of this research later in this chapter, after examining more closely the basic concepts behind each dimension.

Extraversion

Behavioral characteristics and incidence.   Usually, two out of every three people will score in the "average" range on the extraversion dimension, thus making them clinically uninteresting ambiverts. Roughly 16 percent of the population are extraverts and another 16 percent introverts.

According to Eysenck, the typical extravert is sociable, impulsive, optimistic, and has high needs for excitement and for a varied, changing environment. Extraverts tend to lose their temper quickly, become aggressive easily, and be unreliable. They like to have people around, they enjoy parties, and they are usually very talkative. The typical introvert, on the other hand, is reserved, quiet, and cautious. He or she keeps feelings under close control and generally tries to avoid excitement, change, and most social activities. Introverts tend to be reliable and unaggressive and to place great value on ethical standards (Eysenck & Rachman, 1965). Ambiverts exhibit some features of both extraversion and introversion, but not to the same degree or consistency as extraverts and introverts.

Think of the extraversion dimension as a continuum representing a progressive need for stimulation, which can be defined as the impact stimuli have on areas of the brain. The impact is analogous to the taste of food. Some people have a relatively consistent tendency to prefer spicy, hot foods that have more impact on their taste centers (Szechuan cuisine), while others more often choose bland foods (macaroni and cheese) because they do not desire the high taste impact. Some people prefer and actively seek out more stimulation or stimulus impact from other areas of their lives as well—they like rousing music, perpetual bustle, psychedelic drugs. Eysenck maintains that people at the extraversion end of the dimension *require* high levels of stimulation from their environment because of their biological makeup.

If you conceptualize the dimension this way, you may find that the popular term *extrovert* (note the spelling) takes on added meaning. Extroverts are sociable creatures who like to be around people and to be immersed in activity because of the stimulation this provides them. It is important to note, though, that our everyday usage of the nouns *extrovert* and *introvert* are *not* identical to Eysenck's polar classifications.

Because extraverts have higher needs for excitement and stimulation to break the daily boredom, they are also most likely to run counter to the law. They tend to be impulsive, fun-loving, thrill-seeking people who are willing to take chances and stick their necks out. They enjoy pranks and practical jokes and find challenge in opportunities to do the unconventional or even the antisocial. In addition, some features of the extraverted nervous system not only encourage stimulation seeking, but also inhibit the acquisition and internalization of society's rules, as we will see shortly.

Physiological bases of extraversion-introversion. Eysenck (1967) hypothesized that people differ along the extraversion-introversion axis because of genetic differences in certain mechanisms in their central nervous system, particularly the tiny but complex network of neurons located in the central part of the brain stem called the reticular activating system (RAS) (see Figure 2-3). The RAS, which we will discuss in detail in chapter three, is believed to act as a sentinel that awakens and keeps alert the portion of the brain called the cerebral cortex. All higher-level functions, like thinking, memory, and decision making, occur in the cerebral cortex (French, 1957). The RAS arouses the cerebral cortex and keeps it alert to incoming stimuli. Nerve pathways communicating information to the cerebral cortex branch off into collateral pathways travelling to the RAS. In effect, these collaterals "tell" the RAS to alert the brain to incoming information.

Eysenck postulates that both extraverts and introverts inherit an RAS that handles cortical arousal in a unique way, differently from the RAS of the general population. The extravert's RAS does not seem to *generate* cortical excitation or arousal effectively. In fact, it appears to reduce the impact of stimulation and the arousal properties of stimuli before they can reach the cortex. The introvert, on the other hand, apparently has inherited an RAS that *amplifies* stimulation input, keeping cortical arousal at relatively high levels. So we have the extravert, who is cortically under-

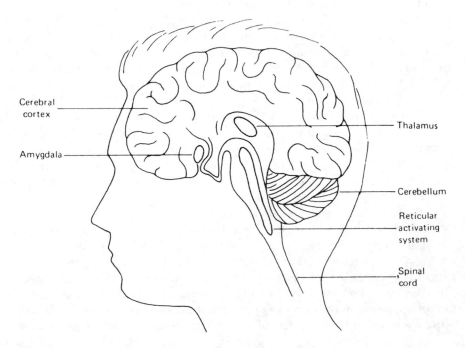

FIGURE 2-3 Location of the reticular activating system relative to other brain structures.

aroused, seeking additional stimulation to achieve an optimally aroused cortex, and the introvert, who is cortically overaroused, trying to avoid stimulation. The ambivert, who obtains an intermediate level of arousal, is generally content with moderate amounts of stimulation.

In chapter three we will also discuss the concept of optimal level of stimulation or cortical arousal. One motivation behind human behavior is the desire to achieve a just-right level of stimulation and cortical arousal. Too much stimulation becomes aversive and even painful, while too little results in boredom and eventual sleep. It is assumed that the extravert, because of the dampening effect of the RAS, needs higher levels of stimulation to maintain that just-right or optimal level of cortical arousal. The introvert, because of the amplifying effect of the RAS, desires relatively lower levels of stimulation. This explains the typical extravert's attraction to spicy foods, loud music, and vividly colored objects and the introvert's preference for bland foods, soft music, and cool or dark-colored objects.

The extravert's stimulation needs are well documented (see Eysenck, 1967, 1981). As mentioned previously, the greater tendency of extraverts to seek sensation is presumably more likely to put them in conflict with the law. Eysenck suggests that most people involved in criminal activity are cortically underaroused and have a strong drive to obtain stimulation or sensation from their environment. They are thus drawn to risk taking, joy riding, and illegal activities that have high stimulation value. Put quite simply, most criminals are extraverts.

Before leaving the section on extraversion, let's digress for a moment on the effects of alcohol on cortical arousal. Alcohol is a general central nervous system depressant. It lowers cortical arousal to the point where one may pass out or fall asleep. The extravert without alcohol is already "half in the bag," and with alcohol he or she is even less alert. For introverts, however, alcohol has the effect of lowering a normally high cortical arousal to a point where they become more extraverted, behaviorally and physiologically. Thus, the usually quiet, reserved person may become boisterous or perform a soft shoe routine on the coffee table after a few drinks. The drunk introvert now has an extraverted arousal level and seeks more stimulation.

Eysenck supposes that the active, aroused cortex is a better inhibitor of activity than the poorly aroused one. Therefore, high cortical arousal leads to inhibition, while low cortical arousal allows subcortical regions of the central nervous system to function without restraint. Alcohol lowers the alertness of the cortex, which presumably lessens its censorship over the primitive, subcortical regions of the nervous system. This facilitates inappropriate, antisocial behaviors usually held in check by the cortex. Thus, according to the Eysenckian perspective, under the influence of alcohol, introverts will do things they normally would not do. On the other hand, even relatively small quantities of alcohol influence the extravert, who already functions at a low level of cortical arousal, toward even more unin-hibited behavior. The correlation between alcohol and crime is a strong one and will be discussed in greater detail in chapter twelve.

By now, you should have a basic understanding of one of Eysenck's personality dimensions. We will now move on to consider the second di-mension, which is equally important.

Neuroticism

Incidence and behavioral characteristics.   Like extraversion, neuroticism is a significant variable in the relationship between personality and crime. Sometimes called emotionality, this dimension reflects an innate biological predisposition to react bodily to stressful events. Basically, neuroticism deals with the intensity of emotional reactions. It is believed to occur in the general population in the same frequencies as extraversion, with 16 per-cent of the population falling above and below one standard deviation from the mean.

A person high on the neuroticism scale reacts intensely and lastingly to stress. In fact, even under low-stress conditions, the person is likely to be moody, touchy, sensitive to slights, anxious, and to complain of various physical ailments like headaches, backaches, and digestive problems. He or she tends to overreact to stress and have difficulty returning to a normal, calm state. People high in emotionality also have a strong propensity to develop neurotic features such as phobias and obsessions. Their opposites, persons at the other ends of the continuum, display emotionally stable, calm, and even-tempered behavior. They tend to keep their wits about them under stress and intense excitement and to select appropriate reac-tions to emergencies. Researchers testing Eysenckian theory refer to high emotionality individuals as *neurotics* and their counteropposites as *stables*.

Physiological bases of neuroticism-stability.   Whereas the extraversion-in-troversion dimension is linked to the central nervous system, the neu-roticism-stability continuum relates to the autonomic nervous system, which can be divided into the sympathetic and parasympathetic nervous systems (see Figure 2-4). The *sympathetic system* activates the body for emergencies by increasing heart rate, respiration flow, blood flow, pupil dilation, and perspiration. The *parasympathetic system* counterbalances the sympathetic; it brings the body back to its normal arousal state. According to Eysenck, differences in emotionality are due to variances in the sen-sitivity of these subdivisions, which are both under the control of the so-called visceral brain or *limbic system*. In addition to a complicated array of neuronal circuitry, the limbic system includes the neurological structures known as the hippocampus, amygdala, cingulum, and hypothalamus. The hypothalamus appears to exert the greatest amount of control over the

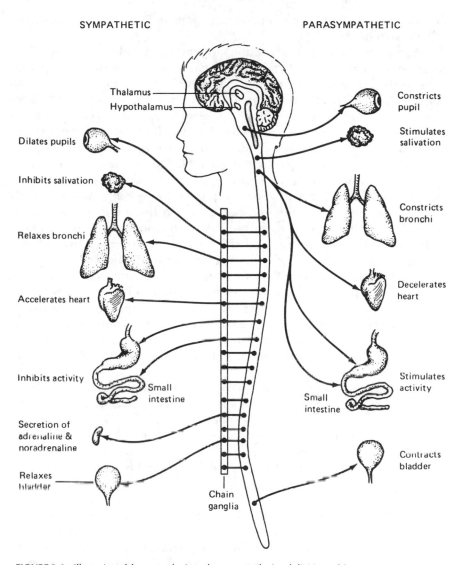

SYMPATHETIC   PARASYMPATHETIC

Thalamus
Hypothalamus

Constricts
pupil

Stimulates
salivation

Dilates pupils

Inhibits salivation

Constricts
bronchi

Relaxes bronchi

Accelerates heart

Decelerates
heart

Inhibits activity

Small
intestine

Small
intestine

Stimulates
activity

Secretion of
adrenaline &
noradrenaline

Relaxes
bladder

Chain
ganglia

Contracts
bladder

FIGURE 2-4   Illustration of the sympathetic and parasympathetic subdivisions of the autonomic nervous system.

autonomic nervous system and thus represents the central mechanism in emotionality.

Neurotics are believed to have unusually sensitive limbic systems, so they achieve emotionality quickly, and it lasts longer. (The term *neurotic* as used here should not be confused with the neurotic classification of mental disorders, which will be discussed in chapter six). Theoretically, it may be that their sympathetic system is activated quickly while their parasympathetic system is slow in counterbalancing this. Stables, low in emotionality, may possess an underactive sympathetic system and an overactive parasym-pathetic system.

Although autonomic activation appears to produce a generalized arousal state in everyone, there is good reason to believe that each person reacts to the stress in unique ways. Some of us tense the muscles in our neck, forehead, or back; others breathe more heavily; for others, the heart pumps faster. This tendency for response specificity may account for the various forms of neurotic behaviors displayed by humans reacting to stress. Some complain of headaches, others of digestive problems or backaches. (Obviously, we are not suggesting that all backache sufferers are neurotics.)

Eysenck assumes that the person high on emotionality is more likely to engage in criminal activity than the person low on that dimension. He bases this assumption on the consistent research finding that emotionality can serve as a drive, pushing an individual to resort to habitual ways of behaving. Under high emotionality (high drive) a person is more vulnera-ble to his or her habits—good or bad. Thus, if the individual has acquired antisocial habits, he or she will be more driven to commit them under high drive than low drive conditions. Neuroticism, therefore, encourages what-ever mindless or habitual behaviors the person has acquired. Furthermore, because habits are usually not as well ingrained in the young as they are in the old, we would expect neuroticism to be an important factor with respect to adult criminals, less so with adolescents, and least so with young children (Eysenck, 1983).

The two dimensions we have looked at thus far are usually combined in classifying an individual's personality. That is, based on Eysenck's per-sonality inventories, a person will be a neurotic introvert, a stable extravert, a neurotic ambivert, and so forth. If we accept Eysenck's views up to this point, we should agree that the neurotic extravert is the most likely of the possible personality types to be involved in criminal behavior.

Psychoticism

No physiological mechanism has yet been suggested to explain the characteristics of psychoticism, Eysenck's most recently formulated dimen-sion. However, psychoticism seems to be highly similar to primary psycho-pathy, which we will discuss in chapter three. Behaviorally, psychoticism is characterized by cold cruelty, social insensitivity, unemotionality, disregard for danger, troublesome behavior, dislike of others, and an attraction to the unusual. "Psychotics" are hostile toward others and enjoy duping or ridicul-ing them. It is important here that we distinguish between Eysenck's psy-chotics and persons who are psychotic in the clinical sense of being out of touch with reality. Although this latter label is losing favor among clini-cians, it appears frequently enough in literature to warrant making the distinction. Psychosis as a classification of mental disorder and abnormality will be dealt with in chapter six.

Eysenck's psychoticism dimension has not received the research attention that extraversion and neuroticism have. However, he hypothesizes that, like extraversion and neuroticism, psychoticism will prove to be a striking characteristic of the criminal population. He suggests that psychoticism will be especially prominent in hard-core, habitual offenders convicted of crimes of violence (Eysenck, 1983). Furthermore, unlike neuroticism, it apparently is important at all stages of development, from childhood through adolescence to adulthood.

Thus far, we have only defined Eysenck's dimensions and, in the case of neuroticism and extraversion, we have isolated the physiological mechanisms that control them. None of this explains, however, why neurotics, extraverts, and psychotics are more likely to be criminal. The reason has to do with some very basic psychological principles to which we now turn our attention.

Crime and Conditionability

A basic premise of this text is that criminal behavior is learned. Traditionally, psychologists have delineated three major types of learning: classical or Pavlovian conditioning, instrumental or operant learning, and social learning. It is important now to examine these processes more carefully if we are to approach an understanding of why some people engage in crime.

The student with a background in introductory psychology will recall Ivan Pavlov's famous experiments with dogs who learned to salivate at the sound of a bell. Pavlov discovered that pairing a neutral stimulus (in this case a bell) with a significant stimulus (for example, food) would result in the dogs' eventually learning to associate the sound of the bell with the food. How do we know the dogs learned to make that association? Because they salivated at the mere sound of the bell, a response they usually reserved for food. The process of learning to respond to a formerly neutral stimulus (bell) which has been paired with another stimulus that already elicits a response (salivation) is basically *classical* or *Pavlovian* conditioning. In classical conditioning, animals (or persons) have no control over the situation, even over what happens to themselves. The animal is "forced" to take the consequences. The bell will ring and food will appear shortly afterward, regardless of what the animal does. In anticipation, and without any effort on its part, the animal salivates. This learning occurs not because of any reward or gain, but merely because of the *association* between the bell and the food.

In *instrumental learning*, the process is quite different. The learner must do something to the environment in order to obtain a reward or, in some cases, to avoid punishment. Instrumental learning is based on learning the consequences of behaving a certain way: If you do something, there is some probability that a certain rewarding event (or at least an avoidance of punishment) will occur. A child may learn, for example, that one parent will give her a piece of candy to quell a temper tantrum; the other parent will not yield. The child will eventually learn to use temper tantrums when Dad's around, but not to use them in front of Mom (or vice versa).

One important aspect of instrumental learning should be stressed: There must be a goal driving the animal or person to operate on the environment. That is, the individual must have a purpose or expectation for his or her behavior, must expect a reward for the response. A reward or reinforcement is the event that increases the likelihood of a response. Classical conditioning, by contrast, results from an association between stimuli and takes place without reward.

Social learning is more complex than either classical conditioning or instrumental learning, because it involves learning from watching others and organizing social experiences in the brain. Since Eysenck did not deal directly with social learning principles, we will reserve this topic for chapter four.

Eysenck (1977) turns the question of criminal behavior around from the usual, "Why do people become criminal?" to, "Why don't more people engage in criminal behavior?" To answer this with the adage, "Crime doesn't pay" is nonsense, since there is evidence that for much of the criminal population, crime *does* pay. After all, one of the chief motivators of behavior may be the desire to gain reward and pleasure (referred to as *hedonism*). "It would seem . . . that a person may, with a fair degree of safety, indulge in a career of crime without having to fear the consequences very much" (Eysenck, 1964, p. 102). According to Eysenck, those detected, convicted, and incarcerated often represent that portion of the criminal population who are of lower intelligence, poorly taught, unable to afford an influential attorney, or simply unlucky. So, if instrumental learning is a major factor, there should be substantially more crime, because people would be more often than not rewarded for operating criminally on their environment. Moreover, when punishment does occur, it is so long in coming that it cannot reasonably be considered a deterrent. Eysenck suggests, in fact, that delayed and sometimes arbitrary punishment may actually encourage criminal activity.

To explain why more people do not become criminal, Eysenck contends that classical conditioning has a stronger effect on most people than instrumental learning. That is, most people behave themselves because they have been classically conditioned during childhood about the rules of society. That guiding light, superego, conscience, or whatever it is that makes us feel uncomfortable before, during, and after a socially and morally disapproved act is, according to Eysenck, a *conditioned reflex*. In a traditional family environment, the children are verbally reprimanded or physically punished for behavior that is against the social mores. Immediately after engaging in a socially or morally frowned-upon act, say punching a friend, a child finds that punishment quickly follows.

Let's return to Pavlov's dog experiments for a moment and substitute the food with painful shock. Immediately following the sound of the bell, the dog receives a severe electrical shock (punishment) through the grids in the floor of the cage. After a number of trials (bell followed by shock) the dog, rather than salivating at the bell, begins to shake in fear. The animal has been classically conditioned to fear the sound of the bell, even when shock no longer follows it. The dog now *associates* shock with the bell rather than food.

Eysenck asserts that basically the same sequence occurs in child-hood—inappropriate behavior followed by reprimand. For example, child punches, mother reprimands. Following a few repetitions of this sequence, the thought of punching stimulates fear of the consequences. In essence, "by punishing antisocial behavior numerous times, parents, teachers, and others concerned with the upbringing of the child, including his or her peers, perform the role of the Pavlovian experimenter" (Eysenck, 1983, p. 60). The child associates punching with punishment, and this bonding between the behavior and the aversive consequences should deter him or her from performing the act. Moreover, the closer the individual comes to performing the act, the stronger the association (fear) becomes.

Most people, Eysenck believes, do not participate in criminal activity (he prefers the term *antisocial behavior*) because after a series of trials they have made strong connections between deviant behavior and aversive con-sequences. On the other hand, those persons who have not made adequate connections, either because of poor conditionability (e.g., extraverts) or because the opportunity to do so was not presented (socialization), are more likely to display deviant or criminal behavior. According to Eysenck, these people do not anticipate aversive events strongly enough to be de-terred; the association has not been sufficiently developed.

Pavlov observed that dogs differ widely in their conditionability to the sound of a bell and theorized that these differences come from properties of their nervous systems. Eysenck also makes this observation, commenting that "German Shepherds are very law abiding: they are easily conditioned and are well known to animal fanciers and shepherds for this property. Basenjis, however, are natural psychopaths, difficult or almost impossible to condition, disobedient and antisocial" (Eysenck, 1983, p. 61). Eysenck makes the same observation concerning humans: Extraverts condition less readily than introverts due to biological differences in their nervous sys-tems. Introverts condition better and therefore are less likely to engage in behavior contrary to society's laws and mores.

The principles of conditioning have been firmly established in the field of psychology as a valid explanation for many forms of behavior. The conditioning process appears to be a powerful force in the socialization of children, particularly in the suppressing of undesirable behaviors. There is every reason to believe that it may be a critical process in determining who becomes involved in deviant or criminal behavior. However, there is also evidence that conditioning can serve as an *instigator* of such behavior. As we will see in later chapters, the association between *pleasurable* events and specific behavior is also an extremely powerful motivator of criminal activity.

According to Eysenck, the conditioned conscience has two effects on behavior: It may prevent us from indulging in forbidden activities, or it may make us feel guilty after we commit them. The conditioned conscience inhibits us from engaging in antisocial activities by its association with prior adverse consequences. In addition, once we have committed the act we tend to feel uncomfortable about our transgressions. Eysenck (1983) supposes the difference rests in the timing of the aversive consequences. Reprimanding a child before or during an act would produce different effects than reprimanding a child after the act. The former situation would result in feelings of discomfort before the act (or while committing it); whereas the latter would produce discomfort (guilt) after the act.

What part does neuroticism or emotionality play? As noted earlier, Eysenck predicts that neuroticism functions as a drive strongly encouraging the performance of behavior previously acquired during childhood. That is, neuroticism amplifies existing habits in a person's repertoire of responses. If a neurotic extravert has not been properly conditioned to avoid stealing and has engaged in frequent, successful stealing in the past, neuroticism will function as a strong force or drive toward the old habit— stealing. In other words,

> behavior (inappropriate or appropriate) = prior conditioning or learned habits × (intensified by) emotionality.

According to Eysenck (1983, p. 65),

> The general growth in permissiveness in homes, schools, and courts has led to a significant reduction in the number of conditioning contingencies to which children are exposed. It would follow as a direct consequence that they would grow up with a much weaker conscience, and consequently that many more children would be led to engage in criminal and antisocial activities.

In essence, Eysenck is asserting that increases in crime may be traced directly to conditions within the home or schools that are not conducive to the development of a conditioned conscience toward avoiding antisocial conduct.

The Evidence for Eysenck's Theory

Now that we have scrutinized Eysenck's theory of criminality, the relevant question becomes, "Can we find research to support it?" Eysenck's theory of criminality predicts that criminals, as a group, will demonstrate lower levels of cortical arousal (extraversion), higher levels of autonomic (sympathetic) arousal (neuroticism), and be more tough minded (psychoticism). In short, he postulates that criminals will score high on the E, N, and P scales of the Eysenck Personality Questionnaire (EPQ), and that these dimensions are more than merely correlated with crime; they are *causally* related to it.

In some cases the research supports Eysenck's hypothesis, but many studies also refute the hypothesis. Although some research seems to damage the theory, these results do not necessarily mean that Eysenck is wrong. Research findings that fail to support parts of a theory suggest that the theory might be modified to account for the new data, provided the experiments were carefully conducted. The theory as a whole may still be promising and useful.

Passingham (1972) reviewed all literature on Eysenck's theory prior to 1972 and found flaws in the basic experimental design of most of the experiments. He noted that few of the studies used adequate controls to compare criminal and noncriminal populations. A control group, of course, should be matched as closely as possible to the experimental group, with all relevant variables —e.g., socioeconomic class, economic and cultural background, and intelligence—the same. Without an adequate control group, meaningful comparisons and valid conclusions are impossible. For example, suppose we designed a study to determine whether the personalities of criminals are significantly different from those of noncriminals, and suppose we used college students as a control group. If we found a significant difference, we could only conclude that the criminals differ from college students. But a college sample very probably differs from a criminal sample on a number of significant variables, such as socioeconomic class. Since college students are generally middle class or higher, and since criminals studied in the research usually are not, the results might reflect a difference between social classes, not necessarily between criminal and noncriminal personalities. The college group, therefore, is not an adequate control group.

Passingham also found that most researchers explaining Eysenck's theory did not delineate subgroups of offenders. They merely selected a heterogeneous sample of prisoners, administered questionnaires, and made comparisons and conclusions based on responses from a control group, often poorly selected. Prisoners are prisoners for a constellation of reasons and offenses. Eysenck recognized this when he commented (1971, p. 289) that "not all crimes are likely to be equally highly correlated with extraversion, and some types of criminals, such as the recidivist 'old lag,' lacking entirely in the social skills needed to make a success of living outside an institution, may in fact show introverted tendencies." In fact, many murderers and sex offenders do show strong introverted patterns. It is imperative, therefore, that researchers study categories of offenders to determine whether certain personalities are linked to certain offenses. A recent review by Farrington, Biron, and LeBlanc (1982) indicates that some of the aforementioned problems have been corrected, but many still remain.

In general, Eysenck's prediction that the criminal and antisocial populations should score significantly higher on the extraversion scale has *not* been consistently supported (Passingham, 1972; Allsopp, 1976; Feldman, 1977; Farrington, Biron, & LeBlanc, 1982). The results are especially inconsistent for adult male offenders and for delinquents of both sexes. While some studies (e.g., Price, 1968; Buikhuisen & Hemmel, 1972) report high extraversion scores for these two groups, other investigations cite evidence that they score *lower* than the general population (e.g., Hoghugi & Forrest, 1970; Cochrane, 1974). Some researchers found no difference between prisoners and delinquents compared to control groups (e.g., Little, 1963; Burgess, 1972). Other studies found significantly higher E scores (extraversion) for *violent* offenders compared to other types of offenders (Gossop & Kristjansson, 1977). Studies separating the extraversion characteristics that reflect impulsiveness from those that reflect sociability found that adult male prisoners score higher on impulsiveness than do male noncriminals, but score lower than noncriminals on sociability (S. B. G. Eysenck & H. J. Eysenck, 1970, 1971). This may reflect the irrelevance of the sociability questions for incarcerated prisoners, since sociability tendencies may be dampened in a correctional institution.

More recently, Berman and Paisey (1984) examined the relationship between antisocial behavior and personality in convicted American juvenile males. Subjects were divided into two groups: thirty juvenile males convicted of assault or confrontation with a victim—called the assaultive group—and thirty juvenile males convicted of offenses involving property without confrontation with a victim—called the nonassaultive group. These male juveniles were being held in the Dade County Juvenile Detention Center (Miami, Florida) awaiting sentencing. All were English-speaking whites. The assaultive group, compared to the nonassaultive group, scored significantly higher on all three of the Eysenckian personality dimensions, P, E and N, particularly on P.

In Spain, Silva, Martorell, and Clemente (1986) compared the Junior EPQ scores of forty-two delinquent males confined in a reformatory to 102 nondelinquent males. They found that P and N scores were significantly higher in the delinquent group. However, contrary to what Eysenck predicted, E scores were significantly higher in the nondelinquent group. In London, Lane (1987) compared "60 pupils with convictions" with "60 pupils without convictions." The criminal group scored substantially higher on the P scale, whereas the noncriminal group scored higher on the N scale. There were no differences between the groups on the E scale. Lane asserted somewhat discouragingly, "Extraversion . . . for so long the central feature of the theory on conduct disorder and criminality, fails to hold up consistently" (p. 805). Moreover, neuroticism scores were consistently in the opposite direction that Eysenck predicted, with the noncriminal group scoring higher than the criminal group. Psychoticism scores were not significant, neither higher nor lower for either group. Lane concludes, "A way of resolving these variations may be to take the argument outside the narrower conditioning model and place it within a broader multifactorial and interactive concept which links individual differences with behavioural and sociological analyses" (p. 806).

The aforementioned studies used *official* data, comparing EPQ scores of convicted delinquents with nondelinquents, or the scores of one group of convicted delinquents with another group. Some studies have not used officially recognized offenders but have tapped the incidence of offending in the general population through self-report (SR) questionnaires. The most popular SR scale in Great Britain is the Antisocial Behavior Scale (ABS), orginally developed by Gibson (1967) and later revised by Allsopp and Feldman (1976). However, research using the ABS has not been supportive of Eysenck's theory of criminality, either. Jamison (1980), using 1,282 secondary school children (ages thirteen to sixteen) in and around London, found a robust correlation between self-reported antisocial conduct and the P scale but a negligible or weak relationship with N and E, respectively. Powell and Stewart (1983), also using British subjects from the secondary and junior schools, found that self-reported antisocial behavior was strongly related to scores on the P scale, weakly to the E scale, and negligibly to the N scale. Similar results have been reported by Rushton and Chrisjohn (1981) on Canadian college students.

The research results examining the relationship between neuroticism and criminal or antisocial conduct are clear: It is not supported. Moreover, the relationship between extraversion and antisocial conduct is only weakly supported, but the relationship between psychoticism and crime appears to be moderately supported. The failure of E-scale findings to support Eysenck's hypothesis strongly may reflect a weakness in his argument that most criminals are poor conditioners. While many may have "faulty consciences," the poor conditioning perspective seems too limited. It might be more accurate to suggest that some criminals have offended because of poor conditionability, others because they perceived antisocial behavior as one of the few avenues available to them for gaining something, and still others for a combination of both reasons or other reasons. Most inmates are not in prison because of a failure to associate social transgressions with feelings of guilt and anxiety. Rather, they are incarcerated for a variety of offenses, prompted by a variety of motives, and associated with a variety of social situations. Because the E scale, which reflects conditionability, is not sensitive enough to account for this, more prisoner subgroup research is needed.

Bartol and Holanchock (1979) administered the Eysenck Personality

Questionnaire to 398 inmates at a maximum security prison in New York state. Sixty-two percent were black, 30 percent Hispanic, and about 7 percent white. The sample was divided into six offender groups according to conviction history: homicide, aggravated assault and attempted murder, rape and sexual assault, robbery, burglary, and drug offenses. When the inmate had committed offenses in more than one category, he was classified according to the most serious. A control group comprised persons who were in waiting rooms at various state employment agencies in predominantly black and Hispanic areas of New York City. We found 187 males who agreed to fill out the EPQ; from all indications, this control group matched the criminal group in age, race, socioeconomic class, and employment history.

All six criminal groups scored *lower* than the control group on the *E* scale, but there were significant differences among the criminal subgroups. Sex offenders were the most introverted, followed by burglars. Robbery offenders were the most extraverted.

While demonstrating the ability of the EPQ to distinguish among offenders in this particular sample, the aforementioned study does not support Eysenck's position on extraversion. Although there appeared to be many reasons for this lack of support, a dominant one was cultural. Prisoners in our study were generally from the black or Hispanic regions of New York City and had been convicted of violent crimes. Eysenck studied predominantly European white prisoners convicted of property crimes. This observation stresses the importance of considering cultural factors when studying heterogeneous criminal populations.

Farrington, Biron, and LeBlanc (1982) found little support for the Eysenckian theory of criminality in their review of the literature, which included their own recent investigation of antisocial individuals in London and Montreal. "Our conclusion is that, at the present time, it seems unlikely that the Eysenck theory, the Eysenck scales, or the Eysenck items are of much use in the explanation of delinquency" (p. 196).

We should not discard the Eysenckian theory this blithely, however. Enough studies find some support for it to warrant speculation and research on why the results are equivocal. Are they due to cultural differences, sampling differences in either offender or control populations, or the wording of questions on the personality inventory? Also, the *P* scale has been somewhat supported by recent research using both convicted delinquents and SR offenders. This finding suggests that people who engage in antisocial or criminal conduct tend to be insensitive, aggressive, impulsive, tough-minded individuals who are highly self-centered. Obviously, more research should be directed at this personality dimension.

Although Eysenck's theory is in a state of flux, we have given it a considerable amount of attention here for three reasons. First, the theory is one of the few comprehensive statements about the role of genetics in antisocial behavior. We still have much to learn from this attempt, and perhaps some modifications will strengthen its explanatory potential. Second, Eysenck's theory recognizes the interaction of the environment—specifically via classical conditioning—with characteristics of the nervous system. Of particular importance is the attention Eysenck gives to individual differences in the nervous system as a biological basis for personality in general (Nebylitsyn & Gray, 1972). Criminology cannot afford to discount the existence of biological factors in antisocial behavior, even if these factors account for the behavior of only a small percentage of the population. At this point, however, it appears that Eysenck's emphasis on classical conditioning as a primary explanation of criminality and his tendency to ignore other forms of learning and mediational (cognitive) processes may be the theory's most damaging weaknesses. In addition, Gordon Trasler (1987) notes that even the concept of conditionability is fraught with difficulties and encourages much debate among contemporary psychologists. There is even considerable debate about what the term means, and the empirical evidence examining the concept remains elusive and conflicting. Finally, Eysenck's theory is unique because it represents one of the few attempts by a psychologist to formulate a general theory of criminal behavior.

SUMMARY AND CONCLUSIONS

Realizing that crime, like all human behavior, results from an interaction between heredity and environment, we have in this chapter looked at the research on the genetic and biological makeup of persons who become criminal. A pioneer in genetic-biological criminology, Cesare Lombroso, asserted that there is a "born criminal," physically distinct from the general population and *predisposed* to act antisocially. Lombroso's theory was periodically revised, but the final version retained the notion of innate criminal tendencies, at least in some offenders. Lombrosian theory was soon put to rest, but it prompted other theorists to posit that there might be more to crime causation than social and environmental factors alone.

Later theorists studied the relationship of body build (Kretschmer) or body type (Sheldon) to crime. Theirs and later studies supported a *correlation* with crime, but questionable methodology often made it impossible to determine whether a *causal* relationship existed. To what extent genetically determined physical characteristics may influence criminal behavior remains unknown.

The genetic factor has also been explored in twin and adoption studies. Generally, empirical studies have found a high concordance rate between identical twins engaged in crime, lending some credence to genetic predisposition. Even when separated at birth, identicals tend to be similar in their pursuit of criminal careers. There have been few adoption studies, primarily because of the inaccessibility of records. The existing research in this area tends to support the genetic viewpoint, but the researchers admonish that the environment can either stimulate or inhibit any inborn tendency toward criminality.

Eysenck has proposed an interaction theory of crime, seeing it as the result of environmental conditions (primarily classical conditioning) working on inherited features of the nervous system. The essence of Eysenckian theory is that individuals with certain types of nervous systems (introverts) condition better, or learn the mores of society much more readily than individuals with other types (extraverts and ambiverts). In other words, introverts link transgressions with disapproval much sooner than others do. Some people would say introverts have a stronger conscience and experience more fear prior to their transgressions and more guilt after committing them. However, as we will note in chapter nine, this quick associative or conditioning ability also means that introverts are more likely to acquire sexually deviant behavior.

Eysenck hypothesizes that neuroticism or emotionality intensifies existing habits, which in some cases may be antisocial ones. Individuals with high emotionality may be more driven toward antisocial habits than individuals with low emotionality. Psychoticism, a dimension that has received less research attention, appears to correlate with features of the psychopath and frequent offenders.

It is obvious that the Eysenckian position needs considerable revision and refinement. As it now stands, the theory has flaws that could be fatal. One glaring weakness is its reliance on classical conditioning to the exclusion of mediational (cognitive) factors and social learning. Despite these problems, Eysenck's work represents a broad, testable theory of criminality that continues to stimulate international research.

CHAPTER THREE
The Psychopath: A Focus on Biological Factors

In the early nineteenth century, the French psychiatrist Philip Pinel felt a need to distinguish the person who habitually exhibited asocial and anti-social actions (not necessarily criminal), but did not exhibit signs of mental illness as it was then understood. He coined the term *manie sans delire* (mania without frenzy) to describe this behavior disorder, which included such features as cruelty, irresponsibility, and immorality (Rotenberg & Diamond, 1971). In 1837 the British psychiatrist J. C. Pritchard renamed the clinically strange group of disorders "moral insanity," presuming that they manifested a "derangement" and a failure to abide by society's expectations of religious, ethical, and cultural conduct. To Pritchard, this was evidence of a mental disease. His term was accepted and used by both the public and the medical profession for over a half century. In 1888, however, the German psychiatrist J. Koch decided that *moral insanity* had unwarranted negative connotations, and he proposed another designation, "psychopathic inferiority." Our modern conception of the psychopath is derived directly from Koch's label.

Psychopathic inferiority, as conceived by Koch, encompasssed numerous behaviors, some of which are still linked with the psychopathic personality as we recognize it today, but many of which are associated instead with neurotic or personality disorders. The early psychiatrists believed that this disorder was constitutional, likely inbred by a genetic strain that produced a basic flaw in one's personality. There were implications, which in some respects continue today, that psychopaths were evil, human vessels of the devil, bent on destroying the moral fabric of society—"the devil made them do it."

Emil Kraepelin, who had an affinity for classification schemes, delineated seven categories of psychopaths in his *Textbook of Psychiatry* in 1913. The seven subtypes were the excitable, the unstable, the impulsive, the eccentric, the liars and swindlers, the antisocial, and the quarrelsome. All represented constitutional predispositions. Not to be outdone, Kahn (1931) suggested sixteen trait-syndromes for the psychopath. In 1930, G. E. Partridge considered psychopathy an exclusively social rather than mental maladjustment and proposed the term *sociopath* to replace *psychopath* (Pennington, 1966).

To stem the proliferation of symptoms and labels and to check the resulting ambiguity, the American Psychiatric Association in 1952 dropped *psychopath* and officially adopted *sociopath*, or, more specifically, "sociopathic personality disturbance, antisocial reaction." Contemporary researchers and clinicians use the terms interchangeably. The purist, however, considers the sociopath a habitual criminal offender who fails to learn from experience. The psychopath may or may not be criminal, and presumably manifests specific empirically verifiable behaviors and biological predispositions that differ from those of the general population.

In 1968, the American Psychiatric Association again changed its label, this time to "personality disorder, antisocial." The DSM III (1980) and DSM III-R (1987) continue to use the term, and it refers specifically to an individual "in which there are a history of continuous and chronic antisocial behavior in which the rights of others are violated . . . " (DSM III, 1980, pp. 317–318).

Robert Hare (1970) proposed a useful scheme to outline three categories of psychopaths, the primary, the secondary or neurotic, and the dyssocial. Only the primary psychopath is a "true" psychopath. The other two categories meld a heterogeneous group of antisocial individuals who comprise a large segment of the criminal population. Secondary psychopaths commit antisocial or violent acts because of severe emotional problems or inner conflicts. They are sometimes called acting-out neurotics, neurotic delinquents, symptomatic psychopaths, or simply neurotic characters. The third group, dyssocial psychopaths, display aggressive, antisocial behavior they have learned from their subculture, like their gangs or families. In both cases, the label "psychopath" is misleading, because the behaviors and backgrounds have little if any similarity to those of primary psychopaths. Yet both secondary and dyssocial psychopaths are often called psychopaths because of their high recidivism rates.

This text adopts Hare's scheme, considering *primary psychopath* an experimentally and clinically useful designation. It is distinguished from *secondary* or *neurotic* psychopath, concepts that can embrace the borderline and more common behaviors that have been loosely called "psychopathic." From this point on, when we refer to the psychopath, we mean the primary psychopath. He or she is unique: neither neurotic, psychotic, nor emotionally disturbed, as commonly believed. Primary psychopaths are *usually* not volcanically explosive, violent, or extremely destructive. They are more apt to be outgoing, charming, and verbally proficient. They may be criminals—in fact, in general they run in perpetual opposition to the law—but many are not. In contrast, sociopaths are, by definition, always criminals.

The late Ferdinand Waldo Demara, Jr., the "Great Impostor," who forged documents and tried dozens of occupations without stopping to obtain a high school education, is a good example of a primary psychopath. A brief description of some of his exploits may help put the primary psychopath in perspective. (See Critchton, 1959, for a more complete version.)

Demara frequently came into contact with the law, primarily because he persisted in adopting fake identities. He once obtained the credentials of a Dr. French, who held a Harvard Ph.D. in psychology. Demara was in the U.S. Navy at the time, awaiting a commission on the basis of other forged documents, but when he realized he was in danger of exposure via a routine security check, he decided he would prefer the Dr. French identity. He dramatized a successful suicide by leaving his clothing on the end of a pier with a note stating that "this is the only way out." Navy officials accepted his "death," and Demara became Dr. French. With his impressive credentials in hand, he obtained a Dean of Philosophy position in a Canadian college, successfully taught a variety of psychology courses, and assumed administrative responsibilities.

He developed a friendship with a physician, Joseph Cyr, and learned the basics of medicine from their long conversations. He eventually borrowed and duplicated Cyr's vital documents—birth, baptism, and confirmation certificates, school records, medical license—and obtained a commission in the Royal Canadian Navy as Dr. Cyr. He read extensively to nurture his growing knowledge of medicine.

During the Korean War, Demara/Cyr was assigned to a destroyer headed for the combat zone. The ship met a small Korean junk carrying many seriously wounded men, who were brought on board for emergency medical care. Three men were in such critical condition that only emergency surgery could save their lives. Although Demara had never seen an operation performed, he hurriedly reviewed his textbooks. With unskilled hands, he operated through the night. By dawn, he had not only saved the lives of the three men, but also had successfully treated sixteen others.

Demara/Cyr's deeds were broadcast over the ship's radio and disseminated, along with his photo, by the press. The real Dr. Cyr, shocked to see Demara's visage over his own respected name, immediately exposed him.

Demara was discharged from the Canadian Navy which, to save itself from additional embarrassment, allowed him to leave without prosecution.

The exploits of this great impostor are far more typical of the primary psychopath than are violence and bizarre perversions. To the public, the term *psychopathic killer* conjures images of a maniac gone berserk with a lust for wanton murder. Psychopathic rapists supposedly torture and murder their victims because they hated their mothers or want to get back at women for some other reason. In fact, most crimes of primary psychopaths are petty and without apparent rationale. Their criminal actions are often inappropriate and astonishingly immature pranks performed without regard for the embarrassment of others or personal risks. Joyrides, drunken brawls, and spontaneous break-ins are more likely to be part of the psychopath's pattern than are serious offenses.

This is not to say that psychopaths never commit heinous and brutal crimes. They sometimes do. Neville Heath—charming, handsome, and intelligent—murdered two young English women in two of the most brutal and sadistic sexual murders ever uncovered (Critchley, 1951; Hill, 1960). Like Demara, Heath had an extraordinary career, much of it in the armed forces. Unlike Demara, his brushes with the law were serious and occasionally ended in imprisonment. He was commissioned and dishonorably discharged on three separate occasions, once each in the British Royal Air Force, the Royal Armed Service Corps, and the South African Air Force. He flew in a fighter squadron in the RAF until he was court-martialed for car theft at age nineteen. He then committed a series of thefts and burglaries and was sentenced to Borstal Prison. Pardoned in 1939, he joined the Royal Armed Service Corps but was dismissed for forgery. On his way home to England, he jumped ship and eventually managed to obtain a commission in the South African Air Force until his past caught up with him. When not in trouble, Heath was regarded as a daring, confident, and highly charming officer—and a rake. After the third court-martial, he developed a taste for sadistic murder.

You may be able to identify other examples of primary psychopaths at their worst. The notorious Charles Manson, who in the 1960s exhibited an uncanny ability to attract a devout cluster of unresisting followers, is one probable example. Another is Henri Landau, "Bluebeard," born in Paris in 1869 and hanged fifty-one years later. Bluebeard was said to have "loved" 283 women and murdered at least ten of them. He forged, swindled, seduced, and murdered, and he assumed multiple occupations, including toy salesperson, physician, lawyer, and engineer. His modus operandi was to seduce women and charmingly persuade them to hand over their money and property for safekeeping.

Throughout the remainder of this chapter we will examine in more detail the behavior, physiology, and background of the primary psychopath, who will hereafter be called simply the psychopath.

BEHAVIORAL DESCRIPTION

One respected authority on the behavioral characteristics of the psychopath is Hervey Cleckley (1976). His often-quoted text, *The Mask of Sanity*, describes in clear and empirically useful terms the major behaviors demonstrated by the full-fledged psychopath, as distinct from the other psychopathic types referred to previously.

Superficial charm and average to above-average intelligence are two of the psychopath's main features, according to Cleckley, and they are both especially apparent during initial contacts. Psychopaths usually impress others as friendly, outgoing, likeable, and alert. They often appear well-educated and knowledgeable, and they display many interests. Psychometric studies indicate that they usually score higher on intelligence tests than the general population (Hare, 1970), particularly on individually administered tests. In fact, Hare wryly comments, the psychopaths who were the sample for his studies were probably the least intelligent of their ilk, since they were not quite bright enough to avoid being convicted for their offenses. (Hare has conducted much of his research on imprisoned psychopaths.)

Psychopaths also do not seem to be plagued with mental disorders, either mild or severe. They lack any symptoms of excessive worry and anxiety, irrational thinking, delusions, severe depressions, or hallucinations. Even under high-pressure conditions they remain cool and calm, as did Ian Fleming's fictitious James Bond, probably a prime example. Feasibly, the doomed psychopath might enjoy a steak dinner (au poivre) with gusto just before being executed. The infamous multiple murderer Herman W. Mudget, alias H. H. Holmes, retired at his normal hour the evening before his execution, easily fell asleep, slept soundly, and woke up completely refreshed. "I never slept better in my life," he told his cell guard. He ordered and ate a substantial breakfast an hour before he was scheduled to be hanged. Until the moment of death, he remained remarkably calm and amiable, displaying no signs of depression or fear (Franke, 1975).

Other principal traits of the psychopath are selfishness and an inability to love or give affection to others. According to Cleckley, egocentricity is *always* present in the psychopath and is essentially unmodifiable. The psychopath's inability to feel genuine, meaningful affection for another is absolute. Psychopaths may be likeable, but they are seldom able to keep close friends, and they have great difficulty understanding love in others. They may be highly skillful at pretending deep affection, and they may effectively mimic appropriate emotions, but true loyalty, warmth, and compassion are foreign to them. Psychopaths are distinguished by flat emotional reaction and affect. In addition, they do not usually respond to acts of kindness. They show capacity only for superficial appreciation. Paradoxically, they may do small favors and appear considerate. One prototype mowed the lawn for his elderly neighbor and slipped her some schnapps when she was ill—the next morning he stole her car.

Psychopaths have a remarkable disregard for truth and are often called "pathological liars." They seem to have no internalized moral or ethical sense and cannot understand the purpose of being honest, especially if dishonesty will bring some personal gain. They have a cunning ability to *appear* straightforward, honest, and sincere, but their claims to sincerity are without substance.

Psychopaths are unreliable, irresponsible, and unpredictable, regardless of the importance of the occasion or the consequences of their impulsive actions. This pattern is cyclical, however. Psychopaths may, for months on end, be responsible citizens, faithful spouses, and reliable employees. They may experience great successes, be promoted, and gain honors, as did Demara and Heath. Suddenly, as skillfully as they have attained these socially desirable goals, they have an uncanny knack of unravelling their lives. They become irresponsible, may pass bad checks, sabotage the company computer, go on a drunken spree, or steal the boss's car and mate. Psychopaths may later say they are sorry and plead for another chance—and most will probably get it. Invariably, if the psychopath is a young adult, the irresponsible behavior will return.

Even small amounts of alcohol prompt most psychopaths to become vulgar, domineering, loud, and boisterous and to engage in practical jokes and pranks. Cleckley notes that they choose pranks which have no appeal for most individuals, and which seem bizarre, inappropriate, and cruel. They lack genuine humor and, not surprisingly, the ability to laugh at themselves.

Cleckley describes a potentially promising, brilliant physician in his early forties who was loved by his patients and had managed to develop a thriving practice during his "upswing" periods. His negative, psychopath behaviors, however, were colossal blunders:

> This man's history shows a great succession of purposeless follies dating from early manhood. He lost several valuable hospital appointments by lying out sodden or by bursting in on serious occasions with nonsensical uproar. He was once forced to relinquish a promising private practice because of the scandal and indignation which followed an escapade in a brothel where he had often lain out disconsolately for days at a time.
>
> Accompanied by a friend who was also feeling some influence of drink he swaggered into his favorite retreat and bellowed confidently for women. Congenially disposed in one room, the party of four called for highballs. For an hour or more only the crash of glasses, scattered oaths, and occasional thuds were heard. Then suddenly an earnest, piercing scream brought the proprietess and her servants racing into the chamber. One of the prostitutes lay prostrate, clasping a towel to her breast, yelling in agony. Through her wails and sobs she accused the subject of this report of having, in his in-

judicious blunderings, bitten off her nipple. An examination by those present showed that this unhappy dismemberment had, in fact, taken place. Although both men had at the moment been in bed with her, the entertainer had no doubt as to which one had done her the injury.

Feeling ran strong for a while, but, by paying a large sum as recompense for the professional disability and personal damage he had inflicted, the doctor avoided open prosecution. Before a settlement had been made, the guilty man attempted to persuade his companion to assume responsibility for the deed. It would be less serious for the other man, he argued, since his own prominence and professional standing made him a more vulnerable target for damaging courtroom dramatics and for slander. His companion, however, declined this opportunity for self-sacrifice with great firmness.

From Cleckley, Hervey, *The Mask of Sanity*, 5th ed., St. Louis, Mo.: The C. V. Mosby Co., 1976, pp. 206–7.

Although above-average in intelligence, psychopaths appear incapable of learning to avoid failure and situations that are potentially damaging to themselves. Some theorists suggest that the self-destructive, self-defeating deeds and attitudes reflect a need to be punished to mitigate the guilt they subconsciously experience, or more simply, that they are driven by a masochistic purpose. Evidence refuting these explanations will be offered later in this chapter.

When a psychopath drifts into criminal activity, impulsivity will usually prevent him or her from performing like a professional criminal. Psychopaths are more likely to participate in capers and hastily planned frolics, or in spontaneous, serious crimes for immediate satisfaction. The professional criminal has purpose and a plan of action; the psychopath is impulsive and lacks long-range goals.

A cardinal fault of psychopaths is their absolute lack of remorse or guilt for anything they do, regardless of the severity or immorality of their actions and irrespective of their traumatic effects on others. Since they do not anticipate personal consequences, psychopaths may engage in destructive or antisocial behavior—such as forgery, theft, rape, brawls, and fraud—by taking absurd risks and for insignificant personal gain. When caught, they express no genuine remorse. They may readily admit culpability and take considerable pleasure in the shock these admissions produce in others. Whether they have bashed in someone's head, ruined a car, or tortured a child, psychopaths may well remark they did it "for the hell of it."

Psychopaths have little capacity to see themselves as others perceive them. Instead of accepting the facts that would normally lead to insight, they project and externalize blame onto the community and family for their misfortunes. Interestingly, educated psychopaths have been known to speak fluently about the psychopathic personality, quoting the literature extensively and discussing research findings, but they cannot look into their own troublesome antics or mount a reasonable attack on their actions.

They articulate their regrets for having done something, but the words are devoid of emotional meaning, a characteristic Cleckley calls *semantic dementia*. Johns and Quay (1962) remarked that psychopaths "know the words but not the music."

Finally, an important behavioral distinction underlying much of Cleckley's description is what Quay (1965) refers to as the psychopath's profound and pathological stimulation seeking. According to Quay, the actions of the psychopath are motivated by an excessive *physiological* need for thrills and excitement. It is not unusual to see psychopaths drawn to such interests as race driving, skydiving, and motorcycle stunts. We will examine this alleged need for stimulation in the pages to follow.

GENDER DIFFERENCES

There are few statistics on the ratio of male to female psychopaths, but it is generally believed that the males far outnumber their female counterparts. Robins (1966) reports that only 15 percent of the psychopaths in her study were female. Because the known psychopathic population is dominated by men, little research has been directed at the women, although both Hare and Cleckley included female psychopaths in some of their work. The most noteworthy research on female psychopaths was a longitudinal fifteen-year study on women in prison conducted by Guze (1976). Psychopathy, Guze notes, is the most frequent personality diagnosis of women felons. It is often accompanied by diagnoses of alcoholism and "hysteria," an outdated personality disorder attributed to adolescent girls and young women. Guze notes that drug dependence is also significantly more frequent among arrested female psychopaths, appearing in 58 percent of the psychopath population compared to 8 percent of convicted female nonpsychopaths.

Guze found that antisocial symptoms in female psychopaths typically began around age eleven. Forty-two percent of the adult psychopaths had a history of juvenile arrests and runaway status offenses. In a finding reflective of moral biases and discriminatory treatment of women, Guze noted that 65 percent had arrest records for sexual misconduct, such as prostitution. Furthermore, many had a history that included incest, lesbianism, and illegitimate pregnancies. It is difficult to separate the status offenses and so-called victimless crimes from the property or violent crimes in Guze's survey. He notes, for example, that recidivism was greatest among psychopaths under age thirty, but it is unclear whether this figure refers to status offenses, adult sexual offenses, or serious crime. Interestingly, 72 percent of the female psychopaths who had ever married had been married at least once to a psychopath or an alcoholic.

Robins (1966) found that female psychopaths followed the same behavioral patterns as male psychopaths, except that they were more frequently involved in sexual misconduct. In her sample, 79 percent of the females displayed abnormally high sexual activity and "excessive" interest in sexual matters. This finding is common in other female psychopath research. In the absence of other behavioral descriptors, it suggests that the psychopath label may have been attached indiscriminately to women who were believed to engage inappropriately in sexual activity.

Cleckley (1976) describes one female psychopath whose nonsexual behavioral characteristics were clearly in evidence before sexual characteristics appeared. "Roberta," a twenty-year-old patient, began to steal small items from stores and from relatives at age ten. As an adolescent, she obtained dresses, cosmetics, candy, perfume, and other articles by charging them to her father without his knowledge. Her school work was mediocre, but her intelligence was clearly superior. She demonstrated overt kindness to animals, but when her own dog was killed by a car, she did not seem to mind. During her teens, she became truant and began to stay out all night. When her parents expressed alarm, she admitted her errors but continued her erratic behavior. Her parents complained that they could not understand her. "It's not that she seems bad or exactly that she means to do wrong," said her father. "She can lie with the straightest face, and after she's found in the most outlandish lies she still seems perfectly easy in her own mind."

When Roberta was expelled from the local high school for excessive truancy, her desperate parents sent her to a series of boarding schools, from which she was either expelled or ran away. Once back home, she added more antisocial habits to her repertoire. Her father employed her as a bookkeeper in his business, but she managed to embezzle considerable sums of money. Attempts to reason with her did nothing to change her behavior; she seemed totally untroubled.

Up to this time, Roberta had displayed little interest in sex and had experienced only mild kissing and "necking," which she found "vaguely" pleasurable. She eventually ran away from home with no purpose except to wander. At this point, she discovered that prostitution was an effective way to obtain money and lodging. When police officers returned her to her home, she ran to her parents, threw herself into their arms, and expressed her affection. She said she was sorry for the distress she had caused them, but the penitence was devoid of feeling. She was unaffected by the inevitable gossip that surrounded her return to her small town. (Adapted from Cleckley, Hervey, *The Mask of Sanity*, 5th ed., St. Louis, Mo.: The C. V. Mosby Co., 1976, pp. 46–55).

In general, research on possible gender differences in psychopathy is complicated by a tendency to equate sexual activity in women with abnormal stimulation-seeking behavior. When "excessive" or "aberrant" sexual activity is separated from other behaviors, female psychopaths have characteristics similar to their male counterparts. Far fewer female than male psychopaths have been identified, however.

BASIC PHYSIOLOGICAL CONCEPTS AND TERMINOLOGY

Contemporary research favors the view that psychopathic behavior results from a complex interaction between neurophysiological and learning or socialization factors. It is important, therefore, to become familiar with additional neuropsychological vocabulary and basic structures of the nervous system, some of which appeared in chapter two. The concepts presented here will also lay the foundation for topics in later chapters (e.g., chapter seven on aggression and violence, chapter nine on sexual offenses, and chapter twelve on drugs) as well.

The human nervous system can be divided into two major parts, either on the basis of structure or function. The structural division—the way it is arranged physically—is perhaps the clearest distinction.

The central nervous system (CNS) and the peripheral nervous system (PNS) are the two principal parts. The CNS comprises the brain and spinal cord, and the PNS comprises all nerve cells (called neurons) and nerve pathways located outside the CNS (see Table 3-1). In other words, those nerves that leave the spinal cord and brain stem and travel to specific sites in the body belong to the peripheral (outside) nervous system. This includes all the nerves connecting the muscles, skin, heart, glands, and senses to the CNS.

The basic function of the PNS is to bring all the outside information to the CNS, where it is processed. Once the CNS has processed information, it relays the interpretation back to the PNS if action is necessary. When you place your finger on a hot object, the PNS relays this raw datum (it is not yet pain) to the CNS, which interprets the datum as the sensation of pain and, in return, relays a command to the PNS to withdraw the finger. The PNS cannot interpret; it only transmits information to the CNS and carries communications back. In the following pages, we will consider the significance of each of these systems to the diagnosis of psychopathy.

Central Nervous System

Structurally, the CNS consists of the brain and spinal cord. Interpretation, thoughts, memories, and images all occur in the cerebral cortex (the highest center of the brain). It is the processing center for

TABLE 3-1   Divisions of Human Nervous System

I. CENTRAL NERVOUS SYSTEM
   A. Brain
   B. Spinal Cord
II. PERIPHERAL NERVOUS SYSTEM
   A. Skeletal Nervous System (communicates with voluntary muscles)
   B. Autonomic Nervous System
      1. Parasympathetic (relaxes and deactivates after emergencies)
      2. Sympathetic (activates for emergencies)

stimulation and sensations received from the outside world and the body via the PNS. The cerebral cortex, which is the outer surface of the human brain, contains about 10 to 13 billion nerve cells, or neurons. Each neuron has a complicated communication link to numerous other neurons, creating an extremely complex and poorly understood communications network. Although the physical structures of the brain do not directly concern us, the electrical and arousal properties of the cortex are relevant in understanding the electroencephalograms (brain wave patterns) and psychological characteristics of the psychopath.

Electrical activity in the CNS became the subject of serious study in the late 1920s, when the German psychiatrist Hans Berger developed sophisticated equipment enabling him to record oscillatory electrical potentials on the scalps of human subjects. The electrical oscillations recorded from the cortex are electroencephalograms (EEGs); the device which records them is the electroencephalograph. Because of the oscillatory characteristics of the EEGs, they are referred to as brain waves. Berger's technique allowed the study of electrical properties of the brain without discomfort to the subject. His work was not immediately recognized, and it was not until the early 1940s that his discovery accelerated investigations of the brain.

Berger (1929) discovered that when EEG recordings were made of the relaxed adult, usually with eyes closed, the electrical activity generally oscillated between eight and thirteen cycles per second (CPS). He called this brain wave pattern, which appeared with some consistency under relaxed conditions, *alpha rhythms*. Nevertheless, he did not know what brain *function* he was recording. To this day, investigators remain uncertain of the exact meaning of brain rhythms, despite rapid technological advances in recording hardware. Many believe that brain waves represent the synchronous, almost symphonic firing of billions of neurons, the purpose of which remains unknown. We do know, as did Berger, that the EEG is an ever changing reflection of the cortex's arousal levels and is sensitive to various changes in both the external and the internal (mood and thought) environments. By studying alpha rhythms, researchers have learned the characteristics of the cortex during sleep, drug ingestion, development, and malfunction, such as epileptic seizures. EEG patterns have also provided us with partial hints about the way the psychopath's cortex functions. Some of the cortical functions of the psychopath appear to be significantly different from the nonpsychopath.

Subsequent to Berger's findings, researchers delineated several other cortical rhythms. The *delta* rhythm spans one-half to three CPS, has high voltage, and indicates that the cortex is at its lowest stage of activity and arousal. The *theta* rhythm has four to seven CPS, less voltage than delta, and represents a stage slightly higher in cortical arousal. Together, delta and theta are often referred to as *slow-wave activity*, because of their relatively low frequency or oscillation rates. *Alpha* rhythms, which have eight to thirteen CPS, represent a higher level of cortical arousal than slow wave activity and are "normal" rhythms for the relaxed adult. *Beta* rhythms have nineteen to thirty CPS, low voltage, and reflect active cognitive processes, thinking, or general arousal states. Beta rhythms are sometimes referred to as *desynchronic* of alpha, since they occur under conditions which block the occurrence of alpha. For example, if an EEG recording is being made while a person is relaxed with eyes closed and someone suddenly calls out the person's name, there will be an immediate blocking of alpha with resultant beta rhythms. For our purpose, it is important to remember that beta reflects high states of cortical activity and arousal.

EEGs seem to change with age. The delta and theta rhythms that predominate in childhood give way to alpha and beta in normal adulthood, except during sleep, when the delta and theta patterns return. Throughout infancy, childhood, and adolescence, the brain rhythms also become progressively more regular, and the cortex increases its potential for higher states of arousal. At birth, brain rhythms are irregular and often nonexistent. During the first year, delta begins to occur with some regularity on both sides of the brain (Fois, 1961). After the first year, the theta rhythm dominates the EEG pattern, eventually giving way to alpha rhythms, which begin to dominate at about age ten. The alpha gradually becomes regular and usually "matures" at around age fourteen. Beta rhythms develop at around age sixteen. The rhythms in the developing human are particularly susceptible to psychological stress and other factors in the environment. Highly irregular theta rhythms, for example, accompany older children having temper tantrums. They become more regular if the child lies down and calms down. The stages of sleep are also delineated on the basis of brain rhythms, the lighter stages characterized by theta patterns and the deeper stage by deltas. Other things being equal, the more aroused and alert the cortex, the higher the frequency and the lower the voltage of the brain waves.

EEG Research on Psychopaths

When researchers discovered that brain waves could be monitored, they began to hypothesize individual differences in those patterns and to devise experiments to test those hypotheses. In a pioneer study during World War II, Hill and Watterson (1942) investigated the EEG patterns of 151 male British military personnel who were not adjusting to military service and were believed to be psychopathic. The investigators divided the men into three classifications: aggressive, mixed, and inadequate psychopaths. The groups actually represented heterogeneous clusters of personality disorders and obviously failed in many respects to meet Cleckley's criteria as we have presented them. One group, however, the aggressive psychopaths, closely resembled Cleckley's primary psychopath. Men in this group had a history of "violence to others regardless of the consequences, repeated destruction of property, or a combination of such kinds of aggressive impulsive behavior" (Hill & Watterson, 1942, p. 47). The results indicated that 65 percent of the aggressive psychopaths demonstrated abnormal EEGs, compared to 15 percent of a group of "normals" used as controls. Most abnormal EEGs were of a *slow-wave* variety—delta and theta; the control group exhibited the usual adult alpha and beta patterns.

This study prompted many other EEG studies using individuals with various kinds of behavior disorders, including psychopathy. Subsequent studies of psychopaths have consistently revealed significantly higher incidences of EEG abnormality of a slow-wave variety (e.g., Craft, 1966; Hare, 1970). In a series of studies conducted by Knott and his colleagues (1953), between 49 and 58 percent of 700 psychopaths had EEG abnormalities, mostly of a slow-wave variety. It should be noted that between 10 and 15 percent of the general population show abnormal EEGs, with "abnormal" being defined in a number of ways. Additional studies by Ehrlich and Keogh (1956) and Arthur and Cahoon (1964) also found that well over half of the psychopaths measured had abnormal EEGs, with most reflecting slow-wave patterns.

It is unclear why many psychopaths display slow-wave activity (immature brain wave patterns). As noted, it is not even clear what cortical functions the EEG represents. Do EEG abnormalities generate psychopathic behavior, or does psychopathic behavior cause EEG abnormality? The answer is not known. It could be that neither causes the other.

Hare (1970) suggests that slow-wave activity represents delayed brain maturation. Since some evidence indicates that EEG patterns of many psychopaths resemble those of children, it is arguable that the brain and cortical functioning of the psychopath is immature and childlike. Hare refers to this as the *maturation retardation hypothesis,* also known as the "maturation lag hypothesis." It is appealing because the behavioral patterns of the psychopath—self-centeredness, impulsivity, inability to delay gratification, and inordinate stimulation seeking—resemble the behaviors of children.

Interestingly, there is also evidence that, with increasing age, the immature EEG patterns of some psychopaths develop into mature ones, and that there is a corresponding change toward more socially approved behavior (Gibbens, Pond, & Stafford-Clark, 1955). Robins (1966) found support for this observation, discovering that the change was most likely to occur between the ages of thirty and forty. It may be that the psychopath's cortex matures later in life than those of the normal adult. It should be emphasized, however, that the EEG evidence to date is sketchy and fragmented, and considerably more data are necessary before a maturation retardation hypothesis deserves widespread support.

In several cross-sectional and longitudinal studies of the criminal histories of male psychopaths and nonpsychopaths, Hare and his colleagues

(Hare, McPherson, & Forth, 1988; Hare & Jutai, 1983; Hare, 1986) did find that the criminal activities of the criminal psychopath decrease at around age forty. Hare, McPherson, and Forth (1988) further observe that the psychopath's dramatic decline in prison time and conviction rate after age forty is often preceded by an equally dramatic increase in these variables between the ages of twenty-five and thirty. The reasons for these discernible shifts remain unknown and are largely left to speculation. One popular hypothesis is "burnout." That is, the frequent wear-and-tear of convictions and prison time eventually takes its toll on the antisocial activities of the criminal psychopath. Hare, however, finds the burnout hypothesis highly unlikely because the psychopath is relatively free of stress, tensions, anxieties, and conflicts that typically lead to emotional burnout. Of course, another favorite hypothesis is maturational lag, described earlier. Other hypotheses include learned strategies for remaining out of prison, or the cognitive realization that the future is bleak without changes in life style. After all, even the criminal psychopath may eventually learn after a series of aversive consequences for antisocial behavior. In sum, the available evidence does suggest a reduction in offending (although not necessarily a complete termination of offending) at around age forty for most male criminal psychopaths, but the reasons for this career shift remain unknown.

Positive spikes.   In the late 1950s and early 1960s, some researchers (e.g., Niedermeyer, 1963; Kurland, Yeager, & Arthur, 1963) noticed that a brain rhythm of a different variety occurred during sleep in many psychopaths and highly aggressive individuals. Against a background of the usual slow-wave activity found in sleep, spontaneous bursts of brain waves with frequencies of six to fourteen CPS appeared in certain locations of the cortex (the temporal lobe) in 66 percent of the aggressive subjects. These individuals had a history of uncontrollable and violent episodes of destructive urges usually triggered by small, trivial slights. The aggressive explosions often resulted in extensive damage to property and injury or death to others. The brain-wave bursts are called *positive spikes*, and they have also been found to occur in the brain waves of psychopaths during awakened states. Reseachers observe that, following the aggressive episodes, the individual expresses no guilt, but is fully aware of the aggressive or even violent behavior (Hare, 1970).

In sum, contemporary research focusing on central nervous system characteristics reveals definite indications of inordinate amounts of abnormal brain-wave patterns, mostly of a childlike nature, in the EEGs of psychopaths. The data suggest that the psychopathic central nervous system is immature and does not develop fully until around age forty to forty-five.

Hemisphere Asymmetry

The human brain can be divided anatomically into two cerebral hemi-spheres—a right and a left. These two cerebral hemispheres seem to coex-ist in some sort of reciprocally balancing relationship in cortical functioning and information processing. For most individuals, the right hemisphere specializes in nonverbal functions, whereas the left specializes in verbal or language functions. Furthermore, the left hemisphere processes informa-tion in an analytical, sequential fashion. Language, for example, requires sequential cognition, and the left seems to be the best equipped for this operation. The right hemisphere, on the other hand, seems to process information holistically and more globally. For example, the right is in-volved in the recognition of faces, a complicated process requiring the processing of information all at once or simultaneously. Thus, the right and left hemispheres are two functionally differentiated information process-ing systems.

In addition to information processing, research is now finding that these two cerebral hemispheres also make different contributions to human emotions. The right hemisphere appears to be particularly important in the understanding and communication of emotion. The left seems to be closely tied to self-inhibiting processes, in contrast to the right, which ap-pears to be more spontaneous and impulsive (Tucker, 1981). Furthermore, the two hemispheres must have a balance of contribution from each for normal judgment and appropriate self-control (Tucker, 1981).

Hare (Hare & Connolly, 1987; Hare & McPherson, 1984) hypothe-sizes that criminal psychopaths manifest an abnormal or unusual balance between the two hemispheres, both in language processing and in emo-tional or arousal states. Hare notes that criminal psychopaths are often strikingly inconsistent with their verbalized thoughts, feelings, and inten-tions. Criminal psychopaths seem to be highly peculiar in the organization of certain perceptual and cognitive processes. It seems as though their left hemisphere is, in some ways, deficient in linguistic processing because they do not rely on the verbal sequential operations to the extent that a majority of individuals do. Since language plays a very important role in the self-regulation of behavior, one of the contributing factors in the extremely impulsive, episodic behavior of psychopaths may reside in some deficiency in their use of internal language. This characteristic was pointed out some time ago by Flor-Henry (Flor-Henry, 1973; Flor-Henry & Yeudall, 1973), who was convinced that psychopathy is closely linked to left-hemispheric language dysfunction.

Nachson (Nachson, 1983; Nachson & Denno, 1987) points out that many studies have found that a disproportionate percentage of violent, repetitive offenders have left-hemispheric dysfunction. Moreover, several researchers have argued that left-handedness may be an indicator of left-hemispheric dysfunction and have predicted that left-handedness will be overrepresented in the criminal or psychopathic population. Fitzhugh (1973) reported that about one-third of a group of juvenile delinquents were left-handed, while Andrew (1978) found that about one out of five adult male offenders preferred their left hand. However, in a later study, Andrew (1980) reported the left-handers seem to be less violent than right-hand offenders. On the other hand, Nachson and Denno (1987), in their investigation of 1,066 black male children—whose mothers participated in the Philadelphia Collaborative Perinatal Project—found that *nonoffenders* (based on official statistics) showed a significantly higher incidence of left-handedness than offenders. Thus, the research results are far from conclusive. Researchers have used different samples, have not been very definitive about their sample composition, and have used a variety of procedures and methods in obtaining and analyzing the data. Much more needs to be done before we can entertain any conclusions about left versus right preferences or left versus right hemispheric functioning in criminal or psychopathic populations.

Stimulation Seeking

Quay (1965) suggests that the psychopath's behavior represents an extreme form of stimulation seeking. Physiologically, psychopaths do not receive the full impact of sensations from the environment. Therefore, in order to get the optimal amount of stimulation necessary to keep the cerebral cortex satisfied, they must engage more frequently in exciting forms of behavior.

Several studies have supported Quay's hypothesis. For example, Wiesen (1965) found that psychopaths worked harder for visual (colored lights) and auditory (music on a radio) stimulation than did a group of nonpsychopaths. In a second experiment that provided continued bombardment of lights and music, Wiesen also demonstrated that nonpsychopaths worked harder than psychopaths to obtain three seconds of silence and relative darkness.

Skrzpek (1969) delineated psychopaths and "neurotic delinquents" on the basis of a behavior rating list for psychopathy and neuroticism developed by Quay (1964). He found that conditions that increased "cortical arousal" (e.g., where the subject was required to make difficult auditory discriminations) decreased preference for visual complexity in both the psychopathic and neurotic groups, but was most pronounced in the latter. On the other hand, a brief period of stimulus deprivation (presumably low cortical arousal) increased preference for complexity in both groups, but a significantly greater increase was shown by the psychopaths.

In an attempt to test Quay's hypothesis that deficient responsivity of the nervous system might account for pathological stimulation seeking,

Whitehill, DeMyer-Gapin, and Scott (1976) conducted an experiment using 103 boring slides of "concrete facades of a modern college campus building." As subjects, the researchers used fifty-five institutionalized "disturbed" preadolescent boys. The professional staff at the institution rated eight boys psychopathic (antisocial) and eight neurotic. A group of seven "normal" noninstitutionalized adolescent boys, matched with the index subjects for age, were used as controls. The average age was 11.5. Results showed that the psychopathic and normal boys looked at the slides significantly less than the neurotic group. More importantly, the psychopathic preadolescents showed a significant decrease in viewing time earlier than the other groups, suggesting that they became bored more quickly than the other groups. Whitehill concluded that the data support the pathological stimulation-seeking hypothesis and favored a physiological ingredient in the formulation of psychopathy. In another project, Orris (1969) found that, compared to nonpsychopaths, psychopathic boys perfomed more poorly on a boring task requiring continuous attention and that they engaged more in boredom-relieving activities like singing or talking to themselves.

Optimal Arousal of the Cerebral Cortex

A number of theorists have postulated (e.g., Berlyne, 1960; Hebb, 1955; Fiske & Maddi, 1961) that organisms seek to maintain preferred or optimal levels of stimulation, with stimulation referring to the amount of sensation and/or information processed by the cortex. In effect, their theories argue for an inverted U-shaped function, with intermediate levels of stimulation most preferred and the extremes least preferred (see Figure 3-1). Insufficient amounts of stimulation lead to boredom, which can be reduced by an increase in stimulation-seeking behavior. On the other hand, exceptionally high levels of stimulation are also aversive and may promote behavior designed to avoid stimulation in an effort to bring the stimulus input to a more pleasurable level.

Cortical arousal appears to have a direct relationship with the amount of stimulation received by the cortex. Low stimulation produces a relatively low level of cortical arousal, whereas high levels of stimulation initiate high cortical arousal. To fall asleep, we must lower the cortex's arousal level by minimizing external and internal stimulation (noises, lights, thoughts). If we do not wish to fall asleep, but our cortical arousal is low (e.g., during a boring lecture), we seek excitement to increase the arousal level. On the other hand, if stimulation becomes excessive, such as via a blaring radio or the pandemonium of rush hour traffic, we are distressed if unable to control the stimulus input. Some psychologists argue that much behavior can be explained as an attempt by the person to maintain optimal or just-right levels of stimulation—levels that are the most comfortable and pleasurable to the individual.

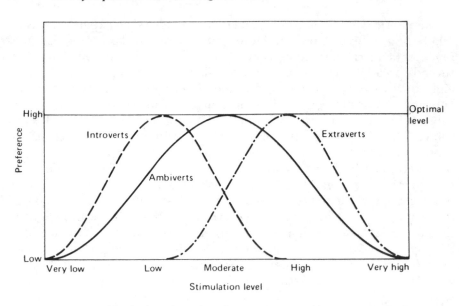

FIGURE 3-1 Optimal levels of stimulation for ambiverts, introverts, and extraverts. Note that introverts reach their optimal level sooner than ambiverts or extraverts do.

It is generally agreed that there are individual differences in the quality and quantity of stimulation necessary for each person to reach the hypothetic optimum. Some of this individual difference may be attributed to certain physiological structures, particularly those found in the brain stem. Eysenck (1967), you will recall, hypothesized that personality differences are largely due to differential needs for stimulation, which are dictated by functional properties of the reticular formation.

The reticular formation can be conveniently divided into several anatomical areas. Chief among these is the reticular activating system (RAS), a tiny but complex nerve network located in the central portion of the brain stem. The RAS underlies our attentiveness to the world and acts as a sentinel that activates the cortex and keeps it alert. Sensory signals or inputs from all parts of the body must travel through the brain stem on their way to the processing center, the cortex. Inside the brain stem, they branch into two major pathways (see Figure 2-3). One major pathway goes through a relay station known as the thalamus; the other travels through the RAS which, in turn, alerts the cortex to incoming information being routed through the thalamic pathway. The RAS-generated arousal is nonspecific in that it energizes the entire cortex and not any specific area. Therefore, any particular stimulation or sensation, from the outside world or from inside the body, has both a coded message (which travels through the thalamus) and a nonspecific arousing effect (which travels through the RAS).

The RAS can also decrease cortical arousal. If certain incoming stimuli are no longer significant or relevant, the cortex "tells" the RAS to filter out that particular group of stimuli. That process is called *adaptation* or *habituation*. Therefore, repetitive and insignificant stimuli are prevented by the RAS from unnecessarily bombarding the cortex with meaningless detail.

Contemporary research and theory *suggest* that the psychopath has a pathological need for excitement and thrills because of some deficiency in or excessive habituation property of the RAS. We emphasize the word *suggest* because, while the research seems consistent in demonstrating that psychopaths appear to have a strong need for stimulation, research has not clearly identified what neurophysiological mechanisms are involved. However, mainstream theory concerning the neurophysiological processes are as follows. The RAS either does not activate the cortex sufficiently to receive the full impact of the incoming information, or else it adapts too quickly, thereby shutting down the cortex's activation before it receives complete information. Either way, the psychopath is unable to reach optimal arousal levels with the same amount of stimulation that normals find adequately arousing. So, the psychopath engages in behaviors that society refers to as thrill-seeking, chancy, antisocial, or inappropriate in order to reach satisfying opitmal cortical arousal.

The general concept of arousal has been used interchangeably with cortical arousal throughout this chapter. In discussing psychopathy, many investigators refer to other forms of arousal, like autonomic (anxiety) or behavior arousal. Basically, these terms mean the same thing. Many states of activation or arousal involve overlapping systems (Korman, 1974). Thus, although there may be slightly different processes and mechanisms involved in different states of arousal, all must involve the heightened arousal levels of the cortex.

In an interesting experiment, Chesno and Kilmann (1975) tested the arousal hypothesis of psychopathy by manipulating stimulation variables (aversive white noise and shock) and personality variables (psychopaths, neurotics, and normals). Ninety male offenders incarcerated in a maximum security penitentiary were selected for the experiment by various criteria. Psychopaths were classified according to Cleckley's criteria. The procedure involved an avoidance learning task, with electric shock being administered for certain incorrect choices by the subject. During the avoidance learning task, each subject received either 35, 65, or 95 decibels of white noise through earphones. (White noise is an auditory stimulus that sounds like a hissing radiator.)

If the arousal hypothesis is correct, the underaroused psychopath under low levels of stimulation should require some form of increased stimulation. Since errors in avoidance learning led to electric shock, psychopaths would be most likely to commit errors and benefit by the stimulation provided by the electric shock. Accordingly, as external stimulation increases (higher levels of white noise), the psychopath should have a decreased need for stimulation and, therefore, should learn to avoid the shock more effectively. The results of the study supported the hypothesis. Psychopaths made significantly more avoidance errors than the other groups as the stimulation *decreased*, which suggests that they prefer punishment to boredom. The finding may explain the well-known inability of psychopaths to benefit from punishment in situations low in stimulation, like prisons or even classrooms. It might even be that imprisoned psychopaths would "learn better" if the conditions under which they were incarcerated were more stimulating.

Peripheral Nervous System

The PNS is subdivided into a *skeletal* division, comprising the motor nerves that innervate the skeletal muscles involved in body movement, and an *autonomic* division, which controls heart rate, gland secretion, and smooth muscle activity. Smooth muscles are those muscles found in the blood vessels and gastrointestinal system; they look smooth under a microscope in comparison to the skeletal muscles, which look striped or textured.

The autonomic segment of the PNS is extremely relevant to our discussion of the psychopath, because here too research has consistently uncovered a significant difference between the psychopath's and the general population's reactivity or responsiveness to stimuli. The autonomic division is especially important, because it activates emotional behavior and responsivity to stress and tension. It can be subdivided into the *sympathetic* and *parasympathetic* segments (see Figure 2-4).

The sympathetic system is responsible for activating or arousing the individual for fight or flight before (or during) fearful or emergency situations. As you will recall, the psychopath displays a James Bond-like coolness, even in stressful situations. We might explain this in one of two ways. Either the sympathetic nervous system does not react sufficiently to stressful stimuli, or the parasympathetic system springs into action in the psychopath more rapidly than in nonpsychopaths. There is research support for both of these positions.

Before discussing in more detail the psychopath's autonomic nervous system, we should note the principles and techniques of measuring autonomic activity. Emotional arousal, which is largely under control of the autonomic nervous system, can be measured by monitoring the system's activity, such as heart rate, blood pressure or volume, and respiration rate. The most commonly used physiological indicator of emotional arousal, however, is skin conductance response (SCR), also known as the galvanic skin response (GSR). Since skin conductance response is the label most advocated by contemporary researchers (Lykken & Venables, 1971), it will be used throughout this chapter.

SCR is simply a measure of the resistance of the skin to conducting electrical current. Although a number of factors in the skin influence its resistance, perspiration seems to play a major role. Perspiration corresponds very closely to changes in emotional states and has, therefore, been found to be a highly sensitive indicator of even slight changes in the autonomic nervous system. Other things being equal, as emotional arousal increases perspiration rate increases proportionately. Small changes in perspiration can be picked up and amplified by recording devices, known as polygraphs or physiographs. An increase in perspiration lowers skin resistance to electrical conductance. In other words, skin conductance increases as emotional arousal (anxiety, fear, and so on) increases.

We noted earlier that psychopaths lack the capacity to respond emotionally to stressful or fearful situations. Essentially, they give the impression of being anxiety-free, carefree, and cool, and they display a devil-may-care attitude. We would expect, therefore, that compared to the normal population, the psychopath has a comparatively underactive, underaroused autonomic nervous system. What has the research literature revealed?

Autonomic nervous system research.   In an oft-cited study, Lykken (1957) hypothesized that since anxiety reduction is an essential ingredient in learning to avoid painful or stressful situations, and since the psychopath is presumed to be anxiety-free, then the psychopath should have special difficulty learning to avoid unpleasant things. Recall that two characteristic features of psychopaths are their inability to learn from unpleasant experiences and their very high recidivism. Lykken carefully delineated his research groups according to Cleckley's criteria. His psychopaths (both males and females) were drawn from several penal institutions in Minnesota and were classified as either primary or neurotic psychopaths. College students comprised a third group of normals.

Lykken designed an electronic maze that subjects were expected to learn as well as possible in twenty trials. There were twenty choice points in the maze, each with four alternatives, with only one being the correct choice. Although three alternatives were incorrect, only one of these would give the subject a rather painful electric shock. Lykken was primarily interested in discovering how quickly subjects learned to avoid the shock (avoidance learning). He reasoned that avoidance learning would be rewarded by the reduction of anxiety on encountering the correct choice point, but since psychopaths are presumably deficient in anxiety, their performance should be significantly worse than that of normals. The hypothesis was supported.

Prior to the maze portion of the experiment, Lykken measured the skin conductance changes of each subject while he or she tried to sit quietly for thirty to forty minutes. During this time, the subjects would periodically hear a buzzer and occasionally receive a slight, brief electric shock several seconds after the buzzer. Eventually, the buzzer became associated with the shock. In normal individuals, the sound of the buzzer itself produced an anxiety response in anticipation of the electric shock (classical conditioning) and was reflected by a substantial increase in SCR. Psychopaths, however, were considerably less responsive to this stress. Furthermore, psychopaths were incapable of learning to avoid the painful electric shocks, while the normals learned significantly better.

Lykken's data indicate that psychopaths do in fact have an under-responsive autonomic nervous system and, as a result, do not learn to avoid aversive situations as well as most other people. Does this provide at least a partial explanation for why psychopaths continue to get into trouble with the law, despite the threat of imprisonment?

Schachter and Latane (1964) followed up on Lykken's work by using similar apparatus and basic procedures, with the exception of one major revision. Each subject was run through the maze twice, once with an injection of a harmless saline solution, once with an injection of adrenaline, a hormone that stimulates physiological arousal. Subjects were prisoners selected on the basis of two criteria: how closely they approximated Cleckley's primary psychopath and how incorrigible they were, as measured by the number of offenses and time in prison. Prisoners high on both criteria were primary psychopaths; prisoners relatively low were normals.

Injections of adrenaline dramatically improved the performance of the psychopath in the avoidance learning task. In fact, with adrenaline injections, the psychopaths learned to avoid shocks more quickly than did normal prisoners with similar injections. On the other hand, when psychopaths had saline injections, they were as deficient in avoidance learning as Lykken's psychopaths.

Since anxiety is presumed to be a major deterrent to antisocial impulses, the manipulation of arousal or anxiety states by drugs may suggest policy implications for the effective treatment of convicted psychopaths. Specific drugs apparently have the potential to increase the emotional level of psychopaths to a point equivalent to the level of the general population.

Subsequent research by Hare (1965a, 1965b) found that primary psychopaths have significantly lower skin conductance while resting than do nonpsychopaths. In a major study, Hare (1968) divided fifty-one inmates at the British Columbia Penitentiary into three groups—primary psychopaths, secondary psychopaths, and nonpsychopaths—and studied them under various conditions, while constantly monitoring their autonomic functioning. The experimental conditions also permitted the observation of a complex physiological response known as the orienting response (OR).

The OR is a nonspecific, highly complicated cortical and sensory response to strange, unexpected changes in the environment. The response may take the form of a turning of the head, a dilation of the eye, or a decrease in heart rate. It is made in an effort to determine what the change is. Pavlov referred to the OR as the "what-is-it" reflex. It is an automatic, reflexive accompaniment to any perceptible change, and it can be measured by various physiological indices. The OR produces, among other things, an increase in the analytical powers of the senses and the cortex.

Hare found that not only did psychopaths exhibit very little autonomic activity (skin conductance and heart rate), but also that they gave smaller ORs than did nonpsychopaths. His data suggest that psychopaths are less sensitive and alert to their environment, particularly to new and unusual events.

Hare later reported intriguing data relating to the heart or cardiac activity of the psychopath. The aforementioned conclusions were based on skin conductance data. When cardiovascular variables are considered, however, some apparent anomalies appear. While skin conductance is consistently low, cardiac activity (heart rate) in the psychopath is often as high as that found in the nonpsychopathic population (Hare & Quinn, 1971). Hare comments, "The psychopaths appeared to be poor electrodermal [skin conductance] conditioners but good cardiovascular ones" (Hare, 1976, p. 135). That is, although psychopaths do not learn to react to stimuli as measured by skin variables, it appears that they learn to react autonomically as well as nonpsychopaths when the heart rate is measured. Hare suggests that the psychopath might be more adaptive to stress when "psychophysiological defense mechanisms" are brought into play, thereby reducing the impact of stressful stimuli.

Hare and his colleagues designed experiments in which the heart rate could be monitored throughout the experimental session. In one experiment, a tone preceded an electric shock by about ten seconds (Hare & Craigen, 1974). In anticipation of the shock, psychopaths exhibited a rapid acceleration of heart beat, followed by a rapid deceleration of heart rate immediately before the onset of the noxious stimulus (a "normal" reaction is a gradual but steady increase in heart rate until the shock). However, their skin conductance remained significantly lower than that of nonpsychopaths. Therefore, psychopaths appear to be superior conditioners when cardiac activity is measured, indicating that they do indeed either learn or inherit autonomic adaptability to noxious stimuli. Hare suggests that this accelerative heart response is adaptive and helps the psychopath tune out or modulate the emotional impact of noxious stimuli. This, he speculates, may be the reason that skin conductance responses are relatively low in the psychopath.

Lykken (1955) also conducted experiments testing the performance of psychopaths on polygraph equipment. If psychopaths are generally underaroused, we would expect that lie detectors would be unable to differentiate their deceptive from their truthful responses, since polygraphs rely on physiological reactivity to questions. Also, psychopaths should have no trouble being deceptive, since they are typically adept at manipulating and deceiving others. Lykken's research confirmed these expectancies. Psychopaths emitted similar skin conductance responses, regardless of whether they were lying or telling the truth. Nonpsychopaths displayed significant differences in reactivity; their lie ratios, reflected by skin conductance, were larger than those of psychopaths. Because of the artificial atmosphere of the laboratory compared to real-life situations, particularly stressful ones, Lykken admonished against uncritical acceptance of his findings until further testing.

Few studies have since directly examined the relationship between psychopathy and lie detection. However, Raskin and Hare (1978) did re-examine the Lykken study, using more sophisticated equipment and better standardization for lie detection. Using twenty-four psychopathic prisoners and twenty-four nonpsychopathic prisoners, they found that both groups were equally easily detected at lying about a situation involving a $20 mock theft. This contradictory finding underscores that fine tuning is still needed if we are to understand the physiological characteristics of the psychopath.

There is evidence, for example, that sufficiently aroused or motivated psychopaths will give physiological responses to interesting events that equal the responses of nonpsychopaths (Hare, 1968). On the other hand, when it comes to highly stressful, serious occasions, psychopaths appear to have incomparable skill at attenuating guilt or fearful reactions (Lykken, 1978). The simulated crime scene in the Raskin-Hare experiment was not only relatively unstressful; it also may have been regarded by the psychopath as an interesting "game." The acid test for the lie detection hypothesis will rest with carefully designed experiments under real-life, highly stressful situations. The present data do not justify firm conclusions.

In summary, the research reviewed thus far allows us to make three tentative conclusions about the autonomic functioning of the psychopath. First, psychopaths appear to be both autonomically and cortically under-aroused, both under rest conditions and under some specific stress conditions. They are much more physiologically "drowsy" than nonpsychopaths. Second, because they lack the necessary emotional equipment, psychopaths appear to be deficient in avoidance learning, which might account partially for their very high recidivism rates. Third, some data suggest that if emotional arousal can be induced, such as by adrenaline, psychopaths can learn from past expereicnes and avoid normally painful or aversive situations, such as prison, embarrassment, or social censure.

We noted earlier that psychopaths are profoundly affected by alcohol, even in small amounts. Alcohol is a general CNS depressant, decreasing arousal levels in the nervous system. Research indicates that underaroused psychopaths are already half asleep and "half in the bag"; alcohol has the general effect of "bagging" them completely. Therefore, we would expect not only that the psychopath would get intoxicated more rapidly than the nonpsychopath of comparable weight, but also would probably pass out sooner. We would also expect the psychopath to have few sleep difficulties. Unfortunately, not enough data have been accumulated in these areas to offer conclusive statements.

CHILDHOOD OF THE PSYCHOPATH

We have discussed the behavioral descriptions and physiological components of psychopaths. Now, how did they get that way? Criminal behavior and other behavior problems are often assumed to be rooted in the home, usually in homes with conflict, inadequate discipline, or poor models. From our discussion of the physiological components of psychopaths, however, it is obvious that the answer is not that simple. Psychopathy seems to be a result of a highly complex interaction of physiological, situational, and learning factors.

Cleckley (1976) is not convinced that any common precursors exist in the family backgrounds of psychopaths, even though relatively homogeneous classifications of psychopathy do exist. However, even if we accept that neurophysiological factors may be causal factors in the development of psychopathy, this does not mean they are hereditary. In fact, there is little evidence to support a strong genetic influence on psychopathy. It *is* possible, though, that psychopaths are born with a *biological predisposition* to develop the disorder, independent of any genetic factors. In line with the Eysenckian view, it could be that psychopaths have a nervous system that interferes with rapid conditioning and association between transgression and punishment. Because of this defect, the psychopath fails to anticipate punishment and, hence, feels no guilt (no conscience). As an alternative to the defect argument, it is possible that certain aspects of the psychopath's nervous system simply have not matured. Another possibility is that a lack of oxygen at birth or early in development adversely affected the RAS.

It appears that psychopathy can be identified early. In a poll of Canadian psychiatrists, 12.7 percent were convinced that the psychopath could be diagnosed prior to age eight, and another 66 percent believed that the disorder could be identified before age eighteen (Gray & Hutchinson, 1964). The DSM III-R (1987) specifies that in order to qualify as having an antisocial personality disorder, certain behavioral patterns must be evident before age fifteen. In a longitudinal study conducted by Robins (1966), clinical records verified that 95 percent of adult psychopaths investigated had demonstrated psychopathic behaviors thirty years previously, as children. After an extensive review of the literature, Quay (1972) notes that psychopathic behaviors in adults are probably labeled "conduct disorders" or "excessive aggressiveness" in children. Childhood behaviors that elicit those labels include extreme disobedience, disruptiveness, fighting, temper tantrums, irresponsibility, and attention seeking.

Some research has linked the psychopath's inordinate stimulation needs with the behavior of the hyperactive child. If the psychopath's physiological underarousal is based on a dysfunction of the nervous system, we would expect to find the same lack of responsivity during his or her childhood. Some hyperactive children, then, may be *candidates* for adult psychopathy.

Hyperactivity

The hyperactive syndrome (also called minimal brain dysfunction, hyperkinesis, or attention deficit disorder) includes a heterogeneity of behaviors, but the central three are: (1) inattention (does not seem to listen, or is easily distracted); (2) impulsivity (acts before thinking, shifts quickly from one activity to another); and (3) excessive motor activity (cannot sit still, fidgets, runs about, is talkative and noisy). Satterfield (1987) notes that, while most childhood disorders are temporary and are not predictive of psychopathology in later life, the hyperactive syndrome presents a different story. "The hyperactive child presents a remarkably immutable syndrome that forecasts an ominous picture of the future. The clinical picture often worsens as the child grows older, with resulting adolescent problems of academic failure and serious antisocial behavior" (Satterfield, 1987, p. 146). Although the common belief is that one eventually outgrows hyperactivity, the evidence is that the key symptomatic features of hyperactivity persist into adulthood (af Klineberg, Magnusson, & Schalling, 1989; Thorley, 1984).

In a thirty-year follow-up of children seen in a child guidance clinic, Robins (1966) found that approximately one-third of those children showing hyperactivity symptoms were diagnosed psychopathic. Similar to neurophysiological features of the psychopath, hyperactivity appears to be closely linked to low levels of cortical arousal (Satterfield, 1978, 1987).

Stimulant drugs are often prescribed to relieve the excessive activity. You might expect that stimulants would increase rather than decrease motor activity. However, they appear to have a specific influence on the RAS and other brain-stem structures, improving their efficiency and allowing more arousal and/or information to reach the cortex (e.g., Bartol, 1975). Thus, the use of stimulant drugs to control hyperactive children has a paradoxical effect.

If hyperactive children have low cortical arousal, they will require greater amounts of stimulation to reach their optimal level of arousal. Cantwell (1975) notes that hyperactive children do not display greater amounts of motor activity on the playground but rather in such places as the classroom, where they are required to control stimulus input. In these situations, it is likely that the arousal level drops below their normal requirement. Thus, the underaroused child will seek increased amounts of stimulation and excitement. One way of getting this is to "cut up" in the classroom and upset others, behavior which is very similar to that of the adult psychopath, who "cuts up" in society.

If children receive adequate stimulus input, such as would be provided by stimulant drugs affecting the activity of the RAS, they no longer need the surplus activity, stimulation, or personal attention. This explanation may account for the fact that behavior modification techniques have been largely ineffective for treating classroom hyperactivity.

After an extensive review of the literature on hyperactive children, Cantwell (1975) found a common thread in adult psychopathy and childhood hyperactivity. Note in the following quote, however, that he uses *sociopath* as a synonym for *psychopath*, which we have warned against doing earlier in this chapter.

> Recent research on waking autonomic functions and EEG patterns in sociopathic adults and in hyperactive children suggest that both groups may have the same underlying neurophysical abnormality: lower levels of basal resting physiological activation than age-matched normals. . . . It would also suggest that . . . there may be a genetically transmitted neurophysiological abnormality that leads to hyperactivity in childhood and sociopathy in adulthood. (Cantwell, 1975, p. 199)

The problem with the Cantwell review, of course, is the equation of psychopathy and sociopathy. It is impossible to tell whether the literature he cites was based on true psychopaths or antisocial individuals with a long history of criminal behavior (sociopaths).

Mendelson, Johnson, and Steward (1971) interviewed the mothers of eighty-three children, ages twelve to sixteen, who had been diagnosed hyperactive several years earlier. Seventy-five percent of the children were still exhibiting hyperactive behavior at follow-up. Mothers complained that the children had a "rebellious attitude" and were generally incorrigible. According to Mendelson, 22 percent of the children continued to demonstrate excessive antisocial behavior and seemed destined to become psychopaths. About 60 percent had had contact with the police, 17 percent on at least three occasions. Twenty-five percent of this group had been referred to juvenile court. More than a third of the eighty-three children had threatened to kill their parents, 7 percent carried weapons, and 15 percent had set fires.

Similar findings were reported by Weiss et al. (1971) in a five-year follow-up study of adolescents who had earlier been diagnosed hyperactive. A great majority of mothers (70 percent) complained that "emotional immaturity" was their child's biggest problem. Thirty percent of the children had no steady friends at follow-up. Twenty-five percent continued to exhibit antisocial behavior regularly. Sixteen percent had been referred to court, and 3 percent were in a reform school at the time of the follow-up study.

In a more recent study, Satterfield (1987) examined the relationship between official arrests and hyperactivity. The study was an eight-year longitudinal analysis of 150 hyperactive and eighty-eight normal children. The data revealed that hyperactives were far more likely to have been arrested for serious crimes than normal children. Moreover, hyperactives were twenty-five times more likely to have been institutionalized for antisocial behavior than normals.

Research on neurophysiological factors in hyperactive children also supports a link between psychopathy and hyperactivity. Several studies have found that 40 to 50 percent of hyperactive children have abnormal EEGs (Satterfield, 1973; Capute, Niedermeyer, & Richardson, 1968; Hughes et al., 1971), especially reflected in abnormal slow-wave activity. You may recall that this cortical feature is common in adult psychopathy. In another series of studies, Satterfield and colleagues (Satterfield & Dawson, 1971; Satterfield et al., 1974) found that many hyperactive children consistently demonstrated low skin conductance levels. The lower their skin conductance level, the greater their restlessness, hyperactivity, and impulsiveness as reported by their teachers. The children showing the lowest arousal (lowest skin conductance and cortical arousal as measured by EEGs) were most responsive to stimulants (specifically, methylphenidate). Following the drug treatment, the children showed a significant increase in arousal as measured by skin conductance and EEGs and a decrease in motor activity.

From his research, Satterfield hypothesized that hyperactivity results from "low arousal and insufficient inhibitory controls over motor outflow and sensory input" (Satterfield, 1975, p. 78). He believes that this lack of inner control results in an overwhelming increase in sensory activity reaching the cortex. Thus, the highly aroused cortex is overloaded by both relevant and irrelevant stimuli, and the individual loses control over what stimuli should dictate his or her behavior.

It is difficult to accept this hypothesis, however, in view of the conceptual gap between consistent findings of *underarousal* and Satterfield's contention of *overarousal*. Moreover, the evidence that stimulant drugs arouse the RAS and cortical arousal is inconsistent with Satterfield's hypothesis. Hyperactivity clearly seems related to stimulus deprivation rather than to overstimulation.

Recent research has focused on developing a more refined classification system of the hyperactive syndrome (Satterfield, 1987; af Klinteberg, Magnusson, & Schalling, 1989). Much of the study has been directed at distinguishing between "pure" hyperactivity, characterized by a high degree of impulsivity, and "aggressive" hyperactivity, characterized by hostility and aggressiveness. In fact, af Klinteberg, Magnusson, & Schalling,

(1989) suggest that impulsivity may be a better predictor of adult criminal behavior than aggressiveness.

From the aforementioned research, it appears likely that *some* childhood hyperactivity is a precursor of *some* adult psychopathy, a finding that underscores the physiological factors in psychopathy. In general, however, with the exception of the work on hyperactivity, few studies have been directed at the neurophysiological components of potential psychopaths during early childhood.

Parental Loss

Research literature often suggests that psychopathy results primarily from a faulty family environment, with researchers offering various interpretations of precisely what the "fault" was. In a background study on outpatients at a psychiatric clinic in Perth, Western Australia, Greer (1964) identified parental loss as a major factor. Parental loss was defined as the complete loss or continuous absence of one or both natural parents for at least twelve months before the child had reached age fifteen. Greer found that 60 percent of seventy-nine patients identified as psychopaths had suffered parental loss. That figure compared to 28 percent of the 387 neurotic subjects and 27 percent of 691 normals.

Greer's results should be viewed cautiously, since the psychopaths were classified according to the American Psychiatric Association 1952 guidelines. The sample, therefore, probably included a rather heterogeneous group of psychopaths. Nevertheless, three findings are particularly interesting. First, significantly more female than male psychopaths had experienced parental loss. Second, a large proportion of the psychopaths had lost a parent before they reached the age of five. Third, psychopaths as a group were much more likely to have lost both parents.

It has also been reported that parental loss in psychopaths is more likely to be paternal than maternal (Oltman & Friedman, 1967), and that the more severe the psychopathic behavior, the more likely there is to be parental loss in the individual's background (Craft, Stephenson, & Granger, 1964). Parental rejection or loss have been found in many other studies, but criteria for defining psychopathy have been too varied to draw meaningful conclusions. Hare (1970) also notes that most of the studies have relied on biased and retrospective data, obtaining background information either from the psychopath (who is a far from reliable source), or from parents, relatives, and friends. The information thus gathered is after the fact and likely to be distorted so facts will fit the behavior.

Buss (1966) described two types of parental behavior he felt are conducive to psychopathic patterns. In the first type, parents are cold and distant to the child, allowing no close relationship to develop. In the second type, discipline, rewards, and punishment are inconsistent and capricious.

Instead of learning right from wrong, the child learns to avoid blame and punishment by lying or by other manipulative means.

After an extensive overview of the research on the causes of psychopathy, McCord and McCord (1964) concluded, "Extreme emotional deprivation or moderate rejection coupled with other environmental conditions or with neural damage to inhibitive centers, best account for the development of psychopathy" (McCord & McCord, 1964, p. 87). According to this view, extreme emotional deprivation by itself can account for some psychopathy, but the McCords noted that a substantial number of deprived psychopaths also have some undefined malfunction in the nervous system. In addition, all psychopaths have experienced parental rejection to some degree.

Cleckley (1976) rebels at this approach, asserting that the theory of parental loss and rejection has been oversold. He is skeptical about any consistent family background pattern emerging from the research, noting that a large percentage of psychopaths in his studies had family backgrounds that seemed happy and conducive to excellent adjustment. According to Cleckley, if there is a negative element in the family background, it must be extremely subtle and abstruse, out of the parents' awareness, and therefore something they should not be blamed for. As a possibility, he suggests an incapacity on the part of the parents for simple warmth, for the "true intimacy that seems to be essential for biologic soundness (substantiality) in some basic relationships" (Cleckley, 1976, p. 411). Parents may be fair, kind, and genial and demonstrate other superior qualities, but they may lack that one subtle but essential ingredient necessary to develop basic warmth and feeling in the child. Moreover, that one special quality may be nearly impossible to isolate for purposes of experimental study.

Phares (1972) believes that one plausible family background explanation of psychopathy is parental pampering and overindulgence. Some children are allowed to escape punishment for antisocial and aggressive behavior by apologizing or by promising not to do it again. They learn to be exceptionally skillful at manipulating others with suitable verbalizations and by being "cute." Phares contends that parents actually reinforce antisocial behavior by allowing children to receive rewards and escape punishment (also highly rewarding) for psychopathic behaviors. In addition, such children rarely have to endure frustration or delayed gratification, since parents cater to their every whim. The children will likely carry these useful behaviors into adulthood.

In the Robins (1966) longitudinal study, most psychopaths were found to have fathers who were either themselves psychopathic or were alcoholic. Robins notes that three of the consequences of having an antisocial, ineffectual father are the inconsistent discipline he provides, marital discord in the family, and a faulty model for the child. Robins did not find a significant relationship between parental rejection and loss and psychopathic behavior, however.

The research on family background, although equivocal, suggests that parental responses to a physiologically based need for stimulation may be crucial. The fact that a child has inordinate stimulation needs does not destine him or her to psychopathy. If parents are effective models, consistent in discipline, and use consistent reinforcement techniques rather than avoidance learning, the child's chances of developing into a moral, sensitive adult are increased. On the other hand, if parents are absent from the home, ineffectual, or inconsistent in discipline, the child will probably not learn appropriate behavior.

However, it appears likely that certain temperamental dispositions of activity, reactivity, emotionality, and sociability that exist at an early age render a child a high risk to engage in behaviors that run counter to society's rules. Highly active children move into (and often against) their environments at a higher pace and more impulsively than less active children. Moreover, children with highly irritable, nasty temperaments are apt to create decidedly different responses from parents and the social environment than children who are temperamentally more relaxed and pleasant. Parents able to tolerate hyperactivity and deal with it effectively provide a better emotional fit than those unable to tolerate a child moving at a high pace toward his or her environment. Parents unable or unwilling to deal with the fast-paced, irritable child may provide an inadequate home environment for "normal" development.

A typical developmental pattern would be hyperactivity in early childhood, perhaps accompanied by a learning disability, a behavioral problem in the middle school years, juvenile delinquency as an adolescent, and a psychopathic or antisocial personality disorder in adulthood. While this pattern is emerging, the psychopathic personality learns, by reward, how to manipulate others verbally. The words "I'm sorry" or "I won't do it again" take on strong reinforcing properties, despite their insincerity.

SUMMARY AND CONCLUSIONS

The primary psychopath should be distinguished from people who may be classified as psychotic, neurotic, or emotionally disturbed. The psychopath should also be distinguished from the sociopath, who in many ways is similar. However, *sociopath* (sometimes called the criminal psychopath) usually refers to a person who habitually violates the law and who does not learn from past experience. The psychopath as discussed here may or may not run afoul of the law.

Psychopaths most often function in society as charming, daring, witty, intelligent individuals, high on charisma but low on emotional reaction and affect. They appear to lack moral standards or to manifest genuine sensitivity toward others. *If* criminals, they become the despair of law enforcement officials because their crimes appear to be without discernible or rational motives. Even worse, they show no remorse or ability to be rehabilitated.

We reviewed much of the physiological research suggesting that the psychopath is different from the rest of the population on a number of physiological measures. The psychopath seems to be underaroused, both autonomically and cortically, a finding which may account for his or her difficulty in learning the rules of society. Recalling our discussion of Eysenck's theory in chapter two, it is clear that the psychopath would be a stable extravert with high psychoticism. The psychopath, like the extravert, apparently is not aroused enough to profit as easily from the classical conditioning that perhaps sets most of us on the straight and narrow path in childhood. If, in addition to this physiological lack, the psychopath's family situation leaves him or her without appropriate models, then he or she is doubly cursed.

Many psychopaths also apparently have abnormal brain-wave patterns, mostly of a slow-wave childlike variety, which suggests that their nervous system is immature, at least until middle age. There are indications of more than the usual amounts of positive spikes, which are brain-wave bursts that correlate with aggressive episodes and impulsivity. Research has failed to discover, however, whether these abnormalities engender psychopathic behavior or vice versa. There is also little evidence to support a strong hereditary influence, although we should not overlook the possibility that psychopaths may be born with a biological predisposition to the disorder.

Studies on the childhood of psychopaths suggest that they may have followed the hyperactive syndrome as children, causing chaos for parents and teachers. It would be folly to maintain, though, that the hyperactive child of today is the psychopath of tomorrow. Perhaps because they are physiologically underaroused, psychopaths do not respond as well to admonishments, threats, or actual punishment as do their nonpyschopathic peers. They do not learn society's expectations and the rules of right and wrong, possibly because anxiety-inducing disciplinary procedures are not that anxiety-producing for them.

There are still numerous gaps in our knowledge of the psychopath, one being in the area of sex differences. Research on female psychopaths is scant. The available data suggest that behavioral characteristics for females are similar to those of male psychopaths, with slightly more emphasis among females on sexual acting-out behavior. This probably reflects a cultural bias, however, since women have been traditionally chastised more than men for behavior deemed inappropriate according to sexual mores.

One feature of psychopaths is abundantly clear, however. They do not seem to think like mainstream society. They appear to perceive situations and approach life differently than most people. This variation in cognitive style is characteristic of many deviant individuals, whether or not they are criminal. We will discuss this phenomenon again in the chapters on homicide and violence and sexual offenses.

CHAPTER FOUR
Origins of Criminal Behavior: Learning Factors

People do not come into situations empty-headed. They have an infinite store of living experiences and an extensive repertoire of strategies for reacting to events. Up to this point, we have not acknowledged these strategies, concentrating instead on heredity and neurophysiology and the significant roles they may play in the development of criminal behavior. These biological factors appear to account in part for individual differences in susceptibility to classical conditioning. Since the capacity to be conditioned strongly affects fear of reprisal, it determines the degree of inhibition of socially undesirable criminal behavior. However, classical conditioning presumes that the human being is an automaton. Pair a neutral stimulus with a closely following painful event and the alert, intact robot will eventually, and automatically, connect the stimulus with the pain. This sequence is probably a very powerful factor in many behaviors, but certainly not in all. Conditioning is only one of several factors involved in the acquisition of criminal behavior.

To understand criminal behavior, it is crucial that we regard all individuals—whether or not they violate the rules of society—as active problem solvers who perceive, interpret, and respond to their environments uniquely. For the moment, consider unlawful behavior as *subjectively adaptive* rather than deviant. In this sense, unlawful conduct is a response pattern that a person has found to be effective, or thinks will be effective, in certain circumstances.

Violent crimes like aggravated assault and homicide are sometimes called "irrational," "uncontrollable," "explosive," or "motiveless," and therefore are believed to resist or defy analysis (e.g., President's Commission on Law Enforcement and Administration of Justice, 1967). Later in this text, we will find, however, that different types of violence can be placed into different theoretical frameworks. The decision to act violently may be a quick one, but the violent behavior is usually *not* irrational or uncontrollable, although in a very small percentage of cases it may be. Even behavior that may arise out of a severe mental disorder, however, may be adaptive, even when it is not legally culpable.

Engaging in criminal behavior might be one person's way of adapting or surviving under physically, socially, or psychologically dire conditions. Another person might decide that violence is necessary to defend honor, protect self, or reach a personal goal. In either case, the person is choosing what he or she *believes* is the best alternative for that particular situation. It is not, of course, necessarily the alternative that others would choose, nor what society condones. What, besides susceptibility to classical conditioning, accounts for the difference? In a very general sense, learning—both operant (or instrumental) and social learning—is an extremely important component in the equation. In the following pages, we will expand the concept of conditioning to include these two distinct forms of learning, which play a major role in the acquisition and maintenance of criminal behavior. Later, we will introduce situational factors that appear to affect the learning process. Since each of these topics springs from the school of psychological thought called behaviorism, we will begin our discussion there.

BEHAVIORISM

Behaviorism "officially" began in 1913 with the publication of a landmark paper by John B. Watson (1878–1958), "Psychology as the Behaviorist Views It." The paper, which appeared in *Psychological Review*, is considered the first definitive statement on behaviorism, and Watson is thus acknowledged as the school's founder. However, Watson was by no means the first to discuss the basic elements of behaviorism. Its roots can be traced back at least to Aristotle (Diserens, 1925), and ingredients are also found in the positivism of both Auguste Comte (1838) and Antoine Cournot (1858) (Titchener, 1914). The point is that Watson's behaviorism represents a recurring phase in the cyclical history of psychology. A psychology of consciousness or mind is followed by a psychology of action and behavior (behaviorism), from which a psychology of mind and consciousness re-emerges. Today, psychology is beginning to move once again toward a psychology of mind, especially cognitive processes. But that's another story, one we will cite periodically throughout this text. For the moment, let's return to Watsonian behaviorism, which has heavily influenced psychological interpretations of criminal behavior.

Watson frequently declared that psychology was the *science* of behavior. He believed that psychologists should eliminate the *mind* and all of its related "vague" concepts from scientific consideration because they could not be observed or measured. He was convinced that the fundamental goal of psychology was to understand, predict, and control human behavior and that only a rigidly scientific approach could accomplish this.

Greatly influenced by Pavlov's research on classical conditioning, Watson thought that psychology should focus exclusively on the interplay between stimulus and response. A stimulus is an object or event that elicits behavior. A response is the elicited behavior. Watson was convinced that all behavior—both animal and human—was controlled by the external environment in a way similar to that described by Pavlov in his initial study—stimulus produces response (sometimes called S-R psychology). Therefore, for Watson, classical (or Pavlovian) conditioning was the key to understanding, predicting, and controlling behavior, and its practical applicability was unlimited.

Today, the chief spokesperson for behaviorism is B. F. Skinner (1904–), who has been the most influential psychologist in the United States during the twentieth century. The Skinnerian perspective especially dominates the application of behavior modification or behavior therapy in the correctional system and in many institutions for the mentally handicapped or disturbed. Some contemporary theories about criminal behavior (e.g., Akers, 1977, 1985) try to integrate Skinnerian behaviorism with sociological perspectives. It is worthwhile, therefore, to spend some time sketching the Skinnerian approach to human behavior in general before assessing its impact on criminology.

Like Watson, Skinner believes that the primary goal of psychology is the prediction and control of behavior. And like Watson, he believes that environmental or external stimuli are the primary—if not the sole—determinants of all behavior, both human and animal. The environmental stimuli become *independent variables* and the behaviors they elicit the *dependent variables*. In the behavioral sciences, a variable is any entity that can be measured. A behavior (or response) is called "dependent" because it is under the control of (or dependent on) one or more independent variables. The consistent relationships between independent and dependent variables (stimulus and response) are scientific laws. Thus, according to Skinner, the aim of behavioristic psychology is to uncover these laws, making possible the prediction and control of human behavior.

Unlike Watson, Skinner does not deny the existence and sometimes usefulness of private mental events or internal stimuli. He emphasizes, however, that these stimuli are not needed by a science of behavior, since the products of mental activity can be explained in ways that do not require allusion to unobserved mental states. Specifically, mental activity can be explained by observing what a person *does,* and it is what a person does that counts. Watson, remember, insisted that consciousness and mind simply do not exist. Thought, to Watson, was little more than tiny movements of the speech apparatus.

At this point, we must emphasize the need to distinguish between behaviorism as a philosophy and method of science, and where behaviorism stands on the central issue of human nature. As a philosophy and method of science, behaviorism posits that knowledge about human behavior can be best advanced if scientists use referents that have a *physical* basis and can be *publicly* observed by others. Since private events that happen inside our heads cannot be seen by others, they cannot be subjected to the rules of science. According to Skinner, behavioral science data must be comparable to be verified or disconfirmed. Otherwise, psychology would remain a philosophical exercise steeped in armchair speculation and untestable opinions. Self-proclaimed experts could continue to assert that shoplifting is an addiction, just like alcoholism, without being taken to task about the validity of their statements. Only a well-executed, systematic study where the terms *shoplifting* and *addiction* are clearly spelled and rigorously tested will advance our knowledge about the accuracy of the shoplifting-addiction statement. Therefore, every psychological experiment, every sentence written into a psychological report, should be anchored to something that we all can observe. Rather than merely saying that someone is anxious or angry, we must identify the precise behaviors that prompt us to make these interpretations. This offers a basis for others, including the person being observed, to agree or disagree with us. "You're twitching in your chair. You must be apprehensive." "No, I'm not! It's that damned woolen underwear my aunt sent from Vermont."

Skinner, and a majority of psychologists with a strong behavioristic leaning, embrace the view that humans differ only in degree from their animal ancestry. The behavior of humans follows the same basic natural laws as that of all animals. Like Darwin, Skinner sees no radical differences between humans and animals. Even human language and conceptual thinking are nondistinctive. Verbal behavior "is a very special kind of behavior, but there is nothing by way of processes involved that would distinguish it from non-verbal behavior and hence [verbal behavior] would not distinguish man from the [other] animals" (Skinner, 1964, p. 156). To Skinner, therefore, research on subhumans like monkeys, rats, and pigeons has great value; if carefully done it will reveal lawful relationships between all organisms and their environments.

Skinner is also clearly a strong *situationist*. All behavior is at the mercy of stimuli in the environment, and individuals have virtually no control or self-determination. Independent thinking and free will are myths. Animals and humans alike *react*, like complicated robots, to their environments. The environmental stimuli and the range of reactions are complex and infinite, but with careful research, this complexity is not unmanageable. Complex human behavior can be broken down into more simple behavior, a procedure sometimes referred to as *reductionism*. In other words, complicated behavior can be best understood by examining the simplest stimulus-response chains of behavior. This point brings us to the issue of *operant* conditioning.

Skinner accepts the basic tenets of classical conditioning but asserts that we need an additional type of conditioning to account more fully for all forms of behavior. Recall Pavlov's experiments with the hungry dogs. The dogs did not operate on their environments to receive rewards; the event (food) occurred regardless of what they did. Skinner calls this "responding conditioning" and contrasts it to a situation in which a subject does something that affects the situation. In other words, subjects behave in such a way that reinforcement is forthcoming. To uncover this operant conditioning principle, Skinner established an association between behavior and its consequences. He trained pigeons (apparently less troublesome and less expensive than dogs) to peck at keys or push levers for food. The pecking or pushing are operations on the environment. The operation should not be construed to imply self-determination, however. It is simply a *reaction* to stimuli in order to receive a certain consequence or reward. In this sense, the behavior that emerges from operant conditioning—although not automatic—is no more indicative of free will than is the behavior that emerges from classical conditioning.

The learning that comes about through operant conditioning was described before Skinner's time, but he is credited with drawing contemporary attention to it. In the early nineteenth century, for example, the philosopher Jeremy Bentham observed that human conduct was controlled by the seeking of pleasure and the avoidance of pain. In essence, this is what is meant by operant learning. It assumes that people do things solely to receive rewards and avoid punishment. The rewards may be physical (e.g., material goods, money), psychological (e.g., feelings of importance or control over one's fate), or social (e.g., improved status, acceptance).

Skinner calls rewards *reinforcement*, defining that term as anything that increases the probability of future responding. Furthermore, reinforcement may be either positive or negative. In *positive reinforcement*, we gain something we desire as a consequence of certain behavior. In *negative reinforcement*, we avoid an unpleasant event or stimulus as a consequence of certain behavior. For example, if as a child you were able to avoid the unpleasantness of certain school days by feigning illness, your malingering was negatively reinforced. Therefore, you were more likely to engage in it again at a future date, under similar circumstances—high school dress-up day, class discussion day in a difficult college course, or the day the district supervisor was scheduled to visit the office. Thus, both positive and negative reinforcement can increase the likelihood of future behavior.

Negative reinforcement is to be distinguished from punishment and extinction. In punishment, an organism receives noxious or painful stimuli as consequences of behavior. In extinction, a person or animal receives neither reinforcement nor punishment. Skinner argues that punishment is an ineffective way to eliminate behavior, because it merely suppresses it temporarily. At a later time, under the right conditions, the response is very likely to reoccur. Extinction is far more effective, because once the organism learns that a behavior brings no reinforcement, the behavior will be dropped from the repertoire of possible responses for that set of circumstances.

According to Nietzel (1979), C. R. Jeffery (1965) was one of the first behaviorists to suggest that criminal behavior was learned according to principles of Skinnerian operant conditioning. Shortly afterwards, Burgess and Akers (1966) agreed with this, and further hypothesized that criminal behavior was both *acquired* and *maintained* through operant conditioning. But, as Nietzel points out, most of the direct evidence for this claim comes from experiments with animals. Evidence that the same occurs in humans is scarce and replete with possible alternate interpretations.

The premise that operant conditioning is the basis for the origin of criminal behavior is deceptively simple: Criminal behavior is learned and strengthened because of the reinforcements it brings. According to Skinner, human beings are born neutral—neither good nor bad. Culture, society, and the environment shape behavior. Therefore, behavior will be labeled good, bad, or indifferent, as society chooses. What is judged "good" behavior in one society or culture may be labeled "bad" in another. Members of a fundamental religious group may believe that it is "bad" for a child to pretend that a block of wood is a toy truck and "good" to hit the child with a rod to stop that behavior. To others, the behavior of the adults who hit the child is "bad." Depending on the severity of the punishment, it may also be criminal assault.

Skinner is convinced that searches for individual dispositions or personalities that lead to criminal conduct are fruitless, because people are ultimately determined by the environment in which they live. He does not completely discount the role of genetics in the formation of behavior, but he sees it as a very minor one; the dominant player is operant conditioning. According to Skinner and his followers, if we wish to eliminate crime, we must change society through behavioral engineering based on a "scientific conception of man." Having agreed on rules and regulations (having defined what behaviors constitute antisocial or criminal offenses), we must design a society in which members learn very early that reinforcement will not occur if they transgress against these rules and regulations, but will occur if they abide by them.

This is a tall order, since the reinforcements for behavior are not always obvious and may actually be highly complex. Property crimes like shoplifting and burglary, or violent crimes like robbery, appear to be motivated in many cases by a desire for physical rewards. However, they may also be prompted by a desire for social and psychological reinforcements, such as increased status among peers, self-esteem, or feelings of competence. It is a safe bet that much criminal behavior is undertaken for reinforcement purposes, positive or negative. The problem then becomes, how do we identify those reinforcements, and how do we prevent them from happening, or at least minimize their value?

Contemporary psychology still embraces a behavioristic orientation toward the scientific study of behavior, but it is growing cool toward the Skinnerian perspective. All behaviorists are not Skinnerians. Many find Skinner's brand of behaviorism too limiting (e.g., Bandura, 1978, 1983). While they agree that a stimulus can elicit a reflexive response (classical conditioning) and that a behavior produces consequences that influence subsequent responding (operant conditioning), they are also convinced that additional factors must be introduced to explain human behavior.

This brings us to the topic of mental states and brain-mediational processes, which Skinner urges us to shun. In recent years, many psychologists have been examining the roles played by self-reinforcement, anticipatory reinforcement, vicarious reinforcement, and all the symbolic processes that occur within the human brain. To avoid confusion, we must now begin to distinguish Skinnerian behaviorism from other forms, including social behaviorism (social learning) and differential association-reinforcement theory.

SOCIAL LEARNING

Early learning theorists worked in the laboratory, using animals as their primary subjects. Pavlov's, Watson's, and Skinner's theories, for example, were based on careful, painstaking observations and experiments with animals. The learning principles gleaned from their work were generalized to a wide variety of human behaviors. In many cases, this was a valid process. Few psychologists would dispute the contention that the concept of reinforcement is one of the most soundly established principles in psychology today.

However, behaviorists also suggested that, since all human behavior is learned, it can also be changed using the same principles by which it was acquired. This generated a plethora of behavior therapies or behavior modification techniques. Use learning principles to establish conditions that change or maintain targeted behaviors and *voila*! therapeutic success! The apparent simplicity of the procedures and methods was especially appealing to many clinicians and other professionals in the criminal justice system, and behavior modification packages sometimes guaranteed to modify criminal behavior were rushed to correctional institutions.

But oversimplification is dangerous when we deal with human complexity. Humans beings *do* respond to reinforcement and punishment, and behavior therapy based on learning principles *can* change certain elements of behavior. Moreover, humans *can* be classically conditioned, although there are individual differences in their susceptibility. When we lose sight of the person and overemphasize the environmental or external determinants of behavior, however, we may be overlooking a critical level of explanation. Remember that human beings are, in part, active problem solvers who perceive, encode, interpret, and make decisions on the basis of what the environment has to offer. Thus, internal factors, as well as external ones, may play significant roles in behavior. This is the essence of social learning theory, which suggests that to understand criminal behavior we must examine perceptions, thoughts, expectancies, competencies, and values. Each person has his or her own version of the world and lives by that version.

To explain human behavior, social learning theorists place great emphasis on cognitive variables, which are the internal processes we commonly call thinking and remembering. Classical and operant conditioning ignore what transpires between the time the organism perceives a stimulus and the time it responds or reacts. Skinnerian behaviorists claim, "If we can account for the facts by using observable behavior, why worry about the labyrinths of internal processes?" Social behaviorists, however, counter that this perspective offers an incomplete picture of human behavior.

The term *social learning* reflects the theory's strong assumption that we learn primarily by observing and listening to people around us—the social environment. In fact, social learning theorists believe that the social environment is the most important factor in the *acquisition* of most behavior. They do accept the necessity of reinforcement for the *maintenance* of behavior, however. Criminal behavior, for example, may be *initially* acquired through association and through observation, but whether or not it is maintained will depend primarily on reinforcement (operant conditioning). For example, if a boy sees someone he admires (i.e., a role model) successfully pilfering from the local sporting goods store, the boy may try some pilfering of his own. Whether he continues that behavior, however, will depend on the personal reinforcement or value it assumes. If no reinforcement is forthcoming (he fails to pocket a baseball because someone else walked into the store, or he finds that the gym shorts he stole do not fit), then the behavior will probably drop out of his response repertoire (extinction). If the behavior brings aversive results (punishment), this will inhibit or suppress future similar behavior.

Several clusters of psychologists are enrolled in the social learning school of thought. We will focus first on the work of two prominent representatives, Julian Rotter and Albert Bandura, since they seem to have the most to offer to the study of criminal behavior from the social learning perspective.

Expectancy Theory

Julian Rotter is best known for drawing attention to the importance of expectations (cognitions) about the consequences (outcomes) of behavior, including the reinforcement that will be gained from it. In other words, before doing anything, we ask, "What has happened to me before in this situation, and what will I gain this time?" According to Rotter, whether a specific pattern of behavior occurs will depend on our expectancies and how much we value the outcomes. To predict whether someone will behave a certain way, we must estimate that person's expectancies and the importance he or she places on the rewards gained by the behavior. Often, the person will develop "generalized expectancies" that are stable and consistent across relatively similar situations (Mischel, 1976).

The hypothesis that people enter situations with generalized expectancies about the outcomes of their behavior is an important one for students of crime. Applying Rotter's theory to criminal behavior, we would say that when people engage in unlawful conduct, they *expect* to gain something in the form of status, power, security, affection, material goods, or living conditions. The violent person, for example, may elect to behave that way in the belief that something will be gained. The serial murderer might believe that God has sent him on a mission to eliminate all "loose" women; the woman who poisons an abusive husband looks for an improvement in her life situation. Simply to label a violent person impulsive, crazy, or lacking in ego control fails to include other essential ingredients in the act. Although self-regulation and moral development are involved—concepts we will discuss in later chapters—people who act unlawfully perceive and interpret the situation and select what they consider to be the most effective behavior under the circumstances. Usually, when people act violently, they do so because that approach has been used successfully in the past (at least they believe it has been sucessful). Less frequently, they have simply observed someone else gain by employing a violent approach, and they try it for themselves. This brings us to Bandura's imitational model of social learning.

Imitational Aspects of Social Learning

An individual may acquire ways of doing something simply by watching others do it; direct reinforcement is not necessary. Bandura (1973b) introduced this idea, which he called *observational learning* or *modeling*, to the social learning process. Bandura contends that much of our behavior is initially acquired by watching others, who are called *models*. For example, a child may learn how to shoot a gun by imitating TV characters. He or she then rehearses and fine-tunes this behavioral pattern by practicing with toy guns. The behavior is likely to be maintained if peers also play with guns and reinforce one another for doing so. Even if the children have not pulled the triggers on real guns, they have acquired a close approximation of shooting someone. It is likely that just about every adult and older child in the United States knows how to shoot a gun, even if they have never actually done so: "You aim and pull the trigger." Of course, shooting safely and accurately is much more complicated, but the rudimentary know-how has been acquired through *imitational learning* (also called modeling or observational learning). The behavioral pattern exists in our repertoires, even if we have never received direct reinforcement for acquiring it.

According to Bandura, the more significant and respected the models, the greater their impact on our behavior. Relevant models include parents, teachers, siblings, friends, and peers, as well as symbolic models like literary characters or TV or movie personages. Rock stars and athletes are modeled by many young people, which is one reason we are exposed to so many public figures touting everything from cosmetics to a drug-free life to draft registration. Interestingly, the commercial and public service advertisements often miss the point. In observational learning, it is not so much what the model says as what the model does that is effective. If football stars actually avoided the use of drugs in their daily lives, their messages to youth might be more effective.

The observed behavior of the model is also more likely to be imitated if the observer sees the model receive a reward. Conversely, it is less likely to be imitated if the model is punished. Bandura believes—much like Rotter—that once a person decides to use a newly acquired behavior, whether he or she performs or maintains it will depend on the situation and the expectancies for potential gain. This potential gain may come from outside (the praise of others, financial gain) or it may come from within (self-reinforcement for a job the individual perceives as well done).

Much of Bandura's research was directed at the learning of aggressive and violent behavior. We will be returning to his theory, therefore, in chapter seven. At this point, however, be aware that a substantial body of experimental findings gives impressive support to his views. For example, pre-school children who watched a film of an adult assaulting an inflated plastic rubber doll were significantly more likely to imitate that behavior than were a comparable group who viewed more passive behavior (Bandura & Huston, 1961; Bandura, Ross, & Ross, 1963). Many studies employing variations of this basic procedure report similar results, strengthening the hypothesis that observing aggression leads to hostility in both children and adults (Walters & Grusec, 1977). Apparently, people who observe aggressive acts not only imitate the observed behavior but also become generally more hostile.

To some extent, social learning as it is discussed by Rotter and Bandura humanizes the Skinnerian viewpoint, since it provides clues about what transpires inside the human brain (or mind). It draws our attention to the cognitive, mediational aspects of behavior, while classical and operant conditioning focus exclusively on the environment. Social learning theorists use *environment* in the social sense, which includes the internal as well as the external environment. Skinnerians prefer to limit relevant stimuli to external surroundings.

Differential Association-Reinforcement Theory

Ronald Akers (1977, 1985; Burgess & Akers, 1966) proposes a social learning theory of deviance that tries to integrate the core ingredients of Skinnerian behaviorism, the social learning theory as outlined by Bandura, and the differential association theory of criminologist Edwin H. Sutherland. Akers calls his theory *differential association-reinforcement* (DAR). Briefly, the theory states that people learn to commit deviant acts through interaction with their social environment.

To understand DAR theory, we must grasp Sutherland's differential association theory, which has dominated the field of sociological criminology for over four decades. It was first set forth in the third edition (1939) of Sutherland's *Principles of Criminology* and restated in 1947. Although Sutherland died in 1950, the theory has been left intact in Donald R. Cressey's subsequent revisions of the original text.

Sutherland believed that criminal or deviant behavior is learned the same way that all behavior is learned. The crucial factors are who a person associates with, for how long, how frequently, how personally meaningful the associations, and how early they occur in the person's development. According to Sutherland, in our intimate personal groups we all learn definitions, or normative meanings (messages), favorable or unfavorable to law violation. A person becomes delinquent or criminal "because of an excess of definitions favorable to violation of law over defintions unfavorable to violation of law. This is the principle of differential association" (Sutherland & Cressey, 1974, pp. 80–81).

Note that criminal behavior does not invariably develop out of association or contacts with "bad companions" or a criminal element. The messages, not the contacts themselves, are crucial. Furthermore, deviant messages must outweigh conventional ones. Therefore, Sutherland also believed that criminal behavior may develop even if association with criminal groups is minimal. For example, law-abiding groups—such as parents—may communicate subtly or bluntly that it is all right to cheat, or that everyone is basically dishonest. This is an extremely important point that will be reiterated when we discuss moral development.

Sutherland's theory is probably popular among social scientists because, as one writer put it, "it attempts a logical, systematic formulation of the chain of interrelations that makes crime reasonable and understandable as normal, learned behavior without having to resort to assumptions of biological or psychological deviance" (Vold, 1958, p. 192). However, the theory is also ambiguous; because of this feature it has not drawn much empirical research (see Gibbons, 1977, pp. 221–228). How are a person's contacts to be measured and weighed? Also, as Cressey (Sutherland & Cressey, 1974) admits, the theory does not specify what kinds of learning are important (e.g., operant, classical, modeling). Neither does it adequately consider individual differences in the learning process.

Akers (1985) tries to correct some of the problems with differential association theory by reformulating it to dovetail with Skinnerian and social learning principles. He proposes that most deviant behavior is learned according to principles outlined in Skinner's operant conditioning, with classical conditioning playing a secondary role. Furthermore, the strength of deviant behavior is a direct function of the amount, frequency, and probability of reinforcement the individual has experienced by performing that behavior in the past. The reinforcement may be positive or negative, in the Skinnerian meanings of the terms.

Crucial to the Akers position is the role played by *social* and *nonsocial* reinforcement, the former being the more important. "Most of the learning relevant to deviant behavior is the result of social interactions or exchanges in which the words, responses, presence, and behavior of other persons make reinforcers available, and provide the setting for reinforcement" (Akers, 1985, p. 45). It is also important to note that most of these social reinforcements are symbolic and verbal rewards for participating or for agreeing with group norms and expectations. For example, doing something in accordance with group or subcultural norms is rewarded with "Way to go!", "Great job," "Good going," a pat on the back, or a friendly grin. Nonsocial reinforcement refers primarily to physiological factors or material acqusition that may be relevant for some crimes, such as drug-related offenses or burglary.

Deviant behavior, then, is most likely to develop as a result of social reinforcements given by significant others, usually within one's peer group. The group first adopts *normative definitions* about what conduct is good or bad, right or wrong, justified or unjustified. These normative definitions become internal, cognitive guides to what is appropriate and will most likely be reinforced by the group. In this sense, normative definitions operate as *discriminative stimuli*—social signals transmitted by subcultural or peer groups to indicate whether certain kinds of behavior will be rewarded or punished within a particular social context.

According to Akers, two classes of discriminative stimuli operate in promoting deviant behavior. First, *positive* discriminative stimuli are the signals (verbal or nonverbal) that communicate that certain behaviors are encouraged by the subgroup. Not surprisingly, they follow the principle of positive reinforcement: The individual engaging in them gains social rewards from the group. The second type of social cue, *neutralizing* or *justifying* discriminative stimuli, neutralize the warnings communicated by society at large that certain behaviors are inappropriate or unlawful. According to Akers, they "make the behavior, which others condemn and which the person himself may initially define as bad, seem all right, justified, excusable, necessary, the lesser of two evils, or not 'really' deviant after all" (Akers, 1977, p. 521). Statements like "Everyone has a price," "I can't help myself," "Everyone else does it," or "She deserved it" reflect the influence of neutralizing stimuli.

The more people define their behavior as positive or at least justified, the more likely they are to engage in it. If deviant activity (as defined by society at large) has been reinforced more than conforming behavior (also defined by society), and if it has been justified, it is likely that deviant behavior will be maintained. In essence, our behavior is guided by the norms we have internalized and for which we expect to be continually socially reinforced by significant others.

Akers accepts the validity of Bandura's modeling as a necessary factor in the initial acquisition of deviant behavior. But its continuation will depend greatly on the frequency and personal significance of social reinforcement, which comes from association with others.

Akers's social learning theory has received its share of criticism. Some scholars consider it tautological: Behavior occurs because it is reinforced, but it is reinforced because it occurs. Kornhauser (1978) points out that there is no empirical support for the theory. Still, the theory remains a very popular one within sociological criminology.

FRUSTRATION-INDUCED CRIMINALITY

Several learning investigators (e.g., Amsel, 1958; Brown & Farber, 1951) have noted that when organisms—including humans—are prevented from responding in a way that had previously produced rewards, their behavior often becomes more energetic and vigorous. Animals bite, scratch, snarl, and become irritable; humans may snarl and become irritable and rambunctious (and may also bite and scratch). Researchers assume that these aroused reponses result from an aversive internal state of arousal which they call *frustration*.

Thus, when behavior directed at a specific goal is blocked, arousal increases and the individual experiences a drive to reduce it. Behavior is energized, but more significantly, the responses which lead to a reduction in the arousal may be strengthened or reinforced. This suggests that people who employ violence to reduce frustration will, under extreme frustration, become more vigorous than usual, possibly even resorting to homicide. It also suggests that violent behavior directed at reducing frustration will be reinforced, since it reduces unpleasant arousal by altering the precipitating event or stimuli.

Leonard Berkowitz (1962) conducted numerous studies relating frustration to criminality. He divided criminal personalities into two main classifications: the socialized and the individual offender. You have already met socialized offenders. We have discussed them throughout this chapter as products of learning, conditioning, and modeling. The individual offender, by contrast, is the product of a long, possibly intense series of frustrations resulting from unmet needs. According to Berkowitz, both modeling and frustration are involved in the development of criminal behavior, but one set of life experiences favors a particular criminal style. "Most lawbreakers may have been exposed to some combination of frustrations and aggressively antisocial models, with the thwartings being particularly important in the development of 'individual' offenders and the antisocial models being more influential in the formulation of the 'socialized' criminals" (Berkowitz, 1962, p. 303).

Berkowitz adds an important dimension to frustration, suggesting that it is particularly intense if an individual has high expectancy of reaching a goal (Berkowitz, 1969). People who anticipate reaching a goal and who feel they have some personal control over their lives are more likely to react strongly to interference than those who feel hopeless. In the first case, delay or blockage may generate intense anger and even a violent response if the frustrated individual believes that type of response will eliminate the interference. The power of frustration may well have been what Maslow (1954) was referring to when he stated that crime and delinquency represent a legitimate revolt against exploitation, injustice, and unfairness. The frustration hypothesis also fits neatly into theories offered by radical or conflict criminologists. Individuals who feel suppressed by the power elite and feel they have a right to reap society's benefits may well experience intense frustration at continuing domination.

The frustration-induced theory helps to explain the behavior of looters during unexpected events like floods, fires, or blackouts. The theory would suggest that individuals who commit larceny under these situations have materialistic goals (e.g., their fair share of middle-class goods) which they have not yet attained. Society blocked the goals, and the individuals became impatient and frustrated. When the opportunity to loot arises, they are there to take it. Demographic profiles of the 2,706 adults arrested and charged with looting during the New York City blackout of 1977 support this theory. The defendants had "stronger community ties" and higher incomes than the average defendant in the criminal justice system (*New York Times*, August 14, 1977). Only about 10 percent were on welfare; approximately half were gainfully employed. Sixty-five percent of those arrested were black and 30 percent were Hispanic. These data suggest that these defendants were, in general, eager to eliminate further delays in meeting their expectancy for a better life.

On the other hand, a good argument could also be made for a modeling or social learning explanation. The data may represent nothing more than the naive response of a group of lower-middle-class violators who modeled seemingly rewarding behavior but lacked the street-wise knowledge to escape detection. The more sophisticated groups, perhaps more representative of larceny suspects as a group, may have looted early and fled. The others, imitating the early groups, were still looting when the police arrived.

Berkowitz hypothesizes that the more intense and frequent the thwartings or frustrations in a person's life, the more susceptible and sensitive the person is to subsequent frustration. Thus, the individual who frequently strikes out at society in unlawful or deviant ways may have encountered numerous severe frustrations, especially during early development, but has not given up hope. In support of this argument, Berkowitz cites the research findings on delinquency (e.g., Glueck & Glueck, 1950; Bandura & Walters, 1959; McCord, McCord, & Zola, 1959), revealing that delinquent children, compared to nondelinquents, have been considerably more deprived and frustrated during their lifetime. Berkowitz also suggests that parental neglect or failure to meet the child's needs for dependency and affection are internal, frustrating circumstances that germinate distrust of all others within the social environment. This generalized distrust is carried into the streets and school, and the youngster may exhibit a "chip on the shoulder." The frustration of not having dependency needs met prevents the child from establishing emotional attachments to other people. The individual may thus become resentful, angry, and hostile toward other people in general.

SITUATIONAL INSTIGATORS AND REGULATORS OF CRIMINAL BEHAVIOR

Most contemporary theories and research support the view that human behavior results from a mutual interaction between personality and situational variables. However, several behavioral and social scientists (e.g., Goldstein, 1975; Gibbons, 1977; Petersen, 1977) complain that much crime research and theory neglects situational variables in favor of dispositional factors. They contend that criminality in many cases may simply reflect being in the wrong place at the wrong time with the wrong people. For example, Gibbons comments: "In many cases, criminality may be a response to nothing more temporal than the provocations and attractions bound up in the immediate circumstances out of which deviant acts arise" (Gibbons, 1977, p. 229). Skinner, of course, exemplifies the position that behavior is controlled by environmental contingencies and events.

Haney (1983) discusses "fundamental attribution error," which refers to a common human tendency to discount the influence of the situation and explain behavior by referring to the personality of the actor instead. He believes that personality or internal states account very little for how we act. The important determining influence is the situation in which we find ourselves. In essence, Haney is arguing that, given the appropriate circumstances, anyone might engage in culpable criminal behavior, that we all have our price.

Situations are rarely static. Our behavior influences them to some extent, and they in turn influence our behavior. This reciprocal interaction between person and environment is one reason why students of crime are beginning to pay more attention to victimology—victims often influence the course of criminal actions, particularly violent ones. At this point we will turn our attention to two situational factors that seem to play a particularly important role in antisocial behavior, authority and deindividuation.

Authority as an Instigator of Criminal Behavior

Sometimes people behave a certain way because someone with power told them they must, even though the actions do not "set right" with their own principles. Kelman and Hamilton (1989) refer to this phenomenon as "crimes of obedience." "A crime of obedience is an act performed in response to orders from authority that is considered illegal or immoral by the larger community" (Kelman & Hamilton, 1989, p. 46). The classic example of the influence of authority is the military order to kill indiscriminately or to commit some other atrocity, such as Lieutenant William Calley's carrying out the massacre of villagers at My Lai in Vietnam. Other examples abound. An example of crimes of obedience in a political/bureaucratic context is the Watergate scandal, where on June 17, 1972, a group of men under the auspices of the White House broke in and tried to bug the Democratic National Headquarters in the Watergate apartment complex. The Iran-Contra scandal provides another example. Crimes of obedience appear to be widespread in the corporate world, an issue we will deal with in more detail in chapter eleven.

In an attempt to delineate some of the variables involved in obedience to authority, Stanley Milgram (1977) designed a series of experiments, using as subjects persons who volunteered (for money) in response to a newspaper ad. The experiments, which eventually received intensive public scrutiny and are now cited in nearly every introductory psychology textbook, studied the amount of electrical shock people were willing to administer to others when ordered to do so by an apparent authority figure.

The subjects were adult males, ages twenty to fifty, who represented a cross section of the socioeconomic classes. They were told that the researchers were studying the effects of punishment on memory. The experiment required a "teacher" and a "victim." Unknown to the volunteers, the victim was part of the experiment, a confederate who had been trained to act in a certain manner as part of the experimental design. In a rigged coin toss, the naive subject (the volunteer) always became the teacher and the confederate the victim. The victim-learner was taken to an adjacent room and strapped into an "electric chair" in the presence of the "naive" teacher.

Next, the teacher was led back to a room where he saw a simulated shock generator—a frightening apparatus with thirty switches presumably capable of delivering thirty levels of electric shock to the learner in the adjacent room. Each level was marked in volts ranging from 15 to 450 and accompanied by a switch. In addition, labels indicated "slight shock," "danger: severe shock," and beyond, to an "XXX" level. Each time the learner gave an incorrect answer to a learning task, the teacher was instructed to administer a stronger level of shock. The victim, who did not of course receive any shock at all, purposefully gave incorrect answers; he had also been trained to scream in agony, plead with the subject to stop, and pound on the wall when the higher levels of shock were administered.

Milgram wanted to discover how far people would go under the orders of an apparent authority figure (the experimenter). He may have found more than he bargained for. Almost two-thirds of the subjects obeyed the experimenter and administered the maximum shock levels. In subsequent experiments, using similar experimental conditions but different subjects (including both males and females), Milgram continued to find similar results.

Many of Milgram's subjects, while obeying the experimenter's instructions, demonstrated considerable tension and discomfort. Some stuttered, bit their lips, twisted their hands, laughed nervously, sweated profusely, or dug their fingernails into their flesh, especially after the victim began pounding the wall in protest (Milgram, 1963). After the experiment, some reported that they wanted to stop punishing the victim but continued to do so because the experimenter would not let them stop. Milgram (1977, p. 118) concluded: "The individual, upon entering the laboratory, becomes integrated into a situation that carries its own momentum."

In subsequent studies Milgram modified the procedure to determine more precisely what conditions inhibited or promoted this extreme obedience. For example, he varied the psychological and physical distance between the subject and the victim. To increase the psychological distance between the two, Milgram eliminated the cries of the victim that had been programmed into the original experiment. In another experiment, to minimize the physical and psychological distance between them, the subject sat next to the victim.

In general, Milgram found that the subjects obeyed the experimenter less as physical, visual, and auditory contact with the victim increased. However, the nearer the *experimenter* got to the "teacher," the more likely the teacher was to obey. Milgram found no evidence of significant personality or sex differences in the studies where shocking behavior was concerned, but he did find that female teachers were more distressed about their task than their male counterparts.

The psychological and physical distance variable suggests some interesting implications. If we were to analogize between Milgram's studies and violent actions, we would expect that the more impersonal the weapon or situation (psychological and physical distance) the greater the *likelihood* for destruction and serious violence. Certainly, killing someone with a firearm at a distance versus killing someone point blank are two different tasks. And both methods differ from choking someone to death with one's bare hands. It would appear that the firearm offers a more impersonal and possibly easier way to eliminate someone, and thus is more likely to lead to violent behavior. Admittedly, this suggestion makes some quantum jumps from a psychological experiment in an artificial setting, but it is a point worth considering when we discuss the relationship between weapons and violence in chapter eight.

In assessing the profound influence of commands from an authority figure, we should also pay close attention to the reactions of the subjects in Milgram's study. Individual differences were noted in the way the subjects reacted to the situation, but not in their actual willingness to shock. Although some subjects refused to continue with the experiment when they believed that they were hurting the victim, most administered the full range of shock levels. Most also displayed anxiety and conflict. Milgram noted a curious dissociation between words and action. Many subjects *said* they could not go on, but they nevertheless did. Some justified their action by concluding that the experimenter would not permit any harm to come to the victim. "He must know what he is doing." Other subjects expressed different interpretations and expectancies, such as the belief that the scientific knowledge gained in the experiment justified the method. It is interesting to note that people who have not undergone the ordeal are quite convinced that they would be members of the defiant group who refused to deliver the extreme levels of shock. Later studies conducted both in the United States and abroad confirmed Milgram's findings, however (Penrod, 1983).

Milgram suggests that our culture may not provide adequate models for disobedience to authority. He admonishes (1977, p. 120) that his studies

> raise the possibility that human nature or, more specifically, the kind of character produced in American democratic society cannot be counted on to insulate its citizens from brutality and inhuman treatment at the direction of

malevolent authority. A substantial proportion of people do what they are told to do, irrespective of the context of the act and without limitations of conscience, so long as they perceive that the command comes from a legitimate authority.

Milgram's theory may account to some extent for irrational acts committed under the influence of authority. Milgram would probably explain the refusal of the Attorney General to fire the Watergate prosecutor as a refusal to perceive the President as a legitimate authority figure. Alternately, there may have been a psychological affinity to the prosecutor. In either case, Milgram would probably find personality factors irrelevant. Other theorists would argue that it is precisely such factors that account for resistance to authority.

Deindividuation

Philip Zimbardo designed a number of studies testing the influence of deindividuation, the process of losing one's identity and becoming part of a group, as a situational variable. Deindividuation apparently follows a complex chain of events. First, the presence of many other persons encourages feelings of anonymity. Then, the individual feels he or she loses identity and becomes part of the group. Under these conditions, he or she can no longer be singled out and held responsible for behavior. Apparently, this feeling then generates a "loss of self-awareness, reduced concern over evaluations from others, and a narrowed focus of attention" (Baron & Byrne, 1977, pp. 581–582). When combined, these processes lower restraints against antisocial criminal behavior and appear to be basic ingredients in mass violence.

In one experiment, Zimbardo (1970) purchased two used cars, left one abandoned on a street in New York City (Manhattan; see Figure 4-1), the other on a street in Palo Alto, California (about 55,000 population). Zimbardo's deindividuation hypothesis predicted that, due to the large population of New York, people would more likely lose their identity and feel less responsible for their actions. Consequently, New Yorkers would be more likely to loot the abandoned vehicle. This is exactly what happened.

FIGURE 4-1 Middle-class white looters systematically stripped the above abandoned car within twenty-six hours in Manhattan. In Palo Alto, a similar car was left untouched during a seven-day period.

Within twenty-six hours, the New York car was stripped of battery, radiator, air cleaner, radio antenna, windshield wipers, side chrome, all four hub-caps, a set of jumper cables, a can of car wax, a gas can, and the only tire worth taking. Interestingly, the looting was not done by delinquents or members of a criminal subculture; all the looters were well-dressed, mid-dle-class whites. On several occasions the looting was done by entire fami-lies: children and parents together in a family enterprise.

On the other hand, the car in Palo Alto was untouched during the seven days it was left abandoned. At one point during a rainstorm, a passer-by actually lowered the hood to prevent the motor from getting wet. Why such a dramatic difference?

Zimbardo suggests that the anonymity of the New York residents worked in combination with situational cues implying that they could get by without repercussions. Zimbardo's hypothesis contends that in high popu-lation areas, who cares what you are doing as long as you are not bothering others or damaging a concerned party's property? Passersby in New York even stopped and chatted with the looters. In Palo Alto, people could be more easily identified. Moreover, a person engaging in this kind of behav-ior would expect to be the target of social disapproval or gossip.

Deindividuation is not necessarily associated with crowds or massive populations, however. The effect may be achieved by a disguise, a mask, or a uniform also worn by others, or it may be achieved by darkness (Zimbar-do, 1970). Research data indicate that people tend to be more abusive, aggressive, and violent when their identity is hidden. This phenomenon might explain why, throughout history, war paints, masks, and costumes have been donned by warriors preparing for battle (Watson, 1973). Even contemporary soldiers, guerillas, and military advisers are deindividuated by their uniforms. Deindividuation also helps explain the apparent ease with which members of groups such as the Ku Klux Klan regress from being apparently respectable citizens by day to violent, hooded terrorizers by night. Again, however, it is too simplistic to assume that no dispositional or other factors are at work.

The disguise aspect of deindividuation was vividly illustrated in an-other sobering Zimbardo experiment (1973) known as the Stanford Prison Experiment. Zimbardo and his colleagues simulated a prison environment in the basement of the psychology building at Stanford University, with all the physical and psychological trappings of an actual prison: bars, prison uniforms, identification numbers, uniformed guards, and other features that encouraged identity slippage. Student volunteers were screened through clinical interviews and psychological tests to ensure that they were emotionally stable and mature. According to Zimbardo, the subjects finally selected were "normal," intelligent college students from middle-class homes throughout the United States and Canada. They were paid $15 a day for participating.

The experiment required two roles, guard and prisoner, which were assigned by random coin toss. The randomization assured that there were no significant differences between the two groups. The "prisoners" were unexpectedly "arrested" and brought to the simulated prison in a police car. There they were handcuffed, searched, fingerprinted, booked, stripped, "deloused," given a number, and issued a prison uniform. Each prisoner was then placed in a 6' × 9' cell with two other inmates.

The guards wore standard uniforms and mirrored sunglasses to encourage deindividuation. In addition, they carried symbols of power: a night stick, keys to the cells, whistles, and handcuffs. Before the prisoners could do even routine things (e.g., write a letter, smoke a cigarette), they had to obtain permission. Guards drew up their own formal rules for maintaining law and order in the prison (sixteen rules in all) and were free to improvise new ones.

Within six days, both guards and prisoners had completely absorbed their roles:

> In less than a week the experience of imprisonment undid (temporarily) a lifetime of learning, human values were suspended, self-concepts were challenged and the ugliest, most base, pathological side of human nature surfaced. We were horrified because we saw some boys (guards) treat others as if they were despicable animals, taking pleasure in cruelty, while other boys (prisoners) became servile, dehumanized robots who thought only of escape, of their own individual survival and of their mounting hatred for the guards. (Zimbardo, 1973, p. 163)

Three prisoners had to be released during the first four days because of hysterical crying, confusion in thinking, and severe depression. Many others begged to be paroled, willing to forfeit the money they had earned for participating in the experiment.

About a third of the guards abused their power and were brutal and demeaning. Other subjects did their jobs as tough but fair correctional guards, but none of these supported the prisoners by urging the brutal guards to ease off. The realism of the prison was apparently striking. "The consultant for our prison . . . an ex-convict with sixteen years of imprisonment in California's jails, would get so depressed and furious each time he visited our prison, because of its psychological similarity to his experiences, that he would have to leave" (Zimbardo, 1973, p. 164). The situation became such that Zimbardo decided to terminate the experiment during the sixth day, instead of proceeding through the planned two weeks.

The experiment prompted him to conclude: "Many people, perhaps the majority, can be made to do almost anything when put into psychologically compelling situations—regardless of their morals, ethics, values, attitudes, beliefs, or personal convictions" (1973, p. 164). Much the same conclusion had been reached by Milgram with respect to the influence of authority figures.

Although the Stanford Prison Experiment underscores the crucial importance of situational variables in determining behavior, there were still significant individual differences in the way the subjects responded to the conditions. For example, only one-third of the guards became brutally enthralled with their power. Rather than making far-reaching conclusions on the basis of how a total of twenty-one subjects (both guards and prisoners) responded, it would be much more fruitful to give some attention to individual variables. For example, it would have been helpful to examine the values, expectancies, competencies, and moral development of the participants, in combination with the situational factors. What developmental factors most likely predisposed individuals to act the way they did, and exactly how did they perceive the situation? What did they expect to gain by their behavior? We will return to the deindividuation issue when we discuss mass violence in chapter eight and offer other perspectives of what happens to people caught up in the excitement of the crowd.

Contemporary Values

We mentioned in chapter one that scientists, especially behavioral and social scientists, rarely design, conduct, and interpret research independently of their own (and society's) biases about human nature. We also noted that the Darwinian perspective dominates Western civilization's thinking. "It is an integral part of the Western tradition to designate humans as animals, to recognize an absolute continuity in all nature, to seek information about human beings by observing animals, to find moral guidance in the example of animals, and to accept—indeed to treasure—the idea that humans are in many ways inferior to animals" (Bock, 1980, p. 9). The Darwinian perspective considers humans, like all animals, innately selfish and ultimately interested only in themselves. Therefore, it should come as no surprise that each theory thus far reviewed asserts that our actions are directed toward obtaining personal gains and minimizing personal losses. We are all ultimately only interested in improving our balance sheet of personal outcomes. We are biologically, innately selfish, taking care of number one. People therefore engage in criminal action simply because it provides reinforcement. Given the right opportunity and a guarantee of nondetection, more of us would do so. As Zimbardo (1979, p. 159) declared, "We are all potential assassins."

Modern, Western society strongly advocates self-actualization, self-realization, self-growth, and self in general. A recent book, *Psychology's Sanction for Selfishness* (Wallach & Wallach, 1983), underscores this trend. Psychology, the authors charge, has endorsed contemporary society's view that the proper mode of living is to be oneself, discover oneself, and let no one and nothing interfere with self-realization. "Submergence of self in the fulfillment of larger loyalties and responsibilities is viewed with suspicion;

the rest of the world is less important, if not downright oppressive" (Wallach & Wallach, 1983, p. 15). To have freedom in today's society is to be free from commitment. "Self-gratification abounds, not only as fact but also as recommended ideal" (Wallach & Wallach, 1983, p. 9). The notion of dedication to a higher purpose or larger goal *outside* of oneself is becoming increasingly quaint and out of date.

To what extent this exclusive self-orientation nurtures criminal behavior is an open question. But certainly the high crime rates, the extensive cruelty of humans toward other humans, and the continued violence, selfishness, self-centeredness, lack of empathy, and pettiness may be due in part to our contemporary perspectives on human nature, which we apply to ourselves as well as to others. Surveying 1,000 students, Mansson (cited by Wallach & Wallach, 1983) found that 90 percent thought there will always be people who are more fit to survive than others (Darwinianism). Ninety-one percent agreed that it is entirely just to eliminate those judged dangerous to the general welfare.

The many theories and proposals directed at the elimination of crime seem to have had little effect on American society. Perhaps it is because they explicit or implicitly endorse the cynical view that anything humans do is intended to advance their personal gain or satisfy their animal urges. This cynical attitude can be seen in the recent research on altruism, where researchers hypothesize (e.g., Wallach & Wallach, 1983) that humans do not usually come to the aid of a stranger unless they expect to gain something or are afraid of social sanction if they do not. Most psychologists argue that behind every altruistic act is a selfish motive. It may be nonmaterialistic, such as wanting to feel good or meet one's quota of good deeds, but it is self-centered nonetheless. It is interesting that most us find it extremely difficult to imagine that an altruistic act was done out of truly genuine concern for another human being.

The foregoing statements are not meant to detract from the theories we have reviewed thus far, which are probably fair descriptions and partial explanations of much human behavior. Biology interacting with learning, or learning interacting with the environment may well account for why we do many of the things we do, but there seems to be something lacking. Perhaps we are misleading ourselves in assuming that human behavior, particularly aggressive, violent, and unlawful behavior, is a residue from our distant past, following the same universal, human-construed laws of all living organisms. Perhaps the human mind follows a different course from the brains of other organisms—and not necessarily a better one. Perhaps these continual assumptions that answers to criminal behavior lie somewhere in our animal ancestry are deflecting us from the "truth" about ourselves. Maybe we are selfish, violent creatures because this is the way we think we should be.

SUMMARY AND CONCLUSIONS

We have reviewed Skinnerian behaviorism, the social learning theories of Rotter and Bandura, the semi-social learning theories of Akers and Hogan, and the Berkowitz frustration theory in this chapter. Each emphasizes to varying degrees the importance of learning in the development and maintenance of criminal behavior.

Our perspective of human nature influences what factors we consider paramount in the acquisition of criminal behavior, such as learning factors or the biological determinants discussed in chapters two and three. Until now, we have focused on the possible *origins* of criminal behavior: biological factors, classical conditioning, operant conditioning, and observational learning. We have also introduced some of the *external* reinforcements involved in the *maintenance* and *regulation* of criminal behavior. They include tangible rewards as well as social and psychological ones. Collectively, external reinforcements that bring us material, social, or psychological gain are called *positive* reinforcements. Behaviors that enable us to avoid unpleasant circumstances are *negatively* reinforced.

Also included in the regulation of behavior is *vicarious* reinforcement, which consists of both observed reward and observed punishment. When we observe others (models) receiving rewards or punishments for certain behavior, we tend to alter our behavior correspondingly. Models are extremely important in the acquisition and regulation of criminal behavior. They are reference points for what we should and can do in a particular set of circumstances. Therefore, models may act as inhibitors or facilitators of behavior. People internalize the actions and philosophies of significant models, thereby making them part of their own behavioral repertoire and cognitive structure. In the next chapter we will elaborate further on the influences of models.

Finally, we discussed some situational *instigators* of crime, such as authority figures and the environmental factors involved in the process of deindividuation. In some instances, people engage in illegal or violent conduct because they are told or ordered to do so. In other instances, the personal sense of identity appears to be lost in the excitement of the crowd. Under these deindividualized conditions, people may do things they normally would not do. We will return to these topics in chapters seven and eight.

CHAPTER FIVE
Juvenile Delinquency

Juvenile justice was officially ushered into the United States on the last day of the 1899 session of the Illinois legislature, when that body passed the seminal Juvenile Court Act. This comprehensive child welfare law defined a delinquent as a child under the age of sixteen who violated a state law or any village or city ordinance. It also established this country's first juvenile court and regulated juvenile institutions within the state. The philosophy underlying the law was that juvenile offenders should not be given the same punitive and retaliatory treatment as adults but rather be given individual attention for their own protection as well as that of society (Chute, 1949). In addition, the law included provisions for dealing with dependent and neglected children.

Although other states had adopted various procedures and regulations relevant to their wayward and neglected youth, the Illinois Act was the first comprehensive attempt at codification. It rapidly became the model for juvenile justice, and by 1911 twenty-two states had adopted similar measures. By 1925, all but two states had established juvenile courts (Tappan, 1949). Today, they exist in some form in every state, either separately or as part of a family court system.

Most programs directed at preventing or treating juvenile delinquency in the early twentieth century were created and managed by psychiatrists, psychologists, or social workers. Not surprisingly, they called for individual counseling and therapy for youthful offenders, usually by a social caseworker or a clinical practitioner. Illinois was also a pioneer in this area, since the first clinic established to provide psychiatric diagnoses to juvenile courts, the Juvenile Psychopathic Institute, opened its doors in Chicago in 1909. Shortly thereafter, the Judge Harvey H. Baker child guidance clinic was established in Boston (Chute, 1949).

In 1930, however, a monumental project was undertaken—again in Chicago—by sociologists proposing a different approach to the prevention of juvenile offenses. Called the Chicago Area Project, it paved the way for a reassessment of existing treatment and preventive programs for delinquents. It also represented the first systematic challenge by sociologists to the domination of psychologists and psychiatrists in both private and public juvenile programs (Schlossman & Sedlak, 1983).

The Project, which lasted thirty years, has been amply described, lauded, and criticized in the sociological and criminal justice literature. Essentially, it immersed researchers and volunteers, including erudite sociologists from the Chicago School, into communities with higher than average rates of delinquency. The researchers obtained oral histories and accounts of juvenile activities, organized recreational programs, offered "curbstone counseling," and mediated with police and juvenile justice agencies on behalf of community youth. The Project de-emphasized the individualized casework approach and drew attention to the role of the community as an agent of informal social control to prevent delinquency. Readers interested in more detail about the Project might refer to Schlossman and Sedlak's (1983) instructive history and assessment.

Ohlin (1983) traces three major shifts in federal policy regarding youth offending during the past two decades. He attributes the first shift to the Chicago Project and others like it. In the early 1960s, Ohlin notes, federal policymakers drew on community organization strategies to foster community responsibility for juvenile misbehavior and funded a variety of social programs toward that end. The programs in general were not successful, however, partly due to naiveté and partly to the massive social changes in society that were occurring during the 1960s. "We are much more aware today that juvenile justice depends on the successful operation of a *broad formal and informal* network of social relationships that guide youth development" (italics added) (Ohlin, 1983, p. 464). Ohlin notes that "the growing gap between expectation and achievable results fostered disillusionment, alienation, social unrest, and ultimately, abandonment of the programs themselves" (Ohlin, 1983, p. 464). He also suggests, however, that we can learn valuable lessons from the failure of those early community programs.

The second shift in social policy was spearheaded by a series of Presidential Commissions studying the broad problems of crime and violence.

In 1967 the first of these Commissions, the President's Commission on Law Enforcement and Administration of Justice, set the tone. Its primary task was to recommend ways to identify and control delinquents and status offenders. The Commission recommended six major strategies: (1) *decriminalization* of status offenses (such as running away from home); (2) *diversion* of youth from court procedures into public and private treatment programs; (3) extension of *due process* rights to juveniles in the same spirit as they had been extended to adult offenders; (4) *deinstitutionalization*, whereby delinquents would be cared for in group homes or small treatment centers instead of the traditional large institutions, reform schools, or training schools; (5) *diversification* of services; and (6) *decentralization* of control of juvenile proceedings and care. Ohlin notes that, although the Commission's recommendations were well received, implementation of the strategies has been "spotty."

In addition, implementation has been somewhat overshadowed by a third change in social policy, which began in the mid-1970s with a nationwide shift toward a law-and-order commitment. Apparently in response to a rapidly growing fear of crime and serious juvenile delinquency, the public began to demand quicker punishments and mandatory sentencing procedures, first for adults and eventually for juveniles. Ohlin notes that this new focus reflects in part a strong conservative reaction to the liberal policies advocated by the National Crime Commissions of the 1960s.

In recent years, those calling for reform of the juvenile justice system have spurred legislation in a variety of states lowering the age whereby youths may be tried as adult offenders for serious violent offenses like rape or murder. There is also a greater preoccupation with chronic, violent offenders, who actually comprise a very small proportion of the juvenile offender population. Ohlin writes (1983, p. 467),

> We are now in one of those periods of conservative reaction where the prevailing views about crime express beliefs about retribution, deterrence, and incapacitation that are deeply rooted in our religious and cultural heritage. . . . Our policies are now being developed by those who believe that the traditional system of punishment can be fine-tuned to control offenders by increasing the predictability and certainty of punishment.

The material in the following pages should help you to decide whether this third shift is justified.

DEFINITIONS

Juvenile delinquency is an imprecise, nebulous legal and social label for a wide variety of law- and norm-violating behavior. Legally, a juvenile delinquent is one who commits an act defined by law as illegal and who is adjudicated delinquent by an appropriate court. The legal definition is usually restricted to persons under eighteen, but states vary in their age distinctions. At this writing, three states (Connecticut, New York, and North Carolina) have laws which allow criminal courts to gain jurisdiction of young offenders at age sixteen, and seven states set the age at seventeen. All states allow juveniles to be tried as adults in criminal courts under certain conditions and for certain offenses.

Juvenile courts are part of the civil court system and differ significantly from criminal courts in both terminology and procedure. For example, juvenile courts accept petitions of delinquency rather than criminal complaints; conduct hearings, not trials; adjudicate juveniles delinquent rather than criminal. In general, juvenile court proceedings are not open to the public. However, juveniles are still protected by many due process safeguards associated with criminal trials, such as written notice of charges, legal representation, the right to confront and cross-examine witnesses, and protection against self-incrimination.

It is helpful to assign unlawful acts committed by delinquents into five major categories: (1) those against persons; (2) those against property; (3) drug offenses; (4) offenses against the public order; and (5) status offenses. Most referrals to juvenile court are for crimes against property (46 percent), followed by offenses against the public order (21 percent), status offenses (17 percent), crimes against persons (11 percent), and drug offenses (5 percent). The first four categories are comparable in definition to crimes committed by adults. Status offenses are acts which only juveniles can commit and which can be adjudicated only by a juvenile court (U.S. Department of Justice, 1978). Typical status offenses range from misbehavior, such as violations of curfew, running away from home, and truancy, to offenses that are interpreted very subjectively, such as unruliness and unmanageability. The judicial system historically has supported differential treatment of male and female status offenders. Adolescent girls, for example, have often been detained for incorrigibility or running away from home when the same behavior in adolescent boys was ignored or tolerated. Until recently, about three times as many girls were held for status offenses as boys (U.S. Department of Justice, 1983). In recent years, as a result of suits brought on behalf of juveniles, many courts have put authorities on notice that this discriminatory approach is unwarranted, and the practice appears to be diminishing. Moreover, under the federal law, juveniles are no longer overtly punished for status violations. Nevertheless, some research indicates that officials circumvent the rules by reaching for ways to bring adolescents, particularly girls, under the aegis of juvenile courts (Chesney-Lind, 1986).

It has been argued that, because status offenses lend themselves to so much subjectivity, they should be removed from the purview of all state juvenile courts (American Bar Association, *Juvenile Justice Standards Project,*

1979). Some states are clearly moving in this direction. On the other hand, many have de-emphasized status offenses or replaced them completely with statutes allowing the detention and/or supervision of youngsters who are presumably in need of protection either from their own rash behavior or the behavior of others. These statutes are usually referred to as PINS or CHINS laws (person or child in need of supervision). Under these laws, runaways or incorrigible youngsters are subject to juvenile court jurisdiction, often at the instigation of their parents, and even though they may not have committed an act comparable to a crime.

The juvenile justice system is fraught with inequities, and scholars have proposed numerous philosophical, structural, and procedural changes to better balance the interests of society, the child, and the parent (e.g., Schultz & Cohen, 1976; American Bar Association, 1979). It is not our purpose here to deal with these problems at any length or to evaluate the recommendations for change. They only serve to provide a backdrop for our main topic, which is the behavior of youths adjudicated delinquent and how serious criminal behavior in youths is acquired and maintained. Our focus throughout this chapter is on the chronic, repetitive offender who moves from adolescence to adulthood in a continuing cycle of offending and reoffending.

Serious versus Nonserious Juvenile Crime

Recent research and legal literature suggests that a useful way of classifying juvenile crime is to distinguish between serious and nonserious acts and between serious and nonserious offenders. The term *serious* can have multiple definitions, however. It may refer to the value of property, frequency of offenses, degree of physical injury, social distance between offender and victim, degree of official intervention, recidivism rates, and so forth (Weis & Sederstrom, 1981). In 1978, Zimring proposed that the serious offender was one who engaged in criminal activity involving serious threats to life or to personal safety and security. According to this definition, serious juvenile offenses would include rape, homicide, aggravated assault, robbery, and arson, but not property crimes. However, the 1980 Amendments to the Juvenile Justice and Delinquency Act of 1974 define serious juvenile crime as "criminal homicide, forcible rape, mayhem, kidnapping, aggravated assault, robbery, larceny or theft punishable as a felony, motor vehicle theft, burglary or breaking and entering, extortion accompanied by threats of violence, and arson punishable as a felony." Thus, the Amendments consider juvenile crime "serious" if it involves serious property offenses as well as violence. *Mayhem*, for example, is defined as malicious injury to person *or* property, which would include felonious vandalism.

The issue of seriousness is crucial in criminology. It affects not only the gathering and interpretation of statistics, but also important decisions about sentencing, probation, and parole. For juveniles, seriousness may affect whether the individual is initially detained and whether the proceedings will be transferred to criminal court.

In an effort to clarify the concept, Sellin and Wolfgang (1964) developed a seriousness scale, which recognizes that both violent and property crimes can be serious. Various offenses are assigned weighted values according to an estimated threat to bodily injury or damage to property. Murder is given the highest ranking of seriousness, with a weighted value of 26. An aggravated assault after which the victim was hospitalized is weighted 7; when the victim is treated but immediately discharged, the weighted value is 4. Forcible rape is rated 10; if a weapon was used in the incident, two more points are added. If property damage is involved, weighted values are assigned according to the total damage in dollars. For example, property damage totalling over $80,000 is weighted 7; damage totalling $2,000 is weighted 3. The seriousness of the offense is thus graded according to the offense and the manner in which the offense is committed.

For each criminal event, an additive procedure is used to determine its seriousness. For instance, consider the following example cited by Sellin and Wolfgang (1964, p. 407). "A holdup man forces a husband and his wife to get out of their automobile. He shoots the husband, gun whips and rapes the wife (hospitalized) and leaves in the automobile (value $2,000) after taking money ($100) from the husband. The husband dies as a result of the shooting. . . ." The event is scored as follows, with the numbers in parentheses being the weights assigned. "The husband was killed (26); the wife was raped (10), threatened with a gun (2), and sustained injuries requiring hospitalization (7). The car was stolen (2). The total value of the property loss, car and money, was $2,100 (4)." In this example, the Sellin-Wolfgang seriousness scale evaluates the event as 51, a very serious offense.

So far we have only presented issues related to the seriousness of the *offense*. Researchers have added another dimension, related to the seriousness of the *offender*. This usually hinges on whether the person has committed the offense or other offenses previously. Thus, if an offender murders twice, regardless of the amount of time between the two crimes, his or her seriousness rating would be 52. Both Strasburg (1978) and Wolfgang, Figlio, and Sellin (1972) recommend that a juvenile with five or more violent or serious offenses be considered a serious juvenile offender. Smith et al. (1980) conclude that a serious juvenile offender is one whose offense history includes adjudication for five or more serious offenses—as defined by the Sellin-Wolfgang scale—or one who is adjudicated for one or more offenses whose severity is equal to homicide or forcible rape.

The Sellin-Wolfgang scale is imperfect, especially since it cannot take into consideration an offender's intentions or the fact that every event takes unpredictable twists. The scale does, however, represent a well-conceived way of attempting to deal with the label "seriousness" for both offenses and offenders in a measurable manner.

Smith and his colleagues (1980) recommend that the following offenses be considered serious juvenile offenses, in accordance with the Sellin-Wolfgang scale. All other offenses are considered nonserious.

1. Homicide or vountary manslaughter
2. Forcible sexual intercourse
3. Aggravated assault
4. Armed robbery
5. Burglary of an occupied residence
6. Larceny/theft of more than $1,000
7. Auto theft without recovery of the vehicle
8. Arson of an occupied building
9. Kidnapping
10. Extortion
11. Illegal sale of dangerous drugs

To a large extent, the first eight offenses listed correspond to the index crimes reported by the FBI in the Uniform Crime Reports (UCR). Index crimes are serious offenses that occur frequently. The list changes periodically. For example, arson was not considered an index crime until 1978 when the FBI recognized that arson incidents had risen dramatically.

In the following section on the incidence of juvenile offending, we will accept Smith's recommendations to delineate seriousness adequately. Furthermore, we will label "violent" those serious offenses against persons that result in bodily injury or death. Serious property offenses will be those presumably (but not necessarily) committed for material gain, such as larceny-theft, motor vehicle theft, and robbery without assault.

INCIDENCE

The nature and extent of delinquent behavior—both what is reported and unreported to law enforcement agencies—is essentially an unknown area (Krisberg & Schwartz, 1983), even more so than adult crime. We simply do not have complete data on the national incidence of juvenile delinquency. We do have statistics collected by law enforcement agencies, the courts, and facilities for delinquents, but the figures are often incomplete and inaccurate.

Like criminal statistics in general, delinquency data are collected from three primary sources: (1) official records of police arrests, such as the FBI's UCR; (2) self-reports of victimization, such as the National Crime Survey; and (3) self-reports of delinquent involvement, where national samples of youth are asked to complete questionnaires about their own behavior. An illustration of this last source is the National Youth Survey (Elliot, Ageton, & Huizinga, 1980).

Although each of the three sources of data is imperfect, most contemporary researchers interested in the correlates and causes of juvenile delinquency prefer self-report survey research (Hindelang, Hirschi, & Weis, 1981) for several reasons. First, they are highly skeptical about the validity of official government data such as UCR reports. Second, victimization surveys are limited, because victims often do not know the age of the offender. Therefore, while these surveys may provide important information about crime in general, they may not accurately reflect the involvement of juveniles. Third, self-report data seem consistent with modern theories of delinquency and crime, many of which were formulated before self-report measures were even adequately developed. In other words, self-report procedures appear more valid than either official reports or victim accounts. Addressing one criticism of self-report studies, Hindelang and his fellow researchers (1981) noted that adolescents generally did not resist reporting their own unlawful behavior, although there were of course exceptions. Blacks and adjudicated delinquents tended to reveal less about themselves than whites and nondelinquents.

In spite of these advantages, self-report surveys are a relatively new development in juvenile justice research and as such do not adequately estimate the incidence of juvenile offending. They may be quite accurate as far as they go, but they do not yet reach enough young people to provide a valid assessment. Moreover, they have traditionally focused on trivial offenses rather than serious law-violating behavior, although designers of the National Youth Survey have made promising strides toward controlling for this problem. Official data, by contrast, offer *extensive*—often nationwide—information on the type of delinquency that concerns law enforcment officials. Yet they are limited in the sense that, like all official data, they may reflect errors in reporting and discretionary treatment. Therefore, although we refer to one type of official data—arrest records—in the following pages, it is with the caveat that these data may not be truly representative of delinquent behavior.

Juvenile arrest figures are gathered from four main sources: (1) UCR; (2) juvenile court processing, as reported by the National Center for Juvenile Justice (NCJJ); (3) juvenile corrections, as reported in the monograph *Children in Custody* (CIC); and (4) probation and parole statistics, as reported in various governmental publications. The last three sources of information have the major disadvantage of greatly underestimating the number of actual offenses, since even more than in the criminal system, a very high proportion—perhaps a majority—of cases are either undetected or are dismissed before reaching the courts. In other words, because of parental involvement, negotiations, and compromises, many offenders do not require adjudication. To add to the problem of obtaining statistics on juvenile offenders, juvenile court dockets do not always reflect *serious* offending. Referrals by parents, schools, probation officers, and other courts, either for status offenses or for supervision, make up much of a court's delinquency workload. Because of this confusion, Smith and his colleagues (1980) argue that the most complete nationwide compilation of juvenile offenses today remains the UCR, despite its serious shortcomings.

Many people today believe that serious juvenile offenses are increasing at a steady and alarming rate. Whether this perception is correct depends in part on what is meant by *serious*. If we consider all the offenses comparable to index crimes reported in the UCR, the public's perception is not supported (see Figure 5-1). If we consider violent and property crimes separately, we see that these crime rates also have levelled off in recent years. Figures 5-1 and 5-2 are based on the juvenile arrest *rate* reported by the UCR for the years 1964 to 1988 and adjusted for fluctuations in the youth population between the ages of eleven and seventeen. The rate trend is also adjusted, as recommended by Smith et al. (1980), for annual variations in the number of jurisdictions reporting. That is, for various reasons, there are yearly differences in the number and location of law enforcement agencies reporting data to the FBI. Any equation calculating arrest rates, therefore, must take this variance into account.

As noted previously, official juvenile statistics do not support the public perception of an overall rising juvenile offending rate. Neither do victimization data obtained by the National Crime Survey (NCS). Both show that *overall*, serious juvenile offenses (defined in accordance with the Sellin-Wolfgang scale) have remained steady or have declined over the past dec-

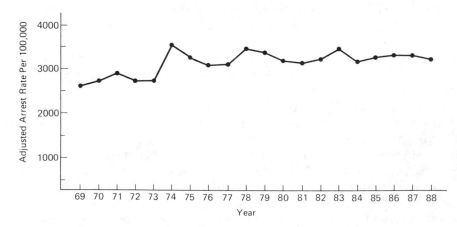

FIGURE 5-1   Adjusted rate of arrests for index crimes (excluding arson): ages eleven through seventeen (1969–1988).

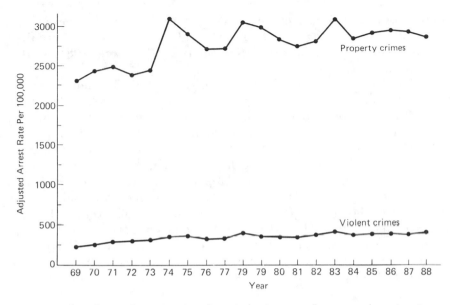

FIGURE 5-2   Adjusted national arrest rates for index violent and property offenses: ages eleven through seventeen (1969–1988).

ade (Laub, 1983; Galvin & Polk, 1983). True, the serious offense rates, which peaked during the mid-1970s, are substantial, but they have *not* increased. In fact, the UCR data indicate that between 1979 and 1988, the number of persons under eighteen arrested for index crimes dropped by nearly 18 percent (U.S. Department of Justice, 1989a). Delinquency self-report studies, since their inception in the late 1950s, also do not indicate that serious delinquency is increasing (Kelley, 1983). Furthermore, both self-report studies and official data suggest that only a small percentage of the juvenile population engages in serious delinquent behavior. It is important to note, however, that only about 3 to 15 percent of serious offenses ever result in "police contact," again according to to some self-report studies (Weis & Sederstrom, 1981). Research utilizing self-report surveys by Elliott, Dunford, and Huizinga (1987), however, suggested that serious, repetitive juvenile offenders escaped detection 86 percent of the time over a five-year period. These figures indicate that the incidence of offending may be substantially underestimated by official arrest data. In other words, a small percentage of youth are committing a substantial amount of undetected offenses, or offenses for which they are not adjudicated.

It is revealing, however, to split UCR index offenses into violent and property categories. If we look only at rates of juvenile *violent* offending, we find a *slight* increase until 1983, then a levelling off (see Figure 5-2). Moreover, when researchers compare the violent offenses of juveniles to violent crimes of adults, they find that the juvenile behavior is less serious in three important ways: (1) Juveniles are less likely to use weapons; (2) they are less successful in completing acts of robbery; and (3) they do not injure their victims as severely as adults do (McDermott & Hindelang, 1981; Weis & Sederstrom, 1981).

How does violent juvenile crime compare with the incidence and rate of property offenses—burglary, larceny-theft, and motor vehicle theft? In 1988 UCR data, the four violent index categories (murder and voluntary manslaughter, forcible rape, robbery, and aggravated assault) represent only 4 percent of all juvenile arrests. If we consider all eight index offenses (adding larceny-theft, motor vehicle theft, burglary, and arson), we find that 88 percent of juvenile arrests were for larceny-theft, motor vehicle theft, and burglary, indicating that a vast majority of juvenile crime is acquisition crime.

But even though the overwhelming percentage of all juvenile offending is directed at property acquisition, the *aggregate* juvenile arrest rates for property offenses show a levelling off, not an increase in recent years. This reflects another trend worth noting. Juveniles are apparently stealing different kinds of property. For example, between 1973 and 1982, the number of arrests for larceny-theft increased 8.5 percent, while motor vehicle theft decreased nearly 50 percent. Juvenile robbery, involving threat and intimidation, decreased slightly. These statistics suggest that juveniles are turning more to theft from homes and businesses and away from theft of vehicles or robbery.

In sum, national arrest rates, victimization studies, and self-report data generate different estimates of the incidence of delinquency. Nevertheless, none support an overall increase in the rate of juvenile offending over the past decade. A series of longitudinal and self-report studies conducted in recent years show that most serious property and violent offenses are being committed by a small but significant segment of the youth population, and that this segment tends toward high recidivism (Bartol & Bartol, 1989). Moreover, *frequent* offenders do not specialize in any one particular kind of offending, such as theft or larceny. Instead, they tend to be involved in a wide variety of offenses, ranging from minor property crimes to highly violent ones. Longitudinal research also indicates that repetitive offenders were unusually troublesome in school, earning poor grades, and have inadequate or inappropriate social skills. In addition, these troublesome behaviors began at an early age, and the more serious the offender, the earlier these childhood patterns appeared. With these observations in mind, we will now turn our attention to a topic directly relevant to the psychological nature of this text, namely the social and psychological factors that appear to be correlated with delinquent behavior among young people.

PREDICTORS OF JUVENILE DELINQUENCY

Contrary to statements found in many crime and delinquency textbooks, few contemporary psychologists believe that delinquent offenders, as a whole, are emotionally disturbed or psychologically maladjusted youths in need of conventional psychotherapy. Rather, mainstream psychology views delinquency, including frequent offenders, as a learned behavior, acquired and maintained like all other human behavior. Most psychologists consider behavior a function of the environment interacting with the person, although, as we noted in chapter one, they tend to weight one more heavily than the other.

Over the past two decades, the psychological study of crime has shifted away from accepting personality traits as major determinants of criminal and delinquent behavior toward a more interactive cognitive and moral development focus. The personality traits or dispositional approach is still viable and will be considered in the next chapter. In the present chapter, we will discuss some of the current cognitive and moral developmental theories of delinquency. First, we will describe major predictors of delinquency most frequently cited in the research literature.

The term *predictor* may be misleading. Predictors do not foretell whether a person will be delinquent, but only estimate the *statistical probabilities* that it will happen. More specifically, a predictor signals a relationship between two or more factors. In empirical research, these relationships are described by *correlations*, calculated by mathematical formulae. It is crucial to remember that correlations only tell us there is a relationship between one thing and another; they do not tell what is causing what. For example, school grades seem to be a predictor of juvenile delinquency, since there is a modest relationship between academic achievement and delinquency. As grades go down, the likelihood of delinquency tends to increase. We *cannot* conclude, however, that low grades *cause* delinquency. For example, we could state with equal conviction that as involvement in delinquency increases, grades will decrease. We simply cannot determine the *direction* of cause from a correlation.

Another danger in the application of correlations based on group data is the *ecological fallacy*. The ecological fallacy is the error of assuming that relationships, or correlations, based on group data will hold in a similar fashion at the individual level. Relationships found for groups are not necessarily identical to relationships for each individual, even though the individuals are part of the group. For example, if we discover that 30 out of 100 individuals up for parole will recidivate within a year, we cannot predict which *particular* individuals will recidivate based on group data. We can only predict with some confidence that 30 percent will. Likewise, if we know that there is a relationship between grades and delinquency, we cannot determine which particular individuals will follow this pattern. Grades may be predictors, but their usefulness is primarily restricted to groups, not particular individuals.

Early Youth Behavior as a Predictor of Later Delinquency

There is good evidence that delinquency patterns begin in early childhood (Bartol & Bartol, 1989). Learning experiences begin early and build on themselves. Researchers have noted differences in impulsiveness, social skills, and feelings for others between children who ultimately became serious delinquents and nondelinquents during their early school years. Even at an early age, aggressive, belligerent children are unpopular and are excluded from peer groups (Hartup, 1983; Patterson, 1982; Olweus, 1978). As a group, highly aggressive, troublesome children demonstrate social and interpersonal skills that are below average. Those children who continue offending into adolescence and young adulthood are troublesome in school, beginning as early as the first grade (Farrington, 1987), and perform below average in most school achievement tasks (Schafer & Polk, 1967; Kelly, 1980; Wilson & Herrnstein, 1985). Low achievement, low vocabulary, and poor verbal reasoning have been found to correlate significantly with later delinquency (Farrington, 1979). As school becomes increasingly aversive for the delinquents, they apparently rely on alternative behaviors, especially attention-getting ones. By the end of the ninth grade, many are engaging in the more common delinquent acts: vandalism, theft, and the status offenses of running away and incorrigibility. By this time also, consideration and empathy for others has not advanced much beyond the early childhood stage. Moreover, the delinquent youngsters become increasingly antagonistic toward authority and resentful of school rules and regulations.

Stealing is another early predictor of delinquency. In fact, in a literature review by Loeber and Dishion (1983), habitual stealing—as reported by parents and teachers—emerged as one of the strongest predictors of later delinquency. Furthermore, youngsters who engaged in stealing, even at the elementary school level, also tended to be simultaneously demonstrating other problem behaviors such as lying, truancy, and running away. Frequent dishonesty appears to be another behavioral pattern that predicts quite early a tendency toward repetitive offending (Loeber & Dishion, 1983; Farrington, 1979).

In sum, the available data suggest that youngsters who become serious, repetitive offenders usually demonstrate antisocial behaviors at least from their early school years on. After surveying the evidence on early childhood behaviors and later criminal behavior, Farrington (1987, p. 71) wrote, "In a very real sense, there appeared to be continuity between childhood troublesomeness and adult criminal behavior." Furthermore, these behaviors are not specialized in that the child does not simply exhibit one problem behavior. The child who eventually becomes delinquent is not only truant or light-fingered; rather, he or she displays a variety of asocial and antisocial acts across many different situations. This pattern is consistent with both official and self-report data, indicating that most serious offenders do not specialize in certain offenses.

Family Background Predictors

It is estimated that over 10 million American children now live with only one parent (Flynn, 1983). Studies based on official data have traditionally found that delinquents come from homes where parents are divorced or separated more often than do nondeliquents (Glueck & Glueck, 1950; Monahan, 1957; Eaton & Polk, 1961; Rodman & Grams, 1967; Flynn, 1983). This has led to conclusions that the broken home could be blamed for much delinquency. Since the 1970s, with the emergence of self-report data, these conclusions have been questioned.

The relationship between the broken home and delinquency carries excessive baggage in that it is confounded with so many other variables and influences. For example, there appears to be an inverse relationship between divorce rates and social economic class or status (Belsky, Lerner, & Spanier, 1984). Couples at the lower end of the socioeconomic status spectrum have the highest divorce rates, while couples in the upper-middle and upper classes have the lowest rates. Thus, it may not be the broken home or single-parent situation per se that is directly contributing to delinquency, but perhaps some combination of socioeconomic class, educational level, or other interacting variables is the causal factor.

Also, the term *broken home* is ambiguous. Homes may be broken by a wide variety of circumstances—death, desertion, divorce, or separation. In addition, we cannot assume that all these separations affect families the same way. For example, there is some evidence that children from broken but conflict-free homes are less likely to be delinquent than children from conflict-ridden but "intact" homes (Gove & Crutchfield, 1982). Furthermore, the composition of the broken homes must be considered. That is, who is living in the broken home—grandparents, stepparent, relatives, or friends?

While the relationship between broken homes and delinquency is a commonly reported one, we are far from explaining it. It is clear that, if the broken home is a predictor, it is probably confounded by a complex of other interacting variables. However, as Flynn (1983, p. 13) asserts: "One point is undisputably clear in the literature: a stable, secure, and mutually supportive family is exceedingly important in delinquency prevention."

Parental discipline also appears related to delinquency. Inconsistent or physically harsh discipline in the home may result in more delinquency than consistent and reasoning forms of discipline. Button (1973) found high correlations between the severity of physical punishment and the amount and severity of antisocial aggression displayed during adolescence. Hirschi (1983) notes that the correlation between violent physical child abuse and delinquency is consistent and strong (this observation will be more carefully examined in chapter eight). The social learning position helps us to explain the relationship between punishment and acting-out behavior. Physical punishments of slapping, hitting, and punching provide a pattern to be modeled when youngsters are themselves frustrated and disenchanted. However, we must be *very* careful not to suggest that physical abuse inevitably produces delinquency nor to overlook the contributions of other parental patterns. Brown (1984) cites evidence that emotional abuse and neglect may play an even more critical role in the development of delinquency. Emotional abuse includes such behaviors as frequently screaming at the child, calling the child insulting names, excessively criticizing, or generally ignoring the child. Neglect usually refers to a gross lack of proper supervision and physical care. We will discuss the various forms of child abuse and their effects in more detail in chapter eight.

Delinquents repeatedly complain that their parents were unfair and nonobjective in administering discipline (McCord, McCord, & Zola, 1959; Glueck & Glueck, 1950), a complaint voiced much less frequently by nondelinquents. Again recalling the social learning position on acquiring behavior, we should easily see why this type of discipline is a problem. First, it yields inconsistent dispensation of reinforcement. This means that socially desirable behaviors, if engaged in, will not be strengthened in the home environment. If a nine-year-old plays a spirited game of hide-and-seek with her younger sister, she may be ignored by the parent on one occasion and chastised for being too noisy the next. Second, punishment contingent on the whim and mood of a parent rather than on any specific behavior on the part of the child contributes to an extremely unpleasant and unpredictable environment.

With the possible exception of Hirschi's (1983) conclusion about physical abuse, the aforementioned family predictors, taken individually, show only weak relationships with delinquency. They allow us to predict the probability of delinquency, but often barely better than chance. After reviewing the recent research literature, however, Loeber and Dishion (1983) found that they could increase the power of prediction by using a combined or composite measure. In other words, if no *single* characteristic is a strong predictor, several in combination—like family size, quality of parental supervision, parental drinking habits, employment history, and criminality—are more impressive, particularly with reference to male delinquency. Loeber and Dishion concluded that children from large families that are characterized by employment problems, disorganization and instability, inadequate supervision, conflict and disharmony, and poor parent-child relationships are at much greater risk of becoming delinquent than children from families without these features.

Peer Association

Adolescents live in two separate worlds: one for the family and the other for friends (Berndt, 1979). Adolescents—especially those in the middle class—often seek advice from family in matters of finance, education, and career plans, but in making decisions about their social lives—dress, drinking, dating, drugs, recreational activities—adolescents overwhelmingly want to be attuned to the opinions of their peers (Sebald, 1986).

Consistently, the research literature finds peer association one of the strongest and most consistent *single* predictors of delinquency (Loeber &

Dishion, 1983; Lanza-Kaduce, Radosevich, & Krohn, 1983; Hindelang, Hirschi, & Weis, 1981). A national, longitudinal self-report survey conducted by Elliott, Huizinga, and Ageton (1985) also reports that association with delinquent peers is one of the strongest predictors of deliquency. Those adolescents reporting having delinquent friends were more likely to report delinquent offending themselves.

However, peer influence is a complicated process. It is highly unlikley that peer influence by itself provides a complete picture of the development of serious delinquency and crime. Serious delinquency is the end product of many influences, including peers, family, and the social environment in general. For example, there is no evidence in the research literature that association with delinquent peers *precedes* or *encourages* offending (Farrington, 1987). In other words, the adolescent may have been prone to frequent antisocial behavior prior to the association with delinquent friends. Therefore, we cannot assert that delinquent peers *cause* other peers who associate with them to become delinquent, but serious delinquents do tend to associate with delinquent friends. In fact, Farrington (1987) notes that those delinquents who associate with delinquent friends over extended periods of time persist in offending as adults. In sum, long-term association with delinquent friends is a good predictor for delinquency and crime.

Delinquency and Intelligence

Criminologists (and many psychologists) have been eager to label the relationship between intelligence and delinquency invalid and spurious. Even to mention the connection may prompt a derisive reaction reserved only for Lombroso's classical born criminal theory. Hirschi and Hindelang (1977, p. 572) write: "Today, textbooks in crime and delinquency ignore IQ or impatiently explain to the reader that IQ is no longer taken seriously by knowledgeable students simply because no differences worth considering have been revealed by research." As Hirschi and Hindelang note, these textbooks are wrong, since one of the most consistent findings in the delinquency literature is that delinquents do, as a group, score lower on standard intelligence tests than nondelinquents do. The essential point that Hirschi and Hindelang made was that the inverse relationship between IQ scores and delinquency continues to be documented by the research, *for whatever reason*. Why this difference exists should be at the heart of the controversy.

In their 1977 article, Hirschi and Hindelang hypothesized that an *indirect causal* relationship exists between IQ and delinquency. By *indirect* they meant that a low IQ leads to poor performance and negative attitudes toward school, which in turn leads to delinquency. A high IQ, on the other hand, leads to good performance and positive attitudes toward school, which in turn leads to the internal acceptance of conventional values and conformity (nondelinquency). Therefore, Hirschi and Hindelang saw school performance and attitudes as "intervening variables" that mediate between IQ and deliquency.

However, one fundamental flaw in the Hirschi and Hindelang argument is the common assumption that IQ reflects intelligence. The term *IQ* is an abbreviation of the *intelligence quotient* derived from a numerical score on a so-called intelligence test. Satisfactory performance on a vast majority of intelligence tests depends greatly on language acqusition and verbal development. Usually, a person must have considerable experience using and defining words—particularly English words. The examinee must be able to make conventional connections and see distinctions between verbal concepts. The examinee must also know the facts that the test designer deems important to know within mainstream culture. At the very least, almost all intelligence tests measure some aspect of academic skills that are taught in school or that predict success in school. A vast majority of psychologists today would agree that IQ scores are strongly influenced by social, educational, and cultural experiences. In short, all intelligence tests are culturally biased.

More importantly, IQ scores and the concept of intelligence should *not* be confused. The term *IQ* merely refers to a standardized score from a test. Intelligence, on the other hand, is a broad, all-encompassing abililty that defies any straightforward or simple definition. It means many things to different people. Intelligence includes ability ranging from musical talent to logical-mathematical skills. The term may also include wisdom, intuition, judgment, and even humor. It is therefore extremely important to make a distinction between IQ and intelligence. While delinquents, as a group, *do* score lower on intelligence tests, this observation should not be construed as documenting that delinquents are less intelligent than nondelinquents. IQ scores are crude indices of mainstream language skills that are heavily influenced by experience. IQ scores are also strongly influenced by the type of test used, its content, the many characteristics of testing situations, and the training and skill of the examiner.

Still, even with these many variations, the inverse relationship between IQ scores and the tendency toward delinquency are frequently reported. As IQ scores go down, the probability of misconduct increases, and vice versa. What does the relationship between IQ scores and delinquency mean? It probably means that delinquents as a group, particularly serious delinquents, have had limited experiences in mainstream society, as well as poor school experiences, but more research is necessary before further explanation is advanced.

Impulsiveness as a Predictor

Impulsive is one of the most shopworn descriptors of the juvenile delinquent. This frayed concept implies that youths as a whole are more inclined to act on sudden urges than on thought. It suggests that delinquents do not think about what they are doing; they are reflexive creatures who respond to the urge of the moment, unpredictably, irrationally, and uncontrollably. This is a limited approach that does not account for the numerous young people who are not impulsive. Social learning theorists suggest instead that delinquents have not learned to delay gratification and thus may not appreciate the consequences of their behavior.

There is good evidence that delinquents as a whole seek immediate gratification instead of waiting for larger but delayed rewards (e.g., Quay, 1965; Ross, 1974; Mischel, 1961; Rosenquist & Megargee, 1969; Stumphauzer, 1973). As a group, delinquents may have found it most expedient to take what is available and not wait for future possibilities. In part, this strong orientation to the present may reflect broken promises or lack of reinforcement for working toward future goals. It is not surprising, therefore, that some delinquents' backgrounds often show academic failure. The reinforcements for academic achievement are not readily apparent and are too far into the future to be of major concern. Moreover, while waiting for the promised future dividends from education, the individual may find the delay aversive and punishing.

Mischel (1976) sees delay of gratification as a two-part process. First, the individual must *decide* to wait for more attractive rewards sometime in the future. This decision-making process is partly influenced by the person's expectancy of actually getting a promised reward. If, from past experiences, he or she has learned that delayed rewards do not materialize, it is unlikely that he or she will decide to wait. If the decision *is* made to wait, however, the second step in the process requires the individual to *maintain self-control* throughout the waiting period. This second step, according to Mischel, requires an ability and skill to generate distractions (both cognitive and behavioral) in order to reduce the frustration and aversiveness of waiting. It also requires trust in one's social environment. Someone who grows up in an environment that offers little opportunity for developing this two-stage process will likely want immediate gratification of needs. Dropping out of school might win out over tolerating the grind; "earning" money through thievery might win out over spending time in a job-training program.

Children probably exhibit the same degree of self-control and delay of gratification as the model or models to which they have been exposed (Bandura & Walters, 1963). Parents and other adults who verbalize the need for delaying gratification but display little self-control themselves provide poor social models for their children. "Listen to what I say and don't do what I do" is a faulty parenting adage.

Also, inconsistent discipline and reinforcement create an atmosphere of noncontingencies, where behavior is interpreted as unrelated to its social consequences. In an environment where reinforcing and punishing events are often unpredictable and inconsistent, children may feel they have no control over their fate. They have little appreciation for the consequences of their own actions, whether antisocial or socially desirable. Threat of punishment becomes ineffective, since it is not guaranteed that the punishment will really be forthcoming. Therefore, the children learn to take their chances and develop a "get-what-you-can-now-and-don't-worry-about-the-unpredictable-consequences" philosophy to life.

People who do not appreciate delayed consequences are not usually deterred from antisocial behavior by threats of punishment, prison, or even death. The delinquent who is viewed as impulsive is actually getting reinforcement from antisocial behavior, not from self-direction toward some future goal. When the antisocial behavior takes the form of violence, it becomes a formidable challenge to society and law enforcement.

In summary, early troublesome behavior, impulsiveness, poor school performance, consistent delinquent peer associations, erratic parental discipline, parental conflict, and low IQ scores are all significant predictors in forecasting high-rate offending in young adulthood. There is very little evidence, however, that any of these factors work in isolation and/or become unitary casual agents in the development of criminal behavior. It is far more likely that these and other factors work in dynamic interaction in the development of serious, repetitive offending patterns.

The predictors discussed so far have been observable behaviors. Cognitive processes also provide crucial information about the development of criminal behavior, a topic we will now turn our attention to.

COGNITIVE AND MORAL DEVELOPMENT

How people acquire, internalize, and develop personal values is a key question in the study of delinquent and criminal behavior. Some philosophers and social scientists argue that we develop our morality and belief system, our concepts of right and wrong, through a series of cognitive stages, with the highest levels being reached through logic and self-discovery. They contend that through the principles of logic and continual learning, humans can discover and cognitively construct ethical and moral principles of fairness, justice, responsibility, and empathy toward others. At these highest stages of cognitive and moral development, direct reinforcement, punishment, and modeling lose their importance.

Among the first major psychological research on moral character was a series of studies conducted by Hartshorne and May (1928–1930), in which they examined such qualities as honesty, generosity, and self-control in children. Their findings devastated those who believed that people—including children—displayed consistent personality traits of morality and immorality across a variety of situations. According to the Hartshorne-May data, moral behavior was situation-specific; children conducting themselves morally or honestly in one situation did not necessarily act commendably in different situations. In fact, the researchers found that a child who was dishonest or ruthless under one set of circumstances was *very likely* to respond differently under a different set of circumstances.

The disappointing conclusion that a situation appears more important in determining moral behavior than does personality temporarily slowed efforts to delineate a personality theory of moral development. However, later statistical analyses of the Hartshorne-May data revealed that the original conclusions may have been unjustified (Burton, 1963, 1976; Eysenck, 1977). Today, after numerous researchers have studied the issue, personality factors and individual differences in development are believed to play a significant role in determining moral behavior. The current data continue to suggest that situational factors do exert a very potent influence, however. Recall the Milgram experiments discussed in chapter four and the role of such factors as authority and deindividuation on human behavior.

Investigations of moral development have focused primarily on moral *judgment* and *reasoning*. The Swiss psychologist Jean Piaget (1948) was a pioneer in studying how we symbolize and organize social rules and make judgments based on that organization. He hypothesized that morality develops in a series of steps or stages, each one depending on previous stages and on the intellectual or cognitive equipment and social experiences of the individual. The developmental psychologist Lawrence Kohlberg (1976) revised Piaget's theory substantially and revived research interest in moral development.

Like Piaget, Kohlberg postulates that moral development evolves in stages. The sequence is invariant. Furthermore, the individual must develop the features and skills of a lower moral stage before attaining a higher one. It is important to note that individuals proceed through the stages at different rates, although Kohlberg provides age guidelines for each stage. He identifies three primary stages: *preconventional, conventional,* and *postconventional* morality. Each primary stage is divided into substages, which we will refer to here as *early* and *late*.

During the *early preconventional* stage, the person acts solely to obtain rewards and avoid punishment. He or she has not yet developed any notion of right or wrong and, therefore, is essentially amoral. This orientation toward reward and punishment and an unquestioning deference to those in power characterize children below age seven, but it may be seen in adults as well.

During the *late preconventional* stage, the right action is that which satisfies one's own needs. This stage reflects a selfish orientation which considers the needs of others only to the extent that favors will be returned: "You scratch my back and I'll scratch yours." According to Kohlberg (1976, 1977), human relationships at this stage are viewed as in a marketplace, not with loyalty, gratitude, or justice, but with the goal of using others to obtain something. The person develops some understanding that in order to obtain rewards one must work with others. The emphasis, however, is still very much on meeting one's own needs.

The *early conventional* stage is referred to as the "good boy" or "nice girl" orientation. The individual's behavior is directed toward gaining social approval and acceptance, especially from peers, and there is much conformity to a stereotyped image of what the majority or peer group regards as acceptable behavior. To obtain social rewards and avoid punishment one has to be "nice." During this stage the conscience, or the ability to feel guilt, begins to emerge.

At the *late conventional* stage, the person does things out of duty and respect for the authority of others. Certain rules and regulations are acknowledged as necessary to ensure the smooth functioning of society; if one is derelict in performing duty, dishonor and blame will result. This late conventional stage is often labeled "law-and-order" morality because of its strong emphasis on unquestioning respect for authority, conventionalism, and rigid rules of conduct.

The final and highest stage of moral development—the postconventional—is probably reached by very few people. To reach these stages, one must have the cognitive ability to abstract and to perceive issues in gray rather than in black and white. During the *early postconventional* stage, correct action is determined by principles which reflect an appreciation for the general rights of individuals as well as the standards which have been critically examined and agreed on by society. This requires a balancing of individual and societal rights. In addition to taking into consideration what is democratically agreed on, the early postconventional person relies on personal values to consider the rightness and wrongness of behavior. These personal values may not be in agreement with those of society. Kohlberg believed that this stage reflects considerable emphasis on the "legal point of view," but with the understanding that unjust laws can be changed.

The *late postconventional* person demonstrates an orientation "toward the decisions of conscience and toward self-chosen ethical principles appealing to logical comprehensivenss, universality, and consistency" (Kohlberg, 1977, p. 63). The moral principles are highly abstract and ethical, and they reflect universal principles of justice and of the reciprocity and equality of human rights. The person relies on his or her own personally developed ethical principles and shows respect for "the dignity of human beings as individual persons."

According to Kohlberg, people progress through the stages at different rates and thus reach them at different ages in their lives. Some never go beyond the preconventional stage, and many never reach the postconventional stage. The development of moral judgment depends on the person's intellectual capacity and life experiences. Thus, someone may possess the cognitive ability to develop high stages of moral development but lack sufficient social experiences. On the other hand, despite adequate moral upbringing, the individual may lack the cognitive ability to abstract and generalize the moral principles involved at the higher stages. It is unclear, however, what constitutes adequate moral upbringing or adequate life experiences. Kohlberg contends, however, that the judgment of a large majority of juvenile delinquents is at the early preconventional and late preconventional stages (Kohlberg & Freundlich, 1973).

Furthermore, Kohlberg did not suppose that most people's moral judgments fit neatly into one stage. Rather, he believed that people often demonstrate a wide range of moral judgments, with most clustering around a single stage. This seems to recognize that situational factors can have an influence on a person's immediate judgments.

It is important to realize that Kohlberg's theory is specifically related to moral *judgment* and the person's rationale for his or her behavior. What may appear to the observer to be unethical or antisocial behavior may, in fact, have a morally sound reason to it, at least from the actor's perspective. Therefore, according to Kohlberg, we should try to understand intentions before we make conclusions about another's behavior.

Kohlberg's hypothesis is important because it suggests that the effort to understand criminality should include attention to individual cognitive development as well as learning and external environmental factors. However, Kohlberg's is certainly not a well-established, validated theory. Research testing it has raised many critical questions. For example, Kohlberg doubts the influence of deviant subcultures on moral development, whereas other researchers show evidence of it. Kohlberg also embraces the idea of universal morality, a concept which troubles his critics. Nevertheless, in the process of questioning these and other elements of moral development theory, other researchers have expanded it and proposed intriguing alternative schema.

Bandura (1977) cites research evidence to document his observation that moral behavior can be acquired and modified through imitative and observational learning processes, including the powerful influence of peer models. There is little doubt that peers exert a strong influence on adolescents. The degree of peer group influence may depend on the individual's stage of moral development, however. Peers may have their strongest influence on individuals at the conventional stage, and decidedly less influence at the preconventional and postconventional stages. Yet Kohlberg suggests that most juvenile delinquents are at the preconventional stage.

The Kohlberg model also suggests that universal moral principles are naturally learned during the course of human development. The logically correct thing to do in any situation is indicated by a set of increasingly abstract rules based on *fairness*. Eventually, persons at the highest stage of moral development would reach the same conclusions about what is just. But although Kohlberg's scheme emphasizes principles of fairness, it does not explain fair behavior. In other words, you may know something is the just thing to do, but this does not mean you will do it.

Researchers like Gilligan (1982), Haan (1977, 1978), and Morash (1983) have all theorized that an additional dimension—an other-oriented one—is needed to explain behavior. Gilligan calls this dimension "contextual relativism," Haan calls it "interpersonal morality," and Morash says it is "other-oriented reasoning." Regardless of the label used, each dimension focuses on the extent to which a person has developed responsibility, concern, and care for others.

Consider the following dilemma. What would you do if you found an unmarked envelope with $100 in it? Would you try to find the owner? The money may be a drop in the bucket to the person who lost it, or it may represent a half year's scrimping. Would your behavior be different if the envelope contained $1,000? You undoubtedly know what is fair and just, but will you behave fairly and justly? To what extent does concern for the person who lost the money enter into your decision?

According to proponents of an other-oriented dimension, the more you can feel for the other person, the more likely you will be to try to return the money. Thus, rather than explaining delinquent or criminal behavior as faulty abstract reasoning or lack of a sense of fairness, the other-oriented dimension emphasizes the extent to which a person has developed empathy for others. The more emphathetic one is, the less violent or harmful to others one will be—or at least the more difficult it will be to justify harmful behavior to oneself.

Researchers studying this other-oriented dimension have reported interesting findings. It appears, for example, that boys develop an ethic of care for others at a later time than girls, usually sometime after adolescence (Morash, 1983). Research by Hoffman (1977), in fact, suggests that empathy is better developed among females than males at all stages, although Eisenberg and Lennon (1983) point out that this conclusion may be due to the method of measurement used. Self-report questionnaires consistently indicated that females were more empathetic, but behavioral observations showed few sex differences. Males may be more reluctant to admit that they care. On the other hand, if there *are* sex differences, it might help explain the fact that male violent crime rates are proportionately higher than female rates. Clearly, more research is needed in this important area of other-orientation.

At this point, however, it seems clear that the quality of the family environment is critical in the development of delinquency. Morash (1983) notes that the family is especially important in developing concern, empathy, and an other-oriented perspective in its young members. While it also develops morality, fairness, and justice, outside institutions such as the school or the church appear to be highly influential as well.

Disorganized, unstable families with parents whose own sense of fairness and empathy are not highly developed are more likely to produce future generations with similar orientations toward others. Such families, of course, cut across all economic lines. Moreover, even if the parents are not criminal, their communications may subtly condone delinquent behavior. Frequent admonitions to "Take what you can get when you can get it" and "Look out for number one because no one else will" suggest that the individual's needs are of prime consideration. The family with the maxim "There's a sucker in every crowd" is unlikely to encourage or reinforce empathetic behavior in its members.

Related to moral development is still another theory, first proposed by Sullivan, Grant, and Grant in 1957. It is called *interpersonal-maturity* theory or, more generally, *I-theory*. Through the efforts of Warren (1983) and others, it has gained attention as a viable psychological theory of delinquent behavior.

I-theory separates personality development into seven stages of interpersonal maturity. Although space does not allow us to describe and explain each stage here, interested readers are encouraged to study Warren's (1983) summary. For our purposes, we will focus on aspects of the theory most pertinent to juvenile behavior.

I-theory research reveals that most delinquents cluster around three of the seven stages: stages I-2, I-3, and I-4. People at maturity level I-2 demand that the world take care of them; they see others primarily as givers or withholders of punishments and rewards. They also have little ability to explain, understand, or predict the behavior or reactions of others. They are not interested in things outside themselves, except as a source of supply. People at maturity level I-3 see the world in an oversimplified fashion. They cannot understand the needs, feelings, and motives of others and why these should be different from their own. They perceive the social environment only as an arena in which they manipulate others for personal gain. Moreover, everyone is out to manipulate everyone else. At the next level—I-4—people are primarily concerned about status and are strongly influenced by those they admire. Hence, they are especially susceptible to the influences of models. They see things as either good or bad, with no inbetweens. Because of their rigidity in their standards and rules, they are also most susceptible to guilt and self-criticism when they fail to meet their primitive and rigid rules of conduct. Warren believes that very few juvenile offenders, less than 1 percent, are beyond maturity stage I-3.

Like Kohlberg's theory, I-theory argues that cognitive development is the result of an interaction between the cognitive ability with which one is born and one's experiences with the social environment. From this interaction, a person develops a consistent set of expectations that constitutes a large segment of the mental component of personality. Therefore, interpersonal maturity theory is grounded on how an individual perceives the world and those within it (Quay, 1987). Although I-theory continues to be used in treatment planning by many juvenile agencies and correctional facilities, it appears to have limited practicality beyond providing a rough estimate of maturity (Harris, 1988).

DIFFERENTIAL SUSCEPTIBILITY TO CRIMINAL BEHAVIOR

The interpersonal-maturity theory and the work of Gilligan, Haan, Morash, and their colleagues suggest more ideas for explaining individual differences in delinquent behavior. Specifically, they stress that we should consider a person's level of cognitive moral development when we try to decide which has the greater influence on conduct, the social environment or the personality. At certain stages in a person's development, he or she may be especially susceptible to peer pressures and expectations. At early stages, parents and family background may play a more crucial role. At later stages, personality factors independent of most environmental pressures may be critical.

The relative importance of classical conditioning and social learning may also depend on cognitive development. Direct reinforcements and punishments may be more important during earlier stages than at later stages. In fact, classical conditioning may well explain behavior during early childhood, but it may become less of a factor as we grow older. Like subhumans who have powers of perceptual thinking but lack conceptual thinking, infants and young children might be especially susceptible to classical conditioning. However, as they develop, conceptual thinking begins to play a more dominant role, and classical conditioning becomes less likely to determine behavior. Operant conditioning and social learning become critical. Social learning may be important during the peer association phase so typical of adolescence, and therefore may be particularly relevant in explaining delinquency, especially gang delinquency. For those few individuals who continue to develop to higher stages of cognitive and moral development, the environment diminishes in importance. Instead, the internal mediational processes that determine the person's notions of fairness and concern for others are likely to dominate.

A concept like differential susceptibility helps explain individual differences in delinquent and criminal behavior, such as why one woman engages in unlawful behavior while her sister, one year older and raised in the same environment, does not. It helps explain why many delinquents outgrow their antisocial conduct while others do not. Furthermore, differential susceptibility encompasses most of the theories of deviance and criminality as well as principles of classical and operant conditioning, social learning, personality traits, and cognitive and moral development. Which theory or principle best explains an individual's delinquent or criminal behavior may primarily depend on which stage of cognitive development the individual has reached.

SUMMARY AND CONCLUSIONS

We have seen that the early development of individuals prone to persistent offending is frequently characterized by considerable failure, adversities, and frustrations. Generally speaking, the backgrounds of persistent offenders are littered with numerous impediments for normal development. Moreover, there is a growing body of evidence that people who experience a series of failures and lack personal efficacy tend to view many aspects of their environments as fraught with danger (Bandura, 1989). Lacking interpersonal skills and personal efficacy, and living in a social environment that fails to provide suitable opportunity to develop competence, many youths resort to a mean, bitter, I-don't-care approach to life. They begin to affect all their social environments with this antisocial approach, and the social environments react similarly in an ongoing, bidirectional interaction. Of course, not all youths react this way to this set of circumstances. Some, because of a certain temperament interacting with a myriad of experiences, acquire interpersonal competencies, academic skills, and effective strategies to avoid a pattern of persistent offending as a way of life.

This chapter has also underscored the importance of an internal code of conduct as guidance for one's behavior. The psychological perspective on juvenile delinquency is becoming increasingly cognitive. Research and theory are focusing on how youthful offenders acquire, internalize, and develop personal values and beliefs. They are interested in studying how juvenile offenders think and how they got to think that way. Included in this psychological study is moral thinking, with emphasis on Kohlberg's theory of moral development. The latest moral development theories focus on empathy and an other-orientation, suggesting that these factors might explain individual differences in behavior toward others.

Social environments and normative groups are important in the development of internal standards, but the point that must be emphasized is that people do not automatically model actions. They extract and process their own standards from the multiplicity of actions and reactions of individuals around them. From all this divergent information, people develop personal standards against which they measure and evaluate their own conduct. These codes of conduct form part of the *self-regulatory mechanisms* we will refer to in later chapters.

Throughout the remainder of this text, it will be obvious that theories emphasizing cognitive processes (i.e., beliefs, values, thoughts) are favored in contemporary psychological explanations of crime and delinquency. Classical and operant conditioning are assuming a more secondary role, although they remain very important in understanding certain offenses. Our beliefs, values, images of ourselves, and our philosophies are the primary guides of our behavior. They are reference points for justifying our conduct to ourselves and others. Most people try to live according to their internal standards and respond to others according to their perspectives of human nature. If our friends, models, and heroes perceive life and the human condition in a certain way, we may well do the same. If cruelty, insensitivity to others, and a selfish orientation is the norm, this may be reflected both in our approach to life and in our perceptions of criminal behavior. Moreover, if we believe that "everyone does it," we have neutralized the stigma attached to the conduct. Youth is a time when we begin to formulate basic philosophies of life. In most instances, delinquency seems to be an expression of the values the juvenile has either adopted or has been exposed to through significant models in the environment.

CHAPTER SIX
The Mentally Disordered Offender

Scientific investigations of abnormal behavior and criminal behavior have much in common. When we differentiate either one from "normal" behavior, we encounter vague definitions, classifications that invite numerous exceptions, and unwieldy and complex variables. In addition, both abnormal and criminal behavior are deviant in the sense that they stray from what is considered normal, expected, and average conduct in society. In this sense, the criteria for determining what behaviors constitute normality may fluctuate according to the dominant economic, social, and political philosophies. With regard to criminal behavior, this point is easily illustrated by both past and present laws governing the use and sale of alcoholic beverages and other drugs. With abnormal behavior, it is easily illustrated by the fact that homosexuality was considered a mental disorder until 1973. In our discussion of deviant behavior, therefore, we are necessarily constricted by the boundaries established in society at this point in time.

Despite complexities in definition and criteria, psychologists have made some progress toward understanding the deviant human mind. Researchers have learned, for example, that most deviant behavior (both abnormal and criminal) is probably acquired through the same fundamental processes as nondeviant behavior. Deviant behavior seems to represent learned response patterns for coping with perceived threats, fears, and stress, and generally, for surviving in one's world (real or imagined). Problems arise when we try to classify and simplify these response patterns, since so many factors go into each individual's discovery of what works best for him or her. As many clinicians are too well aware, human behavior rarely follows a set, predictable pattern to correspond neatly to textbook descriptions or guidelines in a diagnostic manual. Toch and Adams (1989) note that classifications of people are often by-products of resource allocation. That is, classification systems are often implemented for funding purposes and for the determination of staff needs.

In the psychological study of both criminal and abnormal behavior, labels are of limited use. With respect to criminal behavior, they inform us about conduct but not about motivations. We know that a person who has committed petty larceny stole an item or items of relatively nominal value, but we have no idea what led to that conduct. In abnormal behavior, labels are even more of a problem, since they are based on response patterns that may not be manifested in outward behavior. When we say a person is schizophrenic, for example, we may be referring to hallucinations that may not be clearly obvious to an observer. In behavior that is both criminal and abnormal, the problem is, of course, greater.

Since labels explain nothing, the psychological study of the criminal behavior that is presumably abnormal must go beyond them and try to explain its principal causes. In this chapter, therefore, we focus on the mental disorders and their alleged relationship with crime. In doing so, we will find that this relationship is not as strong as is often assumed. We will begin with a brief presentation of the concepts traditionally used by the psychiatric, psychological, and legal profession to describe and predict abnormal behavior. Next we will examine criminal responsibility, competence to stand trial, and the issues of determinism and free will, which are viewed by the legal and psychiatric profession from very different perspectives. Finally, we will examine the concept of dangerousness as it applies to clinical prediction.

MENTAL DISORDERS AND CRIME

It is a popular misconception that the brutal, violent, and apparently senseless crime is usually committed by someone who is mentally ill or sick. A man who sexually assaults, tortures, and kills a four-year-old child *has* to be sick. How else could he do this? An alternate explanation focuses on the subhuman perspective: If not sick, the person is an animal. Although this second approach is gaining ground, perhaps reflecting public impatience with perceived insanity loopholes in the criminal justice system, there is still wide public subscription, mirrored in popular literature, to a presumption of mental illness, particularly when outrageous, inexplicable crimes are at issue.

Throughout the history of civilization there has been a strong tendency to forge this link between mental illness and violent behavior (Monahan, 1981). Most societies and their legal systems have been confused about and often frightened by mental disorder. In fact, the first mental hospital in the American colonies was established after Benjamin Franklin argued forcefully that the mentally ill were prone to violence and should be confined, involuntarily if need be, to protect society (Monahan & Geis, 1976).

The acceptance of this link centers on the assumption that mentally ill people do not play by the rules of society, are unpredictable, and cannot control their own actions. Since they are apt to do anything at any given time, these "crazy people" are potentially dangerous. On the other hand, we also assume that people who commit senseless or incomprehensible violent acts are obviously crazy and sick. Thus, mentally ill people are dangerous, and people who commit bizarre crimes are mentally ill.

Before we can examine the validity of these beliefs, we must define our terms. Mental illness is a disorder of the mind that is judged by experts to interfere substantially with a person's ability to cope with life on a daily basis. It presumably deprives the person of freedom of choice, but it is important to note that there are degrees to this deprivation. Mental illness is manifested in behavior that deviates notably from normal conduct. Use of the term *illness* encourages us to look for etiology, symptoms, and cures and to rely heavily on the medical profession both to diagnose and treat. More importantly, it encourages us to excuse the behavior of persons plagued with the "sickness." If we use the term *mental disorder*, however, we are not so conceptually limited. Mental disorder need not imply that a person is sick and to be pitied or less responsible for his or her actions. Therefore, although *mental illness* is widely used in the psychological, psychiatric, and legal literature and is the term favored in both civil and criminal law, we prefer the less restrictive *mental disorder*.

Mental disorders are manifested in a variety of behaviors, ranging in severity from what Morse (1978) calls "crazy behavior" to conduct that is essentially innocuous. Crazy behavior is that which is obviously strange and unusual and cannot be logically explained. A nineteen-year-old male skipping along the sidewalk with a pie plate on his head and reciting "Wee Willie Winkle" is exhibiting strange behavior. If it is fraternity initiation week on the local campus, there may be a logical explanation. In the absence of such an explanation, the behavior becomes "crazy." In this instance, clinicians might call the behavior *psychotic*, symptomatic of a severe mental disorder. It is not necessarily dangerous, however—a crucial distinction.

The concept of mental disorder, therefore, may connote bizarre, dramatic, harmful, or mildly unusual behaviors whose classifications are published in the *Diagnostic and Statistical Manual of Mental Disorders* (DSM). Compiled by a committee appointed by the American Psychiatric Association, the DSM is the guidebook for clinicians who seek to define and diagnose specific mental disorders. It is reviewed and revised periodically to conform to the contemporary, mainstream thinking of psychiatrists and other mental health professionals. Thus, until 1973, as we noted earlier, homosexuality was considered a mental disorder; today it is no longer so. In a sense, then, mental disorders are whatever the psychiatric profession wishes them to be.

The DSM-III—the current manual published in 1980—differs substantially in content from the DSM-II, which appeared in 1968. The DSM-III-R published in 1987 has made some changes but does not affect the disorders described in this chapter. For our purposes, three major changes between the DSM-II and DSM-III are important: (1) a shift in focus from the *causes* of mental disorders to their behavioral indicators; (2) a reclassification of what were formerly called *neuroses*; and (3) an expansion of the subcategories of psychosis.

The previous DSM was steeped in psychoanalytic, psychodynamic traditions and etiology. Its categories were based on assumed psychodynamic causes. The DSM-III tries to eliminate theory and etiology and concentrate on description and classification, although it is debatable to what extent this has been accomplished (Charney, 1980; Shacht, 1985). If there is substantial research or clinical agreement on the causes of a disorder, this information is included; otherwise, there is generally no speculation. Instead, clinicians are offered more detailed, concrete bases for making diagnoses. Each category is described extensively, and its observable behaviors are carefully outlined.

The second major difference is reflected in the Committee's decision to drop the label "neurosis," because there was little agreement about its meaning. Neurosis has been replaced by three separate major categories: (1) anxiety disorders, which include phobias, generalized anxiety disorders, and obsessive compulsive disorders; (2) somatoform disorders, which include somatization and conversion disorders; and (3) dissociative disorders, including amnesias, fugues, and multiple personality. Since *neurosis* has been traditionally used to encompass all these categories, the Committee recommended that they could be subsumed under the term *neurotic disorders*. It is preferable, however, to use the distinct categories.

When we refer to "crazy behavior," we are not usually talking about neurotic disorders. Generally, these disorders do not result in major problems or discomfort to others in society; only the person affected feels the discomfort. In essence, a neurotic disorder is an emotional reaction that distresses the individual (and perhaps indirectly those closest to him or her) and that the individual finds unacceptable. However, the person maintains contact with reality, and the behavior does not typically violate social norms.

For example, although agoraphobia (an abnormal fear of open spaces) is a mental disorder from a professional point of view, it is not the type of "crazy behavior" that concerns the public. The neurotic disorders may be relatively enduring and recurrent, but they are generally regarded as mild, even by clinicians. Furthermore, since these disorders are rarely associated with violent, frightening actions, they do not play a role in discussions of responsibility for criminal behavior.

A third change in the new edition of the DSM revolves around the subcategories of psychosis. In DSM-II, psychosis was a major section comprising schizophrenia, paranoid states, and major affective disorders (severe depression). Psychosis as a separate category does not appear in DSM-III. Instead, schizophrenic disorders, paranoid disorders, mood disorders, and "psychotic disorders not elsewhere classified" appear as separate major categories. For our purposes, since much of the research we will be discussing was conducted before this change, we will retain the labels "psychosis" and "psychotic behavior," which should be viewed as generic terms covering each of the four categories just cited.

Although many other changes characterize the DSM-III, the aforementioned are of greatest concern to us here. Changes in other categories, such as in psychosexual disorders, will be alluded to as they pertain to the topics being discussed later in this text. For the present, the three categories of mental disorders most relevant are (1) schizophrenic disorders, (2) paranoid disorders; and (3) the personality disorder called antisocial personality disorder. Note that the first two fall into the "psychotic" category; the third is a separate category under the general label "personality disorders." They are relevant because they are most likely to be associated with violent or antisocial behavior and are most often cited to support an insanity defense to criminal charges. We will review each of these disorders and then assess their relevance to criminal behavior.

Schizophrenic Disorders

Schizophrenia is the mental disorder that people most often associate with "crazy behavior," since it frequently manifests itself in highly bizarre actions. Severe breakdowns in thought patterns, emotions, and perceptions are common. Spells of extreme social withdrawal from others are also typical. The thoughts and cognitive functioning of the schizophrenic person become disorganized and fail to correspond to reality, and his or her speech will reflect this. The most common example is a loosening of associations, in which ideas shift between totally unrelated or only obliquely related subjects. Thought becomes fragmented and bizarre, and delusions—false beliefs about the world—are common. For example, a schizophrenic may believe that everyone is plotting to destroy him or her, or that God has sent him on a mission to kill all red-haired prostitutes.

Typical features of the schizophrenic's emotions or affect include inappropriateness (e.g., indiscriminate giggling or crying) or emotional flatness, where no emotional reaction is exhibited. The voice is monotonous, the face immobile and expressionless. The major disturbances in perception are various forms of hallucinations, which involve sensing or perceiving things or events that others do not sense or perceive. The most common hallucinations are auditory, with the individual hearing voices or sounds that no one else can hear.

The DSM-III recognizes five types of schizophrenia: (1) disorganized; (2) catatonic; (3) paranoid; (4) undifferentiated; and (5) residual. Following is a brief summary of the essential features of each type.

1. *Disorganized*: Inappropriate affect (flat, incongruous, or silly emotional responses) and marked incoherence and disorganization in thought patterns. Associated features include grimaces, strange mannerisms, complaints of nonexistent physical ailments, extreme social withdrawal, and other oddities of behavior.

2. *Catatonic*: Severe disturbances in muscular and voluntary movement. Extended periods of mutism are common. The catatonic may assume a bizarre posture for long periods of time (usually several hours) and then fly into an overactive, agitated state of screaming and throwing things.

3. *Paranoid*: Characterized by delusions and hallucinations. Paranoid schizophrenics may be convinced that the FBI is following them with the intent of capturing them and leading them to their death. Or, the paranoid schizophrenic may believe that the world is inhabited by extraterrestrials who are plotting to take over the world. Of all the schizophrenic types, the paranoid is the most frequently represented in criminal behavior.

4. *Undifferentiated*: This type shows psychotic symptoms that cannot be classifed into any of the foregoing categories.

5. *Residual*: These individuals have had at least one episode of schizophrenia, and there is evidence that some of the symptoms are continuing. For example, the person may still display blunted emotions or illogical thinking, but no other symptoms.

Paranoid Disorders

The paranoid disorders do not have clear boundaries, since they often accompany other disorders like schizophrenia, organic mental disorder, paranoid personality disorder, and depressions. The essential feature of all paranoid disorders is the delusional system, which most often includes persecutory beliefs about being spied on, cheated, conspired against, followed, drugged, maliciously maligned, harassed, or obstructed. Generally, these false beliefs are accompanied by anger, resentment, and sometimes violence. Suspiciousness, either generalized or directed at one or more persons, is common. Sometimes the delusional system is grandiose; the person is convinced that he or she possesses great power or is especially important.

Antisocial Personality Disorder

The essential feature of an antisocial personality disorder is a history of continuous behavior in which the rights of others are violated. According to the DSM-III, the antisocial history must date at least as far back as the age of fifteen for males and anytime during adolescence for females. Lying, stealing, fighting, truancy, and resisting authority are the typical childhood symptoms. During adolescence, the person with an antisocial personality disorder frequently exhibits precocious and aggressive sexual behavior, excessive drinking, and the use of illicit drugs. During adulthood, the individual demonstrates a poor work history with an inability to hold onto a good job over a period of several years. Furthermore, there is a marked impaired capacity to sustain lasting, close, warm, and responsible relationships with family, friends, or sexual partners. Overall, antisocial persons fail to become independent, self-supporting adults. They spend most of their lives in institutions (usually correctional facilities) or remain highly dependent on their families. Other accompanying features include restlessness, an inability to tolerate boredom, and a belief that the world is hostile. Antisocial personalities often complain of tension and depression. They are often impulsive and unable to plan ahead.

Antisocial personality disorder occurs more frequently in males than females. It is estimated that about 3 percent of the American male population and about 1 percent of the American female population fall into this category (DSM-III, p. 319). Furthermore, the disorder is more common in lower-class populations, partly because it is connected with impaired earning capacity and partly because of the greater likelihood of being raised in an one-parent family with inadequate models and resources. Finally, the DSM-III concludes that the disorder runs in families, possibly due to a genetic link that predisposes the child.

The validity of the antisocial personality disorder as a meaningful concept has been debated. Blackburn (1988) contends that there is no single type of abnormal personality that is prone to chronic rule violation. Furthermore, the diagnostic label "antisocial personality disorder" remains "a mythical entity" that fails to be meaningful for theory development, research, clinical communication, or prediction. "Such a concept is little more than a moral judgment masquerading as a clinical diagnosis. Given the lack of demonstrable scientific or clinical utility of the concept, it should be discarded" (Blackburn, 1988, p. 511).

MENTAL DISORDERS AND VIOLENCE

Long-term inpatient care or hospitalization of the mentally disordered is a practice that has largely disappeared. Consequently, the mentally disordered have become a more visible presence within the community. When problems arise, often it is the responsibility of law enforcement officials to handle the situation. "As a result, the jails and prisons may have become the long-term repository for mentally ill individuals who, in a previous era, would have been institutionalized within a psychiatric facility" (Teplin, 1984, p. 795).

However, the research literature consistently supports the position that severely mentally disordered individuals are no more likely to commit serious crimes against others than the general population (Brodsky, 1973, 1977; Henn, Herjanic, & Vanderpearl, 1976a; Rabkin, 1979; Monahan, 1981). Media portrayals of a killer driven berserk by bloodthirsty delusions are sensational, frightening, and perhaps entertaining, but in reality this phenomenon is rare.

Henn and his colleagues conducted an extensive series of investigations on all defendants referred by a St. Louis, Missouri court for psychiatric assessment over a ten-year period (Henn, Herjanic, & Vanderpearl, 1976a). Of the nearly 2,000 persons arrested for homicide between 1964 and 1973, only about 1 percent qualified as psychotic, supporting the view that psychotics are no more likely to be violent than the rest of the population. Recall that under the old DSM, psychosis comprised several of the severe mental disorders we have just discussed. Data comparable to the Henn results were also reported by Hafner and Boker (1973) on the German population, and by Zitrin et al. (1975) and Rappeport and Lassen (1965) on the American population.

Focusing on a separate sample of 1,195 defendants accused of a variety of crimes and again referred for psychiatric assessment, Henn learned that the most frequent diagnosis was personality disorder, accounting for nearly 40 percent of all the diagnoses. Two-thirds of those classified as personality disorders were specifically designated antisocial personality. The second most frequent diagnosis was schizophrenia (which also included those labeled probable schizophrenia), comprising 17 percent of the total. The other diagnostic labels (based on DSMs I and II) were evenly distributed and of low frequency.

It is interesting to note that 93 percent of the defendants were diagnosed *something*, which may reflect, in part, a perceived obligation on the part of the evaluation team to tag on a diagnosis of some sort. Of course, this could also reflect sophistication on the part of the referring judges, who were able to detect a likely mental disorder.

Henn also found frequent references to alcoholism, primarily as a secondary diagnosis, in the diagnostic reports. Alcoholism cut across all diagnostic categories, with the notable exception of schizophrenia, where only a few cases were reported. The combination of alcoholism and drug addiction as a secondary diagnosis was common in persons labeled antisocial personality. These findings support those reported by Guze (1976), who found the diagnosis of alcoholism prevalent among offenders with a diagnosis of antisocial personality disorders.

Rabkin's (1979) review of the criminal behavior of discharged mental patients sheds further light on the relationship between crime and mental disorders. A significant number of studies in her literature review found that the arrest rate for discharged mental patients was *higher* than the rate for the general population, especially for assaultive behavior. On its face, this finding contradicts earlier conclusions, but close examination reveals that the data are still consistent. Rabkin suggested two explanations for the disproportionate arrest rates, one derived after separating patients with prior criminal records from those without, and one based on diagnostic technique.

First, a small subset of patients who had criminal records prior to hospital admission continued their antisocial ways soon after discharge from the mental institution. These habitual offenders significantly inflated the arrest rates for all mental patients. Patients without prior criminal records were substantially *below* the arrest rates for the general population. Rabkin suggests that the upward trend in arrest rates is partly due to policy and procedural changes in many mental institutions which allowed patients to return to the community much sooner than in the past, and partly due to the increasing tendency of courts to refer habitual offenders for psychiatric diagnosis. In other words, courts—at least during the period under review—were likely to refer for psychiatric diagnoses people who were criminally prone and who, in a less psychiatrically conscious era, would have been standardly processed through the criminal justice system. And as we might suspect, diagnosticians probably cooperated by tagging on a label that would facilitate, although not guarantee, a commitment to a mental institution.

The other factor accounting for the disproportionate arrest rates is diagnostic. Rabkin found that most criminal offenses after discharge were committed by individuals who had been diagnosed alcoholics, addicts, or personality disordered. The first two diagnostic categories appear consistently in the research. It has also been suggested that so-called personality disorders are often only classified as such because the clinician could find no other way to label a person acting antisocially. Alcoholism and addiction are in the fringe areas of traditional diagnoses because they do not represent what are considered serious or typical mental disorders. When these three categories were omitted, Rabkin found that the arrest rates among the discharged patients were comparable to those reported in the general population.

Teplin (1984) conducted a well-executed study on the tendency of police officers to arrest mentally disorderd individuals. Trained graduate students in psychology observed 1,382 police-citizen encounters (involving

2,555 citizens) and evaluated the mental status of the citizens according to specific criteria (a symptom checklist that listed the major characteristics of severe mental disorders). The police determined that 506 citizens qualified as suspects and arrested 148. The graduate students classified 30 of the 506 suspects and 14 of the 148 of the suspects arrested as exhibiting definite symptoms of mental disorders. Therefore, the police arrested 20 percent more individuals with symptoms than those without symptoms. However, considering that many disordered individuals tend to have annoying symptoms, such as verbal abuse, belligerence, and disrespect, the slightly higher probability of arrest is hardly surprising. In addition, the police officers failed to recognize the behavior as representing a mental disorder in a large number of cases, believing the individuals were simply being disrespectful and asking for trouble.

In summary, the research literature fails to support the widespread and enduring myth that the severely mentally disturbed tend to be killers or unpredictable violent offenders. It is possible, however, as some clinicians believe, that the more bizarre violent offenses are committed by the mentally disordered, particularly those categorized as schizophrenic or paranoid. Yet, there has been no research delineating bizarreness in crime and studying it as a function of mental disorders. Until this is done, the link between severely mentally disordered individuals and egregious crimes remains speculative.

Research does indicate, however, that alcoholism, substance abuse, and antisocial personality disorders are overrepresented in criminal offenses. In the case of alcoholism and substance abuse, the evidence may be clearcut. In the case of personality disorders, it may reflect clinician subjectivity. An evaluating agency may assume at the outset that the individual referred for evaluation is antisocial because he or she has already had contact with the criminal justice system. Add this to the belief that the court is expecting a label of some sort, and the final result may well be a contaminated diagnosis.

Mental disorders in those incarcerated in prison are sometimes cited as evidence of a link between crime and abnormal behavior. The incidence and nature of disorders among the convicted are difficult to determine, however. For one thing, inmate populations are considered different from the population at large because they have been filtered through the criminal justice sytem. For another thing, it is likely that prison conditions have some deleterious effects on mental states. Therefore, an individual may become mentally disordered after being institutionalized, and that fact may not be reflected in the research.

Nevertheless, when Brodsky (1973) reviewed nine studies on prisoner populations, he found that the overall incidence of psychosis was small, occurring in only 1 or 2 percent of the entire population. Neurotic reactions also appeared infrequently, occurring in about 4 to 6 percent of the inmate population. Personality disorders, on the other hand, were diagnosed very frequently. Schands (1958) found that 56 percent of 1,720 North Carolina prisoners could be classified as having a personality disorder of some variety.

If we remove antisocial personality disorders from consideration, the incidence of serious mental disorders in prison populations appears to be small. This may be misleading, because until recently, many prison inmates exhibiting psychotic or "crazy behaviors" were routinely transferred to institutions for the criminally insane. These transfers would therefore not be included in the prison population statistics. In 1980, the U.S. Supreme Court limited this practice (*Vitek* v. *Jones*) by requiring administrative hearings before such transfers could be effected. This decision will likely be reflected in future research on mentally disordered inmates.

THE MENTALLY DISORDERED OFFENDER AND CRIMINAL RESPONSIBILITY

The term *mentally disordered offender*, for purposes of our discussion, refers to the person believed both to be mentally disordered and to have committed a serious criminal act. In some cases, mentally disordered offenders have only been charged with, not convicted of, a crime. In that sense, *offender* is used loosely. Four categories of individuals are included: (1) those found incompetent to stand trial (IST); (2) those found not guilty of a crime by reason of insanity (NGRI); (3) mentally disordered sex offenders (MDSO); and (4) those administratively transferred from a prison to a mental hospital ("transfers"). The first three categories have been adjudicated by the courts. Most mentally disordered offenders have been committed involuntarily to a security section of a mental hospital (or hospital prison), presumably for psychotherapeutic reasons. Occasionally, mentally disordered offenders, specifically ISTs, are allowed to remain in the community but are subjected to a regimen of outpatient therapeutic services.

Steadman and his colleagues (1982), in a national survey that will be cited extensively throughout this section, found that 20,143 persons were admitted to state and federal institutions in the United States during 1978 as mentally disordered offenders. Transfers from prisons to mental institutions accounted for 54 percent of the total. ISTs represented about 32 percent, NGRIs about 8 percent, and MDSOs another 6 percent. The Steadman figures indicate that the national admission rates for mentally disordered offenders have remained about the same at least since 1967, despite some changes in state and federal statutes during the period. In view of the *Vitek* decision mentioned earlier, we might expect some changes in these percentages, a point we will return to shortly.

The Insanity Defense

The best known of the mentally disordered offender categories, due to the wide publicity it attracts, is the judicial determination of not guilty by reason of insanity (NGRI). *Insanity* is a legal term, not a psychiatric or psychological one; it should be used only in the context of a criminal offense. Insanity refers to a person's state of mind at the time an offense was committed. A finding of insanity means that the person was mentally ill at the time of his or her offense, which might be months prior to a psychiatric evaluation and recommendation. The law assumes that mental disorder *can* rob an individual of free will or the ability to make appropriate choices. If this is the case, the individual *may* not be responsible for crimes committed while suffering from the mental disorder. Note that insanity should not be equated with mental illness or serious mental disorder. That is, the evidence that a person was mentally ill at the time of the crime will not necessarily result in a determination of insanity.

Insanity defenses, especially if they are successful, receive extensive media coverage and commentary. When John Hinckley, charged with an attempt on the life of President Reagan, was found NGRI by a federal jury, there was widespread public indignation accompanied by numerous demands for repeal of the insanity plea in federal law. For our purposes, the controversy surrounding the Hinckley case centered on the prosecution's burden to prove that Hinckley was *not* insane. This relates to a complex issue in criminal law that is only tangential to our discussion. It is important to note, however, that insanity pleas are rare compared to the total number of criminal cases. Researchers estimate that defendants use the insanity defense in only about 4 or 5 percent of all United States criminal cases (Steadman & Braff, 1983; Steadman & Cocozza, 1974; Kanno & Scheidemandel, 1969). It is also estimated that acquittals on the basis of insanity (actual NGRIs) occur in only 22 percent of all cases invoking the plea (Steadman & Braff, 1983; Burton & Steadman, 1978).

Defense attorneys have generally not recommended that their clients plead insanity unless they were charged with a serious offense and the evidence against them was overwhelming. When the possible penalty is capital punishment, life imprisonment, or even a lengthy prison sentence without possibility of parole, an insanity defense becomes more palatable. In many jurisdictions, however, insanity acquittees were automatically confined to mental institutions, even without a finding of present mental illness. They might be confined for as long as necessary to produce substantial improvement in their condition. Furthermore, agents administering treatment of NGRI individuals were entitled to use a wide range of therapeutic devices to remedy the deviant condition.

In the 1970s, the insanity defense became slightly more attractive to defense attorneys, because courts began to strike down statutes authorizing automatic and indeterminate commitment and forced treatment of persons found NGRI (Wexler, 1981). A recent decision by the U.S. Supreme Court supports automatic confinement, however, and may have a wide-ranging effect on the insanity defense. In *Jones* v. *U.S.* (1983), the Court ruled that insanity, once found, could be presumed to continue. Therefore, a person could not only be committed automatically, but could also be confined in a mental institution until he or she recovered sanity, regardless of the nature of the offense.

The insanity defense has been recognized in English courts for over 700 years (Simon, 1983). Since the American legal system is derived from British law, American courts have generally recognized it as well. Standards or tests to determine insanity vary widely among the states, but they usually center around one of three broad models of criminal responsibility: the M'Naghten rule, the Brawner rule, or the Durham rule.

M'Naghten has been around in some form since at least the eighteenth century. The rule was formulated in 1843 when Daniel M'Naghten, a Scottish woodcutter, was accused of killing a man he believed to be the Prime Minister. M'Naghten thought he was being persecuted by the Tories and their leader, Prime Minister Sir Robert Peel. He fired a shot into a carriage transporting Peel's secretary, Edward Drumond, thinking Peel himself was in the carriage. There was no question that M'Naghten had committed the act, but the court believed he was so mentally deranged that it would be inhuman to convict him, since he was not in control of his faculties. He was found not guilty by reason of insanity and was committed to the Broadmoor Mental Institution, where he remained until his death twenty-two years later.

In 1851, the M'Naghten rule was adopted in the federal and most state courts in the United States. It is deceptively simple, and therein lies its popularity. It states that a person is not responsible for a criminal act if, "at the time of committing the act, the party accused was labouring under such a defect of reason, from disease of the mind, as not to know the nature and quality of the act he was doing; or if he did know it, . . . he did not know he was doing what was wrong" (M'Naghten, 1843, p. 718). Essentially, the rule states that if a person, because of some mental disease, did not know right from wrong at the time of an unlawful act, or did not know that what he or she was doing was wrong, that person cannot be held responsible for his or her actions.

Some states supplement M'Naghten with an "irresistible impulse" test. This test recognizes or assumes that people may realize the wrongfulness of their conduct, be aware of what is right or wrong in a particular set of circumstances, but still be powerless to do right in the face of overwheming pressures from uncontrollable impulses. In other words, there are conditions under which people presumably cannot help themselves. The M'Naghten test alone would not cover those circumstances, since it requires that the person did not know right from wrong.

The Brawner rule, which is largely based on an insanity rule suggested by the Model Penal Code (MPC), is another rule for determining insanity. The Model Penal Code was proposed in 1962 by a group of legal scholars called the American Law Institute. The Code was drafted to serve as a model for legislatures seeking to modernalize and rationalize their criminal statutes. According to the Brawner rule, "A person is not responsible for criminal conduct if at the time of such conduct as a result of mental disease *or defect* (italics added), he lacks substantial capacity either to appreciate the criminality [wrongfulness] of his conduct or to conform his conduct to the requirements of the law" (*U.S.* v. *Brawner*, 1972, p. 973). It must be demonstrated that the disease or mental defect (1) directly influenced the defendant's mental or emotional processes, or (2) impaired his or her ability to control behavior. The Brawner rule, unlike M'Naghten, recognizes *partial* responsibility for criminal conduct as well as the possibility of an irresistible impulse beyond one's control. It also excludes from the definition of mental disease or defect any repeated criminal or otherwise antisocial conduct. Thus, psychopathic or antisocial personality disorder would not excuse a person under that rule.

The Durham rule was created in 1954 in *Durham* v. *U.S* by the same court that later rejected it in favor of the Brawner rule. Monte Durham, a twenty-six-year-old resident of the District of Columbia, had a long history of mental disorder and petty theft. His crime of the moment was burglary, but he was acquitted because his unlawful act was considered to be "the product of a mental disease or mental defect" (*Durham* v. *U.S.*, 1954, p. 874). While the M'Naghten rule focuses on knowing right from wrong (the mental element in a crime), Durham assumes that one cannot be held responsible if an unlawful action is the *product* of mental disease or defect. There is nothing in the rule that relates directly to the person's mental judgment. If the person has a disease or defect, lack of culpability is easily assumed. Many states were attracted to this simple rule, since it seemed more straightforward and comprehensible to juries. However, it soon became apparent that virtually any defendant could be excused, once mental disease or defect had been established, and the Durham rule quickly lost its popularity.

Incompetency to Stand Trial

Some persons charged with a crime are considered so intellectually and/or psychologically impaired that they are unable to understand the charges or the judicial process, or unable to cooperate rationally with their attorneys in their own defense. In that event, they are adjudicated IST and remitted to a mental institution, or less frequently to an outpatient therapeutic program, until rendered competent. In 1978, an estimated 20,000 IST evaluations were requested by state and federal courts (Steadman et al., 1982), but accurate figures concerning the actual number who were evaluated IST (on a national level) are presently unavailable.

Incompetency to stand trial has no direct relevance to insanity, and the two determinations must be viewed distinctly. Criminal responsibility, which is at the core of the insanity defense, and competency to stand trial refer to a defendant's mental state/capacity at two different points in time. In an insanity claim, the law asks, "What was the defendant's state of mind at the time the offense was committed?" In competency considerations, the question becomes, "What is the defendant's state of mind at the present time, or at the time of the trial?" An individual who was seriously mentally disordered at the time of an offense may have enough mental stability by the time of the trial to be competent to stand trial. On the other hand, a person may be of sound mind during the unlawful act, but may later become disordered or disoriented and be evaluated IST. Furthermore, the competency issue can be raised at any time during the actual proceedings.

Persons found IST, therefore, have not been convicted of any crime, but they may nevertheless be institutionalized for treatment. In recent years, however, ISTs have asserted constitutional rights in connection with their status, including the right to the "least restrictive or drastic alternative" in treatment (Winick, 1983). They have been successful to some extent in lower courts, but the U.S. Supreme Court has not ruled on this matter.

Research on persons found IST indicates that they are highly similar in background characteristics. Most have limited social and occupational skills and a history of prior criminal charges and psychiatric hospitalizations (Williams & Miller, 1981). Compared to the general population, ISTs are disproportionately unmarried, black, and poorly educated (less than ninth-grade education) (Steadman, 1979). Moreover, a vast majority faced serious criminal charges before being adjudicated IST. In fact, the seriousness of the criminal charges against them seems to play a greater role in determining the length of their confinement than the severity of the mental disorder. Furthermore, the IST recidivism rate appears significantly higher than the recidivism rate of comparable offenders not adjudicated mentally disordered (Steadman & Hartstone, 1983). The overall picture indicates that ISTs are marginal individuals with low educational attainment, poor job skills, and a propensity for running afoul of the law. They appear to shuttle back and forth between mental hospitals, and they have few employment or family ties (Steadman, 1979). The IST route, which is often used by criminal defense attorneys as a delaying tactic until community outrage over a heinous crime dissipates, may also represent a tendency to shunt off defendants with little social influence.

In an extensive study of mentally disordered offenders housed in New York state institutions in the mid-1960s, Steadman and Cocozza (1974) found that approximately 40 percent were IST defendants. The latest survey by Steadman and his colleagues (1982) indicates that the IST figure has declined to about 32 percent, although these data are incomplete since only a portion of the institutions surveyed kept records of the actual number of ISTs confined. Thus, about one-third of those involuntarily confined to security mental hospitals for an indefinite period until somehow rendered "competent" were only *charged with*, not convicted of, a crime. Steadman and Cocozza also discovered (as have other investigators) that a shockingly large number of IST defendants had been confined against their will, sometimes for periods far exceeding the maximum sentence for their alleged offense. More significantly, the Steadman-Cocozza data showed that ISTs had not received any treatment which would enable them to achieve competency; in fact, there were often no guidelines or criteria for determining such competency.

Until the 1970s, the typical procedure for determining incompetency required that defendants be confined within a maximum security institution for a lengthy psychiatric-psychological evaluation (usually sixty to ninety days). Following evaluation, the defendant was granted a hearing on the matter of competency. If the court found the defendant unable to understand the charges or the judicial proceedings, or to help counsel in his or her defense, then the defendant would be automatically committed to a security hospital for an indefinite period of time—until competent. Theoretically, this indefinite time period could extend—and sometimes did—into a lifetime of involuntary commitment. Effective treatment was either not provided or could not be offered, and it was anyone's guess what actually constituted competency.

To dramatize the inadequacy of treatment for the ISTs, Schwitzgebel (1977) cites the case of a defendant who received a suspended sentence for third degree assault, but then violated parole by allegedly committing a misdemeanor. He was found IST and was dispatched to a state mental hospital, where he spent the next 14.5 years, waiting to be rendered competent. During that time the defendant received a fractured nose, a fractured right leg, fractured ribs, an injured back, burns on his face and chest, and numerous other injuries as a result of beatings administered by other patients and hospital personnel. He also suffered rectal bleeding and headaches. His hospital files indicated that he received no psychotherapy during his years of confinement; the only "treatment" he received was petroleum jelly and rectal suppositories. And yet, the hospital ultimately discharged him as "improved," with the approval of the court.

Mentally disordered offenders, as a group, receive very little psychotherapy, and when it is provided, its effectiveness is very debatable. In fact, no consistently effective therapy has yet been developed for many serious mental disorders. The traditional form of "talk" psychotherapy is effective primarily for intelligent and articulate individuals plagued with neurotic disorders and motivated to change. Almost all presently existing forms of psychotherapy are ineffective for people demonstrating bizarre or antisocial behavior, especially if they have limited intelligence or education.

Psychoactive drugs do not seem to change a patient's mental state permanently, only render them more manageable temporarily. Many psychotherapists are willing to admit that if they cannot produce marked improvements within the first six months of treatment, they will not do so thereafter, however long they try (Walker, 1978).

Courts are beginning to ameliorate the many injustices perpetuated against mentally disordered offenders, injustices often promoted by the numerous disparities between criminal law and mental health law (Wexler, 1977, 1981). The U.S. Supreme Court restricted both the length of time for IST evaluation and the limits of legal confinement (*Jackson* v. *Indiana*, 1972), and has protected prisoners being transferred to mental institutions without benefit of a hearing on the issue of their mental condition (*Vitek* v. *Jones*, 1980). On the other hand, the Court has not been sympathetic to claims that persons found NGRI should be confined automatically and indefinitely without evidence of a continuing mental disorder.

Transfers

A third way a person may attain mentally disordered offender status is by exhibiting severely disturbed behavior while incarcerated in a prison or correctional facility. The Steadman-Cocozza 1974 analysis revealed that 40 percent of the mentally disordered population were "mentally ill" inmates who had been transferred out of prison and into security mental hospitals. The most recent Steadman survey (1982) found that that number had increased to over 54 percent of the mentally disordered population. About 96 percent of transfers from a prison to a mental hospital were male. Roth (1980) estimates that between 15 and 20 percent of prison inmates exhibit sufficient psychological "pathology" to warrant psychiatric attention, although this does not mean they warrant transfer. According to Roth, about 5 percent of the disorders would qualify as psychosis.

Because states differ greatly in the transfer options they provide for mentally disordered prisoners, it is difficult to distinguish a general pattern in either the disorders or the circumstances surrounding the transfers. However, in 1980, the U.S. Supreme Court began to address the transfer practice, in *Vitek* v. *Jones*. The Court ruled that the transfer of an inmate to a mental health hospital requires, at a minimum, an administrative hearing to determine whether such transfer is appropriate. The Supreme Court recognized the special nature of confinement in a mental health facility and the stigma that often accompanies a commitment (Churgin, 1983). Furthermore, transfer to a mental institution not only entails forced treatment of almost any variety but also may substantially reduce chances for parole, since parole boards may be reluctant to release into the community a prisoner who was recently in a mental hospital setting.

The Mentally Disordered Sex Offender

At this writing, about twenty states and the District of Columbia have statutes dealing with the mentally disordered sex offender (MDSO) (Favole, 1983). The legal literature often refers to these laws as "sexual psychopath statutes," but the term *psychopath* is not really appropriate for a vast majority of these offenders. Other than the label, the statutes have little in common. In most cases, the legislative intention was to provide special dispositional procedures for persons who exhibit a tendency to commit sex offenses, but each state has developed its own set of procedures and definitions. Either explicitly or implicitly, the statutes depict the sexual psychopath as a mentally disordered individual who is particularly *dangerous* to children, women, or both.

In 1937, Michigan became the first state to enact a sexual psychopath statute. It was joined by California in 1939. At one time nearly thirty states had sexual psychopath statutes. In 1963, the change in terminology to "mentally disordered sex offender" took place (Dix, 1983). The earlier statutes sought to "intercept" the "sexual psychopath" even before he was convicted of a crime (Morris, 1982). Today, statutes generally require a conviction, usually of a sex crime, which may range from indecent exposure to forcible rape. Morris (1982, p. 136) notes that the early statutes represented "immediate legislative reactions to sensational sexual crimes," and that they illustrated "a legislative capacity to conceal excessive punitiveness behind a veil of psychiatric treatment. . . . At base lies the false assumption of a connection between sexual offenses and mental illness. . . ." The statutes were also based on the equally false premise that sexual offenders start with minor sexual offenses (e.g., indecent exposure, voyeurism) and move on to more serious ones (e.g., forcible rape).

In recent years there has been a strong move to repeal and abolish MDSO statutes (Dix, 1983). This shift in policy is likely due in part to the many constitutional challenges to discriminatory procedures, inadequate treatment, indeterminate sentencing, and the frequently vague terminology of the statutes. This state of flux with regard to MDSO statutes creates problems for the researcher. There is too little consistency and such a lack of uniformity that it is almost impossible to reach valid conclusions about who gets legally labeled MDSO.

Some studies have made the effort, however. The Steadman project, for example (Steadman et al., 1982), found that virtually all MDSOs are male. In 1978, state and federal courts filed approximately 3,600 requests for clinical evaluations for possible MDSO status. The major determining factor as to whether an offender received this status appeared to be past criminal record. Those with prior sex-related criminal records (other than the current offenses) were far more likely to be evaluated MDSO than those with no prior sex-related criminal record or with a non-sex-related record (Konecni, Mulcahy, & Ebbesen, 1980). Dix (1976) found that 85 to 90 percent of the MDSOs committed to California's Atascadero State Hospital had a prior history of sex offenses. The available evidence suggests that courts rely heavily on the offender's social history and prior criminal record to make their determinations, rather than on facts surrounding the current charge.

Sturgeon and Taylor (1980) compared 260 MDSOs to 122 offenders convicted of sex crimes but not adjudicated MDSO. White sex offenders were more likely to be found MDSO and referred for treatment in a mental health facility, while black and Hispanic sex offenders were nearly twice as likely to be sent to prison. Similar results were reported by Pacht and Cowden (1974), who also found that MDSOs tend to be older and have more prior sexual offenses on their records than other persons convicted of a sexual offense. MDSOs are usually committed to a mental institution for an indeterminate length of time. If the 1978 Steadman survey (Steadman et al., 1982) is representative, MDSOs are also committed for a longer period of time than other mentally disordered offenders.

The procedures used by the law to assign MDSO status as well as the treatment of offenders once they have been so assigned raise ethical, philosophical, and legal issues that are beyond the scope of this text. To some extent, these same issues relate to adjudication and treatment of mentally disordered offenders in general. Cohen (1980) offers a comprehensive legal assessment of the areas in civil and criminal law that represent questionable deprivations of individual liberty in the name of the individual's or society's best interest.

For our purposes, however, we should reiterate that the mentally disordered offender classifications are usually based on the assumption that these individuals are dangerous to the community, often more so than persons convicted of crimes but not mentally disordered. This presumably justifies more extensive—and in some cases indefinite—confinement. MDSOs are considered especially dangerous to women and children. NGRIs and ISTs are presumed dangerous because they have already committed a criminal act, regardless of its nature, although they have not been convicted. Transfers are dangerous to the prison community and must be confined elsewhere. Dangerousness has a variety of implicit meanings, however, and is seldom defined adequately in the statutes. Furthermore, researchers and clinicians have a very difficult time not only defining it, but more importantly evaluating and predicting it. This is not to suggest that mentally disordered offenders are never a threat to society. Those who are should be identified and confined, and a bona fide effort made to provide them with treatment. On the other hand, as we will discover in the next section, dangerous behavior is almost always overpredicted.

DANGEROUSNESS

In August 1966, Charles Whitman, a University of Texas student majoring in architectural engineering, murdered his wife and his mother. Shortly thereafter, he carried his personal arsenal in a footlocker to the observation deck of the 307-foot-tall University Tower. He proceeded to load a number of high-powered, scope-equipped rifles and began randomly shooting at people near the observation deck and on the ground far below. Whitman managed to shoot forty-four people, killing fourteen, before a police officer and a citizen climbed to the tower and ended the tragedy by shooting Whitman himself.

An investigation revealed that the twenty-five-year-old Whitman had consulted a psychiatrist five months before the incident and, during a two-hour interview, had described "overwhelming violent impulses" and great fear of his inability to control them. He had also revealed a compelling need to "go up on the tower with a deer rifle and start shooting people." Whitman did not return for further consultation after the initial two-hour session. Nevertheless, when the news of his contact with a psychiatrist was disseminated, there was public outcry and many questions about why he was not treated, confined, or referred to the proper authorities. Similar questions were raised when the public learned that James Huberty, who killed twenty-two fast-food restaurant patrons in the summer of 1984, had also had contact with a mental health clinic. In Huberty's case, social workers had apparently tried without success to return his telephone calls.

Are clinicians obligated to notify others of the dangerousness of their clients? This issue was raised in a California suit charging that a University psychologist failed to do just that (*Tarasoff* v. *Regents of the University of California*, 1974). Prosenjit Poddar was a voluntary outpatient at a University of California, Berkeley clinic. During his therapy sessions with a clinical psychologist, Poddar articulated fantasies of harming, or perhaps even killing, Tatiana Tarasoff, whom he had met at a dance. The psychologist, who learned from one of Poddar's friends that he planned to purchase a gun, became increasingly concerned. When the patient discontinued therapy, clinic officials wrote to the police requesting their help in getting Poddar committed to a mental institution. Police investigated the case, interviewed Poddar, warned him to stay away from Tatiana, but did not pursue the commitment, apparently because California's new civil commitment law was difficult to interpret. Two months later, Poddar killed Tarasoff by stabbing her, though he was carrying his newly purchased gun. He was charged with first degree murder. Tarasoff's family sued the university clinic, claiming the psychologist had been negligent in not warning the young woman or the family of the danger.

The Tarasoff case, undoubtedly familiar to all clinicians, addressed very directly the question of what duty therapists owe to third parties in warning them of possible harmful behavior from their clients. The California Supreme Court ruled that a psychotherapist has an obligation to use reasonable care to protect intended victims. We will set aside the many implications of the decision with regard to patient-therapist confidentiality as well as the numerous questions it poses about precisely what type of warning is sufficient. Implicit in the duty found by the California court is the capacity to predict dangerousness.

The court apparently believed that mental health professionals can predict with considerable accuracy who is or will be dangerous and who will not. Yet researchers and clinicians have long struggled both to define dangerousness and to predict its occurrence. After the Tarasoff case, dangerousness generated more controversy than even the insanity defense (Simon & Cockerham, 1977). The concept is a crucial one, because both criminal and civil statutes provide for the incarceration or involuntary confinement of those believed to be dangerous. In criminal law, persons convicted of serious crimes are confined in part to protect society from further harm. Furthermore, both adults and juveniles are subject to detention even before being convicted of a crime or adjudicated a delinquent if they are believed dangerous. Decisions whether to parole prisoners are largely based on whether they are dangerous. In involuntary civil commitment, persons believed to be dangerous to themselves or to others because of a mental disorder may be confined until that disorder is corrected.

There is no question that a person is dangerous who has been violent in the past and indicates by word or deed that he or she plans to do serious harm to others. Someone who has committed a series of murders, mutilations, or rapes, and who attests to planning to do more of the same, is certainly—by anyone's definition—a dangerous individual. If a person has no history of violence and threatens harm, however, the situation becomes more problematical. Clinicians have difficulty reaching a consensus on whether this is indeed evidence of dangerousness. If you are asked to list whatever you consider dangerous behavior, your list will very probably differ in both length and content from your next door neighbor's. Some lists will include behavior that promotes psychological harm, such as terrorizing or threatening others, while others will include behavior that produces damage to property, like defacing a valuable stamp collection. As Nigel Walker (1978) points out, some people have very long lists, others quite short ones.

Definition of Dangerousness

The problem of defining dangerous behavior is shared by legislatures and courts as well as by clinicians. All states and all courts recognize that behavior which is likely to result in *physical* harm is dangerous. They begin to differ when behaviors that lead to property damage or psychological injury are involved. One example of psychological injury is the effect on a young woman produced by a person who continually shadows her, observes her public movements, perhaps even photographs her. Some courts have ruled that this type of behavior can cause irreparable emotional damage. They conclude that a threat of "psychological trauma is . . . as much a menace to the health or safety of others as is possible physical injury" (Developments in the Law, 1974, p. 1237; henceforth called Developments). At this writing, the states of Iowa and Hawaii allow behavior "likely to inflict emotional or psychological harm" as evidence of dangerousness to others.

Some state statutes and courts also permit damage to property to qualify as dangerous behavior. The extensive legal protection afforded property ownership in our society supports the reasonableness of this conclusion (Developments, 1974). In the aforementioned *Jones* v. *United States* (1983) case, which supported the automatic and indefinite confinement of a NGRI individual whose offense was petty larceny, the Supreme Court reflected this view. It noted that "crimes of theft frequently may result in violence from the efforts of the criminal to escape or the victim to protect property or the police to apprehend the fleeing criminal" (*Jones* v. *U.S.*, 1983, p. 3050, footnote 14). In this and other cases, the Court has apparently accepted the argument that dangerousness to property is a proper standard to use in evaluating the need for confinement.

Psychologists and psychiatrists are not generally involved in dangerousness predictions unless some type of mental disorder is at issue. That is, in most criminal law, individuals like judges, juries, and parole board members make decisions about dangerousness without any help from clinicians. In civil commitments and in situations involving the insanity plea, competency to stand trial, or mentally disordered sex offenders, psychologists and psychiatrists are more likely consulted. Many clinicians believe that when the possible outcome is confinement, only behavior that leads to, or is likely to lead to, *bodily injury* should be considered dangerous. Possible damage to property should not qualify, and psychological damage is far too elusive to form the basis for legal judgments, clinical evaluation, or empirical conclusions. Currently, most jurisdictions agree that a *substantial probability or risk of serious bodily harm* to self as well as to others constitutes dangerousness, and that risks to property and emotions do not.

Even if we accept this limitation, two hurdles remain: the need to define clearly both seriousness and substantial risk or probability of bodily harm. Neither problem has been resolved to the satisfaction of most students of the legal system. Some incidents of bodily harm are clearly serious—murder, mutilation, rape, and bodily injury requiring lengthy hospitalization. What about a broken arm, a black eye, a cut requiring several stitches? Is the mentally disordered person who periodically engages in fist fights a dangerous individual? Note that the problem here is not in charging a person with assault after he or she has committed an act; rather, it is in deciding to what extent the possibility of such an assault justifies involuntary commitment. Furthermore, seriousness may be influenced by such fortuitous factors as the victim's sense of balance, what the victim strikes when falling, and the victim's general health (Developments, 1974).

Predictions of Dangerousness

The psychological research literature consistently concludes that clinicians are unable to specify the type or severity of harm an individual may cause, or to predict with great accuracy the probability of harm even occurring. Alan Stone (1975, p. 33) writes:

> It can be stated flatly on the basis of my own review of the published material on the prediction of dangerous acts that neither objective actuarial tables nor psychiatric intuition, diagnosis, and psychological testing can claim predictive success when dealing with the traditional population of mental hospitals. The predictive success appropriate to a legal decision can be described in three levels of increasing certainty: Preponderance of the evidence, 51 percent successful; clear and convincing proof, 75 percent successful; beyond a reasonable doubt, at least 90 percent successful.

Stone asserts that mental health professionals have failed to predict dangerous behavior by even the lowest criterion, a preponderance of the evidence. The U.S. Supreme Court, however, has ruled that preponderance is too loose a standard to use in committing presumably dangerous mentally disordered individuals and has found that clear and convincing proof of the likelihood of dangerousness, at the least, is required. We will return to this decision (*Addington* v. *Texas*, 1979) shortly. In line with Stone's conclusion, Cocozza and Steadman (1976) assert that "any attempt to commit an individual solely on the basis of dangerousness would be futile if psychiatric testimony were subjected to any of these three standards of proof" (p. 1101). They add that the psychological research has demonstrated "clear and convincing evidence of the inability of psychiatrists or anyone else to predict dangerousness accurately" (p. 1099).

Wexler (1981) is not so pessimistic, however. He believes that clinicians are asked only to testify to the potential likelihood of dangerousness, and that is perfectly possible on the basis of characteristics of the individual such as age, sex, clinical diagnosis, history of violence, use of drugs, or verbal threats. He comments, "It may well be possible in a given case to prove *even beyond a reasonable doubt* the existence of given characteristics and their probabilistic association with violent behavior" (1981, p. 61).

Although Wexler's point seems well taken, we must still be concerned about the tendency of clinicians to overpredict dangerousness, which may occur even with a clear and compelling standard. In other words, even a variety of factors that might convince a court that the evidence is clear and compelling lend themselves to overprediction. As Monahan (1981) notes, studies of clinical predictions of dangerousness show a strong tendency to overpredict. At a minimum, the most sophisticated predictive methods yield 60 to 70 percent false positives (people who were predicted to be dangerous but did not engage in harmful behavior) (Rubin, 1972; Kozol, Boucher, & Garofalo, 1972; Wenk, Robison, & Smith, 1972). In a ten-year follow-up investigation of 592 convicted male offenders (mostly sex offenders) by Kozol, Boucher, & Garofalo (1972), two of every three persons predicted dangerous were false positives, even after extensive background data and results of independent clinical exams by psychiatrists had been made available to those doing the predicting. Moreover, because of some flaws in the design of the study, the odds for accurate prediction were very much in their favor (Monahan, 1976; Steadman, 1976; Dix, 1980). A continuing body of research in the area of dangerousness prediction with respect to the mentally disordered continues to find that false positives outnumber true positives by a margin of 2 to 1 (Wettstein, 1984).

The ratio of false to true positives deserves some attention. False positives is a descriptor we use for persons who are labeled dangerous (positive), but who do not engage in harmful behavior during a specific period of time after release from custody. True positives are persons predicted to be dangerous and who do engage in subsequent harmful behavior (see Table 6-1). For example, assume a team of mental health professionals concludes that ten persons are dangerous. If during a two-year period following release, six do engage in harmful behavior, we have a 60 percent rate of true positives and a 40 percent rate of false positives. On the other hand, the team may predict that ten people will not engage in violent behavior (negatives). If some of them do, they are called false negatives. True negatives are those predicted not to engage in harmful behavior within a certain period of time and who do not. Thus, if the team predicts that seven out of ten people will not engage in harmful behavior, and five of the ten do not, the team was wrong in two cases. We therefore have a ratio of 20 percent false negatives to 50 percent true negatives.

In many ways it is clearly advantageous for mental health professionals to predict more positives than negatives, especially if there is some

TABLE 6-1   Four Possible Outcomes of Prediction

		CRITERION BEHAVIOR	
		Did	Did not
Prediction	Will	True positive	False positive
	Will not	False negative	True negative

question about whether a person is dangerous. The Tarasoff decision also encourages this trend. Clinicians who fail to warn and protect the community by not detecting persons who eventually commit violent or harmful acts will likely pay a higher social and professional price than clinicians who overpredict dangerousness.

A 1966 U.S. Supreme Court decision, *Baxstrom* v. *Herold*, faciliated extensive social science research on the accuracy of dangerousness prediction. Johnnie Baxstrom had been convicted of second degree assault and sentenced to a 2.5 to 3-year term in a New York State prison. After two years, prison psychiatrists found him dangerous and mentally disturbed, and he was transferred to Dannemora State Hospital for the criminally insane. Despite his requests to be transferred to a civil mental health institution, based on the fact that his prison term was near its expiration date, the Department of Mental Hygiene determined that Baxstrom could not be cared for in a civil hospital because he was potentially dangerous. He remained institutionalized at Dannemora for long after his maximum prison term had expired (by three years). The Supreme Court, with Chief Justice Warren writing the opinion, ruled that Baxstrom had been denied equal protection of the law by being confined in an institution for the criminally insane beyond the expiration of his maximum criminal sentence and without the benefit of a hearing to evaluate his "potentially dangerous" classification. The Court therefore ordered that "in order to accord the petitioner the equal protection of the laws, he was and is entitled to a review of the determination as to his sanity [and dangerous propensities] in conformity with proceedings granted all others civilly commmited . . . " (p. 109).

The Court's ruling directly influenced the confinement of at least 967 other patients held under similar circumstances in secure institutions for the mentally disordered throughout New York State. These "Baxstrom patients," who on the average had spent eight years in involuntary confinement *beyond* the expiration of their criminal sentences, were quickly provided hearings. Against the advice of corrections psychiatrists and physicians, many were released. The Baxstrom patients were predominantly nonwhite, lower socioeconomic class, middle-aged males. Although a vast majority had arrest records and many had previous convictions, only 58 percent had been convicted of violent crimes (Steadman, 1976). On the average, the patients had been institutionalized continuously for fourteen years.

The Baxstrom patients were considered some of New York's most dangerous mental patients, but follow-up reports found that predicted dangerousness had been grossly overstated (false positives)(Monahan, 1976). Steadman and Cocozza (1974) followed up eighty-five Baxstrom patients and discovered that 20 percent were rearrested, but only 7 percent were convicted, usually for minor violations such as vagrancy and public intoxication. An examination of both in-hospital and community behaviors revealed that only 20 percent of the "extremely dangerous" patients were assaultive toward others during the four-year follow-up period (Steadman, 1976). A prominent variable predicting whether Baxstrom patients demonstrated assaultive behavior was age: The younger the patient, the more likely he or she was to engage in assaultive behavior. Even using the Legal Dangerousness Scale (Cocozza & Steadman, 1974), a measure of four criminal background characteristics, there were two false positives for every three patients predicted to be violent, again underscoring the inaccuracy of clinical prediction.

The Baxstrom decision also affected a similar group of mentally disordered offenders in Pennsylvania (*Dixon* v. *Attorney General of the Commonwealth of Pennsylvania*, 1971). Dixon patients were transferred to civil mental hospitals for re-evaluation and treatment or release, after a court ruled unconstitutional a state statute that permitted the indefinite confinement of civilly and criminally committed patients without periodic hearings.

The Dixon patients had notable past histories of mental problems and criminal offenses. Forty-three percent had been hospitalized in the past, and 90 percent were diagnosed psychotic on current admission. Over 80 percent had prior arrest records, 64 percent had previously served jail and prison sentences, and 39 percent had committed five or more offenses in the past. The patients were institutionalized indefinitely at Fairview on the basis of presumed dangerousness. The Dixon patients were followed over a number of years by Thornberry and Jacoby (1979). After their court ordered transfer to civil and less secure mental hospitals, only 19 percent were involved in some kind of violence within the hospital setting. Two-thirds of the Dixon patients were discharged from the civil hospitals within nine months of the transfer. During a four-year follow-up, about 24 percent were arrested, and only one-quarter of these arrests were for violent offenses. Overall, the incidence of false positives—where clinicians had predicted harmful or violent behavior which did not occur—was 67 percent, or two out of every three predictions.

Criminal justice personnel have tried a variety of measures to predict dangerousness. In 1965, in an effort to predict violent recidivism among parolees, researchers in the California Department of Corrections developed a violence-prediction scale based on background information like age, prior offenses, drug usage, and length of imprisonment. Each offender released on parole was evaluated according to this scale (Wenk, Robison, & Smith, 1972). Researchers isolated about 3 percent of the parolees as most violent, but only 14 percent of this most violent group actually violated parole by engaging in violent or harmful acts. Five percent of the entire parolee sample violated parole with violent actions. Although the most violent group were nearly three times more likely to be violent, it should be stressed that a majority (86 percent) of the "dangerous" parolees did not display violent behavior while on parole, nor did 95 percent of the entire parolee population.

In another procedure developed by the California Department of Corrections, all parolees released into supervision were classified into one of six categories, based on aggressive behavior and psychiatric evalution of violence potential (Wenk, Robison, & Smith, 1972). The categories ranged from serious aggressive (those who had committed one or more acts of major violence) to low-level aggressive (no recorded history of aggression). Results of the study involving 7,712 parolees revealed that those regarded as most potentially aggressive (two highest aggressive groups) were no more likely to be violent than the less potentially violent groups (two lowest aggressive groups). The rate of conviction and imprisonment for crimes involving violence for the potentially aggressive groups was 3.1 per thousand parolees, compared to 2.8 per thousand parolees for the potentially least aggressive groups, an insignificant difference. Furthermore, for every correct identification of a potentially aggressive individual, there were 326 incorrect ones.

In a third project, Wenk and his colleagues (1972) studied 4,146 youthful offenders admitted to the Reception Guidance Center at Deuel Vocational Institute, California, during a two-year period. The researchers wanted to determine which background data were most useful in predicting violence during a fifteen-month parole period after the offenders' release from the institution. During the fifteen-month period, 104 or 2.5 percent of the youths violated parole by displaying violent (assaultive) behavior.

To isolate predictive variables of violent behavior, the researchers combined and divided the background data in a number of ways. One procedure revealed that general recidivism (any violation of parole) and violent recidivism (violation of parole by violence) were highest for multiple offenders, youths who had been admitted to the institution on several occasions. In another procedure, youthful offenders with a history of actual violent behavior (which may or may not have resulted in institutionalization) were found to be three times more likely to be involved in violent recidivism during the fifteen-month parole period. It is tempting to jump to the conclusion that multiple offenders and youths with histories of violence are dangerous. Yet Wenk and his collegues admonish that if they were to make predictions based on the same background data, they would still only be accurate only once in twenty predictions. Only a small proportion of youths with violent backgrounds engaged in violence during parole. We should emphasize that the violent behavior was defined as a *conviction* for a violent crime. More recent studies have shown that when *arrest* records for violent crimes are used, the accuracy of prediction gets better (Monahan, 1981). However, even with this increase in accuracy, the false positive rate continues to hover around 60 percent.

It is quite clear that clinicians tend to overpredict dangerous behavior, under the premise that it is better to be safe than sorry. It is also quite clear that predictions of dangerousness, in general, are inaccurate. What accounts for this inaccuracy?

First, the behavior being predicted, violence, occurs relatively infrequently in the daily lives of even the most frequent offender. Therefore, the prediction of an infrequent behavior is akin to finding a needle in a haystack of behaviors. Violent behavior happens (or is reported) so infrequently that if you say it will happen, the odds are already against you. Secondly, while human behavior is generally consistent across time (temporal consistency), it is often inconsistent across situations (trans-situational consistency). More specifically, people tend to act the same way during their lifetimes *if* the situations eliciting this behavior are basically the same. However, if the situations are different, as is so characteristic of life, people are unlikely to act the same way. For example, most of us act differently with our parents than we do with our friends, or we act one way with members of the same sex, but another way with members of the opposite sex. Thus, mental health professionals would be substantially more accurate if they could be certain that the social environment remained the same. In reality, the social environment is always changing, rendering the predictions based on one situation inapposite for another.

Overall, the best predictor of future behavior is past behavior. Past violence will suggest a *probability* of future violence. Furthermore, the more the behavior has occurred in a variety of situations, the more accurate will be the predictions. A person who manifests violence frequently and across many different situations will be far more easy to predict than a person who is only occasionally violent in some situations. If clinicians were able to modify Wexler's (1981) suggested approach and base the likelihood of dangerousness strictly on those characteristics associated with age and past behavior, their predictions might be more accurate.

SUMMARY AND CONCLUSIONS

In this chapter, we focused on the relationship between mentally disordered individuals and crime. In order to begin to understand this relationship, we must go beyond labels, which do not explain why someone behaves in a certain way. Furthermore, labels are assigned by the psychiatric profession and, along with definitions, may change with each edition of the DSM, the standard "cookbook" used by most clinicians.

With the exception of persons with an antisocial personality disorder, individuals with mental disorders are no more likely than the general population to commit crimes, including violent crimes. Furthermore, when crimes are connected with the mentally disordered, they tend to be committed by individuals with a history of antisocial behavior. In other words, the same persons tend to repeat criminal acts; most mentally disordered people are not criminally prone. The same may be said of the general population.

We also reviewed the various categories of mentally disordered offenders, including those found not guilty by reason of insanity, incompetent to stand trial, mentally disordered sex offenders, and transfers. Legal determinations of these categories vary from jurisdiction to jurisdiction. Furthermore, in recent years, many court decisions have affected the way mentally disordered offenders are adjudicated, confined, and treated.

Finally, we reviewed the complex literature on the dangerous offender. Traditionally, clinicians have overestimated the potential violence of mentally disordered populations, engendering debate about the proper criteria for assessing dangerousness. How many persons are forcefully confined, on the basis of dangerousness, without justification? Accurate predictions of dangerousness are extremely elusive. Overall, the best predictor available is past behavior. Those who were violent in the past, compared to those without such a history, are more likely to offend in the future.

CHAPTER SEVEN
Human Aggression and Violence

There is ample evidence of the long history of human involvement in aggression and violence. The 5,600 years of recorded human history, for example, include 14,600 wars, a rate of more than 2.6 per year (Baron, 1983; Montagu, 1976). Some writers argue that aggression has been instrumental in helping people survive. Through centuries of experience, humans learned that aggressive behavior enables them to obtain material goods, land, and treasures; to protect property and family; and to gain prestige, status, and power. In fact, we might wonder whether the human species could have survived had it not used aggression.

Aggression warrants an entire chapter because it is the basic ingredient in violent crime. Furthermore, by studying aggression, psychologists have made substantial contributions to society's effort to understand violence and crime. Is human aggression instinctive, biological, learned, or some combination of these characteristics? If it results from an innate, biological mechanism, the methods designed to control, reduce, or eliminate aggressive behavior will differ significantly from methods used if aggression is learned.

Perspectives of human nature emerge very clearly from the scholarly and research literature on aggression. Some writers and researchers believe that aggressive behavior is basically physiological and genetic in origin, a strong residue of our evolutionary past. This physiological, genetic contention is accompanied by compelling evidence that explanations of human aggressive behavior may be found in the animal kingdom from which it originated. On the other hand, researchers who subscribe to the learning viewpoint believe that, while some species of animals may be genetically programmed to behave aggressively, human beings *learn* to be aggressive from the social environment. The learning position also offers cogent evidence to support its theory. Other researchers remain on a theoretical fence, accepting and rejecting some aspects of each argument.

If aggression and violence represent a built-in, genetically programmed aspect of human nature, we may be forced, as Baron (1983) suggests, toward a pessimistic conclusion. At best, we can only hope to hold our natural, aggressive urges and drives temporarily in check. Furthermore, we should design the environment and society in such as way as to discourage violence, including administering immediate and aversive consequences (punishment) when it is displayed. Even better—and setting aside ethical or legal considerations for the moment—we might consider psychosurgery, electrode implants, and drug control—all effective methods for the reduction, if not the elimination, of violence.

If, on the other hand, we believe that aggression is learned and is influenced by a wide range of situational, social, and environmental variables, we can be more optimistic. Aggression is not an inevitable aspect of human life. Once we understand what factors play major roles in its acquisition and maintenance, we will be able to change human behavior by manipulating these factors.

By most accounts, animal aggression reflects the biological programming carried in the genes to ensure the survival of the species. Humans, with their enormously complex and sophisticated cerebral cortex, rely heavily on thought, associations, beliefs and learning; these become primary determinants of behavior. Theorists differ over the degree to which genetic programming contributes to human behavior. Are people aggressive and violent because their animal instincts continue to promote this particular behavior? The difference-in-degree perspective discussed in chapter one would certainly assume this. And, if the evolutionary aggressive drives still reside within the subcortical structures of the brain (below the cortex in the "old" brain), as some writers tell us they do, are they modifiable? If not, how can we best prevent people from attacking and killing one another? On the other hand, a difference-in-kind perspective suggests that genetic predispositions or biological precursors of aggression have a minimal influence on human behavior, if they have any influence at all. After defining aggression, we will return to these different points of view.

DEFINING AGGRESSION

The task of defining human aggression is surprisingly difficult, as many social psychologists have discovered. Forcibly jabbing someone in the midsection is certainly defining it by example—or is it? Now what about jabbing someone more softly, in jest? Would everyone consider football and boxing aggressive behaviors? If someone pointedly ignores a question, is that an example of aggression? What if someone spreads malicious gossip? If a burglar breaks into your home and you reach for your trusty but rusty rifle, aim it at the intruder, and pull the trigger, is yours an act of aggression? Is it any less so if the rifle does not fire? If someone sits passively on a doorstep and blocks your entry, is this aggression?

Some social psychologists define aggression as the intent and attempt to harm another individual, physically or socially, or, in some cases, to destroy an object. This definition seems adequate for many situations, but it has several limitations. Refusing to speak does not fit well, since it is not an active attempt to harm someone. The person blocking entry also is not trying to injure anyone. Most psychologists place these two behaviors in a special category of aggressive responses and call them passive-aggressive behaviors, since they are generally interpreted as aggressive in intent, although the behavior is passive and indirect.

As fascinating as passive-aggressive behavior may be, it is generally irrelevant when we discuss crime, since the aggression we are concerned about is the type that manifests itself directly in violent or antisocial behavior. We might stretch the point by suggesting that the doorstep sitter is trespassing, in which case he or she might be charged with a criminal offense. In general, however, the aggressive behavior we wish to focus on in this chapter will not be of the passive-aggressive kind.

In an effort to conceptualize the many varieties of human aggression, Buss (1971) tried to classify them based on the apparent motivation of the aggressor (see Table 7-1). You may easily find exceptions and overlapping categories in the Buss scheme, but that emphasizes how difficult it is to compartmentalize human aggressive behavior. It also epitomizes the many definitional dilemmas that hamper social psychologists studying aggression.

Before trying to settle on a satisfactory definition of aggression, it may be useful to recognize two types, *hostile* (or *expressive*) and *instrumental*

TABLE 7-1   Varieties of Human Aggression

	ACTIVE		PASSIVE	
	DIRECT	INDIRECT	DIRECT	INDIRECT
Physical	Punching the victim	Practical joke booby trap	Obstructing passage, sit-in	Refusing to perform a necessary task
Verbal	Insulting the victim	Malicious gossip	Refusing to speak	Refusing consent, vocal or written

Source: Buss, A. H. Aggression Pays. In J. L. Singer (ed.), *The Control of Aggression and Violence.* New York: Academic Press, 1971, p. 8.

aggression, a distinction first made by Feshbach (1964). They are distinguished by their goals or the rewards they offer the perpetrator. Hostile (or expressive) aggression, which we are most concerned with in this chapter, occurs in response to anger-inducing conditions, such as insults, physical attacks, or personal failures. The aggressor's goal is to make a victim suffer. Most homicides, rapes, and other violent crimes directed at harming the victim are precipitated by hostile aggression. The behavior is characterized by the intense and disorganizing emotion of anger, with *anger* defined as an arousal state elicited by certain stimuli, particularly those evoking attack or frustration. Angry at the economic system which deprived him of a job, a sniper may take potshots at passing motorists and feel satisfaction at having lashed out "successfully" at society.

Instrumental aggression begins with competition or the desire for some object or status possessed by another person—jewelry, money, territory. The perpetrator tries to obtain the desired object regardless of the cost. Instrumental aggression is usually a factor in robbery, burglary, larceny, and various white-collar crimes. The thief's obvious goal in a robbery is to obtain cash-value items. Usually, there is no intent to harm anyone. However, if someone interferes with the thief's objective, he or she may feel forced to harm that person or risk losing the desired goal. Instrumental aggression is usually also a feature of calculated murder committed by a hired, impersonal killer.

Bandura (1973a) notes that most definitions of aggression imply that it is solely concerned with behaviors and intentions residing within the perpetrator (or performer). Going a step further, he suggests that the adequate definition of aggression must consider *both* the "injurious behavior" of the perpetrator and the "social judgment" of the victim. Thus, a soft poke in the belly may qualify as aggression if it is done derisively and if the recipient interprets it that way. A textbook on criminal behavior, however, must focus on aggression as manifested in conduct, not as it is perceived by a victim. For our purposes, therefore, we define aggression as *behavior perpetrated or attempted with the intention of harming another individual physically or psychologically* (as opposed to socially) *or to destroy an object*. This definition encompasses all the behaviors described in Buss's typology. Aggressive behavior, of course, will not always qualify as criminal. Furthermore, we will define violence as *destructive physical aggression intentionally directed at harming other persons or things*. Violence may be methodical or random, sustained or fleeting, intensive or uncontrolled. It always destroys the recipient or is intended to do so (Daniels & Gilula, 1970).

THEORETICAL PERSPECTIVES ON AGGRESSION

Behavioral and social scientists have debated for over a half century whether humans are born aggressive and naturally violent or born relatively free of aggressive tendencies. This debate, part of a wider controversy about the respective merits of nature and nurture, touches every school of thought in human behavior. According to the first perspective, humans are programmed aggressive to defend themselves, family, and territory from intruders. According to the second, humans become violent by acquiring aggressive models and actions from society.

Psychoanalytic Viewpoints

Sigmund Freud, the father of psychoanalysis, was convinced that human beings are susceptible from birth to a build-up of aggressive energy, which must be dissipated or drained off before it reaches dangerous levels. This is known as the *psychodynamic* or *hydraulic* model, since it bears a close resemblance to pressure build-up in a container. If excessive pressure accumulates in the container—the human psyche—an explosion is likely to occur, as demonstrated by tirades that may involve violence. According to the traditional Freudian perspective, people who have tirades are blowing off the excess steam of aggressive energy.

Freud suggested that violence in all of its forms is a manifestation of this aggressive energy discharge. Internal energy accumulates to dangerous levels when people have not discharged it appropriately through a process called *catharsis*, one of the most important concepts in psychoanalytic psychotherapy. Catharsis may be accomplished by actual behavior (playing football, for example) or may occur vicariously (watching football). The Freudian-psychodynamic position predicts that children who participate in or avidly watch school sports will ultimately be less aggressive than children who do not. Freudian psychodynamic followers also maintain that people who engage in violent crime (hostile aggression) have not had sufficient opportunity to "blow off steam" and keep their aggressive energies at manageable levels.

Psychodynamic theorists assume that humans, by their very nature, will always be prone to aggressive impulses. Therefore, if violent crime is to be controlled, the human animal must be provided with multiple but appropriate channels for catharsis (e.g., adequate recreational facilities). In this way, children and adults presumably learn to dissipate aggression in socially approved, appropriate ways. Psychotherapy is one such channel, encouraging catharsis under the guidance of a therapist.

Ethological Viewpoints

Ethology is the study of animal behavior in relation to the animal's natural habitat and compares that behavior to human behavior. In the mid-1960s, a number of ethologists published books and articles about aggression which interested and appealed to the general public. Three especially popular books were Konrad Lorenz's *On Aggression* (1966), Robert Ardrey's *The Territorial Imperative* (1966), and Desmond Morris's *The*

Naked Ape (1967). Lorenz (1903-1989) has been the chief spokesperson for a theoretical formulation of ethology as it relates to aggression.

A Nobel laureate in biology, Lorenz believes that aggression is an inherited instinct of both humans and animals. One of its principal purposes is to enable the animal—and also the human being—to defend and protect "staked out" territory, a territory which ensures sufficient food, water, and space to roam and reproduce. If this space is violated, Lorenz argues, the instinctive or genetically programmed response is to attack, or at least to increase aggressive behavior toward the intruder, thus preventing further territory violation. The tendency to attack space violators is referred to as *territoriality*. Lorenz believes it is an innate propensity developed through the lengthy, complex process of evolution. This innate aggressive behavior among members of the same animal species (intraspecific aggression) prevents overcrowding and ensures the best and most powerful mates for the young.

The more deadly the animals' evolutionarily developed weaponry (e.g., fangs, claws, physical size, and strength), the more intense the innate inhibitions *against* engaging in physical combat with members of its own species. This innately programmed inhibition is a form of insurance for species survival, Lorenz believes, since constant intraspecific physical combat would eventually extinguish the species. Intraspecies aggression is accomplished, therefore, not by actual combat, but by complicated displays of force and superiority, such as a show of teeth, size, or color array. These displays are referred to as *ritualized aggression*. Through an intricate communication system not yet clearly understood by scientists, the animals transmit signals, after which the more powerful, dominant one generally wins out. The losing animal demonstrates defeat by various appeasement behaviors, such as rolling over on its back (characteristic of puppies), lowering its tail or head, and emitting cries of defeat. The weaker animal then leaves the territory of the dominant one.

What does all of this have to do with human aggression? Lorenz and other ethologists believe that it is important to understand animal aggression before we can understand human aggression, since humans are part of the animal world and probably follow many of its basic principles. In other words, ethologists subscribe to the difference-in-degree Darwinian perspective. Efran and Cheyne (1974), for example, observed after studying invasion of personal space among humans that "human society may operate through mechanisms which are less uniquely human than is currently fashionable to suggest" (p. 225).

Lorenz raises another issue that, if valid, is more significant to criminal behavior, however. He maintains that human beings have outdistanced the evolutionary process of inhibiting aggression. Instead of developing natural weapons and the species-preserving function of ritualized aggression, humans have developed technological weaponry. Thus, he and many other ethologists believe they can provide at least a partial answer to why human beings wantonly maim and kill members of their own species: They have not developed the ability to engage in the species-preserving behavior of ritualized aggression. Instead, through superior learning ability, they have developed the capacity to annihilate.

The ethological position is intriguing, but it has not been supported by human aggression research (Bandura 1983; Zillman, 1983; Montagu, 1973). Zoologists, biologists, and psychologists have tried with little success to apply the Lorenzian tenets to humans. One problem is that the ethological position relies on a strong analogy between animals and humans. Lorenz argues, for example, that the Greylag goose is remarkably similar to the human species (Berkowitz, 1973). However, the human brain makes us remarkably unlike the Greylag goose and considerably less likely to rely on instinct for determining behavior. Research has yet to delineate any instinctive or *invariant* genetically programmed behavior determinant in humans. Furthermore, "the capacity to exercise control over one's own thought processes, motivation, and action is a distinctively human characteristic" (Bandura, 1989, p. 1175).

Ethologists also fail to acknowledge and interpret the vast body of existing scientific research that has tested their position and found it wanting. This curious response—or nonresponse—undermines the validity of their whole presentation. Some critics have referred to ethological theorizing as "scientific-sounding misinformation" (Leach, 1973). To date, therefore, there is little evidence to justify portraying humans as innately dangerous and brutal or as controlled by instinct.

Frustration-Aggression Hypothesis

Around the time of Freud's death in 1939, a group of psychologists at Yale University proposed that aggression is a direct result of frustration (Dollard et al., 1939). According to John Dollard and his colleagues, people who are frustrated, thwarted, annoyed, or threatened will behave aggressively, since aggression is a natural, almost automatic response to frustrating circumstances. Moreover, people who exhibit aggressive behavior are frustrated, thwarted, annoyed, or threatened. "Aggression is always a consequence of frustration" (Dollard et al., 1939, p. 1).

Because of its simplicity and important implications, the frustration-aggression hypothesis drew much research along with much criticism. Psychologists found it difficult not only to decide what frustration was, but also to determine how it could be measured accurately. Researchers also learned that aggression was a much more complex phenomenon than Dollard and his associates had postulated. Frustration does not always lead to aggression, and aggressive behavior does not always signify frustration. Experiments indicated that people respond to frustration and anger differently.

Some do indeed respond with aggression, but others display a wide variety of responses.

Led by Leonard Berkowitz (1962, 1969, 1973), whose general views on some of the causes of criminality were presented in chapter four, researchers began to propose a revised, contemporary version of the frustration-aggression hypothesis. According to Berkowitz, frustration increases the probability that an individual will become angry and soon act aggressively, with *aggression* defined as a behavior whose goal is to inflict damage or injury on some object or person. In short, frustration facilitates the performance of aggressive behavior. The behavior may be overt (physical or verbal) or implicit (wishing someone dead). Anger, however, is not the only potentially aggressive emotion. Aversive conditions, such as pain, or pleasant states, such as sexual arousal, also may lead to aggressive behavior (Berkowitz, 1973). We will return to this subject shortly.

An important component of the revised frustration-aggression hypothesis is the concept of anticipated goals or expectations. When a behavior directed at a specific goal is thwarted, frustration is likely to result. Thus, the person must have been expecting or anticipating the attainment of a goal or achievement. Mere deprivation of goods will not necessarily lead to frustration. People who are living under deprived conditions may not be frustrated unless they actually expect something better. "Poverty-stricken groups who have never dreamed of having automobiles, washing machines, or new homes are not frustrated because they have been deprived of these things; they are frustrated only after they have begun to hope" (Berkowitz, 1969, p. 15).

Aggression, Berkowitz says, is only one possible response to frustration. The individual may learn others, like withdrawal, doing nothing, or trying to alter the situation by compromise. With this approach, Berkowitz not only emphasizes the importance of learning but also stresses the role of individual differences in response to frustrating circumstances.

The revised frustration-aggression hypothesis, therefore, suggests the following steps: (1) The person is blocked from obtaining an expected goal; (2) frustration results, generating anger; and (3) anger *predisposes* or readies the person to behave aggressively. Whether the person actually engages in aggressive actions will depend in part on his or her learning history, interpretation of the event, and individual way of responding to frustration. It will also depend, however, on the presence of aggression-eliciting stimuli in the environment.

Berkowitz notes that the presence of aggressive stimuli in the external environment (or internal environment represented by thoughts) increases the probability of aggressive responses. A weapon is a good example of such a stimulus. Most people in our society associate firearms with aggression. Berkowitz (1983) likens the firearm to a conditioned stimulus in that the weapon conjures aggressive associations, facilitating overt aggression.

A gun, even when not used, is more likely to generate aggressive action than is a neutral object. "The mere sight of the weapon might elicit ideas, images, and expressive reactions that had been linked with aggression in the past. . . . " (Berkowitz, 1983, p. 124).

In one experiment designed to test this hypothesis (Berkowitz & LePage, 1967) angry male subjects were more likely to engage in aggressive action in the presence of a gun than a comparable group of angry subjects in the presence of a badminton racket. This suggests that a visible weapon (such as a law enforcement officer might carry) may actually facilitate rather than inhibit a violent response in some people.

The Berkowitz-LePage finding generated much controversy as to whether weapons actually do provoke aggressive behavior. A number of studies tried to replicate the finding but failed to find evidence of a weapons effect (Penrod, 1983). However, other studies support the effect (see Berkowitz, 1983; Turner et al., 1977). It should be mentioned that the aggressive-eliciting stimuli need not be aggressive or violent in appearance (i.e., a gun, knife, or bomb) but can be seemingly neutral stimuli. That is, the stimuli need only be associated with aversive events or have a decidedly unpleasant meaning to an individual to intensify aggressive reactions.

More recently, Berkowitz (1989) emphasized two important components to the frustration-aggression equation. Aggressive behavior will be generated (1) to the extent that a person perceives the mistreatment as intentional; and (2) to the degree that the frustration experienced is aversive. According to Berkowitz, people become angry and aggressive at being kept from reaching a desired goal if they *think* someone had intentionally blocked them from achieving that goal or deliberately and wrongly tried to hurt them. "They are much more likely to become openly aggressive at someone's blocking their goal attainment if they believe their frustrater had deliberately and unjustifiably attempted to keep them from reaching their goal than if they think the thwarting had not been intentional or had not been directed at them personally" (Berkowitz, 1989, p. 68). Thus, self-restraint comes into play when people think they have not been deliberately mistreated or that the blocking of the goal was legitimate. On the other hand, people become angry and aggressive when they perceive they have been treated unfairly or were personally attacked.

Berkowitz also postulates that thwartings or frustrations generate a negative affect, which refers to an emotional state people typically seek to lessen or eliminate. Furthermore, an unexpected interference is more apt to provoke an aggressive reaction than is an anticipated barrier to goal attainment, because the former is usually much more unpleasant. That is, it has more negative affect.

In his more recent reformulation of the frustration-aggression hypothesis, Berkowitz has emphasized the importance of cognitive factors. Currently, it is called the *cognitive-neoassociation model*. It operates in the following manner. During the earlier stages, an aversive event produces a negative affect. This negative affect may be due to physical pain or psychological discomfort. Physical pain as an aversive circumstance is clear, but psychological discomfort needs further elaboration. Being verbally insulted is a good example. While there is no physical pain, personal insults or demeaning comments engender anger, depression, or sadness in just about everyone—all negative affects. Unpleasant feelings or negative affects presumably then give rise, almost automatically, to a variety of feelings, thoughts, and memories that are associated with flight (fear) and fight (anger) tendencies. During this early stage, mediating cognitive processes have little influence beyond the immediate appraisal that the situation is aversive. Some people may act quickly on the basis of these initial emotions without further deliberation or forethought, sometimes engaging in violence. During the later stages, however, cognitive appraisal may go into operation and substantially influence the subsequent emotional reactions and experiences after the initial, automatic responses. These cognitions mediate and evaluate a proper course of action. They make causal attributions about the unpleasant experience, think about the nature of their feelings, and perhaps try to control their feelings and actions.

Berkowitz emphasizes that any unpleasant feeling or arousal can evoke aggressive, even violent responses. A depressed person can murder his or her family, or a thwarted teenager may violently lash out at authority.

Social Learning

Why do some people behave aggressively when intensely frustrated while others change their tactics, withdraw, or seem not to be affected? One major factor may be past learning experiences. The human being, as we noted in chapter four, is very adept at learning and maintaining behavior patterns that have worked in the past, even if they only worked occasionally. This learning process begins in early childhood. Children develop many behaviors merely by watching their parents and signficant others in their environment, a process we have called modeling or observational learning. A child's behavior pattern, therefore, is often acquired through the modeling or imitation of other people, real and imagined, in the child's environment (Bandura, 1973a). In fact, available research reveals that the conditions most conducive to the learning of aggression are those in which (1) the child has many opportunities to observe aggression, (2) is reinforced for his or her own aggression, or (3) is often the object of aggression (Huesmann, 1988).

Suppose Harris's father returns home harried after a hot and humid day during which he accomplished nothing (frustration). He finds an official-looking letter from the IRS in the mailbox. He opens it, perhaps muttering mild obscenities under his breath, and finds that the IRS apparently suspects he has shortchanged the U.S. government by several hundred dollars, although he knows he has not (more frustration). He is invited for an audit (even more frustration). In response, he slams his fist on the table, exclaims "Damn it!" or some colorful variation, and kicks the nearest chair (just enough not to damage his toe, since he has learned the painful consequences from past similar episodes). Unknown to father, Harris has observed this whole scenario. Several hours later, when his block tower crumbles, little Harris pounds his fist, kicks the living room chair, and curses, "Damn it!"

When a child's imitative behavior is reinforced or rewarded by praise and encouragement from significant models, the probability that the behavior will occur in the future is increased. There is evidence that American parents (consciously or inadvertently) encourage or reinforce aggressive behavior in their children, particularly in their sons. For example, Harris's behavior might have been reinforced if Dad or Mom drew attention to it—"Isn't that cute?"—or if they laughed. In a future episode, the kicking behavior might be directed at the family cat. Many Harrises in our society are expected or encouraged to be hard-hitting linebackers and to hold their own against neighborhood bullies, providing they are approximately the same size. They often learn that the child who aggresses successfully against others is often rewarded by status, prestige, and the most attractive toys or material goods.

Bandura (1983) identifies three major types of models: family members, members of one's subculture, and symbolic models provided by the mass media. As we noted in chapter five, family members, particularly parents, can be very powerful models up until early adolescence. Beginning in early adolescence, peer models are likely to dominate. Not surprisingly, the highest incidence of aggression is found in communities and groups in which aggressive models abound and fighting prowess is regarded as a valued attribute (Bandura, 1983; Short, 1968; Wolfgang & Ferracuti, 1967).

The mass media, including television, movies, magazines, newspapers, and books, provides abundant symbolic models. Television pervades the life of the growing child, even the very young one, and offers hundreds of potentially powerful aggressive and violent models in a variety of formats, ranging from Saturday morning cartoon film festivals to triple-X-rated cable movies. The effects these models have on children is a highly debated issue and one we will cover later in this chapter.

Since parents are powerful models, we would expect aggressive or antisocial parents to have aggressive or antisocial children. In an old but classic study, Sears, Maccoby, and Levin (1957) interviewed 400 mothers of kindergarten children about their disciplinary techniques, their attitudes about children's aggressiveness, and the children's expressions of aggression toward peers, siblings, and parents. One of the major findings was that physical punishment by parents was related to aggressiveness in the children. This was especially true when physical discipline was supplemented by high permissiveness toward aggression. In support of this finding, some researchers found that preschoolers played more aggressively when they were watched by a permissive adult than when no adult was visible (Siegel & Kohn, 1959).

Bandura (1973a) argues persuasively that aggressive behavior can be most productively understood and modified if we give attention to the learning principles like those alluded to earlier. As psychologists learn more about human behavior, many are beginning to agree with him.

Social learning theory hypothesizes that the rudiments of aggressive behavior are initially acquired through observing aggressive models or on the basis of direct experience. Then, aggression is gradually refined and maintained by reinforcement. Therefore, people may have an aggressive behavioral pattern but may rarely express it if it has no functional value or is not condoned by significant others in their social environment. The social learning system acknowledges that biological structures can set limits on the types of aggressive responses that can be learned, and that genetic endowment influences the rate at which learning progresses (Bandura, 1973a). Biology does not program the individual to specific aggressive behavior, however. These behaviors are learned by observation, either deliberately or inadvertently; they become refined through reinforced practice.

In addition, mere exposure to aggressive models does not guarantee that the observer will try to engage in similar aggressive action at a later date. First, a variety of conditions may prevent observational learning from even taking place. Individuals differ widely in their ability to learn from observation. Some people may fail to notice the essential features of the model's behavior or may have a poor symbolic or visual memory. Alternately, they may not wish to imitate the model. Bandura suggests also that one important component of observational learning may be the motivation to rehearse what has been observed. He notes that a mass murderer, for example, may get an idea from descriptive accounts of another mass killing. The incident remains prominent in his mind long after it has been forgotten by others. He continues to think about the crime and to rehearse the brutal scenario mentally until, under appropriate conditions, it serves as script for his own murderous actions.

Another restriction on observational learning is what happens to the observed model. If the model is reprimanded or punished either during or immediately after an aggressive episode, this will probably inhibit the observer's behavior. The "bad guy" should not get away with violence if we are to discourage antisocial behavior via the entertainment media.

If aggressive behavior is to be maintained, it needs periodic reinforcement. According to social learning theory, aggression is maintained by instrumental learning. In the *initial* stage of learning, observation is important, but in the later stages, reinforcement is essential. The reinforcement may be positive, as when the individual gains material or social rewards, or it may be negative, if it allows the individual to alter or avoid aversive conditions. If aggressive behavior brings rewards in either of these ways, the person is likely to continue it. A youngster subjected to unmerciful harrassment because of his unusual name may be able to stop the teasing with his fists. The reinforcement he gets from his newly found aggressive behavior is negative, but it is still rewarding. Aggression also often allows the individual to feel in control of a situation, if things are not going his or her way. The psychological reinforcement offered by feeling in control is an extremely powerful component in any human behavior.

Cognitive Scripts

Recent cognitive models for learning aggression have hypothesized that, while observational learning is important in the process, the individual's cognitive capacities and information processing strategies are equally important. According to Rowell Huesmann (1988), social behavior in general and aggressive behavior in particular are controlled largely by *cognitive scripts* learned and memorized through daily experiences. "A script suggests what events are to happen in the environment, how the person should behave in response to these events, and what the likely outcome of those behaviors would be" (Huesmann, 1988, p. 15). Each script is different and unique to each person, but once established they become resistent to change and may persist into adulthood. For a script to become established, it must be rehearsed from time to time. With practice, the script will not only become encoded and maintained in memory, but it will be more easily retrieved and utilized when the individual faces a problem. Furthermore, the individual's "evaluation of the 'appropriateness' of a script plays an important role in determining which scripts are stored in memory, in determining which scripts are retrieved and utilized, and which scripts continue to be utilized" (Huesmann, 1988, p. 19). The evaluation process includes the confidence that one has in predicting outcomes of the script, the extent to which an individual judges himself or herself capable of executing the script, and the extent to which the script is seen as congruent with the person's self-regulating internal standards. Scripts that are inconsistent or violate one's internalized standards are unlikely to be stored or utilized. An individual with poorly integrated internal standards against aggression or who is convinced that aggressive behavior is a way of life is more likely to incorporate aggressive scripts for behavior. The aggressive child, for example, is apt to instigate aggressive reactions from others, confirming his or her beliefs about the aggressiveness of human nature in a circular, perpetuating fashion.

Furthermore, aggression is a *simple*, *direct* way of solving immediate conflicts. If something is not going your way, approaching the social environment in a threatening, hostile manner is the most direct way (not necessarily the most effective in the long run) of confronting your tormentors. On the other hand, prosocial solutions and alternative nonaggressive scripts are less direct and more complex than aggressive solutions. In essence, they are more difficult to apply. Theoretically, the more cognitively "simple" individuals would be more inclined to pursue simplistic and direct solutions to their problems. In addition, because prosocial solutions are more complicated and more difficult to apply, they also require effective social skills. However, the development of effective social skills takes time. Consequently, they will have a spotty reinforcement history until perfected. Aggressive behavior, on the other hand, often receives immediate reinforcement for the aggressor and therefore is more likely to be retained in one's arsenal of strategies for immediate solutions of conflictful situations. After a twenty-two-year longitudinal study, Eron and Huesmann (1984) concluded that diminished intellectual and poor social skills have an early effect in increasing the likelihood that a child will adopt characteristically more aggressive styles of behavior to conflict resolution. Further, the evidence indicates that this aggressive style will persist across situations and time and become a preferred style throughout adulthood. But the relationship is simply not one-way, with limited intellectual competence and inadequate skills causing aggressive behavior. Rather, it appears to be interactive. Aggressive behavior may interfere with positive social interactions with teachers and peers for intellectual and social advancement, perpetuating a chain of mutually influencing events: aggressive behavior influencing the social environment, and the social environment, in turn, influencing aggressive behavior.

Dolf Zillman (1988) proposes a similar idea to the cognitive script theory but, like Berkowitz, emphasizes the importance of physiological arousal and its interaction with cognitions. Zillman agrees with Hebb (1955, p. 249) that arousal "is an energizer, but not a guide, an engine but not a steering gear." Cognition provides the steering and direction to the energizing effects of anger, fear, or frustration. A long-standing observation in the study of animal and human aggression is that when the organism recognizes or perceives a threat to its welfare and well-being, it can either fight or flee. Following this "recognition of endangerment," physiological arousal quickly sets in, preparing the organism for fight or flight. The "recognition of endangerment," Zillman reminds us, can be immediate, and the response can be reflex-like. What happens then is also highly dependent on cognition, especially in humans. Very likely, this is when cognitive scripts come in. If the arousal is moderate, the individual with skills and well-integrated standards of prosocial values will probably pursue nonaggressive scripts, although the person may have been angry or threatened at first. However, very high levels of arousal interfere with the complex cognitive processes that mediate our consideration of our internal codes of conduct as well as our ability to assess the intentions of others and the mitigating circumstances around the incident (Zillman, 1988). Think of a very stressful or frightening situation that has happened to you and how difficult it was to think clearly. Or think of a time when you became extremely angry and said or did things you wish you hadn't. At high levels of arousal, our cognitions seem to become narrower and more restricted, almost incapacitated at times. Generally, under these high states of arousal, we resort to strongly established habits to guide and dominate our behavior. In essence, we become "impulsive" and largely unthinking, and cognitions that mediate the diminution of hostile or even violent actions are substantially reduced. However, if we have practiced or rehearsed nonviolent or nonaggressive behaviors as solutions, they are likely to be the habits we resort to under high stress, fear, and high arousal.

Environmental cues are also important in cognitive scripts and strategies we employ for various situations. Which script we employ is dependent on which environmental cues are present.

ENVIRONMENTAL FACTORS

Population Density

Closely related to the ethological point of view is one that sees aggression as a result of population density or overcrowded conditions. In areas of high population concentration, personal space is constantly violated. In urban areas, crowded mass transit systems and apartment complexes teeming with people infringe on personal space and territory. Might this overcrowding be a principal factor in crimes of violence and perhaps in personal property offenses?

John B. Calhoun (1961, 1962) conducted a series of provocative studies using domestic rats and suggesting analogies between the rats and humans. He first allowed groups of rats to propagate freely in a limited physical space with adequate quantities of rat chow and water. Eventually, the rat colonies became overpopulated to such an extent that the rodents demonstrated abnormal behaviors.

Normally, male rats find one or more mates, build a nest, and, together with their mates, produce and raise offspring. Although they roam freely, they rarely show interest in another nest. In Calhoun's crowded conditions, however, the males either no longer cared about building a nest or could not defend it from bands of marauding male rats. The marauders entered the nests, attacked the females, and tore up the surroundings. Females were so harrassed by these marauders that they lost interest in caring for the young. The marauding rats were those who could not build nests of their own because of lack of space. They developed a life style that revolved around attacking other males and females, physically and sexually.

Calhoun also discovered a group of "juvenile delinquents"—male and female rats without nests who were usually too weak to defend one or to find a mate. These young rats would gather in large clusters and spend their day milling around the floor of the cage, sometimes fighting, sometimes sleeping, sometimes harrassing other rats in the vicinity. Rather quickly, the rat society deteriorated and the population declined. Calhoun's studies have been replicated by other researchers using other animals, with generally similar results.

Can we analogize from rats to humans? The research concerning the effects of crowding on human behavior is far from clearcut. At present, there is no evidence of a relationship between overcrowding and *crime* among humans, but some work suggests a link between overcrowding and *aggression*.

Some investigators have exposed people to crowded conditions combined with various room temperatures (Griffith & Veitch, 1971). In general, as population density and temperature increased, so did subjects' negative feelings toward one another. Other investigations (Freedman et al., 1972) found sex differences in response to overcrowding. Males in same-sex, overcrowded groups were more aggressive and hostile than males in same-sex, uncrowded groups. The reverse was true for females. In mixed groups, the sex differences did not occur. This evidence could suggest that men are uncomfortable and hostile in crowded same-sex conditions, while women tend to become more affable and friendly. However, the data also lend themselves to other interpretations. Mueller (1983), for instance, finds that the Freedman data indicate that men in the *low*-density condition were actually *less* competitive and aggressive, and only slightly more punitive than women. The issue of sex differences in aggressive behavior as a function of crowding or density is far from resolved.

Freedman (1975) conducted a number of correlational studies in various geographical areas throughout the United States and found no relationship between population density and crimes of violence like murder, rape, and aggravated assault. When populations were matched for socioeconomic class and other relevant variables, crimes of violence actually decreased in proportion to the population as density increased. Freedman attributed this finding to the large number of potential witnesses in high-density areas.

Population density studies, therefore, do not clearly support a relationship between overcrowding and aggression (Mueller, 1983; Harries, 1980; Kirmeyer, 1978). While density may play a significant role in engendering aggressive behavior in animals, in the human population the situation is far more complicated. Overall, the available evidence at this point does not support the view that a city's or a neigborhood's density has a significant influence on crime. However, there is some tentative evidence that density within the home may play a role in aggression and crime (Mueller, 1983; Gove, Hughes, & Galle, 1977; Roncek, 1975).

Aggression and Ambient Temperature

As temperature increases, violence increases. Or does it? This heat-of-the-night assumption was proposed as a partial explanation for riots and civil disturbances during the late 1960s and early 1970s (Baron, 1977). Later, research spearheaded by Robert Baron (Baron & Ransberger, 1978; Baron & Bell, 1975; Baron & Lawton, 1972; Bell & Baron, 1977) found support for a relationship between ambient temperature and aggression. The relationship seems complex, however. According to Robert Baron, extremely low and high temperatures tend to inhibit aggression, while intermediate levels tend to be associated with it. Baron suggests that when the temperature becomes very unpleasant (too hot or too cold), the person's major concern is to do something self-protective, such as getting a cold drink or donning thermal clothing. In other words, the individual is attempting, as Berkowitz (1989) suggests, to escape aversive circumstances (negative reinforcement). Slightly lower levels of discomfort tend to enhance the likelihood of aggression in some people, however. Picture yourself on an uncomfortably hot, but not excessively humid, summer day. Baron would maintain that your discomfort, compounded by unpleasant odors and other environmental variables, may induce irritability; in potential aggressors, it may produce hostility.

Baron's proposal suggests that collective or individual violence may be prominent at uncomfortable intermediate temperatures, rather than at extremely hot or bitterly cold ones. He hypothesized a similar curvilinear or inverted U-shaped relationship between noise levels and aggression (Baron, 1977). (See Figure 7-1.) As Penrod (1983) notes, however, these studies do not consider adequately the possible influence of other environmental or situational factors that might be associated with hot weather, such as seasonal unemployment. Recent research by Anderson and Anderson (1984) failed to yield the predicted curvilinear relationship. They found that the number of daily violent crimes increased directly as a function of temperature in two different cities. As temperature increased, violent crime increased in a *linear* fashion. In another study, Anderson (1987) discovered that overall violent crime in the U.S. was more prevalent in the hotter summer months as well as in the hotter years. The study also revealed that hotter cities have higher violent crime rates than the cooler cities. These relationships also exhibited a linear function rather than a curvilinear one.

Other investigators have found that a combination of high tem-

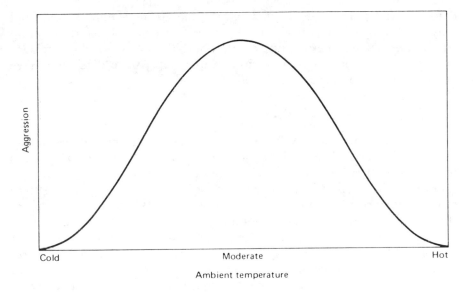

FIGURE 7-1 Hypothesized relationship between aggression and ambient temperature.

perature and air pollution is highly related to family disturbance and violent behavior (Rotton & Frey, 1985). Kenrick and MacFarland (1986) also found a strong linear relationship between horn honking and ambient temperature, at least up to 106 degrees Fahrenheit. The researchers designed a field study where a car (a 1980 Datsun 200SX) was purposely stalled during a green light at an intersection in the Phoenix metropolitan area. Phoenix, of course, is a city where daily temperatures in excess of 90 degrees are quite common. Results indicated that horn honking was directly linked to the temperature-humidity index. That is, the frequency of horn honking increased as temperature increased. The relationship was particularly strong for those honkers who had their windows down (presumably they did not have an air conditioner on or did not have one). In addition to frequency of horn honking, the amount of time spent leaning on the horn also increased as a function of the temperature-humidity index, often accompanied by verbal and nonverbal signals of hostility. The researchers also observed that the highest levels of horn honking were from young male drivers.

Available data also indicate that hotter regions of the world yield more violence, such as murder, rape, assaults, riots, and spouse abuse. In reviewing the research literature on the relationship between violence and temperature in various contexts, Anderson (1989) concludes that there is little doubt of a strong connection between hot temperature and violent crime. However, though the relationship seems to be a strong one, it is also likely to be a very complex one. For example, people may be more inclined to drink alcoholic beverages during high temperatures. Therefore, alcohol may be playing a very critical role in the incidence of violence rather than strictly the ambient temperature itself. There are many possible explanations for the temperature-aggression relationship, but to date none have been strongly supported.

Other Environmental Factors

The relationships between aggression and other environmental factors, such as noise, air pollution, and even erotica, are relatively new areas of inquiry. With reference to air pollution, for example, some studies indicate that individuals exposed to cigarette smoke are more aggressive than individuals in clean-air conditions (Jones & Bogat, 1978). Some people are even more aggressive when someone is simply smoking (inappropriately) around them (Zillman, Baron, & Tamborini, 1981), even if the air is not heavily infiltrated with smoke. Other investigators (e.g., Rotton, 1983) report that malodorous pollution also encourages hostile aggressive behavior. There is also some evidence to suggest that loud, unpredictable, or complex noises may influence aggressive tendencies. For example, Konečni (1975) found that angry subjects exposed to loud or complex noise became more aggressive than angry subjects exposed to soft and simple noise. Apparently, the additional arousal instigated by the noise adds to the arousal effects of anger already felt by the subject. This increase in arousal level presumably facilitates aggressive behavior.

The effects of erotica on aggression and violence, and particularly on sex crimes, is an important topic that has received much research attention in recent years. However, because erotica may be conceptually linked with sexual offenses, we will postpone that topic until chapter nine.

EFFECTS OF MASS MEDIA

In early September 1984, a news item reported that the movie *Red Dawn* had earned the dubious distinction of being the most violent film ever produced. It was said to contain over 100 scenes of violence for each of its two hours.

By the age of sixteen, the average child has spent more time watching television than sitting in a classroom and has probably witnessed more than 13,000 killings (Walters & Malamud, 1975).

In 1979, the movie *Born Innocent* was shown on television. It included a scene in which a teenage girl was sexually assaulted with a broomstick by other teenagers in a juvenile correctional institution. The following day a fourteen-year-old girl was raped by a group of boys using a bottle. According to court records, at least two of the boys had watched the movie the night before.

There are four scenes of violence portrayed on network television to every one scene expressing affection.

It is not surprising that many people are disturbed by media violence and that social science researchers are intrigued by its possible relationship with the violence in our society. In general, experimental studies reveal that television violence in particular has a significant effect on the frequency and type of aggressive behavior expressed by some adults and some children. In addition, there appears to be a *correlation* between violence portrayed in the print media, including pornographic literature, and the occurrence of violent crime. However, researchers to date have not established a causal link. Let us look at this research in more detail.

In a classic study by Bandura (1965), sixty-six nursery school children were divided into three groups and shown one of three five-minute films. All three films depicted an adult verbally and physically assaulting a "BoBo," a large inflatable doll with a sand base. One group saw the adult model being rewarded with candy and a soft drink after displaying aggressive behavior. A second group observed the model being spanked and reprimanded verbally. A third group witnessed a situation in which the model received neither punishment nor reward.

After the children saw the film, they were permitted to free-play for ten minutes in a playroom of toys, including a BoBo doll. The group which had witnessed the adult model being rewarded for the aggressive behavior exhibited more aggression than the other two groups. In addition, boys were more aggressive than girls. The group which saw the adult model being punished exhibited the lowest amount of aggression in the playroom.

Bandura's research, which included variations on the aforementioned basic design, consistently demonstrated this modeling effect. Furthermore, numerous follow-up studies not only replicated his findings but also suggested that media violence may have a strong influence on real-life violence in many situations (Baron, 1977). There has also been some suggestion that even news reports of violence may have a *contagion effect*, a tendency in some people to model or copy an activity portrayed by the entertainment media. Contagion effect is said to occur when action depicted in the media is assessed by certain individuals as a good idea and then mimicked. For example, an ingenious bank robbery, dramatized on television, might be imitated.

Exposure to media-portrayed violence does not, of course, automatically promote aggression. Some individuals are affected more than others. Children from low-income families are apparently more influenced by media violence than middle-class children (Eisenhower, 1969); it is not clear whether this reflects exposure to the violence itself or other factors as well. Researchers have found evidence that positive parental models are likely to override violent models on television (Chaffee & McLeod, 1971; Goldstein, 1975). Moreover, television violence seems to have substantially less effect on families where the parents do not rely on aggressive behavior for solving problems (Chaffee & McLeod, 1971).

Researchers have found that aggressive children watch more media violence, identify more with violent characters, and believe more that the violence they observe reflects real life than nonaggressive children (Lefkowitz et al., 1977; Huesmann, 1988; Huesmann & Eron, 1986). Does this mean that they learned their aggressive styles from the media? The answer is not that clear. Berkowitz (1970) suggests that people who rely heavily on aggression for getting their needs met are more influenced by media violence than are people who do not usually seek violent solutions. Studies have also shown that extremely aggressive adolescents are most strongly attracted to violence portrayed in media entertainment (Berkowitz, 1970; Eron, 1963; Halloran, Brown & Chaney, 1969).

Repeated exposure to violence on television may habituate heavy viewers to violence. It may also distort one's perception of the world. Heavy television viewers respond to violence with less physiological arousal than do light viewers, suggesting that repeated exposure has desensitized them to violent events (Cline, Croft, & Courrier, 1973). Furthermore, television is heavily populated with villainous and unscrupulous people, portrayals that may give frequent viewers a jaded view of the world. There is some evidence that heavy viewers, compared to light viewers, are less trustful of others and overestimate their chances of being criminally victimized (Gerbner & Gross, 1976).

VICTIM-PRECIPITATED AGGRESSION

So far we have maintained that aggression is principally a learned behavior. Although it may be influenced by a number of variables—temperature, frustration, and situational cues, for example—it basically occurs because an individual has learned that aggression works. Social learning theory postulates that most aggressive behavior is acquired through modeling and maintained through various forms of reinforcement, especially social reinforcement. However, we have not yet given attention to another parameter, the victim of the aggression. Often, a specific aggressive act is either provoked or facilitated by the behavior of the person who eventually becomes the victim. Specifically, what begins as a heated argument develops into a physical, violent brawl—a process called *escalation*.

Research reviewed by Baron (1977) indicates that most people respond to provocation in kind (e.g., Taylor, 1967; Epstein & Taylor, 1967; Hendrick & Taylor, 1971; O'Leary & Dengerink, 1973). Furthermore, the reciprocated response approximates in intensity the provocation received. The first person then reacts by *increasing* the provocation. In this way, verbal attacks often lead to physical retaliation and violence. The implication is that in some crimes, the behavior of the victim plays a role in escalating the offender's actions.

The concept of escalation is consistent with social learning theory. That is, we influence our social environment, and the social environment influences us in turn. There is mutual interaction in any interpersonal encounter. Many violent incidents occur between family members or between persons who know one another well. An investigation often reveals escalating anger and arousal between the participants, often ending in serious injury or even death. We will return to this topic in chapter eight.

THE PHYSIOLOGY OF AGGRESSION

Although most aggressive behavior reflects a learned way of responding to situations, some theorists and students of aggression argue that physiological factors play a significant role. In recent years, the relationship between physiology and aggression has been broached during discussions of an alleged premenstrual syndrome, drug treatment for sex offenders, and presumed relationships between certain mental or physical defects (schizophrenia, epilepsy) and crimes of violence. While evidence of a strong relationship between aggression and physiological variables does appear to exist for some species of animals, for humans the evidence is far less compelling.

There is experimental evidence that the nervous and endocrine systems of animals contribute significantly to their aggressive behavior. The endocrine system secretes hormones into the blood or lymph. Differential roles played by male and female hormones have been connected with differential tendencies toward aggressive behavior. Thus, the male hormone testosterone is believed to facilitate aggression in both the male and female (Moyer, 1971; Goldman, 1977). In animals, the female hormone progesterone, when administered to correct hormonal imbalances, may alleviate symptoms of irritability and tension. There is some dated evidence that women taking birth control pills containing progesterone demonstrate less irritability and hostility than do women not on any pill (Hamburg, Moos, & Yalom, 1968).

Some researchers believe that the differential hormonal effects may *partly* explain why human males overwhelmingly commit more violent crimes than do human females. In addition, the relationship between the secretion rate of testosterone and the level of overt hostility correlates well in young men, but not older men (Goldman, 1977). The relationship is especially notable in male adolescents with a history of assault or attempted murder. Testosterone may be released in greater quantities when males are younger than when they are older. We underscore, however, that learning and social expectations and cognitions play an extremely powerful role in any statistics that indicate gender differences in criminal behavior.

PMS

At this point, it is relevant to discuss premenstrual syndrome (PMS), which refers to the cyclic physiological and psychological changes that occur prior to the onset of menstruation, usually four to seven days before. Although there is considerable debate about whether premenstrual symptoms are validated and present in enough women to merit diagnosis as a syndrome (Sommer, 1983), the fact that some physiological changes do occur is rarely questioned. These changes may include increased tension, irritability, depression, emotional lability, anxiety, swelling of the extremities and breasts, fatigue, and headaches. On the other hand, some researchers have also reported positive symptoms associated with PMS, such as increased creativity and physical energy.

The symptoms are believed to be due to changes in the hormonal balance between estrogen and progesterone (Moyer, 1976; Tasto & Insel, 1977). During the preovulation phase (menstrual onset to day fourteen) progesterone dominates over estrogen, a dominance which peaks at approximately day fourteen (ovulation) when the estrogen level begins to increase and eventually dominate. Decreases in progesterone have been associated with high risks of suicide, especially violent suicide (Wetzel, McClure, & Reich, 1971), hospital admissions related to depression and schizophrenia (Tasto & Insel, 1977), and female crime (Dalton, 1964; Moyer, 1971). Because the physiological changes can presumably have a strong influence on behavior, PMS has been used successfully as a criminal defense in British courts. In the United States, a New York case that might have put the syndrome to the test was plea-bargained before it reached the trial stage (Carney & Williams, 1983).

Resistance to a connection between PMS and female criminal behavior is understandable. First, there is too little agreement about whether or not such a syndrome actually exists. Second, if society were to accept PMS as an excusing condition for even a portion of the crime committed by women, the social implications would be shattering. What standards would be used to determine which women were susceptible to PMS, and could any woman be trusted during the premenstrual period? Although these questions may seem overly dramatic, they are not irrelevant if one assumes that, during a significant part of their lives, some women are at the mercy of their biology.

The relationship between the premenstrual syndrome and violent crime has yet to be convincingly documented. The first heavily quoted study on the subject was that of Morton and colleagues (1953), and it appears to have a number of serious methodological flaws (Parlee, 1973). Using a sample of female prisoners, Morton reported that 62 percent of their violent crimes had been committed during the premenstrual week.

Another 17 percent had been committed during menstruation itself. The study, however, has not been replicated.

Dalton (1961) interviewed 156 newly convicted women in British prisons on their first weekend after sentencing. She reported that 22 percent had committed crimes during their premenstrual period, and another 26 percent during menstruation. However, *crime* in her study did not refer to violence, but rather to shoplifting, burglary, embezzlement, forgery, and prostitution. If the increased tension, irritability, and moodiness sometimes accompanying the premenstrual period is related to crime, violent or nonviolent, we need considerably more well-designed research to verify it.

In summary, there is no evidence to date that PMS or, for that matter, excessive testosterone levels in men, cause, facilitate, or encourage criminal behavior. Still, the criminal justice and judicial systems continue to debate whether hormonal balances or imbalances should excuse violent behavior or at least mitigate responsibility (Carney & Williams, 1983) or should have no relevance whatsoever. Although some researchers would have society accept PMS as a substantive defense in crimes of violence (that is, an excusing condition absolving the individual of moral culpability), others believe that such an approach would undermine gains in women's struggle for economic, social, and political equality.

Physiological Control through Surgery and Drugs

Another controversial issue relating to the physiology of aggression is the treatment of violent offenders. Although treatment in the broad sense can mean psychotherapy or psychoanalysis, in the narrow sense it takes on a medical connotation. Those who are violent are administered drugs to dull their senses or overcome the effects of presumably overactive aggression hormones. More drastically, they may be submitted to psychosurgery or castration. The former procedure modifies aggressive centers in the brain; the latter excises the testicles, which contain testosterone, or demolishes their functioning.

It is fairly well documented that castration lessens the tendency for animals to be aggressive. In rare instances, castration of prisoners convicted of sex crimes may have significantly reduced their aggressive episodes (Le Maire, 1956; Hawke, 1950). It may surprise you to learn that compulsory castration was legal in the United States until as late as the 1960s. For example, over 370 "voluntary" bilateral orchidectomies (excision of both testes) were performed on mentally disordered sex offenders in San Diego as a "judicial mandate" (Reiss, 1977).

Treatment with drugs that mimic the chemical composition and action of sexual hormones is more common. For example, medroxyprogesterone (Depo-Provera), which is chemically similar to the female hormone progesterone, is apparently highly effective in lowering testosterone levels

(Moyer, 1976). Lowered levels of the aggression-inducing male hormone testosterone presumably lessen the male drive to engage in sexual activity. Depo-Provera, the reasoning goes, will inhibit the excessive and impulsive sexual and aggressive behaviors of sex offenders. There is some evidence to support this assumption. Blumer and Migeon (1973), for example, found that ingestion of high levels of Depo-Provera successfully reduced sexual arousal and the need to engage in sexual "deviations." However, much research needs to be done before researchers recommend widespread usage. Moreover, the use of drugs—like psychosurgery—raises numerous legal questions, many of which have not yet been addressed by the courts.

Recent work in the neuropyschological sciences has provided additional information about aggressive behavior. Advances in technology and instrument sophistication have allowed neuropsychologists to study the potential influence of molecular components, especially substances known as *neurotransmitters*, in facilitating and inhibiting aggression. Neurotransmitters are biochemicals directly involved in the transmission of neural impulses. Without them, communication within the mammalian nervous system would be impossible. Researchers have learned that some of these neurotransmitters—namely norepinephrine, acetylcholine, and serotonin—may significantly influence the cortical and subcortical mechanisms reponsible for aggression and violence. No *single* neurotransmitter solely excites or inhibits aggression, however. Norepinephrine and acetylcholine appear to be especially important in exciting aggression, while serotonin seems to play a part in inhibiting it (Goldman, 1977).

If certain neurotransmitters are implicated in aggressive behavior, it is not too far-fetched to consider drug regimens for control. Neurotransmitters are strongly affected by drugs. However, since neurotransmitters are the basic chemicals for all behavior, any modification of their levels in the nervous system is likely to affect a large range of behavior and emotions, not only the behavior that researchers are seeking to control. Therefore, although the considerable potential of drugs in controlling and reducing aggression cannot be overlooked, their peripheral effects must be considered.

Some physiologists concentrate their research on trying to identify aggression centers in the brain. Presumably, if the part of the brain that controls or facilitates aggressive or violent behavior could be located, it might be manipulated. The research to date indicates that if an aggression center exists, it is most likely in the general area of the brain stem known as the limbic system, which consists of a diverse group of complicated brain structures and circuitry. Specifically, a small, almond-shaped group of nerve cells in the stem called the amygdala, another structure called the hypothalamus, and a portion of the brain itself called the temporal lobe have been the focus of scientific research. To date, however, we know too little about *how* our brain works, and we do not know where behavioral centers are located (Chorover, 1980).

When researchers examine the relationship between aggression and brain centers, they usually use *stereotaxic* procedure, which many researchers believe has great potential for the control of hostile aggression. By drilling a small hole in the skull, researchers are able to penetrate the brain with small insulated wire electrodes for electrical stimulation. They may also insert minute glass hollow tubes (cannulae) to allow them to stimulate chemically specific sites in the brain and stem. The needle electrode, once properly implanted, may be permanently attached to the skull with screw fittings, allowing a small segment of the electrode to protrude from the skull for the attachment of wires or to receive radio transmission from a distance (see Figure 7-2). This procedure of wireless communication is known as *telemetry*. The external part of the electrode is small enough so that it can be covered with hair and thus not be noticeable. The individual feels no pain from the procedure.

Small electric currents are passed through the electrodes to the brain

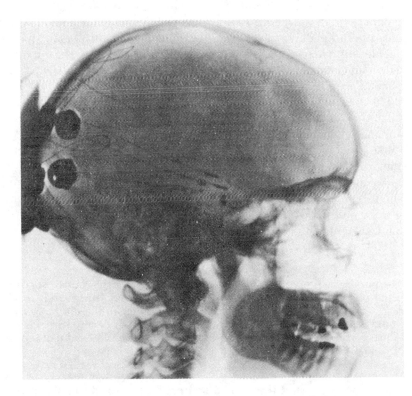

FIGURE 7-2 Diagrammatic representation of electrode implants into the amygdala for control of aggression.

site, stimulating the brain structure (or destroying it, if necessary, with direct current or high-frequency alternating current). In this way, aggressive and violent behavior may be stimulated or inhibited, depending on whether the site has an excitatory (facilitating) or inhibitory effect on aggressive behavior. If the researcher applies low-frequency alternating current to an area with a facilitating function, the individual will probably behave aggressively; conversely, when current is applied to an inhibitory area, the person will be mild-mannered.

As a result of the aforementioned type of research, it is now possible for scientists to implant electrodes into a specific region of the human brain and monitor brain-wave patterns by computer, even when the individual is some distance away from the laboratory. When a brain-wave configuration known to be associated with violent behavior in that particular individual occurs, the computer activates an electrical stimulation to the brain site.

Violence may also be controlled by producing *permanent* alterations of brain tissue (lesions) by surgical, electrical (direct current), or chemical means (collectively called *psychosurgery*). Lesions in the temporal lobe of the brain were performed on several prisoners in California (Valenstein, 1973). The Japanese neurosurgeon Hirataro Narabayashi claims success with amygdala operations on a diversity of patients plagued by aggressive, uncontrollable, destructive, and violent behavior. He reports that about 68 percent of his patients showed a signficant decline in aggressive, violent behavior (Valenstein, 1973).

What are the social implications of such scientific practices? To what extent are they justified? Some investigators assert that we should control the antisocial elements in our society by any perfected biochemical, electrical, or surgical means necessary. In the early 1970s, the then-President of the American Psychological Association, Kenneth B. Clark, urged his colleagues to make full use of these breakthroughs in biological research, which he referred to as *psychotechnology*. Assuming that no individual would choose to be a criminal if he or she were "not impelled by some forms of internal, biochemical, or external, social forces—or some combination of both" (1971, p. 1056), Clark commented:

> The implications of an effective psychotechnology for the control of criminal behavior and the amelioration of the moral insensitivities which produce reactive criminality in others are clear. It would seem, therefore, that there would be moral and rational justification for the use of compulsive criminals as pretest subjects in seeking precise forms of intervention and moral control of human behavior.

Clark also suggested that world leaders be required to submit themselves to perfected forms of psychotechnological and biochemical intervention so that their potentially aggressive, hostile impulses could be controlled.

This would be justified since it would prevent the mass destruction of civilization.

Since Clark's widely quoted address, few psychologists have called for similar drastic interventions, although biochemical intervention and surgical techniques on the human brain (psychosurgery) are increasingly more sophisticated. The medical, legal, moral, and ethical ramifications if Clark's proposals were to be carried out on a large scale would be overwhelming, and the questions posed would be unanswerable. Who would decide which technique should be used on whom? Which individuals would be required to submit to psychosurgery, and which would be encouraged to? What are the constitutional rights of the subjects? Although some courts have already begun to answer some of these questions with respect to institutionalized individuals, there remain numerous unsettled issues that are not within the scope of this text.

Furthermore, biological alleviation of aggressive behavior would undoubtedly affect socially desirable behaviors as well. There is evidence to suggest that aspects of a person's emotional, cognitive, and intellectual functioning may be significantly affected by biological manipulation of the brain. Neuronal networks in the central nervous system do not function in physiological isolation. It is estimated that the brain contains between 10 and 13 billion brain cells (neurons) whose interconnecting pathways form the most complex intercommunication network in the known universe. Each nerve cell or neuron may play some role in behavior. Scientists talk about areas or structures in the brain that may account for some type of behavior, but they know that each of these areas contains numerous neurons and supportive cells that contribute to a variety of functions. Thus, surgical, electrical, or chemical intervention to affect aggression may also incidentally affect other behaviors that need not and should not be changed.

Brain Pathology and Aggression

Routine postmortem examinations on chronically antisocial, violent persons generally find no noticeable lesion or malformation in the limbic system or other areas of the central nervous system (Goldman, 1977). This does not necessarily mean there was no physiological abnormality. The instruments used in the postmortem analysis may not have been sophisticated enough to detect them. Alternately, the individual's violent behavior might have reflected biochemical or neurotransmitter substances rather than malformation or damage to neural structures. In some instances, however, individuals were found to have symptoms of serious brain diseases. Richard Speck, who murdered eight student nurses in Chicago, reportedly displayed such symptoms (Valenstein, 1973). Charles Whitman, who killed passersby from the top of a University tower, was found in an autopsy to have a large tumor in the area of the amygdala (Mark & Ervin,

1970). Even so, it is not clear that these abnormalities directly affected Speck's and Whitman's violent behavior.

Furthermore, it is extremely unlikely that a majority of criminals in our society suffer from brain pathology or significant dysfunction. A small proportion of violent crime may be committed by people with brain diseases, but disease does not account for an appreciable portion of the aggression in our society.

Abnormal brain-wave patterns, introduced in chapter three, are more common, however. A significant number of prisoners who have committed violent crimes apparently display these patterns (Valenstein, 1973; Mark & Ervin, 1970). You may recall that one category of abnormal brain-wave patterns, slow-wave activity, is especially apparent in the temporal lobe region of the brain. Hare (1970) estimates that 2 percent of the general population exhibits this phenomenon, compared to 8.2 percent of the convicted murderer population and 14 percent of aggressive psychopaths. A second type of abnormal brain-wave activity, positive spike activity, occurs in less than 2 percent of the general population. However, it has been estimated that anywhere between 20 and 40 percent of individuals with a history of impulsive, aggressive, and destructive behavior display positive spikes (Hare, 1970). The destructive and violent responses are often precipitated by relatively mild provocations, but they can result in severe damage to property and injury or death to others. Do abnormal brain waves cause violent behavior? Or does violent behavior cause abnormal brain waves? It is impossible to tell. At present, the research on brain-wave patterns has uncovered only correlations, which do *not* signify cause and effect. The evidence to date only indicates that some forms of brain pathology or dysfunctions are found in a very small percentage of those who are violent—nothing more.

Heredity and the XYY Chromosome

Some early investigators believed that criminal behavior and predispositions to be violent were a result of heredity. The most prominent proponent of this view was Lombroso, who was convinced that a criminal "type" could be identified by specific physical characteristics, such as an unsymmetrical head and jaw, a low forehead, protruding ears, and bushy, connected eyebrows.

More contemporary inquiries on the relationship between genetics and criminality have focused on the so-called XYY chromosomal syndrome. The impetus for this research was a study by Jacobs and his associates (1965), who reported that the presence of an extra Y chromosome in the male is significantly associated with the triad of tall stature, mental retardation, and an unusually high level of aggressive behavior. After the Jacobs study was released, some investigators hypothesized that the XYY chromosomal anomaly was closely related to violent criminal activity in males.

Chromosomes are chains of genetic material known as DNA, which contains hereditary instructions for the growth and production of every living cell in the organism. Chromosomes control physical traits such as eye and hair color and height, and they may have substantial influence on many psychological predispositions and temperaments. For example, chromosomes may account for a predisposition to depression. Each cell in the human body normally possesses forty-six chromosomes, or twenty-three pairs. One pair in each cell is responsible for sex determination and sex characteristics. One member of the pair is always an X, but the other member may be either an X or a Y, depending on the sex of the individual. They are named after their appearance under a microscope. Each cell of the normal woman has two X chromosomes, while each cell of the normal man has an X and a Y. In rare instances, however, a genetic anomaly occurs in males in that two Y chromosomes pair with a single X—hence the phenomenon XYY. Rather than the usual forty-six chromosomes, the individual has forty-seven.

The principal characteristics associated with the presence of an extra Y chromosome include unusual height, episodes of violent aggression, and borderline intelligence—although there are many exceptions. Severe acne or scars from acne are also a characteristic.

A number of infamous murderers apparently had the XYY abnormality. One was Robert Peter Tait, who was convicted of beating to death a seventy-seven-year-old woman in Australia (Fox, 1971). The XYY characteristic was discovered after his trial but did not delay his execution. The XYY genotype was first used as a basis for criminal defense in 1968, at the trial of Daniel Hugon in Paris. Hugon was charged with the brutal murder of an elderly prostitute. Although convicted, he received only seven years imprisonment. It is not certain that the court considered the XYY abnormality a mitigating factor in determining his sentence, however (Fox, 1971). In the United States, criminal defendants have not used the defense successfully. "Big Bad John" (Sean) Farley, a 6'8" 240-pound giant who murdered and mutilated a Queens, New York woman in 1969, was convicted in spite of his plea of insanity due to chromosomal imbalance. Finally, Richard Speck, who murdered eight student nurses, possessed some of the physical features associated with the XYY chromosome. After his conviction, researchers examined his chromosomal structure. Although there was considerable confusion at the time the results were released, it has been concluded that Speck's genetic structure does not include the abnormality.

Although XYY has not been used as a criminal defense, there is some empirical support for its relationship with crime. So far, however, there is little evidence that *violence* and XYY go hand in hand. After an extensive review of the world literature, Jarvik, Klodin, and Matsuyama (1973) concluded that the presence of the XYY configuration in the general population averages between 0.11 and 0.14 percent; among mental patients it is significantly higher, averaging between 0.13 and 0.20 percent. However, in criminal populations, Jarvik found that XYY occurred in 1.9 percent of the cases. Jarvik's research combined information from twenty-six studies including 5,066 criminal subjects. The 1.9 percent figure for the presence of the XYY chromosome, however, constitutes a very small percentage of the total prison population and seems to represent very little of the violence in our society. In another study, XYY prisoners were found to have fewer assault incidents than comparable groups of "normal" XY prisoners (Price & Whatmore, 1967). A great majority of the XYY crimes were against property.

Epilepsy and Violence

Between 1889 and 1970, there were only fifteen court cases in the United States in which epilepsy had been used as a defense against charges of murder, homicide, manslaughter, or disorderly conduct (Delgado-Escueta, 1981). However, during the 1970s medical researchers implied that there was a causal relationship between temporal lobe epilepsy and violence (Goldstein, 1974; Pincus, 1980). This implied relationship resulted in a rash of diminished responsibility or insanity defenses for violent acts beginning in 1977. Presumably, the person plagued with this disorder is prone to uncontrollable periods of violence and destruction. Available research fails to support any relationship between violence and epilepsy in general or violence and psychomotor epilepsy, however (Valenstein, 1973; Blumer, 1976).

Although angry, irritable behavior between seizures is commonly reported in chronic temporal lobe epileptics, they rarely inflict physical harm (Blumer, 1976). In rare cases, some violence may occur in the confusional state which takes place immediately after an epileptic seizure if the individual is provoked. During this brief rage attack, the person appears to lose control and may even destroy some furniture or strike a family member. Rarely is there actual physical injury, and rarely are criminal charges brought. Furthermore, it is not clear whether aggression occurs because of the seizure itself, associated brain damage that often accompanies psychomotor seizure activity, or is independent of the seizure itself (Herzberg & Fenwick, 1988). Available evidence indicates that if violence does occur during the seizure episode, the violent behavior is probably due to a long-standing response pattern of the individual and is not directly related to the seizure itself.

SUMMARY AND CONCLUSIONS

In this chapter we reviewed the major psychological perspectives on aggression and violence. Answers to what can be done about aggression and violent crime rest ultimately on one's perspective of human nature. If one believes that aggression is innate and part of our evolutionary heritage, a position held by mainstream psychoanalytic and ethological thought, then the conclusion must be that aggression is part of life and that little can be done to alter this basic ingredient of human nature. Clues for reducing aggression are found in the behavior demonstrated throughout the animal kingdom. If, on the other hand, one believes that human aggression is acquired, then the key becomes principles of human learning and thought, and hope that one can change this acquired behavior for the betterment of humankind. The distinction between the innate and learning viewpoints has been somewhat oversimplified, but most contemporary theories on aggression fall within one or the other camp. At this point, the learning perspective has garnered more empirical support.

However, as more research data are published, the learning perspective becomes increasingly more complex, and additional factors must be considered. For one thing, physiological arousal certainly plays a major role in aggressive and violent behavior, as suggested by Berkowitz (1989). High levels of arousal seem to facilitate (not cause) aggressive behavior in certain situations. Extremely high arousal seems to interfere with our sense of self-awareness and internal control, rendering us more susceptible to environmental cues and to mindless or habitual behaviors. In this sense, under very high arousal, we may not stop to consider the consequences of our violent behavior. This point raises serious questions about the value of capital punishment or life sentences as general deterrents to violent crime.

Situational and other physiological factors also contribute significantly to aggressive behavior. Aggressive stimuli, crowds, pollution, temperature, smells, and central nervous system pathology all must be entertained as possible contributors. Social learning theorists also note that the media and the models they provide substantially affect our attitude, values, and overall impressions about violence. Attitudes, beliefs, and thoughts refer to the cognitive processes that are beginning to emerge as contenders for a leading role in the psychological explanation of criminal behavior. Operant and classical conditioning remain important, but they do not adequately address the many intricacies of criminal behavior.

CHAPTER EIGHT
Criminal Homicide and Assault

If the news and entertainment media are reasonably decent barometers of human interest, homicidal violence must be one of Western civilization's most fascinating subjects and, along with sex, the most marketable. Usually, the more bizarre, senseless, or heinous the murder, the more it receives extensive press coverage, followed shortly thereafter by books, television specials, and movies. Unusual mass murders and so-called motiveless killings are especially popular. Yet, on a national level, homicides consistently account for only about 2 percent of all violent crimes reported in the FBI's UCR and other surveys (U.S. Department of Justice, 1988).

The disproportionate amount of attention paid to criminal homicides may be explained in a variety of ways. One way might be to draw a parallel to the popularity of the occult, the mysterious, and the macabre. We crave our science fiction, our tales of terror, even our haunted houses. Perhaps we need a certain amount of excitement and arousal to prevent our lives from becoming too mundane and boring. Psychologists have long known that novelty produces arousal and excitement and breaks monotony (Berlyne, 1960). This human need for stimulation—which as we learned in chapter two is greater in some people (extraverts) than others (introverts)—may partly explain the appeal of roller coasters, sky jumping, race car driving, and gambling. These same people may enjoy films featuring vampires, werewolves, psycho-murderers, or torture chambers. Or, these vicarious pleasures might be enjoyed by individuals not wishing to seek out excitement directly. In either case, they add zest to life.

The marketability of murder might also be explained by curiosity or exploratory behavior, which is very closely related to excitement and arousal. One purpose of curiosity is to allow organisms to adjust to their environments (Butler, 1954). An individual or an organism explores a new situation to satisfy this curiosity—which is theorized to be a physiological drive state—and in the process of discovering information, adapts to the new situation. Curiosity about murder might help us prepare for the possibility that a similar event might happen to us. Reading about bizarre, seemingly irrational homicides might help us to identify danger signals. Information about the incident gives clues about who murders, who gets murdered, and under what circumstances.

Extensive exposure to violence may immunize us from its horror, however. Many social commentators have advanced cogent arguments that Western civilization has become conditioned or jaded to cruelty and inhumane behavior.

To speculate about why we are attracted to accounts of murder and violence or to wonder about the effects of repeated exposure may not seem to address the main focus of this chapter, which is the violent offender. Speculation becomes relevant, however, when we shift the focus to the individual who is part of a society that seems to have an inordinate need to seek out stimulation or to know details of crimes. When that individual is insensitive to suffering and begins to create his or her own excitement by torturing and murdering, we have a social problem. Psychology, as we will see in this chapter, can offer some suggestions for understanding and solving it.

After defining our terms, we will examine situational and dispositional factors that occur consistently in homicide and aggravated assault, beginning with data gathered by sociological researchers. We should emphasize that the statistics are offered only to provide a broad perspective of the incidence, prevalence, and sociological correlates of violent crime. We will then consider specific types of violence, including family violence, multiple murder, and prison homicide, and then turn to recent psychological research relevant to violent crime.

Thus far in this text, theoretical issues have been introduced with minimum application to specific offenses. Beginning here and throughout the remainder of this text, we will interweave the theories and concepts previously outlined with specific categories of criminal behavior.

DEFINITIONS

Criminal homicide is causing the death of another person without legal justification or excuse. Legally, the term *murder* is reserved for the "felonious killing of one human being by another with malice aforethought"

(Nettler, 1982, p. 3). The UCR, however, includes both murder and non-negligent manslaughter under the rubric *criminal homicide* for reporting purposes. Nonnegligent manslaughter is the willful killing of another human being "without premeditation in heat of passion or while unreasonably resisting an unlawful attack or threatened attack" (*Wingfield* v. *State*, 1960, p. 945). In other words, the offender's original intent was not to kill the victim; however, he became so agitated and emotionally upset in a particular situation that he lost partial control of his self-regulatory system. Since we are concerned with both murder and nonnegligent manslaughter, we will use the general term *homicide*. We are not concerned with suicides, accidental deaths, negligent manslaughter, or justifiable homicide (the killing of a person by a law enforcement officer in the line of duty or the killing of a person in the act of committing a felony by a private citizen).

Assault is the intentional inflicting of bodily injury on another person, or the attempt to inflict such injury. It becomes *aggravated assault* when the intention is to inflict *serious* bodily injury. Aggravated assault is often accompanied by the use of a deadly or dangerous weapon. *Simple assault* is the unlawful, intentional inflicting of less than serious bodily injury without a deadly or dangerous weapon, or the attempt to inflict such bodily injury, again without a deadly or dangerous weapon.

Criminologists generally study aggravated assault and homicide together, primarily because they view many aggravated assaults as failed homicide attempts (Doerner & Speir, 1986; Doerner, 1988). Dunn (1976) challenges this practice. He notes that the aggravated assault rate is at least twenty times that of homicide. "Given this disparity in rates, it is difficult to imagine that even one-quarter of all aggravated assaults were attempted homicides or would have been homicides except for the intervention of medical care" (Dunn, 1976, p. 10). Therefore, it may be unwarranted to consider aggravated assault as being in the same league as homicide; the two may differ in important variables, perhaps even including the motives of the perpetrator. A purist, therefore, would try to maintain an aggravated assault-homicide distinction.

For our purposes, it is neither realistic nor desirable to do so. Not realistic, since much of the relevant research on offender characteristics collapses the categories into one, under the rationale that people who kill usually have a history of assaultive behavior. It is not desirable since, from a psychological point of view, the two types of behavior are very comparable. Often, the type of weapon used determines the final outcome. The high-powered bullet, as an obvious example, is in most cases far more lethal than the knife (Gillin & Ochberg, 1970; Block, 1977). A stabbing or even a beating may represent behavior similar to that displayed in homicide with a Saturday night special. In law, the distinctions between murder and aggravated assault are crucial; in psychology, they are less so.

Block (1977) contends that death is a highly plausible outcome of any violent crime, including robbery and rape. Criminal homicide, then, is violent behavior carried too far. In general agreement with Block, we will designate criminal homicide and aggravated assault as one form of violent behavior, although the statistics section will separate them briefly. In later chapters, we will discuss other forms of violent behavior, including rape, armed robbery, and arson.

SOCIOLOGICAL CORRELATES OF HOMICIDE

Race

One the most consistent findings reported in the sociological criminology literature is that blacks in the United States are involved in criminal homicide at a rate that far exceeds their numbers in the general population. Wolfgang (1958, 1961) studied 588 homicides reported in Philadelphia from 1948 to 1952 and found that about 73 percent of the offenders and 75 percent of the victims were black. Furthermore, in 94 percent of all the reported cases, blacks killed blacks or whites killed whites, indicating that most homicide is *intraracial*.

Subsequent studies have continued to report the preponderence of black offenders and the intraracial nature of homicide (Pokorny, 1965; Voss & Hepburn, 1968; Munford et al., 1976; Zimring, Mukhergee, & Van Winkle, 1983; Humphrey & Palmer, 1987; Hewitt, 1988). Most of the studies have focused on various geographical areas, especially urban areas. In a nationwide study, Riedel, Zahn, and Mock (1985) report that blacks are still more likely to be offenders in at least 50 percent of all homicides, and that generally homicides tend to be intraracial.

In a ten-year study of criminal violence in Chicago between 1965 and 1974, Richard Block (1977) found that the incidence of homicide more than doubled, but the proportion of involvement by race changed very little. In 1965, 78 percent of all offenders and 72 percent of all homicide victims were black; in 1974, the figures were 78 percent and 70 percent, respectively. In 1965, 90 percent of the homicide victims and offenders were members of the same race; this compared to an 88 percent intraracial incidence rate reported in 1974.

Blacks constitute about 12 percent of the U.S. population, but they account for nearly 50 percent of all arrests for violent crimes. About 50 percent of those arrested for murder and about 35 percent arrested for assault are black. In general, blacks comprise on the average about 40 percent of the prisoners in local jails and nearly 50 percent of prisoners in state and federal facilities. Hispanics constitute about 6 percent of the U.S. population and account for about 12 percent of the arrests for violent crimes. However, only about 1 percent of those arrested for homicide are

Hispanic. In addition, Hispanics make up only about 7 percent of the state and federal prison population.

Black males have a 1 in 30 chance of becoming a homicide victim during their lifetime. White males, on the other hand, have a 1 in 179 chance. In fact, murder is the leading cause of death for black males between the ages of twenty-five and forty-four (Rice, 1980; Humphrey & Palmer, 1987). Black females have a 1 in 132 chance of becoming a homicide victim, while white females have a 1 in 495 chance.

Obviously, these figures may reflect a variety of societal inequalities, including lack of opportunities, racial oppression in its many forms, and possible discriminatory treatment by the criminal justice system. For example, a similar pattern exists for native Canadians in Canada. While Canadian Indians constitute only 3 to 3.5 percent of the total population of Canada, they represent 9 percent of the penitentiary population in the country (Hartnagel, 1987). In the prairies and northern sections where the populations of native Canadians are higher, they make up over 40 percent of the jail and penitentiary population. The sociological literature abounds with explanations for the racial disparity in crime rates. Psychological theories offer different viewpoints, including those that focus on social learning and cognitive styles.

Gender

The relationship between homicide and gender is also very strong, although not quite as strong as that between homicide and race. Wolfgang reported that 82 percent of the murderers and 76 percent of the victims in his Philadelphia sample were male. Specifically, the homicide offender rate per 100,000 was 41.7 for black males, 9.3 for black females, 3.4 for white males, and only 0.4 for white females. Notice how the race factor emerges strongly in combination with the gender factor. That is, the group displaying by far the highest incidence of homicide is the black males.

UCR data consistently reveal that the annual arrest rates for murder run about 90 percent male, 10 percent female. Studies in Houston (Pokorny, 1965), Chicago (Voss & Hepburn, 1968; Block, 1977), Atlanta (Munford et al., 1976), North Carolina (Humphrey & Palmer, 1987), Muncie, Indiana (Hewitt, 1988), England (Gibson & Klein, 1961), Israel (Landau, Drapkin, & Arad, 1974), nine different U.S. cities (Zahn & Rickle, 1986), and across the U.S. in general (U.S. Department of Justice, 1988) have also confirmed the very high ratio of males to females when homicide is at issue. Furthermore, there are substantial situational and victim differences between murders committed by males and by females, a topic that will reappear in chapter ten.

Interesting cultural differences also emerge when we examine victim statistics. The English study, for example, found that 60 percent of the victims were females; U.S. studies hover around a 25 percent figure for female victims. In the Israeli study, 51 percent of the victims of Jewish homicide offenders were female, compared to only 34 percent of the victims of non-Jewish offenders. These data illustrate the importance of considering possible cultural determinants and the nature of interpersonal relationships when homicide rates are examined.

Age

With monotonous regularity, national statistics from all sources continue to underscore the fact that about half of all those arrested for violent crime are between the ages of twenty and twenty-nine. In the U.S., the median age of homicide offenders is twenty-nine (Riedel, Zahn, & Mock, 1985). By far the highest rate of offending occurs among young, black males, aged eighteen to twenty (U.S. Department of Justice, 1988; Hindelang, 1981). Recently, however, there is some evidence of a small increase in violent crime committed by the elderly, a phenomenon just beginning to attract research attention (Newman, Newman, & Gewirtz, 1984). Most criminal careers tend to be short, usually dropping off dramatically somewhere between adolescence and early adulthood. However, some have long, protracted careers, involving a series of petty and serious crimes well past young adulthood, although even a majority of these "career criminals" burn out soon after age forty.

Socioeconomic Class

Criminologists have long assumed that crime, including violent crime, is found primarily among the lower socioeconomic class. Recent research (e.g., Williams, 1984; Smith & Bennett, 1985; Bailey, 1984; Blau & Blau, 1982; Hawkins, 1985) continues to support the observation that violence appears to be associated with the lower class or with economic and social discrimination.

Research and commentary by Tittle (Tittle & Villemez, 1977; Tittle, 1983) challenges both the theory and empirical research based on class distinctions in criminal activity, however. Tittle argues that criminologists have established their theories and conducted their research on the basis of unfounded assumptions about the lower class. After reviewing thirty-five self-report studies, Tittle and Villemez (1977) asserted that the supposed link between social class and crime was a myth.

Other criminologists believe that a rejection of the relationship is premature. Brathwaite (1981) reviewed over 100 studies and disagreed with Tittle's conclusions, finding considerable support for the view that individuals in the lower class commit more crime than those in other classes. Elliott, Ageton, and Huizinga (1980), after analyzing data from their self-report youth survey, emphasized the importance of distinguishing between serious crime against persons and property and nonserious offenses. They noted that lower-class youth are proportionately more involved in serious crimes than other youth.

Thornberry and Farnworth (1982) propose a reorientation toward social *status* rather than social *class*. A person's own social status, they argue, is more relevant to criminal activity than the social class of his or her family. Using data from a birth cohort study, they found few class differences in the delinquent activity of youth. However, the same individuals as adults were significantly more likely to be involved in criminal activity if they had low social status.

For the moment, there is little doubt of a relationship between socioeconomic position in society and adult criminal activity, particularly for violent offenses. When nonviolent but still serious offenses are at issue, however, the relationship is not as clearcut.

Victim-Offender Relationship

Until about a decade ago, research consistently indicated that in at least two-thirds of all homicides the offender and the victim knew one another well (Wolfgang, 1958; Bullock, 1955; Svaslastoga, 1956; Driver, 1961; Hepburn & Voss, 1970; Wong & Singer, 1973). In the Wolfgang data, the victim and offender were strangers in only about 14 percent of the cases. In a Chicago investigation, Hepburn and Voss (1970) reported a slightly higher victim-offender unfamiliarity figure, 19 percent.

There are indications that this is changing, however. Apparently, more people are now being killed by strangers than in the past. In Chicago during 1974, murderers and their victims were acquainted in only 58 percent of the incidents (Block, 1977). One explanation for the dramatic increase in the number of people being murdered by strangers is the very rapid increase in street crimes like armed robberies, where victims are killed.

Recent UCR data (U.S. Department of Justice, 1989a) show that over half the murder victims in 1988 were either related to the offender (15 percent) or acquainted with the offender (40 percent). Among all female murder victims in 1988, 31 percent were slain by husbands or intimates, while only 5 percent of the male victims were killed by wives or intimate friends.

Men are victimized by violent strangers at an annual rate more than double that of women (U.S. Department of Justice, 1988). The chance of becoming the victim of a violent crime perpetrated by a stranger increases with age for women, but remains about the same across all ages for men (U.S. Department of Justice, 1989b).

While the homicide offender and his or her victims frequently have similar demographic characteristics, this observation holds primarily for family and acquaintance homicide. When it comes to stranger homicide, there is a clear tendency for the offender to be younger and of a different race than the victim (Riedel, Zahn, & Mock, 1985).

Weapons

Guns and knives are the two preferred instruments for inflicting death, but this preference is somewhat influenced by sex, race, geography, and other parameters. For example, in Philadelphia during the early 1950s stabbing was the most common lethal method (Wolfgang, 1958), whereas in Chicago during the 1960s and early 1970s, shooting was preferred (Hepburn & Voss, 1970: Block, 1977). Later, firearm-related homicides in Chicago increased almost threefold (Block, 1977). However, death inflicted by other weapons increased only slightly.

Nationwide data now indicate that firearms are used in over 60 percent of all homicides, while knives are used in about 20 percent (U.S. Department of Justice, 1988). Half of all homicides are committed with *handguns*. Furthermore, about three-quarters of the law enforcement officers killed each year in the line of duty are killed by persons wielding handguns.

Other Factors

Several other factors associated with violent crime are reported consistently in the research:

1. *Temporal factors.* Homicides tend to increase during the summer months, although some recent research (e.g., Cheatwood, 1988) suggests that the month of December has the highest incidence of homicide in the U.S. Weekends, especially the hours between 8 P.M. Saturday and 2 A.M. Sunday, are clearly when homicides most often occur (Wolfgang, 1958; Hepburn & Voss, 1970; Block, 1977).

2. *Prior arrests.* According to the Wolfgang data, two-thirds of all homicide offenders had previous arrest records. More importantly, when offenders had prior records, they were likely to involve offenses against persons rather than against property, and they were usually violent offenses. Recall that the past track record of the offender is perhaps the single most useful factor for predicting future offenses. The Wolfgang study suggested that many homicidal offenders had patterns of engaging in violent behavior to resolve conflicts.

3. *Victim precipitation.* Wolfgang also found that about 26 percent of the cases were victim-precipitated: The victim contributed in some significant way to his or her own demise. Hepburn and Voss (1970) found that about 38 percent of Chicago homicides seemed provoked by the victim. Studies do suggest that offender motives for killing are often based on minor altercations and domestic quarrels in which both parties were actively aggressive. Recall the phenomenon of escalation presented in the previous chapter, where we noted that some people tend to retaliate in kind to insults or blows. Moreover, verbal

quarrels very often escalate to physical altercation. Separated from the context in which they took place, the precipitating factors of violent behavior are often pitifully trivial. Victim precipitation figures may change as more homicides are committed with strangers as victims, however.

4. *Alcohol.* This continually emerges as a factor associated with homicide. Wolfgang reported that in nearly two-thirds of the cases, either the victim, the offender, or both had been drinking immediately prior to the slaying. The noteworthy relationship between alcohol and violence will be discussed in detail in chapter twelve.

SOCIOLOGICAL CORRELATES OF ASSAULT

Assault has not drawn nearly the amount of research, publication, or popular interest that homicide has. And yet, aggravated assault is the most common type of violent crime, accounting for nearly 50 percent of all violent crimes reported to police. On the average, approximately 2 million incidents of aggravated assault and 3.3 million of simple assault are reported annually. Furthermore, about 5 out of every 1,000 Americans age twelve or older are victims of aggravated assault each year (U.S. Department of Justice, 1989b). About 7 out of every 1,000 are victims of simple assault.

Blacks make up about 40 percent of those arrested for assault, aggravated or simple. Like homicides, assaults are overwhelmingly intraracial (Dunn, 1976; Block, 1977).

The victim and offender know one another or are relatives in at least 50 percent of the reported assault cases (U.S. Department of Justice, 1988, 1989b). As might be expected, the lethal firearm is significantly less often employed in assault than in homicide. In his Chicago study, Block (1977) found that the weapons most commonly used in assault incidents were hands, fists, or feet. Dunn (1976) found similar results in a project undertaken in New York's Westchester County.

About half of those arrested for assault are young. A vast majority are below the age of twenty-five. In addition, males outnumber females 7 to 1 in total arrests for assault.

We will now turn to the major topical areas of violent crime, beginning with family violence. We will then discuss the multiple murderers and prison homicide. The rest of the chapter will concentrate on the psychological characteristics of violent offenders.

FAMILY VIOLENCE

About one of every five murders and nonnegligent manslaughters in the United States involves a family member killing another family member, with a majority (about 50 percent) involving spouse killing spouse. Similar statistics have also been reported in Canada (Silverman & Mukherjee, 1987). Homicide within the family accounts for 45 percent of all murders in England and Wales (Home Office, 1986; d'Orban & O'Connor, 1989). Approximately 7 percent of all *arrests* made for simple or aggravated assaults involved family members (U.S. Department of Justice, 1989a). However, self-report victimization studies suggest that at least 20 percent of simple or aggravated assault involve family members (U.S. Department of Justice, 1989b). Although these official statistics are woefully incomplete, they still underscore the considerable magnitude of family violence.

Some variant of family violence has probably existed since the primordial beginnings of family life. However, with the notable exception of intrafamilial homicide, family violence has not been traditionally regarded as serious crime or worthy of criminal prosecution in this country. State governments and the courts have long claimed that family relationships require or deserve special immunity, including the views that parents have a right to discipline children physically; that a husband possesses the divine right to have sexual access to his wife; or that nagging women or disobedient children often provoke and deserve the beatings they receive (Pleck, 1989). This view has been energetically challenged in recent years by various interest groups attempting not only to acquaint the public about the problem but to activate lawmakers and the criminal justice system toward more stringent legal and social sanctions.

The modern era of family violence interest and research began in 1962 when a Denver pediatrician (C. Henry Kempe) and four of his medical colleagues published a paper in the *Journal of the American Medical Association* entitled "The Battered Child Syndrome" (Kempe et al., 1962). The paper documented evidence of repeated multiple bone fractures of children suspected of being abused, and the article *gradually* became instrumental in the "rediscovery" of serious child abuse. The article was certainly not the sole precipitating factor in prompting the reexamination of child abuse. During the 1960s a very large and influential child welfare movement, bent on drawing public and professional attention to the plight of abused and neglected children, was also taking hold.

In the early 1970s, the Women's Movement was highly influential in the rediscovery of wife beating and shortly thereafter drew attention to marital rape. What began as a women's rights issue soon picked up support as a law-and-order issue (Pleck, 1989). The Women's Movement spawned legislation to increase or establish penalities for wife beating, to strengthen civil remedies, and to make it easier for women victims to file criminal charges against their assailants (Pleck, 1989). During the 1980s, several other types of family violence, from sibling violence to parental abuse of the elderly, have been acknowledged and empirically investigated. Thus, family violence includes spouse abuse, child abuse, sibling violence, abuse of the elderly, and child-to-parent violence. Currently, child abuse research is the most advanced, sophisticated, and extensive in the field of family violence (Finkelhor & Lewis, 1988). The problem of child abuse has also has been the most widely publicized. Nationwide polls in 1976 revealed that only 10 percent of the general population considered child abuse a serious problem. In 1983, however, over 90 percent of the population considered it a serious problem (Wolfe, 1985).

However, despite the current interest and public concern about family violence, we still know very little about it. Systematic study of family violence is new and often poorly designed. Even definitions, terms, and concepts in the field are excessively broad, ambiguous, and applied inconsistently, jeopardizing the comparability, generalizability, and reliability of the research findings (Weis, 1989). For example, it is unclear what behaviors should be included under the rubric *family violence*. Should verbal threats, shouting, slapping, aggressive gestures, intimidation, or spanking be included as examples of violence? Or only the more serious, physical forms of violence such as punching, stabbing, striking, shooting, and burning? Surveys conducted during the 1960s and 1970s, for example, indicated that between 84 to 97 percent of all parents used physical punishment at some time to discipline their children (Gelles, 1982). Surely we cannot conclude that 90 percent of the American parents were abusive during that era. Rather, this high incidence of corporeal punishment was due to the widespread and firmly held tradition that a spanking now and then did the child some good. Although that tradition is currently shifting toward less corporeal punishment, there still remains considerable controversy as to whether parental spankings and slaps constitute abuse.

It is also unclear how the term *violence* differs from abuse, maltreatment, neglect, and emotional and social deprivation. As noted by Gelles (1982), "the battered-child syndrome" quickly gave way to the terms *child abuse, child abuse and neglect,* and *child maltreatment*. Child abuse, once restricted to physical violence by Kempe and his associates, has become increasingly broad, encompassing an extensive range of behaviors and misbehaviors by parents and caretakers. Futhermore, it also remains unclear what relatives or intimates should be included in family violence. Should lovers, intimate friends, common-law spouses, distant relatives, ex-spouses, or separated spouses also be included? Therefore, a troubling aspect of family violence research is that terms are defined differently and often unclearly, and an assortment of family members are included in the sample, making reliable comparisons between studies difficult and valid conclusions nearly impossible to come by. In addition, each study collects data from a variety of sources and often uses substantially different procedures and methodology to tabulate and analyze the data.

For our purposes, research on family violence will be divided into four major questions: (1) How much family violence is there; (2) what are the common characteristics (or correlates) of the offenders and victims; (3)

is family violence fundamentally different from other kinds of violence (such as street violence); and (4) what are the causes of family violence? We will explore the research in these four areas, keeping in mind the critical problems in definition, sampling, and methodology just described. It should be pointed out that intrafamilial sexual abuse, although mentioned in the following sections, will be discussed in greater detail in chapter nine.

Incidence and Prevalence

Estimates on the prevalence and incidence of family violence differ widely. The term *incidence* in this section will refer to the total number of cases (frequency) per year. *Prevalence* will refer to the proportion or ratio of the population involved, such as the number of children experiencing abuse per 1,000 children in the general population.

In 1967, Gil (1970) found only 6,000 confirmed annual cases of child abuse in the United States. However, Light (1973) reanalyzed Gil's data and concluded that between 200,000 to 500,000 children are physically abused in the United States every year. Light further estimated that between 465,000 to 1,175,000 children are severely neglected or sexually abused annually. Nagi (1975), based on nearly 2,000 interviews with all relevant public and private agencies throughout the state of Florida, surmised that about 167,000 cases of physical child abuse are reported each year nationwide. He further speculated that another 91,000 cases remain unreported. The National Incidence Study (NIS), sponsored by the National Center on Child Abuse and Neglect, estimated that 625,000 American children were neglected or abused during 1980 (U.S. Department of Health and Human Services, 1982). Approximately 208,000 of this total were physically assaulted children, with fatal injuries occurring in about 1,000 cases and serious injury occurring in another 137,000 cases.

In 1986, a second National Incidence Study (NIS-2) was conducted. As in 1980, information was gathered from state or local child protective service agencies as well as from the public schools, children's hospitals, police and sheriff's departments, mental health agencies, probation departments, and county health departments. However, the definitions for abuse and negect were broader and more inclusive in the NIS-2, as we will see. The NIS-2 found that between 1980 to 1986 the number of child abuse and neglect cases increased dramatically, even when the original NIS-1 definitions were used. In 1986, 1,025,900 children were abused or neglected, an increase of over 400,800. When the revised definitions were applied, the number of those maltreated swelled to 1,584,700 children. Of this total, 675,000 were found to be abused children, including 358,300 physically abused children, 155,900 sexually abused children, and 211,100 emotionally abused children. Emotional abuse is comprised of three kinds of maltreatment: (1) close confinement; (2) verbal or emotional assault; or

(3) other. Close confinement refers to incidents where the child was tied or bound, or confined in a closet or very small enclosure for long periods of time. Verbal or emotional assault refers to cases where the child was *habitually* belittled, denigrated, scapegoated, or threatened with sexual or physical abuse. *Other* refers to cases where the basic necessities of food, water, shelter, or sleep were withheld for extended periods, or where an attempted physical or sexual assault took place.

The NIS-2 also delineated physical abuse cases according to the severity of the injury. Approximately 1,100 cases of physical injury resulted in the death of the child. Another 160,000 cases (2.5/1,000 children) were classified as serious because the injuries were evaluated as life-threatening, such as loss of consciousness, breathing cessation, broken bones, third degree burns, or extensive second degree burns over the child's body. Another 952,600 children (15.1/1,000 children) received moderate injury from physical abuse. Moderate referred to injury or pain which persisted for at least forty-eight hours, including bruises, burns, depression, and observable emotional distress. Female children were subjected to more abuse of all three kinds (physical, sexual, and emotional) than male children.

The NIS-2 admonishes, however, that the dramatic increase in the incidence and prevalence of child abuse and neglect between 1980 and 1986 may be more a reflection of better recording procedures and more awareness of child maltreatment by public and private social agencies (and the general public) than any explosion of maltreatment. "The NIS-2 study indicates that the increase of incidence of child abuse and neglect between 1980 and 1986 is probably due more to an increase in the recognition of child maltreatment by community professionals than it is due to an increase in the actual occurrence of maltreatment" (U.S. Department of Health and Human Services, 1988, p. xv).

The American Humane Association, or AHA (1987), collects data on the abuse and neglect of children from child protective service agencies in all fifty states, the District of Columbia, Puerto Rico, the U.S. Virgin Islands, Guam, and the Marianas. The Association defines *abuse* as a report of intentional, nonaccidental injury, harm, or sexual assault inflicted on a child. *Neglect* is defined as any caretaker not providing essential care to a child, such as food, clothing, shelter, medical attention, education, or supervision. In 1986, a total of 2,086,112 children were abused or neglected in the United States and its territories, a statistic substantially higher than the one reported by NIS-2 for the same year. Three percent of these children received a serious or major physical injury and another 18 percent received a "minor" physical injury annually. Thus, according to the AHA data, the prevalence of child abuse and neglect is approximately 32 out of every 1,000 American children compared to the NIS-2 rate of 24 per 1,000.

The discrepancy between the NIS-2 and the AHA figures is probably due to a number of things. As noted earlier, each agency defines things differently, collects data from different sources, and varies significantly in procedures and methodology. The AHA data, for instance, includes cases that have been substantiated on further investigation as well as cases that were determined to be unfounded. NIS-2 data were based on more substantiated or documented cases.

Some of the best-designed research has come out of the Family Research Laboratory at the University of New Hampshire. In a 1975 survey, based on interviews with 2,143 married (or cohabiting) couples, Straus, Gelles, and Steinmetz (1980) concluded that 36 out of every 1,000 American children (ages three through seventeen) experienced a "serious assault" during the year. Nationwide, this amounts to about 1.7 million seriously abused children annually. Moreover, the New Hampshire group discovered that most children (94 percent of those abused) were not assaulted just once but repeatedly over the course of a year, with an average of over ten serious assaults per year. In 1985 the New Hampshire group (Straus & Gelles, 1986) conducted a similar study, although rather than relying on face-to-face interviews as in the earlier study they interviewed 6,002 couples via telephone. Surprisingly, they discovered that the incidence of child abuse, although still distressingly high, had actually decreased 47 percent between 1975 and 1985. They attributed this decrease to enhanced public awareness, increased social and legal sanctions, better resources, and more extensive and knowledgeable social services during the ten-year period.

Studies estimating the prevalence and incidence of spousal violence also differ dramatically in their figures. Steinmetz (1977) estimated that out of a population of 47 million couples, 3.3 million wives and over a quarter of a million husbands are subjected to severe beatings by their spouses. In a national survey conducted in 1975 by the New Hampshire group (Straus, Gelles, & Steinmentz, 1980), 28 percent of the married persons interviewed said they had experienced marital violence at some point in the marriage. Sixteen percent reported some kind of *physical* violence between spouses during the year of the survey. Interestingly, in a 1975 national survey and in a later one (1985) (Straus & Gelles, 1986), no significant differences were found between men and women in overall self-reported rates of aggressing against their spouses. In fact, in more recent surveys, women were reported as engaging in all forms of aggression against their spouses at rates equal to or greater than those for men (O'Leary, 1988; O'Leary et al., 1989). Furthermore, some of this aggression apparently is not reciprocated by husbands but is initiated and continued by the wife alone. However, a strong caveat must be inserted here. Adult women respondents tend to overreport—both perpetration and victimization—in surveys of this type, while men generally underreport (Weis, 1989). Furthermore, *severely* battered women, especially those who have been victimized over a long period, tend to *underestimate* both the frequency and severity they experience

(Frieze & Browne, 1989). Therefore, conclusions about the extent of partner abuse must remain very tentative. The most common forms of aggression for both men and women appear to be pushing, grabbing, or shoving. However, the impact of men's physical aggression on women is usually more deleterious than women's physical aggression toward men (O'Leary, 1988).

The 1985 New Hampshire survey also suggests that wife physical abuse decreased by 27 percent between 1975 and 1985. Thus, contrary to reports of an epidemic of wife beating during the 1970s and 1980s, the UNH data refute this claim. The available evidence also suggests that much spousal abuse does not begin during the marriage. Some research indicates, for example, that over one-third of women about to be married have been victims of physical violence from their fiances (O'Leary & Curley, 1986).

Estimates of the proportion of elderly persons (persons sixty-five or older) who are abused range from 4 to 10 percent, but it is difficult to make confident estimates because of a lack of reliable statistics (Pagelow, 1989; Pillemer & Suitor, 1988). Best incidence estimates suggest that between 500,000 and 2.5 million elderly persons are abused by their caretakers each year (Pagelow, 1989). Pillemer and Finkelhor (1988) focused on the Boston metropolitan area and found that three percent of the elderly suffered from one of three kinds of abuse: physical abuse, chronic verbal abuse, or neglect. The researchers extrapolated that about 1 million elderly persons are similarly abused throughout the United States.

Violence between siblings is believed to be the most common form of intrafamilial violence, but surprisingly little is known about it (Gelles, 1982; Ohlin & Tonry, 1989). While professionals may recognize intrafamilial violence of parent-to-child, spouse-to-spouse, they still may find it difficult to recognize sibling violence and abuse. Steinmetz (1981) reported that two-thirds of the adolescent siblings in the family sample she studied used physical violence to resolve conflict. Families having only sons consistently experience more sibling violence than do families that have only daughters (Straus, Gelles, & Steinmetz, 1980). It is estimated that 3 children in 1,000 used a gun or knife on a sibling in the United States (Gelles, 1982). The victims of the more extreme forms of sibling violence tend to be younger siblings. For example, Fehrenbach et al. (1986) reported that over 40 percent of the victims of adolescent rape were younger siblings, usually less than twelve years of age.

Child-to-parent abuse has also become an important topic. Three teenagers (ages fifteen to seventeen) in 100 (3.5 percent) were reported as kicking, biting, punching, hitting with an object, beating up, threatening, or using a gun or knife against a parent (Gelles, 1982). The killing of parents (parricide) is usually committed by sons (Lubenow, 1983; Pagelow, 1989), but is the rarest form of intrafamily homicide. Mothers are killed (matricide) far more often than fathers (patricide) by both adolescents and adult sons and daughters. Female parricide is exceptionally rare in all countries of the world (d'Orban & O'Connor, 1989). When daughters are involved in parricide, they often secure the help of a male friend or sibling to commit the violence. In Britain, boys most often kill a parent (or parents) with explosive violence in response to prolonged provocation and parental brutality and abuse (d'Orban & O'Connor, 1989).

According to recent statistics, at least 7 percent of all intact families are multiassaultive (Hotaling & Straus, 1989). That is, some families are characterized by continual cycles of intrafamily physical aggression and violence. Siblings hit each other, spouses hit each other, parents hit the children, and the older children hit the parents. Findings support the notion that assault is a generalized pattern in interpersonal relations that crosses setting and is used across targets (Hotaling & Straus, 1989). Men in families in which children and wives are assaulted are five times more likely to have also assaulted a nonfamily person than are men in nonassaultive families. A similar pattern holds for women from multiassaultive families, although the relationship is not as strong. Sibling violence is particularly higher in families in which child assault and spouse assault are present, with boys displaying significantly more assaultive behavior (Hotaling & Straus, 1989). Moreover, children from multiassaultive families have an inordinately high rate of assault against nonfamily members (Hotaling & Straus, 1989). These children are also more likely to be involved in property crime, to have adjustment difficulties in school, and to be involved with police (Hotaling & Straus, 1989). Since a vast majority of the studies have been correlational in design, it is not possible to determine causal directions. It is simply extremely difficult to tell what is causing what in this complicated web of interrelated variables. However, it is quite clear that multiassaultive family members are violent and antisocial across a variety of settings, including toward both family members and society in general, and may demonstrate this behavioral pattern throughout most of their lifetimes.

Correlates

For some time, the scholarly and popular literature have concluded that both abusive parents and abusive spouses have themselves been the victims of family violence during their childhoods (Megargee, 1982). Individuals grow up to be abusive because they were abused themselves, a belief referred to as the cycle-of-violence hypothesis. However, the consequences of physical assault of children are neither so simple nor so absolute as many public pronouncements would have us believe (Garbarino, 1989). Publications supporting the cycle-of-violence hypothesis rarely present empirical data to support their claim (Gelles, 1982; Pagelow, 1989). When data are presented they are based on small case studies and correlations are marginal or, at best, modest. Much of the literature, however, suffers from the "woozle effect." The woozle effect, a term first used in a Winnie-the-Pooh story, and later adopted by Houghton (1979), refers to the tendency of one study to cite another study's data or conclusions, but without the qualifications and problems inherent in the first study (Gelles, 1982). For example, one study might conduct a self-report survey of a nonrepresentative sample of battering husbands (who were forced by the courts to attend a battering husband workshop in Apples, Wisconsin). Many of these battering men, perhaps mindful of the social sanctions and legal consequences facing them, and hoping to reduce culpability, assert they were victims of severe physical abuse as children. Since no control group was used (nonbattering husbands) and the sample was nonrepresentative (husbands convicted and assigned by the court within a single geographic and cultural area of the country), the researchers make modest or tentative conclusions, stressing the limited external validity of their findings. The woozle effect occurs when other writers or researchers cite this flawed and highly tentative study, without mentioning its acknowledged limitations, as *conclusive* evidence for the cycle-of-violence hypothesis.

In short, the cycle of violence and the overall consequences of abuse and neglect are *not* well documented, and the resilience of human beings rules out any simple cause and effect relationship between maltreatment and future behavior (Garbarino, 1989). In many cases, rather than finding that abusive parenting is the logical consequence of being being victimized as children, the opposite sequence is likely to take place. Realizing and sensitive to the enormous psychological and social costs of family violence, many victims of child abuse may be less likely than their nonabused peers to commit aggressive acts as adults within their families. Garbarino (1989, p. 222), for example, writes, "Many victims of child abuse, probably most, survive it and avoid repeating the pattern in their own child rearing."

Another traditional belief is that battered women allow themselves to be battered (Frieze & Browne, 1989). Others have argued that victims of spouse abuse are masoschistic, consciously and unconsciously precipatating the violence to which they are subjected (Megargee, 1982). Still others have depicted battered wives as lacking self-esteem, being highly passive and dependent on their husbands, and willing to place greater value on maintaining the marriage above their safety (Megargee, 1982).

Abusive husbands have been depicted as extremely possessive and unreasonably jealous men who treat their wives like property coveted by other men. This depiction led to other assumptions about the inadequacy, incompetence, and low self-esteem of these abusive husbands who saw threats to their masculinity everywhere. Alcohol abuse is also often seen as part of the clinical picture. Similarly, men who abuse their children were seen as incompetent, immature individuals, overwhelmed and frustrated by the responsibilities of parenting. The violence of both the abusive hus-

band and the abusive father was seen as irrational and expressive, precipitated by frustration and extreme anger. Some professionals have suggested
that street violence is generally rational and instrumental, whereas family
violence is predominately irrational and expressive (see Megargee, 1982;
Hotaling & Straus, 1989).

The empirical evidence for these depictions is meager, equivocal, and
confusing. Some studies find some support for these correlates, others
provide no support. Despite several attempts at psychological typologies
for wife and child abusers (Megargee, 1982), there does not seem to be any
evidence for "typical" psychological profiles for either wife batterers or
child abusers. The search for demographic variables has been equally
mixed and inconclusive (Weis, 1989; Hotaling & Straus, 1989). Wife and
child abuse appears to cut across socioeconomic, religious, and ethnic lines.
Even current research on gender does not reveal clear trends for women or
men as assaulters of spouse, child, or parent.

Alcohol and drug abuse seem to play a role as an exacerbater but not
as a cause of the family violence. Abusive men with severe alcohol or drug
problems are apt to abuse their partners *both* when drunk and when sober.
However, abusive husbands who drink heavily are violent more frequently,
and inflict more serious injuries on their partners than do abusive men who
do not have a history of alcohol or drug problems (Frieze & Browne, 1989).
A similar pattern also holds for men who abuse their children. Many use
alcohol as an excusing agent that allows them to escape some culpability for
their antisocial or violent actions as well as to avoid the full impact of legal
sanctions.

Once violence has occurred, it tends to be repeated (Frieze & Browne,
1989). Over time, violence, if not adequately sanctioned, may also become
more severe and more frequent. Furthermore, being violently victimized
by an intimate over a extended period of time may result in emotional
reactions and psychological scars decidedly different than those seen in
victims of violent crime by strangers. We need more research on the patterns of abuse over the life course of a family before we can offer
conclusions.

The elderly appear to be maltreated in much the same way that children are maltreated—with one notable exception: financial exploitation
(Pagelow, 1989). The likeliest candidates for elder abuse appear to be white
women between the ages of seventy-five and eighty-five, middle to lower
class, Protestant, and suffering from some form of physical or mental impairment (Pagelow, 1989). Only five percent of the elderly are placed in
institutions or rest homes, although 85 percent of them have at least one
chronic illness (Hudson, 1986). Most are living at home. Abusive caretakers
tend to lack resources, feel trapped, and may be abusing drugs or alcohol.
Two-thirds of abusive caretakers are forty years old or older, and most are
sons and daughters of the victims. Spouses constitute the second largest
abuser category. Male caretakers are more likely to abuse the elderly phys-

ically, while women caretakers are prone to abuse them psychologically or neglect them. However, both men and women are equally likely to exploit them financially. The most common abuse is a combination of psychological abuse and neglect (Pagelow, 1989). Elder abuse victims do not ask for help and may refuse assistance.

Is Family Violence Different from General Violence?

As noted earlier, some clinicians and writers have suggested that family violence is fundamentally different from general (or street) violence and thus should be examined separately (Megargee, 1982). Physical violence against children and spouses are "special" cases of violence that require family-based theories to explain them. Wife abusers are psychologically distressed, and their violence is irrational. As also mentioned earlier, child abusers are depicted as incompetent and immature, unable to cope with the responsiblities of parenting, and hold unrealistic expectations of children. Similarly, child abusers are extremely emotional and irrational in their assaults. Street offenders, on the other hand, presumably use violence in a deliberate, rational way to to gain things, such as material goods, status, or other social reinforcements. General violent offenders utilize violence for a purpose, whereas family violent offenders are lashing out in anger and without discernible purpose.

Empirical evidence for differences between criminal violence in the streets and family violence is weak and equivocal, with most of the studies being unsystematic or seriously flawed methodologically (Hotaling & Straus, 1989). The evidence we have so far, however, strongly suggests that the etiology of violent behavior may be very similar, whether it is used against a family member or a nonfamily member. Violent people tend to be violent generally, both within and outside the family context. They are aggressive and assaultive toward a large variety of targets and across a wide array of settings.

Theoretical Explanations for Family Violence

The development of theory requires well-designed and executed research. Without theoretical testing through sound research, speculations and free-floating explanations abound without empirical anchoring. This describes what is happening in the field of family violence. Gelles and Straus (1979), for example, were able to identify fifteen different theories attempting to explain family violence. Weis (1989, p. 123) observes that "the field is, with few exceptions, characterized by descriptive work, with little hypothesis testing, causal modeling, or attempts to construct and test integrated theories of the different types of family violence."

The systematic study of family violence, however, is a new undertaking. Thus, it suffers from a constellation of uncoordinated research and a matrix of poorly integrated theory, as all new sciences do. Furthermore, the family is a difficult social situation to study. It is a complex social system consisting of many roles and is a private social group where interactions and behaviors are invisible to outsiders. Social interactions are more intense, emotional, and consequential than other interactions (Weis, 1989). In addition, family influences do not flow in one direction; they are apt to be multidirectional, a process called "reciprocal influence" (Bartol & Bartol, 1989). For example, while the parents affect the development of the child, the child also affects the development and psychological growth of the parents, including their marital relationship, relationships with friends, and even the level of job satisfaction. Reciprocal influence implies that the social enviroment influences the individual, and the individual, in turn, has an impact on the social environment. Therefore, theories that are sensitive to the reciprocal interactionism of family dynamics are the best candidates to advance our knowledge about family violence.

Cessation of Family Violence

Although theories of family violence are underdeveloped, the effectiveness of various procedures or strategies to reduce family violence can still be tested. Unfortunately, there have been very few systematic evaluations of the effectiveness of particular strategies in combating family violence (Elliott, 1989).

One of the more influential investigations examining the effectiveness of police responses to spouse abuse was the Minnestoa Domestic Violence Experiment (Sherman & Berk, 1984). The police officers participating in this project handled marital conflict one of three ways: arrest, separating the parties, or advising (or mediating) the parties. Follow-up of the effectiveness of these approaches over a six-month period indicated that arrest was the most effective police response for reducing misdemeanor family assaults. However, the study has serious design problems that undermine both its external validity and internal validity. Moreover, there is some evidence that the impact of an arrest wears off over a relatively short period of time (eight to twelve months) and the assaults return to their original level (Elliott, 1989).

The effectiveness of the legal sanctions of prosecution, conviction, and sentencing in deterring subsequent family violence is also questionable. There are also many unanswered questions about the effectiveness of community services and care for family violence victims (Saunders & Azar, 1989).

Much of the contemporary work and commentary has been directed at reducing wife abuse. Fagan (1989) hypothesizes that a large segment of the rewards and a support men receive for abusing their wives derives from a long-standing cultural stereotype that men must be dominant and show women who is boss. One very "masculine" way of achieving and maintaining this expected dominance is through physical aggression and, if necessary, some violence. Some of the reinforcement comes from the satisfaction of maintaining this physical dominance and the postive social status that accompanies domination over wives advocated by one's peer group and subculture. Accordingly, men subscribing to this subculture socialize together, drink together, and participate in male-oriented recreation activities, generally excluding their wives from these activities. This male subculture provides a social milieu that supports and encourages traditional male dominance in male-female relationships, even if it requires violence now and then. Frequent contacts with this exclusive male subculture by the husband, combined with increasing social isolation of the wife, are particularly associated with the more severe forms of wife abuse (Bowker, 1983; Fagan, 1989). Presumably, the more deeply immersed into this subculture a man is, the more likely he is to batter his wife. To what extent some women also support this male-dominating tradition is largely unknown, but knowledge about the degree to which women explicitly or implicitly favor this belief system may be extremely important in a deeper understanding of the dynamics of the relationship. This is not to imply that a subculture that supports male domination in a marriage necessarily advocates violence in carrying out this dominance, but research *does* suggest that many wife batterers manage to isolate their families socially while receiving considerable encouragement and support for physical aggression from their social network of friends. It is not unusual in rural areas, for example, for abusive husbands to see to it that their wives and children are physically isolated in small mobile homes in the woods, while they continually go hunting, fishing, and drinking with their friends.

An effective way of breaking the wife-abuse cycle, therefore, is to change the abuser's attitudinal system and social network of friends that support or at least condone physical male domination of family relationships. Obviously, this strategy will not be easy to apply in many abusive behavioral patterns. Abusers have had a life-long learning experience in developing belief systems and probably have had considerable reinforcement history for their aggressive actions toward women from their subculture. "Leaving the subculture is not unlike leaving the world of the addict or the alcoholic" (Fagan, 1989, p. 408).

To *initiate* a motivation to change a behavioral pattern of wife abuse often requires establishing a series of situations where the psychological costs for the abuse outweigh its psychological benefits. Legal sanctions may be one way, but many batterers realize that these sanctions are normally weak and without teeth. However, serious attempts by the criminal justice system to put some bite into these legal sanctions (such as arrests, criminal charges, and conviction) may begin to prove effective over the long haul. It is important to note that it is unlikely that any one arrest or single event will promote a wish to change. It is more likely that a series of aversive and costly events, such as strong legal sanctions combined with social sanctions from the community (public disclosure, visits by social agencies) and emotional sanctions from the victim (reporting the abuse to authorities, leaving the home, separating, threatening divorce) will wear the abuser down to a point where he makes a decision to change his behavioral patterns.

However, the more severe and protracted the violence is, the more difficult it may be to stop, despite formal external interventions—legal or otherwise (Fagan, 1989). Legal and social sanctions for spouse abuse may work for less chronic and severe situations. However, legal sanctions, regardless of the nature and strength of the sanction, may not only be ineffective for the more serious cases, but could possibly lead to escalation in violence. Therefore, social, legal, and emotional sanctions may be more effective with individuals who do not have an extensive history of repetitive and serious violence.

As we will see in the next chapter, it is one thing to get a person to *decide* to stop acting a certain way. It is quite another for an individual to *continue* to avoid that behavior. Research clearly demonstrates that the maintenance of positive behavior is far more difficult to achieve than stopping the negative behavior.

MULTIPLE MURDERERS

One of the most frightening and perhaps incomprehensible types of homicide is the random killing of groups of people, either in one episode or individually over a period of time. Although mass and serial murders are still rare occurrences, when they do happen they cannot escape attention, and they remain etched in the public consciousness. Who today cannot recall the slaughter of twenty-one patrons of at a San Diego McDonald's in July 1984 by James Oliver Huberty, or the planned separate murders of thirty-three young men and boys in the cellar of the suburban Chicago home of John Wayne Gacy during the late 1970s. The crimes of David Berkowitz, known as the infamous "Son of Sam," and those of the "Hillside Strangler," the "Boston Strangler," and Theodore Bundy are all classic multiple murders in the United States that have received extensive media coverage. In England, we have had "Jack-the-Ripper" in earlier times and more recently, Peter Sutcliffe, the "Yorkshire Ripper" who killed thirteen women in the red-light districts of Northern England. Dennis Nilsen became England's first serial killer to prey on the homosexual subculture, committing at least fifteen known murders (Jenkins, 1988). More recently in the United States, there has been a rash of multiple murders where an individual goes into a school building or business establishment and begins shooting randomly with a semiautomatic firearm at anyone.

Serial murder is usually reserved for incidents where an individual (or individuals) kill a number of individuals (usually a minimum of three) over time. The time interval is usually days, weeks, but more likely months or years. *Mass murder* normally refers to the killing of a number of individuals within one occurrence, usually at the same location. Thus, an individual who kills victims over a number of hours in a local business establishment qualifies as a mass murderer rather than a serial murderer. *Spree murder* involves a number of killings at two or more locations with almost no time between murders and are the result of a single event. A bank robber who kills some individuals within the bank, flees with hostages, and kills a number of people while in flight over a state-wide chase would be an example of a spree murderer. In this section, our attention will be directed at serial and mass murderers.

Serial murders seem to be on the increase in the United States and England. In the U.S. during the 1950s and 1960s there were only two cases of an individual killing ten or more victims over a period of time. Since 1970, however, there have been at least forty known individuals who qualify as serial murderers (Jenkins, 1988). The U.S. Department of Justice concluded that there were about thirty-five serial murderers active at any given point in the U.S. during the 1970s and 1980s (Jenkins, 1988). Mass murderers also seem to be on the increase in the U.S., although the phenomenon remains rare in England. Available estimates indicate that as many as 3,500 to 5,000 victims are slain by serial or mass murderers in the United States each year (Holmes & Deburger, 1988).

Jenkins (1988) notes that victims of serial murderers tend to be young women, especially active prostitutes. Children of both sexes (ages eight to sixteen) are the second largest category of serial murder victims. Jenkins also finds that serial murderers tend to find their victims in environments with many transients where a stranger is likely to pass unnoticed, such as red-light districts, or skid-rows.

Unlike the typical violent individual who demonstrates a propensity for violence at an early age, serial murderers generally begin their careers of repetitive homicide at a relatively late age. Jenkins (1988) concludes that most start their careers between the ages of twenty-four and forty. Interestingly, the median age of arrested serial murderers is thirty-six. The arrest typically occurs about four years after they begin killing. While serial murderers have extensive police records, the records reflect a series of petty theft, embezzlement, forgery, rather than a history of violence (Jenkins, 1988). Surprisingly, they also do not have extensive juvenile records. Jenkins concludes that the English cases do not provide any early indicators or predictors of eventual murderous behavior. When British serial murderers committed their first murder, about half were married, had a stable family life, and usually lived in the same house for many years. A majority had stable jobs, and, disconcertingly, a good number had been former police officers or security guards.

Serial murderers kill about four people per year, an average that seems to be characteristic of both British and American offenders. However, the evidence does not support any notion that they kill on the basis of some compulsive or irresistible urge. Rather, the murder appears to be more a result of opportunity and the random availability of a suitable victim.

Holmes and Deburger (1988) have recently analyzed the characteristics of serial killers in the United States. In general, the patterns and characteristics of the British sample correspond closely to the American. However, while the British serial murderers generally stay in the same neighborhood, many of their American counterparts prefer to move around the country, committing murders in a number of states and jurisdictions. Holmes and Deburger also note that serial murder is predominately white males killing white females. Victims, both in the British and American samples, tend to be strangers or individuals who the killer met only briefly before, a pattern that makes it particularly difficult for law enforcement agencies to identify the assailant. Moreover, the motive for the killing is usually aberrant and extremely difficult to understand to those who seek the murderer's arrest.

Holmes and Deburger make a gallant attempt to classify serial murderers into a typology based on motive. They identify four major types: (1) visionary; (2) mission-oriented; (3) hedonistic; and (4) power/control-oriented. The visionary type is driven by voices or visions that demand that a particular group of people be destroyed, such as prostitutes, homosexuals, or derelicts. The visionary often operates on the basis of a "directive from God." In many instances, this type qualifies as psychotic or crazy. The mission-oriented type determines that there are a particular group of people that must be destroyed or eliminated. He sees no visions, hears no voices, and functions on a day-to-day basis without demonstrating crazy or psychologically aberrant behavior. The hedonistic type strives for pleasure and thrill seeking, and people are objects to use for one's own enjoyment. Reportedly, the hedonistic killer gains considerable pleasure from the murder event itself. The power/control type strives to get satisfaction by having complete life-or-death control over the victim. Sexual components may or may not be present, but the primary motive is the extreme power over the helpless victim.

Based on clinical observations and experience, Lunde (1976) summarizes the characteristics of both serial and mass murderers which he considers, from a psychiatric perspective, the same. Thus, he uses the term "mass murderer" as a collective term to include both types.

According to Lunde, mass murderers are almost always psychotic and kill either for no apparent reason or for an apparent but perverse (often sexual) reason. He compares mass and single murderers on a number of factors. Mass murders in the United States are almost always performed by white males, while single murders are most often committed by blacks. The mass murderer is rarely intoxicated during the episode, while single murders are often associated with alcohol consumption by the offender, victim, or both. Lunde also notes that mass murderers rarely know their victims well. The choice of victims is usually not random or coincidental, however. The offender usually selects victims possessing specific attributes; there is a significant physical, social, or psychological feature about the victim that attracts the offender. Even mass murderers who randomly shoot into a group of people are making some deliberate choice of victims. James Oliver Huberty, the "McDonald's killer," selected a fast-food restaurant in a Hispanic community and was said to have disliked Hispanics and children. Other mass killers have preyed on young black boys, college women, or prostitutes.

Lunde believes that most mass murderers fall into two psychiatric classifications: *paranoid schizophrenia* or *sexual sadism*. We have already discussed the salient features of paranoid schizophrenia in chapter six, and we will not review that particular syndrome here. We might suggest, however, that Lunde would probably place Huberty in this category, along with Jim Jones, who orchestrated the deaths of some 900 members of his "Church of God" in Jonestown, Guyana.

Sexual sadism, the second category, in its extreme form is "a deviation characterized by torture and/or killing and mutilation of other persons in order to achieve sexual gratification" (Lunde, 1976, p. 48). Unlike the offender exhibiting paranoid schizophrenic patterns, the sexual sadist usually does not manifest psychotic behavior. He also tries to avoid detection, and is therefore not likely to "play games," like sending cryptic messages that draw attention. Of all types of murderers, sexual sadists are the most likely to murder again, Lunde warns. Characteristically, they are males under age thirty-five who have very few normal social and sexual relationships. Their victims, who are apparently viewed as objects to be used as sources of pleasure, are almost always women, but homosexual serial murders have also occurred.

Brittain (1970), a British psychiatrist, concentrates on the sadistic murderer and basically agrees with Lunde's observations. Sadistic murderers are typically shy, withdrawn, quiet, and mild-mannered, he notes. They rarely show anger. They have very few friends and prefer solitary pursuits, like reading and listening to music. They are usually fascinated by the occult, black magic, werewolves, vampires, and portrayals of horror in both print and electronic media. They often demonstrate strong attraction for objects that have sexual meaning for them—women's shoes, handbags, stockings, and lingerie. As we will see in chapter nine, however, it would be incorrect to assume that this tendency leads to sadistic murder. More often than not, sadistic murderers have no prior criminal record. They are drawn to semiskilled employment and generally have a poor work history.

These individuals become dangerous when they have suffered a loss of self-esteem, such as being laughed at by a woman, mocked by acquaintances, or demoted or discharged from employment. Their murders are usually carefully planned, perhaps weeks in advance. They seem unconcerned about the moral implications of their brutal acts and treat their victims as objects. According to Brittain, the sight of suffering and the helplessness of the victims increasingly excites sadistic offenders. They usually kill by strangulation, apparently because of the total control over the victim this method offers them. Shooting is too quick and too kind. Following death, victim mutilation is common. After the macabre murder, the sexual sadist may return home calmly and display little if any distress or guilt.

When sadistic murderers are arrested, Brittain notes, they continue to display little tension or guilt. They may even enjoy describing the incident in detail. They appear to bask in all the attention they receive; it is not uncommon to see them smiling into television and still cameras. They have turned a once-mundane existence into excitement, and they may even feel they have made their mark on history.

Brittain does not try to shape his observations into a causal theory. His stated purpose is to provide a factual description for practical use. He does emphasize, as does Lunde, that given the opportunity the sadistic offender will most likely murder again.

What are we to make of these unpalatable descriptions, which are based on years of clinical observations? Although Lunde and Brittain provide valuable information, they have neither offered a satisfactory explanation for mass murder nor presented a testable theory. Furthermore, since classification schemes are continually falsified by the evidence, there are probably many maximum security facilities housing at least one nonwhite, extraverted mass murderer. Nevertheless, perhaps due to the rarity of this crime and its distasteful elements, psychological researchers have not flocked to study it.

It is a mistake, however, to assume along with Lunde that almost all mass murderers are seriously mentally disordered in the clinical sense of that term. While their thought patterns may be considered to be extremely aberrant when it comes to sensitivity and concern for other human beings, a vast majority of serial killers fail to qualify as psychotic or crazy in the traditional scheme of mental disorders. Serial killers have developed versions of the world characterized by values, beliefs, perceptions, and general cognitive processes that facilitate repetitive murder, often in a brutal, demeaning, and cold-blooded manner. They commit the type of murders that draw interest, send spine-chilling fear into the community, and appear incomprehensible. They draw considerable expenditure from law enforcement agencies in both time and money in their detection and arrest. Motives are difficult to determine and seem to be based on psychological rewards rather than material gain. But the labels "sick," "crazy," or "psychotic" explain little and offer little hope in the quest for understanding the processes involved in the development of this behavior.

Jenkins (1988) makes some important points about what happens to serial murderers once taken in custody. Almost inevitably they attempt a defense of insanity or diminished responsibility, but very rarely succeed. The public, in Britain, Canada, and the United States, is consistently highly reluctant to attribute insanity to extremely violent offenders, particularly in the case of serial or mass murderers.

PRISON HOMICIDE

Another area that has received little research attention is the homicide that occurs within the walls of a correctional facility. According to Toch (1977), violence rates in most correctional facilities are increasing at a rate higher than violence outside of prison. A comparison of prison and nonprison homicides might offer us clues about homicide in general.

Sylvester, Reed, and Nelson (1977) examined homicides in state and federal prisons housing 200 or more adult felons in 1973. Killings of correctional personnel as well as inmates were included. The researchers analyzed the homicide event itself and background variables of both victims and offenders. They obtained information on 128 prison homicides; seventy-eight involved inmates killing inmates, ten involved an inmate killing staff, three involved staff killing an inmate, and one incident involved one member of the correctional staff killing another member of the correctional staff. In thirty-five of the inmate death incidents, the assailant was not known. One staff member was killed by an unidentified assailant.

Correctional staff were more likely to be killed by groups of assailants, whereas inmates were more likely to be murdered by a single individual. Stabbing was the method most frequently used to inflict death (about 75 percent of the incidents). Eight percent of the victims died of strangulation, 5 percent were beaten to death, 5 percent were killed by firearms, and about 4 percent were victims of fire. A notable feature of prison homicide is the severity of the beatings and stabbings, often exceeding the force necessary to inflict death. Half of the victims died instantly or within an hour of the assault, and another 20 percent died within two hours.

When the researchers examined apparent motives, they found that fifteen incidents were a direct result of conflicts surrounding homosexuality, while in six additional instances homosexuality was judged to be a secondary motive. Toch (1977) has also called attention to homosexuality as a motivating factor in prison violence. Like heterosexual relationships, homosexual affairs inspire jealousy, feelings of rejection and dishonor, and a refusal to accept the end of a relationship. These are all motivating circumstances which seem to play significant roles in instigating violent episodes.

Revenge toward someone who had informed on others was a primary motive in sixteen homicides, while arguments (a catch-all category) precipitated fifteen others. Specific disagreements over money, personal property, or drugs accounted for another twenty-five killings. Racial tension was the principal factor in seven cases. In about a quarter of the incidents, no apparent motive could be ascertained.

The homicides occurred in proportion to the racial composition of the facility, suggesting that interracial conflicts and tensions within the prison may not be as dramatic as is often assumed. Incidents of blacks killing blacks and whites killing whites were more frequent than interracial ones, a finding consistently reported in the general homicide literature. The Sylvester project did find evidence that black assailants were more likely than white assailants to be disciplined, referred for prosecution, and indicted for homicide. Once cases were brought to court, however, the conviction rate was about the same, whether the accused was black or white.

The study reported interesting differences between single-assailant and multiple incidents. The three leading motives for single-assailant violence were homosexuality, arguments, and unpaid debts; the leading motives for multiple-assailant killings were "snitching," power struggles between groups, and drug quarrels. The researchers observed that single-assailant events appeared to be associated with personal relationships between two individuals, while multiple-assailant incidents were induced by a need to maintain "inmate social order." More than half of the single-assailant situations appeared to have been victim-precipitated. In most multiple assailant events, the victim appeared to play a more passive role. Multiple assailants were more likely to kill in the victim's cell, while single assailants killed in a variety of other prison locations. Finally, single assailants (compared to multiple) used a wider variety of weapons in killing their victims. Multiple assailants relied heavily on stabbing. These data suggest that in prison, multiple-assailant homicides are planned, purposeful acts, while single-assailant events are more spontaneous actions prompted by interpersonal conflict.

Psychological features of the offenders and victims were not included in Sylvester's analysis, apparently because of a number of deficiencies in the methods used to make those assessments. Of considerable interest, however, is the criminal history of the assailants. About half were serving time for serious violent crimes at the time of the prison homicide; one-quarter of these violent inmates were currently imprisoned for murder. Once in prison, they continued to be violent. Sixty percent of the assailants had been disciplined for assault prior to the prison homicide. Individuals who killed correctional personnel had been especially violent. Ninety-one percent of these assailants were serving time for serious violent crime, and 80 percent had been cited for assaultive behavior while in prison. These findings underscore the importance of considering the past behavioral history of a person in judging the likelihood of future violence. The fact that individuals who engage in violent acts in the outside world continue to engage in violence in the inside world of prison emphasizes the point that there is indeed some trans-situational consistency in human behavior when it comes to violence.

PSYCHOLOGICAL FACTORS IN VIOLENT CRIME

Impulsive Violence

Violent crime is often seen as resulting from the impulsive, spur-of-the-moment, and unpredictable acts of enraged individuals. The person who savagely assaults and sometimes kills is operating on impulse, slashing out at a victim without much forethought or planned strategy. This point of view, of course, partly supports the argument for gun control. If the gun were not available, the perpetrator would not have wounded or killed the victim—at least not as easily. The availability of a weapon, however, is only part of the story.

Some theorists believe that certain personalities or dispositions are more likely to react violently under certain circumstances than others. In *Violent Men*, Toch (1969) theorizes that most violent episodes can be traced to well-learned, systematic strategies of violence that some people have found effective in dealing with conflictful, interpersonal relationships. Thus, violence is not simply the act of a person acting on impulse; it is the act of one who has *habitual* response patterns of reacting violently in particular situations. It is Toch's impression that, if we examine the history of violent persons, we will discover surprising consistency in their approaches to interpersonal relationships. They learned, probably in childhood, that violence works for them. They used violent responses effectively to obtain positive and negative reinforcement. They got what they wanted or avoided unpleasant situations by being violent.

Toch posits that humiliating affronts and threats to reputation and status are major contributing factors to violence. A blow to the self-esteem of the person who has few skills for resolving disputes and conflicts (such as verbal skills) may precipitate violence. This is especially true if the person's subculture advocates that disputes be settled through physical aggression.

In a similar vein, Berkowitz hypothesizes that people sometimes react violently, not because they anticipate pleasure or displeasure from their actions, but because "situational stimuli have evoked the response (they) are predisposed or set to make in that setting" (Berkowitz, 1970, p. 140). That is, individuals have been conditioned—specifically, classically conditioned—to react violently by prior experiences in similar situations. In some instances, according to Berkowitz, powerful environmental stimuli essentially produce impulsive behavior. Under these conditions, one's "thinking" becomes highly simplified, responding "mindlessly" to stimuli in a well-learned manner. Thus, some people "fall into" a rage, impulsively striking out automatically in response to unpleasant feelings brought on by aversive or noxious stimuli. Aversive or noxious stimuli can be anything from a face one "doesn't like" to physical abuse by another. Nevertheless, the individual is not *likely* to strike out unless he or she has been in a rage in past situations.

A similar view is expressed by Zillman (1979, 1983), who believes that cognitive or thinking processes are greatly impaired at extreme levels of emotional arousal. Under high excitement, such as anger, behavior normally controlled by thought becomes controlled by mindless habits. Therefore, at very high levels of emotional upset, hostile or aggressive behaviors are likely to become "impulsive," a term Zillman associates with habit strength. The behaviors have been so well learned that they appear quickly and without thought on the part of the individual. In other words, they seem to be "mindless" actions. Impulsive behavior, then, is not unusual, out-of-character behavior; it reflects habitual responses that might be rejected by the individual under low arousal or normal conditions.

Toch, Berkowitz, and Zillman all suggest that when experiencing powerful emotional reactions, many people become incapable of considering the consequences of their violent acts. High arousal inhibits cognitive processing to the point where they may not think before acting. The environment and the relevant external stimuli take control over the internal mediation processes that have been weakened by extremely high levels of arousal.

Overcontrolled and Undercontrolled Offenders

One of the most heuristic explanations of violence was advanced by Edwin Megargee (1966), who identified two distinct personalities in the highly assaultive population: the *undercontrolled* and the *chronically overcontrolled* aggressive types. The undercontrolled aggressive person has few inhibitions against aggressive behavior and frequently engages in violence when frustrated or provoked. Aggression is a behavioral pattern that becomes the habitual response when the person is upset or angry.

By contrast, the chronically *overcontrolled* person has well-established inhibitions against aggressive behavior and rigidly adheres to them, even in the face of provocation. This person has learned (or been conditioned) about the consequences (real, imagined, or implied) of engaging in violence. The overcontrolled individual is the socialized, or perhaps over-socialized, person who readily associates violations of social mores and regulations dictated by others with potentially punishing consequences. Even more than others, he or she will often say, "If I violate the rules, I will be punished." Recalling Eysenck's dichotomy, we might posit that the introvert is much like the overcontrolled personality, while the extravert exhibits many features of the undercontrolled.

According to Megargee, however, there may come a time when frustration and provocation overwhelm the overcontrolled person. If this happens, he or she may strike out violently, perhaps even exceeding the violence exhibited by the undercontrolled person. The undercontrolled-overcontrolled typology, therefore, suggests that the more brutal and unexpected slayings are often performed by usually inhibited, restricted individuals. Thus, neighbors, friends, and relatives are shocked by a homicide committed by a "nice, quiet, well-mannered boy":

> A 16-year-old choir boy described as a "hell of a nice kid" was arraigned here Thursday as funeral services were held for three girls he is accused of stabbing to death. The girls' bodies were found Monday, face down in a stream in deep woods about a quarter of a mile from their homes. The state medical examiner said two of the girls were stabbed 40 times each and the third eight times. The death weapon was believed to be a hunting knife. (Tom Stuckey, Associated Press release, October 14, 1977)

In an empirical test of Megargee's hypothesis, Blackburn (1968) divided a group of violent offenders into extreme assaultives and moderate assaultives. *Extreme assaultives* were defined as those convicted of murder, manslaughter, or attempted murder. *Moderate assaultives* included persons who had wounded with intent to cause serious bodily harm, or who had maliciously wounded or assaulted. On the basis of personality measures, extreme assaultives were significantly more introverted, conforming, and overcontrolled and less hostile than moderate assaultives. Moreover, their extreme aggressive behaviors had occurred only after prolonged or repeated provocation (real or imagined).

In another study (Tupin, Mahar, & Smith, 1973), convicted murderers with a history of violent offenses were found to have a much higher incidence of hyperactivity, fighting, temper tantrums, and other extraverted features during childhood than a comparable group of murderers without previous criminal records of violence. These "sudden murderers"—those without a previous record—were also found in other clinical studies to be introverted and plagued by feelings of inadequacy, loneliness, and frustration (e.g., Weiss, Lamberti, & Blackburn, 1960; Blackburn, Weiss, & Lamberti, 1960). These are all features of the overcontrolled personality type.

Lee, Zimbardo, and Bertholf (1977) reported a limited but pertinent study using a small group of nineteen murderers. Ten were classified as "sudden murderers" because their background reflected no other criminal offenses, while nine were regarded as habitual offenders with prior arrests for violent acts. The Stanford Shyness Survey and Minnesota Multiphasic Personality Inventory (MMPI) were administered to both groups. Eight of the ten sudden murderers indicated they were "shy" on the Stanford Scale, compared to only one of the nine habitual offenders. According to MMPI results, the sudden murderer group tended to be significantly more over-controlled and passive than the habitual offender group, who tended to be more undercontrolled and assertive. These results combined with other observations suggested to the researchers that people who are overcontrolled are capable of more extreme violence when "inner restraints" break down than are individuals who hold their behavior under looser controls.

At present, there is some evidence to suggest that violent offenders may differ along a continuum of undercontrolled-overcontrolled, with most at the polar ends of the continuum. Moreover, we could further hypothesize that undercontrolled violent offenders will be the habitual criminals. Overcontrolled offenders, who usually do not have criminal records, are more likely to engage in one quick, highly violent or murderous episode.

More recent evidence indicates that undercontrols and overcontrols are found in the nonviolent populations about as often as found in violent populations, however (Henderson, 1983). This finding implies that the Megargee schema may not offer as much in explaining the various types of violence as originally expected. Furthermore, the over- and undercontrolled dimension does not fully account for the role of situational parameters. For example, persons who are passive and unassertive are more likely to experience intense frustrations and to find themselves in many situations where they feel threatened, insecure, and powerless. The Lee-Zimbardo-Bertholf group (1977) tried to relate this lack of social and verbal skills to the sudden murderer, who is typically a shy individual without the necessary interpersonal skills to assert himself or herself in social situations. Obviously, however, most shy people do not become sudden murderers.

When people lack the skills and strategies to modify at least some of their social situations, feelings of helplessness usually result. These feelings are in turn likely to provoke one of two response patterns: approach (attack) or avoidance (withdrawal). The withdrawal response, as theorized by Martin Seligman (1975), is often called reactive depression or hopelessness. The person feels there is nothing that can be done about his or her predicament, so why bother? This response pattern is vividly illustrated by powerless people living under dire poverty conditions, who perceive that they have little opportunity for change—a life without hope.

On the other hand, an alternative response is to attack, to lash out in desperation, especially if a person believes this response pattern will be effective in improving his or her circumstances. The sudden murderers, who have been passive and pushed around all their lives, may be resorting to one final attempt to change what is happening to them. Their homicidal violence may be a very desperate response to gain immediate control over their lives, without consideration for the future consequences of their act. An interesting question might be poised at this point: Which is more adaptive under seemingly hopeless conditions, remaining depressed and hopeless, committing suicide, or doing something violent in a desperate attempt to change things?

Cognitive Self-Regulation and Violence

The subject of impulsive behavior brings us to what some social learning and cognitive theorists call *self-regulatory capabilitites*. Psychological research is finding that this may be an extremely important factor in violent behavior. According to social learning theory (e.g., Bandura, 1983) and social cognition theory (Bandura, 1986, 1989), we are able to exercise considerable cognitive control over our behavior. Cognitive capacity enables us to transcend the present and think about the future as well as the past, even in the absence of immediate environmental cues. This conceptual thinking ability lets us guide our own behavior by thinking about its possible outcomes. However, circumstances sometimes weaken cognitive control and facilitate impulsive actions. Under certain conditions, therefore, our actions are directed more by external stimuli than by cognitive self-regulatory mechanisms.

The self-regulatory process presumes the development and refinement of cognitive structures and concepts, which is learning. As we stated earlier, the world as we know it is based on our cognitive structures, which are nonspecific but organized representations of prior experiences. Some people possess more structures than others, and some deviate from what the social mainstream regards as "accurate" structures of the world and human nature. People with many sophisticated structures can evaluate behavior in more complex ways than can people with few, crude structures. For example, someone with a large storehouse of sophisticated concepts would be less inclined to label a murderer simply as "sick" or "an animal."

Under normal circumstances, we perceive, interpret, compare, and act on the basis of these structures, which we will refer to as *personal standards*. If we do not like what we are doing, we can change our behavior, justify it, or try to stop thinking about it. We can also reward and punish ourselves for our conduct. Self-punishment is expressed as guilt or remorse following actions we consider foreign to our standards. In most instances, however, we prefer self-reinforcement to punishment; therefore, we behave in ways that correspond to our cognitive structures. We anticipate the feelings of guilt we will experience for alien actions, and thus we restrain ourselves. "Anticipatory self-condemning reactions for violating personal standards ordinarily serve as self-deterrents against reprehensible acts" (Bandura, 1983, p. 30). Therefore, each of us develops personal standards or codes of conduct that are maintained by self-reinforcement or self-punishment, as well as by external reinforcement and punishment.

Our standards may be built around simplistic beliefs that "There is a sucker in every crowd," or "People are basically mean and brutal," or "The surest route to success is to take care of number one." People who have adopted the "me first" approach and are convinced that rigorous competition and aggression are the best strategies for achieving success may find that aggression—even violent behavior—is a source of self-reinforcement and pride (Toch, 1977). In the extreme, "number one" individuals lack self-reprimands for aggression and harmful conduct. Their personal standards about human nature are a built-in justification for their cruel acts.

Standards are not confined to individuals, but may be characteristic of entire cultures and societies. Some cultures, subcultures, or groups try to develop ethical and moral standards of conduct in their members. We might ask at this point to what extent American society cultivates nonviolent behavior.

Relating all of this specifically to aggression and violence, we can see that personal and group standards dictate much of our behavior. If one's philosophy is that "life is cheap" and if insensitive conduct is the norm, violence can become a way of life. Some people, therefore, are cruel and violent not necessarily to receive reward from the external environment, but because violence reflects their internal standard and implicit theory of human nature. Others, perhaps the majority, have adopted standards and have built cognitive structures that do not condone hurtful or reprehensible conduct.

To some extent, we have oversimplified self-regulatory mechanisms theory in an effort to introduce some of its concepts. Self-regulation does not invariably operate across all situations. Otherwise, how do we explain destructive and reprehensible conduct perpetrated by apparently decent, moral people over the centuries in the name of religious principles and righteous ideologies? What, if anything, justifies deliberate, planned large-scale violence such as bombing or war? How do we explain mob violence, where seemingly good people appear to be swept along by their emotions or by the crowd? Why don't self-regulatory mechanisms operate then, when they are so needed?

Social learning theory explains some of this by hypothesizing that under certain circumstances self-regulatory processes become *disengaged* from conduct. "In the social learning analysis, moral people perform culpable acts through processes that disengage evaluative self-reactions for such conduct . . . " (Bandura, 1983, p. 31). This disengagement may be what takes place in impulsive violence. As described by Berkowitz (1983) and Zillman (1983), high levels of emotional arousal take our attention away from our internal mechanisms of control. When we become extremely angry, for example, we often say and do things we later regret. We feel upset, remorseful, and guilty, and we wish we could take back our words and actions. If we had carefully considered and evaluated the consequences of our behavior, we would probably have acted differently. But under the heat of emotion, our self-regulatory system, with all its standards and values, was held in abeyance. As we get older, however, we generally learn from experience to pay closer attention to our internal control mechanisms, and we engage in fewer impulsive outbursts. This "mellowing" feature may partly account for the lower rates of impulsive violence as age increases.

Regardless of our personal standards against violence or doing harm to others, therefore, we all may occasionally engage in harmful or even violent conduct. When this happens, we use several approaches to convince ourselves of the "rightness" of our actions. We may feel, for example, that under certain conditions some people need to be taught a lesson. An errant child may be hit; an experimental subject may be shocked; a murderer may be executed in the service of justice. The problematical logic of these explanations becomes evident when they are turned about. From a political terrorist's perspective, acts of violence are justified if they accomplish a greater good, like freeing society from a tyrant. Ideally, then, we should very narrowly define conditions under which physical aggression and violence might be justified (e.g., to save another human life).

We may also neutralize our internal standards to some extent by concluding, "Others are doing it, many of them much more than I am." "Most people cheat on their income tax returns. It's part of the game." Certainly, this perspective is relevant to participants engaged in corporate or white-collar crime, a topic we will return to in chapter eleven. In addition, as we saw in the chapter on juvenile delinquency, some groups neutralize their criminal conduct by removing from it the onus of "badness." In fact, engaging in the "bad" conduct may increase one's status within the group.

Another way in which we may downplay our internal standards, especially those against violence, is by convincing ourselves that some individuals are less than human, more animal-like than most. This approach works nicely if we accept the difference-in-degree position on human nature. In other words, we may *dehumanize* people who commit terribly cruel and heinous murders, in effect seeing them as closer to animals than most other people. Some people justify capital punishment on the basis that some criminals are subhuman. Dehumanization helps explain the numerous black lynchings in U.S. history and the treatment of the Jews in Nazi Germany. In war, we dehumanize the enemy by using derogatory epithets. Like justifying the "rightness" of violence, however, dehumanization also works from both perspectives. Thus, the mass or serial murderer and the individual who continually engages in assaultive behavior, as we have seen, views victims as objects divested of humanity. The offender feels little remorse for any suffering inflicted and does not worry about anticipatory self-punishment. Research has shown, however, that it becomes more difficult to behave cruelly toward others as they become personalized and humanized (Bandura, Underwood, & Fromson, 1975). In other words, if an assailant becomes acquainted with a potential victim, there is less likelihood that he or she will be cruel. This would seem especially true of crimes where killing the victim is not the primary goal.

Finally, we also may disengage our personal standards from our conduct when we are told to do something reprehensible by a legitimate authority. When someone who possesses legitimate power commands us to do something, we are, in a sense, relieved of personal responsibility for the conduct, even if the conduct is alien to our personal standards. The Milgram obedience study discussed in chapter four is a good illustration of this.

In sum, the self-regulatory system we develop is not invariant or automatic, but dynamic and subject to certain experiences and circumstances. Moreover, many events are ambiguous and do not fit readily into our existing cognitive templates. Under these conditions, we are more likely to seek clues from outside sources. Nevertheless, the value of the self-regulatory system is its tendency to guide our behavior toward what we believe is the right thing to do in a particular situation. The more we believe in our internal standards, the less prone we will be to rely on outside sources, even under stress or pressure situations. This suggests that the best internal standards are those we have developed ourselves, rather than those imposed or advocated by an external group and which we embrace only for convenience or for appearances.

Fortunately, most people have developed an internal standard that to wantonly harm another person is wrong. Therefore, the reason why a vast majority of people do not engage in violent behavior is not simply because of a classically conditioned reflex. Rather, it is most likely because they have adopted a belief system that subscribes to the view that it is wrong to harm another human being, at least without *just* cause. Of course, the human tendency to justify one's behavior—the just-cause argument—is often inseparable from the most heinous violence in human history. We justify large-scale organized violence (wars), claiming we must protect ourselves, family, and way of life from the brutal (less-than-human) enemy.

The next section focuses on mob behavior and what happens to the self-regulatory mechanisms of normally gentle people caught up in a madding crowd. The crowd, it seems, often robs the individual of his or her identity and, consequently, his or her usual reliance on personal standards of conduct. Some of the most violent behavior is exhibited, not by single individuals, but by excited groups, especially large ones. Physical assaults that occur in the midst of riots or demonstrations, vigilante-instigated lynchings or beatings, gang rapes, and public stonings all illustrate this mob violence.

Deindividuation and Crowd Violence

The powerful effects of crowds on individual behavior has interested social scientists since the early 1900s. Crowd influence is usually studied under the rubric *collective behavior*, which includes riots, gang rapes, panics, lynches, demonstrations, and revolutions. For our purposes we are concerned with collective behavior only as it affects the instigation and maintenance of violence.

One of the first theorists of collective behavior was Gustave LeBon, whose 1896 book *The Crowd* is regarded as the classic study of groups. Because his views were colored by the French Revolution, LeBon did not take kindly to individual behavior swayed by the crowd. Humans in a crowd are like a herd of animals, he said, easily swayed or spooked. LeBon believed that those who normally are nonviolent and law-abiding are capable of the kind of violence, intolerance, and general cruelty found in the most primitive savages. The person enmeshed in the mob loses sensibility and the ability to reason and forfeits his or her own mind to the crowd. The collective mind is dangerously brutal and destructive to people and property. According to LeBon, even educated people become simple-minded and irrational under its influence. Essentially, LeBon claimed, each person comes under the control of the reflexive "spinal cord" rather than the cerebral cortex.

Most of us have seen dramatizations of a "berserk" mob clamoring for the destruction of some political, social, or physical institution or for swift "justice" for an individual or group. Descriptions of mob actions often liken them to brush fires which grow in intensity and are quickly out of control. However, since true mob actions are naturally occurring and spontaneous events, it is difficult to place them under the scrutiny of scientific, systematic investigation. The processes involved in mob action are still not well understood, therefore. Some social psychologists (e.g., Zimbardo, 1970; Diener, 1980) have attempted laboratory studies of mob or group violence, generally by approximating conditions that might bring out aggression and positing that, if allowed to continue, the aggression would likely result in violence. Obviously, they must stop far short of actual violence, so whether it would have occurred remains speculative. The procedure of trying to mimic an event under laboratory conditions is called a *simulation*.

Zimbardo (1970) believes that deindividuation accounts for much of the tendency of otherwise "tame" individuals to engage in antisocial, violent behavior. Recall from chapter four that deindividuation includes a reduction in feelings of personal distinctiveness, identifiability, and personal responsibility. Furthermore, in a crowd the threshold of normally restrained behavior is lowered. In other words, people feel anonymous, less responsible for their behavior, and less inhibited. According to Zimbardo, these conditions encourage the antisocial behavior associated with selfishness, greed, hostility, lust, cruelty, and destruction.

In one widely cited experiment, Zimbardo manipulated two variables, feelings of anonymity and features about the victim. He randomly assigned female college students to deindividuation and "identifiable" groups. Subjects in the deindividuation group wore shapeless white lab coats and hoods over their heads and worked in dimly lit conditions (see Figure 8-1). The experimenters avoided using their names. By contrast, participants in the identifiable groups felt anything but anonymous. They wore large name tags, were greeted by name, worked under fully illuminated conditions, and wore their own clothes with no added lab coats or hoods.

Subjects were told the project was set up to study empathy. The real purpose, of course, was to study the relationship between deindividuation and aggression. Each subject listened to a five-minute recorded interview between her future "victim" and the experimenter. Some victims were portrayed as warm, sincere, honest persons, while others were obnoxious, self-centered, conceited, and critical. After each interview, the subjects were allowed to administer shock to the interviewees they had heard on tape. They were allowed to observe the reactions of their victims by way of a one-

FIGURE 8-1 Three subjects used in Zimbardo's experiment on deindividuation listen to the tapes of their soon-to-become "victims."

way mirror. Aggressive behavior of the subjects was measured by the length of time a painful electical shock was administered. "Victims"—who actually received no shock—were trained to writhe, twist, and grimace.

Recall now that Zimbardo was manipulating two variables, anonymity (loss of personal identity) and features of the victim (environmental stimuli). Thus, some *subjects* were hooded, others were well identified. Some *victims* were pleasant and likeable, others were obnoxious. Zimbardo reasoned that members of the deindividuation group would administer shocks of longer duration because of the diffusion of responsibility and loss of personal identity. He also hypothesized that victim features would be irrelevant, because the heightened arousal experienced under deindividuation would interfere with ability to discriminate between the victims. Put another way, the excitement and resulting arousal engendered by shocking someone without the threat of any repercussions would prevent discernment of the target (the person receiving the shock).

One additional hypothesis was tested. Zimbardo predicted that subjects in the deindividuation group would administer longer shocks as the experiment progressed. He believed the act of administering shock without responsibility would be exciting and reinforcing for its own sake (what he called "affective proprioceptive feedback"). In brief, the person finds that doing the antisocial behavior feels "so good" each time she does it that the behavior builds on itself in intensity (vigor) and frequency.

Results of the experiment supported all three hypotheses. The deindividuation group shocked victims twice as long as the identifiable group. The dindividuation group also administered the same levels of shock, regardless of the victim's personality features. And finally, this group shocked for longer periods as the experiment progressed. "Under conditions specified as deindividuating, these sweet, normally mild-mannered college girls shocked another girl almost every time they had an opportunity to do so, sometimes for as long as they were allowed, and it did not matter whether or not that fellow student was a nice girl who didn't deserve to be hurt," Zimbardo concluded (1970, p. 170).

Essentially, Zimbardo argues that deindividuated aggression is not controlled by the social environment; it is unresponsive to both the situation and the state or characteristics of the victim. That is, the high arousal generated by the excitement of a crowd reduces both (1) a person's private self-awareness, and (2) his or her ability to discriminate among external stimuli, such as victim characteristics. The participant is no longer guided by self-regulatory mechanisms and is "blind" to such stimuli as the victim's distress or discomfort. The aggressor loses individuality to the collective mind of the crowd; he or she neither feels compassion nor considers the circumstances. The victim may plead, beg, cry, or scream, but these stimuli will have little effect on the crowd behavior. Even a prestigious and powerful authority figure may be unable to stop the violence once self-identity is obliterated by the furor of the crowd.

Zimbardo's research design, like that of Milgram, has been criticized extensively for its questionable use of subject deception and shock (albeit simulated) and its focus on the negative aspects of human behavior. In a sense, these types of experiments constitute a form of psychological entrapment; would people really act this way if not prompted by an experimenter? In the wake of such experiments, the National Institute of Mental Health, the American Psychological Association, and other organizations have adopted ethical guidelines that are applied to the funding and approval of research. Experiments like Zimbardo's, therefore, are unlikely to be replicated. Nevertheless, their possible implications cannot be ignored.

Diener (1980) disagrees with the tenets of Zimbardo's deindividuation theory, postulating that deindividuated behavior *is* responsive to situational or victim characteristics. He believes that a person's normal self-regulatory behavior is reduced by the unusual and exciting activity of the crowd, and that this reduced private self-awareness creates an *internal* state of deindividuation. Since the individual has trouble retrieving his or her standards of appropriate conduct, he or she becomes more responsive to environmental cues (Prentice-Dunn & Rogers, 1982, 1983). In crowds, people do report a strong loss of individual identity, an overwhelming tendency to concentrate on the moment rather than the future, and substantially altered thinking and emotion (Prentice-Dunn & Rogers, 1983). They become less aware of thoughts, moods, bodily states, and other internal processes. Think of the athlete caught up in the excitement of the game, who continues to play while seriously injured. After the game, the athlete might exclaim about a fractured arm, "It didn't feel that serious!"

According to Diener, because deindividuated individuals do not pay attention to their internal processes, including their self-regulatory capabilities, they depend more on environmental cues for behavioral direction. Thus, when aggressive and violent cues are present, they are far more likely than usual to engage in violence. It is Diener's contention that if the victim of a mob action could, in some way, be "humanized," the crowd might stop its brutality. In other words, perpetrators' attention should be directed toward the victim rather than the violence being displayed by other actors. Dierner also believes that participants in a mob action can be made to pay closer attention to their internal regulation norms. His hypothesis deserves to be tested by further research. Of course, whether the cries and pleas of the victim during an attack actually could alter the crowd behavior is a question unlikely to be answered by laboratory research. Furthermore, because the theories of Zimbardo and Dierner are based on laboratory studies, we cannot conclude that they generalize to actual situations. They do, however, suggest possible explanations for violent mob behavior.

SUMMARY AND CONCLUSIONS

In this chapter, we began to narrow our focus to consider specific offenses. Previous chapters were broader, in that they dealt with general theoretical orientations to çrime. Here, we reviewed the major sociological data on violence, summarized the four major issues on family violence, discussed the rare phenomenon of multiple murder, touched on prison homicide, and presented the principal psychological theories and research on violence.

Sociological data indicate that homicides are rare compared to the total incidence of violent crime. They are generally committed by young males, usually black, living in environments that implicitly or explicitly advocate violence for the resolution of conflict. While assaults are far more common than homicide, the same sociological features appear, particularly for aggravated assault.

The psychological perspective suggests that three central issues surround violence: (1) self-control, as dictated by self-regulatory mechanisms; (2) emotional arousal; and (3) individual reference points for behavioral guidance, which may be either internal or external. Violence is most often committed while the participants are under very high levels of emotional arousal, particularly anger. High arousal seems to reduce the ability to attend to internal standards of conduct and general self-awareness. Furthermore, high arousal seems to make people feel less responsible for their actions; they often claim, "I don't know what came over me," or "I couldn't help it." In short, high arousal renders people more susceptible to "mindless" behaviors and places them under the influence of external stimuli or events.

Self-regulatory mechanisms develop through socialization and personal beliefs about what is right or appropriate, wrong or inappropriate. Under normal conditions, self-regulatory mechanisms control behavior by providing cognitive templates for what is proper behavior for a specific situation. The effect of arousal on these self-regulatory mechanisms appears especially important in explaining street or domestic violence, where the violence is spontaneous, highly charged, and often used as a way of settling personal conflicts.

Individual construct systems are highly similar to the self-regulation process, but refer in this context to the human ability to justify or neutralize conduct, no matter how reprehensible. Self-regulation refers to behavioral control; the construct system enables a person to perform an act and deal with it later. Human beings, with their intricate cognitive equipment, have an uncanny knack for neutralizing, disregarding, minimizing, rationalizing, and misjudging their deeds. We have an enormous capacity for disengaging our beliefs and our internal standards from our actions. Bandura (1983) lists six common disengagement practices we use for dealing with our own reprehensible, antisocial conduct. It is instructive to examine each of these strategies here.

First, people do not ordinarily engage in antisocial conduct until they have justified to themselves the rightness or morality of their actions. Reprehensible acts can be made honorable through cognitive restructuring. Thus, a distressed father, convinced that he must save his family from the evil of the world, kills his children, his wife, and then himself. In essence, he reconstructed his construct system to fit what we believed was the right thing to do under the circumstances. Another example would be where a moral young man who believes killing is wrong voluntarily goes to war to protect his country. At first, these two actions may seem to have nothing in common. However, they both represent cognitive restructuring.

A second disengagement practice—related to the first—is where people convince themselves that their violent acts are really trivial and not all that bad compared to what others have done. In war we convince ourselves that the atrocities committed by the enemy are far worse than anything we do. A rapist might convince himself that rape is not really that serious, since no "real" physical harm comes to the victim.

A third strategy involves the power of language. One of the costs of human intellectual ability is the considerable power of words; they allow us to justify our actions with relative ease. We use euphemisms to neutralize reprehensible behavior. For example, intelligence (spy) manuals use words like *neutralize* and *terminate* instead of *assassinate* and *kill*. The euphemisms carry less onus and cause less disruption to moral beliefs. In the chapter on juvenile delinquency, we noted that youth subcultures employ various euphemisms to neutralize their antisocial acts.

A fourth strategy—one most commonly found in group violence—is the diffusion of responsibility. Statements that best typify this practice include: "I was just following orders," "I was just following the crowd," and "The executive board decided that it was in the best interest of the economy (and the company) to continue production, despite some risk to the health of others." These assertions have the effect of displacing responsibility for one's actions to others, or to forces outside oneself.

A fifth strategy is not even to think about the consequences of one's actions. Here, people convince themselves that the consequences are not important. Alternately, they manage to detach themselves from the aftermath of violent actions. For example, the bombardier or the person who pushes the button that will release lethal chemicals onto a civilian population is not only following orders (diffusion of responsibility) but also is probably not allowing himself to think about the tragedy that will result.

Finally, the sixth practice is to dehumanize the victim. "She was loose and got what she deserved." "He was scum." The enemy are labeled "gooks" or something akin to vicious animals. Dehumanization removes all the human, dignifying qualities from the victim or intended victim. As Bandura (1983, p. 32) points out: "Many conditions of contemporary life are conducive to dehumanization. Bureaucratization, automation, urbanization, and high social mobility lead people to relate to each other in anonymous, impersonal ways." These impersonal, dehumanizing aspects of life facilitate violence and make living with it possible.

CHAPTER NINE
Sexual Offenses

Sexual behavior in many societies is a subject fraught with moral codes, taboos, norm expectations, religious injunctions, myths, and unscientific conclusions. In the United States, the daring venture of Albert Kinsey and his colleagues in publishing the scientific evidence they had gathered at the Institute for Sexual Research dispelled numerous myths and corrected fallacies about sex. Many still linger, however, especially with reference to the sex offender, for whom society has little tolerance. Moreover, society often does not distinguish between types of sex offenses. "Degenerates" who expose themselves to passersby or watch unsuspecting women undressing are as likely to be feared or to attract disgust and anger, as are rapists and child molesters. Often, the community clamors for the strict and speedy prosecution of the offender, who is considered a deranged or evil person (or animal) driven by some inner sinister force, and from whom citizens must be protected.

Sexual offenders are frequently viewed as a homogeneous class of individuals. Research shows, however, that they vary widely in the frequency and type of sexual activity they engage in, and they differ in personal attributes like age, background, personality, race, religion, beliefs, attitudes, and interpersonal skills (Knight, Rosenberg, & Schneider, 1985). The features of their crimes also differ markedly among offenders, including time and place, the sex and age of the victim, the degree of planning the offense, and the amount of violence used or intended (Knight, Rosenberg, & Schneider, 1985).

The causes of sexual offending are neither simple nor straightforward. As the knowledge from systematic study accumulates, it is clear that this behavior is influenced by multiple, interactive factors. Past learning experiences, cognitive expectations and beliefs, conditioning, environmental stimuli, and reinforcement contingencies (both rewards and punishments) are all involved. In this chapter we will review the major research findings on potential causal factors involved in the crimes of rape, child molestation, and exhibitionism. We will also discuss the phenomenon of fetishes which sometimes leads to minor criminal activity.

Some studies (e.g., Revitch & Schlesinger, 1988) reveal that many sex offenders are not prone to violence or physical cruelty, but rather are timid, shy, and socially inhibited. While this may be correct for a large segment of pedophiles, it is not for many rapists whose attacks often have strong aggressive features. In fact, their sexual aggression can be divided into at least two major categories: instrumental and expressive. Instrumental sexual aggression is when the sexual offender uses just enough coercion to gain compliance from his victim. In expressive sexual aggression, the offender's *primary aim* is to harm the victim physically as well as psychologically. In some cases the expressive aggression is "eroticized" in that the offender becomes sexually aroused in the presence of physical or psychological brutality.

Regardless of the sex offender's characteristics, motivations, and method of attack or coercion, the social and psychological costs to victims and their families are immeasurable and often devastating. A recent survey of 3,132 households in the Los Angeles Epidemiologic Catchment Area (ECA) study illustrates this very well. Researchers found that over 13 percent of the individuals interviewed had been victims of sexual assault at least once in their lifetimes (Burnam et al., 1988; Sorenson et al., 1987; Siegel et al., 1987). Two-thirds of the sexually assaulted subjects reported two or more assaults. Moreover, lifetime sexual assault was more frequently reported by women (16.7 percent) than men (9.4 percent). Thirteen percent of the victims were first assaulted between the ages of six and ten, 19 percent between eleven and fifteen, 34 percent between sixteen and twenty, and 15 percent between twenty-one and twenty-five. The experience of being sexually assaulted was associated with substantially higher risks for later onset of serious, self-destructive depression, substance abuse, numerous fears and inhibiting anxieties, and a variety of major interpersonal problems. Overall, the ECA project found that both male and female victims of sexual assault are two to four times more likely to develop serious psychological problems than nonvictims. In this chapter we will focus on the two sexual offenses that are most troubling to society and most tragic to victims—rape and child molestation (pedophilia)—and we will briefly discuss other sexual deviations that may lead to criminal activity.

RAPE

Definitions of rape vary widely from state to state; in many states the term *sexual assault* has replaced *rape* in the criminal statutes. According to the U.S. Department of Justice, rape is "unlawful sexual intercourse with a female, by force or without legal or factual consent" (U.S. Department of Justice, 1988, p. 2). The UCR defines rape somewhat differently, distinguishing *forcible* from statutory rape or rape by fraud. Forcible rape is "the carnal knowledge of a female, forcibly and against her will." It includes rape by force, assault to rape, and attempted rape. Statutory rape is the carnal knowledge of a girl, with or without her consent. The critical factor is the age of the victim, an arbitrary legal cutoff point below which a girl is believed not to have the maturity to consent to intercourse or understand the consequences. Age limits vary from state to state, but most set the limit at sixteen or eighteen. Thus, if an adult male engages in sexual relations with a minor female, he may be convicted of statutory rape. Rape by fraud is having sexual relations with a consenting adult female under fraudulent conditions. Among the most frequently cited example is that of the psychotherapist who has sexual intercourse with a patient under the guise of offering treatment.

Many in the general population (including the victims themselves) do not define sexual attacks as rape unless the assailant is a stranger. Thus, if the victim is sexually assaulted by a husband or a boyfriend, she may not report the incident. Criminal justice officials as well as the general public often feel marital or date rape is unimportant because they are believed to happen so rarely, compared to stranger rape, or to be less psychologically traumatic to the victim. Criminal prosecutors, for example, admit they are reluctant to prosecute marital or date rape cases because of concerns that juries will not believe that a woman could be raped by a husband or male friend (Kilpatrick et al., 1988). However, in a survey of the general population conducted by Kilpatrick et al. (1988), subjects who had been raped identified their husbands as assailants in 24 percent of the cases and male friends in 17 percent of the cases. These data suggest that over 40 percent of the rapes were committed by husbands or dates, a significant and frequently overlooked statistic in the tabulation of rape.

The classification and study of rape offenses is also hampered by the fact that jurisdictions vary widely in their definitions of rape, often disagreeing with the Department of Justice or UCR guidelines. In the mid-1970s, the National Institute of Law Enforcement and Criminal Justice funded extensive surveys of law enforcement agencies that illustrate these differences

(Chappell, 1977a, 1977b). Most agencies reported that vaginal penetration was the *minimum* criterion for an alleged offense to qualify as rape. Over half of the law enforcement agencies surveyed also required evidence of both penetration and force, while another third required evidence of penetration, force, a weapon, and/or resistance by the victim. As might be expected, the average number of rapes reported by the latter agencies was significantly lower than the average number reported by other law enforcement agencies accepting less demanding criteria.

Prosecutors require more stringent evidence than law enforcement agencies before accepting an incident as a probable rape. Most of the 150 prosecutors polled in the Chappell survey set four threshold criteria for filing a complaint of forcible rape: (1) evidence of penetration; (2) lack of victim consent; (3) threat of force; and (4) female sex of the victim. It is intriguing to note, however, that 92 percent of the prosecutors sampled did not have formal guidelines for filing a charge of forcible rape. Therefore, their survey responses were more likely to reflect their own judgments about the minimum threshold requirements for initiating action against an alleged offender.

Although some agencies follow the UCR guidelines for classifying rape, many adopt different classification systems. About one-third have more stringent requirements, one-fifth less stringent. Some jurisdictions distinguish between attempted rape and forcible rape. Many, especially the larger ones, include different degrees of forcible rape (e.g., first and second degree). In addition, the term *sexual assault* may be used rather than *rape*. In cases involving multiple offenses (e.g., rape plus burglary, homicide, or robbery), the offense considered the more "serious" takes precedence and is more likely to be tabulated in the offense statistics, while the "lesser" crime committed at the same time is not reported. For instance, since homicide is considered to be a more serious crime than forcible rape, homicide-rapes traditionally are tabulated under homicide and not under rape. Therefore, because of these wide variations, we must view statistical comparisons and information pertaining to the "average" rape very cautiously.

Incidence and Prevalence

From all indications, the United States has the highest incidence of rape in the world. During the past decade and according to the UCR, "official" incidence of reported rape in the United States has been about 65 to 75 for every 100,000 women. This rate represents 6 to 8 percent of the total violent crime rate. Of course, we must recognize that the actual rape rate is greatly underestimated, partly because of some of the problems listed in the previous section and partly because of the ordeal women must go through just to report the incident. Victimization studies offer a revealing contrast to the official rates. Russell (1983) selected at random and interviewed 930 women living in the San Fransciso area. She learned that

175 of them (19 percent) reported at least one completed extramarital rape and 284 (13 percent) reported at least one attempted extramarital rape. Fifty percent of those reporting these incidents said they had been raped or attacked more than once, and only 8 percent said they had reported any rape incident to law enforcement authorities. A study by Hindelang and his associates (Hindelang et al., 1976), designed to gather victimization rates on randomly selected households, found that only about one out of every four forcible or attempted rapes was reported to law enforcement agencies. A study of hitchhike rape estimates that over two-thirds go unreported (Nelson & Amir, 1975). Based on a national sample of college students from thirty-two U.S. colleges and universities, Koss and her colleagues (Koss, Gidycz, & Wisniewski, 1987) discovered that about 28 percent of the college women had been victims of rape or attempted rape (as defined by the UCR). More startling, however, was the finding that virtually none of the incidents were reported to the police and thus were not recorded in official crime statistics. Based on their data, Koss estimates that the victimization rate for women is 3,800 per 100,000, a rate drastically different from the official rates of 65 to 75 per 100,000.

Additional victimization data indicate that there is approximately a 1 in 5 chance that a woman will be raped at some time during her lifetime (Furby, Weinrott, & Blackshaw, 1989). If we include *attempted* rape, the odds may be 3 to 1 (Russell & Howell, 1983). As mentioned previously, a surprising number of women are sexually victimized while on a date. Approximately 22 percent of college women surveyed indicated they had been subjected to a forced sexual encounter (e.g., fondling, oral sex, or intercourse) by a *date* at some point in their lives (Yegidis, 1986; Dull & Giacopassi, 1987). Rapaport and Burkhart (1984) found that 15 percent of a sample of college men acknowledged that they had obtained sexual intercourse against their dates' will. Koss, Gidycz, & Wisniewski (1987) report that about 8 percent of their sample of nearly 3,000 college men admitted raping or attempting to rape their dates.

Some data suggest that reporting may be on the increase. Chappell (1977a) found that rates of reported rape more than doubled over a ten-year period, and others note that they continue to increase steadily (U.S. Department of Justice, 1988). During the interval from 1978 to 1988, for example, the incidence of reported forcible rape increased 21 percent. This continuing increase in reporting probably reflects a higher level of commmunity awareness about rape, the influence of the women's movement, increased training and sensitivity of law enforcement officers, and the gradual revision of statutes and procedures that make the gathering of legal evidence less stressful for the victim. In Chappell's national survey of 150 prosecutors' offices (Chappell, 1977b), 61 percent of the respondents believed that the increased reporting rape rate reflected a change in public attitude toward crime. Another third of the prosecutors felt that the increase was a result of the heightened sensitivity of the criminal justice system. It is interesting to note, however, that a vast majority of the prosecutors felt that the increased rape rate also reflected to some extent a "general pattern of increased violence" in America.

The psychological effects on the rape victim, both during and after the assault, are often severe and incalculable. She is frequently victimized twice—by the assailant and by the criminal justice process. Upon reporting the assault, she is expected to recall and describe personally stressful and humiliating events in vivid detail for law enforcement personnel, who often are men. She is also required to undergo a medical examination to establish physical evidence of penetration and use of physical force.

If the victim is able to withstand these stressful conditions, which are sometimes exacerbated by negative reactions from parents, husband, friends, and even by threats from the assailant, she then must prepare for the courtroom, where her privacy is invaded and her credibility may be attacked. Rape trials are usually covered extensively by the press, although most news organizations do not reveal the victim's name or photograph her. Her reputation, however, is especially vulnerable. Ninety-two percent of the prosecutors surveyed by Chappell asserted that victim credibility was one of the most important elements in convincing juries to convict for forcible rape. Therefore, the defense often has concentrated on the victim's prior sexual history to destroy her credibility and to portray her as a demirep. The strategy of disparaging the victim in this way has come under attack in recent years, and many states have revised their evidentiary rules in an attempt to limit the use of a victim's sexual history. Approximately forty states have enacted "rape shield" laws which restrict, to varying degrees, the admissiability of the victim's sexual history into the courtroom (Borgida, 1980). In addition, victim assistants, whose function it is to offer support, give direct services, and advocate for victims, have been instrumental in easing her burden.

Although criminal justice agencies are beginning to be more sensitive to the painful ordeal a victim must go through, the costs are still high. If the woman reports the sexual assault to the police, it means she must devote many hours to the process of the investigation and the subsequent court proceedings (Burt & Katz, 1985). She must bear the costs of missed days of work, child care, medical expenses for the physical and psychological trauma, and transportation. She may feel a need to change life styles, move, and install expensive security systems and locks. Sleeplessness, anxiety, and depression must also be factored into the cost equation. We will discuss these issues in more detail shortly.

Situational and Victimization Characteristics

The Chappell surveys (1977a, 1977b) found that rapes in large cities are most likely to occur in the victim's residence or, less frequently, outdoors. In cities under 100,000 population, and especially in rural areas, they are most likely to occur in motor vehicles, a fact which may reflect the higher frequency of hitchhiking in smaller communities. In fact, hitchhiking (by the victim) accompanied 20 percent of all rapes reported in small cities, compared to 10 percent in large metropolitan areas.

The use of alcohol and other disinhibiting substances is common in rapists. The substance abuse is apparent both in the personal history of the rapist and at the time of the offense. Anywhere between 42 to 90 percent of convicted rapists admit they were under the influence of a disinhibiting substance at the time of the sexual assault, and between 58 to 90 percent exhibit a history of substance abuse (Marques & Nelson, 1989; Pithers et al., 1989).

Women's fears about being physically harmed in rape are not unfounded. While weapons, especially firearms and knives, are used in only about 25 percent of the reported assaults (U.S. Department of Justice, 1988), about one-fourth of all rape victims sustain injury serious enough to warrant medical attention or hospitalization. *Severe physical* injury, however, is relatively rare, with about 5 percent receiving serious, lasting injury (Williams & Holmes, 1981). Another 39 percent receive minor injury, and 23 percent receive a variety of cuts and bruises (Williams & Holmes, 1981). A recent study suggests that women receive more physical and psychological trauma from sexual assault by husbands than by strangers (Kilpatrick et al., 1988). Furthermore, the psychological damage is apparently longer lasting and more damaging, resulting in serious depression, extensive fears, and problems of sexual adjustment.

Victim surveys also indicate that the most commonly used methods of force during date rapes are verbal persuasion, alcohol, or drugs. While weapons are rarely used, physical overpowering (similar to a wrestling match) is commonly reported (Kanin, 1984). Furthermore, data suggest that date rapes occur most frequently in the male's apartment or room, with the next likely location being the female's apartment or room. Very few occur in a car or outside.

Rapists often expect more than vaginal intercourse. In approximately 25 percent of the rapes Chappell studied, the assailant also demanded oral sexual acts; in about 10 percent he demanded both oral and anal sexual acts; in about 6 percent, anal sexual acts only; and in 4 percent other sexual actions. Amir (1971) reported similar patterns.

Offender Characteristics

What kind of a person rapes? How did he get that way? Why does he do it? Can the "rapist personality" be easily identified? Are rapists mentally disordered? In this section, we should keep in mind that many studies addressing these questions are based on information obtained from convicted offenders located in prisons, forensic evaluation clinics, or secure psychiatric facilities, a very biased sample, since less than 3 percent of reported rapes in the United States result in a conviction (Battelle Law and Justice Study Committee, 1977).

The most consistent demographic finding is that rapists tend to be young. According to UCR data, over half of those arrested are under age twenty-five, and 80 percent are under age thirty. Henn and his colleagues (Henn, Herjanic, & Vanderpearl, 1976a) reported that 75 percent of those accused of rape and referred to a mental health evaluation team in St. Louis between the years 1952 and 1973 were under age thirty. The Queen's Bench Foundation (1978) found that 70 percent of its sample of seventy-three convicted rapists were under age twenty-five. The National Crime Survey estimates that nearly one-quarter of the rapes or attempted rapes in any given year are committed by offenders between the ages of twelve and twenty. Davis and Leitenberg (1987) found that when both arrest statistics and victim surveys are considered, about 20 percent of all rapes and about 30 to 50 percent of all cases of child sexual abuse can be attributed to adolescent offenders. In fact, 50 percent of all adult sex offenders report that their first sexual offense occurred during adolescence (Abel, Mittelman, & Becker, 1985).

Another consistent finding is that men accused of and convicted of rape have been in perpetual conflict with society, long before the current rape offense. About one-fourth of those arrested for forcible rape have raped previously, and about one-third have a prior arrest history for violent offenses other than rape (Chappell, 1977a). In a sample of 114 convicted rapists studied by Scully and Marolla (1984), 12 percent had a previous conviction for rape or attempted rape, 39 percent had previous convictions for burglary and robbery, 29 percent for abduction, 25 percent for sodomy, and 11 percent for first or second degree murder. Overall, 82 percent had a prior criminal record, but only 23 percent had been convicted of sexual offenses. Gebhard et al. (1965) reported that 87 percent of their sample of sexual offenders (mostly rapists) had been convicted of some other crime besides their sexual offense prior to age twenty-six.

Occupationally, people arrested for rape tend to come from the so-called blue-collar working class (about 50 percent) and from the ranks of the unemployed (approximately 30 percent). In the Scully and Marolla (1984) study, only 20 percent of all convicted rapists had a high school education or better, and 85 percent came from working-class backgrounds. Very few individuals from the professional or white-collar occupational fields are arrested for rape. A study conducted in England (Wright, 1980) reports that 75 percent of those arrested for rape were in the unskilled working class, and only 2 percent were classified as professional or managerial. Interestingly, when professional people are accused in the U.S., their numbers drop precipitously when the rape charge gets to the prosecutor's office, while the other occupational groups remain about the same. At face value, these data suggest that the more affluent or privileged offender is more likely to be filtered out early in the judicial process than the less privileged, less powerful offender.

According to prosecutors, about one-fourth of those accused of rape admitted that the incident was planned and premeditated (Chappell, 1977b). The problem with this statistic, of course, is that most suspects are unwilling to admit premeditation, since it makes the case against them that much stronger. Therefore, it is highly probable that the number of premeditated rapes is substantially higher than those reported by prosecutors. On the basis of an analysis of reported rapes in Philadelphia, Amir (1971) claims that 71 percent were planned. In the Queen's Bench Foundation study (1978), over two-thirds of the convicted rapists interviewed admitted that they had clearly set out to commit a rape.

Traditionally, the rapist has been considered by many clinicians the victim of "uncontrollable urges" (Edwards, 1983) or the recipient of a "disordered personality" (Scully & Marolla, 1984). Psychiatric criminology has, for a long time, dominated the popular literature on the sexual offender and continues to have substantial impact on the thinking of Western civilization. As Scully and Marolla (1985) observe, the psychiatric literature as well as the general public have traditionally attributed four fundamental causes for rape behavior. They are: (1) uncontrollable impulses or urges; (2) mental illness or disease; (3) momentary loss of control precipitated by unusual circumstances; and (4) victim instigation. Further, Scully and Marolla assert that each of these statements attribute the cause of the rape behavior to parameters *outside* of the rapist himself, often to the victim. In other words, the traditional psychiatric literature has consistently attributed the causal factors of sexual deviations to circumstances beyond the offender's direct or immediate control. Empirical research has *not* supported these assumptions, however. After discussing each in brief, we will outline what researchers *have* been finding.

Uncontrollable or *irresistible impulse* attribution refers to a psychological state where the normal restraints of self-control are substantially reduced or virtually eliminated by an overwhelming sex drive. The major argument from this perspective maintains that high levels of sexual deprivation may cause a bubbling over of an innate, natural sex drive of such intensity that the individual loses control of his behavior and consequently can no longer help himself. Driven by this powerful, biological force his only release is immediate sexual gratification. Symons (1979), for example, writes that men's sexual impulses are part of human nature and that men innately seek "no-cost, impersonal copulations."

Mental illness or *disease* attribution contends that rape—and most other sexual deviations—is symptomatic of some deep-seated sickness or mental aberration. All sexual offenders are basically "sick" and in need of help. Inherent in this perspective is the conviction that sexually deviant behaviors are similar in causation and represent a single type of psychopathology, usually some form of character disorder (Lanyon, 1986). According to Lanyon (1986, p. 176), this belief "tends to be the view held by the judicial system, by social service agencies, and by the general public." And as Scully and Marolla (1985) point out, "belief that rapists are or must be sick is amazingly persistent" (p. 298). Also related to this perspective is the contention that many rapists are actually latent homosexuals who sexually assault a female to prove their masculinity to themselves and others.

A recent development within the disease model perspective is the contention that sexual offending represents an addiction (e.g., Carnes, 1983). This sexual-addiction approach is persuasive and appealing because sex offending has some obvious and compelling similarities to other forms of addiction, such as alcoholism, overeating, gambling, shoplifting, and drug abuse. Interestingly, the approach relies heavily on the same treatment strategies advocated by Alcoholics Anonymous (AA) and emphasizes the "twelve steps to recovery." Consequently, various self-help groups have appeared, such as Sex and Love Addicts Anonymous, Sexaholics Anonymous, Sexual Addicts Anonymous, and Sexual Abuse Anonymous. The basic text for Sex and Love Addicts Anonymous (Augustine Fellowship, 1986), for example, states that one's need for a close relationship with another "could be debased by addiction into a compulsive search for sex and romance, or obsessional entrapment in relationships characterized by personal neediness and hyperdependency—in patterns that could forever prevent really meeting the underlying need for authentic experience of self and other" (p. viii). These groups and approaches should not be confused with Relapse Prevention (RP), a new treatment regimen that shows considerable promise in the reduction of sexual offending. We will be discussing this form of treatment near the end of this chapter.

A third popular belief, *drug attribution*, argues that one can momentarily lose control of one's urges in certain circumstances, such as through the use of drugs or alcohol. Alcohol, for example, is believed to remove social and moral constraints, leaving some men at the mercy of their sexual appetites. This desire simply becomes overwhelming, causing some men to attack the most convenient victim. In one study, two-thirds of the men who raped their dates attributed their assaults to excessive drinking (Kanin, 1984). They claimed the date rape was caused by their own inebriation together with a loss of judgment due to high levels of sexual excitement. One-fifth were convinced that there was no way the attack would have occurred had they been sober.

The fourth perspective, *victim attribution*, contends that the victim has, in some way, led the perpetrator into temptation. Rape, according to this view, is a sexual act that is promoted unconsciously by the female. "Nice girls don't get raped" or at least they don't "let it get out of hand." Hitchhike rape, for example, is, according to this view, probably victim-precipitated rape. Because of their unconscious desires, women unwittingly cooperate with the rapist by making themselves available to him various ways. In the Kanin (1984, p. 96) date rape study, two-thirds of the men said "that although it was probably rape in the legal sense, the fault for the incident resided with the female because of her sexual conduct. According to these males, the sexual demeanor of their victims literally absolved them of guilt so that we are now confronted with something akin to justifiable rape, an analogue to justifiable homicide." Several major surveys conducted on a wide section of the American population strongly suggest that many people continue to believe a victim is at least partially responsible for her rape and that only certain girls get raped (Lottes, 1988).

As noted earlier, empirical study has *not* supported the validity of these four fundamental assumptions; it does, however, support their persistence. In other words, people continue to believe that rape is caused by drugs, precipitated by the victim, or is the product of mental illness or the offender's uncontrollable urges or addiction. These misconceptions are held by offenders as well as others. Scully and Marolla (1984) interviewed 114 convicted rapists to obtain information about their perceptions, motivations, and afterthoughts and found that most could be divided into two major groups, "admitters" and "deniers." Admitters essentially corroborated the story told by police and victims. Deniers' versions differed significantly from those of police and victims. The researchers identified forty-seven admitters and thirty-two deniers. Apparently, the remainder could not be classified into either category.

Deniers justified their rape behavior primarily by making the victim blameworthy. Five themes ran through these justifications: (1) Women are seductresses; (2) women mean yes when they say no; (3) most women eventually relax and really enjoy it; (4) nice girls don't get raped; and (5) the act was a minor wrongdoing, since the victims were not physically hurt. Thirty-one percent of the deniers said the victim was the aggressor: a seductress who lured them, unsuspecting, into sexual action. About 22 percent said the victim had not resisted enough or that her no had really meant yes. As one offender put it, despite some struggle, "deep down inside I think she felt it was a fantasy come true." Sixty-nine percent of the deniers justified their behavior by claiming not only that the victim was willing, but also that she enjoyed herself, in some cases to an immense degree. Most of the deniers (69 percent) were convinced that "nice girls don't get raped." Their victims, they said, had dressed seductively, were hitchhiking, or were generally known to be "loose."

The belief that bad things happen to bad people and good things happen to good people is called by psychologists the *just world hypothesis* (Lerner, 1980), mentioned in chapter one. It is the simplistic belief that one gets what one deserves and deserves what one gets. Just-worlders—people who are most apt to adopt this hypothesis—believe that victims of misfortune or crime deserve their fate. Deniers noted that their victims should not have been in the bar alone, should not have been hitchhiking, or should have worn a bra. The deniers, in this sense, were just-worlders.

A majority of the deniers said that their actions were not reprehensible since they believed they had not physically harmed the victim. Many felt that, although their behavior was not completely proper, it should not have been considered a serious criminal offense, despite the fact that they had threatened their victims with lethal weapons.

Admitters, in contrast to deniers, regarded their behavior as morally wrong and as a serious, harmful attack on their victims. However, most of them tried to diminish their own culpability by asserting that they could not help themselves or were compelled by forces outside their control. Three themes ran through the admitters' justifications: (1) the use of alcohol and drugs; (2) emotional problems; and (3) a "nice guy" self-image. Over three-fourths said they had been under the influence of alcohol or drugs at the time of the attack and that the substance had influenced their judgment and behavior. They were convinced that the ingested substance had, in effect, reduced their awareness as well as their self-control. Normally, they said, they would not have engaged in such a disgusting act.

Forty percent of the admitters said they believed emotional problems were at the root of their rape behavior, and 33 percent specifically cited an unhappy, unstable childhood or a marital-domestic situation. Furthermore, 80 percent of the admitters described an upsetting problem or anger-inducing event that occurred prior to the attack. Consistently, Scully and Marolla (1984) found that these men described themselves as being in a rage because of an incident involving a woman with whom they believed they were in love. By contrast, only about 20 percent of the deniers described such problems.

Most of the admitters described themselves as "nice guys," who under normal circumstances would never dream of doing such a violent thing to a woman. In other words, their actions during that violent episode did not represent their true selves. Many expressed regret and sorrow for their victim and apologized to the researchers. We will return to these justifications and excuses later in this chapter.

Classification of Rape Patterns

Since such a wide variety of sexual offenders are involved in rape, some interesting attempts have been made to categorize rapists according to their behavioral patterns. Researchers at the Massachusetts (Bridgewater) Treatment Center (Cohen, Seghorn, & Calmas, 1969; Cohen et al., 1971; Knight & Prentky, 1987; Prentky & Knight, 1986) recognized that rape involves both sexual and aggressive features and tried to formulate a behavioral classification system that takes these elements into consideration.

Before we proceed, however, it is important to realize that classification systems are permeated with numerous problems and drawbacks. One obvious problem is that individuals do not fit neatly into a category. Furthermore, there may not be *many* who do. As astutely noted by Gibbons (1988), classification systems or typologies generally consist "of criminological foundations that assume that real life persons can be found in significant numbers who resemble the descriptions of offenders in the various typologies that have been put forth. . . . Researchers have often failed to uncover many point-for-point real-life cases of these hypothesized types of offenders" (p. 9). However, typologies or classification systems are valuable in organizing an otherwise confusing array of behaviors. They are also useful in correctional facilities for risk management, such as deciding where to a place an inmate, or in treatment programming, such as deciding what particular treatment modality might be most beneficial for an inmate. It should be stressed, however, that rape is *not* a unified behavior pattern but rather is a complicated, often poorly understood, individualized behavior that appears to be precipitated by a variety of internal and external stimuli.

The Massachusetts Treatment Center (MTC) has identified four major categories of rapists: (1) displaced aggression, (2) compensatory, (3) sexual aggressive, and (4) impulsive rapists. *Displaced aggression* rapists (also called in other classification systems *displaced anger* or *anger-retaliation* rapists) are primarily violent and aggressive in their attack, displaying minimum or total absence of sexual feeling. These men use the act of rape to harm, humiliate, and degrade the woman. The victim is brutally assaulted and subjected to sadistic acts like biting, cutting, or tearing. In most instances, the victim is a complete stranger who happens to be the best available object or stimulus for the violence, although she may possess characteristics that attract the assailant's attention. The assault is not sexually arousing for the displaced aggression rapist, and he often demands oral manipulation or masturbation from the victim to become tumescent. Available evidence suggests that resisting this type of rapist only makes him more violent.

According to Knight and Prentky (1987), an offender must demonstrate the following characteristics during the attack in order to be assigned to the displaced aggression category:

1. The presence of a high degree of nonsexualized aggression or rage expressed either through verbal and/or physical assault that clearly exceeds what is necessary to force compliance of the victim.
2. Clear evidence, in verbalization or behavior, of the intent to demean, degrade, or humiliate the victim.
3. No evidence that the aggressive behavior is eroticized or that sexual pleasure is derived from the injurious acts.
4. The injurious acts are not focused on parts of the body that have sexual significance.

Although many of these rapists are married, they are usually ambivalent toward the women in their lives (Cohen et al., 1971), and their relationships with women are often characterized by frequent irritation and periodic violence. They perceive women as being hostile, demanding, and unfaithful. In addition, they often select as their targets for sexual assault women whom they consider active, assertive, and independent. The occupational history of these assailants is stable and often shows some level of success. Usually, the work is "masculine," such as truck driving, carpentry, construction, or mechanics. The attack typically follows an incident that has upset or angered the rapist, particularly about women and their behavior. The term *displaced aggression* is derived from the fact that the victim rarely has played any direct role in generating the aggression and arousal. This offender often attributes his offense to "uncontrollable impulses."

Compared to other rapists, the childhood of the displaced aggression offender is often chaotic and unstable. Many were physically and emotionally neglected. A large number were adopted or placed in foster homes. About 80 percent were brought up in single-parent homes.

Compensatory rapists rape in response to an intense sexual arousal initiated by stimuli in the environment, often quite specific stimuli. This type of rapist is sometimes referred to in the clinical and research literature as the "power-reassurance," "sexual aim," "ego dystonic," or "true" sex offender. Aggression is not a significant feature here; the basic motivation is a desire to prove sexual prowess and adequacy. In their day-to-day lives, compensatory rapists tend to be extremely passive, withdrawn, and socially inept. They live in a world of fantasy that centers on images of eagerly yielding victims who will submit to pleasurable intercourse and find the rapist's performance so outstanding that they will plead for a return engagement. The compensatory rapist's fantasies or personal versions of the world may so distort his view of the victim that he may seek further contact with her, even if she strongly resisted the sexual assault.

Although his victim is usually a stranger, the compensatory rapist has probably seen her frequently, watched her, or followed her. Specific stimuli associated with her probably excite him. For example, he may be drawn to college women but may feel the attraction would not be mutual if he approached them via a socially accepted route. He cannot face the prospect of rejection. However, if he can prove his sexual prowess, the victim will appreciate his value. If the victim vigorously resists the compensatory rapist, he is likely to flee; if she submits passively, he will rape without much force or violence. This sexually aroused passive assailant will often ejaculate spontaneously, even on mere physical contact with the victim. In general, he does not demonstrate other kinds of antisocial behavior.

The compensatory rapist is often described by others as a quiet, shy, submissive, lonely "nice man." Although he is a reliable worker, his withdrawn, introverted behavior, lack of self-esteem, and low levels of need for achievement usually preclude academic, occupational, or social success. His rapes—or attempts at rape—are an effort to compensate for his sense of inadequacy, hence the category to which he is assigned. More recent research by Knight and Prentky (1987) questions the incompetence issue. They found that, compared to the other rapist types, the compensatory rapist evidenced the best heterosexual adaptation and achieved the highest employment skill level. If this finding is replicated, the very term *compensatory rapist* would become misleading.

The *sexual aggressive* or *sadistic* rapist is the one in whom sexual and aggressive features seem to coexist at equal or near-equal levels. In order for him to experience sexual arousal, it must be associated with violence and pain, which excite him. He rapes, therefore, because of the combination of violence and sexual features in the act. He is convinced that women enjoy being forcefully raped and being dominated and controlled by men. This, he believes, is part of woman's nature. Anger and aggression are not always present during the early stages of the assault, which may actually begin as a seduction. In this sense, the sexual aggressive rapist considers the victim's resistance and struggle a game, a form of protesting too much; what she really wants is to be sexually assaulted and raped. This belief appears deeply ingrained and widely accepted in many Western societies (Edwards, 1983). Consider the following remarks made by a Scottish attorney general: "M.P.s would do well to remember that rape involves an activity which was normal . . . it was part of the business of men and women that they hunted and were hunted and said 'yes' and 'no' and meant the opposite" (Edwards, 1983, p. 114).

Sexual aggressive offenders are often married, but because they display little commitment or loyalty, they also often have a history of multiple marriages, separations, and divorces. They also may be frequently involved in domestic violence. In fact, their backgrounds include antisocial behaviors beginning during adolescence or before and ranging from truancy to rape-murder. They have been severe management problems in school. Throughout their childhood, adolescence, and adulthood, they exhibit poor behavior controls and a low frustration tolerance. Their childhoods are characterized by physical abuse and neglect.

In the extreme, these rapists engage in sexual sadism much like the displaced aggression rapists: Their victims may be viciously violated, beaten, and even killed. The difference between the two types is that the sexual aggressive rapist derives intense sexual satisfaction from aggression, pain, and violence. In order to qualify for assignment to the sexual aggressive category, the offender needs to demonstrate (1) a level of aggression or violence that clearly exceeds what is necessary to force compliance of the victim; and (2) the explicit, unambiguous evidence that aggression is sexually exciting to him.

A fourth type of rapist, the *impulsive* or *exploitative* type, demonstrates neither strong sexual nor aggressive features, but engages in spontaneous rape when the opportunity presents itself. The rape is usually carried out in the context of another crime, such as robbery or burglary. The victims simply happen to be available, and they are sexually assaulted with minimum extra-rape violence or sexual feeling. Generally, this offender has a long history of criminal offenses other than rape. In order to be assigned to this group, the offender must show (1) callous indifference to the welfare and comfort of victim; and (2) the presence of no more force than is necessary to gain the compliance of the victim.

The Massachusetts Treatment Classification scheme offers a rough framework for conceptualizing and simplifying the behaviors and motives involved in rape. Although the categories may need refinement and reconstruction, they represent a beginning toward understanding important individual differences in men who rape. The classifications also underscore the multiple strategies and cognitive beliefs possessed by rapists and discourage dogmatic proclamations about why rape occurs. Finally, they suggest alternative strategies to women who may wonder to what extent they should resist a rapist. It seems fairly clear that compensatory rapists—and possibly also impulsive rapists—will be deterred by a victim who struggles. The displaced aggression rapist, and probably the sexual aggressive one, are apt to respond with more violence.

Groth (1979) has developed a typology with many similarities to the MTC scheme. The Groth proposal is based on the presumed motivations and aims that underlie almost all rapes. Rape is seen as a "pseudo-sexual act" in which sex serves merely as a vehicle for the primary motivations of power and aggression. Groth—rather dogmatically—asserts, "Rape is never the result simply of sexual arousal that has no other opportunity for gratification. . . . Rape is always a symptom of some psychological dysfunction, either temporary and transient or chronic and repetitive" (p. 5). Later, he states, "Rape is always and foremost an aggressive act" (p. 12). Consequently, Groth divides rape behavior into three major categories: anger rape, power rape, and sadistic rape.

In *anger rape*, the offender uses more force than necessary for compliance and engages in a variety of sexual acts that are particularly degrading or humiliating to the female (such as sodomy, fellatio, or even urinating on her). He also expresses his contempt for the victim through abusive and profane language. Thus, for the anger rapist, rape is an act of conscious anger and rage toward women, and he expresses his fury physically and verbally. Sex is actually dirty, offensive, and disgusting to him and this is why he uses it to defile and degrade the victim. Very often his attacks are prompted by some previous conflict or humiliation by some significant female (often a wife, a boss, or a mother). The assault is characterized by considerable physical brutality.

In *power rape*, the assailant seeks to establish power and control over his victim. Thus, the amount of force and threat used depends on the degree of submission shown by the victim. "I told her to undress and when she refused I struck her across the face to show her I meant business" (Groth, 1979, p. 26). His goal is sexual conquest, and he will try to overcome any resistance. Sexual intercourse is his way of asserting identity, authority, potency, mastery, and domination rather than strictly sexual gratification. Often the victim is kidnapped or held captive in some fashion, and she may be subjected to repeated assaults over an extended period of time. The sexual assault is sometimes disappointing to the power rapist because it fails to live up to his frequent fantasies of rape. "Everything was pleasurable in the fantasy, and there was acceptance, whereas in the reality of the situation, it wasn't pleasurable, and the girl was scared, not turned on to me" (Groth, 1979, p. 27).

The third pattern of rape, *sadistic rape*, includes both sexual and aggressive components. In other words, aggression is eroticized. The sadistic rapist experiences sexual arousal and excitement in the victim's maltreatment, torment, distress, helplessness, and suffering. The assault usually involves bondage and torture, and he directs considerable abuse and injury on various areas of the victim's body. Prostitutes, women he considers promiscuous, or women representing symbols of something he wants to punish or destroy often incur the wrath of the sadistic rapist. The victim may be stalked, abducted, abused, and sometimes murdered.

Groth (1979) reports that over half of the offenders evaluated or treated by his agency (Connecticut Sex Offender Program) were power rapists, 40 percent were anger rapists, and only 5 percent were sadistic rapists. The similarities between Groth's scheme and the MTC typology are multiple. The anger rapist is similar to the displaced aggressive rapist, the sadistic rapist is similar to the sexual aggressive rapist, and the power rapist shows many commonalities with the compensatory rapist.

Etiology

Generally speaking, sexual socialization plays a crucial role in the rapist's perceptions of what the rape accomplishes and what is "masculine." It is important to realize that sexual socialization (or sexual training) is rarely acquired entirely from home or school; much of it comes from peers, friends, the entertainment media, and experimentation. Most of us, even as children, were fed misconceptions, taboos, and strategies for dealing with the opposite sex. Males often learn it is "manly" to take the sexual initiative and to persist, even against resistance. Details of a sexual conquest, related to buddies, represent the badge of masculinity and self-worth. On the other hand, if attempts to conquer turn into a comedy of errors, they are seen as personal failure and sexual inadequacy. In addition, many people (both men and women) learn that a woman cannot be raped unless she wants to be. Others learn that women want to be dominated and controlled and that successful lovers demonstrate the "I'm-the-boss" syndrome. It is interesting to note in this context that some victims actually receive marriage proposals from their assailant (Russell, 1975). Other rapists ask their victims to evaluate their performance during or after the act.

Some researchers have proposed an immaturity hypothesis to account for much rape. Goldstein (1977) found that a sample of convicted sex offenders (who were mostly rapists) continued in adulthood to derive most of their sexual pleasure from fantasizing sexual stimuli they had derived from the media or from their own imagination. Average males (controls), by contrast, drew much of their sexual pleasure from real-life sexual encounters. Goldstein also discovered that many rapists have pervasive and obsessive preoccupations with sexual matters, to the point where the sexual preoccupation permeates their lives, and where normally nonerotic material becomes vividly incorporated into sexual fantasies.

Goldstein found that rapists, compared to the average male, relied substantially more on masturbation during adulthood, and that this was frequently accompanied by erotic material derived from the entertainment media. Furthermore, *all types* of sexual offenders had on the average *fewer* contacts with erotica during their formative years than did most other males. In addition, sexual curiosity was often repressed because of a punitive parental approach to matters sexual. Together, these factors provide a conducive setting for sexual misconceptions and ignorance.

Koss and Dinero (1988) conducted a well-designed survey of approximately 3,000 male students at thirty-two U.S. colleges and universities. Students were asked questions about the extent of verbal coercion and physical force they had used to become sexually intimate with women without their consent. They were also questioned about attitudes and habits. The results indicated that highly sexually aggressive men expressed greater hostility toward women, frequently used alcohol, frequently viewed violent and degrading pornography (in contrast to Goldstein's finding), and were closely involved with peer groups that reinforce highly sexualized and dominating views of women. In addition, the more sexually aggressive the student, the more likely he was to believe that force and coercion are legitimate ways to gain compliance in sexual relationships. The researchers concluded: "In short, the results provided support for a developmental sequence for sexual aggression in which early experiences and psychological characteristics establish conditions for sexual violence" (p. 144).

In summary, most rapists seem to subscribe to attitudes and ideology that encourage men to be dominant, controlling, and powerful, whereas women are expected to be submissive, permissive, and compliant. Such an orientation seems to have a particularly strong disinhibitory effect on sexually aggressive men, encouraging them to interpret the ambiguous behavior of females as come-ons, to believe that women are not really offended by coercive sexual behaviors, and to perceive rape victims as desiring and deriving gratification from being sexually assaulted (Lipton, McDonel, & McFall, 1987).

Additional evidence of rapists' deviant attitudes and beliefs comes from physiological research. Abel and his associates (Abel et al., 1977; Abel et al., 1978) have found that rapists show high and nearly equal sexual arousal to audiotaped portrayals of both rape and consenting sexual acts. The degree of sexual arousal was indicated by the subject's penile tumescence, which is measured by a device called a plethysmograph. Male non-rapists, on the other hand, show significantly less penile tumescence to rape depictions. In fact, convicted rapists became highly aroused by rape depictions in which the victim experiences abhorrence and pain rather than sexual pleasure. Encouraged by these findings, Abel developed a physiological measure called the "rape index." The index is arrived at by dividing the average percent of full penile erection to rape stimuli by the average percent of full penile erection to consenting sexual stimuli. Avery-Clark and Laws (1984) have developed a similar indicator for pedophiles called the "Dangerous Child Abuser Index." Today, many investigators use this measure in the diagnosis and treatment of rapists as well as child molesters. Generally, research suggests that rapists tend to have a higher rape index than nonrapists. The overall accuracy of the penile plethysmograph and its sensitivity to extraneous factors and faking remain very much in question, however.

Abel and his group also discovered that some rapists became highly sexually aroused even to scenes of *nonsexual* aggression, such as a man beating a woman with his fists. Thus, it appears that some men strongly associate aggression and violence toward women with sexual arousal, a pattern very similar to that of the sexual agressive rapist described earlier. In fact, in rapists the intensity of this deviant arousal has been found to be positively related to the number of rapes committed and the degree of injury inflicted on victims (Abel et al., 1978). Some rapists apparently find scenes that show women being beaten exciting and pleasurable. In addition, male spouse abusers may, in part, be motivated by such arousal. On the other hand, a majority of men (70 percent) in the general population find the presence of aggression inhibiting to sexual arousal (Malamuth, Check, & Briere, 1986). Interestingly, men in the general population who are sexually aroused by force also are more accepting of an ideology that justifies male aggression against and dominance over women. These men also admit that they would probably rape if the opportunity were presented.

The role played by fantasy and imagination in the development of sexually aggressive behavior is becoming an increasingly important topic (Laws & Marshall, in press). Self-reports by sexual offenders find that frequent imagery and fantasy of sexually aggressive scenes is extremely important in motivating and guiding overt sexual aggression. Aggressive fantasies are particularly exciting to men convicted of rape (Abel et al., 1977). Interestingly, in a SR survey of 114 college men conducted by Greendlinger and Byrne (1987), over one-third indicated they fantasize about aggressively raping a woman, and 54 percent fantasize about forcing a woman to have sex.

Related to the role played by fantasy in the development of sexual deviance is the role played by masturbation. The intrinsically physiological pleasure and arousal generated by masturbation can serve as a strong bonding agent, particularly if paired repeatedly with some fantasized object or person. Also, it is important to realize that there are two powerfully reinforcing processes in masturbatory activity: sexual arousal and the reduction of that arousal at orgasm. Fantasized or actual behaviors which are sexually arousing and which result in sexual satisfaction (i.e., orgasm) are likely to increase in strength and frequency. This process is known as "masturbatory conditioning" (Marshall & Barbaree, 1988). On the basis of clinical studies (e.g., Groth, 1979; Marshall, 1988; George & Marlatt, 1989), it appears that masturbatory conditioning may play a very integral part in the development of both normal and deviant sexual behavior.

In sum, the evidence to date indicates overwhelmingly that rapists learn to be rapists and that much of the teaching is done by equally naive peers, parents, significant social models, and the entertainment media. Rape springs from a culture, characterized by violence, which communicates a dominant ideology that degrades women and justifies coercive sexuality. Fortunately, most males eventually acquire a close approximation of sexual sophistication and some understanding of the needs of others. Many rapists, however, seem to remain sexually and, in some ways, socially immature.

Attitudes that promote the denigration of women may be widespread, however. There is distressing evidence that rapists may reflect the explicit and implicit beliefs held by many others. For example, in a recent study, 35 percent of male college students on several different campuses felt there was some likelihood that they would rape if they could be sure of getting away with it (Malamuth, 1981). In another study, 60 percent of a group of 352 male undergraduates indicated there was some likelihood they would rape or force a female to perform a sexual act against her will if given the opportunity (Briere, Malamuth, & Ceniti, 1981).

Malamuth (1989) cautions, however, that one does not conclude that subjects who indicate they would sexually force a woman are necessarily "potential rapists." The scale used in his research, Attraction to Sexual Aggression (ASA), is designed to measure the *belief* that actually engaging in sexual aggression would be an arousing, attractive experience. Whether they would act on that belief is dictated by a myriad of factors across a wide spectrum of influences, including the degree of motivation to commit the act, the internal and exernal inhibitions present, and the opportunity to commit the act.

Rape and Pornography

The relationship between rape and pornography is shrouded with confusion and surrounded by debate. Two Presidential Commissions established to study the effect of pornography on crime and human behavior reached opposite conclusions. The first and most comprehensive, established in 1967, was directed not to issue recommendations unless the effects were clearcut. Because of the complexity it uncovered, the Commission could not conclude whether explicit sexual material contributed significantly to sex crimes, prompting then President Richard M. Nixon to remark that the Commission was "morally bankrupt." Many have used this conclusion to support their contention that pornography is not harmful. The second National Commission on Obscenity and Pornography, which issued a report in 1984, recommended widespread restrictions of pornographic material. This Commission has been extensively criticized for its lack of scientific objectivity.

Research evidence has suggested that under certain conditions pornography facilitates aggressive, sexual behavior toward women. Studies by Donnerstein (1983) and Malamuth (Malamuth, Haber, & Feshbach, 1980; Malamuth, Heim, & Feshbach, 1980; Malamuth & Check, 1981) indicate, for example, that a general statement that pornography does *not* negatively influence people needs several qualifiers. In a series of ongoing experiments, Donnerstein finds evidence that three factors influence the relationship between erotica and human aggression: (1) the level of arousal elicited by erotic films; (2) the level of aggressive content; and (3) the reactions of the victims portrayed in these films and photographs. Donnerstein and others (e.g., Meyer, 1972; Zillman, 1971) angered male subjects in a variety of ways, then found that erotica shown to these aroused subjects significantly increased their aggressive behavior toward others. Because of their arousing properties, the erotic stimuli apparently may promote aggression under certain conditions. This finding accords with Berkowitz's theory (discussed in chapter seven) on the relationship between arousal and aggression. Anything—sexual or not—that increases the arousal level of an already aroused subject will increase aggressive behavior in situations where aggression is the dominant behavior. The increased arousal may also draw the subject away from his own internal control or self-regulatory mechanisms, thereby allowing him to be less concerned about the consequences of his behavior. Furthermore, pornography investigations reveal that if the subject was angered by a woman, he would be even more aggressive toward other women after being exposed to the erotic film. These findings corroborate the frequent clinical observation that prior to a rape many rapists had been angered, upset, humiliated, or insulted, often by a female (e.g., Groth, 1979).

Extremely violent stimuli, both erotic and nonerotic, can also facilitate aggression toward women even in nonangered males under certain conditions. The level of violence in the film appears significant. Portrayals of women being assaulted, even nonsexually, can increase subsequent aggressive behavior by males toward women, even when the males are not angry. Therefore, highly aggressive and violent acts depicted in the media may facilitate the rape act for some males. Since many rapists regard their act as a direct aggressive attack on women, seeing films where women are physically abused may encourage and support their own violent inclinations.

The reactions of the victims portrayed in films also seem crucial. Films or photographs that depict the female victim enjoying rape (common in pornography) encourage acceptance of the rape myth and promote violence against women (Malamuth & Check, 1981). If, on the other hand, the victim finds the rape both painful and abhorrent (negative aggressive erotica), male observers are disinclined to act aggressively. However, several qualifiers must be attached to this finding. If the male observer is already angered (aroused), seeing the victim suffer may make him more aggressive, since any arousal increase in an already aroused subject will increase subsequent aggressive behavior. The specific content of the film becomes irrelevant, as long as it meets the minimum criterion of being somehow arousing. On the other hand, males who are not upset or aroused before seeing a female victim suffer are less likely to aggress against women.

For some individuals, however, due to their conditioning history, pain cues are reinforcing if they are repeatedly associated with sexual gratification. Precisely how they react to various erotic portrayals is unclear, but it seems reasonable to suggest that they would find depictions of pain both highly arousing and supportive of their belief that pain and sexual gratification go together. They might also conclude that the pain-pleasure relationship is inherently characteristic of everyone's sexual gratification and that women really enjoy being "roughed up."

The relationship between violent pornography and sexual aggression remains complex and troubling. Although sexually arousing nonviolent pornography should be available in a free society and arguably has social value, violent pornography has no redeeming value. Its harmful effects, however, are difficult to document except as they relate to a subgroup of individuals. If all violent pornography were eradicated today, sex crimes would likely decrease. The same argument could be made to support confiscation of handguns and rifles, or random, unannounced drug testing of the citizenry. The extent to which a society should be asked to barter freedom in exchange for security remains a topic about which reasonable people consistently disagree.

PEDOPHILIA

Pedophilia, commonly known as "child molestation" or child sexual abuse, is defined in a variety of ways. The DSM-III (1980) defines the term as a condition where an adult fantasizes or engages in sexual activity with pre-pubertal children (age ten or less) as a repeatedly preferred or exclusive method of achieving sexual gratification. According to Finkelhor and Araji (1986), pedophilia is when a male adult has a conscious sexual interest in prepubertal children. One of two behaviors signifies that interest. Either the adult has had some sexual contact with a child (touched the child or had the child touch him with the purpose of his becoming sexually aroused), or the adult has masturbated to sexual fantasies involving children. The last definition recognizes that a male adult may have very strong sexual interest in children and be blocked only by circumstances from acting on it more directly. With the exception of the DSM-III, the term *prepubertal* usually refers to children under the age of thirteen. Occasionally, researchers ex-tend the definition to include ages thirteen through fifteen, but most liter-ature reserves the term *hebephilia* for sexual contact by adult males with young adolescents. Traditionally, most definitions of pedophilia were re-stricted to sexual contact between an adult and child who are not closely related. Sexual acts between members of a family when at least one partici-pant is a minor were typically labeled "incest." More recent research and commentary, however, have placed all sexual contacts between an adult and a child into the pedophilia category. For purposes of clarity, we will use *pedophilia* and *child molestation* interchangeably as umbrella terms for all categories of child sexual abuse.

Incidence and Prevalence

As with sexual offenses in general, a caveat pertaining to the statistics is necessary. Data on pedophilia are difficult to obtain, since there are no central or national objective recording systems for tabulating sexual of-fenses against children. Also, as just noted, offenders may be arrested and prosecuted under a variety of statutes and for a variety of offenses, includ-ing child rape, aggravated assault, sodomy, incest, indecent exposure, or lewd and lascivious behavior. Although the UCR lists sex offenses, it does not differentiate pedophilia from the mixture of other possible sexual of-fenses. However, a variety of retrospective surveys of the general popula-tion indicate that from a quarter to a third of all females and a tenth or more of all males were molested during childhood (Finkelhor & Lewis, 1988; Peters, Wyatt, & Finkelhor, 1986). Moreover, only 35 percent of the children who are sexually victimized report it to anyone (Finkelhor, 1979). Russell (1984) found that in her sample only 2 percent of all incestuous abuse cases and 6 percent of all cases of extrafamilial abuse of females under eighteen had ever been reported to the police. From a national survey of about 1,200 American males (Finkelhor & Lewis, 1988), it is estimated that between 5 and 10 percent of the male population has engaged or will engage in child sexual abuse at some time in their lives. It is important to note, however, that this figure may include a one-time incident which—although still to be condemned—may not represent the offender's usual behavior and would not qualify him as a pedophile for purposes of this chapter.

In the Russell (1984) survey, 930 randomly selected female residents of San Francisco were interviewed throughout the summer of 1978. The purpose of the project was to obtain an estimate of the incidence and prevalence of rape and other forms of sexual assault, including the amount of sexual abuse respondents experienced as children. Twelve percent of the women said they had been sexually abused by a relative before the age of fourteen. Twenty-nine percent reported at least one experience of sexual abuse by a nonrelative before reaching the age of fourteen. Overall, 28 percent of the 930 women reported at least one incident of sexual abuse before reaching the age of fourteen.

Frisbie (1965) gathered data on nearly 2,000 male sex offenders (including rapists) referred to California's Atascadero State Hospital for psychiatric evaluation. He estimated that 5 out of every 1,000 adult males in the U.S. general population are arrested for child sexual abuse.

Situational and Victimization Characteristics

The offender, or pedophile, is almost always male, but the victim may be of either sex. Heterosexual pedophilia—male adult with female child—appears to be the more common type, with available data indicating that three-quarters of pedophiles choose female victims exclusively (Lanyon, 1986; Langevin, 1983). Homosexual pedophilia—male adult preference for male child—appears to be substantially less frequent (about 20 to 23 percent of the reported cases). A small minority of pedophiles choose their victims from both sexes. The behavior of the pedophile or child molester is usually limited to caressing the child's body, fondling the child's genitals, and/or inducing the child to manipulate his or her genitals. Heterosexual penetration is apparently involved in only a small proportion of the total number of offenses.

The offender and the victim know one another in most instances, often very well (McCaghy, 1967; Virkkunen, 1975; Schultz, 1975). Many victims were actively seeking natural affection from their offenders, as a child seeks to be hugged or cuddled. Some victims feel kindly and lovingly toward the offender, who sometimes interprets this behavior as "seductive." Clinical observations suggest that pedophiles, as a group, tend to have positive feelings toward their victims, generally perceive them as being willing participants, and frequently victimized children living in their immediate households (Miner, Day, & Nafpaktitis, 1989). It is not uncommon for the sexual behavior between the offender and victim to have gone on for a sustained period of time.

The form of the sexual contact seems to depend on three factors: the degree to which the offender had previous nonsexual interactions with children, the nature of the relationship between the child and the offender, and the age of each. Offenders who have had limited interaction with children are more likely to perform or expect genital-genital and oral-genital contact, rather than to indulge only in caressing or fondling. Furthermore, the more familiar the offender and the victim are with one another, the greater the tendency for genital-genital or oral-genital contact.

There is some disagreement about the extent to which child molesters harm the child physically or use physical force. According to most research, pedophiles do not usually use overt physical coercion. McCaghy (1967) found no evidence of any kind of coercion, verbal or physical, in three-fourths of the child molestation cases he examined. Research by Groth and his colleagues (Groth, Hobson, & Gary, 1982) supports these findings. Lanyon (1986), summarizing the research, concluded that violence is involved in about 10 to 15 percent of child sexual abuse cases. However, Hall, Proctor, and Nelson (1988) report that 28 percent of a sample of convicted pedophiles (122 nonpsychotic patients of a state mental hospital) were officially identified as having used physical force or the threat of force beyond what was necessary to gain the victim's compliance. Marshall and Christie (1981) found that in a sample of forty-one pedophiles incarcerated in Canadian federal penitentiaries, twenty-nine had used physical force. In an earlier study of 150 pedophiles, Christie, Marshall, and Lanthier (1979) had reported that 58 percent used excessive force in their attack, and 42 percent of the child victims had sustained notable injury. The researchers suggested that the offenders in their sample were highly sexually aroused by physical violence, significantly more so than other nonaggressive sex offenders. The reported differences in the use of violence and force by pedophiles appears to be explained by the sample used. Studies reporting a high incidence of violence or aggression focus on incarcerated, relatively hard-core offenders, while those reporting little or no violence sampled less-criminal or nonincarcerated pedophiles, generally those on probation.

Groth, Hobson, and Gary (1982) recommend that the few offenders using violence or force and causing physical harm to the child should be labeled "child rapists." On the other hand, those offenders only using psychological pressures should be considered child molesters or pedophiles. Although Groth's suggestion has merit, researchers in this area have used *pedophile* or *child molester* as umbrella terms to cover all child sexual abusers.

Recent research offers strong support for the assumption that sexual abuse in childhood (both violent and nonviolent) produces long-term psychological problems in many children (Briere, 1988). Reports of depression, guilt, feelings of inferiority, substance abuse, suicidality, anxiety, chronic tension, sleep problems, and fears and phobias are common. Depression is the symptom most commonly reported among adults who were molested as children. The extent of psychological damage to the child produced by sexual abuse is dependent on several factors. Groth (1978) contends that the greatest trauma occurs in children who have been victims for long periods of time, are victimized by a closely related person (such as a stepfather), when the victimization involves penetration, and when it is accompanied by aggression. In their careful review of the research literature on pedophilia, Browne and Finkelhor (1986) concluded that: (1) Younger children appear to be somewhat more vulnerable to trauma than older children; (2) the closer the relationship between offender and victim the greater the trauma; and (3) the greater the force used the greater the trauma. They also concluded, however, that there is no conclusive support for the contention that the longer and more frequent the abuse the greater the trauma. Nor is there any clear evidence that trauma is related to the *type* of sexual abuse (intercourse, fondling, fellatio, cunnilingus, etc.). This suggests that "mild" abuse may be as traumatizing as intercourse, especially if the victim is young and closely related to the offender. The Browne and Finkelhor review also suggests that, for some unexplained reason, victims of child sexual abuse are more likely than nonvictims to be sexually assaulted again as adults.

Offender Characteristics

Pedophilia is primarily committed by males, but it is not exclusively a male offense. The National Center on Child Abuse and Neglect (1981) reported that 46 percent of the abusive sexual experiences encountered by children included a female perpetrator. This figure is misleading, however, in that it includes any female caretaker who "permitted acts of sexual abuse to occur" (Russell & Finkelhor, 1984). In other words, leaving the child with a boyfriend as a babysitter who in turn molests the child would be considered sexual abuse by the mother. The mother who fails to report her suspicions that her husband is sexually abusing her daughter may also be included in the statistic. If only those women who actually *committed* child sexual abuse are included, the percentage of female offenders drops to 13 percent in the case of female victims and 24 percent in the case of males (Russell & Finkelhor, 1984). On the basis of their research, Russell and

Finkelhor (1984) suggest that females are involved in about 5 percent of the sexual abuse of girls and about 20 percent of the cases of boys. Because sexual abuse of children by females is so little explored, we will concentrate in the remainder of this chapter on what is known about male pedophiles.

Although there is considerable age variability, the average age of *convicted* male child molesters ranges between thirty-six and forty. While about 75 percent of convicted rapists are under thirty, about 75 percent of convicted child molesters are over that age (Henn, Herjanic, & Vanderpearl, 1976b). Groth (1978), however, notes that all the child molesters he and colleagues have worked with had committed their first child molestation offense before age forty. Over 80 percent were first offenders by age thirty, and about 5 percent had committed their first sexual assault before they reached adolescence. However, despite the statistical finding that child molesters tend to be older than most other sexual offenders, there seems to be a pattern of victim preference as a function of age. Older pedophiles (over fifty) seek out immature children (ten or younger); younger pedophiles (under age forty) prefer girls between the ages of twelve and fifteen (Revitch & Weiss, 1962). The latter are technically classified as hebrophiles.

Perhaps because of the extremely negative attitude society displays toward child molesters, pedophiles almost always resist taking full responsibility for their offenses (McCaghy, 1967). Many claim that they went blank, were too drunk to know what they were doing, could not help themselves, or did not know what came over them. They show a strong preference to attribute the cause of their behavior to external forces or motivating factors largely beyond their personal control.

However, those charged with child molestation rarely manifest any serious or pronounced behavioral or emotional problems other than the pedophilia (Henn, Herjanic, & Vanderpearl, 1976b). When clinical diagnoses are made, they are most often organic brain syndrome (damage) or mental retardation, but still these represent only a small percentage of the total pedophile population. Since pedophilia and exhibitionism are the most common sexual offenses committed by senile and arteriosclerotic men (Coleman, 1976), the organic brain syndrome classification is not really surprising.

Many aggressive pedophiles demonstrate a large number of similarities with rapists and the prison population in general (Knight, Rosenberg, & Schneider, 1985). The most notable commonalities are: (1) They have problems with alcohol; (2) they have a high rate of high school failure and dropout; (3) they tend to have unstable work histories in unskilled occupations; and (4) they tend to come from the low socioeconomic class.

Alcohol abuse is frequently a problem in sex offenders. While about one-third to one-half of convicted rapists have serious problems with alcohol, about one-quarter to one-third of convicted pedophiles have such problems (Knight, Rosenberg, & Schneider, 1985). Research also indicates that a large segment of pedophiles do not progress much beyond the eighth grade in school (Christie, Marshall, & Lanthier, 1979), and many show signs of mental deficiencies on traditional IQ tests (Knight, Rosenberg, & Schneider, 1985; Swanson, 1968).

About two-thirds of those arrested and convicted for child molestation offenses come from the unskilled or semiskilled occupational groups (McCaghy, 1967; Gebhard et al., 1965). However, other occupational groups may handle the incident quite differently to prevent additional trauma for the victim and social embarrassment for their families during the legal investigation and process. In the 1980s, the media were filled with accounts of the alarming increase in child sex abuse rates. These same accounts note that it knows no economic or social barriers: Child offenders exist in all levels of society and among all occupational groups.

Classification of Child Offender Patterns

The Massachusetts Treatment Center (MTC) (Cohen, Seghorn, & Calmas, 1969; Knight, Rosenberg, & Schneider, 1985; Knight, 1988) has been developing a widely cited typology of pedophile behavioral patterns, similar to the rape typology presented earlier. Four major pedophiliac patterns have been identified: (1) the fixated type, (2) the regressed type, (3) the exploitative type, and (4) the aggressive or sadistic type.

The *fixated* (or immature) child molester demonstrates a long-standing, exclusive preference for children as both sexual and social companions. He has never been able to develop a mature relationship with his adult peers, male or female, and he is considered socially immature, passive, timid, and dependent by most people who know him. He feels most comfortable relating to children, whom he seeks out as companions. Sexual contact usually occurs only after the adult and child have become well acquainted. Fixated pedophiles rarely marry, and their social background lacks much evidence of dating peers or even any sustained, long-term friendship with an adult (outside of relatives). This pedophile wishes to touch, fondle, caress, and taste the child. He rarely expects genital intercourse, and very rarely does he use physical force or aggression.

The fixated pedophile generally has average intelligence. His work history is steady, although it is often work that is below his ability. His social skills are adequate for day-to-day functioning. Probably most troubling about the fixated or immature pedophile is that he is not concerned or disturbed about his exclusive preference for children as companions, nor can he see why others are concerned. Therefore, he is difficult to treat and is most likely to recidivate.

The *regressed* pedophile had a fairly normal adolescence and good peer relationships and heterosexual experiences, but later developed feelings of masculine inadequacy and self-doubt. Problems in the individual's occupational, social, and sexual lives followed. The regressed child offender's background commonly includes alcohol abuse, divorce, and a poor employment record. Each pedophilial act is usually precipitated by a significant jolt to the offender's sexual adequacy, either by female or male peers. For example, the pedophile may perceive other males as being more successful with women. Unlike the immature child offender, the regressed child offender usually prefers victims who are strangers and who live outside his neighborhood. The victims are nearly always female. Unlike the fixated pedophile, he seeks genital sex with his victim. Because he feels remorseful and expresses disbelief after that act, clinicians usually find him a good prospect for rehabilitation. As long as stressful events are kept to a minimum and he learns to cope adequately with those he does have, he is unlikely to reoffend.

The *exploitative* pedophile seeks children primarily to satisfy his sexual needs. He exploits the child's weaknesses any way he can, and tries various kinds of strategies and tricks to get him or her to comply. He is usually unknown to the child and commonly tries to get the child isolated from others and his familiar surroundings. If necessary, he will use aggression and physical force to get the child to comply to his wishes. The exploitative offender does not care about the emotional or physical well-being of the child, but only sees the victim as a sexual object.

The exploitative offender exhibits a long history of criminal or antisocial conduct. His relationships with peers are unpredictable and stormy. He is unpleasant to be around and is often avoided by others who know him. He tends to be highly impulsive, irritable, and moody. His markedly defective interpersonal skills may be the principal reason why he chooses children as victims (Knight, Rosenberg, & Schneider, 1985). Clinicians find him difficult to treat as his deficiencies extend to all phases of his daily life.

The *aggressive* (or sadistic) pedophile is drawn to children for both sexual and aggressive reasons. Pedophiles in this group are apt to have a long history of antisocial behavior and poor adaptation to their environments. Most prefer victims of the same sex (homosexual pedophilia). Since the primary aim is to obtain stimulation without consideration for the victim, this group often assaults the child viciously and sadistically. The more harm and pain inflicted, the more this offender becomes sexually excited. Aggressive or sadistic pedophiles are most often responsible for child abductions and murders. Clinicians find this type not only dangerous to children but among the most difficult to treat. Fortunately, this type is rare.

An example of an aggressive child molester was Albert Fish (1870–1936), whose background is discussed by Nash (1975). Fish, called the "moon maniac," admitted sexually molesting more than 400 children over a span of twenty years. In addition, he confessed to six child murders and made vague reference to numerous others. He was eventually convicted of murdering a twelve-year-old girl and was electrocuted in 1936. A more contemporary example might well be John Wayne Gacy, Jr., who sadistically murdered thirty-three teenage boys and young men and buried their bodies in the cellar of his suburban Chicago home.

Fish thought the conditions of his childhood led to a "perverted" life of crime. He was abandoned at an early age and placed in an orphanage, where he first witnessed and experienced brutal acts of sadism. Fish was quoted as saying, "Misery leads to crime. I saw so many boys whipped it ruined my mind." He apparently began his career of child molesting in earnest when his wife deserted him for another man. This suggests that, like regressed offenders, aggressive offenders may begin their crimes in response to precipitating events involving rejection and feelings of sexual inadequacy.

In a classification system similar to that of the Massachusetts Treatment Center, Groth (1978; Groth & Burgess, 1977) classifies child offenders on the basis of the longevity of the behavioral patterns and the offender's psychological aims. If the sexual preference for children has existed persistently since adolescence, he is classified an *immature* or *fixated* child offender. Like the MTC classification system, the fixated child offender has been sexually attracted primarily or exclusively to significantly younger people throughout his life, regardless of what other sexual experiences he has had. Groth believes that this fixation is due to an arrestment of psychological maturation, resulting from unresolved formative issues that persist and underlie subsequent development. On the other hand, if the offender has managed to develop some normalcy to his relationships with adults but resorts to child offending when stressed or suffers a devastating blow to his self-esteem, he is called a *regressed* child offender.

Based on his clinical research, Groth also has subdivided child offenders according to their intentions or psychological aims. He identifies two basic categories: (1) sex pressure offenders, and (2) sex force offenders. In sex pressure offenses, the offender's typical modus operandi is to entice children into sexuality through persuasion or cajolement, or to entrap them by placing them in a situation in which they feel indebted or obligated. A child may feel he owes something to the person who taught him to swim or bought him a bike. The sex force offense, on the other hand, is characterized by threat of harm and/or the use of physical force in the commission of the offense. The offender either intimidates the child by exploiting the child's relative helplessness, naivete, and awe of adults, or attacks and physically overpowers his victim.

Groth finds he can further subdivide the sex force group into the *exploitative* type in which the *threat* of force is used to overcome victim resistance, or the *sadistic* type who derives great pleasure in hurting the child. The exploitative type typically employs verbal threats, restraint, manipulation, intimidation, and physical strength to overcome any resistance on the part of the child. His intent is not necessarily to hurt the child but to obtain compliance. The sadistic type, which fortunately is rare, eroticizes physical aggression and pain. He uses more force than is necessary to overpower the victim and many commit a so-called lust murder. Therefore, the physical and psychological abuse and/or degradation of the child is necessary for him to experience sexual excitement and gratification. Often, the child is beaten, choked, tortured, and violently sexually abused.

Certainly the Groth typology has strong commonalities with the MTC typology. The immature and the regressed child offenders display features of the sex pressure offender, and the aggressive child offender shows strong similaritites to the sex force offender. It may be more appropriate for the present to classify the child offender according to the degree of coercion or force he uses rather than according to personality features. The first method focuses on offender behavior, a criterion which is both more objective and clearcut. The second focuses on "understanding" the behavior by assuming a variety of personal cognitive constructs. We have too little information about child offenders at this point to do that with much confidence.

Recidivism

If pedophilia is learned, we would expect a fairly high incidence of recidivism. Like the national recidivism rates for most offenses, however, pedophile recidivism rates are difficult to confirm. Moreover, the second time around the pedophile is undoubtedly more careful about detection. In the California study by Frisbie (1965), recidivism rates over a five-year period were reported to be 18.2 percent for heterosexual pedophiles and 34.5 percent for homosexual pedophiles. However, as Schultz (1975) noted, most pedophile offenses go unreported. Abel and colleagues (1981) reported that incarcerated homosexual pedophiles had, on the average, thirty-one victims, while heterosexual pedophiles had an average of sixty-two victims. A Dutch study (Bernard, 1975) reported that at least half of its repondents claimed sexual contacts with at least ten or more children. Fourteen percent of the sample—which included both arrested and unarrested pedophiles—admitted to sexual contacts with more than fifty, and 6 percent to contacts with between 100 and 300 children. Fifty-six percent of this sample indicated they had one or more "regular" sexual contacts with children. Fully 90 percent asserted that they did not want to stop their pedophilial activities.

Abel et al. (1988) report that of the 192 nonincarcerated child offenders who voluntarily participated in a treatment program, the men most likely to drop out of treatment were those with a history of considerable and varied pedophilic behavior. That is, 70 percent of the frequent child offenders who demonstrated no age preference (child or adolescent) nor gender preference (male or female) dropped out of treatment, usually early in the process. The treatment program consisted of thirty ninety-minute group sessions given weekly and directed at decreasing deviant arousal, developing cognitive restructuring of distorted sexual attitudes and beliefs, and increasing subjects' social competence with adults. In addition, those subjects who managed to complete the program and who had varied child offending behavior and multiple victims were the ones who were most likely to recidivate within one year after treatment.

Further indications of recidivism rates of child offenders can be garnered from the thirteen-year outpatient treatment program described by Marshall and Barbaree (1988). This Canadian project offered psychological treatment of deviant sexual behavior on a voluntary basis to a variety of sexual offenders. Forty percent of the child offenders refused treatment. The project had access to official records (charges and convictions) throughout North America as well as to information from "unofficial" files of local police departments and Children's Aid Societies in the towns where the offenders lived. Thirty-two percent of the untreated child offenders reoffended compared to 14 percent of the treated offenders. The average follow-up period for both groups was approximately three and a half years. In reference to the twenty-six men who recidivated, only eleven were identified "officially" (charges and convictions), whereas the remainder were identified through the "unofficial" information. Even so, the unofficial measures of recidivism were still official in that they were collected by public agencies, which leaves us still wondering how high the "unofficial" recidivism rates for child offenders really are.

Etiology

Most explanations of pedophilia focus on a single factor as the principal cause of sexual and social preferences for children by adults. One clinical hypothesis, for example, suggests that pedophiles select children as sex objects because they are haunted by feelings of masculine and sexual inadequacy in adult relationships (e.g., Groth, Hobson, & Gary, 1982). They are terrified of being ridiculed in their sexual and social behavior by the adult world. In the world of the child, they can be safely curious, awkward, and inexperienced. This observation might help explain why pedophiles rarely engage in heterosexual intercourse. Although this inadequacy hypothesis appears to have some validity, it fails to explain the full range and diversity of pedophilic behavior.

Finkelhor and Araji (1986) find four basic explanations for pedophilia in the research and clinical literature: emotional congruence, sexual arousal, blockage, and disinhibition theories. The most common is what they call *emotional congruence* theories. These theories try to explain why a person would find relating sexually to a child to be emotionally gratifying and congruent with their needs. Finkelhor and Araji refer to these explanations as emotional congruent theories since they convey the idea of a fit between the adult's emotional needs and the child's characteristics. Most congruence theories are psychoanalytic in origin and focus on "arrested psychological development." According to this perspective, pedophiles see themselves as children with childish emotional needs and dependency, and consequently feel most comfortable with children. A similar version focuses on the low self-esteem and a loss of efficacy pedophiles experience in their daily lives. Relating to a child is congruent because the inadequate adult finally feels powerful, omnipotent, and in control of a relationship. In short, relating to a child provides a sense of mastery and control in their lives.

The second group of theories tries to explain why pedophiles become sexually aroused by certain characteristics of children. Sexual arousal is typically measured by penile tumescence to the presence of children or to sexual fantasies of children. Called *sexual arousal* theories, this perspective contends that pedophiles become sexually aroused to stimuli (features of children) that, for a variety of reasons, do not generate sexual arousal in normal males. One set of theories within this group posits that it is a common childhood experience to engage in sexual play with playmates. For the pedophile, the childhood sexual play may have been particularly vivid, rewarding, stimulating, and even possibly the most sexually exciting experience he has ever had. Adult sexual play, by comparison, was less arousing, satisfying, or rewarding, perhaps even nonexistent. The pedophile's shyness, for example, may have precluded adult sexual contacts. Under these conditions, he probably took the most available sexual avenue, masturbation. As noted earlier, the powerful reinforcing role of masturbatory behavior (masturbatory conditioning) has been demonstrated in clinical studies of most sexual offenses (Marshall, 1988). During masturbation, the pedophile's fantasies may focus on the satisfying sexual experiences he had during childhood. Repetitive masturbatory activity, therefore, reinforces the immature level of sexual behavior associated with childhood. Whereas masturbation of itself may be a normal outlet for sexual tension, for the pedophile it becomes an act that reinforces his attraction to children. Continual association between the pleasurable masturbatory activities and fantasies about childhood sexual experiences results in a strong bond between sexual arousal and children. Eventually, the children become sexual stimuli capable of arousing high levels of sexual excitation.

Another version of the sexual arousal perspective links traumatic sexual victimization to pedophilic behavior. Many researchers have found unusually high amounts of childhood sexual victimization in the background of pedophiles (Bard et al., 1987). It is unclear, however, how sexual trauma, which is supposedly aversive, becomes conditioned or associated with the sexual pleasures of pedophilia.

Blockage theories assume that pedophilia is the result of blockage of normal sexual and emotional gratification from adult relationships. Frustrated in his quest for normal channels of sexual gratification, the offender seeks the company of children. Blockage theories emphasize the unassertive, timid, inadequate, and awkward personalities of the pedophile, arguing that these social deficiencies make it nearly impossible for him to develop normal social and sexual relationships with adult females. When the marital relationship breaks down, for example, the pedophile may turn to his daughter as a substitute.

The fourth set of explanations focus on the loss of self-control and personal constraints on behavior. *Disinhibition* theories outline a variety of circumstances that presumably propel the offender to his deeds. Poor impulse control, excessive use of alcohol and drugs, and an assortment of stressors could all lead him over the brink to his favorite deviant sexual practices. As mentioned earlier, many pedophiles refuse to take blame but attribute the cause of their pedophilic behavior to forces outside of themselves. "I couldn't help myself" or "I don't know what came over me" are frequent pleas.

Which theoretical perspective has the inside track for the explanation of pedophilia? By themselves none can account for the multiple causes and the full range of learning experiences, beliefs, motivations, and attitudes of pedophiles.

EXHIBITIONISM

Exhibitionism is the deliberate exposure of the genitals to another person to achieve sexual gratification. Several authors have reported that in some parts of the world exhibitionism—often called indecent exposure—is the most frequent sexual offense known to the police (e.g., Wincze, 1977; Coleman, 1976). In Canada and the United States, exhibitionism—usually called lewd and licentious behavior in the legal system—accounts for about one-third of all sex crimes (Evans, 1970; Rooth, 1974), and in the United Kingdom it accounts for one-fourth (Feldman, 1977). Bancroft (1976) estimates that exhibitionism is the second most common sexual deviation treated at mental health facilities in England. Rooth (1973, 1974) argues that the practice of exposing oneself is primarily a Western phenomenon, however. In India, extensive surveys have failed to uncover a single case (Rooth, 1974). In Japan, the incidence for one year was fifty-nine convicted cases, compared to 2,767 in England and Wales during the same year. Rooth (1973) also supposes that exhibitionism is rare in Latin America and Third World countries.

To what extent exhibitionism is exclusively a Western phenonmenon remains open to debate. Much depends on the culture and police discretion in each country. In Latin American countries, for example, it is a common sight to see men and women openly urinating in public (Rhoads & Borjes, 1981). If a society reacts so casually to nudity or exposure of sexual organs, exhibitionism will lose its shock value. In an effort to determine comparable rates of exhibitionism, Rhoads and Borjes asked working women in both the United States and Guatemala how often men had exposed themselves to them in public. The survey indicated no difference in number of incidences, but the *official records* of the two countries were drastically different. This may reflect a reluctance of the part of the Guatemalian women to report exhibitionism, since officers are likely to ridicule the victims.

Exhibitionists are almost always males who delight in surprising and shocking their audiences. They differ from "strippers"—both male and female—in that the former expose themselves for economic gain rather than sexual gratification. In addition, of course, persons watching strippers do so deliberately and voluntarily. Exhibitionists sometimes masturbate during the exposure, but most prefer to do so in private, immediately following their exposure.

Situational Characteristics

If the offender is not particularly brazen, he may habitually hide behind the curtain of a window in his home when school lets out and, as young girls walk by, tap on the window, quickly expose himself, and make a fast retreat behind the curtain. This is risky, however, since his identity is easily traceable. Another favorite procedure is to use a car, drive slowly by a female or group of females, open the car door, show himself, and quickly drive away. The bolder exhibitionist is often the "street flasher" who opens his coat to a selected victim, makes certain the impression registers, and then runs or walks away.

Favorite locations for exposure vary, but most exhibitionists prefer public places like parks, theaters, stores, or relatively uncrowded streets. A Toronto study (Mohr, Turner, & Jerry, 1964) reported that 74 percent of a sample studied preferred open places, and most displayed themselves from a parked car. The remainder of the sample generally preferred their own home, often exhibiting themselves through windows or doorways.

The overwhelming majority of exhibitionists prefer strangers for victims and rarely expose more than once to the same victim. Although the preferred victim is usually female, an exhibitionist will occasionally expose himself to adult males and male children. Exhibitionists who prefer adult women will usually expose to them individually, while those who prefer female children will generally expose to small groups of two or three (Evans, 1970; Mohr, Turner, & Jerry, 1964). Most adult female victims are in their late teens or early twenties, usually unmarried. This supports the theory that most exhibitionists deliberately select their victims on the basis of specific stimuli. For example, an exhibitionist may have a definite preference for exhibiting to young girls between the ages of nine and eleven who look "naive." Another may search for a pretty face, dark hair, shapely legs, or various other physical features. Exhibitionists also tend to be consistent in the setting and time of day they choose for exposure. In fact, many are so predictable that, once the incidence is reported, they are easily detected and arrested.

Offender Characteristics

Most exhibitionists begin their behavior at puberty, with a peak period occurring between ages fifteen and thirty (Evans, 1970). Contrary to popular belief, onset after age thirty is extremely rare, except in men with mental impairment due to organic brain damage or senility. Compared to the general population, exhibitionists usually have at least average intelligence, educational levels, and vocational interests (Blair & Lanyon, 1981). The majority also appear to have a reliable work record (Mohr, Turner, & Jerry, 1964).

Psychosis or other mental disorders are found no more frequently in exhibitionists than in the general population (Blair & Lanyon, 1981). However, exhibitionists show an above-average incidence of previous sexual offenses other than exhibitionism, including voyeurism and even attempted rape. In the main, however, exhibitionists neither assault their audience physically nor desire sexual intercourse with them. It is highly probable that if victims expressed interest in sexual activity, most exhibitionists would be frightened and confused and would flee. In most cases, the primary motive behind the exhibitionism is the sexual excitation (reinforcement) the offender receives from shocking, surprising, or mildly frightening his victims. These reactions generate considerable sexual arousal. Later, he will probably masturbate to that image. On the other hand, if his exposure fails to engender the anticipated fright or surprise, and produces instead a disinterested, noncommittal facial expression, the offender is disappointed and suffers some loss of self-esteem.

Although many exhibitionists are married, most are considered socially and sexually inadequate both by themselves and those around them. Many are introverted, shy, socially reserved individuals who feel uncomfortable in most social situations. Generally, they are described as unassertive, self-effacing, timid, and passive. A majority of exhibitionists feel the urge to expose following a blow to their fragile self-esteem, which prompts heightened feelings of inadequacy and stress.

Therefore, like other sexual offenses, exhibitionism is a learned behavioral pattern reinforced by sexual arousal and the subsequent tension reduction achieved through masturbation. Many exhibitionists indicate that their behavior was initially acquired through some preadolescent sex play or by chance. For example, the history of most exhibitionists includes a vivid memory of a young girl expressing amazement or fear at their penis, viewed either acidentally or during sexual play. Characteristically, this attention was sexually exciting to the male, and he masturbated to the imagery of the incident. This not uncommon incident by itself is usually not sufficient enough to establish exhibitionism. However, a repeated pairing of the memory of the event with the sexual arousal derived from masturbation may lead to a proclivity for exhibitionism in individuals who lack sufficient self-control or self-regulatory mechanisms. That is, pleasurable, repetitive masturbatory activities in the presence of this mental imagery strongly encourage eventual exposure of the penis to victims who are perceived as similar to the initial observer. If the first, real-life exposure is sexually arousing, a strongly reinforcing chain of events is established. Each time the exhibitionist exposes and receives this sequence of rewards, the behavior pattern becomes that much more firmly entrenched.

During subsequent periods of stress and inadequacy, exposure becomes an increasingly effective way of dealing with uncomfortable emotions, especially when preferred victims are available. Therefore, because exhibitionism is a learned response, it continues to be repetitive and resistant to extinction. Furthermore, exhibitionists may expose themselves many thousands of times without complaints from victims. Irate adults do not report an incidence of exhibitionism unless the victim was their offspring. Even then they may not report in order to protect the child from having to describe the incident to police.

It is important to note that exhibitionists, in contrast to many pedophiles, often express a desire to change their behavior. Although they may expose themselves numerous times, once detected they are more likely to seek therapeutic help. Moreover, it is also not uncommon for an exhibitionist to seek professional help prior to being arrested for his behavior.

VOYEURISM AND FETISHISM

Voyeurism, also known as scotophilia or inspectionalism, is the tendency to gain sexual excitement and gratification from observing unsuspecting others naked, undressing, or engaging in sexual activity. The term *fetishism* refers specifically to a sexual attraction to inanimate objects rather than to people. It is distinct from *partialism*, which is an exaggerated sexual interest in some part of the human anatomy not usually associated with sexual arousal, such as the knee. The individual with a fetish may become sexually aroused at the sight of boots, handbags, nylons, panties, fur, or even tailpipes on motor vehicles. The fetish object may be kissed, fondled, tasted, smelled, or just looked at.

Both voyeurism and fetishism are little more than minor sexual offenses, since they usually do not seriously harm the community. They are often, of course, egregious violations of other people's privacy because "victims" are being observed without their knowledge, or their possessions are appropriated for "deviant" purposes. The voyeur or the fetishist runs afoul of the law when he harasses, trespasses, burglarizes, damages property, or steals objects.

Recall that the voyeur is sometimes an exhibitionist, and vice versa. However, the voyeur is less likely than the exhibitionist to become involved in serious forms of antisocial behavior, such as rape or other forms of violence. He does not harm his victims physically, and, like the exhibitionist, he is often described as a passive, shy, introverted, submissive, and harmless person. Clinical studies reveal that he suffers from strong heterosexual anxieties and immaturity.

One observation made in the Queen's Bench Foundation study (1978) demands attention. About 10 percent of the convicted rapists interviewed stated that they had watched their victim through a window observation before attacking her. The authors suggested that, in view of this finding, some "peeping Toms" should be watched for possible rape tendencies. However, some distinguishing aspects about voyeurism should be noted. All but one offender had intentions of raping before observing. The one rapist who said that he did not intend to rape when he watched his victim admitted that he did intend to "have sex" with her. In addition, all but one of these offenders had weapons in their possession at the time of their arrest (knives, guns, meat fork), even though they ordinarily did not carry them. Also, forceful entry into the victim's apartment was the common approach, and the victim was often raped with extreme violence.

These rapists, therefore, probably had little in common with the typical voyeur. Their intention from the outset was to attack the victim violently. They apparently watched the victim to determine her habits, whether anyone else was at home, and the best way to get into her residence. In other words, they were stalking their victims. The typical voyeur gets his satisfaction from watching, imagining, and eventually masturbating, with no intention of having sexual contact, forced or other otherwise, with the victim.

Voyeurism, like other forms of sexual deviation, is a learned behavior. Although each individual has a unique approach to viewing, many voyeurs report the preadolescent experience of becoming sexually aroused while watching an unsuspecting woman undress. A common theme running through clinical studies is that the mental imagery of that scene is later coupled with sexual arousal, again perhaps satisfied through masturbation. Eventually, this conditioning produces a desire to observe different, realistic sexual scenes. Keep in mind that an important component of the sexual excitement experienced by the voyeur is his victim's unawareness of his presence. Erotic films or pornography, by themselves, are not likely to serve his purpose.

Fetishism is principally a male phenomenon pursued in the privacy of one's home, without interference in the lives of others. "The essential feature is the use of nonliving objects (fetishes) as a repeatedly preferred or exclusive method of achieving sexual excitement" (DSM-III, 1980, p. 268). Sexual activity may involve the fetish by itself or be integrated into sexual behavior with a human partner. Through classical conditioning, virtually any object may assume sexual significance. Gosselin and Wilson (1984) describe a study of a man who was strongly attracted to safety pins. From the age of eight, he had experienced extreme sexual pleasure from gazing at these shiny objects in the privacy of his bathroom. "When he was 23 his wife observed the complete sequence, which began with him staring at the safety pin for about a minute. This was followed by a glassy-eyed appearance, vocal humming noises, sucking movements of the lips and total immobility for another minute or two" (Gosselin & Wilson, 1984, p. 104).

Most fetish objects, however, are those worn by the female, such as undergarments, shoes, boots, or hosiery. Chalkley and Powell (1983) found that underwear, stockings, and other types of lingerie were most popular for British fetish collectors. Next most common were rubber and certain rubber articles such as Mackintoshes, tubes, dolls, and paraphernalia for giving enemas.

In an excellent if controversial demonstration of fetish conditioning, Rachman (1966) showed male subjects a slide of a pair of women's black boots, followed immediately by slides of attractive, naked women (sexual arousal). After a number of such trials, the subjects became sexually excited, as measured by penile circumference, in reponse to the boots slide itself. There were also indications that the subjects not only became aroused by the particular boots, but also by slides of other boots and shoes as well.

Fetishism merits attention here primarily because the person with a strong attachment to an object might commit larceny or burglary to get it. One of the major avenues for obtaining fetishes is to steal, and, since clothes dryers are more in vogue in modern society than clotheslines, the fetishist's traditional method of stealing from the backyard clothesline has been replaced by more daring techniques. Chalkley and Powell (1983), in their British sample of forty-eight cases of fetishism, found that 38 percent experienced considerable excitement and sexual arousal when stealing the fetish. In this sense, it is conceivable that an indeterminant number of unexplained burglaries (when minor things are taken but more valuable items remain untouched) are a result of an impatient quest for fetishes! Some fetish burglars find sexual excitement just being in someone's house without their knowledge and presence. It is also not unusual for the fetish burglar to take valuable objects along with his fetish, however, either to throw off suspicion or to offer a face-saving "reasonable" explanation for the burglary if he is apprehended.

TREATMENT OF SEXUAL OFFENDERS

Sexual offenders are often highly resistant to changing their deviant behavior patterns. Although a wide variety of treatment programs have been tried, very few have been successful in eradicating sexual offending. After careful review of the research and clinical literature, Furby, Weinroth, and Blackshaw (1989, p. 27) concluded: "There is as yet no evidence that clinical treatment reduces rates of sex reoffenses in general and no appropriate data for assessing whether it may be differentially effective for different types of offenders." The Furby review included *all* variants of therapeutic approaches. Despite this pessimistic appraisal, behavioral approaches continue to offer the most effective technique in the temporary cessation of deviant sexual behavior in motivated individuals. Behavior therapy argues that maladaptive sexual behaviors are learned according to the same rules as normal sexual behavior by means of classical and/or instrumental conditioning, modeling, reinforcement, generalization, and punishment. They are, therefore, modifiable. Behavioral therapy, compared to traditional verbal, insight-oriented therapy, has demonstrated short-term effectiveness in eliminating exhibitionism and fetishism (Kilmann et al., 1982), some forms of pedophilia (Marshall & Barbaree, 1988), and sexual aggression and arousal (Quinsey & Marshall, 1983).

The major problem, however, is not with getting the motivated offender to stop his deviant sexual pattern, but with preventing his relapse across time and situations. It is analogous to dieting. Most diet regimens do work in getting the motivated individual to lose weight. However, they offer little help in preventing people from eventually relapsing into old eating habits.

A treatment approach showing much promise in the treatment of sex offenders is called *Relapse Prevention* (RP). "RP is a self-control program designed to teach individuals who are trying to change their behavior how to anticipate and cope with the problem of relapse" (George & Marlatt, 1989, p. 2). The program emphasizes self-management; clients are considered responsible not for the cause but for the solution of the problem. And as the name implies, the program concentrates on preventing a *relapse* of deviant sexual. Therefore, RP distinguishes treatment from maintenance. As stated earlier, behavior therapy is effective in cessation of the behavior, but RP is specifically designed to be effective in helping the individual *maintain* the "cure." Distinctions are made between the terms *relapse* and *lapse*. "Relapse is a violation of a self-imposed rule or set of rules governing the rate or pattern of a selected of a selected target behavior" (George &

Marlatt, 1989, p. 6). A lapse, on the other hand, refers to "a single instance of violating the rule" (p. 6). "With sex offenders, the term *relapse* will refer to any occurrence of a sexual offense, thus connoting full scale reestablishment of the problematic behavior. The term *lapse* will refer to any occurrence of willful and elaborate fantasizing about sexual offending or any return to sources of stimulation associated with the sexual offense pattern, but short of performance of the offense behavior" (p. 6).

RP, as a system of maintenance-oriented principles and interventions, has two central objectives: It teaches individuals (1) to cope effectively with "high-risk situations" (HRSs); and (2) to identify and respond to early warning signals of urges and "apparently irrelevant decisions" (AIDs). An HRS is any situation that poses a threat to the individual's sense of control over his behavior and consequently increases the probability of lapse or relapse. Examples of HRSs that may predispose an individual toward relapse include negative emotional states, such as anger and depression, interpersonal conflict, and various social pressures (George & Marlatt, 1989). Research by Pithers and associates (Pithers et al., 1988; Pithers et al., 1989) has found that rapists often experience anger and use alcohol or other drugs before engaging in sexual aggression. Pedophiles, on the other hand, often experience anxiety or depression before seeking a child. A feeling of low self-esteem is experienced by both groups. These precursors reflect the beginning stages of an HRS. In other words, they psychologically predispose the individual toward a relapse.

Relapse seems to follow a sequence of events, all representing HRSs (Pithers et al., 1983; George & Marlatt, 1989). First, an urge, fleeting thought, or dream about committing an offense occurs. This is followed by elaborations of fantasies about committing the offense. Then, the aroused individual engages in masturbation coupled with fantasies and/or pornography related to the imagined sexual activity. The individual then plans how he is going to commit the act. Finally, the individual engages in the act. RP provides a framework within which a variety of behavioral, cognitive, educational, and skill-training techniques are used to train sex offenders to recognize and interrupt these chain of events (Marshall & Barbaree, 1988).

If the individual does not know how to cope with these HRSs, there is a high probability that he may lapse or relapse. On the other hand, if he learns how to cope and he successfully manages to get through the HRS without violating his newly adopted rules, perceived control strengthens and the probability of relapse declines. The individual experiences a sense of mastery and self-efficacy and is better prepared for the next bout with an HRS.

The second component in PR intervention is AIDs—apparently irrelevant decisions. What at first glance seems to be a innocuous decision, unrelated to an HRS, may well be the first step toward relapse. For example, a pedophile's decision to take walks by parks and school yards at times when they are predictably crowded with children might be an early warning sign. It is important, therefore, that the individual learn to recognize and interrupt these apparently irrelevant decisions.

Critical to PR treatment intervention is the motivation of the offender. Without motivation, the program will not work. Remember, another key feature is that PR is for *maintaining* a cessation of the deviant behavior, not cessation itself. Therefore, a behavior therapy program or other conventional treatment intervention that stops the behavior must precede PR. The treatment phase normally takes a relatively short period of time. Another important point outlined by George and Marlatt (1989) is that incarceration without treatment will not prevent reoffending. They offer three reasons for this. First, externally imposed, forced control does little to encourage an offender to seek help in changing his ways. Second, the offender can still maintain attachment to his offense pattern through fantasy. Third, it is conceivable that an offender could continue to actually engage in some semblance of his offense patterns even during confinement.

A volunteer outpatient treatment program for child molesters described by Marshall and Barbaree (1988) illustrates very well some of the procedures used to *stop* the behavior. The program uses a variety of behavior techniques. First, clinicians utilize aversive conditioning by linking electric shock to an offender's deviant visual and verbal images. Second, they reduce the attraction of deviant fantasies during masturbation through satiation therapy. Satiation therapy attempts to reduce the sex drive by having the patient masturbate at a frequency that will substantially reduce urges and cravings. Third, they eliminate the occurrence of deviant thoughts elicited by children or by daydreams during their day-to-day living pattern through smelling salts. That is, each patient carries smelling salts, and each time a deviant thought occurs, the patient is instructed to place the salts close to his nose and to inhale deeply. Through aversive conditioning, deviant thoughts are soon strongly associated with the experience of unpleasant smelling salts. Currently, there is no evidence that this aversive therapy has a negative impact on "normal" sexual thoughts and behavior.

The program also enhances the social competence of the child molester by training him in the skills of conversation with adult partners as well as reducing the anxiety in the presence of adult partners. The treatment also addresses training in assertiveness, and counsels the patient in financial management, use of leisure time, and alcohol or drug use. So far, Marshall and Barbaree have been able to do a three-and-a-half-year follow-up on 117 patients, some of whom received the treatment described and some who did not. While 32 percent of the nontreatment group has reoffended, only 14 percent of the treated group has reoffended. In another PR project, Pithers et al. (1988) found a 10 percent relapse rate for rapists, and a 3 percent relapse rate for pedophiles during a short follow-up (less than one year).

PR is a very recent development and its long-term success has yet to be established. However, it does have substantial promise for the elimination of deviant behavior in offenders motivated to change.

SUMMARY AND CONCLUSIONS

Rape is committed for a variety of reasons by a variety of offenders. A major motivation appears to be to harm, derogate, or embarrass the victim. In some situations, the rapist may interpret his behavior as harmless, believing that his victims enjoy being "roughed up." Nevertheless, the effect is invariably the opposite. The psychological and social damage to the victim are incalculable. Sexual assault by husbands, dates, and intimate friends is more frequent than commonly supposed.

Most rapists are young and often show a history of rape and other violent actions. Several attempts at typologies or classification systems of sex offenders have been tried, the most notable being those developed by the Massachusetts Treatment Center and Groth.

Rape behavior appears due, in part, to the type of socialization experiences the offender has had. He has constructed, from information received from a variety of sources and models, a belief and value system that encourages and justifies the rape behavior. Further, most rapists have attitudes and an idelology that encourage men to be dominant, controlling, powerful while expecting women to be submissive, permissive, and compliant. This attitudinal pattern may be much more prevalent in society in both men and women than commonly realized.

We also learned that under very high levels of arousal, any consideration of the rightness of a sexual assaulter's behavior or its consequences may be obliterated. As we saw with reference to homicide and assault, high levels of arousal reduce attention to private self-awareness and personal standards of appropriate conduct. Under high levels of excitement, *some* normally law-abiding persons *may* become rapists, or at least use the high excitement as a justification for their rape behavior. Of course, some people possess a value system that justifies rape or the resolution of interpersonal conflict through violence, regardless of their arousal level.

Pedophilia, also potentially a very serious offense from the victim standpoint, appears to involve less aggression and violence, except, of course, for the pedophilia that includes rape and assault. Pedophilia appears to be motivated by both sexual desire and an expectation of sexual adequacy. Like rape, it is engaged in for a variety of reasons by a variety of offenders. Each has his own construct system and beliefs about his behavior and motivations. Some offenders, for whatever reason, are vicious and violent; others are passive, relatively meek people who enjoy the companionship of children. Most pedophiles are the latter. They appear to see themselves as sexually and interpersonally inept adults who feel more comfortable interacting with children. Classical conditioning also appears to play a prominent role in the development of pedophilia, perhaps much more so than in rape.

We closed this chapter with some attention to the minor sexual offenses of exhibitionism, voyeurism, and fetishes. Classical conditioning, particularly masturbatory conditioning, also appears to play a crucial role in the development of these sexual deviations. Sexual arousal repeatedly linked with objects and persons seems especially important.

Treatment of sexual offenses can be highly successful if the offender's motivation to change is evident. Successful treatment strategies must not only focus on the cessation of the antisocial sexual conduct, but on maintenance as well.

CHAPTER TEN
Property Crimes and Crimes Against the Public Order

Property crimes generally involve the illegal acquisition of money and material goods or the illegal destruction of property. Crimes against the public order are actions against public or moral decency or other conduct which is interpreted as a threat to the orderly operations of a given society. Examples include adultery, prostitution, pornography, gambling, vagrancy, disorderly conduct, public drunkenness, and drug use. Often, these violations are called "victimless crimes" because of the difficulty pinpointing an identifiable victim of the offense. Later in this chapter we will concentrate on the public order crime of prostitution. In the next chapter we will turn our attention to drug use and its relationship to criminal behavior. Most of this chapter will focus on the various kinds of property offenses.

Property crimes are similar to the violent offenses discussed in earlier chapters in one important psychological aspect. Most of them involve a dehumanization of the victim, although in a different sense from the dehumanization that often occurs in violence. In most property crimes (such as larceny and burglary), the offenders avoid confronting their victims directly. Therefore, they do not directly observe or experience the economic, social, and psychological discomfort of their victims. In the victim's absence, internal values and social constraints are less effective, allowing the offender to repress, deny, or justify the crime more easily. As Gresham

Sykes (1956) puts it, the individual's internal sentiments are more easily neutralized by the physical absence of the victim. The offender does not have to think of the effects his or her actions have on the victim, because the offender does not know the victim as a human being, only as a target. The exception, of course, is robbery, but even in this case, victim contact is usually fleeting.

We will focus specifically on the property crimes of robbery, burglary, shoplifting, larceny-theft, and auto theft. Figure 10-1 provides a percentage breakdown of the UCR index crimes for 1988. As you can see, larceny-theft, burglary, and motor vehicle theft account for 88 percent of the total index crimes, with larceny-theft accounting for a large majority. In addition, offenses subsumed under the label "white-collar" crime will also be covered. Finally, we will touch on hostage taking (kidnapping), bombings, and arson, which could also be classified as violent offenses. Because they are often motivated by the desire to acquire property, social status, or psychological rewards, they are included here. Robbery is also considered a violent crime, but in most cases the primary motive again is the desire for material gain.

Obviously, most people engage in property crime for the money or for other tangible rewards that meet biological and material needs. Sykes notes, however, that this does not tell us why some people commit offenses

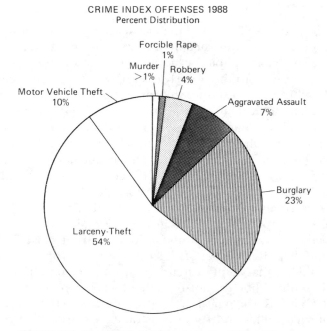

CRIME INDEX OFFENSES 1988
Percent Distribution

FIGURE 10-1   Source: U.S. Department of Justice UCR, 1989.

against property under certain social conditions while others do not. Explanations based strictly on economic necessity and the satisfaction of basic human needs do not go far enough. Sykes proposes the concept of *relative deprivation* as one additional factor. To assess the economic want associated with property crime, we should consider not what the person has or is making in personal income, but rather how great is the discrepancy between what he or she has and would like to have. Specifically, relative deprivation is the psychological distance between what people perceive they have now and what they feel they can realistically attain—their goal. Goals are strongly influenced by the social groups to which people belong or reference group with which they identify.

From a psychological perspective, property crimes cannot be simply explained by biological needs, material wants, or even in terms of relative deprivation. Powerful cognitive motivators must also be considered. These cognitive factors are in the form of outcome expectations and the capacity to predict and appreciate future consequences of one's behavior. Furthermore, the cognitive forces may be relatively independent of external reinforcements like tangible rewards or even social and status rewards. Self-reinforcements, including self-rewards and self-punishments, may represent a major motivating factor in many property crimes.

Cognitive factors are also extremely important in another sense: They allow the offender to justify his or her behavior. A strong theme of this chapter is the tendency of property offenders to minimize, distort, or deny misconduct or reprehensible behavior. The aforementioned psychological separation from the victim helps them to do this. We will expand on these psychological issues of motivation and justification throughout the following pages.

BURGLARY

Burglary is the unlawful entry of a structure, with or without force, with intent to commit a felony or theft. About 7 percent of all U.S. households are burglarized at least once each year, and about 42 percent of these household burglaries do not involve forced entry. That is, the offenders entered through an unlatched window or unlocked door or used a key "hidden" in an obvious place, such as under a doormat. Sixty-seven percent of all reported burglaries involve residential property, while the remaining third involve commercial establishments. Burglaries are more likely to occur during the warmer months, apparently because people are more likely to be outdoors or away on vacation and are more likely to leave doors and windows open, making their residences vulnerable.

A study by Langer and Miranksy (1983) reveals that a surprisingly large segment of the population does not take responsibility for burglary prevention. Approximately half of the New York City residents questioned admitted they did not lock all their doors when away from home, even if they had been burglarized before. Interestingly, while 66 percent believed that burglary could be prevented, 61 percent of these subjects did not use all their locks. They believed that it was the responsibility of others (e.g., the police, the landlord, the building superintendent) to guard the premises, rather than their own personal reponsibility. Furthermore, those who thought their neighborhoods were unsafe and burglary-prone were less likely to use locks than those who considered their neighborhoods safe and less burglary-prone. Possibly, people in burglary-prone areas are convinced that if someone decides to burglarize their homes, there is not much they can do about it, locks or no locks.

Like other criminal offenses, burglary seems to be primarily a crime committed by the young; over eight of every ten persons arrested annually are under twenty-five, with the average age being about twenty-two. To some extent, this arrest ratio may reflect the lack of sophistication of younger burglars who, because of their inexperience, are more likely to be detected. Burglary is also a male enterprise, with only 5 percent of those arrested being female. Although 70 percent of those arrested are white, nonwhites are overrepresented in proportion to their numbers in the general population (Eskridge, 1983).

As noted earlier, about two of every three burglaries are residential. Burglary of residences usually occurs during the daytime and on weekdays, whereas commercial establishments are usually burglarized late at night and on weekends (Pope, 1977b). This is not surprising, since burglary is a passive crime; the offender selects times and places that will minimize the possibility of an encounter with victims. Of all crimes, burglary also offers the greatest probability of success with the least amount of risk. Not only is it a crime without victim contact and probability of identification, but it also does not require weapons. Furthermore, the penalties usually are less severe than those for robbery. Juvenile offenders are more likely than their older counterparts to burglarize during the daytime hours (Pope, 1977c). In fact, a prime time for many juvenile burglaries is at the end of the school day, often between 3 P.M. and 6 P.M.

The identification of situational cues are especially important in successful burglary. Nee and Taylor (1988) found that there are at least four broad categories of relevant cues used by experienced residential burglars. They are:

1. occupancy cues, such as letters or newspapers visible in mailbox, motor vehicles present, windows, blinds, and curtains shut or open;
2. wealth cues, such as the appearance of the house, the neighborhood, the quality of the landscaping, the make of car driven, and visible furnishings;
3. layout cues, such as how easy it would be to gain access into the house or building, as well as escape; and

4.   security cues, such as alarm systems, window locks, and deadbolt locks.

Taylor and Nee (1988) designed a study that tested the possible differences in identifying these cues between burglars and homeowners. The burglars consisted of a group of fifteen experienced burglars serving time in Cork Prison, and the homeowners consisted of fifteen Irish homeowners. Each subject was requested to explore a simulated environment made up of slides and a map of five different houses. The researchers found that burglars were better able to discern security provisions and were more concerned about escaping successfully from the scene than were homeowners. Most surprising, however, was the high amount of agreement between burglars and homeowners on which houses were most vulnerable to burglary. More research needs to be done in this area and the range of relevant cues better identified.

Bennett and Wright (1984) conducted an extensive three-year project on convicted burglars confined in various prisons throughout southern England. The researchers' primary interest was to learn the decision-making processes and perceptions of the residential burglars at the time of the crime. The principal method of data collection in the study was through semistructured interviews with the burglars themselves. Although a majority of the burglars had committed a variety of other property crimes, almost all of them considered burglary their main criminal activity. Therefore, most of them probably qualify as professionals rather than amateurs.

Bennett and Wright discovered that almost all the burglaries were planned. Very few of the burglaries were the result of a spur-of-the-moment decision, nor were there any constant or irrepressible urges to burglarize. The two main aspects that went into the planning were the situational cues of surveillability and occupancy. Surveillability cues were related to the amount of cover or openness around the house, whether it was overlooked by neighboring houses, the availability of access to the rear, and the presence or proximity of neighbors. Occupancy cues were similar to the ones reported by Nee and Taylor, such as a car in the driveway, lights on in the house, the presence of mail, whether the walks were shoveled or the lawn was cut, and so forth. Experienced burglars said that "occupancy proxies" were the major deterrents in attempts to burglarize. Specifically, burglar alarms and dogs were extremely important in the prevention of burglary. Security locks, deadbolts, increased police patrols, and other such strategies had little influence in their decisions to burglarize, or their success in doing so.

National research data on arrested burglars in the U.S. indicate that a large proportion commit the offense near their own residence. This seems especially true for juvenile offenders (Pope, 1977a). The Santa Clara Criminal Justice Pilot Program (1972) found that over one-half of the apprehended offenders traveled no more than a mile from their own home to commit the offense. It is difficult to generalize from this statistic, however, because *apprehended* burglars are presumably less skillful and thus more detectable than burglars who succeed. It is possible that successful burglars operate farther away from home. Eskridge (1983) found that those who burglarized commercial establishments were more willing to travel much greater distances.

Over half the apprehended burglars worked with an accomplice (Chimbos, 1973; Pope, 1977a). Eskridge (1983), who conducted a survey of crime in Lincoln, Nebraska, reports that nearly two-thirds of the identified burglars worked in groups of two or more. On a national level, groups of two or more are responsible for just under half (42 percent) of all burglary incidents. National data also suggest that very few burglars work with more than three accomplices. Younger offenders and females are more likely to use accomplices than older males (Pope, 1977a). However, this pattern also depends to some extent on the sophistication of the offender. Experienced, competent offenders who realize the formidable challenge presented by protection instruments (alarms or safes) may also be more likely to take on assistants (Shover, 1972). Also, if the Santa Clara project sample is representative of burglaries in general, burglars are rarely under the influence of alcohol and other drugs at the time of their crime. Less that 1 percent of those apprehended were under the influence of those substances.

As for other criminal offenses, the best predictor of burglary is an offender's record. In a California analysis, 80 percent of the offenders studied had a prior arrest record (Pope, 1977c). Of these, 58 percent had a prior burglary arrest and 47 percent had prior drug arrests, usually selling. Males were far more likely to have a previous criminal record than females.

Amateur burglars usually take money or personal items that they need, whereas the professional takes items with excellent resale value, like stereos, cameras, television sets, jewelry, and furs (Vetter & Silverman, 1978). The professional usually has access to a "fence," whereas the amateur rarely has that kind of contact. A fence, an integral component in the professional burglary cycle, is a person who knowingly buys stolen merchandise for the purpose of resale. Professional burglars also have individually distinctive methods and not infrequently leave their mark to goad the investigators they have foiled.

As you might expect, the motives for burglary are varied, but the primary factor for professionals is undoubtedly monetary gain. When performed competently, burglary is a lucrative business with low risks and with monetary rewards far surpassing those the burglar might earn in the "straight" world. David (1974) learned that a husband and wife team he interviewed made, on the average, $400 to $500 a day; a solitary offender in his sample made about $500 per week. Many professionals also conceive of their behavior as a challenging skill to be continually developed and refined. In this sense, burglary is highly adaptive and represents an instrumental behavior supported by strong reinforcement.

Shover (1972) discusses some of the outstanding features of the competent professional burglar, whom he calls the "good burglar." This burglar demonstrates technical skill, maintains a good reputation for personal integrity among colleagues in the criminal subculture, gets most of his income from burglary, and has been at least relatively successful at the crime. A good reputation means that the burglar is closed-mouth, stands up to police, and is sympathetic to the criminal way of life.

The professional burglar, then, is primarily motivated by money but also by self-satisfaction and accomplishment. When self-satisfaction and self-reinforcement are conditioned on certain accomplishments, people are motivated to expend the effort needed to attain the desired goal, perhaps even independently of monetary gain. Thus, a burglar who takes great pride in developing ingenious techniques and stumping police is even more likely to continue his illegal conduct. While external reinforcements (tangible rewards) are important, internal reinforcement may be a very powerful motivating and regulating factor.

Larceny and Motor Vehicle Theft

McCaghy (1980) refers to the larceny category as a "garbage can" because it is heterogeneous and unwieldy to classify. Larceny is defined as the "unlawful taking or attempted taking of property other than a motor vehicle from the possession of another . . . " (U.S. Department of Justice, 1988, p. 3). It differs from burglary in that it does not involve unlawful entry. Larceny includes pickpocketing, purse snatching, shoplifting, stealing from vending machines or from motor vehicles, and theft of property left outdoors (bicycles, pedigreed dogs, lawnmowers), and so forth. Over 50 percent of all property crimes fall into the larceny category. Figure 10-2 provides a percentage distribution of the more common types of theft.

Motor vehicle theft refers to the "unlawful taking or attempted taking of a self-propelled road vehicle owned by another, with the intent of depriving the owner of it permanently or temporarily" (U.S. Department of Justice, 1983, p. 3). Motor vehicle theft accounts for about 8 percent of all property crimes.

Although larceny and motor vehicle theft are common and widespread offenses, research reporting specifically on these areas is rarely available. To some extent, the motivating factors that apply to burglary apply here as well. On the other hand, larceny is more likely to be committed by the nonprofessional and the desperate.

Shoplifting

Shoplifting comprises about 15 percent of all arrests for larceny-theft in 1988 (Figure 10-2). Traditionally, it has been assumed that shoplifting is a crime committed primarily by adolescent girls and women. Several explanations have been offered for women's greater involvement in shoplifting,

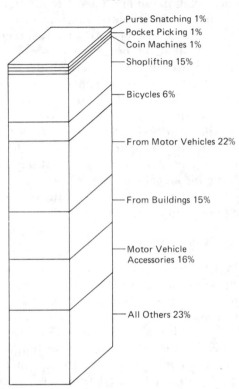

LARCENY-THEFT
Percent Distribution by Type of Theft
1988

Purse Snatching 1%
Pocket Picking 1%
Coin Machines 1%

Shoplifting 15%

Bicycles 6%

From Motor Vehicles 22%

From Buildings 15%

Motor Vehicle
Accessories 16%

All Others 23%

FIGURE 10-2   Source: U.S. Department of Justice UCR, 1989.

the most common being that women have greater opportunity to steal small items from merchants than men. Gibbens (1981) notes that women are more likely to be in stores where detectives are stationed. As men join the ranks of frequent shoppers, however, their shoplifting rates are beginning to increase, and the gap between men and women is narrowing (Moore, 1984). Baumer and Rosenbaum (1984), in an extensive review of the available research, conclude that gender ratio appears to be about 50/50 today. Interestingly, although women apparently shoplifted more than men in the past, more men than women were actually *convicted* (Smart, 1976).

There has also been widespread belief that a vast majority of shoplifters are juveniles under age eighteen. Currently, most studies indicate that although juveniles make up a large portion of shoplifters, they are by no means the majority (Baumer & Rosenbaum, 1984). Moreover, about 70 percent of apprehended juvenile offenders were working in groups, compared to about 20 percent of apprehended adult shoplifters (Baumer & Rosenbaum, 1984). It should also be noted that shoplifting by juveniles is more likely to be evenly proportioned among males and females (Russell, 1973; Baumer & Rosenbaum, 1984). This is also apparently true for shoplifting by the elderly, a phenomenon on the increase and engaged in by both men and women in nearly equal numbers (Fyfe, 1984).

A majority of apprehended shoplifters are in the middle-income bracket and generally carry enough money or credit cards to pay for the items stolen (Baumer & Rosenbaum, 1984). Males tend to favor concealing stolen merchandise in pockets or clothing, while females generally prefer purses or shopping bags. The method of concealment, however, depends considerably on the merchandise, the gender of the offender, and the type of store. In clothing stores, shoplifters would more likely attempt to walk out wearing the clothing after leaving the fitting room, for example. Males prefer to hide items beneath their clothing in supermarkets, while pockets are preferred in drug and discount stores. Females tend to prefer purses for concealment in supermarkets or grocery stores, and packages and bags in drug and discount stores. The item most commonly stolen in supermarkets or grocery stores is meat, while in drug stores clothing tends to be the more common, followed by health and beauty aids.

Baumer and Rosenbaum outline some of the psychological characteristics and behavioral patterns of shoplifters. They note that such things as extreme nervousness, aimless walking up and down the aisles, looking around frequently, glancing up from the merchandise frequently, and leaving the store and returning a number of times are some of the indicators that suggest shoplifting.

In spite of its traditional prominence in female crime, shoplifting has received little psychological research attention. The most heavily quoted source on the subject, Cameron's *The Booster and the Snitch: Department Store Shoplifting* (1964), reported data accumulated in the 1940s and early 1950s. Cameron divided her shoplifters into two groups: commercial shoplifters were "boosters," and amateur pilferers were "snitches." All of her data were subsequently explained with reference to this dichotomy. The boosters were professionals, accepted members of the criminal subculture: They stole for substantial financial gain by choosing items from preselected locations. Boosters used a wide range of techniques such as "booster boxes," packages designed for concealing items inserted through hidden slots or hinged openings, or "stalls," containers with hidden compartments (large handbags, coats with hidden pockets). Snitches, on the other hand, were "respectable" persons who rarely had criminal records. They did not consider themselves thieves, and the idea that they may actually be arrested and prosecuted rarely crossed their minds. Very often, once apprehended, they claimed they stole the item on impulse and did not know what came over them.

The motives behind commercial shoplifting may be clearer than those behind the amateur type. Whereas boosters take merchandise of value, snitches tend to take inexpensive items they can use. Some research has noted that male snitches prefer items of more value, such as stereo equipment, records, and jewelry. Women snitches seem to take clothing, cosmetics, and food. The boosters shoplift for the money; the snitches for more obscure reasons.

Theories concerning the intentions of snitches range from economic ones, like attempts to stretch the family budget (Cameron, 1964), to emotional ones, like attempts to satisfy needs centering around matrimonial stress, loneliness, and depression (Russell, 1973). In recent years, some "experts" have even concluded that most shoplifting is an addiction, much like gambling and alcoholism. The notion of shoplifting as a means of alleviating unmet needs or addiction is weak and poorly documented, however. The behavior gains attention, but it also becomes aversive. On the other hand, the contention that shoplifting has primarily an economic motivation seems oversimplified. Shoplifting is pursued by different people for different reasons.

Moore (1984), studying 300 convicted shoplifters referred for presentence investigation, identified five patterns of offending. Although no shoplifters were considered professional to the degree of Cameron's booster category (the professionals may have escaped detection), 11.7 percent were semiprofessional, reporting shoplifting behavior at least once a week. Their "take" amounted to approximately $1,250 a year.

The most frequent type of shoplifter in Moore's study was the "amateur" (56.4 percent), who stole small personal items when the opportunity arose. The methods used by amateurs were less sophisticated than those of the semiprofessionals and, unlike the semiprofessionals, the amateurs admitted that their behavior was morally wrong or illegal. Both types of shoplifting were premeditated, habitual, and directed toward financial gain. Persons in the amateur category were more likely to exhibit mild personality disorders or to be plagued by psychosocial stressors associated with interpersonal problems such as family disruption.

Approximately 17 percent of Moore's offender population were impaired by mental or emotional problems. However, very few individuals (1.7 percent) had severe mental or emotional problems that were directly related to their shoplifting. The persons in this category were called "episodic" offenders.

Fifteen percent of the sample were "impulse" shoplifters, and another 15 percent were "occasional" offenders. Impulse shoplifters typically had seen an item that they desired but were unable to afford. They had picked it up and pocketed it or carried it around the store, often in a daze, trying to decide whether to steal it. Eventually they tried to walk out but were detected. Later, they could not recall at what point they had made the decision to shoplift. Occasional offenders were less impulsive but more likely to steal for excitement or a dare. Both impulse and occasional offenders were extremely embarrassed when detected, pleaded with officials to give them another chance, and were considered unlikely to shoplift again.

Although Moore found no significant gender differences in overall shoplifting, 68 percent of the teenage offenders were male, whereas 56.5 percent of the adult offenders were female. Moore also found interesting differences between males and female adult offenders with respect to psychological stress. Women were exposed to stress significantly more than men (28.9 percent of the women compared to 13.5 percent of the men). Substance abuse was more common among men (52 percent to 26 percent). Mental disorders, found only in a small percentage of the total shoplifter population, appeared twice as often in women as in men. There were no gender differences in the incidence of milder mental disorders, however.

Recently, some social science research has focused on elderly shoplifters. Feinberg (1984) found that shoplifting was neither a female-dominated offense nor was undertaken for subsistence purposes. Elderly shoplifters, he notes, are neither indigent, lonely, nor victims of poor memory. He attributes their criminal offenses to changes in status that separate the elderly from mainstream society. Often, they must re-evaluate their past values and try out different selves and meanings. To what extent Feinberg's research may be generalized to other age groups is an open question.

One thing does appear clear, however. Clinicians and researchers have been unable to substantiate evidence of *kleptomania*, the neurotic compulsion to steal. Some have even questioned its very existence as a behavior pattern. A strong argument against kleptomania is that shoplifters display exceedingly low recidivism rates. Once apprehended, the amateur rarely shoplifts again (Cameron, 1964; Russell, 1973). If kleptomania were an important ingredient, we would expect the individual to steal repeatedly.

Complicating the dearth of information on shoplifting is the usual problem in obtaining valid statistics. Data acquisition with regard to shoplifting offenses is especially difficult, since store personnel exercise wide discretion in even reporting offenses. Hindelang (1974) found that whether charges were filed depended on the retail value of the stolen object, what was stolen, and the manner in which it was taken rather than demographic and personality characteristics of the shoplifter. Specifically, it did not seem to matter whether the offender was male or female, black or white, poor or middle class. What determined referral for arrest was whether the item was expensive, had resale value, or was stolen in a professional, skillful manner. Fyfe (1984) suggests that merchants have become impatient with shoplifting and are now less reluctant to prosecute, however. He notes that store detectives not uncommonly have police powers, which means they are able to initiate steps toward prosecution without involving local police agencies. This more discreet method of handling offenders encourages merchants to be less lenient and less likely to allow a shoplifting to go unpunished.

ROBBERY

Robbery is taking or attempting to take anything of value from a person by force or threat of force. Like many other crimes, it is primarily an offense of the young male. Over half of those arrested for robbery are under twenty-one, and three out of every four are under twenty-five. Over 90 percent are male.

Robbery accounts for only about 4 percent of all arrests for property crimes. However, because of its potential physical harm to victims, it is among the crimes most feared by the American population (Garofalo, 1977). It involves a high probability of physical harm from a *stranger*, and it can happen to anyone. One in three victims are injured in robbery (also called stickup, holdup, mugging), and one in ten so seriously that they require medical attention (U.S. Department of Justice, 1988). Furthermore, robbery offenders are more likely to use weapons that other violent offenders. In fact, firearms are discharged in about one-fifth of all robberies. Yet, is is among the least studied criminal offenses. One reason for this is that robbery seems so obvious and straightforward: People rob to obtain money. The process is quick, and the potential returns are substantial. Compared to burglary, however, the risks are great and the penalties substantial. Much of this may be true, but as we have seen, human behavior should not be oversimplified. The motives of offenders may be extremely varied. People behave a certain way because they have convinced themselves that is what works best for them.

The major distinctions between robbery and other property crimes are the direct contact between the offender and the victim and the threat or use of force. The offender threatens bodily harm if the victim resists or impedes the offender's progress; usually this threat is backed up by a clearly visible lethal weapon, such as a firearm.

The combination of taking property and threatening physical harm to a victim creates problems for the researcher or criminologist classifying the offense. Should robbery be considered a property crime or a violent crime? Wolfgang and Ferracuti (1967) argue that robbery—like homicide, rape, and aggravated assault—develops within a subculture of violence and should be classified as a violent crime. Normandeau (1968), on the other hand, contends that robbers are generally not violent and are associated with a subculture of theft rather than one of violence. Normandeau bases his judgment on a study of Philadelphia robberies, in which he discovered that 44 percent involved no physical injury to the victim. While 56 percent of the victims did sustain some injury, only 5 percent needed to be hospitalized.

If Wolfgang and Ferracuti are correct in saying that robbery is a crime of violence springing from a violent subculture, the backgrounds of offenders should support this. We would expect to find criminal records and a social history peppered with violent incidents. In a study of Boston robberies during 1964 and again during 1968, Conklin (1972) found no "excessive amount" of prior criminal violence in the backgrounds of robbery offenders compared with the "general criminal populations of the country." In addition, fewer than one-third of the robbery victims had sustained injuries in the incidents. Similar findings are reported by Normandeau (1968) and Spencer (1966), neither of whom found that robbers had high conviction rates for violent conduct. However, research does suggest that robbers who did rely on violence in the past are more likely to use it in the future, whether in robbery or in other crimes.

One way to solve the problem of classifying robbery is to consider it both a property crime and a violent crime. In fact, Vetter and Silverman (1978) suggest that it is more accurately catalogued as a violent property crime. Most robbers, they point out, try to intimidate and frighten victims through threats of violence. The offender rationalizes that the more fear can be induced (without panic) the less resistance will be encountered. If the offender feels his or her control over the situation is weakening, he or she may flee, exert greater threat, or become more violent.

Strong-arm robbery (without a weapon) is more likely to result in injury to the victim than is robbery with a firearm or knife. Presumably, victims are less fearful (and thus more daring) when confronted by an unarmed individual. In the absence of a gun or other weapon, the victim's resistance to losing valuable personal property is stronger, and he or she is more apt to hamper the progress of the strong-arm offender. The tendency to resist, therefore, may partly account for the higher rates of victim injury in these no-weapon situations. Furthermore, the offender is likely to feel more confident, powerful, and in control of the incident when he or she has a weapon. Because of this increase in confidence, the offender is less likely to be anxious and disorganized in response patterns, and thus is better able to think clearly and evaluate the consequences of actions.

Assessing skilled robbery, Peter Letkemann (1973) offers pertinent remarks about the successful robber's confidence and victim "management." First, he or she analogizes between the technical skills of the burglar and the mechanic, and between the professional skills of the robber and the clinician. Burglars do not have to be concerned with people, but professional robbers must be able to maintain control and handle their victims at all times. Bank robbers, for example, assert that the keys to a successful heist are confidence and the ability to control people under high stress. Confidence, they believe, is reflected in the robber's tone of voice and general behavior. High levels of self-confidence are crucial if they are to maintain control of the situation. Successful robbers also note that the posture and physical location of the victims are deliberately designed to enhance the offender's control over them.

According to Letkemann, professional robbers often express dismay over media treatment of robbery. Television and movies generally downplay the seriousness of bank robbery, for example; the offenders therefore must work harder to convince their victims that they mean business. The entertainment media also encourages some victims to be heroes; robbers consider heroes irrational and extremely dangerous.

WHITE-COLLAR CRIME

The term *white-collar crime* was coined in 1939 by Edwin H. Sutherland in his presidential address to the American Sociological Society. He also was one of the first researchers to conduct an empirical study of illegal corporate behavior, in 1949. Following Sutherland's lead, a considerable amount of pioneering research was done on white-collar crime between 1939 and 1963 (Geis, 1988). However, during the second period, from 1964 to 1975, there was a discernible decline in interest in white-collar crime. Fortunately, the area has experienced a strong revival of interest since 1975.

White-collar crime is an extremely vague term, however. It is not at all clear what kinds of conduct should be included. Should embezzlement, computer fraud, arson for profit, bribery, theft of trade secrets, forgery, tax evasion, and corporate obstruction of justice all be encompassed by the term? Furthermore, we should recognize that organizations can be both offenders and victims. While large corporations are dumping their toxic wastes illegally, their employees may be pilfering materials from the company. Do both the toxic dumping and the theft of paperclips qualify as white-collar crime?

Horning (1970) proposed a tripartition to distinguish the various behaviors that might be at issue. He reserved *white-collar crime* for acts committed by salaried employees in which the company of their employment is either the victim or the locale for the commission of an illegal act from which they *personally* benefit. *Corporate crime* refers to illegal acts by employees in the course of their employment and for which the company is the primary benefactor. *Blue-collar crime* refers to the whole array of illegal acts committed by *nonsalaried* workers where the place of employment is the victim. Examples of blue-collar crime include the theft of company materials, the destruction of company property, or the falsification of production records. To some extent we will adopt Horning's classification. However, *white-collar crime* will encompass all three offenses, since it is the commonly preferred term throughout the literature. We will use *profes-*

sional crime to refer to the illegal but personally beneficial conduct of management and executives. Corporate and blue-collar crime will be defined in accordance with Horning's classifications.

The extent of white-collar crime is unknown, both in terms of frequency and dollar amounts. Very rarely do professional, corporate, or blue-collar crimes find their way to criminal court. When the organization is the victim, it usually handles the situation informally by demanding restitution and/or firing the employee or forcing a resignation. It does not benefit the company's public image to file a criminal complaint. When the organization is the violator (corporate crime), civil suits are often preferred to criminal charges. Alternately, administrative agencies of government may hold hearings and ultimately fine the corporation. The word *crime* is one that corporate decision makers would quibble with, since they do not perceive of a majority of their "violations" as criminal. The fact that the questionable conduct of organizations and their employees may be handled in such a variety of ways adds to the great difficulty in obtaining data about the extent of white-collar crime.

Blue-Collar Crime

Studies of blue-collar crime generally focus on two problems: employee theft and counterproductive behavior. The first involves direct illegal activity; the second involves conduct that hurts the business less directly, but perhaps as seriously.

Employee theft is an enormous drain on American business, costing business and industry an estimated 5 to 10 billion dollars each year (Clark & Hollinger, 1983). We lack information to help us understand the nature and extent of employee theft and to improve methods for preventing and controlling it. In one survey of employees from forty-seven retail, manufacturing, and service organizations, one-third admitted stealing company property (Clark & Hollinger, 1983). The property included merchandise, supplies, tools, and equipment. In addition, almost two-thirds of the employees surveyed reported other types of misconduct, such as sick leave abuse, drug or alcohol use on the job, long lunch and coffee breaks, slow and sloppy workmanship, and falsifying time sheets. Collectively, these are the aforementioned counterproductive behaviors. They do not involve actual removal of material goods from the organization, but they do reduce production and services. Theft and counterproductive behaviors appear to go together, since those who pilfer company materials also tend to be engaged in counterproductive behavior.

Explanations for employee theft and counterproductive behaviors are multiple, but most cluster around the themes of age, dissatisfaction, and one's normative group at the workplace. The highest levels of theft and counterproductive behaviors are reported by younger, unmarried

male employees (age sixteen to the mid-twenties). Apparently, these younger employees do not feel any commitment or loyalty to the organization,
probably because they do not expect to spend their lives in that situation.
Many are college and high school students working only until they graduate. High levels of theft and counterproductive behaviors are also found
among employees expressing dissatisfaction with some aspect of their employment, especially with their immediate supervisor. Another component
of job dissatisfaction is the workers' perception of the company's attitude
toward them. If the workers perceive the organization as caring little about
them, job dissatisfaction and the concomitant theft and counterproductive
behaviors tend to follow.

While age and job dissatisfaction are highly correlated with theft and
counterproductive behavior, normative support offers a viable *explanation*
for blue-collar crime. Normative support refers to the standards, perceptions, and values the work group has established for itself, with or without
the organization's implicit (or explicit) approval. In short, normative support refers to group norms. For example, the group may consider pilfered
material a supplement to one's hourly wages, a fringe benefit. "It goes with
the job." "The company expects you to take a little on the side." Another
example is where the work group verbally neutralizes the societal and
organizational prohibitions against theft. "Everyone does it." "No one cares
if we take a few things." "These items are not of significant value." "This is
not really stealing." Sieh (1987) found that garment workers took "only
what was owed them" and rarely stole items of substantial value. Cressey
(1953) refers to these justifications as "vocabularies of adjustment."

Whether the group considers it acceptable to take something or decides where the line should be drawn ("You can help yourself to ballpoint
pens, but staplers are hands off") depends on many variables. For example,
the size of the organization is likely to be a factor. Smigel (1970) found that
when workers were "forced" (in a questionnaire) to select an organization
they would be most inclined to victimize, they first chose large businesses,
then government, and lastly small businesses. They considered large corporations and big government impersonal bureaucratic giants able to ab-
sorb losses more easily than smaller organizations.

Another variable in determining what is acceptable is the value or
type of property. Horning (1970) tried to learn which property was most
likely to be pilfered at a midwestern electronics plant. Three kinds of
property were identified: personal, company, and property of uncertain
ownership. Examples of personal property were lunch pails, wallets, jewelry, marked clothing, and modified tools. Company property included instruments and expensive supplies that clearly belonged to the company. In
addition to fixtures, heavy machinery, and equipment, the "hard-core"
company property included power tools, bulky and expensive components,
and any components, parts, materials, or tools on which the company had

placed special value (e.g., by using a checkout system or an established accounting procedure). Property of uncertain ownership included scraps, waste, junk parts, screws, nails, nuts, bolts, and other items that were plentiful and of little value by themselves. Although 91 percent of the workers admitted pilfering, a vast majority of the items stolen were of uncertain ownership. In fact, the vast majority of the workers believed that taking either personal or company property was wrong, whereas taking items of uncertain ownership was not.

Regardless of the explanation, blue-collar crime seems to require some subjective *justification* on the part of the worker. He or she does not perceive his or her conduct as illegal or even unethical, either because the behavior is in line with group norms, in line with internal standards, or both. From the group's or worker's perspective, the theft or the counterproductive behavior are either expected or they adjust the imbalances inherent in working for the company. It is interesting to note that employee theft diminishes when an organization clarifies for the work force precisely what constitutes misconduct and what is expected (Clark & Hollinger, 1983). This approach, combined with working conditions that convince employees their organization cares about them, seems to be the most effective in reducing employee theft and counterproductive behavior. Furthermore, improvement in the work environment functions both ways; the worker is also expected to demonstrate loyalty and commitment to the organization, setting up appropriate models for new workers. But loyalty to a company may also go too far, as when it represents a higher obligation than commitment to law and ethics. Individual blind loyalty often leads to corporate crime. According to Geis:

> The record suggests . . . that unharnessed power is not to be trusted, at least in social systems where the desire for personal gain is operative and where the opportunity to secure such gain at the expense of others is readily available. Human beings, particularly those with a strong organizational force behind them, are much too artful in constructing benign, personally lulling explanations for evil actions to be allowed to operate beyond scrutiny. (1988, p. 27)

Corporate Crime

Corporate crime is a broad category, covering offenses ranging from price fixing to failure to correct a serious defect on an aircraft (or even notify the user of the defect). The estimated costs of corporate crime—both financial and from a human suffering standpoint—are staggering. The financial cost of corporate crime is estimated to be between $20 and $40 billion a year (Kramer, 1984). Kramer (1984) estimates that over 100,000 deaths a year may be attributed to occupationally related diseases, most caused by the knowing and willful violation of occupational health and safety standards by businesses and industries. Commercial manslaughter kills more people than are murdered by acts listed in the official crime statistics (Geis & Monahan, 1976; Kramer, 1984). Annually, 20 million serious injuries are associated with unsafe and defective consumer products—unsafe foods and drugs, and defective autos, tires, or appliances. About 110,000 of these injuries result in permanent disability, and 30,000 result in death (Schrager & Short, 1978). Obviously, all of these accidents, injuries, and deaths are not due directly or even indirectly to corporate neglect or illegal action, but the data suggest that many are (Hochstedler, 1984).

Some writers have argued that law breaking in American business (as well as government) is normative, in that the social climate of many organizations encourages illegal and unethical behavior (e.g., Conklin, 1977). The former head of the Employment Division of the Securities and Exchange Commission, for example, stated bluntly: "Our largest corporations have trained some of our brightest young people to be dishonest" (Kohlmeier, 1976, p. 58). The constitution of unethical or dishonest practices in business is a matter of dispute. Often, executives believe that some dishonesty or deceit has to be tolerated in the best interest of the company, the organization, or even the country. Conklin (1977, p. 91) quotes one executive who asserted that in business, whatever is normal practice is ethical. It may not be legal, but from a business standpoint, if it is normal practice, it is ethical.

Therefore, company and organizational norms allow and encourage their decision makers to deny criminal intent and to maintain a non-criminal self-concept. The norms also encourage them to restructure their personal values and beliefs about what is reasonable and appropriate conduct.

You may recall that in the summary section of chapter eight, we referred to sets of strategies people use to neutralize some of their violent conduct and separate it from their personal codes. The strategies, proposed by Bandura (1978) are worth repeating here. Although they operate with reference to a wide range of reprehensible conduct, they are particularly relevant to the discussion of corporate crime. The strategies may be used individually or in combination.

One set operates at the level of behavior. What is culpable is made honorable through moral justifications and euphemistic jargon. A normally reprehensible act becomes personally and socially acceptable when it is associated with beneficial or moral ends. "We did it in the best interest of the company, the employees and their families, and the country." Similarly, corporate decision makers may regard the laws they are violating as unfair, unjust, or simply not in keeping with good business practices. Under this set of practices, vocabularies of adjustment may be brought into play. Conklin (1977) asserts that vocabularies of adjustment may even play a more crucial role in corporate crime than in juvenile delinquency.

A second set of neutralizing or dissociative strategies obscures or distorts the relationship between actions and their effects. In this group of strategies, people do not see themselves as personally responsible or accountable for their actions. They may disregard or deny the consequences of their actions—"It simply didn't happen the way the press reported it." Alternately, they may displace responsibility to the victim—"Consumers often don't use the appliance properly"—or diffuse the responsibility among the decision-making group—"After careful deliberation the board decided this would be the right decision."

A third set of strategies addresses the effects of the action on the recipients. Here, the dignifying qualities of the victims are removed. "Most consumers are greedy and stupid." "Third World countries are overcrowded anyway." We saw this strategy in action earlier in this text, when aggressors regarded their victims as less than human. This dehumanizing approach also seems to be a hallmark of prejudice and scapegoating.

The social climate surrounding executive and managerial offices may be similar to that found among nonsalaried workers, in that norms are established and maintained to permit internal self-justification for misconduct. However, executive and managerial decisions are presumably made in the best interest of the company (and ultimately of the individuals themselves), while blue-collar crimes are performed for immediate self-benefit. Also, corporate conduct is usually learned from supervisors, whereas blue-collar conduct is usually acquired from peers.

In sum, through cognitive restructuring supported by corporate norms, decision makers can justify and rationalize behavior that appears reprehensible to outsiders. The restructuring process prevents the manager or executive from labeling him or herself "criminal." In fact, in some corporations, the extent to which the norms and justifying mechanisms are embraced may well determine how far up the corporate ladder one climbs.

Professional Crime

Professional crime, like blue-collar crime, is illegal behavior pursued primarily for the benefit of the individual rather than the organization. Unlike blue-collar crime, however, the conduct usually does not fit a group or corporate norm. Professional crime is largely a solitary pursuit, with the offender guided primarily by his or her own personal justifications and reasoning. The embezzler, for example, is operating outside both corporate and group norms, although he or she may justify the behavior in much the same way as other white-collar crimes are justified. In other words, an embezzler may convince herself that the activity really is not a crime since she is merely borrowing the money temporarily and will put it to good use. Later, she will reimburse the company (secretly, of course). Other examples of professional crime include bribery, computer fraud, and theft of services.

A major difference between white-collar crimes in general and conventional property crimes is that the white-collar offenders are less inclined to label themselves "criminal." In general, they have convinced themselves that they are not engaging in serious misconduct. They believe that their conduct goes with the job, is in the best interest of the company, or will not hurt anyone. Conventional property offenders, as a group, are more willing to admit that their offenses are criminal and that their actions do cause some grief to victims.

White-collar offenders also seem to engage in more cognitive restructuring of values and beliefs than conventional property offenders. Moreover, for blue-collar and corporate offenders, there is strong normative support from peers, which is less likely to happen for conventional property offenders.

Let's now turn our attention to three offenses that are somewhat outside the realm of property crimes, but nonetheless have many of the same features.

HOSTAGE-TAKING OFFENSES

The hostage taker holds victims against their will and uses them to obtain material gain or personal advantage. Typically, this offender threatens to take the lives of the victims if certain demands are not met within a specified time period. Included in the broad hostage-taking category are abductions and kidnappings, skyjackings, and some acts of terrorism.

Miron and Goldstein (1978) divide hostage-taking offenses into two major categories based on the offender's primary motivation: *instrumental* and *expressive* conduct. In instrumental hostage-taking, the offender's goal is recognizable, material gain. An example is kidnapping a child and holding him or her for ransom. The goal in expressive hostage-taking is psychological: The offender wants to become significant and to take control over his or her fate. Expressive offenders generally feel that they have little control over events in their lives. They want to become important, and they believe the media coverage accompanying their hostage-taking will help them to achieve this goal. To the observer, the conduct of the expressive offender often seems senseless and even suicidal. A skyjacker who demands that a pilot fly an aircraft full of passengers from one continent to another, with no apparent reason, is an example.

Hostage-taking offenses sometimes begin as instrumental acts but develop into expressive ones. An offender who initially kidnaps someone for material gain may find that his demands are unrealistic and not likely to be met; in this case, the person may decide to play out the scenario for the attention, significance, and control it affords. Sometimes both instrumental and expressive motives are clearly involved from the beginning. That is, the offender expects both material and psychological gain from the abduction.

Miron and Goldstein suggest strategies for dealing with hostage takers. First, they should be denied the excitement and stimulation they hope to initiate; this requires that a potentially chaotic situation be handled as calmly as possible, with minimum media attention. As noted in chapter four, very high levels of arousal tend to promote disorganized response patterns and reduce internal thought processes. Under high excitement and chaos, the offender is more likely to revert to "mindless" behavior, which may include violence. Miron and Goldstein advocate that the police not overreact to hostage takers and only utilize as many law enforcement officers as absolutely necessary. In addition, the media should be asked to avoid overplaying the incident with cameras and commentators.

Second, offenders must be allowed to *feel* that they are in some control of the situation. Helplessness and powerlessness may have prompted the offense in the first place. If the captors do not feel they have attained any control, they may take steps to prove the opposite, such as shooting one of the hostages.

Third, in hostage situations *time* can be a strong ally. Once the early stages of a crisis have passed and some stability and calm have been achieved, the passage of time plays a positive role. Time has several effects. After the initial high-arousal state, the body winds down, eventually to a point where the offender feels tired, sluggish, and depressed. Under these conditions the event takes on aversive properties, and the person is likely to begin to wish he were not in this situation. Time also promotes thought and more reliance on internal standards of conduct. If the offender has incorporated some values of society, he may begin to appreciate the ramifications of his behavior. However, he may also begin to construct justifications. Either process, however, may enable him to accede more easily to police requests. Time also affects the relationship with the hostage. According to social psychological research, the more familiar one is with an object or person, the more one tends to become attracted to it (e.g., Freedman, Sears, & Carlsmith, 1978). In many hostage situations, the more the victim and captor get to know one another, the more they begin to accept one another. Furthermore, if the hostage was a stranger to the captor, the hostage takes on human qualities with the passage of time.

The attraction between victim and captor is called the *Stockholm effect*, after a hostage-taking incident in Sweden which resulted in marriage between a female hostage and one of her abductors. Police negotiators have noted that on occasion the hostage will side with the captor in working out demands. Although this may simply reflect a wish to end the terrifying ordeal as quickly as possible, it may also signify some attraction to the abductor. When hostages act this way, experts sometimes maintain that they have been brainwashed. An alternate explanation is that they have developed an attraction for their captors and temporarily identified with their values and goals.

How can a hostage-taking incident, which by its very nature is stressful, generate attraction? We have already noted that mere familiarity can increase attraction to an object or person. There is evidence, also, that unpleasant emotion may intensify attraction (Middlebrook, 1974). Research by Schachter (1971) suggests that when people are physiologically aroused, they may have difficulty labelling the arousal with the appropriate emotion, because several conflicting emotional labels may be available. It does not seem to matter whether the arousal derives from negative or from positive circumstances. For example, sexual deprivation may lead to physiological arousal, which may be labelled love. The same process may operate in a highly charged hostage-taking incident, where familiarity combined with very high arousal leads to mutual attraction. If the victim or kidnapper is deindividualized by a hood or a mask, the incident is much less likely to develop into attraction. Also, ideals and purpose may override any tendency to humanize and be attracted to the victims.

ARSON

It is estimated that 30 percent of all fire losses in the United States may be attributed to arson (Karter, 1982), which officially refers to the "intentional damaging or destruction or attempted damaging or destruction by means of fire or explosion of property without the consent of the owner, or of one's (own) property . . . " (U.S. Department of Justice, 1988, p. 3). Arson is difficult to prove or establish, because the evidence is often destroyed in the fire. Even with evidence that the fire was set, the motive is often unknown. Arson joined the list of FBI index crime in 1978, signifying both its seriousness and its frequency. Over 1,000 civilians and about 120 firefighters die each year in deliberately set fires; an additional 30,000 civilians and 4,000 firefighters are injured (Brady, 1983; Carter, 1980).

There appears to be a wide variety of motives for arson, including profit, revenge, spite, jealousy, crime concealment, intimidation, vandalism, and excitement. Most fires set by juveniles appear to be motivated by wishes to get back at authority or gain status, or prompted by a dare or a need for excitement. The predominant motive for adult arsonists seems to be revenge. Boudreau and his associates (1977) list six primary motives for arson and estimate their relative frequencies:

1. *Revenge, spite,* or *jealousy.* Arsonists in this category include jilted lovers, feuding neighbors, disenchanted employees, and people who want to get back at someone they believe cheated or abused them. Alcohol is often associated with this motive (Inciardi, 1970). Robbins and Robbins (1964) found that

revenge accounted for 47 percent of the fires set by adults compared to only 5 percent of those set by juveniles. In Inciardi's sample, 58 percent were motivated by a desire for revenge.

2. *Vandalism or malicious mischief.* Fires set to challenge authority or to relieve boredom are by far the most common of those set by juveniles. In the Robbins study, 80 percent of the fires set by juveniles stemmed from this motive.

3. *Crime concealment or diversionary tactics.* At least 7 to 9 percent of convicted arsonists are believed to be trying to obliterate evidence of burglaries, larcenies, and murders (Robbins & Robbins, 1964; Inciardi, 1970). The offender in this category expects that the fire will destroy any evidence that a crime was committed. Arson has also been used to divert attention while the offender burglarizes another building or residence.

4. *Profit, insurance fraud.* This is the category most likely to attract professional arsonists, who generally escape detection. Consequently, there is little hard data and few statistics to support this motive. However, since the profits gained from arson of this type are so large and the probability of detection so small, actual incidence is believed to be much higher than reported statistically.

5. *Intimidation, extortion, sabotage.* This category refers to fires set for the purpose of frightening or deterring. Examples are fires set by striking workers or employees to intimidate management or by extortionists to show that they mean business. Another example is the destruction of abortion clinics, presumably set by antiabortionists wishing to intimidate. By most accounts, arson with this motive is extremely rare.

6. *Pyromania* and other psychological motives. Pyromania is a psychiatric term for an "irresistible urge" or passion to set fires along with an intense fascination with flames. Before setting the fire, the individual is said to experience a build-up of tension; once the fire is underway, he or she experiences intense pleasure or release (DSM-III, 1980). Although the fire-setting urge is uncontrollable, the individual often provides many clues about his or her intention before setting the fire. Pyromania is believed to be a motive in only a small percentage of all arsons, but we will discuss it in more detail to illustrate how some crimes lend themselves well to psychoanalytical interpretation.

So-called pyromaniacs are believed to be regular spectators at fires in their neighborhoods and communities. They are also believed to set off false alarms and to show unusual interest in fire-fighting paraphernalia. According to the DSM-III, pyromaniacs are often characterized by lower than average intelligence, chronic personal frustrations, heavy use of alcohol, sexual problems, and resentment of authority.

Pyromania was coined in the early nineteenth century to refer to a form of "insanity" identified by the impulse to set fires without apparent motive (Schmideberg, 1953). In the mid-1800s, clinicians suggested that there was a relationship between firesetting and sexual disturbances, and psychoanalytic and psychiatric literature in particular continued to promote that link. For instance, Gold (1962, p. 416) contends that the roots of arson are "deep within the personality and have some relationship to sexual disturbance and urinary malfunction." Abrahamsen (1960, p. 129) writes: "Firesetting is a substitute for a sexual thrill, and the devastating and destructive powers of fire reflect the intensity of the pyromaniac's sexual desires, as well as his sadism."

Orthodox psychoanalytic thinking draws a connection between pleasurable urination (urethral eroticism) and firesetting. Fenichel (1945, p. 371) concluded: "Regularly deep-seated relationship to urethral eroticism is to be found. . . . In the same way that there are coprophilic perversions based on urethral eroticism, perversions may also be developed based on the derivative of urethral eroticism, pleasure in fire." This theory is based in part on the presumption that many firesetters are or have been enuretic (bedwetters) (Halleck, 1967). The theory does not suggest that enuretic people are likely to be firesetters, only that firesetters have more than their share of bedwetting behavior. Whether this relationship actually exists is still not clear from available research.

The relationship between sexual arousal and firesetting is plausible, since, through the process of classical conditioning, virtually *any* object or event can become associated with sexual arousal and gratification. The fact that some arsonists have fetishes or records of previous arrests for sexual offenses (MacDonald, 1977) lends some support to this possibility. Individuals who are sexually aroused by fire may, in general, be highly conditionable introverts. We may also expect them to be sexually, socially, and vocationally inadequate (as noted by Levin, 1976). Firesetting could be a way of feeling significant and resolving conflicts.

While some firesetters may obtain sexual arousal and gratification from fire, there is very little evidence that a majority do. In an extensive analysis of sixty-eight convicted arsonists imprisoned in Florida, South Carolina, and North Carolina, sexual "abnormality" was no more in evidence than it was in a comparable group of controls (nonarsonist offenders) (Wolford, 1972). Nor is there much evidence for the diagnostic label "pyromaniac." Koson and Dvoskin (1982) were unable to find any arsonists in their sample that met the DSM-III criteria of pyromania. More specifically, even though 38 percent of the sample were repetitive arsonists, none qualified as exhibiting a recurrent failure to resist impulses to set fires compounded by an intense fascination with firesetting and seeing them burn. In Canada, Bradford (1982) found only one individual out of thirty-four repetitive arsonists who even could even remotely qualify as a pyromaniac, and Hill et al. (1982), in another Canadian sample of thirty-eight arsonists, found none. Yesavage et al. (1983) also found no indications that fifty French arsonists were attracted to fire for sexual reasons. Similar findings have been reported for child firesetters (Kuhnley, Hendren, & Quinlan, 1982; Stewart & Culver, 1982).

However, recent research on repetitive arsonists is beginning to identify some common features. The most consistent finding is that adult repetitive arsonists, as a group, experience little control over their environment or personal lives. They are usually from a socially disadvantaged segment of the population (Jackson, Glass, & Hope, 1987). Their plight is usually compounded by an assortment of physical, mental, and psychological handicaps (Koson & Dvoskin, 1982). Compared to other criminal groups, their intellectual level (IQ scores) and educational attainment are low (Wolford, 1972; Lewis & Yarnell, 1951). They also lack social or interpersonal skills for dealing with their social environment and consequently often lack self-esteem (Hurley & Monahan, 1969; Vreeland & Levin, 1980). Depression is commonly reported, sometimes with serious suicide inclinations (Jackson, Glass, & Hope, 1987).

Therefore, the overall picture of the adult repetitive arsonist is one of inadequacy, frequent failure, social passivity, and social isolation. Theoretically, repetitive fire setting *may* be motivated by an attempt to gain some control over their lives and some social recognition. For example, the firesetting seems to be precipitated by events that exacerbate the arsonist's feelings of self-esteem, sadness, and depression (Bumpass, Fagelman, & Birx, 1983). In addition, following a firesetting, many arsonists stay at the scene of the fire, often sound the alarm, and even help fight the fire. In some cases they take heroic action to save lives. The recognition they receive for these actions probably enhances their self-esteem and instills a sense of control in their lives.

Jackson, Glass, and Hope (1987) note that most acts of firesetting by repetitive arsonists progress from small fires to large fires, and the arsonists also become increasingly more involved in fighting the fire. Furthermore, repetitive arsonists set fires alone and in secret, with virtually no one aware of their actions until caught. If caught, their history of firesetting presents an additional opportunity for them to gain attention and recognition from others.

What are the etiological factors in repetitive firesetting? Fascination and experimentation with fire appear to be a common feature of normal child development. Kafrey (1980) discovered that interest and fascination with fire appear to be nearly universal in children between five and seven years old. Furthermore, this fascination with fire begins early, with about one in five children setting fires before the age of three. Fire-setting behavior appears to decline after age seven, probably due to frequent admonishments of its dangers from parents and other adults. Those children who continue to set fires tend to be more mischievous, energetic, adventurous, and impulsive than their peers. Many are considered conduct problems by their teachers. Kafrey (1980) refers to this behavioral patterns as the "rascality pattern." The rascality pattern has also been noted by Kuhnley, Hendren, and Quinlan (1982), Stewart and Culver (1982), and Kolko, Kazdin, and Meyer (1985).

The frequent observation that youthful firesetters are conduct problems, impulsive, more hyperactive, and even more aggressive than their peers appears to be in sharp contrast to the behavior of repetitive adult firesetters, described previously. However, aggressive, acting-out, and hyperactive children are often unpopular with peers (Hartup, 1983; Maccoby, 1986), and demonstrate poor interpersonal and social skills for dealing with others. Patterson (1982) writes that impulsive, hyperactive children with a low frustration tolerance and inadequate social skills tend to be social isolates. Moreover, other research (e.g., Caspi, Elder, & Bem, 1987) indicates that ill-tempered children have considerable personal, marital, social, and financial failure throughout their lifetimes, a pattern very similar to repetitive arsonists. In addition, both the frequent childhood firesetter and repetitive adult arsonist exhibit a continual battle against the social environment as demonstrated by frequent contacts with criminal justice agencies. In their conclusion on child and adult firesetting, Vreeland and Levin (1980, p. 44) write:

> The picture turns out to be one of an individual with several maladaptive behaviour patterns, of which firesetting is one. We have identified social ineffectiveness as a common factor in the general tendency of firesetters to have drinking problems, marital, occupational and sexual problems, and to exhibit a variety of other criminal and antisocial behaviours.

Thus, firesetting may be just one component in the constellation of maladaptive behaviors displayed by these individuals. Firesetting may be among these behaviors because of previous experiences with fire. Ritvo, Shanok, & Lewis (1983) found that a surprising large number of firesetters had been burned and maltreated with fire as children. They describe how one frequent firesetter during his early childhood had his feet severely burned by his father as a punishment for lighting fires. Another boy had been beaten on his buttocks with a hot spatula by his father. Still another had his hands held over a lighted stove burner by his mother until burned for lighting fires. Ritvo, Shanok, and Lewis (1983, p. 266) speculate that these punishments may have "conveyed the message that the use of fire was an acceptable mode of retaliation."

In this section we have concentrated on the repetitive arsonists who set fires primarily for psychological and social gain. This focus is not to imply that a majority of arson fires are set by these individuals. Obviously, arson is committed for a variety of reasons by a variety of offenders, although much of it is probably committed for monetary gain, such as insurance.

BOMBINGS

In 1986, there were 858 reported bombings in the United States, resulting in fourteen deaths and 185 injuries (U.S. Department of Justice, 1987). Explosive incidents accounted for 79 percent and incendiaries (bombs with highly flammable materials) for 21 percent of the overall bombings in 1986. Two out of five bombings were directed at residential property. Vehicular bombings (cars, plans, trains) accounted for 17 percent, commercial establishments 13 percent, schools 6 percent, and postal facilities and equipment 5 percent.

In over half the bombings in 1986, the motives were unknown. In bombings where the motives were identified, the most frequent motive was mischief or vandalism (44 percent). In 23 percent of the incidents, revenge or intimidation was the primary motive. Personal animosity accounted for 15 percent, and sabotage or subversion another 7 percent.

Many of the motives for bombing are believed to resemble those for arson. However, it would appear that some bombers are more intent on destruction and injury than arsonists are, and they do not wish to cover up the cause of the destruction. Moreover, the bombing generally requires more technical knowledge than arson, and it is also more dangerous. The planning, construction, safe transportation, placing, and activating of an explosive device require more skill than dropping a match onto gasoline-soaked rags under a stairwell.

The apparent motives for bombings change with the times. Between the years 1968 and 1971, nearly half of the bombings in the U.S. were a result of "social protest" (Moll, 1974), while in 1975 over a third of the bombings were due to "personal animosity" and another third to "malicious destruction" (U.S. Department of Justice, 1976). In 1975 only 10 percent of the bombings were related to social protest. Since 1977 there has been a fairly steady decline in bombings in this country. The explanation for this decrease is unknown.

While there is certainly no single bomber-type personality, MacDonald (1977) contends that there is a personality pattern drawn to bombing which demonstrates most of the characteristics of the "compulsive fire-setter"; he calls it the "compulsive bomber." *Compulsive* implies that the individual is drawn to the activity again and again, seemingly out of the individual's control.

MacDonald reports that the compulsive bombers he has known exhibited a fascination with bombs from childhood. In addition, he found them keenly interested in discussing explosive devices and various techniques of detonating. Large segments of their life appear devoted to the study, development, and experience of bombing. More importantly, they derive excitement from their actions and are aroused by only one aspect of the explosion: the power, the fire, or the noise. One bomber confessed, "I want to become more than what I am" (MacDonald, 1977, p. 40).

In line with the psychoanalytic tradition, however, MacDonald links sexual gratification with bombing, claiming that one in six compulsive bombers obtain sexual pleasure from their explosions. This is apparently based on his observation that sexual deviation is prominent in many bombers.

One of the more dramatic and perhaps best known bombers was George Metesky, a fifty-six-year-old, known as the "Mad Bomber of New York." Metesky planted thirty-two different pipe bombs between 1940 and 1956, all supposedly designed to draw attention to the unfair labor practices of a major utility. Metesky was working for United Electric (now known as Consolidated Edision, or Con Ed) in 1931 when a gush of hot gas from a boiler knocked him down. At the time he got up and walked away without apparent injury, but he later claimed illness from the accident, inability to work, and he expected compensation. When the company repeatedly denied his requests, Metesky undertook an intense campaign de-singed to bring attention to Con Ed's "dastardly deeds." He planted bombs in locations which would receive heavy press coverage (Macy's Department Store, the New York Public Library, Grand Central Station), but he maintained he did not intend to harm anyone. Fortunately, no one was killed during his bombing missions, but some twenty-two were injured. Although his first bombing attempt failed, he subsequently became more sophisticated, technically competent, and successful.

Metesky at one point wrote a letter to the editor of a New York newspaper:

> Have you noticed the bombs in your city, if you are worried, I am sorry, and also if anyone is injured. But it cannot be helped, for justice will be served, I am not well and for this I will make the Con Edison sorry. Yes, they will regret their dastardly deeds. I will bring them before the bar of justice, public opinion will condemn them, for beware, I will place more units under theater seats in the near future. F.P. (MacDonald, 1977, p. 47)

The phrase *dastardly deeds* eventually spelled Metesky's downfall. Investigators searching the files of Con Ed for evidence of disgruntled employees uncovered it in the file folder of Metesky, who had used it in a letter to the company many years before.

Brussel (1968), the consulting psychiatrist in the Mad Bomber case, wrote a detailed account of the events surrounding the search for the bomber and the arrest, when over a half dozen law enforcement agents closed in on Metesky's home. He greeted them cordially and immediately guessed their purpose. He smiled frequently and appeared to be in a state of high self-satisfaction at capture. Throughout the trial, Metesky beamed and seemed to be enjoying the excitement he had created and the attention he was gaining. In 1957, the court found him "insane" (Brussel contends he was suffering from "paranoia"), and he was committed to Matteawan State Hospital. Metesky was released in 1973.

Although he was considered insane, he displayed a life-long design to draw attention to his plight and the perceived injustice done to him.

Metesky's behavior probably was his way of coping with his feelings about helplessness. Possibly, another principal reason for his bombings was to add excitement to his life or to become famous as the Mad Bomber. Overall, it appears that Metesky was successful in creating some significance for himself.

PROSTITUTION

Prostitution is illegal in all states except Nevada. In the popular literature, it is blamed for decreases in neighborhood property values, increases in drug abuse and violent crime, and deterioration of the American family. On the other hand, cogent arguments have been advanced in favor of its legalization. Some commentators note that prostitutes (especially female prostitutes) are more often victims than offenders, and more than one author suggests that the criminal justice system shares the role of victimizer with pimps and persons who patronize prostitutes (James, 1978). On the other hand, some social scientists and social commentators suggest that adult prostitution is a lucrative career and that the time may be ripe for society to recruit prostitutes as social workers specializing in treating some sexual problems (Adler, 1975).

Because prostitution is presently a crime and one that holds a dominant place in female criminality, it merits our consideration. Obviously, males as well as females become prostitutes. Female prostitutes, however, account for approximately one-third of the female jail and prison population (James, 1978), whereas male prostitutes are rarely incarcerated. In 1988, there were 24,293 arrests of males for prostitution (including "johns"), compared to 52,871 female arrests (U.S. Department of Justice, 1989a). Prostitution also is relevant to this text because it is a "deviant behavior" that lends itself well to psychological examination. Our purpose in discussing prostitution is not to consider its moral and policy implications, but to focus on the sociological and psychological myths and misconceptions that surround it. We will not, however, address the exploitation of juveniles of both sexes for prostitution purposes, a phenomenon quickly gaining the attention of social science researchers.

Prostitution is defined as the offering, agreement to offer, or provision of sexual relations in return for tangible rewards or special favors. It may involve either a heterosexual or homosexual pairing, or it may involve group behavior. Although it most commonly refers to the procurement of sexual intercourse with a woman by a man, a variety of sexual activity may be involved.

It is impossible to estimate the number of commercial prostitutes in the United States, since police agencies interpret the criminality of the behavior very subjectively and arbitrarily. Arrests are often dependent on social and political pressures. It is also generally recognized that prostitutes are often harassed and detained, with or without formal arrest, and for purposes other than the idealized goal of eliminating the practice. Primary clientele are believed to be white, middle class men between the ages of thirty and sixty (Haft, 1976).

Theorists and researchers have traditionally offered biased, subjective generalizations about the female prostitute. They have alternately called her feeble-minded, emotionally disturbed, a latent or manifest homosexual, oversexed, sexually deprived, a primitive creature, or an individual rigidly fixated at her Oedipal (or Electra) stage of psychosexual development. From all indications, none of these labels adequately describes *the* prostitute. Women who become prostitutes appear to come from many different walks of life, possess varied educational and family backgrounds, demonstrate a wide range of personality types, and express a great variety of motives for involvement in prostitution.

Several researchers have brought attention to a system of class structure among prostitutes. At the lower end of the continuum are the streetwalkers who work the streets; at the uppermost level are call girls, who cater to a select clientele and who are rarely arrested. In between are a variety of categories, which may (but do not inevitably) include stag party workers, escorts, masseuses, conventioneers, and circuit travelers. Coleman (1976) found that, as we go up the social class structure, the women are increasingly physically attractive, intelligent, well educated, and sophisticated. Adler (1975) points out that the contemporary prostitute is, in many instances, socially and culturally indistinguishable from women in general.

> The flashy and distinctive styles of dress have either disappeared altogether or have faded into the commonplace as they have been adopted as fashion by the rest of society. It is often no longer possible to distinguish the prostitute from the matrons, college girls, or debutantes who might congregate at any public gathering. (pp. 73–74)

It was generally believed that many prostitutes, especially at the lower status levels, came from lower- or lower-middle-class homes, but even this is now in question. James (1978) noted that a full 64 percent of her sample of streetwalkers reported their childhood family's income as middle or upper class. There seems little doubt, however, that most prostitutes come from conflictful families, where patterns of alienation from a single parent or from both parents are discernible. Many prostitutes also report negative sexual experiences in the home during preadolescence or adolescence. In an oft-cited study, 41 percent of 136 prostitutes reported incestuous experiences, usually with their father (James, 1976). Forty-seven percent reported they had been raped, and 17 percent had been raped more than once, most before reaching the age of sixteen. Studies of juvenile postitutes lend support to these findings. Silberman (cited in Bracey, 1982) interviewed over 200 juvenile prostitutes and reported that 61 percent had been sexually molested by a member of their household. Bracey (1982) found that 50 percent of juvenile prostitutes in her sample reported forcible sexual advances by older men before they reached puberty.

Contrary to popular assumption, a majority of prostitutes do not appear to be lured into the activity by organized crime, brutal pimps, under false pretenses, or to support drug habits. Recruitment by pimps, madames, or organized crime appears to have been a factor for only about 20 percent of the prostitute population. The assumption of heavy drug use among prostitutes also appears questionable. James (1978) suggests that the prostitutes apprehended by police (and who thus end up in the criminal statistics) tend to be the "hypes"—the addicts working as prostitutes to support a drug habit. They "form a special, lower class in the hierarchy of the 'fast life'"(James, 1978, p. 306). Inciardi (1980) surveyed 149 female heroin users and found a high incidence of prostitution (about one-third) among them. However, he did not find evidence for a strong causal link. The women who commited crimes to support their drug habits were much more likely to choose property offenses, like larceny or fraud, rather than prostitution.

What motivates women to engage in prostitution? An obvious, although oversimplistic answer, is money. It is important to distinguish between financial necessity and financial comfort, however. James (1976) found that only 8.4 percent of her sample started prostitution out of economic necessity, but 56.5 percent did out of a desire for money and material goods. They saw prostitution as a lucrative business that offered material rewards they otherwise might not have attained. Social rewards like parties, dancing, and expensive dining were also a factor.

The James study and others like it have dispelled several alleged motives for entering into prostitution—narcissism, frigidity, hatred of men, fears of lesbianism, or an unresolved sexual attachment to one's father (Electra complex). Some studies have reported that prostitutes may be more sexually responsive in their own personal lives than women in general (Pomeroy, 1965; James, 1976). James's finding that only 1 percent of her sample demonstrated hostility toward men damages Gibbens' (1957) "Circe complex" theory, which suggests that prostitutes have burning desires to turn men into swine. Greenwald's (1958) suggestion that prostitution is a way of combating a fear of homosexuality and a way of proving "normality" also seems to be on shaky ground. James found that, although 35 percent of her sample had experienced a lesbian relationship, only 7 percent had frequent homosexual activity. An additional 7 percent considered themselves exclusively lesbian. Although these figures appear high compared to the general female population, it should be emphasized that the prostitution sample was drawn from women who were blasé about so-called deviant behavior. They had ample opportunity for lesbian contact, yet did not apparently pursue it.

Finally, the Freudian theory that prostitution is a result of early sexual love for the opposite-sex parent, and that subsequent sexual partners represent insufficient surrogates, seems weak. According to this theory, the bulk of sexual energy and attraction is directed to the initial love object; later partners are unsatisfactory. Therefore, the sexually promiscuous female endlessly but subconsciously searches for the treasured first love object, the father (or in the case of male prostitutes, the mother). The Freudian perspective sees prostitution as individual psychopathology rather than a social phenomenon. Since a consistent finding in the research literature is that more than half of all prostitutes did not have an available father figure in the home, it is questionable whether they would develop unconscious, imagined incestuous relationships.

To conclude that women go into prostitution and remain there for financial gain is premature, however, and it oversimplifies human behavior. Why do not more women opt for that life style? Furthermore, although material gains may provide an initial incentive, it is widely recognized that most prostitutes—with the possible exception of independent, high-class call girls—do not directly profit much from their work, given the obligatory payoffs to pimps, police, hotel clerks, and taxi drivers.

Human behavior represents an infinite array of learned response patterns, and prostitution as a complex behavior should be no exception. It is frequently observed that most prostitutes find out about prostitution through friends and get started through their efforts and encouragement (James, 1978). These personal contacts provide significant models and opportunities for imitative learning. In addition, the sex-for-sale behaviors offer greater reward possibilities (money, excitement, adventure) than a previous life predicament. For some, prostitution offers a more positive and potentially exciting alternative than the home situation. Furthermore, the relationship with a pimp who often serves as husband, boyfriend, father, lover, agent, and protector (James, 1976) may be considerably more rewarding than the relationship with family.

Once these expectations and potentially rewarding behaviors are acquired, continued involvement depends partly on the actual rewards obtained. Do the positives of prostitution outweigh the negatives? Even given "good money" and an ideal situation in which the prostitute is relatively independent, few personalities would seem suited for long-term prostitution. To be habitually used solely as a sexual object would appear to require, among other things, a learned method of detachment and the availability of other sources of self-esteem.

Prostitution appears to be an emotionally stressful and psychologically draining occupation. James found that at least 50 percent of her sample listed emotional stress, worry about physical harm at the hands of a customer, or low self-esteem as major disadvantages. Another 20 percent listed the stress of worrying about venereal disease, reactions of family and society, personal vulnerability, and feelings of helplessness as primary disadvantages.

Legalization may alleviate some of the stress, but it is unlikely that it would change the situation substantially. As one prostitute interviewed by Millett (1974) remarked: "The worst part about prostitution is that you're obliged not to sell sex only, but your humanity. That's the worst part of it: that what you're selling is your human dignity. Not really so much in bed, but in accepting the agreement—in becoming a bought person" (p. 140).

SUMMARY AND CONCLUSIONS

The main theme of this chapter centers on the ways property offenders minimize, neutralize, deny, and justify their actions to themselves and others. We have reviewed the property crimes of burglary, larceny, motor vehicle theft, shoplifting, robbery, white-collar crime, and the tangential property crimes of arson, bombing, and hostage taking. Perceived control of one's environment is a secondary theme. We also covered briefly an example of a crime against the public order, namely prostitution. We found that this "victimless" crime is replete with myths and misunderstandings, and is characterized by limited sytematic study, especially in more recent research.

While monetary gain is certainly a powerful motive in property crimes, the cognitive standards against which the offender's behavior is judged and regulated are crucial. These points of reference are strongly influenced by the social context and by one's immediate reference groups, such as fellow workers or peers. Reference groups and the social context are especially powerful influences in white-collar crimes, specifically corporate crime and the blue-collar offenses. By restructuring their cognitions to align them with the social climate, white-collar offenders are able to engage in behavior that they would otherwise perceive as reprehensible. Conventional property offenders are less likely to restructure their cognitions drastically, although they too may do so. White-collar offenders often deny they are doing anything wrong; traditional property offenders are more likely to admit wrongdoing, although like most criminals, they also justify it.

In discussing white-collar crime, we focused on Bandura's strategies for justifying or denying unlawful behavior. Each type of strategy involves either restructuring cognitions or denying consequences of one's conduct. All strategies promote a neutralization of any guilt feelings or self-punishment. The price we pay for the human brain is its powerful ability to justify even heinous and reprehensible actions. It may be that, in the long run, we have more to fear from corporate and organizational behavior than from any collection of conventional crimes.

CHAPTER ELEVEN
Drugs and Crime

In a recent poll (Strasser, 1989a) of 1,000 individuals randomly selected across the continental United States, two-thirds of the respondents felt that the sale and usage of drugs was the key cause of crime. In this chapter we will review the evidence in support or against this public perception.

The relationship between drugs and crime may be viewed from two perspectives: (1) the use, sale, and possession of an illegal drug as a crime; and (2) the effect of drugs on antisocial behavior. Concentrating on drug possession and consumption would require sifting through varied regulations and statistics, many of which are ambiguous and most of which differ from state to state. For our purposes, we are most concerned with the effect various drugs have on the criminal behaviors discussed throughout this text. Is a person more likely to be violent while under the influence of drugs? And if so, which ones? Are people more sexually aroused and aggressive under the influence of certain drugs and thus more likely to rape or otherwise sexually assault? A considerable body of research is available to help answer these questions.

Four major categories of psychoactive drugs will be covered. To keep the chapter within manageable limits, however, we will focus on only one or two representative drugs within each group, usually the one most often associated with crime. The *hallucinogens* or psychedelics, which include LSD (lysergic acid diethylamine), mescaline, psilocybin, phencyclidine, ketamine, marihuana, and hashish, will be our first category. So called because they sometimes generate hallucinations, the hallucinogens are chemicals that lead to a change in consciousness involving an alteration of reality. In some respects they replace the present world with an alternative one, although persons using them can generally attend to their altered state and to reality simultaneously. Marihuana, classified as a hallucinogen, is certainly a mild one for a majority who use it. Because of its widespread use and the public's tendency to mistakingly associate it with crime and bizarre behavior, it will be the main drug covered under the hallucinogens category. We will also include phencylidine (PCP), a powerful drug that has been linked to crime during the 1980s.

Next, we will discuss the *stimulants*, so called because they appear to stimulate central nervous system functions. They include amphetamines, clinical antidepressants, cocaine, caffeine, and nicotine. Again because of an alleged relationship with crime, amphetamines and cocaine will be highlighted.

The third group includes the *opiate narcotics*, which generally have sedative (sleep-inducing) and analgesic (pain-relieving) effects. Heroin will be featured in this section. The heroin addict appears frequently in crime statistics, since it is believed that he or she often turns to crime—particularly property crime—to finance this expensive habit.

Finally, alcohol will represent the *sedative-hypnotic* chemicals that depress central nervous system functions. In most instances, the sedative-hypnotics are all capable of sedating the nervous system and reducing anxiety and tension.

The relationship between drugs and crimes is complicated by a three-fold interaction: (1) the pharmacological effects of the drug, which refers to the chemical impact of the drug on the body; (2) the psychological characteristics of the individual using the drug; and (3) the psychosocial conditions under which the drug is taken. Pharmacological effects include features of the nervous system, such as the amount of neurotransmitter substances within neurons, and body weight, blood composition, and other physiological features that significantly influence the chemical effects of the drug. Psychological variables include the mood of person at the time the drug is consumed, previous experience with the drug, and the person's expectancies about the drug's effects. Psychosocial variables include the social atmosphere under which the drug is taken. The people who are present and their expectations, moods, and behavior all may influence an individual's reactions to a drug.

In order to understand the effects of any drug, therefore, the pharmacological, psychological, and psychosocial variables all must be taken into account. Considering the fact that crime is complex to begin with, deciphering the crime-drug connection becomes very difficult, and the conclusions are necessarily that much more elusive and tentative.

The relationship between drugs and crime is further complicated by the cultural, subcultural, and racial aspects of drug consumption. The use of heroin, illegal methadone, and cocaine, for instance, has traditionally been a black phenomenon; whites have been more inclined to be heavy users of amphetamines and barbiturates (Inciardi, 1981). In recent years, however, cocaine has rapidly gained favor among the middle class, regardless of race. Cultural preferences shift and change depending on drug availability, law enforcement priorities, and changes in cultural attitudes.

Furthermore, certain professional criminal groups often prefer one drug over another. Professional pickpockets, shoplifters, and burglars, for example—when they use drugs—have a distinct preference for those that steady their nerves and provide relief from the pressures of their occupation (Inciardi, 1981). Professional pickpockets often consider opiates instrumental in furthering their careers. To some extent, this may have a cyclical effect, since their material gain from their crimes is often used to obtain the drugs.

Before proceeding, we must distinguish two terms that are consistently used in the drug literature: *tolerance* and *dependence*. Drug tolerance is the "state of progressively decreased responsiveness to a drug" (Julien, 1975, p. 29). Tolerance is indicated if the individual requires a larger dose of the drug to reach the same effects he or she has previously experienced. In other words, the person has become psychologically and physiologically used to or habituated to the drug.

Dependence may be physical or psychological, or both. In simple terms, physical dependence refers to the physiological distress and physical pain a person suffers if he or she goes without the drug for any length of time. Psychological dependence is difficult to distinguish from physical dependence, but it is characterized by an overwhelming desire to use the drug for a favorable effect. The person is convinced that he or she needs the drug to maintain an optimal sense of well-being. The degree of psychological dependence varies widely from person to person and drug to drug. In its extreme form, the person's life is permeated with thoughts of procuring and using the drug, and he or she may resort to crime to obtain it. In common parlance, the person who is extremely psychologically and/or physically dependent is the addict.

Secondary psychological dependence may also develop. While primary dependence is associated with the reward of the drug experience (positive reinforcement), secondary dependence refers to expectancies about aversive withdrawal or the painful effects that will accompany absence of the drug. Thus, to avoid the anticipated pain and discomfort associated with withdrawal, the individual continues to take the drug (negative reinforcement).

THE HALLUCINOGENS: CANNABIS

Marihuana, which apparently originated in Asia, is among the oldest and most frequently used intoxicants. The earliest reference to it was found in a book on pharmacy written by the Chinese emperor Shen Nung in 2737 B.C.

(Ray, 1972). It was called the "Liberator of Sin" and recommended for such ailments as "female weakness," constipation, and absent-mindedness. The word *maihuana* is commonly believed to have derived from "mary jane," Mexican slang for cheap tobacco, or from the Portugueses word *mariguano*, meaning intoxicant.

The drug is prepared from the plant *Cannabis*, an annual which is cultivated or grows freely as a weed in both tropical and temperate climates. There are at least three species of Cannabis—sativa, indica, and ruderalis— each differing in psychoactive potency. The psychoactive (intoxicating) properties of the plant reside principally in the chemical Delta-9 tetrahydrocannabinol (THC), found mainly in its resin. Thus, the concentration and quality of THC within parts of the plant determine the potency or psychoactive power of the drug.

THC content varies from one preparation to another, partly due to the quality of the plant itself, but also due to its environment. The strain of the plant, the climate, and the soil conditions all affect THC content. For example, the resin is believed to retard the dehydration of the flowering elements and thus is produced in greater quantities in hot, tropical climates than in temperate zones (Hofmann, 1975). Consequently, cannabis grown in the tropics (Mexico, Columbia, Jamaica, and North Africa) presumably has greater psychoactive potential than American-grown hemp, a product not highly prized by experienced cannabis users. More recent information suggests, however, that THC potency is more a feature of the species of the cannabis plant than of geographic area or climatic conditions (Ray, 1983).

The cannabis extracts used most commonly in the United States are marihuana and hashish. Marihuana is usually prepared by cutting the stem beneath the lowest branches, air drying, and stripping seeds, bracts, flowers, leaves, and small stems from the plant. There is no evidence that the female cannabis plant contains more THC than the male. Hashish, the arabic word for "dry grass," is produced by scraping or in some other way extracting the resin secreted by the flowers. Therefore, hashish, which is usually sold in this country in small cubes, has more THC content than Marihuana. Hofmann (1975) reports that the THC content in hashish ranges from 5 to 12 percent, while the more potent forms of marihuana (e.g., ganja from Jamaica) contain about 4 to 8 percent THC. Mexican varieties often contain less than 1 percent of THC and American varieties often less than 0.2 percent.

When exposed to air over a period of time, marihuana appears to lose its psychoactive potency, since THC is converted to cannabinol and other inactive compounds (Mechoulam, 1970). Cannabis extracts with higher levels of resin deteriorate more rapidly than those with lower levels.

In the United States, marihuana and hashish are usually smoked, most often in hand-rolled cigarettes. In a national survey conducted in 1979, over 50 million Americans admitted they had at least tried marihuana (Ray, 1983). A common practice in other countries is to consume cannabis as "tea" or mixed with other beverages or food.

Psychological Effects

The psychological effects of cannabis are so subjective and dependent on such a wide range of variables that any generalizations must be accompanied by the warning that there are numerous exceptions. Reactions to cannabis, like all psychoactive drugs, depend on the complex interactions of both pharmacological and extrapharmacological factors. As we noted, these include the mood of the user, the user's expectations about the drug, the social context in which it is used, and the user's past experiences with the drug. The strong influence of these extrapharmacological factors together with the widespread variation in THC content in any sample of cannabis make it exceedingly difficult to obtain comparable research data. Essentially, the effects of cannabis are unique to each individual. Except for increases in heart rate, increases in peripheral blood flow, and reddening of the membranes around the eyes, there are few consistent physiological changes reported for all persons (Hofmann, 1975; National Commission, 1972; Canadian Government Commission of Inquiry, 1971).

Addiction to THC does occur, but only at doses and continued use far above what is now used recreationally (Ray, 1983). Furthermore, the person who uses marihuana must *learn* to use the drug to reach a euphoric "stoned" or "high" state. Ray (1983) reports that a three-stage learning process is involved. First, users must inhale the smoke deeply and hold it in their lungs for twenty to forty seconds. Then, they must learn to identify and control the effects. Finally, they must learn to label the effects as pleasant.

Cannabis and Crime

Public concern about the connection between cannabis and crime was stimulated by a number of articles printed in a New Orleans newspaper as long ago as 1926 (Ray, 1972). In 1931, a popular article concluded that one out of every four persons arrested in New Orleans was *addicted* to cannabis. With public interest activated, a drive to get the "dangerous" drug outlawed was soon underway. It was spearheaded by the then Commissioner of Narcotics, Harry Anslinger, who convinced Congress and many states that marihuana often led to serious crime and was a threat to the moral fabric of American society. During this time (the 1930s), marihuana use was often linked with both violent and "perverted" crime.

In 1937, Congress passed the Marihuana Tax Act, a bill intended to add muscle to antimarihuana laws that by then existed in forty-six states. The Tax Act did not actually outlaw cannabis, but it taxed the grower, distributor, seller, and buyer prohibitively and established so many requirements that it was nearly impossible to have anything to do with any form of cannabis (Ray, 1972). Interestingly, none of the attitudes or regulations were supported by comprehensive scientific investigations or evidence that marihuana was harmful. The information communicated was anecdotal; the "documentation" consisted of testimony of the "I know a case where" variety. The U.S. Supreme Court eventually declared the Marihuana Tax Act unconstitutional.

In 1939, Bromberg published results of a study conducted in New York between the years 1932 and 1937. Out of a total of 16,854 prisoners, only sixty-seven said they were cannabis users and only six of those were indicted for a violent crime. Bromberg concluded that the relationship between marihuana use and crime was not substantiated, but staunch advocates of the marihuana-crime connection were not swayed.

Numerous research projects directed at the effects of cannabis were launched during the 1950s, 1960s, and early 1970s. Many of these studies had methodological shortcomings and did not control for parity of dosage levels, means of administering the drug, and THC content in the drug itself. Psychological factors associated with the subjects were not considered carefully enough, and experimental settings and instructions were haphazard. At first, some of the research suggested a relationship between cannabis use and criminal behavior. However, with more sophisticated statistical analyses that controlled demographic and criminal background variables, the earlier results were found to be spurious (National Commission, 1972). To date, no investigation has established a causal link between the use of cannabis and criminal activity. Of course, this assertion excludes the illegal acts of selling, possessing, or using the drug.

Independent research as well as investigations conducted by government-sponsored commissions strongly indicate that marihuana does not directly contribute to criminal behavior. After an extensive review of available literature, the National Commission on Marihuana and Drug Abuse (1972, p. 470) came to this conclusion: "There is no systematic empirical evidence, at least that is drawn from the American experience, to support the thesis that the use of marihuana either inevitably or generally causes, leads to or precipitates criminal, violent, aggressive or delinquent behavior of sexual or nonsexual nature." The Commission Report (p. 470) adds: "If anything, the effects observed suggest that marihuana may be more likely to neutralize criminal behavior and to militate against the commission of aggressive acts."

One of the predominant effects of THC is relaxation and a marked decrease in physical activity (Tinklenberg & Stillman, 1970). THC induces muscular weakness and inability to sustain physical effort, so that the user wishes nothing more strenuous than to stay relatively motionless. As Tinklenberg and Stillman (1970, p. 341) note, "'being stoned' summarizes these sensations of demobilizing lethargy." It is difficult to imagine "stoned" users engaging in assaultive or violent activity. In anything, THC should reduce the likelihood of criminal activity, particularly aggressive conduct, as the Commission suggested. There is some evidence to support this conclusion.

Tinklenberg and Woodrow (1974) found that drug users who use mainly marihuana seem less inclined toward violence and aggression than their counterparts who prefer other drugs, such as alcohol or amphetamines. After examining drug usage among lower-class minority youth, Blumer and his associates (1967) made the same observation. In fact, they found that marihuana users deliberately shunned aggression and violence; in order to maintain one's status in the group, it was important to remain "cool" and nonaggressive, regardless of provocation.

Although the empirical evidence so far indicates that cannabis does not, as a rule, stimulate aggressive behavior or other criminal actions, whenever we deal with human behavior there will be exceptions. Individuals familiar with the effects of cannabis have heard of occasional negative experiences produced by THC. Although the phenomenon is rare, some people do report feelings of panic, hypersensitivity, feelings of being out of contact with their surroundings, and bizarre behavior. Some individuals have experienced rapid, disorganized intrusions of irrelevant thoughts, which prompted them to feel they were losing control of their mind. Under these conditions, it is plausible that one would interpret the actions of others as threatening. It is also possible that these panicked individuals might attack those surrounding them.

However, those who investigate cannabis effects usually agree that people who act violently under the influence of the drug were probably predisposed to act that way, with or without the drug (National Commission, 1972). The evidence indicates that violent marihuana users were violent prior to using cannabis. In other words, they learned the behavioral pattern independently of cannabis. In addition, they have come to expect that the drug will "bring out" aggression or violence in them.

In summary, there is no solid evidence to indicate that cannabis contributes to or encourages violent or property crime, in spite of continuing beliefs that this relationship exists. In fact, there is evidence to suggest that cannabis users are *less* criminally or violently prone under the influence of the drug than users of other drugs, such as alcohol and amphetamines. There are also no supportive data that cannabis is habit forming to the point where the user must get a "fix" and will burglarize or rob to obtain funds to purchase the drug.

Phencyclidine (PCP)

PCP may be classified as a central nervous system depressant, anesthetic, tranquilizer, or hallucinogen. It has many effects, but most pronounced is its barbiturate-like downer effect, perceptual distortions and hallucinations, and its amphetamine-like upper effects, such as excitation and hyperactivity. An overdosed person, for example, may show signs of both moving from upper to downer effects, while having hallucinations.

PCP was first synthesized in 1957 but, due to its psychotic and hallucinogenic reactions, it was taken off the market for human consumption in 1965 and limited to veterinary medicine as an animal immobilizing agent. Between 1973 and 1979 its popularity increased but then declined briefly between 1979 and 1981. Since 1982, however, it has showed a resurgence in popularity (Crider, 1986). Most users are male, black, and between the ages of twenty and twenty-nine (Crider, 1986). The behavior of *some* individuals under the influence of PCP is highly unpredictable and may lead to life-threatening situations. Under the spell of PCP psychosis, delusions of superhuman strength, persecution, and grandiosity are not uncommon. On occasion, they may use weapons to defend themselves and commit other acts of violence. However, the incidence of violence caused by PCP influence is unknown.

There is wide variation in degree of purity and dosage forms of PCP manufactured in clandestine laboratories. It comes in capsules, tablets, liquids, or powders. It may be administered orally, by inhalation, and at times by intravenous injection. Users usually combine PCP with other drugs, particularly marihuana and alcohol. It can cause death, although the majority of fatal doses were combined with alcohol (Brunet et al., 1985–1986). Because of its adverse and negative effects, the reasons for its popularity remain obscure.

The available evidence clearly indicates that PCP users tend to be multiple illicit drug users (polydrug users). In addition, it continues to be one of the more common drugs found in arrestee populations. Wish (1986) reports that in an urinalysis study of nearly 5,000 male arrestees in Manhattan in 1984, 12 percent showed evidence of PCP. Furthermore, 49 percent of those using PCP were also using other drugs at the time of the arrest, usually cocaine. In a similar project conducted in Washington, D.C., 30 percent of the male arrestees were using PCP. In both studies, the vast majority of the subjects were arrested for goal-oriented, income-generating crimes rather than violent offenses. However, to what extent PCP propels a person toward a life of crime is largely unkown, but it does not seem likely that the PCP user regularly engages in crime to support his or her habit. PCP users are generally polydrug users who have demonstrated a variety of antisocial conduct prior to PCP usage. Polydrug usage is more likely to be one symptom within a complicated matrix of other symptoms found in certain individuals habitually "going against" their environment.

AMPHETAMINES AND COCAINE

Amphetamines and cocaine are classified as central nervous system stimulants and have highly similar effects. Amphetamines are part of a group of synthetic drugs known collectively as *amines*. Cocaine (coke, snow, candy) is a chemical extracted from the coca plant (Erythroxylon coca), native to Peru. The amines in particular produce effects in the sympathetic nervous system, a subdivision of the autonomic nervous system, which arouse the person to action that might include fighting or fleeing from a frightening situation.

Amphetamines are traditionally classified into three major categories: (1) amphetamine (Benzedrine); (2) dextroamphetamine (Dexedrine); and (3) methamphetamine (Methedrine or Desoxyn). Of the three, Benzedrine is the least potent. All may be taken orally, inhaled, or injected, and all act directly on the central nervous system, particular the reticular activating system (Bloomquist, 1970). Once the drug is taken, it is rapidly assimilated into the bloodstream, but it is metabolized and eliminated from the body relatively slowly. Both psychological and physiological reactions to these drugs vary dramatically with the dose; in addition, the effects of massive quantities intravenously injected differ substantially from low doses administered orally. Reactions to the drugs also vary widely among individuals. For our purposes, we will refer to amphetamines in the broad sense, including all three categories.

The common slang terms for amphetamines include bennies, dexies, copilots, meth, speed, white cross, uppers, "A," pep pills, diet pills, jolly beans, black bombers, truck drivers, eye openers, wakeups, hearts, footballs, bombitas, crossroads, cartwheels, coasts-to-coasts, splash, and purple hearts. The slang names are derived from the various effects, the purposes to which the drug is put, the shape and color of the drug, or the trade name of the manufacturers.

The American pharmaceutical industry produces an estimated 8 to 10 billion doses of amphetamines annually (Hofmann, 1975). This figure is believed to be considerably higher than the estimated number of amphetamine prescriptions dispensed during the same period of time. Prescriptions reached an all-time high in 1965 (24.5 million), but this figure has declined steadily since then because of widespread concern about misuse of the drug and its effect. A sizeable portion of all amphetamines produced end up in the black market for distribution. Because the drug is a synthetic compound, unlike cannabis or cocaine, it can be easily produced by self-appointed chemists for large-scale illegal distribution. Therefore, it is exceedingly difficult to estimate the quantity of amphetamines consumed each year in the Unites States.

Cocaine has traditionally been much more expensive than amphetamines, partly because it is a natural organic substance and cannot be produced synthetically. The coca plant from which it is extracted thrives at elevations of 2,000 to 8,000 feet with heavy rainfall (100 inches per year). It is an evergreen shrub, growing to about 3 feet tall, and generally found in the eastern slopes of the Andes. It has long been used by Peruvians living in or near the Andes. Mountain natives chew coca leaves almost continuously and commonly keep them tucked in their cheek (Ray, 1972). Coca leaves are also used for tea. There are at least 200 strains of coca plants, but the vast majority contain little if any cocaine. However, with the increasing appetite of North Americans for cocaine, South American growers and entrepreneurs have not only developed vast new areas for the cultivation of coca but also new, more vigorous strains of the plant (Inciardi, 1986).

In the United States and Canada, cocaine is usually administered nasally (sniffing), inhaling (smoking), or intravenously. Cocaine taken orally is poorly absorbed because it is hydrolyzed by gastrointestinal secretions. Light users normally sniff the drug to obtain their "high," but chronic sniffing can result in nasal irritation and inflammation. The common unit in the black market is the "spoon," which approximates one gram of the diluted drug. In most cases, cocaine is diluted twenty to thirty times its weight. It is estimated that there are 6 million (3% of the population) regular cocaine users in the United States (*National Geographic*, January, 1989, p. 25).

Coca Cola contained cocaine as an active ingredient until 1903, when caffeine was substituted (Kleber, 1988). In fact, around the turn of the century, cocaine was used not only in soft drinks (such as Kos-Kola, Wise-ola, and Care-Cola), but even in cigarettes and cigars, various tonics, foods, sprays, and ointments (including hemorrhoid salves) (Smart, 1986). The famous drink "Vin Mariani" so popular among the wealthy at the time was a combination of French wine and cocaine. However, cocaine began to fall into disfavor when people became concerned about its dangerous and undesirable effects. By 1910, cocaine had fast become the most hated and feared drug in North America (Kleber, 1988). The Harrison Narcotics Act of 1914 in the United States and the Propriety and Patents Medicines Act of 1908 in Canada sharply curtailed or terminated its usage, and the popularity of cocaine correspondingly declined until the 1960s.

In national surveys conducted in the early 1980s in Canada, about 4 percent of the college students and 3 percent of the adults said they used cocaine at least once during the year (Smart, 1986). In the United States, the incidence is higher, with about 16 to 20 percent of the college students using cocaine at least once during the year (Johnson, Bachman, & O'Malley, 1983), and about 28 percent of the adults saying they used the drug at least once in their lifetimes (Miller et al., 1983).

Psychological Effects

In small doses, both amphetamines and cocaine increase wakefulness, alertness, and vigilance, improve concentration, and produce a feeling of clear thinking. There is generally an elevation of mood, mild euphoria, increased sociability, and a belief that one can do just about anything. In large doses, the effects may be irritability, hypersensitivity, delirium, panic, aggression, hallucinations, and psychosis. Injected at chronically high doses, these drugs may precipitate "toxic psychosis," a syndrome with many of the psychotic features of paranoid schizophrenia. With the metabolization and elimination of the drug, the psychotic episode usually dissipates.

Stimulants and Crime

Heavy users of amphetamines typically prefer to inject the drug directly into the bloodstream, cranking up with several hundred milligrams at one time. During these speed "runs" the user may engage in aggressive or violent behavior (Tinklenberg & Stillman, 1970; Hofmann, 1975; National Commission on Marihuana and Drug Abuse, 1973). Ellinwood (1971) studied the case histories of thirteen persons who committed homicide under amphetamine intoxication and found in most instances that the homicidal act was directly related to the effects of the amphetamine itself.

At this point in our knowledge, there is little evidence to support a relationship between stimulants and crime. Both amphetamines and cocaine, in small doses, increase alertness and concentration. In large doses, they generally produce negative psychological effects. However, at this point there is not enough evidence to conclude that they facilitate either property or violent crime.

Crack

The most common form of cocaine smoking in the United States is freebasing. Freebase is prepared by dissolving cocaine hydrochloride in water and then adding a strong base such as ammonia or baking soda to the solution (Weiss & Mirin, 1987). This cocaine freebase is generally dissolved in ether to extract the cocaine, and then the ether is removed by drying. Other methods may be used which bypass the ether method. The result is a product ranging from 37 to 96 percent purity (Weiss & Mirin, 1987).

In recent years, a purified, high-potency form of freebase cocaine known as "crack" has exploded in popularity. Several times more pure than ordinary street cocaine, crack smoking generates a very rapid intense state of euphoria, which peaks in about five minutes. The psychological and physical effects of crack are as powerful as any intravenously injected cocaine. However, the euphoria is short-lived, ending in about ten to twenty minutes after inhalation, and is followed by depression, irritability, and often an intense craving for more. Although most users limit themselves to one or two "hits," some users seek multiple hits.

Some experts regard crack as the most addictive drug currently available on the street (Weiss & Mirin, 1987). Its popularity probably resides in the instantaneous psychological effects it provides, its inexpensiveness, and its wide availability throughout most U.S. major cities. In recent years, about one-third of all arrests made by the New York City Narcotics Division involved cocaine, and over half of them involved crack (Cohn, 1986). Because it is so inexpensive and available, it has become a very popular drug for the young—including preteenagers. It is also extremely dangerous to the user and may result in a rapid, irregular heartbeat, respiratory failure, or a cerebral hemorrhage.

The relationship between crack and crime remains obscure. One thing that does emerge form the research literature is that crack users are often polydrug users. Furthermore, persistent offenders tend to be polydrug users. While it is difficult at this point in our knowledge to determine which comes first, drug use or involvment in crime, the evidence does suggest that persistent offenders have engaged in a variety of illegal activities and troublesome conduct throughout their lifetimes, probably before drug abuse.

NARCOTIC DRUGS

The word *narcotics* usually provokes intense negative reactions and very often is quickly associated with crime. Like the word *dope,* it is widely misused to denote all illegal drugs. In this chapter, narcotic drugs refer only to the derivatives of (or products pharmacologically similar to products of) the opium or poppy plant, *Papaver somniferum.*

The opium plant, an annual, grows to about 3 to 5 feet in height. Today, most opium is grown in two regions: (1) the Golden Triangle: Laos, which produces 70 metric tons of opium per year; Burma, which produces 532 metric tons; and Thailand, which produces 36 metric tons; and (2) the Golden Crescent: Iran, Afghanistan, and Pakistan, which together produce about 865 metric tons annually (Inciardi, 1986). Interestingly, it is estimated that about 150 metric tons of opium per year are sufficient to meet the needs of all the world's narcotic addicts (Ray, 1983).

Narcotic drugs can be divided into three major categories on the basis of the kind of preparation they require: (1) natural narcotics, which include the grown opium; (2) semisynthetic narcotics, which include the chemically prepared heroin; and (3) synthetic narcotics, which are wholly prepared chemically and include methadone, meperidine, and phenazocine. All are narcotics because they produce similar effects: relief of pain, relaxation, peacefulness, and sleep (*Narco,* of Greek origin, means "to sleep"). Narcotics are highly addictive for some individuals, to the point where they develop a relentless and strong craving for the drug. Many heavy narcotic users, however, lead successful, productive lives, without significant interference in their daily routine. There is no single type of opium user.

Heroin

The most heavily used illegal narcotic in this country is heroin. There are an estimated 500,000 heroin addicts in the United States, and perhaps two or three times as many heroin "chippers" (i.e., occasional users) (Ray, 1983). The street scene continually changes with respect to the use of illegal drugs, but heroin use is apparently becoming more popular. Heroin looks like a white, crystalline material and is characterized by the bitter taste of alkaloid. Its appearance is largely dictated by its diluents, which in most cases make up 95 to 98 percent of its total weight. A good "bag" of heroin contains about 300 milligrams of diluents and only 15 milligrams of heroin (Hofmann, 1975).

Heroin is rarely taken orally, because the absorption rate is slow and incomplete. It may be administered intramuscularly, subcutaneously ("skin popping"), or intravenously ("mainlining"), or it may be inhaled ("snorted"). The experienced heroin user strongly prefers mainlining because of the sensational thrill, splash, rush, or kick it provides. The effects of heroin depend on the quantity taken, the method of administration, the interval between administrations, the tolerance and dependence of the user, the setting, and the user's expectations. Effects usually wear off in from five to eight hours, depending on the user's tolerance.

Like all the narcotics, heroin is a central nervous system depressant. For many users, it promotes mental clouding, dream-like states, light sleep punctuated by vivid dreams, and a general feeling of "sublime contentment." The body may become permeated with a feeling of warmth, and the extremities may feel heavy. There is little inclination toward physical activity; the user prefers to sit motionless and in a fog.

Heroin and Crime

No other drug group is as closely associated with crime as the narcotics, particularly heroin. The image of the desperate "junkie" looking for a fix is familiar to everyone. Furthermore, because of the adverse effects of the drug, it is assumed that the heroin user is bizarre, unpredictable, and therefore dangerous. However, high doses of narcotics produce sleep rather than the psychotic or paranoid panic states sometimes produced by high doses of amphetamines. Therefore, narcotics users rarely become violent or dangerous. Research strongly indicates that addicts do not, as a general rule, participate in violent crimes such as assault, rape, or homicide (National Institute on Drug Abuse, 1978; Canadian Government's Commission of Inquiry, 1971; National Commission on Marihuana and Drug Abuse, 1973; Tinklenberg & Stillman, 1970).

Research evidence does suggest a relationship between heroin addiction and money-producing crime. A study in Miami of 573 narcotics users found that they were responsible for almost 6,000 robberies, 6,700 burglaries, 900 stolen vehicles, 25,000 instances of shoplifting, and 46,000 other events of larceny and fraud (Inciardi, 1986). Self-report surveys find that heroin users report financing their habits largely through "acquisitive crime" (Jarvis & Parker, 1989; Mott, 1986). Parker and Newcombe (1987) studied crime patterns and heroin use in the English community of Wirral, located in northwest England. They found that many heroin users were from the poor sections of the community and were young. The researchers were also able to divide their sample into three groups: (1) The largest group consisted of young offenders who were not known to be using heroin but were highly criminally active; (2) heroin users who engaged in considerable acquisitive crime, but were involved in this type of crime prior to their heroin addiction; and (3) heroin users who started engaging in acquisitive crime after their habit in order to support the habit. The Parker-Newcombe investigation suggests that some heroin addicts do support their habit through crime.

Ball, Shaffer, and Nurco (1983) found that heroin addicts committed more money-producing crime when they were addicted compared to times when they were not. Still, it may be misleading to examine the heroin-crime relationship in isolation without considering the possible interactions between polydrug use and crime, or to conclude that heroin addiction causes crime. All we can say with some confidence at this point is that those who use heroin also seem to be deeply involved in money-producing crime. Heroin users, however, may not be driven to crime by the needs of their addiction. Heroin users, particularly polydrug users, *may* represent a segment of society that runs counter to society's rules and expectations in multiple ways, drug use and larceny among them. It may well be that most heroin-addicted criminals were involved in crime before they became addicted. Furthermore, polydrug users tend to switch from drug to drug, depending on what is available and inexpensive at the time, and do not seem physiologically desperate for any one drug. They substitute one drug for the other.

THE DEPRESSANTS: ALCOHOL

Despite the public concern over heroin, opium, marihuana, cocaine (especially crack) and the amphetamines, the number one drug of abuse has been and continues to be alcohol (ethanol, ethyl alcohol, grain alcohol). About two-thirds of all adults in the United States report that they use alcohol regularly (Rosenhan & Seligman, 1984), and surveys estimate that anywhere between 12 to 33 percent of the men and 2 to 5 percent of the women drink heavily (Helzer, 1987). Other surveys indicate that one-third of American families have problems with alcohol (Peele, 1984). Alcohol is responsible for more deaths and violence (it is the third major cause of death) than all other drugs combined. Approximately 25,000 individuals are killed each year, for example, in traffic accidents in which a driver was under the influence of alcohol.

Psychological Effects

The social, psychological, and physical effects of excessive use of alcohol can be just as destructive to the individual, his or her family, and society in general, as heroin abuse. And similar to heroin, the alcoholic can develop a strong psychological and physical dependence on the drug. Society's attitudes toward alcohol are dramatically different from its attitudes toward other drugs of abuse, however. In virtually every part of the United States it is legal and socially acceptable to consume the drug. In public, drinking behavior is generally unregulated unless it involves heavy intoxication and correspondingly unacceptable conduct, like disturbing the peace or operating a motor vehicle. In private, one can get as drunk as one wishes, a privilege not granted with respect to other drugs.

The effects of alcohol are complex, and we can provide only a cursory treatment here. At low doses (2 or 4 ounces of whiskey, for example) alcohol seems to act as a stimulant on the central nervous system. Initially, it appears to affect the inhibitory chemical process of nervous system transmission, producing in the individual feelings of euphoria, good cheer, and social and physical warmth. In moderate and high quantities, however, alcohol begins to depress the excitatory processes of the central nervous system, as well as its inhibitory processes. Consequently, the individual's neuromuscular coordination and visual acuity are reduced, and he or she does not perceive pain and fatigue. The ability to concentrate is also impaired. Very often, self-confidence increases and the person becomes more daring, sometimes foolishly so. It is believed that alcohol at moderate levels begins to "numb" the higher brain centers which process cognitive information, especially judgment and abstract thought. It should be emphasized at this point that the levels of intoxication are not necessarily dependent on the amount of alcohol ingested; as for other psychoactive drugs, the effects depend on a myriad of interacting variables.

Alcohol and Crime

The belief that alcohol is a major cause of crime appears to be deeply embedded in American society. Surveys, for example, suggest that over 50 percent of the population are convinced that alcohol is a major factor in crimes of violence (Critchlow, 1986). This pervasive belief appears to be based on the premise that alcohol instigates aggressive conduct in some individuals or somehow diminishes the checks and balances of nonaggressive, nonviolent behavior.

Coleman (1976) calls alcohol a "catalyst for violence," noting that about one out of every three arrests in the United States results from alcohol abuse. A survey of state prisons in 1974 found that 43 percent of all inmates had been drinking when they committed the crime for which they were serving time (Law Enforcement Assistance Administration, 1976). In a Missouri study, 55 percent of all males charged with capital or first degree murder over a three-year period were taking alcohol, drugs, or a combination of both at the time of the homicide (Holcomb & Anderson, 1983). Cole, Fisher, and Cole (1968) reported that 51 percent of a sample of California women arrested for homicide had been drinking at the time of their offense. Fifty-five percent of those convicted for murder in Britain (Gillies, 1965) and 51 percent of those convicted in France (Derville et al., 1961) were drinking at the time of the violence. Nichol et al. (1973) found that the more severe the drinking problem, the more serious the violent offense. Mayfield (1976) reports that 57 percent of a sample of convicted American murderers were drinking when they killed. Rada (1975) cites evidence that 50 percent of a sample of rapists were drinking at the time of their offense. Tinklenberg (1973) found that 53 percent of a sample of California youths under age nineteen convicted of murder, manslaughter, or assault were under the influence of alcohol at the time of their offense. A national survey of 12,000 inmates indicated that 38 percent of the inmates were daily or almost daily drinkers in the year prior to their incarceration, and approximately 50 percent had been drinking just prior to the offense that resulted in their incarceration (Kalish, 1983). Glaser (1978, p. 275) estimates that "about half of the people arrested on any charge in the United States either are under the influence of alcohol when taken into custody, or are held for acts committed when drunk, or both." In summary, the evidence is quite clear that approximately half of all offenders who commit violent crime were drinking at the time of offense, and many were highly intoxicated.

While the relationship between alcohol and violence has long been suspected, the landmark study by Wolfgang (1958) on 588 Philadelphia homicides brought the alcohol-violence relationship into clear focus and stamped it with some scientific confirmation. The Wolfgang survey reported that in 9 percent of the homicides, the victims had been drinking alcohol at the time of the offense; 11 percent of the offenders had been drinking. More importantly, however, in an additional 44 percent of the cases, alcohol was present in *both* the offender and the victim. The Wolfgang findings suggest that people become volatile under the influence of alcohol and that the danger increases greatly when both parties have been drinking. Research continues to support this finding.

High blood alcohol content (BAC) has often been consistently reported in about 50 percent of homicide victims (e.g., Cleveland, 1955; Fisher, 1951; Bowden, Wilson, & Turner, 1958; Verkko, 1951; Wilentz, 1953; Bensing & Schroeder, 1960; Spain, Bradess, & Eggson, 1951). In a recent study (Welte & Abel, 1989), 46 percent of the homicide victims had significant amounts of alcohol, and many had substantial amounts. Specifically, 70 percent had BAC amounts higher than 0.10. This was especially the case for victims involved in fight-related homicides. The high BAC-victim connection, however, should not be read as simply supporting the conclusion that most victims precipitated their own demise. Although this may be the case in a proportion of violent events, the relationship should also be viewed as underscoring the importance of the social context within which violence occurs. Violence frequently occurs in social situations where drinking is heavy, physiological arousal is high (such as anger), interpersonal conflict is evident, and cognitive processes—especially judgment and abstract reasoning—are impaired.

Research in the psychology laboratory also finds strong evidence that drinking alcohol facilitates physical aggression. In the typical laboratory experiment, subjects are placed in a variety of conditions (independent variables) and can administer "electric shock" (simulated) to another person (the amount and frequency of the shock is the dependent variable). The independent variable may be the drug conditions to which subjects are randomly assigned (e.g., drug, placebo—where subjects believe they are receiving a drug but do not, and nondrug conditions where the subjects believe they are not receiving a drug and do not). To create another common independent variable, researchers may place subjects into aroused (usually anger) and nonaroused conditions.

Research using these paradigms has consistently found that drinking alcohol facilitates aggression, measured by shocking behavior (Taylor & Leonard, 1983; Taylor & Sears, 1988). Furthermore, as the quantity of alcohol consumed increases, so does the tendency to be aggressive, at least up to the point when the subject "passes out." We will return to these two findings shortly.

It should be mentioned that the alcohol-violence connection appears to be strongest in the United States, even though the amount of alcohol consumption in this country is by no means the highest in the world. Many countries, including France, Italy, Spain, West Germany, Portugal, and Russia, consume substantially more alcohol per capita than the United States. In addition to obvious cultural differences between the countries, drinking patterns are also different. In some countries, alcohol consumption is spread out across the day, including meal times, whereas in the United States drinking is generally reserved for the end of the day, particularly during weekends and holidays. Think of the drinking patterns of college students, who traditionally let loose on weekends with heavy consumption of alcohol and "partying." It appears to be this episodic heavy drinking pattern that is most strongly related to aggression, violence, and antisocial behavior.

The relationship between episodic heavy drinking of alcohol and aggression or violence is well supported, but how is it explained? Many models and theories have been proposed during the past twenty years, but a majority can be be subsumed into two major categories: *disinhibitory* models and *social-cognitive* models. Disinhibitory models contend that alcohol, directly or indirectly, influences neurological or psychological mechanisms that normally control aggressive and antisocial behavior. One disinhibitory perspective hypothesizes that alcohol chemically influences the portion of the brain which controls the expression of aggression. The more intoxicated the person, the less control they have of their behavior. Another disinhibitory perspective, and by far the most popular in American society, supposes that certain people have a particular sensitivity or susceptibility to alcohol. This perspective views problem drinking as a biological abnormality or disease. This approach, known as the "American disease model" (Miller & Hester, 1989), is deeply entrenched in American society and forms the fundamental assumption of Alcoholics Anonymous (AA). Polls show, for example, that 79 percent of Americans believe that alcoholism is a disease that requires medical treatment (Peele, 1984).[1] The basic AA version is that chronic problem drinking is a disease reflected in an individual's inability to control alcoholic drinking, a disease that exists within the individual even before the first drink is taken. Furthermore, "The condition is irreversible and progressive and requires complete and utter abstinence." (Peele, 1984, p. 1339).

All disinhibitory models assume that alcohol has the power to disinhibit impulses that are normally held in check, and consequently this disinhibition may result in drink-induced criminal behavior (Critchlow, 1986). Furthermore, alcohol also provides a powerful excuse for undesirable behaviors which are often accompanied by such pleas as "I couldn't help myself" or "Alcohol always does this to me." Peele (1984, p. 1348) writes, "Disease conceptions may be alluring to our contemporary society because they are congruent with general ideas about the self and personal responsibility. Alcoholism viewed as an uncontrollable urge is after all part of a larger trend in which premenstrual tension, drug use and drug withdrawal, eating junk foods, and lovesickness are presented as defenses for murder."

While disinhibitory viewpoints focus on internal influences or predispositions, social-cognitive models emphasize the interactions between subjective belief systems or expectancies and the social environment. They reject the disease or loss of control assumptions of disinhibitory models. Social-cognitive models argue that problem drinking and much of the psychoactive influences of alcohol are learned and situationally determined.

---

[1] The disease conception is not confined to the United States, however. Seventy percent of the general public in Scotland also are convinced that it is a disease (Crawford & Heather, 1987).

The contention that one cannot help oneself or that alcohol directly instigates a loss of control is a subjective, cognitive expectancy that feeds on itself, rather than a disease. A person's expectations or cognitions influence how they respond to alcohol. Alcohol serves as a cue for acting intoxicated and doing things one normally would not do, and you act the way you *believe* alcohol makes you act.

There is considerable empirical support for social-cognitive models of drinking behavior, and actually very little empirical support for disinhibitory models. For example, disinhibitory models advocate total abstinence if alcoholic-prone people are to control themselves, otherwise "one drink leads to one drunk." However, a large body of research shows that the most effective treatment for heavy drinkers is to train them to be responsible light to moderate drinkers rather than have them abstain completely over their lifespans (see Peele, 1984). Research continually shows that total abstinence has a poor track record over the long haul, especially for younger single men, since the abstinence requirement does not dovetail with their life styles and the opportunities and pressures they face to drink (Peele, 1984).

Among the proponents of social-cognitive theory are Marlatt and Rohsenow (1980) and Lang and his colleagues (1975), who found that the amount of alcohol consumed may not be as important as what the person expects from the drug. Independent of the pharmacological effects, some people expect to become giddy, or loud, or boisterous after one or more drinks. Some anticipate acting more aggressively under the influence because alcohol is "supposed" to have that effect. According to Lang, if a person expects alcohol to influence behavior in a preconceived way, it probably will. Moreover, as mentioned earlier, the person avoids blame for some of his or her actions, because society tends to accept the "I was drunk" explanation. In fact, Sobell and Sobell (1973) suggested that one of the rewarding aspects of heavy drinking is that it provides a socially acceptable excuse for engaging in inappropriate behavior.

In the Lang et al. (1975) experiment, half of the subjects were told they would be drinking alcohol, which actually was either vodka or tonic water. The other half were told they would be drinking tonic water, not alcohol. However, half the members of this second group were actually given vodka, and the other half received the tonic water they expected. Results indicated that "the only significant determinant of aggression was the expectation factor; subjects who believed they had consumed alcohol were more aggressive than subjects who believed they had consumed a non-alcoholic beverage, regardless of the actual alcohol content of the drinks administered" (p. 508).

According to social-cognitive theory, therefore, the consumer's expectancy becomes the crucial factor. As long as consumers believe they drank alcohol, they expect to feel intoxicated. Furthermore, being "intoxicated," they tend to feel less responsible for their behavior, including violent or criminal behavior. Interestingly, convicted murderers who were intoxicated during the crime often claim they cannot remember the incident at all (Schacter, 1986). Whether these claims of amnesia are geniune remain very much in doubt.

Critchlow (1986) asserts that the pharmacological action of alcohol cannot account for the many transformations in social behavior that occur when people drink, as those transformations vary widely from culture to culture and in the same culture across time periods. She argues that the effects of alcohol on social behavior are found largely at the cultural level. Expectations about what alcohol can do behaviorally can be learned through a particular culture by anyone, even before taking the first drink. Critchlow writes,

> On a cultural level, it seems to be the negative consequences of alcohol that hold the most powerful sway over our thinking. . . . Thus, by believing that alcohol makes people act badly, we give it a great deal of power. Drinking becomes a tool that legitimates irrationality and excuses violence without permanently destroying an individual's moral standing or society's systems of rules and ethics. (pp. 761–762)

While cognitive expectancies play an extremely important role, we should not downplay the pharmacological effects of alcohol. Alcohol does affect the neurochemistry of the central nervous system by depressing many functions. Anyone who has tried to act sober with marginal success, no matter how they tried, can attest to this effect. Research confirms that alcohol has a strong pharmacological effect on behavior, somewhat independent of subjective expectancies. For example, Shuntich and Taylor (1972) found that actually intoxicated subjects were more aggressive than both subjects who consumed a placebo beverage (thinking they had consumed alcohol) and subjects who did not consume any beverage. Zeichner and Pihl (1979, 1980) also found that subjects in a nonalcohol condition were as aggressive as placebo subjects who thought they had consumed alcohol.

Social cognitive theory also predicts that the amount of alcohol consumed should make little difference on overall behavior. If subjects believe they are consuming large amounts, they will, correspondingly, act more intoxicated (and hence more aggressive). If, on the other hand, they do not believe they have consumed much alcohol, even though they actually have, they will be less aggressive and less likely to act intoxicated. In other words, the misled subjects will behave at the level of aggressiveness that corresponds with their expectations, regardless of the amount of alcohol they consume.

In evaluating this implication, a series of studies by Stuart Taylor and his associates (Taylor & Gammon, 1975; Taylor, Gammon, & Capasso,

1976; Taylor et al., 1976, 1979) are instructive. The Taylor projects found that small doses of alcohol (e.g., 0.5 ounces of vodka or bourbon per 40 pounds of body weight) tend to inhibit aggression, while larger doses (1.5 ounces per 40 pounds) tend to facilitate aggression. Therefore, depending on the amount, alcohol may either inhibit or facilitate expressions of aggression and violence.

The Taylor experiments are in agreement with the known pharmacological effects of alcohol. At small amounts, alcohol appears to stimulate the central nervous system, generating mild euphoria and a sense of well-being. This good cheer becomes readily apparent at a party when, after the first round of drinks, people tend to take on a happy frame of mind. As alcoholic intake increases, however, the integrating functions of the cortex are depressed, causing some disorganization and impairment of complex cognitive functions. At extreme levels of intoxication, even simple cognitive processes like attention and sustained concentration break down, eventually ending in stupor and sleep. Therefore, violent behavior, if it is to occur, will most likely occur at moderate levels of intoxication.

In the Taylor investigation, when subjects were informed that they would be consuming alcohol, aggression was positively related only to the amount of alcohol actually consumed, not to the amount they thought they had consumed (Taylor & Gammon, 1975). In a later study (Taylor et al., 1979), subjects were informed that they would be consuming one of three drugs: alcohol, marihuana, or a tranquilizer. Therefore, all subjects within each group had the same drug expectancy. They then received either a high or low dose of THC or alcohol. The results demonstrated that the high dose of alcohol faciliated aggression, while the high dose of THC suppressed it.

Overall, Taylor's data strongly suggest that the aggression demonstrated by intoxicated subjects is a joint function of the pharmacological state produced by alcohol and cognitive and situational factors. The researchers maintain that alcohol consumption by itself does not produce aggressive behavior (Taylor & Leonard, 1983). Physiological effects of alcohol do influence behavior, but they also interact with expectancies and with what is happening in the person's environment at any given time.

Emotions may be important also. Jaffe, Babor, and Fishbein (1988) observe that alcoholics exhibit more aggressive, violent behavior than do nonalcoholics, especially when drinking. Beyond this, however, the researchers also noted that alcoholics frequently report highly negative emotions when drinking, such as anger and depression. They concluded, "Thus it is possible that when these states are experienced by alcoholics with a prior history of aggressive behavior, the likelihood of alcohol-related aggression increases and such behavior can be predicted with some degree of reliability" (p. 217). Similarly, unhappy or depressive thoughts presumably activate other negative memories and feelings and therefore are likely to promote aggressive, violent inclinations (Berkowitz & Heimer, 1989).

Situational factors are crucial. In all of Taylor's studies, aggression was not automatically produced by alcohol, even alcohol in large amounts. Rather, subjects were provoked, threatened, or at least were in the presence of aggressive cues before they displayed aggressive behavior. Therefore, in order for aggression to occur, there must be provocative, incitive, or instigative cues along with intoxication. Something or someone must anger, threaten, or in some other way arouse the intoxicated subject. But external cues are certainly not the whole story. Internal cues, such as thoughts, beliefs, or even imagined slights or provocations can serve as instigating cues for aggressive or violent behavior.

SUMMARY AND CONCLUSIONS

This chapter reviewed the relationship between crime and a number of drugs commonly associated with criminal behavior. Four major drug categories were identified: (1) the hallucinogens; (2) the stimulants; (3) the opiate narcotics; and (4) the sedative-hypnotics. Rather than discuss most of the drugs in each category, we considered only those commonly believed to be connected with criminal conduct. Moreover, we did not examine the crimes of drug distribution or possession. We are mainly concerned with whether the substance itself facilitates or instigates illegal action, especially violence. In other words, are persons under the influence of marihuana more violent than they are normally? Or, to what extent does alcohol directly contribute to loss of control or reduce self-regulatory mechanisms?

Cannabis, which includes marihuana and hashish, is a relatively mild hallucinogen with few psychological or physiological side effects. No significant relationship between cannabis use and crime has been consistently reported in the research literature. If anything, marihuana seems to reduce the likelihood of violence, since its psychoactive ingredient, THC, induces muscle weakness and promotes feelings of lethargy.

Amphetamines and cocaine (especially crack) represented the stimulant group. Most illegal users do not participate in crime other than the possession or sale of these drugs. Similar to marihuana, amphetamines are plentiful and inexpensive. However, there some documented cases in which heavy users of amphetamines entered psychological states that presumably predisposed them to violence and paranoia. In addition, several studies have found correlations between violent offenders and a history of amphetamine abuse. As in all correlations, however, it is difficult to determine what contributes to what. Cocaine, a natural drug that grows only in certain parts of the world, has traditionally been quite expensive. In recent years, the drug has become widely available and its cost less prohibitive. There is no hard evidence, however, that cocaine generally renders one more violent, more out of control, or more likely to engage in property crimes.

We discussed heroin as the representative of the opiate narcotics. Like most other narcotics, heroin appears to be highly addictive, particularly in the sense that it creates a strong psychological dependency. Narcotics in general are so addictive and so expensive that substantial funds are needed to support a user's habit. Thus, some researchers have found a moderate correlation between narcotics and various income-generating crimes. On the other hand, others have noted that most addicts turned to drugs after they had developed criminal patterns.

Of all the drugs reviewed, alcohol—representing the sedative-hypnotic group—shows the strongest relationship with violent offenses, such as rape, homicide, and assault. At intermediate and high levels, alcohol appears to impair or disrupt the brain operations responsible for self-control. However, it is likely that violent behavior associated with alcohol use is a joint function of pharmacological effects, cognitive expectancies, and situational influences. If the individual expects that alcohol will make him or her act aggressively, and if the social environment provides appropriate cues, aggression or violent behavior will be facilitated. Furthermore, alcohol offers the user an external justification for his or her conduct. "When I take a few drinks, I become hostile and can't help myself."

However, the relationships between crime and all the drugs discussed in this chapter are complex, involving interactions between numerous pharmacological, social, and psychological variables. Research is beginning to ease some data out of the complexity, but additional studies employing well-designed methodology are greatly needed to understand the many possible influences of psychoactive drugs on human behavior, particularly criminal behavior.

CHAPTER TWELVE
Correctional Psychology

In this text we have concentrated on the genetic, neuropsychological, psychological, and social characteristics of the serious offender. We have seen that persistent offenders engage in various crimes in a variety of ways for a variety of reasons. However, there are some generalizations that can be made. We have learned that the antisocial behavior of persistent offenders often begins early in life. Some demonstrate a discernible pattern of going against the environment as early as the first grade, ranging from lying, stealing, and truancy to bullying and frequent fighting with peers. Most are male. They are often disliked and socially rejected by a majority of their peers, who are not interested in opposing the social environment themselves. In many instances, antisocial children grow up with below-average interpersonal skills for dealing with others in a socially appropriate manner. Their friends tend to be delinquent, antisocial peers.

Antisocial children also often do poorly in school work, a pattern that accumulates in disinterest and dropping out—mentally as well as behaviorally. Their work history tends to be spotty, with extended periods of unemployment followed by unskilled labor. For some unknown reasons, persistent offenders often score below the norm on IQ tests, although in other ways some demonstrate an uncanny "intelligence" or street sense of how to survive.

Persistent offenders, particularly those aggressive and violent, often come from multiassaultive families where physical and other kinds of abuse are commonplace. In addition, they often have family members, especially parents and/or siblings, who are also frequent offenders and antisocial themselves (Blumstein, Farrington, & Moitra, 1985).

As we discussed in the previous chapter, many persistent offenders tend to be polydrug users, using whatever combinations are on the market at an affordable price. They do not specialize in any one type of offending, but tend to demonstrate a wide variety of antisocial behavior, ranging from theft to rape. In fact, the frequency, seriousness, and variety of offending are highly correlated (Farrington, 1987). Moreover, the frequency of offending seems to decline with age, especially around age forty. However, the reasons for this decline are unknown.

Although there are some solid indications that persistent offenders have nervous systems that require high amounts of stimulation, there is little reason to believe that these neurological propensities cannot be overcome by learning and cognitive factors as well as by the influences of the social environment. Human beings are simply not driven by animal instincts, genetic programming, chromosomal anomalies, or primitive biological urges or proclivities from their evolutionary past. They are thinking, active agents with dreams, goals, and unique versions of the world. These versions and goals influence their ongoing behavior, including behavior that violates criminal law. Cognitive processes and constructs can override biology in human action and conduct. Nor is there convincing evidence that any sizeable portion of criminal behavior is propelled by some mental disease, biological abnormality, or addiction. Sexual addiction, alcohol addiction, shoplifting addiction, and all the other variants of addiction portrayed by the media or self-proclaimed experts are not supported by empirical research. Human beings are highly adaptable and changeable, a topic we will review later in this chapter.

The focus of this chapter will be on the work of correctional psychologists in predicting and changing criminal behavior patterns. The three main services provided by correctional psychologists are: (1) diagnosis and classification; (2) treatment or intervention; and (3) research, planning, and evaluation. A majority of correctional psychologists are located in assessment or reception centers that operate centrally or regionally to screen and classify newly received offenders (Clements, 1987). Some psychologists also provide treatment services at these centers. Other correctional psychologists treat inmates diagnosed as having mental disorders or adjustment problems within the correctional facility itself. In fact, psychologists make up about half of the professionally trained mental health staff in prisons and outnumber psychiatrists by at least 5 to 1 (Clements, 1987). Some correctional psychologists are involved in administration, research, planning, and evaluation of existing programs. Since diagnosis, classification, and treatment are increasingly guided by research evaluation, the need for psychologists in research areas is expanding rapidly. We will review each of these functions in the remainder of this chapter. Before we do, however, it is important that we have some familarity with the correctional system as a whole.

THE CORRECTIONAL SYSTEM

In the United States, detained, accused, and convicted persons are housed in three types of facilities: jails, community-based facilities, and prisons. Jails are operated by local (or sometimes state) governments to hold persons temporarily detained, awaiting trial, or sentenced to confinement for less than one year. Therefore, jails house a mixture of persons at various stages of criminal justice processing. About 50 percent of the jail population have not been convicted. It is estimated that over 8 million jail admissions occur annually in this country (U.S. Department of Justice, 1988).

Community-based facilities are operated by public or private organizations (under governmental contract). They hold persons for less than twenty-four hours of each day to allow them limited opportunity to work, attend school, or make other community contacts. This plan is an option in lieu of continuing prison or jail confinement. Overall, community-based facilities house about 4 percent of of all those confined in the correctional system.

Prisons are operated by state and federal governments to hold persons sentenced under state and federal laws to terms of more than one year. Prisons are often classified according to three levels of security: maximum, medium, and minimum security. Maximum or close security prisons are typically surrounded by a double fence or wall (usually 18 to 25 feet high) guarded by armed correctional officers in observation towers. About 40 percent of this country's maximum security prisons were built before 1925. Medium security prisons typically are enclosed within double fences topped with barbed wire. About 90 percent of medium security prisons were built after 1925. Minimum security prisons usually do not have armed guards and may or may not have fences surrounding the buildings. More than 60 percent of these prisons were built after 1950.

In the United States, about 40 to 50 percent of all prison inmates are housed in maximum security facilities (U.S. Department of Justice, 1988). Thirty-seven to 40 percent are housed in medium security facilities and the remainder in minimum security facilities.

Between 475,000 and 525,000 inmates are housed in state and federal prisons in any given year in this country. At any given time, the total is affected by changes in judicial and legislative philosophies about deterrence and incapacitation, the amount of space available, law enforcement practices, and economic conditions. In recent years, there has been a sub-

The Prison Population is at an All-Time High.

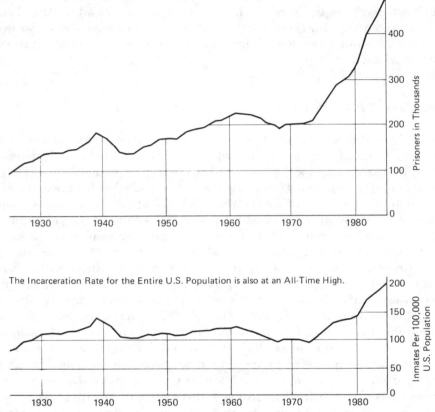

FIGURE 12-1   Source: State and Federal Prisoners, 1925–1985, BJS Bulletin, October 1986.

stantial increase in prison and jail populations (see Figure 12-1). Moreover, the inmate population for women appears to be increasing at a rate higher than for men (Deconstanza & Scholes, 1988). In 1987, for example, the male inmate population in state prisons increased by 6.6 percent, while the female inmate population increased by 9.3 percent. These increases probably reflects a judicial and societal change in attitude about what should be done about offenders rather than any dramatic increase in crime rates. For example, the dramatic increase in women inmates during the 1980s appears to be primarily due to substance abuse (Decostanza & Scholes, 1988).

Nearly 64 percent of all adult inmates have experienced prior incarceration—either in juvenile facilities, adult institutions, or both. After release from prison, about 12 percent are likely to be back in prison within one year. After three years, about 24 percent of the parolees return to prison. Decostanza and Scholes (1988) estimate that one out of every three women inmates return to prison at some point in their lives. More than half of all prison returns are for technical violations of parole. The remainder are for new, major convictions. When former inmates reach age thirty, there is a high probability that they will not return to prison. The reasons are multiple, but one viable explanation is that the justice system, in effect, physically "wears down" offenders (U.S. Department of Justice, 1988). The process of repeatedly being arrested, appearing in court, and adjusting to prison life eventually is perceived by offenders as an exhausting ordeal.

Societal Rationale for Imprisonment of Offenders

Four fundamental considerations are usually in operation when offenders are sentenced: (1) protection of other members of society, frequently called *incapacitation*; (2) *rehabilitation*; (3) *punishment*; and (4) *deterrence*. The first is the most straightforward justification for confining convicted individuals against their will. If the criminal is believed dangerous to society, on the basis of past conduct, it is obvious that society must be protected from future injury. However, if we rely heavily on incapacitation to remove the offender from the streets, we are in danger of increasing the inmate population dramatically and far beyond the present capacity of correctional facilities. On the other hand, we have seen that only a small percentage—around 8 to 10 percent—of the criminal population commit, by far, an inordinate amount of the crime—perhaps more than 50 percent of the total. For example, Peterson, Braiker, and Polich (1981) reported that the average prisoner committed about three serious crimes per year of street time, while the most frequent offender (about 8 percent of the inmate population) committed over sixty serious crimes per year of street time. Incapacitation directed at this 8 percent might be a more effective means of reducing crime, a strategy called *selective incapacitation*.

In recent years, the effectiveness of incapacitation has been questioned seriously (Blumstein et al., 1986; Cohen, 1983; Visher, 1987). And rehabilitation "is being revived, reaffirmed, and resold" (Visher, 1987, p. 514). Rehabilitation as a justification for confinement often creates heated debate. Rehabilitation is essentially restoring the person to a useful life, either through education, training, treatment (e.g., psychotherapy, behavior modification, plastic surgery) or a combination of these. During the 1970s, rehabilitation lost favor with much of society, including courts and criminal justice practitioners. Contributing to this disenchantment was a provocative article by R. M. Martinson (1974), arguing that the concept of rehabilitation, especially in the form of treatment methods then in operation, did not work. Correctional administrators were put on notice that rehabilitation programs were not efficacious (Adams, 1977). The concept of rehabilitation has yet to regain a comfortable foothold within the correctional system. In the scholarly community, however, rehabilitation remains a viable alternative (Cullen & Gilbert, 1982; Gendreau & Ross, 1983; Greenwood & Zimring, 1985).

Punishment and deterrence are closely linked. Society has for a very long time assumed that some form of punishment—defined as aversive consequences for one's behavior—is an effective method of behavior control. With reference to criminal behavior, punishment supposedly works in two ways.

First, it is believed that punishment and its public disclosure reveal to the members of a society what the consequence of criminal behavior will be (the informative role). "If you choose to violate this rule, this is what will happen." Thus, the threat and fear of punishment should act as a potent deterrent. Second, punishment applied directly to the offender should deter him or her personally from future violations (the inhibitory role). It is usually assumed that direct application of aversive stimuli is more effective than the observation or knowledge of punishing consequences. In other words, many shoplifters are not deterred from a first offense by signs that warn them of possible prosecution, or by reading or hearing about other offenders. However, the embarrassment of having one's name published in the local newspaper and the pain of paying a fine or spending time in confinement is much more likely to prevent future violations. This theory does not hold as easily for more serious offenses, however.

Theoretical discussions on the effectiveness of punishment as a deterrent often revolve around the aforementioned dichotomy. The term *general deterrence* is used for the threat of punishment on the public at large; *special deterrence* refers to the actual experience of punishment by the offender (Andenaes, 1968). The long-debated question surrounding the relationship between deterrence and criminal conduct has never been satisfactorily answered. It is reasonable to assume, however, that general deterrence or the threat of punishment does prevent a significant number of people from violating the law.

The general deterrence associated with the legal system may not be as powerful as the threat of punishment established through socialization and moral development, however. It is reasonable to assume that a very large segment of the population will not engage in serious criminal activity, even if there is no police officer at the elbow. For most people, fear of social, parental, or self-disapproval operate as sufficient deterrents. In keeping with our theme of the complexity of human behavior, it is probable that some combination of the aforementioned internal and external checks are operating for most people.

CLASSIFICATION AND PREDICTION

Classification systems do three important things: (1) They simplify and summarize; (2) enhance prediction; and (3) remind us that crime and delinquency are behaviorally and psychologically heterogeneous with multiple causation. The pressures of overcrowding, scarce fiscal resources, and legal challenges have contributed to a renewed interest in classification within the jails and prisons of this country (Brennan, 1987). Inmate classification systems serve a number of important, if not critical, functions within the correctional system. First, they help corrections officials make decisions about inmate placement in order to provide a safe environment for all inmates and staff. Second, they provide information for treatment, intervention, and rehabilitation. If we do not intend to treat all offenders alike and do not intend to behave haphazardly toward them, then some form of classification for treatment is necessary (Sechrest, 1987). Third, classification systems help in making predictions about recidivism and other risks to society.

Although a good many schemes or systems of classification have been proposed and used over the years, their impact has been limited (Sechrest, 1987). The situation is much the same for juveniles and adults, but more emphasis has been placed on classification of juvenile offenders for treatment (Sechrest, 1987). Eleven of the better-known and researched classification schemes are the Megargee system, Toch's Prison Preference Inventory, Risk Assessment, Quay's AIMS, Quay's juvenile typology, the Jesness Inventory Classification System, the Interpersonal Maturity Level Classification System, the Federal Bureau of Prison Classification System, the National Insititute of Corrections Model, The Illinois Adult Classication System, and the California Prison Classifcation System. We will briefly review only Megargee's system and Quay's systems in this section.

The Megargee system was developed and validated on large samples of youthful offenders, ages eighteen to twenty-seven (Megargee & Bohn, 1979). Classification is based on response patterns to questions from the Minnesota Multiphasic Personality Inventory (MMPI), one of the oldest and most widely used personality measurements in the world today. The MMPI is also the most commonly used classification and diagnostic instrument in state and federal correctional facilities (Carlson, 1990). Through years of research, ten types of offenders have been identified on the basis of MMPI profiles. They are (descriptions adapted from Zager, 1988, Sechrest, 1987, and Megargee & Bohn, 1977):

1. well-adjusted individuals who lack conflicts with authorities;
2. well-adjusted underachievers with good interpersonal skills;
3. inadequate individuals who are anxious, constricted, dogmatic, and with a tendency to abuse alcohol;
4. charming individuals who tend to be impulsive, manipulative, and achievement-oriented;
5. submissive and anxious individuals who are hardworking and reliable;
6. hedonistic, manipulative individuals who have poor interpersonal relations with peers and staff;
7. individuals from deprived backgrounds who do better in prison as well as on release than expected;

8. individuals with extensive criminal records who are tough, streetwise, cynical, and generally antisocial;

9. individuals with extensive criminal records, polydrug abuse, who are described as hostile, misanthropic alienated, and antisocial; and

10. individuals characterized as being unstable and emotionally disturbed.

Quay (1984) developed a system called the Adult Internal Management System (AIMS). AIMS classifies male inmates into five categories. Much of the following descriptions of the five groups were taken from a recent study by Levinson (1988). Group I consists of inmates who presently exhibit or have histories of aggressive and sometimes violent behavior. Members of this group are most likely to cause major disturbances within the institution. Group II inmates do not demonstrate the same degree of aggressive behavior as Group I inmates, but they tend to be master manipulators in obtaining things they want as well as causing trouble within the institution. Group III members do not have an extensive criminal history and generally are those the staff can rely on. Group IV represents prisoners who are withdrawn, unhappy, whiny, socially isolated, complaining, and unreliable. They are easily victimized within the institution. Group V inmates follow the characteristics of anxious, maladjusted, depressed, chronically worried, and easily upset. They, too, are easily victimized.

Often the AIMS groups are further classified according to potential for aggressive behavior. Groups I and II are considered the "heavies" in that they are violence-prone and manipulative predators. Group III members are evaluated as "moderates," and Groups IV and V are considered "lights." It is often recommended that "heavies" be housed in the facility's most secure living quarters, while the "lights" should be housed in quarters as distant from the "heavies" as possible. "Moderates" can be placed in either living area without anticipated problems. As the reader can discern, AIMS appears to be more designed for management than treatment purposes. Currently, AIMS has been implemented in Pennsylvania, South Carolina, and some institutions of the Federal prison system (Posey, 1988).

Quay (1987) has also developed a classification system for juvenile offenders that delineates four categories: (1) the undersocialized or unsocialized delinquent; (2) the socialized delinquent; (3) the attention deficit disorder (ADD) delinquent; and (4) the anxiety-withdrawal-dysphoria delinquent. Undersocialized delinquents display aggression, negativism, resistance, and lack of concern for others. Basically, they follow the characteristics of the adult psychopath. Undersocialized youths, as the label implies, have not become adequately socialized to mainstream social values and standards. Youths institutionalized for repetitive, serious offenses tend to be undersocialized, and they also tend to be the group who are constant disciplinary problems and unresponsive to institutional treatment and rehabilitation programs. Socialized delinquents, on the other hand, have become socialized not so much to mainstream societal standards but to the norms and values of a delinquent subculture or group. Compared to the undersocialized group, they tend to be less overtly aggressive, less interpersonally alienated, and more responsive to treatment. The third type is plagued by an attentional deficit (previously labeled hyperactivity). Youths in this category have problems in focusing and sustaining attention and in coming to grips with task demands. The cognitive and social-behavioral correlates of this pattern and the accompanying frustrations leave the child especially susceptible to environmental influences, including those that foster delinquency. The fourth pattern carries the intimidating clinical label anxiety-withdrawal-dysphoria and is characterized by neurotic, overinhibited, anxious, and socially withdrawn behavior. Those following this pattern do not deal competently with the social environment and generally prefer to avoid it by withdrawing from social interactions. Delinquent or deviant acts in this category are motivated by a need to escape or avoid stressful situations. Examples include truancy from school, running away from home, or theft of a motor vehicle.

Classification systems have become useful tools for decision making and placement within the correctional system in recent years. Some have drawn considerable research and evaluation, especially the Megargee MMPI-based system. All current classification systems, however, have their problems and need much more research before they fulfill their missions. Sechrest (1987) asserts that they lack theoretical sophistication, and the methodologies used to develop them have been generally inadequate. Furthermore, the lack of dependable means of treatment or intervention for offenders, both juvenile and adults, makes classification difficult (Sechrest, 1987). Finally, the rapid proliferation of classification systems demands some empirical attempts to integrate and organize them in line with the various philosphies of correctional facilities and administrations.

PSYCHOLOGICAL EFFECTS OF IMPRISONMENT

Clinical case studies on the effects of prison life have often concluded that, for many individuals, imprisonment can be brutal, demeaning, and generally devastating. These studies often describe a variety of psychological symptoms believed to be caused directly by imprisonment, including psychosis, severe depression, inhibiting anxiety, and social withdrawal. However, more recent research (e.g., Toch & Adams, with Grant, 1989; Toch & Adams, 1989; Zamble & Proporino, 1988) raises serious questions about the extent of serious psychological deterioration that is *caused* by imprisonment. Before we continue, it must be emphasized that there are wide individual differences in reactions to imprisonment. Some people do react to imprisonment with severe emotional or mental disorders, but the number appears smaller than originally supposed.

Zamble and Porporino (1988) examined the coping strategies and adjustment characteristics of inmates in Canadian penitentiaries. They found that emotional disruption and adjustment were clearly problems for most inmates during the beginning of their sentences, particularly signs of serious to moderate depression. This deleterious reaction came as no surprise as prison produces a dramatic disruption in customary behavior, compounded by restrictions, deprivations, and constraints. However, these initial reactions soon dissipated for most inmates, and no lasting emotional disturbance was discernible as the inmate became adjusted to his surroundings and prison routine. Toch and Adams (with Grant, 1989) report a similar pattern in their study on American prisoners. The Toch-Adams data suggest that inmates with emotional problems also tend to be disruptive in prison. Furthermore, their data support the frequent observation that age is a consistent correlate of prison violations, with young inmates being much more prone to engage in prison misbehavior than older inmates.

Inmate reactions to prison life appear to follow a curvilinear pattern, with stress indicators increasing at the beginning of the term, then dropping, and then rising again as the end of their term approaches (Bukstel & Kilmann, 1980). Sometimes referred to as the "short-timers syndrome," many inmates exhibit signs of distress, sleeplessness, restlessness, and anxiety, probably in anticipation of the new coping strategies required for the outside.

Zamble and Porporino write, "We conclude that prisons do not produce permanent harm to the psychological well-being of inmates" (p. 149). On the other hand, they did not find positive effects either. "Our data show very little positive behavioral change in prison, just as earlier we could see little evidence for generalized negative effects" (p. 151). Interestingly, Toch and Adams suggest that prison experiences actually temper or even improve inmate misbehavior, most particularly in the young inmate under age twenty-five. "Young inmates, who are presumably more rambunctious and less mature than older inmates, appear to derive some benefit from this forced environment . . . it is encouraging to find that prison inmates who are initially most resistant to restrictions on their personal liberty demonstrate increasingly levels of conformity over time" (pp. 19–20). Why this happens remains largely a mystery, but Toch and Adams (with Grant, 1989) suggest that the maturation process facilitated by *humane* prison environments plays a crucial role. The researchers contend that inmate behavior is likely to improve when inmates learn the association between behavior and its positive or negative consequences within the institution, and when they have psychological support, the opportunity to participate in conventional activities, form attachment bonds, and build relationships.

In summary, a vast majority of inmates do not demonstrate long-lasting psychological impairment or problems as a result of imprisonment. However, there are certain conditions where this conclusion may not hold, namely crowding and isolation.

Psychological Effects of Crowding

Prison crowding has become increasingly an important topic as the prison population reaches critical numbers. Prison crowding has probably always been a concern, but the sheer number of offenders being currently processed through the system is without precedent. Prison officials estimate that the United States is currently at least 11 percent short in bed space in states' prisons and jails, a situation likely to get much worse (Patrick, 1988). While the U.S. has the highest proportion of its population incarcerated, the crowding problem is worldwide (Patrick, 1988). Prison populations everyone appear to be increasing.

Prison and jail overcrowding *does* seem related to a higher incidence of physical illness, socially disruptive behavior, and emotional distress (Bukstel & Kilmann, 1980). Some researchers have suggested that disruptive behavior in correctional facilities increases directly as the available space decreases (Megargee, 1976; Nacci, Prather, & Tetelbaum, 1977). This relationship seems to be particularly pronounced for juvenile institutions (Megargee, 1976), and for women prison inmates (Ruback & Carr, 1984). In most cases, inmates are housed in units with fifty or more inmates with less than 20 square feet of space per person.

In a fifteen-year project on prison crowding, Paulus (1988) concluded that increasing the number of residents in correctional housing units significantly increased the negative psychological (tension, anxiety, depression) and physical reactions (e.g., headaches, high blood pressure, cardiovascular problems) in inmates. The critical factor appears to be the number of residents sharing a space and simply not the amount of space available. For example, providing some privacy and limiting the visual and physical access of other inmates, such as providing cubicles in open dormitories, reduces the negative impact of living there.

Paulus also found that socioeconomic level, education level, and prior prison or jail confinements were related to inmate reactions to crowded conditions. Specifically, the higher the socioeconomic and education level, the more difficult the adjustment to and the lower the tolerance for crowded conditions. Presumably, many members of the lower socioeconomic class are used to living under crowded conditions and therefore are more tolerant of invasions of privacy and other factors involved in crowded environments. Surprisingly, prior confinement *interfered* with adjustment to crowded conditions. Prisoners who had some history of prior imprisonment exhibited more problems in adjustments than those without prior time. A reason suggested by Paulus is that individuals with extensive prison histories are likely to have spent part of their time in single cells or under less crowded conditions. This may have made them particularly sensitive to crowded conditions, such as living in a dormitory setting. Paulus also found that men and women, and blacks and whites, react similarly to variations in social density.

Paulus hypothesizes that crowding has its primary impact through its influence on social interaction. For one thing, crowding reduces one's sense of control over the social environment, and with that many people things become unpredictable and uncertain. Secondly, crowded situations interfere with one's goals, such as carrying out desired activities, restrict freedom and privacy, and expose one to a variety of undesired intrusions. And thirdly, crowded situations produce much more activity, noise, interactions, smells, violations of personal space, and generally excessive stimulation.

In summary, the available research does indicate that crowding is related to negative psychological and physical problems in confinement. However, individuals react differently to crowded conditions, some demonstrating much better adjustment than others. There are many other variables that have to be considered also, such as the type of institution, the institutions's orientation, the type of social milieu, the degree of crowding, and the phase an individual is in his or her sentence.

Psychological Effects of Isolation

In corrections, there are two main types of inmate isolation: solitary confinement and protective custody or protective seclusion. Solitary confinement refers to the complete or highly restricted social isolation of persons for specific or unspecific periods of time, with other necessities of life being provided (Bartol, 1983). The primary purpose is usually punishment. The definition of protective seclusion is similar, except the primary purpose is for the protection of the inmate, either from him or herself, or from the other inmates. For example, correctional staff may be fearful of possible suicide. Under these conditions, the level of social and perceptual-sensory isolation may be even more extreme than solitary because many materials and items must be removed from the cell or else the inmate may use the objects to accomplish the suicide.

Systematic knowledge of the psychological effects of isolation comes primarily from the psychological laboratory using volunteers who allow themselves to be socially isolated, sometimes with sensory restrictions such as a blindfold or earphones, for varying periods of time. The research so far demonstrates that individuals respond differently to solitude; some show great tolerance and often welcome the quiet solitude from the hustle and bustle of daily living. Others experience stress and anxiety, even after relatively short periods of isolation. In general, however, the research shows that most individuals are able to tolerate and even adjust to isolation, if the isolation is short in duration, such as a few days.

In the past, the conditions of solitary or protective custody in institutions have often been deplorable. Offenders have been held in cells without adequate ventilation, heat, clothing, light, sanitary, and bathroom facilities for long periods of time. Since no published research has examined the effects of such adverse conditions, it is difficult to determine what the psychological effects might be. Fortunately, the courts are beginning to set up minimum conditions that must be met during isolation as well as due process requirements. At this time, there is not enough evidence to conclude, one way or the other, whether isolation under deplorable conditions or over extended periods of time causes gross psychological disruption or impairment.

REHABILITATION

One of the fundamental goals of corrections is to inhibit unlawful, antisocial behavior, at the very least by keeping perpetrators confined and away from society. During the 1970s and 1980s, because of a variety of factors including budgetary considerations, widespread disenchantment with the concept of rehabilitation, and a hard-line approach to offenders, the correctional system made punishment and confinement its primary goal. In so doing, however, the system risks promoting more unlawful behavior, since prison confinement per se reinforces learned deviant responses. Unless we opt for a drastic change in our methods of punishment, such as corporal punishment (Newman, 1982) or irreversible banishment, we must somehow reconcile prison confinement with the realities of postconfinement and effective living on the outside.

This brings us to the subject of rehabilitation, whose fundamental goal is to develop lawful alternative behavior that will generalize beyond the institution. If rehabilitation is thought of in terms of training, this goal is difficult—some would say impossible—to achieve. First, the positive, alternative behavior to be developed must be capable of bringing to the individual significant social, psychological, and material rewards. Second, different approaches would be needed for different types of offenders. Training may be inappropriate for the violent or sexual offender; for the property offender, it would involve developing skills that would translate to the outside world and provide better rewards than those obtained from criminal behavior. Third, rehabilitation of this sort necessitates educating the general public, legislators, and professionals about its long-term benefits and the probabilities of success, and there were always many failures.

Alternative behavioral development as a viable rehabilitative goal would likely require large financial investments in facilities, well-trained and motivated staff, offender job placement, elimination of prejudice toward former felons, and long-term, carefully executed research on the effectiveness of the programs. The correctional system as it now operates is a poor setting in which to implement this approach. Furthermore, during the 1970s and 1980s, public expressions of sympathy toward prisoners were very rare.

Yet most would agree that there is a strong relationship between lack of personally meaningful employment and recidivism, particularly in regard to economically motivated crimes (Halleck & Witte, 1977; Kennedy, 1976; Jenkins & Barton, 1973). Individuals engaged in rewarding employment are less apt to be involved in unlawful activity. This requires not only the availability of a job, but also the appropriate social and occupational skills to maintain it. Moreover, the rewards must be greater than the rewards offered by the criminal activity. Too frequently, ex-offenders cannot meet even the first criteria, obtaining a job. Glaser (1964) writes, "Unemployment may be among the principle causal factors involved in the recidivism of adult male offenders" (p. 329). Moreover, it is estimated that the unemployment rate for ex-offenders is three times the rate for the general population, and that most who received "vocational training" are not able to use it (Dale, 1976).

Additionally, the recidivism rate for the unemployed is four times that of the fully employed ex-offender. This relationship does not necessarily *prove* that unemployment is a causal factor. It might be that offenders who are prone toward continuing unlawful behavior are also less likely to find and maintain suitable employment because of personal inadequacy. However, it is difficult to ignore statements like the following:

> An opportunity to live a normal, non-criminal productive life is denied the ex-offender immediately upon his release from the penal institution. We effectively preclude his rehabilitation by failing to train and educate him, by refusing to hire him, by allowing the private bonding industry to intimidate employers, and by enacting restrictive occupational licensing requirements at the behest of self-serving economic groups. (Dale, 1976, p. 336)

If we shift the focus from rehabilitative training to psychological rehabilitation (treatment), we may find some reason for guarded optimism. The dilemma still remains that any type of rehabilitation proposal may sound like an idealized package delivered many times before. Correctional officers exposed to wide varieties of hard-core offenders on a daily basis and under adverse conditions are apt to view the prison population as totally incorrigible and to suspect and resist any notion that offenders can be changed. Many correctional personnel come to view criminals as less-than-human creatures who have few dignifying qualities. The reasons why criminals have become this way are irrelevant; what matters is that little can be done about them now. On the other hand, there is ample evidence that the prison system as it exists dehumanizes many correctional officers as well as prisoners.

Some offenders, especially habitually violent ones, are unlikely to benefit from psychological rehabilitation and should remain in prison for society's protection. Moreover, if you believe that aggression and selfishness are integral features of human nature (the difference-in-degrees perspective), then warehousing prisoners makes good sense. Those who believe in inherent selfishness and violence tend to be strongly pessimistic about what can be done about the crime problem. More prisons, stricter law enforcement, and a more efficient judicial process offer the only solution. Those less inclined to believe that humans are locked in the natural fate of inherent violence, selfishness, and deceit may be more optimistic about whether anything can be done about the crime problem. If humans learn to be criminal, and are guided by changeable construct systems and self-regulatory mechanisms rather than by genetic programming, then creative rehabilitation using learning principles may be extremely effective.

The overwheming bulk of the psychological and social research indicates that humans learn behavior, including deviant and unlawful behavior, from significant members of their society. Furthermore, they are constantly perceiving and interpreting their actions and the actions of others in accordance with internal standards and cognitive constructs. To understand their behavior, it seems most fruitful to examine these mediated processes and the justifying mechanisms that accompany them. To change their actions over an extended period of time, it will be necessary to change the cognitive templates or schema they use to perceive, interpret, and expect.

PSYCHOLOGICAL TREATMENT

Several years ago, Carlson wrote that rehabilitation by means of psychological treatment "is out of fashion today. It is not dead yet, but the literature is littered with death warrants" (1976, p. 32). He implies that behavioral science professionals (e.g., psychologists, psychiatrists, and social workers) are responsible for overselling their goods to the correctional system.

Numerous other practitioners, administrators, and academicians have come to the same or similar conclusions. Martinson (1974), one of the chief critics of rehabilitation, reviewed 231 studies of prison rehabilitative programs and concluded: "With few and isolated exceptions, the rehabilitative efforts that have been reported so far have had no appreciable effect on recidivism" (p. 25). His conclusion that "nothing works," together with growing disenchantment about rehabilitation within the criminal justice system, had a powerful effect on criminal justice administration. There was an immediate shift away from rehabilitation and toward other models of corrections, such as strict punishment with minimal efforts to rehabilitate. Later, the dust settled somewhat and administrators became more reluctant to discard rehabilitative programs in their entirety. Even Martinson eventually reduced his onslaught to "almost nothing works" (Lipton, Martinson, & Wilks, 1975).

One of the first to criticize Martinson's "nothing works" doctrine was Palmer (1975), who noted that Martinson tended to reject any type of rehabilitative treatment that was not *highly* successful. According to Palmer, Martinson was seeking a cure-all approach that would work for everyone, all or almost all of the time. He was not interested in partial success, and he appeared indifferent to the fact that about one-half (48 percent) of his 231 sample studies showed success with at least some subjects.

Adams (1977) pointed out that correctional treatments appear to be as effective as the partial success rate achieved thus far by traditional psychotherapy offered to the general population. Many of the projects that Martinson considered failures demonstrated behavioral improvement during the treatment, but there was regression to original behavior upon return to the original environment (Adams, 1977). In some cases, the return to criminal behavior occurred years after the improved behavior during treatment. Martinson's tendency to accept only the long-term signs of "cure" masks the short-term effect of correctional treatment. If individuals have no sufficient alternatives and skills for coping in the outside world, it is not surprising that they will return to their original deviant ways once back in the social environment from which these ways were acquired and which supports them.

Halleck and Witte (1977) note that Martinson's critique spanned the years 1945 to 1967, when evaluation and research methodology relating to corrections was in its infancy. "Evaluations since 1967 have, in general, been more thorough and more reliable statistically than those before that date" (Halleck & Witte, 1977, p. 376). Halleck and Witte believe that the later evaluations are more promising and cite, as examples, two work-release programs in California which significantly reduced the recidivism rate.

Quay (1977), in a cogent argument against the view that nothing works, noted that evaluations of correctional treatment concentrated too much on the adequacy of the research designs and measurement of outcomes and too little on the integrity of the program being assessed. To evaluate a program, a researcher must consider the rationale and goals of the treatment as well as how that treatment is delivered. Labeling a program "treatment" or "counseling" tells us nothing about what happened in the program. For example, were counseling sessions actually held? How well were they attended? Were inmates coerced into participating in the program, or were they able to volunteer freely without implicit threat?

Quay also advocates scrutinizing the delivery of treatment. Were the "counselors" untrained prison guards or community volunteers? Quay suggests that some evidence of competence to deliver treatment might be measured by the counselors' past educational experience, academic degrees, or similar qualifications. In evaluating rehabilitation programs, we should also examine the nature of the training and orientation given to the counselors, particularly if they were nonprofessionals. Was the training provided in two one-hour lectures by disinterested instructors, or was it provided intensively over a period of weeks by interested personnel? What kind of supervision did the treatment personnel receive?

Finally, Quay asks, how generalizable is a particular treatment approach to all inmates? To be maximally effective, any treatment-rehabilitative program should be formulated in relation to the needs and capabilities of each person, a concept referred to as *differential treatment*.

In his review of the literature, Quay finds that studies evaluating correctional treatment provide little information concerning the foregoing considerations. In one of the two studies that did describe goals, personnel, and treatment procedures in some detail (Kassebaum, Ward, & Wilner, 1971), it was quite evident that the planning, goal definition, and implementation of the program were poorly done.

Before proclaiming correctional psychological treatment per se ineffective and worthless, critics should give it a chance to perform under sophisticated planning, careful and dedicated execution, and well-designed methods of evaluation. It would be a mistake to discard a potentially useful concept because of misunderstanding and poorly conceived evaluation methods, and to wait for the rehabilitative treatment pendulum to swing back several decades later.

Psychotherapy

The main problem with rehabilitative treatment programs, however, might not be so much their evaluation as their validity. In other words, are any forms of psychological treatment effective in changing criminal behavior? Before answering this difficult question, we must describe briefly what is meant by psychological treatment, or psychotherapy.

The terms *psychotherapy*, *therapy*, *counseling*, and *treatment* are used interchangeably by clinicians. Broadly, they refer to a set of procedures or techniques used to help individuals or groups alter their maladaptive behavior, develop adaptive behavior, or both. The behavior must be considered maladaptive by the individual, however. In other words, the person must want to change.

Psychotherapy can be divided into six very broad and overlapping areas: psychoanalytic, behavioral, humanistic-existential, interpersonal, group, and cognitive therapy. Each approach is designed to change a person's way of thinking about the world to some extent. Most psychotherapies try to change cognitive constructs about ourselves, others, or both. Skinnerian behaviorism is probably least inclined to worry about cognitive constructs, since it focuses heavily on overt behavior to the exclusion of the mediational processes. Lately, most behaviorists have shifted to a more cognitive-behavioral approach.

Each variant of the psychotherapies has been tried to some extent within the correctional system under wide variations in method and purpose and different degrees of commitment. Overall, they have been marginally successful or unsuccessful in reducing criminal behavior, depending on one's point of view. To assess the many therapies used is not the purpose of this chapter. We will focus briefly on behavioral therapy, however, since it has drawn considerable attention and controversy over the past decade. Following that, we will give some attention to cognitive therapy, which appears to offer the most realistic approach to rehabilitative treatment.

Behavior Therapy

Behavior therapy was developed from learning-conditioning principles derived from well-controlled, precise laboratory environments or small-scale, well-designed demonstration projects. The social and physical environments are crucial considerations in the planning of any behavior therapy program. Before the treatment program can be effectively implemented, the target behaviors and the environmental events which accompany them must be accurately described and carefully evaluated as to how, when, and where they occur for a particular individual. This information in normally gathered through direct observation of the individual within situations where he or she typically exhibits the target behavior, and through interviews with the individual and acquaintances. In the planning stage, these initial data concerning the target behavior (such as frequency) provide baseline or pretreatment information which is useful for later determinations of how effective the treatment plan has been. Once the target behaviors and the conditions under which they occur are determined, the next step usually involves establishing a twofold plan: (1) The associative or reinforcement bond between the target behavior and the environmental event must be weakened; (2) more desirable behavior must be instituted through reinforcement. When the plan has been implemented, comparing treatment data with baseline data helps to determine whether or not it is working. If the original treatment plan does not work, the conditions will be reassessed and a modified plan will be introduced.

Behavior therapy (also called behavior modification) seems to have a number of advantages. It has been shown to be highly effective in changing and developing specific behaviors under controlled, experimental conditions. Its apparent simplicity and the ease with which it can be applied by paraprofessionals with minimal training are also appealing. Furthermore, it is economical, because it does not require a legion of high-level, expensive professionals, and it can be immediately beneficial for controlling unmanageable behavior within the institution. Finally, because it quantifies observable behaviors, it lends itself very well to evaluation and research.

However, behavior therapy has a number of problems. While it *seems* to offer a simple, straightforward method of alleviating pressing behavior problems, it actually requires sophistication on the part of the therapist, stringent environmental control, and a high degree of cooperation and commitment from those even remotely involved in the program. Transferring behavior techniques from the controlled psychological laboratory to the correctional institution, where there are bound to be numerous constraints, is an extremely difficult task. Another flaw is behavior therapy's lack of demonstrated generalizability to the natural environment outside the prison, where powerful, significant models and reference groups often dilute the short-term effectiveness of many behavior therapy approaches. Finally, and perhaps most important, behavior therapy in the correctional setting raises many questions about the rights of inmates, especially if there is any indication that they are being coerced to participate.

Behavior therapy, well applied and with the inmate's willing participation, may be useful for controlling institutional behavior and can promote the acquisition of specific social and academic skills. Furthermore, when combined with social cognitive therapy, it is beginning to demonstrate its effectiveness in inhibiting or even reducing criminal behavior in the natural environment, such as with sex offenders (discussed in chapter nine).

In all fairness, treatment programs within institutions are often handicapped by inadequate facilities, staff, programs, and financial support. Added to these restraints are legal, political, and social pressures. If some restrictions were reduced, the scientific community might be able to design and formulate effective, generalizable programs that would involve more personal commitment and freedom of choice on the part of the inmate.

Another feature of the prison system that makes treatment and rehabilitation difficult is that two systems are at work—the formal system dictated by authorities and the informal system run by inmates. In the latter, two processes may be identified: *criminalization* and *prisonization*. In criminalization, inmates exchange, share, and support one another's construct systems, beliefs, attitudes, and feelings. The system creates a "deviant" culture where inmates form subgroups and develop friendships, loyalty, and commitment. Prisonization is the process whereby inmates learn the specific rules, general culture, and expectations of the prison community. With these two learning processes at work, which are often in conflict with society, it seems that the longer inmates spend time in prison the more likely will they crystallize their thinking about their deviant life styles and become "better criminals." Research continually reveals that, in general, the longer one spends in prison, the more likely one is to reoffend.

The processes of criminalization and prisonization underscore the traditionally recognized influence of normative or reference groups on human behavior. Criminal behavior, however, is not simply the result of imitating others in the social environment, or even the result of external reinforcement. Recent research in cognitive psychology goes one step further. "If actions were determined solely by external rewards and punishments, people would behave like weathervanes, constantly shifting in different directions to conform to the momentary influence impinging on them. They would act corruptly with unprincipled individuals and honorably with righteous ones, and liberally with libertarians and dogmatically with authoritarians" (Bandura, 1977, p. 128). Instead, most human behavior is motivated and regulated in large part by personally adopted beliefs, values, and expectations.

Cognitive Therapy

During the past two decades, cognitive theories have come to dominate the research on learning, memory, personality, motivation, and social psychology (Mahoney & Lyddon, 1988). The growth of cognition also has been very strong in the areas of counseling and psychotherapy.

One of the forerunners of the cognitive approaches was *reality therapy*, a form of self-control therapy developed by the psychiatrist William Glasser (1965) and still commonly used in corrections today. The basic principles for the approach was developed at the Ventura (California) School for Girls, whose residents were seriously delinquent adolescent girls. The popularity of reality therapy stems partly from its straightfoward approach and easy to understand procedures. Because of its apparent simplicity, paraprofessionals and front line correctional staff can be easily trained to offer personal and group therapy to inmates. Reality therapy is based on the perspective that offenders must face reality—no matter what happened to them in the past—and take full responsibility for their behavior *now*. In essence, the focus is to teach offenders responsible behavior. A major contribution of reality therapy has been to focus attention on the irresponsible nature of crime and delinquency, rather then viewing them as the result of some psychological sickness or disorder.

Other important forerunners of commonly used cognitive treatment approaches are George Kelly's (1955) *personal construct therapy*, Albert Ellis' (1962) *rational-emotive therapy*, and Aron T. Beck's (1970) *cognitive therapy*. All of these early approaches have undergone extensive revision since their initial formulation, and have splintered into many different therapeutic perspectives.

In recent years, *constructivist* therapy has emerged as a viable, rapidly growing approach across a wide area of cognitive therapies. "The basic assertion of constructivism is that each individual creates his or her own representational model of the world. This experiential scaffolding . . . in turn becomes a framework from which the individual orders and assigns meaning to new experience" (Mahoney & Lyddon, 1988, p. 200). The basic idea of the constructivist approach is that individuals do not formulate static templates through which ongoing experience are filtered, but rather develop more *dynamic* constructs that are always subject to change as a result of new experiences. Thus, "the constructivist does not view cognitive structures as static, storage entities but rather as systems of transformation" (Mahoney & Lyddon, 1988, p. 203).

From a constructivist perspective, developing human beings are active information processors, who explore and adapt to the environment, and who continually organize information about the world and oneself into increasingly complex views (Greenberg, 1988). On the other hand, repetitively violent and antisocial individuals may be those who are essentially trapped in an isolated, socially closed-off, and self-constructive cognitive system that relies on simple, straightforward aggressive solutions to survival. Moreover, they continually fall out of mainstream society, which results in their already isolated cognitive systems becoming more narrow, restrictive, and deviant. Instead of becoming more complex and integrative, the world versions of the repetitive offender may stagnate or deteriorate. Many repetitive offenders may become so caught up in their personal versions of the world that they refuse to allow alternative views to pierce their cognitive armor. Yochelson and Samenow (1976), for example, contend that there are 52 basic errors in thinking practiced by the hardcore criminals which must be corrected before there is any hope of change. It would seem that cognitive therapies offer the best hope for changing the thinking and belief systems of the repetitive offender.

We also need to have a better understanding of the relationships among the vast array of swirling systems that affect delinquent and criminal behavior before we can have highly effective treatment or prevention programs. "Human action is . . . regulated by multilevel systems of control" (Bandura, 1989, p. 1181). One such approach is a social systems theory. A social systems approach facilitates a synthesis of what we know across the various disciplines and perspectives, whether we are discussing social class, neighborhood, community, culture, family, siblings, or the individual (Bartol, 1988). Social systems theory assumes that while it is helpful to study personality variables, family, the neighborhood, and the culture in isolation, it is far more effective to study these variables in *relationship* to one another. In order to change criminal behavior over long periods of time, we need to study not only the offenders themselves but also their families, peers, schools, neighborhoods, communities, and cultures, all in relationship to one another. The offender affects the other systems and the systems affect the offender in complex, poorly understood ways. Treatment and preventive approaches that are fully able to appreciate this dynamic interplay are far more likely to be successful than those that only concentrate on one aspect of an individual's life.

Of course, it is easier to describe the factors that might contribute to criminal behavior than to offer a comprehensive, realistic proposal for dealing with it. The primary mission of this text was to propose some explanations for criminal behavior from a psychological perspective. Whether these explanations will be accepted and applied to solving the crime problem remains to be seen. We can only reiterate that the correctional system as it now operates, with its defeatist attitude toward rehabilitation and its emphasis on punishment for its own sake, cannot improve the situation. Undoubtedly, the ideal way of dealing with crime is by attacking its origins; from a psychological point of view this basically means examining the values we communicate to our young. Nevertheless, it is not too optimistic to hope that the psychological principles we have discussed may be applied to at least some offenders presently housed in correctional institutions.

References

ABEL, G. G., BARLOW, D. H., BLANCHARD, E. B., & GUILD, D. (1977). The components of rapists' sexual arousal. *Archives of General Psychiatry, 34,* 895–903.

ABEL, G. G., BECKER, J. V., BLANCHARD, E. B., & DJENDEREDJIAN, A. (1978). Differentiating sexual aggressives with penile measures. *Criminal Justice and Behavior, 5,* 315–332.

ABEL, G. G., BECKER, J. V., MURPHY, W. D., & FLANAGAN, B. (1981). Identifying dangerous child molesters. In R. B. Stuart (Ed.), *Violent behavior: Social learning approaches to prediction, management and treatment.* New York: Brunner/Mazel.

ABEL, G. G., MITTELMAN, M. S., & BECKER, J. V. (1985). Sexual offenders: Results of assessment and recommendations for treatment. In H. H. Ben-Aron, S. I. Hucker, C. D. Webster (Eds.), *Clinical criminology.* Toronto: MM Graphics.

ABEL, G. G., MITTELMAN, M., BECKER, J. V., RATHNER, J., & ROULEAU, J. (1988). Predicting child molesters' response to treatment. In R. A. Prentky & V. L. Quinsey (Eds.), *Human sexual aggression: Current perspectives.* New York: New York Academy of Sciences.

ABRAHAMSEN, D. (1952). *Who are the guilty?* Westport, CT: Greenwood Press.

ABRAHAMSEN, D. (1960). *The psychology of crime.* New York: Columbia Univ. Press.

ADAMS, S. S. (1977). Evaluating correctional treatments. *Criminal Justice and Behavior, 4,* 323–340.

ADLER, C. (1985). An exploration of self-reported sexually aggressive behavior. *Crime and Delinquency, 31,* 306–331.

ADLER, F. (1975). *Sisters in crime.* New York: McGraw–Hill.

ADLER, F. (1981). International concern in light of the American experience. In F. Adler (Ed.), *The incidence of female criminality in the contemporary world.* New York: New York Univ. Press.

ADLER, M. J. (1967). *The difference of man and the difference it makes.* New York: Holt, Rinehart & Winston.

AGNEW, R. (1984). Appearance and delinquency. *Criminology, 22*, 421–440.

AKERS, R. L. (1977). *Deviant behavior: A social learning approach* (2nd ed.). Belmont, CA: Wadsworth.

AKERS, R. L. (1985). *Deviant behavior: A social learning* (3rd ed.). Belmont, CA: Wadsworth.

ALLSOPP, J. F. (1976). Criminality and delinquency. In H. J. Eysenck & G. D. Wilson (Eds.), *A textbbok of human psychology*. Baltimore: Univ. Park Press.

ALLSOPP, J. F., & FELDMAN, M. P. (1976). Personality and antisocial behaviour in schoolboys: Item analysis of questionnaire measures. *British Journal of Criminology, 16*, 337–351.

AMERICAN BAR ASSOCIATION. (1979). *Juvenile justice standards project*. Chicago: American Bar Association.

AMERICAN HUMANE ASSOCIATION. (1987). *Highlights of official child neglect and abuse reporting—1985*. Denver, CO: Author.

AMIR, M. (1971). *Patterns in forcible rape*. Chicago: Univ. of Chicago Press.

AMSEL, A. (1958). The role of frustrative nonreward in noncontinuous reward situations. *Psychological Bulletin, 55*, 102–119.

ANDENAES, J. (1968). Does pusnishment deter crime? *The Criminal Law Quarterly, 11*, 76–93.

ANDENAES, J. (1969). The general preventive effects of punishment. In I. Radzinowicz & M. E. Wolfgang (Eds.), *Crime and justice* (Vol. 2). *The criminal in the arms of the law*. New York: Basic Books.

ANDERSON, C. A. (1987). Temperature and aggression: Effects on quarterly, yearly, and city rates of violent and nonviolent crime. *Journal of Personality and Social Psychology, 52*, 1161–1173.

ANDERSON, C. A. (1989). Temperature and aggression: Ubiquitous effects of heat on occurrence of human violence. *Psychological Bulletin, 106*, 74–96.

ANDERSON, C. A., & ANDERSON, D. C. (1984). Ambient temperature and violent crime: Tests of the linear and curvilinear hypothesis. *Journal of Personality and Social Psychology, 46*, 91–97.

ANDREW, J. M. (1978). Laterality on the tapping test among legal offenders. *Journal of Clinical Psychology, 7*, 149–150.

ANDREW, J. M. (1980). Are left-handers less violent? *Journal of Youth and Adolescence, 9*, 1–9.

ARDREY, R. (1966). *The territorial imperative*. New York: Atheneum.

ARTHUR, R. G., & CAHOON, E. B. (1964). A clincal and electroencephalographic survey of psychopathic personality. *American Journal of Psychiatry, 120*, 875–882.

AUGUSTINE FELLOWSHIP. (1986). *Sex and Love Addicts Anonymous*. Boston: The Augustine Fellowship.

AVERY-CLARK, C. A., & LAWS, D. R. (1984). Differential erection response patterns of sexual child abusers to stimuli describing activities with children. *Behavior Therapy, 15*, 71–83.

BAILEY, W. C. (1984). Poverty, inequality and city homicide rates. *Criminology, 22*, 531–550.

BALL, J. C., SHAFFER, J. W., & NURCO, D. N. (1983). The day-to-day criminality of heroin addicts in Baltimore—A study in the continuity of offense rates. *Drug and Alcohol Dependence, 12*, 119–142.

BANCROFT, H. (1976). Behavioral treatments of sexual deviations. In N. H. Leitenberg (Ed.), *Handbook of behavioral modifications and behavoiral therapy*. Englewood Cliffs, NJ: Prentice-Hall.

BANDURA, A. (1965). Influence of models' reinforcement contingencies on the acquisition of imitative responses. *Journal of Personality and Social Psychology, 1*, 589–595.

BANDURA, A. (1973a). *Aggression: A social learning analysis*. Englewood Cliffs, NJ: Prentice-Hall.

BANDURA, A. (1973b). Social learning theory of aggression. In J. F. Knutson (Ed.), *The control of aggression*. Chicago: Aldine.

BANDURA, A. (1977). *Social learning theory*. Englewood Cliffs, NJ: Prentice-Hall.

BANDURA, A. (1978). The self-system in reciprocal determinism. *American Psychologist, 33*, 344–358.

BANDURA, A. (1983). Psychological mechanisms of aggression. In R. G. Geen & E. I. Donnerstein (Eds.), *Aggression: Theoretical and empirical reviews*. Vol. 1. New York: Academic Press.

BANDURA, A. (1986). *Social foundations in thought and action: A social cognitive theory*. Englewood Cliffs, NJ: Prentice-Hall.

BANDURA, A. (1989). Human agency in social cognitive theory. *American Psychologist, 44*, 1175–1184.

BANDURA, A., & HUSTON, A. (1961). Identification as a process of incidental learning. *Journal of Abnormal and Social Psychology, 63*, 311–318.

BANDURA, A., ROSS, D., & ROSS, S. (1963). Vicarious reinforcement and imitative learning. *Journal of Abnormal and Social Psychology, 67*, 601–607.

BANDURA, A., UNDERWOOD, B., & FROMSON, M. E. (1975). Disinhibition of aggression through diffusion of responsibility and dehumanization of victims. *Journal of Research in Personality, 9*, 253–269.

BANDURA, A., & WALTERS, R. H. (1959). *Adolescent aggression.* New York: Ronald Press.

BANDURA, A., & WALTERS, R. H. (1963). *Social learning and personality development.* New York: Holt, Rinehart & Winston.

BARD, L. A., CARTER, D. L., CERCE, D. D., KNIGHT, R. A., ROSENBERG, R., & SCHNEIDER, B. (1987). *Behavioral Sciences & the Law, 5*, 203 220.

BARON, R. A. (1977). *Human aggression.* New York: Plenum Press.

BARON, R. A. (1979). Aggression and heat: The "long hot summer" revisited. In A. Baum, J. E. Singer, & S. Valins (Eds.), *Advances in environmental psychology.* Hillsdale, NJ: Erlbaum.

BARON, R. A. (1983). The control of human aggression: An optimistic perspective. *Journal of Social and Clinical Psychology, 1*, 97–119.

BARON, R. A., & BELL, P. A. (1975). Aggression and heat: Mediating effects of prior provocation and exposure to an aggressive model. *Journal of Personality and Social Psychology, 31*, 825–832.

BARON, R. A., & BYRNE, D. (1977). *Social psychology* (2nd ed.). Boston: Allyn & Bacon.

BARON, R. A., & LAWTON, S. F. (1972). Environmental influences on aggression: The facilitation of modeling effects by high ambient temperatures. *Psychonomic Science, 26*, 80–83.

BARON, R. A., & RANSBERGER, V. M. (1978). Ambient temperature and the occurrence of collective violence: The "long, hot summer" revisited. *Journal of Personality and Social Psychology, 36*, 361–366.

BARTOL, C. R. (1975). The effects of chlorpromazine and detroamphetamine sulfate on the visual stimuluation preferences of extraverts and introverts. *Psychophysiology, 12,* 22 31.

BARTOL, C. R. (1983). *Psychology and American law.* Belmont, CA: Wadsworth.

BARTOL, C. R. (1988). Understanding delinquency: Causal loops and social systems. *Criminal Justice and Behavior, 15*, 394–401.

BARTOL, C. R., & BARTOL, A. M. (1989). *Juvenile delinquency: A systems approach.* Englewood Cliffs, NJ: Prentice-Hall.

BARTOL, C. R., & HOLANCHOCK, H. A. (1979). A test of Eysenck's theory of criminality on an American prisoner population. *Criminal Justice and Behavior, 6*, 245–249.

BATTELLE LAW AND JUSTICE CENTER REPORT. (1977). *Forcible rape: An analysis of legal issue.* Washington, DC: National Institute of Law Enforcement and Criminal Justice.

BAUMER, T. L., & ROSENBAUM, D. P. (1984). *Combating retail theft: Programs and strategies.* Boston: Butterworth.

Baxstom v. Herold, 383 U.S. 107 (1966).

Beck, A. T. (1970). Cognitive therapy: Nature and relation to behavior therapy. *Behavior Therapy, 1*, 184–200.

BECKER, J. V., ABEL, G. G., BLANCHARD, E. B., MURPHY, W. D., & COLEMAN, E. (1978). Evaluating social skills of sexual aggressives. *Criminal Justice and Behavior, 5*, 357–367.

BELL, P. A., & BARON, R. A. (1977). Aggression and ambient temperature: The inhibiting and facilitating effects of hot and cold environments. *Bulletin of the Psychonomic Society, 6*, 240–242.

BELL, R. R. (1976). *Social deviance: A substantive analysis.* Homewood, IL: Dorsey Press.

BELSKY, J., LERNER, R. M., & SPANIER, G. B. (1984). *The child in the family.* New York: Random House.

BENNETT, T., & WRIGHT, R. (1984). *Burglars on burglary: Prevention and the offender.* Brookfield, VT: Gower.

BENSING, R. C., & SCHROEDER, O. (1960). *Homicide in an urban community.* Springfield, IL: Charles C. Thomas.

BERGER, H. (1929). Uber das Electrenkephalogram des Menschen. *Archiv fur Psychiatrie und Nervenkrank-heiten, 87*, 527–570.

BERKOWITZ, L. (1962). *Aggression: A social-psychological analysis.* New York: McGraw-Hill.

BERKOWITZ, L. (1969). The frustration-aggression hypothesis revisted. In L. Berkowitz (Ed.), *Roots of aggression.* New York: Atherton Press.

BERKOWITZ, L. (1970). The contagion of violence: An S-R mediational analysis of some effects of observed aggression. In W. J. Arnold & M. M. Page (Eds.), *Nebraska symposium on motivation*. Lincoln, NE: Univ. of Nebraska Press.

BERKOWITZ, L. (1973). Words and symbols as stimuli to aggressive responses. In J. F. Knutson (Ed.), *The control of aggression*. Chicago: Aldine.

BERKOWITZ, L. (1983). The experience of anger as a parallel process in the display of impulsive, "angry" aggression. In R. G. Geen & E. I. Donnerstein (Eds.), *Aggression: Theoretical and empirical reviews*. Vol. 1. New York: Academic Press.

BERKOWITZ, L. (1989). Frustration-aggression hypothesis: Examination and reformulation. *Psychological Bulletin, 106*, 59–73.

BERKOWITZ, L., & HEIMER, K. (1989). On the construction of the anger experience: Aversive events and negative priming in the formation of feelings. In L. Berkowitz (Ed.), *Advances in experimental social psychology*. Vol. 22. New York: Academic Press.

BERKOWITZ, L., & LEPAGE, A. (1967). Weapons as aggression-eliciting stimuli. *Journal of Personality and Social Psychology, 7*, 202–207.

BERLYNE, D. E. (1960). *Conflict, arousal, and curiosity*. New York: McGraw-Hill.

BERMAN, T., & PAISEY, T. (1984). Personality in assaultive and non-assaultive juvenile male offenders. *Psychological Reports, 54*, 527–530.

BERNARD, F. (1975). An inquiry among a group of pedophiles. *Journal of Sex Research, 11*, 242–255.

BERNDT, T. (1979). Developmental changes in conformity to peers and parents. *Developmental Psychology, 15*, 608–616.

BLACKBURN, N., WEISS, J., & LAMBERTI, J. (1960). The sudden murderer. *Archives of General Psychiatry, 2*, 670–678.

BLACKBURN, R. (1968). Personality in relation to extreme aggression in psychiatric offenders. *British Journal of Psychiatry, 114*, 821–828.

BLACKBURN, R. (1971). Personality types among abnormal homicides. *British Journal of Criminology, 11*, 14–31.

BLACKBURN, R. (1978). Psychopathy, arousal, and the need for stimulation. In R. D. Hare & D. Schalling (Eds.), *Psychopathic behaviour: Approach to research*. Chichester, England: Wiley.

BLACKBURN, R. (1988). On moral judgments and personality disorders. *British Journal of Psychiatry, 153*, 505–512.

BLAIR, C. D., & LANYON, R. I. (1981). Exhibitionism: An etiology and treatment. *Psychological Bulletin, 89*, 439–463.

BLAU, J. R., & BLAU, P. M. (1982). Metropolitan structure and violent crime. *American Sociological Review, 47*, 114–128.

BLOCK, C. R. (1985). Race/ethnicity and patterns of Chicago homicide 1965 to 1981. *Crime and Delinquency, 31*, 104–116.

BLOCK, R. (1977). *Violent crime*. Lexington: MA: Lexington Books.

BLOOMQUIST, E. R. (1970). The use and abuse of stimulants. In W. G. Clark & J. DelGiudice (Eds.), *Principles of psycho-pharmacology*. New York: Academic Press.

BLUMER, D. (1976). Epilepsy and violence. In D. J. Madden & J. R. Lion (Eds.), *Rage·hate·assault and other forms of violence*. New York: Spectrum Publishers.

BLUMER, D., & MIGEON, C. (1973). *Treatment of impulsive behavior disorders in males with medroxyprogesterone acetate*. Paper presented at the annual meeting of the American Psychiatric Association.

BLUMER, H., SUTTER, A., AHMED, S., & SMITH, R. (1967). *ADD center project final report: The world of youthful drug use*. Berkeley, CA: Univ. of California Press.

BLUMSTEIN, A., COHEN, J., ROTH, J., & VISHER, C. (Eds.), (1986). *Criminal careers and career criminals*. Washington, DC: National Academy Press.

BLUMSTEIN, A., FARRINGTON, D. P., & MOITRA, S. (1985). Delinquency careers: Innocents, desisters and persisters. In M. Tonry and N. Morris (Eds.), *Crime and justice: An annual review of research*. Vol. 6. Chicago: Univ. of Chicago Press.

BOCK, K. (1980). *Human nature and history: A response to sociobiology*. New York: Columbia Univ. Press.

BORGIDA, E. (1980). Evidentiary reform of rape laws: A psychological approach. In P. D. Lipsitt & B. D. Sales (Eds.), *New directions in psycholegal research*. New York: Van Nostrand Reinhold.

BORGSTROM, C. A. (1939). Eine Serie von kriminellen Zwillingen. *Archiv fur Rassenbiologie, 12,* 18–44.

BOUDREAU, J., KWAN, Q., FARAGHER, W., & DENAULT, G. (1977). *Arson and arson investigation.* Washington, DC: U.S. Government Printing Office.

BOWDEN, K. M., WILSON, D. W., & TURNER, L. K. (1958). A survey of blood alcohol testing in Victoria (1951–56). *Medical Journal of Australia, 45,* 13–15.

BOWKER, L. H. (1983). *Beating wife-battering.* Lexington, MA: Lexington Books.

BRACEY, D. H. (1982). Concurrent and consecutive abuse: The juvenile prostitute. In B. R. Price and N. Sokoloff (Eds.), *The criminal justice system and women.* New York: Clark Boardman.

BRADFORD, J. M. W. (1982). Arson: A clinical study. *Canadian Journal of Psychiatry, 27,* 188–193.

BRADY, J. (1983). Arson, urban economy, and organized crime: The case of Boston. *Social Problems, 31,* 1–27.

BRAITHWAITE, J. (1981). The myth of class and criminality reconsidered. *American Sociological Review, 46,* 36–57.

BRENNAN, T. (1987). Classification: An overview of selected methodological issues. In D. M. Gottfredson & M. Tonry (Eds.), *Prediction and classification: Criminal justice decision making.* Vol. 9. Chicago: Univ. of Chicago Press.

BRIERE, J. (1988). The long term clinical correlates of childhood sexual victimization. In R. A. Prentky & V. L. Quinsey (Eds.), *Human sexual aggression: Current perspectives.* New York: New York Academy of Sciences.

BRIERE, J., MALAMUTH, N., & CENITI, J. (1981). *Self-assessed rape proclivity: Attitudinal and sexual correlates.* Paper presented at APA meeting, Los Angeles.

BRITTAIN, R. P. (1970). The sadistic murderer. *Medicine, Science and the Law, 10,* 198–207.

BRODSKY, C. M. (1976). Rape at work. In M. J. Walker & S. L. Brodsky (Eds.), *Sexual assault: The victims and the rapist.* Lexington, MA: Lexington Books.

BRODSKY, S. L. (1973). *Psychologists in the criminal justice system.* Urbana, IL: Univ. of Illinois Press.

BRODSKY, S. L. (1977). Criminal and dangerous behavior. In D. Rimm & J. Somervill (Eds.). *Abnormal psychology.* New York: Academic Press.

BROMBERG, W. (1939). Marihuana: A psychiatric study. *Journal of the American Medical Association, 113,* 4–12.

BROWN, J. S., & FARBER, I. E. (1951). Emotions conceptualized as inter-vening variables—with suggestions toward a theory of frustration. *Psychological Bulletin, 48,* 465–495.

BROWN, S. E. (1984). Social class, child maltreatment, and delinquent behavior. *Criminology, 22,* 259–278.

BROWNE, A., & FINKELHOR, D. (1986). Impact of child sexual abuse: A review of the research. *Psychological Bulletin, 99,* 66–77.

BRUNET, B. L., REICHENSTEIN, R. J., WILLIAMS, T., & WONG, L. (1985–1986). Toxicity of phencyclidine and ethanol in combination. *Alcohol and Drug Research, 6,* 341–349.

BRUSSEL, J. A. (1968). *Casebook of a crime psychiatrist.* New York: Bernard Geis Associates.

BUIKHUISEN, W., & HEMMEL, J. J. (1972). Crime and conditioning. *British Journal of Criminology, 17,* 147–157.

BUKSTEL, L. H., & KILMANN, P. R. (1980). Psychological effects of imprisonment on confined individuals. *Psychological Bulletin, 88,* 469–493.

BULLOCK, H. A. (1955). Urban homicide in theory and fact. *Journal of Criminal Law, Criminology and Police Science, 45,* 565–575.

BUMPASS, E. R., FAGELMAN, F. D., & BIRX, R. J. (1983). Intervention with children who set fires. *American Journal of Psychotherapy, 37,* 328–345.

BURGESS, P. K. (1972). Eysenck's theory of criminality: A test of some objectives of disconfirmatory evidence. *British Journal of Social and Clinical Psychology, 11,* 248–256.

BURGESS, R. L., & AKERS, R. L. (1966). A differential association-reinforcement theory of criminal behavior. *Social Problems, 14,* 128–147.

BURNAM, M. A., STEIN, J. A., GOLDING, J. M., SIEGEL, J. M., SORENSON, S. B., FORSYTHE, A. B., & TELLES, C. A. (1988). Sexual assault and mental disorders in a community population. *Journal of Consulting and Clinical Psychology, 56,* 843–850.

BURT, M. R. (1980). Cultural myths and supports for rape. *Journal of Personality and Social Psychology, 38,* 217–230.

BURT, M. R. (1983). Justifying person violence: A comparison of rapists and the general public. *Victimology, 8,* 131–150.

BURT, M. R., & KATZ, B. L. (1985). Rape, robbery, and burglary. *Victimology, 10,* 325–358.

BURTON, N., & STEADMAN, H. J. (1978). Legal professionals' perceptions of the insanity defense. *Journal of Psychiatry & Law, 6,* 173–187.

BURTON, R. V. (1963). Generality of honesty reconsidered. *Psychological Review, 70,* 481–499.

BURTON, R. V. (1976). Honesty and dishonesty. In T. Lickona (Ed.), *Moral development and behavior.* New York: Holt, Rinehart & Winston.

BUSS, A. H. (1966). *Psychopathology.* New York: Wiley.

BUSS, A. H. (1971). Aggression pays. In J. L. Singer (Ed.), *The control of aggression and violence.* New York: Academic Press.

BUTLER, R. A. (1954). Curiosity in monkeys. *Scientific American* (reprint #426). San Francisco: W. H. Freeman.

BUTTON, A. (1973). Some antecedents of felonious and delinquent behavior. *Journal of Child Clinical Psychology, 2,* 35–37.

CALHOUN, J. B. (1961). Phenomena associated with population density. *Proceedings of the National Academy of Sciences, 47,* 428–429.

CALHOUN, J. B. (1962). Population density and social pathology. *Scientific American, 206,* 139–148.

CAMERON, M. O. (1964). *The booster and the snitch.* New York: Free Press.

CANADIAN GOVERNMENT'S COMMISSION OF INQUIRY. (1971). *The non-medical use of drugs: Interim report.* London: Penguin Books.

CANTER, S. (1973). Personality traits in twins. In G. Claridge, S. Canter, & W. I. Hume (Eds.), *Personality differences and biological variations: A study of twins.* Oxford: Pergamon Press.

CANTWELL, D. P. (1975). A medical model for research and clinical use with hyperactive children. In D. P. Cantwell (Ed.), *The hyperactive child.* New York: Spectrum.

CAPUTE, A. J., NIEDERMEYER, E. F. L., & RICHARDSON, I. (1968). The electroencephalogram in children with minimal cerebral dysfunction. *Pediatrics, 41,* 1104.

CARLSON, K. A. (1990). 1989 survey of psychological testing practices in prisons. *Correctional Psychologist, 22,* 9–11.

CARLSON, R. J. (1976). *The dilemmas of corrections.* Lexington, MA: Lexington Books.

CARNES, P. (1983). *Out of the shadows: Understanding sexual addiction.* Minneapolis: Compcare Publications.

CARNEY, R. M., & WILLIAMS, B. D. (1983). Premenstrual syndrome: A criminal defense. *Notre Dame Law Review, 59,* 253–269.

CARTER, R. (1980). Arson and arson investigation in the United States. *Fire Journal, 74,* 40–47.

CASPI, A., ELDER, G. H., & BEM, D. J. (1987). Moving against the world: Life course patterns of explosive children. *Developmental Psychology, 23,* 308–313.

CAVIOR, N., & HOWARD, L. R. (1973). Facial attractiveness and juvenile delinquency among black offenders and white offenders. *Journal of Abnormal Child Psychology, 1,* 202–213.

CHAFFEE, S. H., & MCLEOD, J. M. (1971). *Adolescents, parents, and television violence.* Paper presented at the meeting of the American Psychological Association, Washington, DC.

CHALKELY, A. J., & POWELL, G. E. (1983). The clinical description of forty-eight cases of clinical fetishism. *British Journal of Psychiatry, 142,* 292–295.

CHAPPELL, D. (1977a). *Forcible rape: A national survey of the response by police* (LEAA). Washington, DC: U.S. Government Printing Office.

CHAPPELL, D. (1977b). *Forcible rape: A national survey of the response by prosecutors* (LEAA). Washington, DC: U.S. Government Printing Office.

CHARNEY, J. (1980). The new diagnostic and statistical manual of mental disorders: Or, what's in a name? *Philosophical Psychology, 1,* 59–71.

CHEATWOOD, D. (1988). Is there a season for homicide? *Criminology, 26,* 287–306.

CHEIN, I. (1962). The image of man. *Journal of Social Issues, 18,* 1–35.

CHESNEY-LIND, M. (1986). Women and crime. *Signs, 12,* 78–96.

CHESNO, F. A., & KILMANN, P. R. (1975). Effects of stimulation intensity on sociopathic avoidance learning. *Journal of Abnormal Psychology, 84,* 144–150.

CHIMBOS, P. D. (1973). A study of breaking and entering offenses in "Northern City," Ontario. *Canadian Journal of Criminology and Corrections, 15,* 316–325.

CHOROVER, S. L. (1980). Violence: A localizable problem? In E. S. Valenstein (Ed.), *The psycho-surgery debate.* San Francisco: W. H. Freeman.

CHRISTIANSEN, K. O. (1977a). A review of studies of criminality among twins. In S. Mednick & K. O. Christiansen (Eds.), *Biosocial bases of criminal behavior.* New York: Gardiner Press.

CHRISTIANSEN, K. O. (1977b). A preliminary study of criminality among twins. In S. Mednick & K. O. Christiansen (Eds.), *Biosocial bases of criminal behavior.* New York: Gardiner Press.

CHRISTIE, M. M., MARSHALL, W. L., & LANTHIER. R. D. (1979). *A descriptive study of incarcerated rapists and pedophiles.* Report to the Solicitor General of Canada.

CHURGIN, M. M. (1983). The transfer of inmates of mental health facilities: Developments in the law. In J. Monahan & H. J. Steadman (Eds.), *Mentally disordered offenders.* New York: Plenum.

CHUTE, C. L. (1949). Fifty years of the juvenile court. In M. Bell (Ed.), *Current approaches to delinquency.* New York: National Probation and Parole Association.

CLARIDGE, G. (1973). Final remarks. In G. Claridge, S. Canter, & W. I. Hume (Eds.), *Personality differences and biological variations.* Oxford: Pergamon Press.

CLARK, J. P., & HOLLINGER, R. C. (1983). *Theft by employees in work organizations.* Washington, DC: U.S. Department of Justice.

CLARK, K. B. (1971). The pathos of power: A psychological perspective. *American Psychologist, 26,* 1047–1057.

CLECKLEY, H. (1976). *The mask of sanity* (5th ed.). St. Louis: Mosby.

CLEMENTS, C. B. (1987). Psychologists in adult correctional institutions: Getting off the treadmill. In E. K. Morris & C. J. Braukmann (Eds.), *Behavioral approaches to crime and delinquency.* New York: Plenum.

CLEVELAND, F. P. (1955). Problems in homicide investigation IV: The relationship of alcohol to homicide. *Cincinnati Journal of Medicine, 36,* 28–30.

CLINE, V. B., CROFT, R. G., & COURRIER, S. (1973). Densitization of children to television violence. *Journal of Personality and Social Psychology, 27,* 360–365.

COCHRANE, R (1974). Crime and personality. Theory and evidence. *Bulletin of the British Psychological Society, 27,* 19–22.

COCOZZA, J. J., & STEADMAN, H. J. (1976). The failure of psychiatric prediction of dangerousness: Clear and convincing evidence. *Rutgers Law Review, 29,* 1084–1101.

COHEN, F. (1980). *The law of deprivation of liberty: A study in social control.* St. Paul, MN: West.

COHEN, J. (1983). Incapacitation as a strategy for crime control. In M. Tonry & N. Morris (Eds.), *Crime and justice: An annual review of research.* Vol. 5. Chicago: Univ. of Chicago Press.

COHEN, M. L., GARAFALO, R., BOUCHER, R., & SEGHORN, T. (1971). The psychology of rapists. *Seminars in Psychiatry, 3,* 307–327.

COHEN, M., SEGHORN, T., & CALMAS, W. (1969). Sociometric study of the sex offender. *Journal of Abnormal Psychology, 74,* 249–255.

COHN, V. (1986). Crack use. *NIDA Notes, 1,* 6.

COLE, K. E., FISHER, G., & COLE, S. S. (1968). Women who kill. *Archives of General Psychiatry, 19,* 1–8.

COLEMAN, J. C. (1976). *Abnormal psychology and modern life* (5th ed.). Glenview, IL: Scott, Foresman.

COLLINS, J. J. (1981). Alcohol use and criminal behavior. In J. J. Collins (Ed.), *Drinking and crime.* New York: Guilford.

COMMISSION ON OBSCENITY AND PORNOGRAPHY. (1970). *The report of the Commission on Obscenity and Pornography.* Washington, DC: U.S. Government Printing Office.

CONKLIN, J. E. (1972). *Robbery and the criminal justice system.* Philadelphia: Lippincott.

CONKLIN, J. E. (1977). *"Illegal but not criminal."* Englewood Cliffs, NJ: Prentice-Hall.

CONNELL, P. H. (1968). Use and abuse of amphetamines. *General Practitioner, 39,* 261–265.

CORTES, J. B., & GATTI, F. M. (1972). *Delinquency and crime: A biopsychosocial approach.* New York: Seminar Press.

CRAFT, M. (1966). The meanings of the term "psychopath." In M. Craft (Ed.), *Psychopathic disorders and their assessment.* Oxford: Pergamon Press.

CRAFT, M., STEPHENSON, G., & GRANGER, C. (1964). A controlled trial of authoritarian and self-governing regimes with adolescent psychopaths. *American Journal of Orthopsychiatry, 34*, 543–554.

CRAWFORD, J., & HEATHER, N. (1987). Public attitudes to the disease concept of alcoholism. *The International Journal of Addiction, 22*, 1129–1138.

CRESSEY, D. R. (1953). *A study in the social psychology of embezzlement: Other people's money.* Glencoe, IL: Free Press.

CRIDER, R. (1986). *Phencyclindine: Changing abuse patterns.* In D. H. Clovet (Ed.), *Phencyclidine: An update.* Rockville, MD: National Institute of Drug Abuse.

CRITCHLEY, M. (1951). *The trial of Neville George Clevely Heath.* London: William Hodge.

CRITCHLOW, B. (1986). The powers of John Barelycorn: Beliefs about the effects of alcohol on social behavior. *American Psychologist, 41*, 751–764.

CRITCHTON, R. (1959). *The great imposter.* New York: Random House.

CROWE, R. R. (1974). An adoptive study of antisocial personality. *Archives of General Psychiatry, 31*, 785–791.

CULLEN, F., & GILBERT, K. E. (1982). *Reaffirming rehabilitation.* Cincinnati, OH: Anderson.

DALE, M. W. (1976). Barriers to the rehabilitation of ex-offenders. *Crime and Delinquency, 22*, 322–337.

DALGAARD, O. S., & KRINGLEN, E. (1976). A Norwegian twin study of criminality. *British Journal of Criminology, 16*, 213–233.

DALTON, K. (1961). Menstruation and crime. *British Medical Journal, 2*, 1752–1753.

DALTON, K. (1964). *The premenstrual syndrome.* Springfield, IL: Charles C. Thomas.

DANIELS, D. N., & GILULA, M. F. (1970). Violence and the struggle for existence. In D. Daniels, M. Gilula, & F. Ochberg (Eds.), *Violence and the struggle for existence.* Boston: Little, Brown.

DAVID, P. R. (1974). *The world of the burglar.* Albuquerque, NM: Univ. of New Mexico Press.

DAVIS, G. E., & LEITENBERG, H. (1987). Adolescent sex offenders. *Psychological Bulletin, 101*, 417–427.

DECOSTANZA, E., & SCHOLES, H. (1988). Women behind bars: Their numbers increase. *Corrections Today, 50*, 104–108.

DELGADO-ESCUETA, A., MATTSON, R., & KING, L. (1981). The nature of aggression during epileptic seizures. *New England Journal of Medicine, 305*, 711–716.

DEMAREST, M. (1981, July 6). Cocaine: Middle class high. *Time*, 56.

DERVILLE, P., L'EPEE, P., LAZARIN, H. J., & DERVILLE, E. (1961). Statistical indications of a possible relationship between alcoholism and criminality: An inquiry into the Bordeaux region. *Revue Alcoholisme, 7*, 20–21.

DEVELOPMENTS IN THE LAW. (1974). Civil commitment of the mentally ill. *Harvard Law Review, 87*, 1190–1406.

DIENER, E. (1980). Deindividuation: The absence of self-awareness and self-regulation in group members. In P. Paulus (Ed.), *The psychology of group influence.* Hillsdale, NJ: Erlbaum.

DION, K. (1972). Physical attractiveness and evaluations of children's transgressions. *Journal of Personality and Social Psychology, 24*, 207–213.

DION, K., BERSCHEID, E., & WALSTER, E. (1972). What is beautiful is good. *Journal of Personality and Social Psychology, 24*, 285–290.

DISERENS, C. M. (1925). Psychological objectivism. *Psychological Review, 32*, 121–152.

DIX, G. E. (1976). Differential processing of abnormal sex offenders. *Journal of Criminal Law and Criminology, 67*, 233–243.

DIX, G. E. (1980). Clinical evaluation of the "dangerous" if "normal" criminal defendants. *Virginia Law Review, 66*, 523–581.

DIX, G. E. (1983). Special dispositional alternatives for abnormal offenders: Developments in the law. In J. Monahan & H. J. Steadman (Eds.), *Mentally disordered offenders.* New York: Plenum.

Dixon v. Attorney General of the Commonwealth of Pennsylvania, 325 F. Supp. 966, 969 (M.D. Pa. 1971).

DOERNER, W. G. (1988). The impact of medical resources on criminally induced lethality: A further examination. *Criminology, 26*, 171–179.

DOERNER, W. G., & SPEIR, J. C. (1986). Stitch and sew: The impact of medical resources upon criminally induced lethality. *Criminology, 24*, 319–330.

DOLLARD, J., DOOB, L. W., MILLER, N. E., MOWRER, O. H., & SEARS, R. R. (1939). *Frustration and aggression.* New Haven, CT: Yale Univ. Press.

DONNERSTEIN, E. (1983). Erotica and human aggression. In R. G. Geen & E. I. Donnerstein (Eds.), *Agression: Theoretical and empirical reviews.* Vol. 2. New York: Academic Press.

D'ORBAN, P. T., & O'CONNOR, A. (1989). Women who kill their parents. *British Journal of Psychiatry, 154,* 27–33.

DRIVER, E. D. (1961). Interaction and criminal homicide in India. *Social Forces, 40,* 153–158.

DSM-II. (1968). *Diagnostic and statistical manual of mental disorders* (2nd ed.). Washington, DC: American Psychiatric Association.

DSM-III. (1980). *Diagnostic and statistical manual of mental disorders* (3rd ed.). Washington, DC: American Psychiatric Association.

DSM-III-R. (1987). *Diagnostic and statistical manual of mental disorders* (Revised ed.). Washington, DC: American Psychiatric Association.

DULL, R. T., & GIACOPASSI, D. J. (1987). Demographic correlates of sexual and dating attitudes: A study of date rape. *Criminal Justice and Behavior, 14,* 175–193.

DUNN, C. S. (1976). *The patterns and distribution of assault incident characteristics among social areas.* Albany, NY: Criminal Justice Research Center, Analytic Report 14.

Durham v. United States, 214, F.2d 862 (D.C. Cir. 1954).

EARLS, C. M. (1988). Aberrant sexual arousal in sexual offenders. In R. A. Prentky & V. L. Quinsey (Eds.), *Human sexual aggression: Current perspectives.* New York: New York Academy of Sciences.

EATON, J., & POLK, K. (1961). *Measuring delinquency.* Pittsburgh: Univ. of Pittsburgh Press.

EBBESEN, E. B., DUNCAN, B., & KONECNI, V. G. (1975). Effects of content of verbal aggression on future verbal aggression: A field experiment. *Journal of Experimental Social Psychology, 11,* 192–204.

ECCLES, J., & ROBINSON, D. N. (1984). *The wonder of being human: Our brain and our mind.* New York: Free Press.

EDWARDS, S. (1983). Sexuality, sexual offenses and conception of victims in the criminal justice process. *Victimology: An International Journal, 8,* 113–128.

EFRAN, M. G., & CHEYNE, J. A. (1974). Affective concomitants of the invasion of shared space: Behavioral, physiological, and verbal indicators. *Journal of Personality and Social Psychology, 29,* 219–226.

EHRLICH, S. K., & KEOGH, R. P. (1956). The psychopath in a mental institution. *Archives of Neurology and Psychiatry, 76,* 286–295.

EISENBERG, L. (1972). The human nature of human nature. *Science, 176,* 123–128.

EISENBERG, N., & LENNON, R. (1983). Sex differences in empathy and related capacities. *Psychological Bulletin, 94,* 100–131.

EISENHOWER, M. S. (CHAIRMAN). (1969). *Commission statement on violence in television entertainment programs.* Washington, DC: U.S. Government Printing Office.

ELLINWOOD, E. H. (1971). Assault and homicide associated with amphetamine abuse. *American Journal of Psychiatry, 127,* 90–95.

ELLIOTT, D. S. (1989). Criminal justice procedures in family violence crimes. In L. Ohlin & M. Tonry (Eds.), *Family violence.* Vol. 11. Chicago: Univ. of Chicago Press.

ELLIOTT, D. S., AGETON, S. S., & HUIZINGA, D. (1980). *The national youth survey.* Boulder, CO: Behavioral Research Institute.

ELLIOTT, D. S., DUNFORD, T. W., & HUIZINGA, D. (1987). The identification and prediction of career offenders utilizing self-reported and official data. In J. D. Burchard & S. N. Burchard (Eds.), *Prevention of delinquent behavior.* Newbury Park, CA: Sage.

ELLIOTT, D. S., & HUIZINGA, D. (1983). Social class and delinquent behavior in a national youth panel: 1976–1980. *Criminology, 21,* 149–177.

ELLIOTT, D. S., HUIZINGA, D., & AGETON, S. S. (1985). *Explaining delinquency and drug use.* Beverly Hills, CA: Sage.

ELLIS, A. (1962). *Reason and emotion in psychotherapy.* New York: Lyle Stuart.

ELLIS, L. (1982). Genetics and criminal behavior: Evidence through the end of the 1970's. *Criminology, 20,* 43–66.

EPSTEIN, S., & TAYLOR, S. P. (1967). Instigation to aggression as a function of degree of defeat and perceived aggressive intent of the opponent. *Journal of Personality, 35,* 265–289.

ERON, L. D. (1963). Relationship of TV violence habits and aggressive behavior in children. *Journal of Abnormal and Social Psychology, 67*, 193–196

ERON, L. D., & HUESMANN, L. P. (1984). The relation of prosocial behavior to the development of aggression and psychopathology. *Aggressive Behavior, 10*, 201–211.

ESKRIDGE, C. W. (1983). Prediction of burglary: A research note. *Journal of Criminal Justice, 11*, 67–75.

EVANS, D. (1970). Exhibitionism. In C. G. Costello (Ed.), *Symptoms of psychopathology: A handbook*. New York: John Wiley.

EYSENCK, H. J. (1964). *Crime and personality*. London: Routledge & Kegan Paul.

EYSENCK, H. J. (1967). *The biological basis of personality*. Springfield, IL: Charles C. Thomas.

EYSENCK, H. J. (1971). *Readings in extraversion-introversion. Volume 2. Fields of application*. New York: Wiley-Interscience.

EYSENCK, H. J. (1973). *The inequality of man*. San Diego, CA: Edits Publishers.

EYSENCK, H. J. (1977). *Crime and personality*. (2nd ed). London: Routledge & Kegan Paul.

EYSENCK, H. J. (1981). *A model for personality*. New York: Springer.

EYSENCK, H. J. (1983). Personality, conditioning, and antisocial behavior. In W. S. Laufer & J. M. Day (Eds.), *Personality theory, moral development, and criminal behavior*. Lexington, MA: Lexington Books.

EYSENCK, H. J. (1984). Crime and personality. In D. J. Miller, D. E. Blackman, & A. J. Chapman (Eds.), *Psychology and the law*. Chichester, England: Wiley.

EYSENCK, H. J., & EYSENCK, S. B. G. (1971). A comparative study of criminals and matched controls on three dimensions of personality. *British Journal of Social and Clinical Psychology, 10*, 362–366.

EYSENCK, H. J., & GUDJONSSON, G. H. (1989). *The causes and cures of criminality*. New York: Plenum.

EYSENCK, H. J., & RACHMAN, S. (1965). *The causes and cures of neurosis*. San Diego, CA: Robert R. Knapp.

EYSENCK, S. B. G., & EYSENCK, H. J. (1970). Crime and personality: An empirical study of the three-factor theory. *British Journal of Criminology, 10*, 225–239.

EYSENCK, S. B. G., & EYSENCK, H. J. (1971). Crime and personality: Item analysis of questionnaire responses. *British Journal of Criminology, 11*, 44–62.

FAGAN, J. (1989). Cessation of family violence. In L. Ohlin & M. Tonry (Eds.), *Family violence*. Vol. 11. Chicago: Univ. of Chicago Press.

FARRINGTON, D. P. (1979). Environmental stress, delinquent behavior, and conviction. In I. G. Sarason & C. D. Spielberger (Eds.), *Stress and Anxiety*. Vol. 6. Washington, DC: Hemisphere.

FARRINGTON, D. P. (1987). Predicting individual crime rates. In D. M. Gottfredson & M. Tonry (Eds.), *Prediction and classification*. Vol. 10. Chicago: Univ. of Chicago Press.

FARRINGTON, D. P., BIRON, L., & LeBLANC, M. (1982). Personality and delinquency in London and Montreal. In J. Gunn & D. P. Farrington (Eds.), *Abnormal offenders, delinquency, and the criminal justice system*. Chichester, England: Wiley.

FAVOLE, R. J. (1983). Mental disability in the American criminal process: A four issue survey. In J. Monahan & H. J. Steadman (Eds.), *Mentally disordered offenders*. New York: Plenum.

FEHRENBACH, P. A., SMITH, W., MONASTERSKY, C., & DEISHER, R. W. (1986). Adolescent sexual offenders: Offender and offense characteristics. *American Journal of Orthopsychiatry, 56*, 225–233.

FEILD, H. S. (1978). Attitudes toward rape: A comparative analysis of police, rapists, crisis counselors, and citizens. *Journal of Personality and Social Psychology, 36*, 156–179.

FEINBERG, G. (1984). Profile for the elderly shoplifter. In E. S. Newman, D. J. Newman, & M. L. Gewirtz (Eds.), *Elderly criminals*. Cambridge, MA: Oelgeschlager, Gunn & Hain.

FELDMAN, M. P. (1977). *Criminal behavior: A psychological analysis*. London: Wiley.

FENICHEL, O. (1945). *The psychoanalytic theory of neurosis*. New York: W. W. Norton.

FESHBACH, S. (1964). The function of aggression and the regulation of aggressive drive. *Psychological Review, 71*, 257–272.

FINKELHOR, D. (1979). *Sexually victimized children*. New York: Free Press.

FINKELHOR, D., & ARAJI, S. (1986). Explanations of pedophilia: A four factor model. *The Journal of Sex Research, 22*, 145–161.

FINKELHOR, D., & LEWIS, I. A. (1988). An epidemiologic approach to the study of child molestation. In R. A. Prentky & V. L. Quinsey (Eds.), *Human sexual aggression: Current perspectives*. New York: New York Academy of Sciences.

FISHER, G., & HOWELL, L. M. (1970). Psychological needs of homosexual pedophiliacs. *Diseases of the Nervous System, 31*, 623–625.

FISHER, R. S. (1951). Symposium on the compulsory use of chemical tests for alcoholic intoxication. *Maryland Medical Journal, 3*, 291–292.

FISKE, D. E., & MADDI, S. R. (1961). *Functions of varied experience*. Homewood, IL: Dorsey.

FITCH, J. H. (1962). Two personality variables and their distribution in acriminal population: An empirical study. *British Journal of Social and Clinical Psychology, 1*, 161–167.

FITZHUGH, K. B. (1973). Some neuropsychological features of delinquent subjects. *Perceptual and Motor Skills, 36*, 494.

FLOR-HENRY, P. (1973). Psychiatric syndromes considered as manifestations of lateralized temporal-limbic dysfunction. In L. V. Latiner & K. E. Livingston (Eds.), *Surgical approaches in psychiatry*. Lancaster, England: Medical and Technical Publishing.

FLOR-HENRY, P., & YEUDALL, L. T. (1973). Lateralized cerebral dysfunction in depression and in aggressive criminal psychopathy. *International Research Communications Systems, 7*, 31.

FLYNN, E. E. (1983). Crime as a major social issue. *American Behavioral Scientist, 27*, 7–42.

FOIS, A. (1961). *The electroencephalogram of the normal child*. Springfield, IL: Charles C. Thomas.

FOX, R. G. (1971). The XYY offender: A modern myth? *Journal of Criminal Law, Criminology, and Police Science, 62*, 59–73.

FRANKE, D. (1975). *The torture doctor*. New York: Avon.

FREEDMAN, J. L. (1975). *Crowding and behavior*. San Francisco: W. H. Freeman.

FREEDMAN, J. L., LEVY, A., BUCHANAN, R. W., & PRICE, J. (1972). Crowding and human aggressiveness. *Journal of Experimental Social Psychology, 8*, 528–548.

FREEDMAN, J. L., SEARS, D. O., & CARLSMITH, J. J. (1978). *Social psychology* (3rd ed.). Englewood Cliffs, NJ: Prentice Hall.

FRENCH, J. D. (1957). The reticular formation. *Scientific American, 196*, 54–60.

FRIEZE, I. H., & BROWNE, A. (1989). Violence in marriage. In L. Ohlin & M. Tonry (Eds.), *Family violence*. Vol. 11. Chicago: Univ. of Chicago Press.

FRISBIE, L. V. (1965). Treated sex offenders who reverted to sexually deviant behavior. *Federal Probation, 29*, 52–57.

FRODI, A., MACAULAY, J., & THOME, P. (1977). Are women always less aggressive than men? A review of the experimental literature. *Psychological Bulletin, 84*, 634–660.

FURBY, L., WEINROTT, M. R., & BLACKSHAW, L. (1989). Sex offender recidivism: A review. *Psychological Bulletin, 105*, 3–30.

FYFE, J. F. (1984). Police dilemmas in processing elderly offenders. In E. S. Newman, D. J. Newman, & M. L. Gewirtz (Eds.), *Elderly criminals*. Cambridge, MA: Oelgeschalger, Gunn & Hain.

GABRIELLI, W. F., & MEDNICK, S. A. (1983). Genetic correlates of criminal behavior. *American Behavioral Scientist, 27*, 59–74.

GALANTER, M. (1974). Why the "haves" come out ahead: Speculations on the limits of social change. *Law & Society Review, 9*, 95–160.

GALVIN, J., & POLK, K. (1983). Juvenile justice: Time for new direction? *Delinquency and Crime, 29*, 325–332.

GARBARINO, J. (1989). The incidence and prevalence of child maltreatment. In L. Ohlin & M. Tonry (Eds.), *Family violence*. Vol. 11. Chicago: Univ. of Chicago Press.

GAROFALO, J. (1977). *Public opinion about crime: The attitudes of victims and nonvictims in selected cities*. Washington, DC: U.S. Government Printing Office.

GEBHARD, P. H., GAGNON, J. H., POMEROY, W. B., & CHRISTENSON, C. V. (1965). *Sex offenders*. New York: Harper & Row.

GEIS, G. (1988). From deuteronomy to deniability: A historical perlustration on white collar crime. *Justice Quarterly, 5*, 7–32.

GEIS, G., & MONAHAN, J. (1976). The social ecology of violence. In T. Lickona (Ed.), *Moral development and behavior*. New York: Holt, Rinehart & Winston.

GELLES, R. J. (1982). Domestic criminal violence. In M. E. Wolfgang & N. A. Weiner (Eds.), *Criminal violence*. Beverly Hills, CA: Sage.

GELLES, R. J., & STRAUS, M. A. (1979). Determinants of violence in the family: Toward a theoretical integration. In W. R. Burr, F. I. Nye, & I. L. Reiss (Eds.), *Contemporary theories about the family*. New York: Free Press.

GENDREAU, P., & ROSS, P. (1983). Correctional treatment. *Juvenile and Family Court Journal*, Winter, 31–39.

GEORGE, W. H., & MARLATT, G. A. (1989). Introduction. In D. R. Laws (Ed.), *Relapse prevention with sex offenders*. New York: Guilford Press.

GERBNER, G., & GROSS, L. (1976). Living with television: The violence profile. *Journal of Communications, 26*, 173–199.

GIBBENS, T. C. (1957). Female offenders. *British Journal of Delinquency, 8*, 23–25.

GIBBENS, T. C. (1981). Female crime in England and Wales. In F. Adler (Ed.), *The incidence of female criminality in the contemporary world*. New York: New York Univ. Press.

GIBBENS, T. C., POND, D. A., & STAFFORD-CLARK, D. (1955). A follow-up study of criminal psychopaths. *British Journal of Delinquency, 5*, 126–136.

GIBBONS, D. C. (1977). *Society, crime and criminal careers*. (3rd ed.). Englewood Cliffs, NJ: Prentice-Hall.

GIBBONS, D. C. (1980). Explaining juvenile delinquency: Changing theoretical perspectives. In D. Schichor & D. H. Kelly (Eds.), *Critical issues in juvenile delinquency*. Lexington, MA: Lexington Books.

GIBBONS, D. C. (1988). Some critical observation on criminal types and criminal careers. *Criminal Justice and Behavior, 15*, 8–23.

GIBSON, E., & KLEIN, S. (1961). *Murder*. London: H. M. Stationary Office.

GIBSON, H. B. (1967). Self-reported delinquency among schoolboys, and their attitudes to the police. *British Journal of Social and Clinical Psychology, 6*, 168–173.

GIL, D. (1970). *Violence against children: Physical child abuse in the United States*. Cambridge, MA: Harvard Univ. Press.

GILLIES, H. (1965). Murder in West Scotland. *British Journal of Psychiatry, 111*, 1087–1094.

GILLIGAN, C. (1982). *In a different voice*. Cambridge, MA: Harvard Univ. Press.

GILLIN, J. C., & OCHBERG, F. M. (1970). Firearms control and violence. In D. N. Daniels, M. F. Gilula, & F. M. Ochberg (Eds.), *Violence and the struggle for existence*. Boston: Little, Brown.

GLASER, D. (1964). *The effectiveness of a prison and parole system*. Indianapolis, IN: Bobbs-Merrill.

GLASER, D. (1978). *Crime in our changing society*. New York: Holt, Rinehart & Winston.

GLASSER, W. D. (1965). *Reality therapy*. New York: Harper & Row.

GLUECK, S., & GLUECK, E. (1950). *Unraveling juvenile delinquency*. New York: Harper & Row.

GLUECK, S., & GLUECK, E. (1956). *Physique and delinquency*. New York: Harper & Row.

GOLD, L. H. (1962). Psychiatric profile of the firesetter. *Journal of Forensic Sciences, 7*, 404–417.

GOLDMAN, H. (1977). The limits of clockwork: The neurobiology of violent behavior. In J. P. Conrad & S. Dinitz (Eds.), *In fear of each other*. Lexington, MA: Lexington Books.

GOLDSTEIN, J. H. (1975). *Aggression and crimes of violence*. New York: Oxford Univ. Press.

GOLDSTEIN, M. (1974). Brain research and violent behavior. *Archives of Neurology, 30*, 1–34.

GOLDSTEIN, M. J. (1977). A behavioral scientist looks at obscenity. In B. D. Sales (Ed.), *The criminal justice system*. Vol. 1. New York: Plenum.

GORING, C. (1913/1972). *The English convict: A statistical study*. Montclair, NJ: Patterson Smith.

GOSSELIN, C., & WILSON, G. (1984). Fetishism, sadomasochism and related behaviours. In K. Howells (Ed.), *The psychology of sexual diversity*. London: Basil Blackwell.

GOSSOP, M. R., & KRISTJANSSON, I. (1977). Crime and personality. *British Journal of Criminology, 17*, 264–273.

GOVE, W. R., & CRUTCHFIELD, R. D. (1982). The family and delinquency. *The Sociological Quarterly, 23*, 301–319.

GOVE, W. R., HUGHES, M., & GALLE, O. R. (1977). Overcrowding in the home: An empirical investigation of its possible pathological consequences. *American Sociological Review, 44*, 59–80.

GRAY, K. G., & HUTCHISON, H. C. (1964). The psychopathic personality: A survey of Canadian psychiatrists' opinions. *Canadian Psychiatric Association Journal, 9*, 452–461.

GREENBERG, L. S. (1988). Constructive cognition: Cognitive therapy coming of age. *The Counseling Psychologist, 16*, 235–238.

GREENDLINGER, V., & BYRNE, D. (1987). Coercive sexual fantasies of college men as predictors of self-reported likelihood to rape and overt sexual aggression. *The Journal of Sex Research, 23,* 1–11.

GREENWALD, H. (1958). *The call girl.* New York: Ballantine Books.

GREENWOOD, P. J., & ZIMRING, F. (1985). *One more chance: The role of rehabilitation in reducing the criminality of chronic serious juvenile offenders.* Rand Report R-3214-OJJDP. Santa Monica, CA: Rand Corporation.

GREER, S. (1964). Study of parental loss in neurotics and sociopaths. *Archives of General Psychiatry, 11,* 177–180.

GRIFFITH, W., & VEITCH, R. (1971). Hot and crowded: Influences of population density and temperature on interpersonal affective behavior. *Journal of Personality and Social Psychology, 17,* 92–98.

GROTH, A. N. (1978). Patterns of sexual assault against children and adolescents. In A. W. Burgess, A. N. Groth, L. L. Holmstrom, & S. M. Sgroi (Eds.), *Sexual assault of children and adolescents.* Lexington, MA: Lexington Books.

GROTH, A. N. (1979). *Men who rape: The psychology of the offender.* New York: Plenum.

GROTH, A. N., & BURGESS, A. W. (1977). Motivational intent in the sexual assault of children. *Criminal Justice and Behavior, 4,* 253–271.

GROTH, A. N., HOBSON, W. F., & GARY, T. S. (1982). The child molester: Clinical observation. *Journal of Social Work and Human Sexuality, 1,* 129–144.

GUNN, J. (1971). Criminality and violence in epileptic prisoner. *British Journal of Psychiatry, 118,* 337–343.

GUZE, S. B. (1976). *Criminality and psychiatric disorders.* New York: Oxford Univ. Press.

HAAN, N. (1977). *Coping and defending: Processes of self-environment organization.* New York: Academic Press.

HAAN, N. (1978). Two moralities in action contexts: Relationships to thought, ego regulation, and development. *Journal of Personality and Social Psychology, 36,* 286–305.

HAFNER, H., & BOKER, W. (1973). Mentally disordered violent offenders. *Social Psychiatry, 8,* 220–229.

HAFT, M. G. (1976). Hustling for rights. In L. Crites (Ed.), *The female offender.* Lexington, MA: Lexington Books.

HALL, C. S., & LINDZEY, G. (1970). *Theories of personality* (2nd ed.). New York: Wiley.

HALL, G. C. N., PROCTOR, W. C., & NELSON, G. M. (1988). Validity of physiological measures of pedophilic sexual arousal in a sexual offender population. *Journal of Consulting and Clinical Psychology, 56,* 118–122.

HALLECK, S. L. (1967). *Psychiatry and the dilemmas of crime.* New York: Harper & Row.

HALLECK, S. L., & WITTE, A. D. (1977). Is rehabilitation dead? *Crime and Delinquency, 23,* 372–382.

HALLORAN, J. D., BROWN, R. L., & CHANEY, D. (1969). *Mass media and crime.* Leicester, England: Leicester Univ. Press.

HALVERSON, C. F., & VICTOR, J. B. (1976). Minor physical anomalies and problem behavior in elementary school children. *Child Development, 47,* 281–285.

HAMBURG, D. A., MOOS, R. H., & YALOM, I. D. (1968). Studies of distress in the menstrual cycle and the postpartum period. In R. P. Michael (Ed.), *Endocrinology and human behavior.* London: Oxford Univ. Press.

HAMMERSLEY, R., & MORRISON, V. (1987). Effects of polydrug use on the criminal activities of heroin-users. *British Journal of Addiction, 82,* 859–906.

HANEY, C. W. (1983). The good, the bad, and the lawful: An essay on psychological injustice. In W. S. Laufer & J. M. Day (Eds.), *Personality theory, moral development, and criminal behavior.* Lexington, MA: Lexington Books.

HARE, R. D. (1965a). A conflict and learning theory analysis of psychopathic behavior. *Journal of Research in Crime and Delinquency, 2,* 12–19.

HARE, R. D. (1965b). Acquisition and generalization of a conditioned-fear response in psychopathic and nonpsychopathic criminals. *Journal of Psychology, 59,* 367–370.

HARE, R. D. (1968). Psychopathy, autonomic functioning, and the orienting response. *Journal of Abnormal Psychology, 73,* 1–24.

HARE, R. D. (1970). *Psychopathy: Theory and research.* New York: Wiley.

HARE, R. D. (1976). Anxiety, stress and psychopathy. In G. Shean (Ed.), *Dimensions in abnormal psychology.* Chicago: Rand McNally.

HARE, R. D. (1980). A research scale for the assessment of psychopathy in criminal populations. *Personality and Individual Differences, 1*, 111–119.

HARE, R. D. (1982). Psychopathy and the personality dimensions of psychoticism, extraversion and neuroticism. *Personality and Individual Differences, 3*, 35–42.

HARE, R. D. (1983). Diagnosis of antisocial personality disorder in a prison population. *American Journal of Psychiatry, 140*, 887–890.

HARE, R. D. (1984). Performance of psychopaths on cognitive tasks related to frontal lobe function. *Journal of Abnormal Psychology, 93*, 133–140.

HARE, R. D. (1986). Criminal psychopaths. In J. C. Yuille (Ed.), *Selection and training: The role of psychology.*

HARE, R. D., & CONNOLLY, J. F. (1987). Perceptual asymmetries and information processing in psychopaths. In S. A. Mednick, T. E. Moffitt, & S. A. Stack (Eds.), *The causes of crime: New biological approaches.* Cambridge, England: Cambridge Univ. Press.

HARE, R. D., & CRAIGEN, D. (1974). Psychopathy and physiological activity in a mixed-motive game. *Psychophysiology, 11*, 197–206.

HARE, R. D., & JUTAI, J. W. (1983). Criminal history of the male psychopath: Some preliminary data. In K. T. Van Dusen and S. A. Mednick (Eds.), *Prospective studies of crime and delinquency.* Boston: Kluwer-Nijhoff.

HARE, R. D., & MCPHERSON, L. M. (1984). Violent and aggressive behavior by criminal psychopaths. *International Journal of Law and Psychiatry, 7*, 35–50.

HARE, R. D., MCPHERSON, L. M., & FORTH, A. E. (1988). Male psychopaths and their criminal careers. *Journal of Consulting and Clinical Psychology, 56*, 710–714.

HARE, R. D., & QUINN, M. (1971). Psychopathy and autonomic conditioning. *Journal of Abnormal Psychology, 77*, 223–239.

HARRIES, K. D. (1980). *Crime and the environment.* Springfield, IL: Charles C. Thomas.

HARRIS, P. W. (1988). The interpersonal maturity level classification system. *Criminal Justice and Behavior, 15*, 58–77.

HART, H. M., JR., & SACKS, A. M. (1958). *The legal process: Basic problems in the making and application of law.* Unpublished manuscript.

HARTL, E. M., MONNELLY, E. P., & ELDERKIN, R. D. (1982). *Physique and delinquent behavior.* New York: Academic Press.

HARTNAGEL, T. F. (1987). Correlates of criminal behaviour. In R. Linden (Ed.), *Criminology: A Canadian perspective.* Toronto: Holt, Rinehart & Winston.

HARTSHORNE, H., & MAY, M. A. (1928–1930). *Studies in deceit.* New York: Macmillan.

HARTUP, W. W. (1983). Peer relations. In P. H. Mussen (Ed.), *Manual of child psychology.* New York: Wiley.

HAWKE, C. C. (1950). Castration and sex crimes. *American Journal of Mental Deficiency, 55*, 220–226.

HAWKINS, D. F. (1983). Black and white homicide differentials: Alternatives to an inadequate theory. *Criminal Justice and Behavior, 10*, 407–440.

HAWKINS, D. F. (1985). Black homicide: The adequacy of existing research for devising prevention strategies. *Crime and Delinquency, 31*, 83–103.

HAYASHI, G. (1967). A study of juvenile delinquency in twins. In H. Misuda (Ed.), *Clinical genetics in psychiatry.* Tokyo: Ogaku Shain.

HEBB, D. O. (1955). Drives and the C.N.S. (Conceptual Nervous System). *Psychological Review, 62*, 243–254.

HELZER, J. E. (1987). Epidemiology of alcoholism. *Journal of Consulting and Clinical Psychology, 55*, 284–292.

HENDERSON, M. (1983). An empirical classification of non-violent offenders using the MMPI. *Personality and Individual Differences, 4*, 671–677.

HENDRICK, C., & TAYLOR, S. P. (1971). The effects of belief similarity and aggression on attraction and counter aggression. *Journal of Personality and Social Psychology, 17*, 342–349.

HENN, F. A., HERJANIC, M., & VANDERPEARL, R. H. (1976a). Forensic psychiatry: Profiles of two types of sex offenders. *American Journal of Psychiatry, 133*, 694–696.

HENN, F. A., HERJANIC, M., & VANDERPEARL, R. H. (1976b). Forensic psychiatry: Diagnosis of criminal responsibility. *The Journal of Nervous and Mental Disease, 162*, 423–429.

HEPBURN, J., & VOSS, H. L. (1970). Patterns of criminal homicide: A comparison of Chicago and Philadelphia. *Criminology, 8,* 19–45.

HERZBERG, J. L., & FENWICK, P. B. C. (1988). The aetiology of aggression in temporal lobe epilepsy. *British Journal of Psychiatry, 153,* 50–55.

HETHERINGTON, E. M., & PARKE, R. D. (1975). *Child psychology: A contemporary viewpoint.* New York: McGraw-Hill.

HEWITT, J. D. (1988). The victim-offender relationship in convicted homicide cases: 1960–1984. *Journal of Criminal Justice, 16,* 25–33.

HILL, D. (1952). EEG in episodic psychotic and psychopathic behavior: A classification of data. *EEG and Clinical Neurophysiology,* 1952, *4,* 419–442.

HILL, D., & WATTERSON, D. (1942). Electroencephalographic studies of the psychopathic personality. *Journal of Neurology and Psychiatry, 5,* 47–64.

HILL, P. (1960). *Portrait of a sadist.* New York: Avon.

HILL, R. W., LANGEVIN, R., PAITICH, D., HANDY, L., RUSSON, A., & WILKINSON, L. (1982). Is arson an aggressive act or a property offense? *Canadian Journal of Psychiatry, 27,* 648–654.

HINDELANG, M. J. (1974). Decisions of shoplifting victims to invoke the criminal justice process. *Social Process, 21,* 580–593.

HINDELANG, M. J. (1981). Variations in sex-race-age-specific incident rate of offending. *American Sociological Review, 46,* 461–474.

HINDELANG, M. J., DUNN, C. S., SUTTON, L. P., & AUMICK, A. (1976). *Sourcebook of criminal justice statistics, 1975.* Washington, DC: U.S. Government Printing Office.

HINDELANG, M. J., HIRSCHI, T., & WEIS, J. G. (1981). *Measuring delinquency.* Beverly Hills, CA: Sage.

HINDELANG, M. J., & McDERMOTT, M. J. (1981). *Juvenile criminal behavior: An analysis of rates and victim characteristics.* Washington, DC: U.S. Government Printing Office.

HIRSCHI, T. (1983). Crime and family policy. *Journal of Contemporary Studies,* Winter, 3–16.

HIRSCHI, T., & HINDELANG, M. J. (1977). Intelligence and delinquency. *American Sociological Review, 42,* 571–587.

HOCHSTEDLER, E. (ED.). (1984). *Corporations as criminals.* Beverly Hills, CA: Sage.

HOFFMAN, M. (1977). Sex differences in empathy and related behaviors. *Psychological Bulletin, 84,* 712–722.

HOFMANN, F. G. (1975). *A handbook on drug and alcohol abuse: The biomedical aspects.* New York: Oxford Univ. Press.

HOGHUGHI, M. S., & FORREST, A. R. (1970). Eysenck's theory of criminality: An examination with approved school boys. *British Journal of Criminology, 10,* 240–254.

HOLCOMB, W. R., & ANDERSON, W. P. (1983). Alcohol and multiple drug abuse in accused murderers. *Psychological Reports, 52,* 159–164

HOLMES, R. M., & DEBURGER, J. (1988). *Serial murder.* Newbury Park, CA: Sage.

HOOD, R., & SPARKS, R. (1970). *Key issues in criminology.* New York: McGraw-Hill.

HOME OFFICE. (1986). *Criminal statistics: England and Wales 1985.* London: HMSO.

HORNING, D. N. M. (1970). Blue-collar theft: Conceptions of property, attitudes toward pilfering, and work group norms in a modern industrial plant. In E. O. Smigel & H. L. Ross (Eds.), *Crimes against bureaucracy.* New York: Van Nostrand Reinhold.

HOTALING, G. T., & STRAUS, M. A. (1989). Intrafamily violence, and crime and violence outside the family. In L. Ohlin & M. Tonry (Eds.), *Family violence.* Vol. 11. Chicago: Univ. of Chicago Press.

HOUGHTON, B. (1979). Review of research on women abuse. *Paper presented at the annual meeting of American Society of Criminology.* Philadelphia.

HUDSON, M. I. (1986). Elder maltreatment: Current research. In K. A. Pillemer & R. S. Wolf (Eds.), *Elder abuse: Conflict in the family.* Dover, MA: Auburn House.

HUESMANN, L. R. (1988). An information processing model for the development of aggression. *Aggressive Behavior, 14,* 13–24.

HUESMANN, L. R., & ERON, L. D. (1986). *Television and the aggressive child: A cross national comparison.* Hillsdale, NJ: Erlbaum.

HUESMANN, L. R., ERON, L. D., LEFKOWITZ, M. M., & WALDER, L. O. (1984). The stability of aggression over time and generation. *Developmental Psychology, 20,* 1120–1134.

HUGHES, R., CRAWFORD, G., BARKER N., SCHUMANN, S., & JAFFE, J. (1971). The social structure of a heroin copping community. *American Journal of Psychiatry, 128,* 554.

HUMPHREY, J. A., & PALMER, S. (1987). Race, sex, and criminal homicide offender-victim relationships. *Journal of Black Studies, 18,* 45–57.

HURLEY, W., & MONAHAN, T. M. (1969). Arson: The criminal and the crime. *British Journal of Criminology, 9,* 4–21.

HUTCHINGS, B., & MEDNICK, S. A. (1975). Registered criminality in the adoptive and biological parents of registered male criminal adoptees. In R. R. Fieve, D. Rosenthal, & H. Brill (Eds.), *Genetic research in psychiatry.* Baltimore: John Hopkins Univ. Press.

HUTCHINGS, B., & MEDNICK, S. A. (1977). Criminality in adoptees and their adoptive and biological parents: A pilot study. In S. A. Mednick & K. A. Christiansen (Eds.), *Biological bases of criminal behavior.* New York: Gardiner Press, 127–142.

INCIARDI, J. A. (1970). The adult firesetter, a typology. *Criminology, 3,* 145–155.

INCIARDI, J. A. (1980). Women, heroin, and property crime. In S. K. Datesman & F. R. Scarpitti (Eds.), *Women, crime and justice.* New York: Oxford Univ. Press.

INCIARDI, J. A. (1981). Crime and alternative patterns of substance abuse. In S. E. Gardner (Ed.), *Drug and alcohol abuse.* Rockville, MD: National Institute on Drug Abuse.

INCIARDI, J. A. (1986). *The war on drugs: Heroin, cocaine, crime and public policy.* Palo Alto, CA: Mayfield Publishing.

JACKSON, H. F., GLASS, C., & HOPE, S. (1987). A functional analysis of recidivistic arson. *British Journal of Clinical Psychology, 26,* 175–185.

JACOBS, P. A., BRUNTON, M., MELVILLE, H. M., BRITTAIN, R. P., & McCLEMONT, W. F. (1965). Aggressive behavior, mental subnormality and the XYY male. *Nature, 208,* 1351–1352.

JAFFE, J. H., BABOR, T. F., & FISHBEIN, D. H. (1988). Alcoholics, aggression and antisocial behavior. *Journal of Studies on Alcohol, 49,* 211–218.

JAFFE, Y., MALAMUTH, N., FEINGOLD, J., & FESHBACH, S. (1974). Sexual arousal and behavioral aggression. *Journal of Personality and Social Psychology, 30,* 759–764.

JAMES, J. (1976). Motivations for entrance into prostitution. In L. Crites (Ed.), *The female offender.* Lexington, MA: Lexington Books.

JAMES, J. (1978). The prostitute as victim. In J. R. Chapman & M. Gates (Eds.), *The victimization of women.* Beverly Hills, CA: Sage.

JAMISON, R. N. (1980). Psychoticism, deviancy, and perception of risk in normal children. *Personality and Individual Differences, 1,* 87–91.

JARVIK, L. F., KLODIN, V., & MATSUYAMA, S. S. (1973). Human aggression and the extra Y chromosome. *American Psychologist, 28,* 674–682.

JARVIS, G., & PARKER, H. (1989). Young heroin users and crime. *British Journal of Criminology, 29,* 175–185.

JEFFERY, C. R. (1965). Criminal behavior and learning theory. *The Journal of Criminal Law, Criminology, and Police Science, 56,* 294–300.

JENKINS, P. (1988). Serial murder in England 1940–1985. *Journal of Criminal Justice, 16,* 1–15.

JENKINS, W. O., & BARTON, M. C. (1973). *Longitudinal follow-up investigation of the post release behavior of paroled and released offenders.* Elmore, AL: Rehabiliation Research Foundation.

JOHNS, J. H., & QUAY, H. C. (1962). The effect of social reward on verbal conditioning in psychopathic military offenders. *Journal of Consulting Psychology, 26,* 217–220.

JOHNSON, L. G., BACHMAN, J. G., & O'MALLEY, P. M. (1983). *Student drug use, attitudes and beliefs: National trends 1975-1983.* Rockville, MD: National Institute on Drug Abuse.

JOHNSON, R. N. (1972). *Aggression in man and animals.* Philadelphia: W. B. Saunders.

JONES, C., & ARONSON, E. (1973). Attribution of fault to a rape victim as a function of respectability of the victim. *Journal of Personality and Social Psychology, 26,* 415–419.

JONES, J. W., & BOGAT, G. A. (1978). Air pollution and human aggression. *Psychological Reports, 43,* 721–722.

Jones v. United States, 103 S. Ct. 3043 (1983).

JULIEN, R. M. (1975). *A primer of drug action.* San Francisco: W. H. Freeman.

KAFREY, D. (1980). Playing with matches: Children and fire. In D. Canter (Ed.), *Fires and human behaviour.* Chichester, England: Wiley.

KAHN, E. (1931). *Psychopathic personalities.* New Haven, CT: Yale Univ. Press.

KALISH, C. B. (1983). *Prisoners and alcohol.* Washington, DC: U.S. Department of Justice.

KANIN, E. J. (1984). Date rape: Unofficial criminals and victims. *Victimology, 9,* 95–108.

KANNO, C. K., & SCHEIDEMANDEL, P. L. (1969). *The mentally ill offender: A survey of treatment programs.* Washington, DC: Joint Information Service.

KARTER, M. (1982). Fire loss in the United States during 1981. *Fire Journal, 76,* 68–86.

KASSEBAUM, G., WARD, D., & WILNER, D. (1971). *Prison treatment and parole survival: An empirical assessment.* New York: Wiley, 1971.

KELLEY, T. M. (1983). Status offenders can be different: A comparative study of delinquent careers. *Crime and Delinquency, 29,* 365–395.

KELLY, D. H. (1980). The educational experience and evolving delinquent careers: A neglected institutional link. In D. Schichor & D. H. Kelly (Eds.), *Critical issues in juvenile delinquency.* Lexington, MA: Lexington Books.

KELLY, G. A. (1955). The psychology of personal constructs. New York: Norton.

KELMAN, H. C., & HAMILTON, V. L. (1989). *Crimes of obedience: Toward a social psychology of authority and responsibility.* New Haven, CT: Yale Univ. Press.

KEMPE, C. H., SILVERMAN, F. N., STEELE, B. B., DROEGEMUELLER, W., & SILVER, H. K. (1962). The battered-child syndrome. *Journal of the American Medical Association, 181,* 17–24.

KENNEDY, R. E. (1976). Behavior modification in prisons. In W. Craighead, A. Kasdin, & M. Mahoney (Eds.), *Behavior modification: Principles, issues and applications.* Boston: Houghton Mifflin.

KENRICK, D. T., & MACFARLAND, S. W. (1986). Ambient temperature and horn honking. *Environment and Behavior, 18,* 179–191.

KILMANN, P. R., SABALIS, R. F., GEARING, M. L., BUKSTEL, L. H., & SCOVERN, A. W. (1982). The treatment of sexual paraphilias: A review of the outcome research. *The Journal of Sex Research, 18,* 193–252.

KILPATRICK, D. G., BEST, C. L., SAUNDERS, B. E., & VERONEN, L. J. (1988). Rape in marriage and in dating relationships: How bad is it for mental health. In R. A. Prentky & V. L. Quinsey (Eds.), *Human sexual aggression: Current perspectives.* New York: New York Academy of Sciences.

KIRMEYER, S. L. (1978). Urban density and pathology—a review of research. *Environment and Behavior, 10,* 247–269.

KLEBER, H. D. (1988). Epidemic cocaine abuse: America's present, Britain's future? *British Journal of Addiction, 83,* 1359–1371.

AF KLINTEBERG, B., MAGNUSSON, D., & SCHALLING, D. (1989). Hyperactive behavior in childhood and adult impulsivity: A longitudinal study of male subjects. *Personality and Individual Differences, 10,* 43–50.

KNIGHT, R. A. (1988). A taxonomic analysis of child molesters. In R. A. Prentky and V. L. Quinsey (Eds.), *Human sexual aggression: Current perspectives.* New York: New York Academy of Science.

KNIGHT, R. A., & PRENTKY, R. A. (1987). The developmental antecedents and adult adaptations of rapist subtypes. *Criminal Justice and Behavior, 14,* 403–426.

KNIGHT, R. A., ROSENBERG, R., & SCHNEIDER, B. A. (1985). Classification of sexual offenders: Perspectives, methods, and validation. In A. W. Burgess (Ed.), *Rape and sexual assault.* New York: Garland.

KNOTT, J. R., PLATT, E. B., ASHBY, M. C., & GOTTLIEB, J. S. (1953). A familial evaluation of the electroencephalogram of patients with primary behavior disorder and psychopathic personality. *EEG and Clinical Neurophysiology, 5,* 363–370.

KOHLBERG, L. (1976). Moral stages and moralization: The cognitive-developmental approach. In T. Lickona (Ed.), *Moral development and behavior.* New York: Holt, Rinehart Winston.

KOHLBERG, L. (1977). The child as a moral philosopher. In CRM, *Readings in developmental psychology today.* New York: Random House.

KOHLBERG, L., & FREUNDLICH, D. (1973). Moral judgment in youthful offenders. Kohlberg & E. Turiel (Eds.), *Moralization, the cognitive development approach.* Holt, Rinehart & Winston.

KOHLMEIER, L. M. (1976, September 26). The bribe busters. *The New York* 58, 91–99.

KOLKO, D. J., KAZDIN, A. E., & MEYER, E. C. (1985). Aggression childhood firesetters: Parent and child reports. *Journal of* ogy, *53,* 377–385.

Koneční, V. J. (1975). The mediation of aggressive behavior: Arousal levels vs. anger and cognitive labeling. *Journal of Personality and Social Psychology, 32*, 706–712.

Koneční, V. J., Mulcahy, E. M., & Ebbesen, E. B. (1980). Prison or mental hospital: Factors affecting the processing of persons suspected of being "mentally disordered sex offenders." In P. D. Lipsitt & B. D. Sales (Eds.), *New directions in psycholegal research.* New York: Van Nostrand Reinhold.

Korman, A. (1974). *The psychology of motivation.* Englewood Cliffs, NJ: Prentice-Hall.

Kornhauser, R. R. (1978). *Social sources of delinquency.* Chicago: Univ. of Chicago Press.

Koson, D. F., & Dvoskin, J. (1982). Arson: A diagnostic study. *Bulletin of the American Academy of Psychiatry and the Law, 10*, 39–49.

Koss, M. P., & Dinero, T. E. (1988). Predictors of sexual aggression among a national sample of male college students. In R. A. Prentky and V. L. Quinsey (Eds.), *Human sexual aggression: Current perspectives.* New York: New York Academy of Sciences.

Koss, M. P., Gidycz, C. A., & Wisniewski, N. (1987). The scope of rape: Incidence and prevalence of sexual aggression and victimization in a national sample of higher education students. *Journal of Consulting and Clinical Psychology, 55*, 162–170.

Kozol, H. L., Boucher, R. L., & Garofalo, P. F. (1972). The diagnosis and treatment of dangerousness. *Crime and Delinquency, 8*, 371–392.

Kramer, R. C. (1984). Corporate criminality: The development of an idea. In E. Hochstedler (Ed.), *Corporations as criminals.* Beverly Hills, CA: Sage.

Kranz, H. (1936). *Lebensschicksale kriminellen Zwillinge.* Berlin: Julius Springer.

Krapelin, E. (1913). *Clinical psychiatry: A textbook for physicians.* New York: Macmillan.

Kretschmer, E. (1925). *Physique and character.* New York: Harcourt Brace Jovanovich.

Krisberg, B., & Schwartz, I. (1983). Rethinking juvenile justice. *Crime and Delinquency, 29*, 333–364.

Kuhnley, E. J., Hendren, R. L., & Quinlan, D. M. (1982). Fire-setting by children. *Journal of the American Academy of Child Psychiatry, 21*, 560–563.

Kurland, H. D., Yeager, C. T., & Arthur, R. J. (1963). Psychophysiologic aspects of severe behavior disorders. *Archives of General Psychiatry, 8*, 599–604.

Kurtzberg, R. L., Mandell, W., Lewin, M., Lipton, D. S., & Shuster, M. (1978). Plastic surgery on offenders. In N. Johnson & L. Savitz (Eds.), *Justice and corrections.* New York: Wiley.

Landau, S. F., Drapkin, E., & Arad, S. (1974). Homicide victims and offenders: An Israeli study. *The Journal of Criminal Law and Criminology, 65*, 390–396.

Landy, D., & Aronson, E. (1969). The influence of the character of the criminal and his victim on the decisions of simulated jurors. *Journal of Experimental Social Psychology, 5*, 141–152.

Lane, D. A. (1987). Personality and antisocial behaviour: A long term study. *Personality and Individual Differences, 8, 799–806.*

att, G. A. (1975). Effects of alcohol on *bnormal Psychology, 84*, 508–518.

rg Thieme Verlag.

prevention. In E. J. Langer (Ed.), *The*

baum.

molestation. *Journal of Consulting and*

(1983). Cogntive moral development, S. Laufer & J. M. Day (Eds.), *Personality* exington, MA: Lexington Books.

ove object: Heterosexual rejection as *rmal Psychology, 89*, 295–298.

minal Justice and Behavior, 10, 485–506.

'6). *Survey of inmates of state correctional* U.S. Government Printing Office.

punishment: Deterrence. Ottawa: Supply

ing theory of the etiology and maintenance of deviant sexual preference and behavior. In W. L. Marshall, D. R. Laws, and H. E. Barabaree (Eds.), *Handbook of sexual assault.* New York: Plenum.

LEACH, E. (1973). Don't say "boo" to a goose. In A. Montagu (Ed.), *Man and aggression* (2nd ed.). London: Oxford Univ. Press.

LeBon, G. (1896). *The crowd.* London: Ernest Benn.

LEE, M., ZIMBARDO, P. G., & BERTHOLF, M. (1977). Shy murderers. *Psychology Today,* November, 68–70, 148.

LEFKOWITZ, M., ERON, L., WALDER, L., & HUESMANN, L. (1977). *Growing up to be violent: A longitudinal study of the development of aggression.* New York: Pergamon Press.

LEGRAS, A. M. (1932). *Psychese en Criminaliteit bij Twellingen.* Utrecht: Keminken ZOON N.V.

LE MAIRE, L. (1956). Danish experiences regarding the castration of sexual offenders. *Journal of Criminal Law and Criminology, 47,* 294–310.

LERNER, M. J. (1970). The desire for justice and reactions to victims. In J. Macaulay & L. Berkowitz (Eds.), *Altruism and helping behavior.* New York: Academic Press.

LERNER, M. J. (1980). *The belief in a just world: A fundamental delusion.* New York: Plenum.

LETKEMANN, P. (1973). *Crime as work.* Englewood Cliffs, NJ: Prentice-Hall.

LEVI, M. (1984). Explaining commercial credit fraud. In D. J. Miller, D. E. Blackman, & A. J. Chapman (Eds.), *Psychology and the law,* Chichester, England: Wiley.

LEVIN, B. (1976). Psychological characteristics of firesetters. *Fire Journal, 70,* 36–41.

LEVINSON, R. (1988). Developments in the classification process: Quay's aims approach. *Criminal Justice and Behavior, 15,* 24–38.

LEWIS, N. D. C., & YARNELL, H. (1951). Pathological firesetting (pyromania). *Nervous and Mental Disease Monographs,* No. 82.

LIGHT, R. J. (1973). Abused and neglected children in America: A study of alternative policics. *Harvard Educational Review, 43,* 556–598.

LINZ, D. (1989). Exposure to sexually explicit materials and attitudes toward rape: A comparison of study results. *The Journal of Sex Research, 26,* 50–84.

LIPTON, D. N., McDONEL, E. C., & McFALL, R. M. (1987). Heterosocial perception in rapists. *Journal of Consulting and Clinical Psychology, 55,* 17–21.

LIPTON, D., MARTINSON, R. M., & WILKS, J. (1975). *The effectiveness of correctional treatment.* New York: Praeger.

LITTLE, A. (1963). Professor Eysenck's theory of crime: An empirical test on adolescent offenders. *British Journal of Criminology, 4,* 152–163.

LOEBER, R., & DISHION, T. (1983). Early predictors of male delinquency: A review. *Psychological Bulletin, 94,* 68–99.

LOMBROSO, C. (1876). *L'uomo delinquente.* Milan, Italy: Torin.

LOMBROSO, C. (1911/1968). *Crime, its causes and remedies.* Montclair, NJ: Patterson Smith.

LOMBROSO, C. (1972). Introduction. In Lombroso-Ferrero, G., *Criminal Man,* Montclair, NJ: Patterson Smith.

LOMBROSO, C., & FERRERO, W. (1895). *The female offender.* London: Fisher Unwin.

LOMBROSO-FERRERO, G. (1972). *Criminal man.* Montclair, NJ: Patterson Smith.

LORENZ, K. (1966). *On aggression.* New York: Harcourt Brace Jovanovich.

LOTTES, I. L. (1988). Sexual socialization and attitudes toward rape. In A. W. Burgess (Ed.), *Rape and sexual assault II.* New York: Garland Publishing.

LUBENOW, G. C. (1983). When kids kill their parents. *Newsweek,* June 27, 35–36.

LUNDE, D. T. (1976). *Murder and madness.* San Francisco: San Francisco Book Co.

LYKKEN, D. T. (1955). *A study of anxiety in the sociopathic personality* (Doctoral dissertation, Univ. of Minnesota). Ann Arbor, MI: Univ. Microfilms, No. 55–944.

LYKKEN, D. T. (1957). A study of anxiety in the sociopathic personality. *Journal of Abnormal and Social Psychology, 55,* 6–10.

LYKKEN, D. T. (1978). The psychopath and the lie detector. *Psychophysiology, 15,* 137–142.

LYKKEN, D. T., & VENABLES, P. H. (1971). Direct measurement of skin conductance: A proposal for standardization. *Psychophysiology, 8,* 856–872.

MACCOBY, E. E. (1986). Social groupings in childhood. In D. Olweus, J. Block, & M. Radke-Yarrow, (Eds.), *Development of antisocial and prosocial behavior: Research, theories, and issues.* New York: Academic Press.

MacDONALD, J. M. (1977). *Bombers and firesetters.* Springfield, IL: Charles C. Thomas.

MacLeod, R. B. (1970). Newtonian and Darwinian conceptions of man; and some alternatives. *Journal of the History of the Behavioral Science, 6,* 207–218.

Mahoney, M. J., & Lyddon, W. J. (1988). Recent developments in cognitive approaches to counseling and psychotherapy. *The Counseling Psychologist, 16,* 190–234.

Malamuth, N. M. (1981). Rape proclivity among males. *Journal of Social Issues, 37,* 138–157.

Malamuth, N. M. (1989). The attraction to sexual aggression scale: Part one. *The Journal of Sex Research, 26,* 26–49.

Malamuth, N. M., & Check, J. V. P. (1981). The effects of violent-sexual movies: A field experiment. *Journal of Research in Personality, 15,* 436–446.

Malamuth, N. M., Check, J. V. P., & Briere, J. (1986). Sexual arousal in response to aggression: Ideological, aggressive, and sexual correlates. *Journal of Personality and Social Psychology, 50,* 330–340.

Malamuth, N. M., Haber, S., & Feshbach, S. (1980). Testing hypothesis regarding rape: Exposure to sexual violence, sex differences, and the "normality" of rape. *Journal of Research in Personality, 14,* 121–137.

Malamuth, N. M., Heim, M., & Feshbach, S. (1980). The sexual responsiveness of college students to rape depictions: Inhibitory and disinhibitory effects. *Journal of Personality and Social Psychology, 38,* 399–408.

Mark, V. H., & Ervin, F. R. (1970). *Violence and the brain.* Hagerstown, MD: Harper & Row.

Marlatt, G. A., & Rohsenow, D. J. (1980). Cognitive processes in alcohol use: Expectancy and the balanced placebo design. In N. K. Mello (Ed.), *Advances in substance abuse: Behavioral and biological research.* Greenwich, CT: JAI Press.

Marques, J. K., & Nelson, C. (1989). Elements of high-risk situations for sex offenders. In D. R. Laws (Ed.), *Relapse prevention with sex offenders.* New York: Guilford.

Marshall, W. L. (1988). The use of sexually explicit stimuli by rapists, child molesters, and nonoffenders. *The Journal of Sex Research, 25,* 267–288.

Marshall, W. L., & Barbaree, H. E. (1988). An outpatient treatment program for child molesters. In R. A. Prentky and V. L. Quinsey (Eds.), *Human sexual aggression: Current perspectives.* New York: New York Academy of Sciences.

Marshall, W. L., & Christie, M. M. (1981). Pedophilia and aggression. *Criminal Justice and Behavior, 8,* 145–158.

Martinson, R. M. (1974). What works—questions and answers about prison reform. *Public Interest, 35,* 22–54.

Maslow, A. H. (1954). *Motivation and personality.* New York: Harper.

Mayfield, D. (1976). Alcoholism, alcohol, intoxication and assaultive behavior. *Diseases of the Nervous System, 37,* 288–291.

McCaghy, C. H. (1967). Child molesters: A study of their careers as deviants. In M. Clinard & R. Quinney (Eds.), *Criminal behavior systems: A typology.* New York: Holt, Rinehart & Winston.

McCaghy, C. H. (1980). *Crime in American society.* New York: Macmillan.

McCandless, B. R., Persons, W. S., & Roberts, A. (1972). Perceived opportunity, delinquency, race and body build among delinquent youth. *Journal of Consulting and Clinical Psychology, 38,* 281–287.

McClearn, G. E., & DeFries, J. C. (1973). *Introduction to behavioral genetics.* San Francisco: W. H. Freeman.

McCord, W., & McCord, J. (1964). *The psychopath: An essay on the criminal mind.* Princeton, NJ: Van Nostrand.

McCord, W., McCord, J., & Zola, I. K. (1959). *Origins of crime: A new evaluation of the Cambridge-Somerville Youth Study.* New York: Columbia Univ. Press.

McDermott, M. J., & Hindelang, M. J. (1981). *Juvenile criminal behavior in the United States: Its trends and patterns.* Washington, DC: U.S. Government Printing Office.

McGurk, B. J. (1981). The validity and utility of a typology of homicides based on Megargee's theory of control. *Personality and Individual Differences, 2,* 129–136.

McReynolds, P. (1968). The motivational psychology of Jeremy Bentham: I.Background and general approach. *Journal of the History of the Behavioral Sciences, 4,* 230–244.

Mechoulam, R. (1970). Marihuana chemistry. *Science, 168,* 1159–1166.

Mednick, S. A., Gabrielli, W. F., & Hutchings, B. (1984). Genetic influences in criminal convictions: Evidence from an adoption cohort. *Science, 234,* 891–894.

Mednick, S. A., Gabrielli, W. F., & Hutchings, B. (1987). Genetic factors in the etiology of criminal behavior. In S. A. Mednick, T. E. Moffitt, & S. A. Stack (Eds.), *The causes of crime: New biological approaches.* Cambridge, England: Cambridge Univ. Press.

MEDNICK, S. A., & VOLAVKA, J. (1980). Biology and crime. In N. Morris & M. Tonry (Eds.), *Crime and justice: An annual review of research* (Vol. 2). Chicago: Univ. of Chicago Press.

MEGARGEE, E. I. (1966). Undercontrolled and overcontrolled personality types in extreme antisocial aggression. *Psychological Monographs, 80,* No. 3.

MEGARGEE, E. I. (1976). Population density and disruptive behavior in prison settings. In A. K. Cohen, F. G. Cole, & R. G. Bailey (Eds.), *Prison violence.* Lexington, MA: Lexington Books.

MEGARGEE, E. I. (1982). Psychological determinants and correlates of criminal violence. In M. E. Wolfgang & N. A. Weinder (Eds.), *Criminal Violence.* Beverly Hills, CA: Sage.

MEGARGEE, E. I., & BOHN, M. J. (1977). Empirically determined characteristics of the ten types. *Criminal Justice and Behavior, 4,* 149–210.

MEGARGEE, E. I., & BOHN, M. J. (1979). *Classifying criminal offenders.* Newbury Park, CA: Sage.

MENDELSON, W., JOHNSON, N., & STEWARD, M. A. (1971). Hyperactive children as teenagers: A follow-up study. *Journal of Nervous and Mental Disease, 153,* 273–279.

MEYER, T. P. (1972). The effects of sexually arousing and violent films on aggressive behavior. *Journal of Sex Research, 8,* 324–333.

MIDDLEBROOK, P. M. (1974). *Social psychology and modern life.* New York: Knopf.

MILGRAM, S. (1963). Behavioral study of obedience. *Journal of Abnormal and Social Psychology, 67,* 371–378.

MILGRAM, S. (1977). *The individual in a social world.* Reading, MA: Addison-Wesley.

MILLER, J. D., CISIN, I. H., GARDNER-KEATON, H., HARRELL, A. V., WIRTZ, P. W., ABELSON, H. I., & FISHBURNE, P. M. (1983). *National survey on drug abuse: Main findings.* Rockville, MD: National Institute on Drug Abuse.

MILLER, W. B. (1980). Gangs, groups, and serious youth crime. In D. Schichor & D. H. Kelly (Eds.), *Critical issues in juvenile delinquency.* Lexington, MA: Lexington Books.

MILLER, W. R., & HESTER, R. K. (1989). Treating alcohol problems: Toward an informed eclecticism. In R. K. Hester & W. R. Miller (Eds.), *Handbook of alcoholism treatment approaches: Effective alternatives.* New York: Pergamon Press.

MILLETT, K. (1974). "J," the life. In E. Goode & R. Troiden (Eds.), *Sexual deviance and sexual deviants.* New York: William Morrow.

MINER, M. H., DAY, D. M., & NAFPAKTITIS, M. K. (1989). Assessment of coping skills: Development of situational competency test. In D. R. Laws (Ed.), *Relapse prevention with sex offenders.* New York: Guilford.

MIRON, M. S., & GOLDSTEIN. A. P. (1978). *Hostage.* Kalamazoo, MI: Behaviordelia.

MISCHEL, W. (1961). Preference for delayed reinforcement and social responsibility. *Journal of Abnormal and Social Psychology, 62,* 1–7.

MISCHEL, W. (1968). *Personality and assessment.* New York: Wiley.

MISCHEL, W. (1973). Toward a cognitive social learning reconceptualization of personality. *Psychological Review, 80,* 252–283.

MISCHEL, W. (1976). *Introduction to personality* (2nd ed.). New York: Holt, Rinehart & Winston.

M'Naghten, 10 Clark & Fin. 200, 210, 8 Eng. Rep 718, 722 (1943).

MOHR, J. W., TURNER, R. E., & JERRY, N. B. (1964). *Pedophilia and exhibitionism.* Toronto: Univ. of Toronto Press.

MOLL, K. D. (1974). *Arson, vandalism and violence: Law enforcement problems affecting fire departments* (LEAA). Washington, DC: U.S. Government Printing Office.

MONAHAN, J. (1976). The prevention of crime. In J. Monahan (Ed.), *Community mental health and the criminal justice system.* New York: Pergamon Press.

MONAHAN, J. (1981). *Predicting violent behavior.* Berverly Hills, CA: Sage.

MONAHAN, J., & GEIS, G. (1976). Controlling "dangerous" people. *Annals of the American Academy of Political and Social Science, 423,* 142–151.

MONAHAN, T. P. (1957). Family status and the delinquent child: A reappraisal and some new findings. *Social Forces, 35,* 250–258.

MONTAGU, A. (1973). *Man and aggression* (2nd ed.). London: Oxford Univ. Press.

MONTAGU, A. (1976). *The nature of human aggression.* New York: Oxford Univ. Press.

MOORE, R. H. (1984). Shoplifting in middle Amercia: Patterns and motivational correlates. *International Journal of Offender Therapy and Comparative Criminology, 28,* 53–64.

MORASH, M. (1983). An explanation of juvenile delinquency: The integration of moral-reasoning theory and sociologocal knowledge. In W. S. Laufer & J. M. Day (Eds.), *Personality theory, moral development, and criminal behavior*. Lexington, MA: Lexington Books.

MORASH, M. (1986). Wife battering. *Criminal Justice Abstracts, 18*, 252–271.

MORRIS, D. (1967). *The naked ape*. New York: McGraw-Hill.

MORRIS, N. (1982). *Madness and the criminal law*. Chicago: Univ. of Chicago Press.

MORSE, S. J. (1978). Behavior, morals, and science: An analysis of mental health law. *Southern California Law Review, 51*, 527–654.

MORTON, J., ADDISON, H., ADDISON, R., HUNT, L., & SULLIVAN, J. (1953). A clinical study of premenstrual tension. *American Journal of Obstetrics and Gynecology, 65*, 1182–1191.

MOTT, J. (1986). Opoid use and burglary. *British Journal of Addiction, 81*, 671–677.

MOYER, K. E. (1971). The physiology of aggression and the implication for aggression control. In J. L. Singer (Ed.), *The control of aggression and violence*. New York: Academic Press.

MOYER, K. E. (1973). The physiological inhibition of hostile behavior. In J. F. Knutson (Ed.), *The control of aggression*. Chicago: Aldine.

MOYER, K. E. (1976). *The psychobiology of aggression*. New York: Harper & Row.

MUELLER, C. W. (1983). Environmental stressors and aggressive behavior. In R. G. Geen & E. I. Donnerstein (Eds.), *Aggression: Theoretical and empirical reviews*. Vol. 2. New York: Academic Press.

MUNFORD, R. S., KAZER, R.,, FELDMAN, R., & STIVERS, R. (1976). Homicide trends in Atlanta. *Criminology, 142*, 213–231.

MURPHY, J. M., & GILLIGAN, C. (1980). Moral development in late adolescence and adulthood: A critique and reconstruction of Kohlberg's theory. *Human Development, 23*, 77–104.

NACCI, P. L., TEITELBAUM, H. E., & PRATHER, J. (1977). Population density and inmate misconduct rates in the federal prison system. *Federal Probation, 41*, 26–31.

NACHSHON, I. (1983). Hemisphere dysfunction in psychopathy and behavior disorders. In M. Myslobodsky (Ed.), *Hemisyndromes: Psychobiology, neurology, psychiatry*. New York: Academic Press.

NACHSHON, I., & DENNO, D. (1987). Violent behavior and cerebral hemisphere function. In S. A. Mednick, T. E. Moffitt, & S. A. Stack (Eds.), *The causes of crime: New biological approaches*. Cambridge, England: Cambridge Univ. Press.

NAGI, S. G. (1975). Child abuse and neglect programs: A national overview. *Children Today, 4*, 13–17.

NASH, J. R. (1975). *Bloodletters and badmen: Book 3*. New York: Warner Books.

NATIONAL CENTER ON CHILD ABUSE AND NEGLECT (NCCAN) (1981). *Study findings: National study of the incidence and severity of child abuse and neglect*. Washington, DC: U.S. Department of Health and Human Services.

NATIONAL COMMISSION ON MARIHUANA AND DRUG ABUSE. (1972). *Marihuana: A signal of misunderstanding*. Appendix, Vol. 1. Washington, DC: U.S. Government Printing Office.

NATIONAL COMMISSION ON MARIHUANA AND DRUG ABUSE. (1973). *Drug use in America: Problem in perspective*. 2nd report. Washington, DC: U.S. Government Printing Office.

NATIONAL INSTITUTE FOR JUVENILE JUSTICE AND DELINQUENCY PREVENTION. (1976). *The link between learning disabilities and juvenile delinquency: Current theory and knowledge* (LEAA). Washington, DC: U.S. Government Printing Office.

NATIONAL INSTITUTE ON DRUG ABUSE. (1978). Drug abuse and crime. In L. D. Savitz & N. Johnson (Eds.), *Crime in society*. New York: Wiley.

NEBYLITSYN, V. D., & GRAY, J. A. (1972). *Biological bases of individual behavior*. New York: Academic Press.

NEE, C., & TAYLOR, M. (1988). Residential burglary in the Republic of Ireland: A situational perspective. *Howard Journal, 27*, 105–116.

NELSON, S. D. (1975). Nature/nurture revisted II. *Journal of Conflict Resolution, 19*, 734–761.

NELSON, S., & AMIR, M. (1975). The hitchhike victim of rape: A research report. In I. Drapkin & E. Viano (Eds.), *Victimology: A new focus*. Vol. 5. Lexington, MA: Lexington Books.

NETTLER, G. (1982). *Killing one another*. Cincinnati: Anderson.

NETTLER, G. (1984). *Explaining crime*. (3rd ed.). New York: McGraw-Hill.

NEWMAN, E. S., NEWMAN, D. J., & GEWIRTZ, M. L. (EDS.). (1984). *Elderly criminals*. Cambridge, MA: Oelgeschlager, Gunn & Hain.

NEWMAN, G. (1982). *Just and painful: A case for the corporal punishment of criminals*. New York: Macmillan.

NICHOL, A. R., GUNN, J. C., GRISTWOOD, J., FOGGETT, R. H., & WATSON, J. P. (1973). The relationship of alcoholism to violent behaviors resulting in long-term imprisonment. *British Journal of Psychiatry, 123*, 47–51.

NIEDERMEYER, A. A. (1963). *Der Nervenarzt, 34*, 168.

NIETZEL, M. T. (1979). *Crime and its modification: A social learning perspective.* New York: Pergamon.

NORMANDEAU, A. (1968). Patterns in robbery. *Criminologica, 1*, 2–13.

OHLIN, L. E. (1983). The future of juvenile justice policy and research. *Crime and Delinquency, 29*, 463–472.

OHLIN, L. E., & TONRY, M. (1989). Family violence in perspective. In L. Ohlin & M. Tonry (Eds.), *Family violence.* Vol. 11. Chicago: Univ. of Chicago Press.

O'LEARY, K. D. (1988). Physical aggression between spouses: A social learning pespective. In V. B. Van Hasselt, R. L. Morrison, A. S. Bellack, & M. Hersen (Eds.), *Handbook of family violence.* New York: Plenum.

O'LEARY, K. D., BARLING, J., ARIAS, I., ROSENBAUM, A., MALONE, J., & TYREE, A. (1989). Prevalence and stability of physical aggression between spouses: A longitudinal analysis. *Journal of Consulting and Clinical Psychology, 57*, 263–268.

O'LEARY, K. D., & CURLEY, A. D. (1986). Assertion and family violence: Correlates of spouse abuse. *Journal of Marital and Family Therapy, 12*, 281–289.

O'LEARY, M. R., & DENGERINK, H. A. (1973). Aggression as a function of the intensity and pattern of attack. *Journal of Experimental Research in Personality, 7*, 61–70.

OLTMAN, J., & FRIEDMAN, S. (1967). Parental deprivation in psychiatric conditions. *Diseases of the Nervous System, 28*, 298–303.

OLWEUS, D. (1978). *Aggression in the schools.* New York: Wiley.

ORRIS, J. B. (1969). Visual monitoring performance in three subgroups of male delinquents. *Journal of Abnormal Psychology, 74*, 227–229.

PACHT, A., & COWDEN, J. (1974). An exploratory study of five hundred sex offenders. *Criminal Justice and Behavior, 1*, 13–20.

PAGELOW, M. D. (1989). The incidence and prevalence of criminal abuse of other family members. In L. Ohlin & M. Tonry (Eds.), *Family violence.* Vol 11. Chicago: Univ. of Chicago Press.

PALMER, T. (1975). Martinson revisited. *Journal of Research in Crime and Delinquency, 12*, 3–14.

PARKER, H., & NEWCOMBE, R. (1987). Heroin use and acquisitive crime in an English community. *British Journal of Sociology, 38*, 331–350.

PARLEE, M. B. (1973). The premenstrual syndrome. *Psychological Bulletin, 80*, 454–465.

PASSINGHAM, R. E. (1972). Crime and personality: A review of Eysenck's theory. In V. D. Nebylitsyn & J. A. Gray (Eds.), *Biological bases of individual behavior.* New York: Academic Press.

PATRICK, A. (1988). The crowding crisis: A global view. *Corrections Today, 50*, 110–111, 114–115.

PATTERSON, G. R. (1982). *Coercive family processes.* Eugene, OR: Castalia Press.

PAULHUS, D. L., & MARTIN, C. L. (1986). Predicting adult temperament from minor physical anomalies. *Journal of Personality and Social Psychology, 50*, 1235–1239.

PAULUS, P. B. (1988). *Prison crowding: A psychological perspective.* New York: Springer-Verlag.

PEELE, S. (1984). The cultural context of psychological approaches to alcoholism. *American Psychologist, 39*, 1337–1351.

PENFIELD, W. (1975). *The mystery of the mind.* Princeton, NJ: Princeton Univ. Press.

PENNINGTON, L. A. (1966). Psychopathic and criminal behavior. In L. A. Pennington & I. A. Berg (Eds.), *An introduction to clinical psychology.* New York: Ronald Press.

PENROD, S. (1983). *Social psychology.* Englewood Cliffs, NJ: Prentice-Hall.

PETERS, S. D., WYATT, G. E., & FINKELHOR, D. (1986). Prevalence. In D. Finkelhor (Ed.), *Sourcebook on child sexual abuse.* Beverly Hills, CA: Sage.

PETERSEN, E. (1977). *A reassessment of the concept of criminality.* New York: Halstead Press.

PETERSON, M. A., BRAIKER, H. B., & POLICH, S. M. (1981). *Who commits crimes?* Cambridge, MA: Oelgeschlager, Gunn & Hain.

PHARES, E. J. (1972). A social learning theory approach to psychopathology. In J. Rotter, J. Chana, & E. J. Phares (Eds.), *Applications of a social learning theory of personality.* New York: Holt, Rinehart & Winston.

PIAGET, J. (1948). *The moral judgment of the child.* New York: Free Press.

PILLEMER, K., & FINKELHOR, D. (1988). The prevalence of elder abuse: A random sample survey. *The Gerontologist, 28,* 51–57.

PILLEMER, K., & SUITOR, J. J. (1988). Elder abuse. In V. B. Van Hasselt, R. L. Morrison, A. S. Morrison, A. S. Bellak, M. & Hersen (Eds.), *Handbook of family violence.* New York: Plenum.

PINCUS, J. H. (1980). Can violence be a manifestation of epilepsy? *Neurology, 30,* 304–306.

PITHERS, W. D., BEAL, L. S., ARMSTRONG, J., & PETTY, J. (1989). Identification of risk factors through clinical interviews and analysis of records. D. R. Laws (Ed.), *Relapse prevention with sex offenders.* New York: Guilford.

PITHERS, W. D., KASHIMA, K. M., CUMMING, G. F., BEAL, L. S., & BUELL, M. M. (1988). Relapse prevention of sexual aggression. In R. A. Prentky & V. L. Quinsey (Eds.), *Human sexual aggression: Current perspectives.* New York: New York Academy of Sciences.

PITHERS, W. D., MARQUES, J. K., GIBAT, C. C., & MARLATT, G. A. (1983). Relapse prevention with sexual aggressives. In J. G. Greer & I. R. Stuart (Eds.), *The sexual aggressor: Current perspectives on treatment.* New York: Van Nostrand Reinhold.

PLECK, E. (1989). Criminal approaches to family violence, 1640–1980. In L. Ohlin & M. Tonry (Eds.), *Family violence.* Vol 11. Chicago: Univ. of Chicago Press.

POKORNY, A. D. (1965). A comparison of homicide in two cities. *Journal of Criminal Law, Criminology and Police Science, 56,* 479–484.

POLLAK, O. (1950). *The criminality of women.* New York: A. S. Barnes.

POMEROY, W. (1965). Some aspects of prostitution. *Journal of Sex Research, 5,* 177–187.

POMEROY, W. A. (1974). *Police chiefs discuss drug abuse.* Washington, DC: The Drug Abuse Council.

POPE, C. E. (1977a). *Crime-specific analysis: An empirical examination of burglary offender characteristics* (LEAA). Washington, DC: U.S. Government Printing Office.

POPE, C. E. (1977b). *Crime-specific analysis: The characteristics of burglary incidents* (LEAA). Washington, DC: U.S. Government Printing Office.

POPE, C. E. (1977c). *Crime-specific analysis: An empirical examination of burglary offense and offense characteristics* (LEAA). Washington, DC: U.S. Government Printing Office.

POSEY, C. D. (1988). Introduction. *Criminal Justice and Behavior, 15,* 5–7.

POWELL, G. E., & STEWART, R. A. (1983). The relationship of personality to antisocial and neurotic behaviours as observed by teachers. *Personality and Individual Differences, 4,* 97–100.

PRENTICE-DUNN, S., & ROGERS, R. (1982). Effects of public and private self-awareness on deindividuation and aggression. *Journal of Personality and Social Psychology, 43,* 503–513.

PRENTICE-DUNN, S., & ROGERS, R. (1983). Deindividuation in aggression. In R. G. Geen & E. I. Donnerstein (Eds.), *Aggression: Theoretical and Empirical Reviews.* Vol. 2. New York: Academic Press.

PRENTKY, R. A., & KNIGHT, R. A. (1986). Impulsivity in the life style and criminal behavior of sexual offenders. *Criminal Justice and Behavior, 13,* 141–164.

PRESIDENT'S COMMISSION ON LAW ENFORCEMENT AND ADMINISTRATION OF JUSTICE. (1967). *The challenge of crime in free society.* Washington, DC: U.S. Government Printing Office.

PRICE, J. B. (1968). Some results on the Maudsley Personality Inventory from a sample of girls in borstal. *British Journal of Criminology, 8,* 383–401.

PRICE, W. H., & WHATMORE, P. B. (1967). Behaviour disorders and patterns of crime among XYY males identified at a maximum security hospital. *British Medical Journal, 1,* 533–536.

QUAY, H. C. (1964). Dimensions of personality in delinquent boys as inferred from the factor analysis of case history data. *Child Development, 35,* 479–484.

QUAY, H. C. (1965). Psychopathic personality: Pathological stimulation-seeking. *American Journal of Psychiatry, 122,* 180–183.

QUAY, H. C. (1972). Patterns of aggression, withdrawal, and immaturity. In H. Quay & J. Werry (Eds.), *Psychopathological disorders of childhood.* New York: Wiley.

QUAY, H. C. (1977). The three faces of evaluation: What can be expected to work. *Criminal Justice and Behavior, 4,* 341–354.

QUAY, H. C. (1984). *Managing adult inmates.* College Park, MD: American Correctional Association.

QUAY, H. C. (1987). Institutional treatment. In H. C. Quay (Ed.), *Handbook of juvenile delinquency* . New York: Wiley.

QUEEN'S BENCH FOUNDATION. (1978). The rapist and his crime. In L. D. Savitz & N. Johnson (Eds.), *Crime in society*. New York: Wiley.

QUINSEY, V. L. (1977). The assessment and treatment of child molesters: A review. *Canadian Psychological Review*, *18*, 204–220.

QUINSEY, V. L., & MARSHALL, W. L. (1983). Procedures for reducing inappropriate sexual arousal: An evaluation review. In J. G. Greer & I. R. Stuart (Eds.), *The sexual aggressor*. New York: Van Nostrand Reinhold.

RABKIN, J. G. (1979). Criminal behavior of discharged mental patients: A critical appraisal of the research. *Psychological Bulletin*, *86*, 1–27.

RACHMAN, S. J. (1966). Sexual fetishism: An experimental analogue. *Psychological Record*, *16*, 293–296.

RADA, R. T. (1975). Alcoholism and forcible rape. *American Journal of Psychiatry*, *121*, 776–783.

RAPAPORT, K., & BURKHART, B. R. (1984). Personality and attitudinal characteristics of sexually coercive college males. *Journal of Abnormal Psychology*, *93*, 216–221.

RAPOPORT, J. L., & QUINN, P. O. (1975). Minor physical anomalies (stigmata) and early developmental deviation. *International Journal of Mental Health*, *4*, 29–44.

RAPPEPORT, J., & LASSEN, G. (1965). Dangerousness-arrest rate comparisons of discharged patients and the general population. *American Journal of Psychiatry*, *121*, 776–783.

RASKIN, D. C., & HARE, R. D. (1978). Psychopathy and detection of deception in a prison population. *Psychophysiology*, *15*, 126–136.

RAY, O. (1983). *Drugs, society and human behavior*. (3rd ed.) St. Louis: C. V. Mosby.

REID, S. T. (1985). *Crime and criminology*. (4th. ed.) New York: Holt, Rinehart & Winston.

REISS, J. (1977). "Voluntary" castration of mentally disordered sex offenders. *Criminal Law Bulletin*, *13*, 30–48.

REVITCH, E., & SCHLESINGER, L. B. (1988). Clinical reflections on sexual aggression. In R. A. Prentky and V. L. Quinsey (Eds.), *Human sexual aggression: Current perspectives*. New York: New York Academy of Sciences.

REVITCH, E., & WEISS, R. G. (1962). The pedophiliac offender. *Diseases of the Nervous System*, *23*, 73–78.

RHOADS, J. M., & BORJES, E. D. (1981). The incidence of exhibitionism in Guatemala and U S. *British Journal of Psychiatry*, *139*, 242–244.

RICE, D. (1980). Homicide from the perspective of NCHS statistics on blacks. *Public Health Reports*, *95*, 550–552.

RIEDEL, M., ZAHN, M., & MOCK, L. F. (1985). *The nature and patterns of American homicide*. Washington, DC: U.S. Government Printing Office.

RITVO, E., SHANOK, S. S., & LEWIS, D. O. (1983). Firesetting and nonfiresetting delinquents. *Child Psychiatry and Human Development*, *13*, 259–267.

ROBBINS, E., & ROBBINS, L. (1964). Arson with special reference to pyromania. *New York State Journal of Medicine*, *2*, 795–798.

ROBINS, L. N. (1966). *Deviant children grow up*. Baltimore: Williams & Wilkins.

ROBINS, L. N., & O'NEAL, P. (1959). The adult prognosis for runaway children. *American Journal of Orthopsychiatry*, *29*, 752–761.

ROCHE, P. Q. (1958). *The criminal mind: A study of communication between criminal law and psychiatry*. New York: Grove Press.

RODMAN, H., & GRAMS, P. (1967). Juvenile delinquency and the family: A review and discussion. In *Task Force Report: Juvenile delinquency and youth crime*. Washington, DC: U.S. Government Printing Office.

RONCEK, D. W. (1975). Density and crime: A methodological critique. *American Behavioral Scientist*, *18*, 843–860.

ROOTH, G. (1973). Exhibitionism outside Europe and America. *Archives of Sexual Behavior*, *2*, 351–363.

ROOTH, G. (1974). Exhibitionists around the world. *Human Behavior*, *3*, 61.

ROSANOFF, A. J. (1934). Criminality and delinquency in twins. *Journal of Criminal Law and Criminology*, *24*, 923–934.

ROSANOFF, A. J., HANDY, L. M., & PLESSET, I. (1941). The etiology of child behavior difficulties, juvenile delinquency and adult criminality with special reference to their occurence in twins. *Psychiatric Monographs*, *1*. Sacramento, CA: Sacramento Dept. of Institutions.

ROSENHAN, D. L., & SELIGMAN, M. E. P. (1984). *Abnormal psychology*. New York: Norton.

ROSENQUIST, C. M., & MEGARGEE, E. I. (1969). Delinquency in three cultures. Austin, TX: Univ. of Texas Press.

ROSENTHAL, D. (1970). Genetic theory and abnormal behavior. New York: McGraw-Hill.

ROSENTHAL, D. (1971). Genetics of psychopathology. New York: McGraw-Hill.

ROSENTHAL, D. (1975). Heredity in criminality. Criminal Justice and Behavior, 2, 3–21.

ROSS, A. (1974). Psychological disorders of children. New York: McGraw-Hill.

ROTENBERG, M., & DIAMOND, B. (1971). The biblical conception of psychopathy: The law of the stubborn and rebellious son. Journal of the History of the Behavioral Sciences, 12, 29–38.

ROTH, L. (1980). Correctional psychiatry. In W. Curran, A. McCorry, & C. Petty (Eds.), Modern legal medicine, psychiatry, and forensic science. Philadelphia: Davis.

ROTTON, J. (1983). Affective and cognitive consequences of malodorous pollution. Basic and Applied Psychology, 4, 171–191.

ROTTON, J., & FREY, J. (1985). Air pollution, weather, and violent crimes: Concomitant time-series analysis of archival data. Journal of Personality and Social Psychology, 49, 1207–1220.

RUBACK, R. B., & CARR, T. S. (1984). Crowding in a women's prison: Attitudinal and behavioral effects. Journal of Applied Social Psychology, 14, 57–68.

RUBIN, B. (1972). Predictions of dangerousness in mentally ill criminals. Archives of General Psychiatry, 27, 397–407.

RUSHTON, J. P., & CHRISJOHN, R. D. (1981). Extraversion, neuroticism, psychoticism, and self-reported delinquency: Evidence from eight separate samples. Personality and Individual Differences, 2, 11–20.

RUSSELL, D. (1973). Emotional aspects of shoplifting. Psychiatric Annals, 3, 77–86.

RUSSELL, D. E. H. (1975). The politics of rape: The victim's perspective. New York: Stein & Day.

RUSSELL, D. E. H. (1983). The prevalence and incidence of forcible rape and attempted rape of females. Victimiology: An International Journal, 7, 81–93.

RUSSELL, D. E. H. (1984). Sexual exploitation. Beverly Hills, CA: Sage.

RUSSELL, D. E. H., & FINKELHOR, D. (1984). The gender gap among perpetrators of child sexual abuse. In D. E. H. Russell (Ed.), Sexual exploitation. Beverly Hills, CA: Sage.

RUSSELL, D. E. H., & HOWELL, N. (1983). The prevalence of rape in the United States revisted. Signs: Journal of Women in Culture and Society, 8, 688–695.

RUTTER, M., & GILLER, H. (1984). Juvenile delinquency: Trends and perspectives. New York: Guilford Press.

SAMPSON, R. J. (1985). Race and criminal violence: A demographically disaggregated analysis of urban homicide. Crime and Delinquency, 31, 47–82.

SANTA CLARA CRIMINAL JUSTICE PILOT PROGRAM. (1972). Burglary in San Jose. Springfield, VA: U.S. Department of Commerce.

SARBIN, T. R. (1979). The myth of the criminal type. In T. R. Sarbin (Ed.), Challenges to the criminal justice system: The perspective of community psychology. New York: Human Services Press.

SATTERFIELD, J. H. (1973). EEG issues in children with minimal brain dysfunction. Seminars in Psychiatry, 5, 35–46.

SATTERFIELD, J. H. (1975). Neurophysiologic studies with hyperactive children. In D. P. Cantwell (Ed.), The hyperactive child. New York: Spectrum Publications.

SATTERFIELD, J. H. (1978). The hyperactive child syndrome: A precursor of adult psychopathy? In R. D. Hare & D. Schalling (Eds.), Psychopathic behaviour: Approaches to research. Chichester, England: Wiley.

SATTERFIELD, J. H. (1987). Childhood diagnostic and neurophysiological predictors of teenage arrest rates: An eight year propsective study. In S. A. Mednick, T. E. Moffitt, & S. A. Stack (Eds.), The causes of crime: New biological approaches. Cambridge, England: Cambridge Univ. Press.

SATTERFIELD, J. H., ATOIAN, G., BRASHEARS, G. C., BURLEIGH, A. C., & DAWSON, M. E. (1974). Electrodermal studies of minimal brain dysfunction in children. In Clinical use of stimulant drugs in children. The Hague, Excerpta Medica.

SATTERFIELD, J. H., & DAWSON, M. E. (1971). Electrodermal correlates of hyperactivity in children. Psychophysiology, 8, 191–197.

SAUNDERS, D. G., & AZAR, S. T. (1989). Treatment programs for family violence. In L. Ohlin & M. Tonry (Eds.), Family violence. Vol. 11. Chicago: Univ. of Chicago Press.

SAVITZ, L. D. (1972). Introduction. In G. Lombroso-Ferrero, *Criminal man*. Montclair, NJ: Patterson Smith.

SCHACHT, T. E. (1985). DSM-III and the politics of truth. *American Psychologist, 40*, 513–521.

SCHACHTER, S. (1971). *Emotion, obesity and crime*. New York: Academic Press.

SCHACHTER, S., & LATANE, B. (1964). Crime, cognition and the autonomic nervous system. In M. R. Jones (Ed.), *Nebraska symposium on motivation*. Lincoln, NE: Univ. of Nebraska Press.

SCHACTER, D. L. (1986). Amnesia and crime: How much do we really know? *American Psychologist, 41*, 286–295.

SCHAFER, W. E., & POLK, K. (1967). Delinquency and the schools. *Task force report: Juvenile delinquency and youth crime*. Washington, DC: U.S. Government Printing Office.

SCHANDS, H. C. (1958). *A report on an investigation of psychiatric problems in felons in the North Carolina prison system*. Chapel Hill, NC: Department of Psychiatry, Univ. of North Carolina.

SCHLOSSMAN, S., & SEDLAK, M. (1983). The Chicago area project revisited. *Crime and Delinquency, 29*, 398–462.

SCHMIDEBERG, M. (1953). Pathological firesetters. *Journal of Criminal Law, Criminology and Police Science, 44*, 30–39.

SCHRAGER, L., & SHORT, J. (1978). Toward a sociology of organizational crime. *Social Problems, 25*, 407–419.

SCHULSINGER, F. (1972). Psychopathy: Heredity and environment. *International Journal of Mental Health, 1*, 190–206.

SCHULTZ, J. L., & COHEN, F. (1976). Isolationism in juvenile court jurisprudence. In M. Rosenhan (Ed.), *Pursuing justice for the child*. Chicago: Univ. of Chicago Press.

SCHULTZ, L. G. (1975). *Rape victimology*. Springfield, IL: Charles C. Thomas.

SCHWITZGEBEL, R. K. (1977). Professional accountability in the treatment and release of dangerous persons. In B. D. Sales (Ed.), *Perspectives in law and pscyhology: The criminal justice system*. Vol. 1. New York: Plenum Press.

SCULLY, D., & MAROLLA, J. (1984). Convicted rapists' vocabulary of motive: Excuses and justifications. *Social Problems, 31*, 530–544

SCULLY, D., & MAROLLA, J. (1985). Rape and vocabularies of motive: Alternative perspectives. In A. W. Burgess (Ed.), *Rape and sexual assault*. New York: Garland Publishing.

SEARS, R., MACCOBY, E., & LEVIN, H. (1957). *Patterns of child rearing*. Evanston, IL: Row, Peterson.

SEBALD, H. (1986). Adolescents' shifting orientations toward parents and peers: A curvilinear trend over recent decades. *Journal of Marriage and the Family, 48*, 5–13.

SECHREST, L. (1987). Classification for treatment. In D. M. Gottfredson & M. Tonry (Eds.), *Prediction and classification: Criminal justice decision making*. Vol. 9. Chicago: Univ. of Chicago Press.

SEGAL, Z. V., & MARSHALL, W. L. (1985). Heterosexual social skills in a population of rapists and child molesters. *Journal of Consulting and Clinical Psychology, 53*, 55–63.

SELIGMAN, M. E. (1975). *Helplessness: On depression, development, and death*. San Francisco: W. H. Freeman.

SELLIN, T. (1970). A sociological approach. In M. E. Wolfgang, L. Savitz, & N. Johnson (Eds.), *The sociology of crime and delinquency* (2nd ed.). New York: Wiley.

SELLIN, T. A., & WOLFGANG, M. (1964). *The measurement of delinquency*. New York: Wiley.

SHAFER, S. (1976). *Introduction to criminology*. Reston, VA: Reston Publishing.

SHELDON, W. H., HARTL, E. M., & MCDERMOTT, E. (1949). *Varieties of delinquent youth: An introduction to constitutional psychiatry*. New York: Harper.

SHELDON, W. H., & STEVENS, S. S. (1942). *The varieties of temperament*. New York: Harper.

SHERMAN, L. W., & BERK, R. A. (1984). The specific deterrent effects of arrest for domestic assault. *American Sociological Review, 49*, 261–272.

SHIELDS, J. (1962). *Monozygotic twins brought up apart and together*. Oxford: Oxford Univ. Press.

SHOEMAKER, D. J. (1984). *Theories of delinquency*. New York: Oxford Univ. Press.

SHORT, J. F. (1968). *Gang delinquency and delinquency subcultures*. New York: Harper & Row.

SHORT, J. F., & NYE, I. (1957). Reported behavior as a criterion of deviant behavior. *Social Problems, 5*, 207–213.

SHOVER, N. (1972). Structures and careers in burglary. *Journal of Criminal Law, Criminology and Police Science, 63*, 540–548.

SHOVER, N. (1983). The later stages of ordinary property offender careers. *Social Problems, 31*, 208–218.

SHUNTICH, R. J., & TAYLOR, S. P. (1972). The effects of alcohol on human physical aggressions. *Journal of Experimental Research in Personality, 6*, 34–38.

SIEGEL, A., & KOHN, L. (1959). Permissiveness, permission, and aggression: The effect of adult presence or absence on aggression in children's play. *Child Development, 30*, 131–141.

SIEGEL, J. M., SORENSON, S. B., GOLDING, J. M., BURNAM, M. A., & STEIN, J. A. (1987). The prevalence of childhood sexual assault: The Los Angeles Epidemiological Catchment Area Project. *American Journal of Epidemiology, 126*, 1141–1153.

SIEH, E. W. (1987). Garment workers: Perceptions of inequity and employee theft. *British Journal of Criminology, 27*, 174–190.

SIGALL, H., & OSTROVE, N. (1978). Physical attractiveness and jury decisions. In N. Johnson & L. Savitz (Eds.), *Justice and corrections*. New York: Wiley.

SILVA, F., MARTORELL, C., & CLEMENTE, A. (1986). Socialization and personality: Study through questionnaires in a preadult Spanish population. *Personality and Individual Differences, 7*, 355–372.

SILVERMAN, R. A., & MUKHERJEE, S. K. (1987). Intimate homicide: An analysis of violent social relationships. *Behavioral Sciences and the Law, 5*, 37–47.

SIMON, R. J. (1975). *Women and crime*. Lexington, MA: Lexington Books.

SIMON, R. J. (1983). The defense of insanity. *Journal of Psychiatry & Law, 1*, 183–201.

SIMON, R. J., & COCKERHAM, W. (1977). Civil commitment, burden of proof, and dangerous acts: A comparison of the perspectives of judges and psychiatrists. *Journal of Psychiatry & Law, 5*, 571–594.

SKINNER, B. F. (1964). Behaviorism at fifty. In T. W. Wann (Ed.), *Behavorism and phenomenology*. Chicago: Univ. of Chicago Press.

SKOGAN, W. G. (1977). Dimensions of the dark figure of unreported crime. *Crime and Delinquency, 23*, 41–50.

SKOGAN, W. G. (1978). Weapon use in robbery. In J. A. Inciardi & A. E. Pottieger (Eds.), *Violent crime: Historical and contemporary issues*. Beverly Hills, CA: Sage.

SKRZPEK, G. J. (1969). The effects of perceptual isolation and arousal on anxiety, complexity preference and novelty preference in psychopathic and neurotic delinquents. *Journal of Abnormal Psychology, 74*, 321–329.

SMART, C. (1976). *Women, crime and criminology: A feminist critique*. London: Routledge & Kegan Paul.

SMART, R. G. (1986). Cocaine use and problems in North America. *British Journal of Criminology, 28*, 109–128.

SMIGEL, E. O. (1970). Public attitudes toward stealing as related to the size of the victim organization. In E. O. Smigel & H. L. Ross (Eds.), *Crimes against bureaucracy*. New York: Van Nostrand Reinhold.

SMITH, C. P., ALEXANDER, P. S., HALATAYN, T. V., & ROBERTS, C. F. (1980). *A national assessment of serious juvenile crime and the juvenile justice system: The need for a rational response*. Vol. 2. Washington, DC: U.S. Government Printing Office.

SMITH, M. D., & BENNETT, N. (1985). Poverty, inequality, and theories of forcible rape. *Crime and Delinquency, 31*, 295–305.

SOBELL, M. B., & SOBELL, L. C. (1973). Individualized behavior for alcoholics. *Behavior Therapy, 4*, 49–72.

SOMMER, B. A. (1983). How does menstruation affect cognitive competence and psychophysiological response? *Women and Health, 8*, 53–90.

SORENSON, S. B., STEIN, J. A., SIEGEL, J. M., GOLDING, J. M., & BURNAM, M. A. (1987). The prevalence of adult sexual assault: The Los Angeles Epidemiological Catchment Area Project. *American Journal of Epidemiology, 126*, 1154–1164.

SPAIN, D. M., BRADESS, F. A., & EGGSON, A. A. (1951). Alcohol and violent death. *Journal of the American Medical Association, 146*, 334–335.

SPENCER, C. (1966). *A typology of violent offenders*. Administrative Abstract No. 23, California Department of Corrections, September.

SPERRY, R. (1983). *Science and moral priority*. New York: Columbia Univ. Press.

SPITZER, R. L. (1985). DSM-III and the politics-science dichotomy syndrome. *American Psychologist, 40,* 522–526.

STAFFIERI, J. R. (1967). A study of social stereotypes of body image in children. *Journal of Personality and Social Psychology, 1,* 101–104.

STEADMAN, H. J. (1972). The psychiatrist as a conservative agent of social control. *Social Problems, 20,* 263–271.

STEADMAN, H. J. (1976). Predicting dangerousness. In D. J. Madden & J. R. Lion (Eds.), *Rage·hate·assault and other forms of violence.* New York: Spectrum Publishers.

STEADMAN, H. J. (1979). *Beating a rap? Defendants found incompetent to stand trial.* Chicago: Univ. of Chicago Press.

STEADMAN, H. J., & BRAFF, J. (1983). Defendants not guilty by reason of insanity. In J. Mohanan & H. J. Steadman (Eds.), *Mentally disordered offenders.* New York: Plenum.

STEADMAN, H. J., & COCOZZA, J. J. (1974). *Careers of the criminally insane.* Lexington, MA: Lexington Books.

STEADMAN, H. J., & HARTSTONE, E. (1983). Defendants incompetent to stand trial. In J. Monahan & H. J. Steadman (Eds.), *Mentally disordered offenders.* New York: Plenum.

STEADMAN, H. J., MONAHAN, J., HARTSTONE, E., DAVIS, S. K., & ROBBINS, D. C. (1982). Mentally disordered offenders: A national survey of patients and facilities. *Law and Human Behavior, 6,* 31–38.

STEINMETZ, S. K. (1977). *The cycle of violence: Assaultive, aggressive, and abusive family interaction.* New York: Praeger.

STEINMETZ, S. K. (1981). A cross-cultural comparison of sibling violence. *International Journal of Family Psychiatry, 2,* 337-351.

STEWART, M. A., & CULVER, K. W. (1982). Children who set fires: The clinical picture and a follow-up. *British Journal of Psychiatry, 140,* 357–363.

STONE, A. (1975). *Mental health law: A system in transition.* Washington, DC: U.S. Government Printing Office.

STONNER, D. (1976). The study of aggression: Conclusions and prospects for the future. In R. Green & E. O'Neal (Eds.), *Perspectives on aggression.* New York: Academic Press.

STRASBURG, P. A. (1978). *Violent delinquents: A report to the Ford Foundation from the Vera Institute of Justice.* New York: Monarch.

STRASSER, F. (1989a). One nation, under siege. *The National Law Journal,* August 7, S2-S3, S15.

STRASSER, F. (1989b). It's not as bad as people think. *The National Law Journal,* August 7, S16-S17.

STRAUS, M. A., & GELLES, R. J. (1986). Societal change and change in family violence from 1975 to 1985 as revealed by two national surveys. *Journal of Marriage and the Family, 48,* 465–479.

STRAUS, M. A., GELLES, R. J., & STEINMETZ, S. K. (1980). *Behind closed doors: Violence in the American family.* New York: Doubleday.

STUMPFL, F. (1936). *Die Ursprunge des Verbrechens om Lebenshauf von Zwillingen.* Leipzig: George Thieme Verlag.

STUMPHAUZER, J. (1973). Modification of delay choices in institutionalized youthful offenders through social reinforcement. In J. Stumphauzer (Ed.), *Behavior therapy with delinquents.* Springfield, IL: Charles C. Thomas.

STURGEON, V., & TAYLOR, J. (1980). Report of a five year follow-up study of mentally disordered sex offenders released from Atascadero State Hospital in 1973. *Criminal Justice Journal of Western State Univ., San Diego, 4,* 31–64.

SULLIVAN, C. E., GRANT, M. Q., & GRANT, J. D. (1957). The development of interpersonal maturity: Applications to delinquency. *Psychiatry, 20,* 272–282.

SUTHERLAND, E. H., & CRESSEY, D. R. (1974). *Criminology.* (9th ed.). Philadelphia: J. B. Lippincott.

SVALASTOGA, K. (1956). Homicide and social contact in Denmark. *American Journal of Sociology, 62,* 37–41.

SWANSON, D. W. (1968). Adult sexual abuse of children: The man and circumstances. *Diseases of the Nervous System, 29,* 677–683.

SYKES, G. M. (1956). *Crime and society.* New York: Random House.

SYLVESTER, S. F., REED, J. H., & NELSON, D. (1977). *Prison homicide.* New York: Spectrum Publications.

SYMONS, D. (1979). *The evolution of human sexuality.* New York: Oxford Univ. Press.

TAPPAN, P. W. (1947). Who is the criminal? *American Sociological Review, 12,* 100–110.

TAPPAN, P. W. (1949). *Juvenile delinquency.* New York: McGraw-Hill.

Tarasoff v. *Regents of the Univ. of California,* 529 p.2d 553 (Cal. 1974), *vac., reheard in bank, & aff'd* 131 Cal. Reptr. 14, 551, P.2d 334 (1976).

TASTO, D., & INSEL, P. (1977). The premenstrual and menstrual syndromes. In S. Rachman (Ed.), *Contributions to medical psychology.* Vol. 1. Oxford: Pergamon Press.

TAYLOR, M., & NEE, C. (1988). The role of cues in simulated residential burglary. *British Journal of Criminology, 28,* 396–401.

TAYLOR, S. P. (1967). Aggressive behavior and physiological arousal as a function of provocation and the tendency to inhibit aggression. *Journal of Personality, 35,* 297–310.

TAYLOR, S. P., & GAMMON, C. B. (1975). Effects of type and dose of alcohol on human physical aggression. *Journal of Personality and Social Psychology, 32,* 169–175.

TAYLOR, S. P., GAMMON, C. B., & CAPASSO, D. R. (1976). Aggression as a function of the interaction of alcohol and threat. *Journal of Personality and Social Psychology, 34,* 938–941.

TAYLOR, S. P., & LEONARD, K. E. (1983). Alcohol and human physical aggression. In R. G. Geen & E. I. Donnerstein (Eds.), *Aggression: Theoretical and empirical reviews.* Vol. 2. New York: Academic Press.

TAYLOR, S. P., SCHMUTTE, G. T., LEONARD, K. E., & CRANSTON, J. W. (1979). The effects of alcohol and extreme provocation on the use of highly noxious shock. *Motivation and Emotion, 3,* 73–81.

TAYLOR, S. P., & SEARS, J. D. (1988). The effects of alcohol and persuasive social pressure on human physical aggression. *Aggressive Behavior, 14,* 237–244.

TAYLOR, S. P., VARDARIS, R. M., RAVITCH, A. B., GAMMON, C. B., CRANSTON, J. W., & LUBETKIN, A. E. (1976). The effects of alcohol and delta-9-tetrahydrocannabinol on human physical aggression. *Aggressive Behavior, 2,* 153–161.

TEPLIN, L. (1984). Criminalizing mental disorder. *American Psychologist, 39,* 794–803.

THORLEY, G. (1984). Review of follow-up and follow-back studies of childhood hyperactivity. *Psychological Bulletin, 96,* 116–132.

THORNBERRY, T. P., & FARNWORTH, M. (1982). Social correlates of criminal involvement: Further evidence on the relationships between social status and criminal behavior. *American Sociological Review, 47,* 505–518.

THORNBERRY, T. P., & JACOBY, J. E. (1979). *The criminally insane: A community follow-up of mentally ill offenders.* Chicago: Univ. of Chicago Press.

TINKLENBERG, J. R. (1973). Alcohol and violence. In P. G. Bourne (Ed.), *Alcoholism: Progress in research and treatment.* New York: Academic Press.

TINKLENBERG, J. R., & STILLMAN, R. C. (1970). Drug use and violence. In D. Daniels, M. Gilula, & F. Ochberg (Eds.), *Violence and the struggle for existence.* Boston: Little, Brown.

TINKLENBERG, J. R., & WOODROW, K. M. (1974). Drug use among youthful assaultive and sexual offenders. In S. H. Frazier (Ed.), *Aggression.* Baltimore: Williams & Wilkins.

TITCHENER, E. B. (1914). On "psychology as the behaviorist views it." *Proceedings of the American Philosophical Society, 53,* 213.

TITTLE, C. R. (1983). Social class and criminal behavior: A critique of the theoretical foundation. *Social Forces, 62,* 334–358.

TITTLE, C. R., & VILLEMEZ, W. J. (1977). Social class and criminality. *Social Forces, 56,* 474–502.

TITTLE, C. R., VILLEMEZ, W., & SMITH, D. (1978). The myth of social class and criminality: An empirical assessment of the empirical evidence. *American Sociological Review, 43,* 643–656.

TOCH, H. (1969). *Violent men: An inquiry into the psychology of violence.* Chicago: Aldine.

TOCH, H. (1977). *Police, prisons, and the problems of violence.* National Institute of Mental Health. Washington, DC: U.S. Government Printing Office.

TOCH, H., & ADAMS, K. (1989). *The disturbed violent offender.* New Haven, CT: Yale Univ. Press.

TOCH, H., & ADAMS, K., WITH GRANT, J. D. (1989). *Coping: Maladaptation in prisons.* New Brunswick, NJ: Transaction Publishers.

TRASLER, G. (1987). Some cautions for the biological approach to crime causation. In S. A. Mednick, E. Moffitt, & S. A. Stack (Eds.), *The causes of crime: New biological approaches.* Cambridge, England: Cambridge Univ. Press.

TROJANOWICZ, R. C., & MORASH, M. (1983). *Juvenile delinquency: Concepts and control.* (3rd ed.). Englewood Cliffs, NJ: Prentice-Hall.

TUCKER, D. M. (1981). Lateral brain function, emotion and conceptualization. *Psychological Bulletin, 89,* 19–46.

TUPIN, J. P., MAHAR, D., & SMITH, D. (1973). Two types of violent offenders with psychosocial descriptors. *Diseases of the Nervous System, 34,* 356–363.

TURNER, C. W., SIMONS, L. S., BERKOWITZ, L., & FRODI, A. (1977). The stimulating and inhibiting effects of weapons on aggressive behavior. *Aggressive Behavior, 3,* 355–378.

U.S. DEPARTMENT OF HEALTH AND HUMAN SERVICES. (1982). *National study of the incidence of child abuse and neglect.* Washington, DC: U.S. Government Printing Office.

U.S. DEPARTMENT OF HEALTH AND HUMAN SERVICES. (1988). *Study findings: Study of national incidence of child abuse and neglect.* Washington, DC: U.S. Government Printing Office.

U.S. DEPARTMENT OF JUSTICE. (1973). *Report to the nation on crime and justice.* Washington, DC: U.S. Department of Justice.

U.S. DEPARTMENT OF JUSTICE. (1976). *Bomb summary—1975.* Washington, DC: U.S. Goverment Printing Office.

U.S. DEPARTMENT OF JUSTICE. (1978). *Children in custody: A report on the juvenile detention and correctional facility census of 1973.* Washington, DC: U.S. Government Printing Office.

U.S. DEPARTMENT OF JUSTICE. (1985). *The risk of violent crime.* Washington, DC: U.S. Government Printing Office.

U.S. DEPARTMENT OF JUSTICE. (1987). *UCR bomb summary—1986.* Washington, DC: U.S. Government Printing Office.

U.S. DEPARTMENT OF JUSTICE. (1988). *Report to the nation on crime and justice: The data.* (2nd ed.). Washington, DC: U.S. Department of Justice.

U.S. DEPARTMENT OF JUSTICE. (1989a). *Uniform Crime Reports.* Washington, DC: U.S. Government Printing Office.

U.S. DEPARTMENT OF JUSTICE. (1989b). *Criminal victimization in the United States, 1987.* Washington, DC: U.S. Government Printing Office.

United States v. Brawner, 471 F.2d 969 (D.C. Cir. 1972).

VALENSTEIN, E. S. (1973). *Brain control.* New York: Wiley.

VASTA, R. (1982). Physical child abuse: A dual-component analysis. *Developmental Review, 2,* 125–149.

VERKKO, V. (1951). *Homicides and suicides in Finland and their dependence on national character.* Copenhagen: C.E.R. Gad.

VETTER, H. J., & SILVERMAN, I. J. (1978). *The nature of crime.* Philadelphia: W. B. Saunders.

VIRKKUNEN, M. (1975). Victim precipitated pedophilia offenses. *British Journal of Criminology, 15,* 175–180.

VISHER, C. A. (1987). Incapacitation and crime control. *Justice Quarterly, 4,* 513–543.

Vitek v. Jones, 445 U.S. 480, 100 S. Ct. 1254 (1980).

VOLD, G. B. (1958). *Theoretical criminology.* New York: Oxford Univ. Press.

VOSS, H. L., & HEPBURN, J. (1968). Patterns in criminal homicide in Chicago. *Journal of Criminal Law, Criminology, and Police Science, 59,* 499–506.

VREELAND, R. G., & LEVIN, B. M. (1980). Psychological aspects of firesetting. In D. Canter (Ed.), *Fires and human behaviour.* Chichester, England: Wiley.

WADSWORTH, M. E. J. (1979). *Roots of delinquency: Infancy, adolescence and crime.* Oxford, England: Martin Robinson.

WALKER, N. (1978). Dangerous people. *International Journal of Law & Psychiatry, 1,* 37–49.

WALLACH, M. A., & WALLACH, L. (1983). *Psychology's sanction for selfishness.* San Francisco, CA: W. H. Freeman.

WALLERSTEIN, J. S., & WYLE, J. (1947). Our law-abiding law breakers. *Probation, 25,* 107–112.

WALSTER, E. (1966). Assignment of responsibility for an accident. *Journal of Personality and Social Psychology, 3,* 73–79.

WALTERS, G. C., & GRUSEC, J. E. (1977). *Punishment.* San Francisco: W. H. Freeman.

WALTERS, H. F., & MALAMUD, P. (1975). Drop that gun, Captain Video. *Newsweek,* March 10, 81–82.

WARREN, M. Q. (1979). The female offender. In H. Toch (Ed.), *Psychology of crime and criminal justice.* New York: Holt, Rinehart & Winston.

WARREN, M. Q. (1983). Applications of interpersonal-maturity theory of offender populations. In W. S. Laufer & J. M. Day (Eds.), *Personality theory, moral development, and criminal
behavior*. Lexington, MA: Lexington Books.

WATSON, R. I. (1973). Investigation into deindividuation using a cross-cultural survey technique. *Journal of Personality and Social Psychology, 25*, 342–345.

WEIS, J. G. (1989). Family violence methodology and design. In L. Ohlin & M. Tonry (Eds.),
Family violence. Vol. 11. Chicago: Univ. of Chicago Press.

WEIS, J. G., & SEDERSTROM, J. (1981). *The prevention of serious delinquency. What to do?* Washington, DC: U.S. Department of Justice.

WEISS, G., MINDE, K., WERRY, J., DOUGLAS, V., & NEMETH, E. (1971). Studies on the hyperactive child: Five-year follow-up. *Archives of General Psychiatry, 24*, 409–414.

WEISS, J., LAMBERTI, J., & BLACKBURN, N. (1960). The sudden murderers. *Archives of General
Psychiatry, 2*, 670–678.

WEISS, R. D., & MIRIN, S. M. (1987). *Cocaine.* Washington, DC: American Psychiatric Press.

WELTE, J. W., & ABEL, E. L. (1989). Homicide: Drinking by the victim. *Journal of Studies on
Alcohol, 50*, 197–201.

WENK, E. A., ROBISON, J. O., & SMITH, G. W. (1972). Can violence be predicted? *Crime and
Delinquency, 18*, 393–402.

WEST, D. J., & FARRINGTON, D. P. (1973). *Who becomes delinquent?* London: Heinemann Educational.

WETTSTEIN, R. M. (1984). The prediction of violent behavior and the duty to protect third
parties. *Behavioral Science & the Law, 2*, 291–316.

WETZEL, R. D., McCLURE, J. N., & REICH, T. (1971). Premenstrual symptoms in self-referrals
to a suicide prevention service. *British Journal of Psychiatry, 119*, 525–526.

WEXLER, D. B. (1977). Criminal commitment contingency structures. In B. D. Sales, (Ed.), *The
criminal justice system*. Vol. 1. New York: Plenum Press.

WEXLER, D. B. (1981). *Mental health law.* New York: Plenum Press.

WHITEHILL, M., DeMYER-GAPIN, S., & SCOTT, T. G. (1976). Stimulation seeking in antisocial
preadolescent children. *Journal of Abnormal Psychology, 85*, 101–104.

WIESEN, A. E. (1965). Differential reinforcing effects of onset and offset of stimulation on the
operant behavior of normals, neurotics and psychopaths. (Doctoral dissertation, Univ.
of Florida). Ann Arbor: MI: Univ. Microfilms, No. 65-9625.

WILENTZ, W. C. (1953). The alcohol factor in violent deaths. *American Practitioner: Digest of
Treatment, 4*, 21–24.

WILLIAMS, J. E., & HOLMES, K. A. (1981). *The second assault: Rape and public attitudes.* Westport,
CT: Greenwood Press.

WILLIAMS, K. (1984). Economic sources of homicides: Re-estimating the effects of poverty and
inequality. *American Sociological Review, 49*, 283–289.

WILLIAMS, W., & MILLER, K. S. (1981). The processing and disposition of incompetent mentally ill offenders. *Law and Human Behavior, 5*, 245–261.

WILSON, E. O. (1975). *Sociobiology: The new synthesis.* Cambridge, MA: Belknap Press.

WILSON, E. O. (1978). *On human nature.* Cambridge, MA: Harvard Univ. Press.

WILSON, J. Q., & HERRNSTEIN, R. J. (1985). *Crime and human nature.* New York: Simon &
Schuster.

WINCZE, J. P. (1977). Sexual deviance and dysfunction. In D. Rimm & J. Somervill (Eds.),
Abnormal psychology. New York: Academic Press.

WINFREY, C. (1979). Why 900 died in Guyana. *The New York Times Magazine*, February 25, 39–
46, 50.

WINICK, B. J. (1983). Incompetency to stand trial. In J. Monahan & H. J. Steadman (Eds.),
Mentally disordered offenders. New York: Plenum.

WINICK, C., & KINSIE, P. (1971). *The lively commerce.* Chicago: Quadrangle Books.

WISH, E. D. (1986). PCP and crime: Just another illicit drug? In D. H. Clouet (Ed.), *Phencyclidine: An update.* Rockville, MD: National Institute on Drug Abuse.

WOLFE, D. A. (1985). Child-abusive parents: An empirical review and analysis. *Psychological
Bulletin, 97*, 462–582.

WOLFGANG, M. E. (1958). *Patterns in criminal homicide.* Philadelphia: Univ. of Pennsylvania
Press.

WOLFGANG, M. E. (1961). A sociological analysis of criminal homicide. *Federal Probation, 25,* 48–55.

WOLFGANG, M. E. (1972). Cesare Lombroso (1835–1909). In H. Mannheim (Ed.), *Pioneers in criminality.* Montclair, NJ: Patterson Smith.

WOLFGANG, M. E., & FERRACUTI, F. (1967). *The subculture of violence.* London: Tavistock.

WOLFGANG, M. E., FIGLIO, R. M., & SELLIN, T. (1972). *Delinquency in a birth cohort.* Chicago: Univ. of Chicago Press.

WOLFORD, M. R. (1972). Some attitudinal, psychological and sociological characteristics of incarcerated arsonists. *Fire and Arson Investigator, 16,* 8–13.

WONG, M., & SINGER, K. (1973). Abnormal homicide in Hong Kong. *British Journal of Psychiatry, 123,* 37–46.

WRIGHT, K. N. (1988). The relationship of risks, needs, personality classification systems and prison adjustment. *Criminal Justice and Behavior, 15,* 454–472.

WRIGHT, R. (1980). Rape and physical violence. In D. J. West (Ed.), *Sex offenders in the criminal justice system.* Cambridge, England: Cambridge Univ. Institute of Criminology.

YEGIDIS, B. L. (1986). Date rape and other forced sexual encounters among college students. *Journal of Sex Education and Therapy, 12,* 51–54.

YESAVAGE, J. A., BENEZECH, M., CECCALDI, P., BOURGEOIS, M., & ADDAD, M. (1983). Arson in mentally ill and criminal populations. *Journal of Clinical Psychiatry, 44,* 128–130.

YOCHELSON, S., & SAMENOW, S. E. (1976). *The criminal personality.* Vol. 1. New York: Jason Aronson.

YOSHIMASU, S. (1961). The criminological significance of the family in the light of the studies of criminal twins. *Acta Criminological et Medicinae Legalis Japanica, 27,* 117–141.

YOSHIMASU, S. (1965). Criminal life curves of monzygotic twin-pairs. *Acta Criminological et Medicinae Legalis Japanica, 31,* 9–20.

ZAGER, L. D. (1988). The MMPI-based criminal classification system. *Criminal Justice and Behavior, 15,* 39–57.

ZAHN, M. A., & RICKLE, W. C. (1986). Murder and minorities: The Hispanic case. Paper presented at the Academy of Criminal Justice Sciences annual meeting, Orlando, FL.

ZAMBLE, E., & PORPORINO, F. G. (1988). *Coping, behavior, and adaptation in prison inmates.* New York: Springer-Verlag.

ZEICHNER, A., & PIHL, R. O. (1979). Effects of alcohol and behavior contingencies on human aggression. *Journal of Abnormal Psychology, 88,* 152–160.

ZEICHNER, A., & PIHL, R. O. (1980). Effects of alcohol and instigator intent on human aggression. *Journal of Studies on Alcohol, 41,* 265–276.

ZILLMAN, D. (1971). Excitation transfer in communication-mediated aggressive behavior. *Journal of Experimental Social Psychology, 7,* 419–434.

ZILLMAN, D. (1979). *Hostility and aggression.* Hillsdale, NJ: Erlbaum.

ZILLMAN, D. (1983). Arousal and aggression. In R. G. Geen & E. I. Donnerstein (Eds.), *Aggression: Theoretical and empirical reviews.* Vol. 1. New York: Academic Press.

ZILLMAN, D. (1988). Cognitive-excitation interdependencies in aggressive behavior. *Aggressive Behavior, 14,* 51–64.

ZILLMAN, D., BARON, R., & TAMBORINI, R. (1981). Social costs of smoking: Effects of tobacco smoke on hostile behavior. *Journal of Applied Social Psychology, 11,* 548–561.

ZIMBARDO, P. (1970). The human choice. Individuation, reason, and order versus deindividuation, impulse, and chaos. In W. J. Arnold & D. Levine (Eds.), *Nebraska symposium on motivation 1969.* Lincoln, NE: Univ. of Nebraska Press.

ZIMBARDO, P. G. (1973). The psychological power and pathology of imprisonment. In E. Aronson and R. Helmreich (Eds.), *Social psychology.* New York: Van Nostrand.

ZIMBARDO, P. G. (1979). The psychology of evil, or the perversion of human potential. In T. R. Sarbin (Ed.), *Challenges to the criminal justice system.* New York: Human Services Press.

ZIMRING, F. G. (1978). The serious juvenile offender: Notes on an unknown quantity. In U.S. Department of Justice, *The serious juvenile offender.* Washington, DC: U.S. Government Printing Office.

ZIMRING, F. G., MUKHERGEF, S. K., & VAN WINKLE, B. (1983). Intimate violence: A study of intersexual homicide in Chicago. *University of Chicago Law Review, 50,* 910–930.

ZITRIN, A., HARDESTY, A., BURDOCK, E., & DROSSMAN, A. (1975). Crime and violence among mental patients. *Scientific Proceedings of the 128th Annual Meeting of the American Psychiatric Association, Abstracts, 142*, 140–141.

ZUCKERMAN, M. (1979). *Sensation seeking beyond the optimal level of arousal.* Hillsdale, NJ: Erlbaum.

Author Index

Subject Index

413